S0-EAU-123

MURDER CAPITAL OF THE WORLD

The Santa Cruz community looks back at the Frazier, Mullin, and Kemper murder sprees of the early 1970s

EMERSON MURRAY

This first edition is limited to one thousand copies, signed by the author.

This is number __457__ / 1,000

Copyright ©2021 by Emerson Murray
All rights reserved.

No part of this book may be reproduced or
transmitted in any form or by any means,
electronic or mechanical, including photo-
copying, scanning, recording, or by any information storage and retrieval system, without
permission in writing from the author.

Published by Emerson Murray
Scotts Valley, California
murdercapitaloftheworld.com

Library of Congress Control Number:
2021900857
Murder Capital of the World / by Emerson
Murray
ISBN 978-1-7364813-0-1
1. United States History. 2. Crime.
Printed in the United States of America

First Edition. Limited to 1,000 copies.

*Right: Adrian Fuhrman, Roger Murray, and Jim
Gianera.*

MURDER

CAPITAL

OF THE

WORLD

CONTENTS

THE ACKNOWLEDGEMENTS & THE FORMAT

My dad was a friend and roommate of Jim Gianera, one of Herbert Mullin's victims. The first photo in this book hung on his wall for years. We talked about the crimes of Frazier, Mullin, and Kemper in our house. I remember spending the night at my friend Steve's house in fourth grade. Same thing. We talked about Kemper and his horrific crimes. My grandmother had saved clippings from the newspaper when Frazier killed the Ohtas and Dorothy Cadwallader. I remember looking at the picture of survivors, Lark and Taura Ohta, and I must have said something because my foster brother, Jamal, teased that I was going to marry them. I was five. I never felt like my family was morbid. These stories were, and still are everywhere in Santa Cruz. Mention the names of the killers in public and someone will have a personal story or remembrance.

This is the story of my community, told by the survivors themselves. I'm afraid that as memories fade and our neighbors pass away, these stories are being lost to time. In 2019 I had a panic about this and was compelled to act. You hold in your hands our rich local history of a very dark time.

The film *The Lost Boys* was filmed here in Santa Cruz under the fictitious name Santa Carlo. The "Welcome to Santa Carlo" billboard in the movie has graffiti scrawled on it, "Murder Capital of the World." That's not fiction. Well into the sprees a reporter from the *San Francisco Examiner* asked District Attorney Peter Chang, "Would you say that Santa Cruz is the murder capital of the world?"

Chang responded, "Right now, we must be the murder capital."

Thank you to everyone who spent time with me, telling their stories and sharing their information. A book like this is a team effort and I'm grateful to be a part of an amazing team of people. It's been a chain of contacts for the last few years. An amazing spider web of incredible, heartbreaking, and fascinating stories. I tried to honor the subjects of each chapter as best as I could, while respecting the living.

Thank you to my family for putting up with my late nights and quick trips and forced smiles as I dragged them off to another morbid location. Best crew ever.

Thanks to my friends and extended family, who have pushed me and encouraged me and inspired me. My brother and his family always had an encouraging word and fresh ideas and notes.

Thanks to Greg Azevedo. We thought, DAMN! Someone needs to do a miniseries or movie about this. Something like David Fincher's *Zodiac*, fact-driven with a blazing pace. We didn't have the skills, but I did what I could.

Thank you to Pete Amos, the Vestal Family, Rita Wright, Austin Comstock, Harold Cartwright, Chris Cottle, Monty Lunde, and everyone else who shared priceless photographs, documents, and recordings with me. Your kindness humbles me. Also, thank you to the Santa Cruz County Sheriff's Office, especially Christopher Shearer and April Skalland.

Special thanks to Lark Ohta who spent hours and hours with me on the project. I hope I have done you proud.

Thanks to the proofreaders and spelll checkers and continuity directors who cleaned up my mess rather well: Amanda Murray, Jessica Beck, Christine Falco, and Matt Widener. The best!

Thanks to my mom and dad for raising me with an appreciation for our local history, dark as it may have been.

THE FORMAT

My book is a big 'ol book of quotes. I call the style primary source non-fiction. I fill in the gaps between quotes, but the style can be discombobulating for some. For me, it is an excellent way to tell a chaotic, quick-moving story with many people, many opinions, and especially differing, and sometimes conflicting, memories. I'm hoping you will feel the whirlwind that Santa Cruz law enforcement and the community felt at the time.

I robbed, swiped, and copied the quotes from every reliable source I could. I added dates to the quotes where I had the information. I have used paragraph breaks for pacing and drama, which makes reading quotes easier and more familiar. If there is an elision (marked by […]) you'll know that an unimportant quotation was removed. I've made every effort to represent the context accurately. My comments and clarifications are in gray.

The modern quotes from Herbert Mullin are from handwritten letters. Mullin's writing includes symbols and formatting that I cannot successfully replicate. I did my best to relay the intent and foundation of his writing.

Because of the various documents referenced in this book, the style conventions are often contradictory.

There is a list of works consulted at the end, but frankly it's a mess, cobbled together from my notes. You'll get no apology from me.

Thank you for picking up yet another book on this subject. I hope you get something new and fresh out of my book, if only an appreciation for the people and community that were terrorized by the madness.

THOSE QUOTED

Allison Ayers: Friend and roommate of John Linley Frazier

Allyn Kemper: Sister of Edmund Kemper

Ami Chandler: Neighbor of the Ohta

Ariadne Symons: Santa Cruz Deputy District Attorney

Arthur Reichstadt: Social Worker, Atascadero

Austin Comstock: Santa Cruz attorney

Barney Barnett: Journalist

Barry Burt: Mullin classmate and local

Bill Tubbs: Private investigator

Bob Lee: Santa Cruz County District Attorney

Bonnie Ring: UCSC Lecturer and friend of Rosalind Thorpe

Byron Stookey Jr.: UCSC Director of Academic Planning

C. Gilbert: Santa Cruz Police Officer

Cameron Smith: UCSC student

Carla Gervasoni: Neighbor of Kemper

Cesar Barber: UCSC Vice Chancellor

Charles Franich: Judge

Charles Morris: Psychiatrist

Charmaine Falcon: Friend of Jim Gianera

Chris Cottle: Santa Cruz County Assistant District Attorney

Chuck Scherer: Santa Cruz Deputy Sheriff

Clark Kerr: University of California President

Clarnell Strandberg: Kemper's mother

Cleo Taylor: Social Worker, Atascadero

Cynthia Schall: Victim of Kemper.

Dan Forbus: Santa Cruz County Supervisor

Dan Righetti: Reporter, *Santa Cruz Sentinel*

Dave Alcorn: Santa Cruz Deputy Sheriff

David Cadwallader: Brother-in-law of Dorothy Cadwallader

David Dozier: Childhood neighbor of Kemper

David Marlowe: Psychologist

David Martinez: Pueblo Police Officer

David O'Neil: Psychology Intern, Atascadero

Dee Shafer: Psychologist

Delores Frazier: Wife of John Linley Frazier

Ditta Oliker: Mother of David Oliker

Don Smythe: Santa Cruz Deputy Sheriff

Don Stewart: Mullin's boxing coach

Donald Lunde: Psychiatrist

Doug James: Santa Cruz County Sheriff

Doug Monroe: Santa Cruz Police Officer

Douglas Liddicoat: Friend of Dr. Ohta

Douglas Roth: Friend of Kemper

Duane Gull: Santa Cruz Deputy Sheriff

Earl Fox: Chief of Police, Fleetwood, Pennsylvania

Edmund Kemper

Edmund Kemper Jr.: Kemper's father

Edmund Kemper's fiance

Edward Lawrence: Friend of Mullin

Edward McGowan: Los Gatos Police Officer

Eleanor Foster: Joan Gianera's mother

Ernest Wicklund: Santa Cruz Mayor

Errol Morris: Filmmaker

F.M. Glenn Wilson: UCSC Provost

Floyd Weber: Scotts Valley reserve police officer

Forrest Robinson: Friend and co-worker with Clarnell Strandberg

Forrest Schall: Brother of Cynthia Schall

Fred Spector: Robert Spector's uncle

Gary Hamby: Childhood friend of Frazier

Gene Dawson: Reverent, Drug Abuse Preventive Center

Geno Pini: Santa Cruz Police Chief

George Gianera: Jim Gianera's brother

Hans Dibbern: Doctor. Performed autopsies

Harold Cartwright: Investigator, Santa Cruz Public Defender's Office

Harold Klonecky: Principal of Torrance High

Harry Brauer: Judge

Henry Mello: Santa Cruz County Supervisor

Herbert Mullin

Holly Harman: Friend of Jim and Joan Gianera

J. Bonar: Santa Cruz Corrections Officer

James Jackson: Santa Cruz Public Defender

James Liu: Alice Liu's father

James McCoy: Pueblo Police Officer

James Sheridan: Santa Cruz Police Officer

Jean Everice Carter: Doctor. Performed autopsies

Jean Mullin: Herbert Mullin's mother

Jeff Esposito: High school friend of Herbert Mullin and Dean Richardson

Jeff Towle: Friend of Mary Guilfoyle

Jeffrey Card: Brother of Brian Scott Card

Jim Conner: Santa Cruz Police Officer

Jim Ingram: Santa Cruz Deputy Sheriff

Joan Stagnaro: Neighbor of Fred Perez

Joe Cole: Neighbor of Frazier

Joel Fort: Psychiatrist

Joey Tranchina: Photographer

John Douglas: FBI Behavioral Science Unit

John Fiorovich: Country Cousin's Sporting Goods

John Hopper: Santa Cruz Deputy Sheriff's Explorer Scout

John J. O'Connor: Priest and Mullin family friend

John Linley Frazier

John Perez: Son of Fred Perez

John Stroud: Psychiatric Consultant, Atascadero

June Aries: Ex-mother-in-law of John Linley Frazier's wife, Delores

Karen Weigel: Employee of Dr. Ohta

Kenneth Pittenger: Santa Cruz Deputy Sheriff

Kenneth Springer: Mullin jury foreman

Kimberly Weiskopf: Frazier's neighbor

Lark Ohta

Lothair Dreibelbis: Father of Mark Dreibelbis

Louis Keller: Santa Cruz Sheriff's Office Administration

Louis Wileman: Associate of Dr. Ohta

Lynn Scott: High school friend of Dean Richardson and Jim Gianera

Marilyn Baker: KQED news host

Marj Von B: Journalist

Maxine White: SLV counselor

Melinda Cadwallader: Daughter of Dorothy Cadwallader

Mercedes Tileston: Social Worker, Atascadero

Michael Madden: Frazier's neighbor

Michael Rugg: Neighbor of John Linley Frazier and owner/operator of the Bigfoot Discovery Museum

Michael Stebbins: Owner of Performance West

Mickey Aluffi: Santa Cruz Deputy Sheriff

Mike Lee: Reporter KPIX

Mike Prizmich: Mullin Parole Board Presiding Commissioner

Mike Wark: Friend of John Linley Frazier

Miriam Finnegan: Friend of Joan Gianera and daughter of Police Detective Dennis Finnegan

Morton Felix: Clinical Psychologist

Nancy Guilfoyle: Mary Guilfoyle's sister-in-law

Pat Bocca: Sister of Herbert Mullin

Pat Liteky: Santa Cruz County Supervisor

Pat O'Brien: Newscaster for KPIX television

Pat Pascal: John Linley Frazier's mother

Paul Dougherty: San Mateo County Criminalist

Paul Tara: Santa Cruz County Undersheriff

Paula Johns: UCSC assistant professor

Pete Amos: Photographer, *Santa Cruz Sentinel*

Peter Chang: Santa Cruz County District Attorney

Randall Kane: Owner, The Catalyst

Raymond Koch: Neighbor of Herbert Mullin

Richard Auwaerter: Psychologist, Atascadero

Richard Foerster: Santa Cruz Police Officer

Richard Koch: Childhood friend of Mullin

Richard Verbrugge: Investigator, Santa Cruz District Attorney's Office

Robert Edgar: UCSC Provost and friend of Alice Liu

Robert Francis: Kathleen Francis' husband

Robert Kinsey: Psychiatrist

Robert Ludlow: Santa Cruz attorney

Robert Mayber: Pueblo Chief of Police

Robert Silva: Pueblo Police Officer

Rod Sanford: Santa Cruz Deputy Sheriff

Roger Krone: Neighbor of Frazier

Roger Murray: My dad

Ronald Rico: Santa Clara County Deputy District Attorney

S. Solomon: Doctor, Atascadero

Sam Munoz: Jury Room owner

Sam Robustelli: Santa Cruz Deputy Sheriff

Sandra Bryson: Frazier Parole Board Presiding Commissioner

Sean Upton: Santa Cruz Police Officer

Skaidrite Rubene-Koo: Aiko Koo's mother

Steven Houtz: Francis family neighbor

Susan Felix: Wife of Dr. Morton Felix

Susan Swanson: Sister of Edmund Kemper

Ted Pound: Fire Chief

Terry Medina: Santa Cruz Deputy Sheriff

Thatcher Hall Clark: Francis family neighbor

Tim Crump: Neighbor of Herbert Mullin

Walt Weiskopf: Frazier's neighbor

Walter Rappaport: Psychiatrist

Ward Damio: Author

Wendy Thorpe: Rosalind Thorpe's sister

Werner Herzog: Filmmaker

William Friedland: UCSC Senior Preceptor

William Helms: Chief Deputy, Madera Police Department

William Henry Mitchell: Doctor. Performed autopsies

William Kelsay: Santa Cruz County Assistant District Attorney

William Mullin: Herbert Mullin's father. Legal name is Martin William Mullin.

Crime Spree Soars–Another Murder

Santa Cruz Sentinel

118th Year NO. 37 TUESDAY AFTERNOON, FEBRUARY 13, 1973 15c 24 Pages

Today's Closing N.Y. Stocks

Weather

MONTEREY BAY AREA — Rain likely continuing at times through Wednesday. High Wednesday in the 50s. Lows in the 40s. Variable winds becoming southerly.

Temperatures for the 24 - hour period ending at 8 a.m. today: High 53. Low 47. Rainfall: 1.16 inches.

'Senseless' Slaying Of SC Man

By TOM HONIG
Sentinel Staff Writer

Another Santa Cruz killing, Fred Perez, 72, 511 Lighthouse Ave., who comes from one of the oldest pioneer families in Santa Cruz, was shot and killed this morning while doing yardwork near his home.

A Police Lt. Chuck Scherer described the slaying as "a senseless, ambush slaying with no motive." He said that the killer fired the shot at Perez from a distance of about 75 yards.

Police have a man in custody in connection with the slaying, which took place at 8 a.m.

Herbert William Mullen, 25, 1541 McClellan Road, Felton, was apprehended by police minutes after the killing as he reportedly was on his way out of town in a blue Chevrolet station wagon. Patrolman Sean Upton nabbed the suspect as he was driving on River Street near Coral Street, and he gave up without a fight, police said.

Police Capt. Dick Overton said that Mullen has not made any statements except to ask police to observe his civil rights.

A neighbor reported the slaying to police. She said that she saw a station wagon leaving the scene of the killing at the intersection of Lighthouse Avenue and Gharkey Street moments after hearing a sound resembling a gunshot.

She said that she looked over and saw Perez lying on the ground.

Perez had reportedly been moving dirt with a shovel before he was shot. The lot on which he was working is located at the corner of Lighthouse Avenue and Gharkey Street. The house on the lot is occupied by renters.

A sheriff's deputy who was returning home following the graveyard shift at work spotted the man down in the yard, and thinking that he was perhaps the victim of a heart attack, he said to the man, "you'll be all right." The deputy said that the man at that point was still alive.

Police responding to the call arrived moments after the shooting, while still more police gave pursuit to the getaway car.

A witness at the scene of the arrest said that police discovered a rifle in the car which Mullen was driving.

The Perez family is one of the oldest in the local fishing business. Malio Stagnaro, a good friend of Perez, said that the man's grandfather and three uncles preceded Perez in the retail end of the business.

Stagnaro said Perez served in China during World War I. After the war, he fought professionally under the name of Freddie Bell for three years.

After he retired a couple years ago, Stagnaro said, he "took things easy" with his wife, Margaret. "He worked around the yard, or went fishing. He had no enemies in the world. Everybody like Fred, he was really a fine person. Everybody on the wharf today is in a state of shock — all the boys are really shook up."

A policeman checks over the spot which Fred Perez fell after being shot and killed this morning. Perez had been moving dirt with a shovel and a wheelbarrow when he was shot. In the background, authorities talk with neighbors and passerbys in an attempt to find out what happened.
(Sentinel Photo By Pete Amos)

Youth Held In Capitola Death

By DON RIGHETTI
Sentinel Staff Writer

A 16 - year - old door - to - door peddler has been charged with the rape slaying of an elederly Capitola woman.

Wilfried Willie Brown, a California Youth Authority parolee, is being held at the Santa Cruz County Probation Center charged with first degree murder and rape of Mrs. Ida Anderson Stine.

Officers said evidence shows Brown was not involved in other cases in the rash of homicides and rapes which has terrorized this area in recent weeks.

District Attorney Peter Chang said rape victims were shown pictures of Brown and they reported he was not their assailant.

Capitola Police Chief Martin Bergthold issued a statement which indicated the intense investigation which incriminated Brown showed that he acted alone and had "flipped out" - turned psychotic - at the time of the crime. Bergthold said Brown's mental state was not drug - induced.

Brown was a resident of the Drug Abuse Preventive Center, but as part of a special rehabilitation program of the youth authority, not as a drug addict.

Both Bergthold and Chang emphasized that "in no way should this incident cast doubt or become a negative reflection of the excellent work...efforts...and achievements of the DAPC."

They said DAPC Director

Wilfried Brown

Gene Dawson and his staff were cooperative and helpful to the investigating officers.

Mrs. Stine, a 79 - year - old widow and a popular Capitola figure, apparently was raped, smothered and then dumped into a water-filled bathtub of her 208 Sacramento Ave. home. Her body was discovered last Tuesday.

Police knew that Brown and two other DAPC residents had been in the area selling soap to raise funds for the drug abuse center. They questioned the three, apparently narrowed the suspects to two, then arrested a Brown.

Chang says Brown has given a statement on the crime, but the district attorney refused to reveal its content. He says "a strong case" has been built against the suspect.

He added that despite Brown's mental condition at the time of the crime, the prosecution will proceed, at least in its initial stages, on the basis of first - degree murder.

Chang siad he doesn't know at this time if Brown will be tried asan adult.

Chang declined to say why Brown originally was sentenced to the CYA, but he said the Capitola murder was "not a drug related action."

Dawson said he was well aware of the criticism the crime will bring to his organization and added he is attempting to gear the agency to weather the storm.

He added that three psychiatrists had deemed Brown to be capable of rehabilitation before he was admitted to to the DAPC program. Dawson said he intends to make the screening tighter than ever.

Lawmen were criticized by newsmen for not announcing the arrest sooner to help ease the jangled nerves of the public in the wake of the crime wave.

Bergthold said word of the arrest , which took place Sunday, was held up in order not to jeopardize the case against Brown.

Mrs. Stine, widowed in 1966, was a long - time worker for the Women's Christian Temperance Union and served several years as state president of the organization.

James Kennedy, Treasurer, Dies

County Treasurer - Tax Collector James A. Kennedy died Monday at his home in Mt. Hermon.

Kennedy, 60, a native of Denver, Colo., was elected to the county post in 1966 and took office the following January. He ran unopposed for a second term in 1970.

Kennedy's main campaign issue in 1966 was his promise to invest county tax dollars, and when he ran again four years later he estimated the county had earned more than $2.5 million in interest on the investments.

Long active in community affairs, Kennedy was appointed to the county planning commission in 1961. He also was president of the San Lorenzo Valley Chamber of Commerce in 1964, was chairman of the governmental affairs task force of the Santa Cruz Area Chamber of Commerce in 1972, was treasurer of the California State Treasurers Assn. in 1970-71, secretary in 1971 - 72 and second vice president in 1972 - 73, was a director of the Santa Cruz chamber, was vice chairman of the Heart Sunday collection in 1970, was a member of the now defunct county board of zoning adjustment, was a trustee of the old Boulder Creek

James A. Kennedy

School District, was on the county public works commission, was a member of the county grand jury, was a member of the Santa Cruz County Grand Jury Assn., was on the original Cabrillo College organization committee, the Cabrillo bond committee and the volunteer fire department.

Kennedy served on various committees of the California State Tax Collectors Assn., was a member of First Baptist Church of Felton, the Soquel Grange and Santa Cruz Elks Lodge 824.

For 15 years he was employed by the Mt. Hermon Assn. in a supervisory capacity and for nine years was the business manager of the Christian conference grounds. He operated his own grading and paving business for three years prior to his election to the county position.

Kennedy, who attended schoolsin Denver, did graduate work, studied business administration and management. During World War II he supervised and inspected submarine

(Continued on Page 2)

News Quiz Starts Today

The first weekly news quiz appears today on Page 7 of The *Sentinel*.

The quiz, a new feature prepared by Visual Education Consultants of Madison, Wis., is being run in conjunction with educational materials furnished 23 local schools, sponsored by The Sentinel.

But the quiz also can be taken by our other readers to refresh their memories and test their understanding of the news of the world in the past week.

Piston Engine goes . . .

BOING BOING BOING!

Mazda Engine goes . . .

m-m-m-m-m-m

TEST DRIVE THE ROTARY ENGINE AT . . .

SANTA CRUZ MAZDA

Dollar Devalued

Nixon Calls For Tough U.S. Trade Legislation

WASHINGTON (AP) — President Nixon today followed up his 10 per cent devaluation of the dollar with a call for tough trade legislation aimed at getting "a fairer shake" for American business.

The devaluation was a dramatic move to calm troubled world money markets and restore confidence in the battered U.S. currency.

It was announced at a late Monday night news conference by Treasury Secretary George P. Shultz. It was the second dollar devaluation in 14 months and it swept aside a world currency agreement reached in December 1971.

Today, the President called Shultz to the White House and there disclosed his intention to seek legislation he said is needed to "get other nations away from their discriminatory policies."

Since Congress is in recess, Nixon can not send any suggested bill to the Capitol until next week.

Although the devaluation was widely expected as a result of tumultuous monetary disruptions on money-exchange markets in the past few weeks, few thought it would be so large.

Shultz told newsmen that the move, combined with two other key trade and monetary actions, would benefit the U.S. consumer, workingman and businessman.

The immediate impact of a devaluation is to raise the price of imports from foreign countries. But, because the dollar is now cheaper in relation to other currencies, prices of U.S. exports will be less.

The devaluation will be achieved formally by raising the official price of gold from

(Continued on Page 2)

U.S., Cuba Agreement On Hijacking Reached

WASHINGTON (AP) — President Nixon indicated Tuesday an agreement has been reached with Cuba on hijacking.

The indication came in off-the-cuff presidential remarks to newsmen at the White House when he said he had just talked to Secretary of State William P. Rogers and discussed "the hijacking agreement with Cuba."

The President added that Rogers "will be able to fill you in at the appropriate time."

The President brought up the subject after telling reporters that Rogers was heading for Florida with Treasury Secretary George Shultz to confer with AFL-CIO president George Meany on devaluation and planned trade legislation.

It was then that he said one of the subjects he had discussed with Rogers "was the hijacking agreement with Cuba."

The comments were volunteered to a small group of reporters who had been allowed into the White House Rose Garden where Nixon was strolling with Donald Rumsfeld, new U.S. ambassador to NATO.

As the President was preparing to re-enter his office, he paused on the steps and dropped the indication that negotiations had been completed.

An agreement on hijacking would be a major breakthrough toward improving U.S.-Cuban relations.

In the last several years many hijackers of airplanes in the United States have forced the pilots to fly to Cuba. A hardening attitude on the part of Cuba has become apparent toward the hijackers.

U.S.-Cuba exchanges, conducted through the Swiss, who represent the United States in Cuba, began in early December.

It has been unofficially reported that the two countries were at odds, during the exchanges, on how broad the antihijacking accord should be.

The United States was said last month to favor an agreement applying only to airplane hijacking.

Students Riot

CAIRO (AP) — Forty policemen were injured in clashes with university students Sunday and an undisclosed number of students were arrested Monday near Ein Shams and Cairo universities, the interior minister reported.

Women Hitchhikers —Why Do They Do It?

By TOM HONIG
Sentinel Staff Writer

"I admit it's getting scary — especially the last couple weeks," admitted a hitchhiking coed shortly after climbing in the car on Mission Street. While riding up to UCSC, she discussed the pros and cons of the matter.

"I hitchhike to school nearly every day from Felton. Luckily I've had no close calls, at least here, but of course I usually get rides from other students. I guess I really should ride the bus, but they don't even run from around Felton to the campus. At least I don't think they do, I've never seen the schedule.

"I had a couple close calls a few years ago. One time a businessman made a grab for me while I was getting out; another time a guy offered me $20 to go to bed with him, and after he got a little aggressive I jumped from the car.

"I try to find out what kind of a guy is driving before I get in the car with him. Of course, if things get tight I could probably kick an attacker in the groin.

"What upsets me more than the rapes and murders we've had lately is the decision not to allow abortions at the hospital... If I got raped on my way up to

(Continued on Page 6)

Body Identified As Cabrillo Coed

The skeletal remains found Sunday afternoon near Bonny Doon have been positively identified as those of Cabrillo College coed Mary Guilfoyle, who had been missing since Oct. 24.

Identification was made Monday by a comparison of dental work and Xrays, according to sheriff's deputies. Dentist Peter Courneen Xrayed the jaw and skull portions found Sunday off Smith Grade Road. The dental work matched records obtained from Miss Guilfoyle's local dentist.

The body was discovered about 125 yards from Smith Grade Road by a group of target shooters. It had not been buried. Clothing fragments found near the remains led deputies to suspect that the body was that of a woman.

It also appeared to have been at that spot for several months, which led to speculation that the body may have been that of Miss Guilfoyle, who was last seen leaving Cabrillo to hitchhike to the Department of Human Resources in Santa Cruz for an appointment which she never kept.

Family hired a private investigator to aid in the search for Miss Guilfoyle.

Miss Guilfoyle, who lived at 2-1681 East Cliff Drive, is survived by her father, William D. Guilfoyle of Kenmore, N.Y. She originally was from Buffalo.

She is the second known Cabrillo coed to have been murdered as the result of hitchhiking. The dismembered body of Cynthia Ann Schall, 18, were discovered in Monterey County and here last month.

Sheriff's Detective Lt. Ken Pittenger said this morning that investigators urgently wish to talk to any woman who has been the victim of rape or attempted rape and who has not previously reported the incident.

Pittenger also repeate[d] lawmen's warning t[o] hitchhikers, saying, "It is t[oo] hazardous to be used as [a] method of transportation. A[ny] young female who sticks h[er] thumb in the air is a potenti[al] rape and-or murder victim."

Four Other Rape Victims Reported

By MARK BERGSTROM
Sentinel Staff Writer

The number of reported rape cases, mostly involving hitchhiking coeds, has grown to 11, according to city police Lt. Charles Scherer. Scherer said at a press conference this morning that over the weekend four more young women reported that they were victims of rapes occurring over a period of the last four months. All came forward, presumably after reading recent stories of violence directed toward hitchhikers.

As reported by police last week, there had been seven rapes and two attempted rapes of young female hitchhikers. They describe their assailant as a male Negro, approximately 6-0, 190-200 pounds, medium hair (not Afro), between 20 and 30 years old.

The four cases reported over the weekend also involve a suspect matching that description.

Scherer also indicated that his department has received "hundreds" of telephone calls from worried relatives of girls thought to be hitchhiking through the Santa Cruz area.

In addition to the reported rape cases, police investigators are searching for clues to the whereabouts of two UCSC coeds who were reported missing just over a week ago. The two missing girls are Rosalind Thorpe, 23, and Alice Helen Liu, 21. Both were last seen on campus

(Continued on Page 2)

Two Booked In Kidnap Ca[se]

RIVERSIDE (AP) — The [...] year-old daughter of a [...] erside super market execu[tive] was kidnaped from her h[ome] and found three days later [han]dcuffed to a bed in Burb[ank], police said today. Two me[n and] a woman were arrested.

The victim, Ellen Ann St[...], a University of Californ[ia] Riverside coed, was found [han]dcuffed to a bed Monday [in the] Burbank home of a ma[n and] wife who were arrested, [said] police Lt. Vic Jones.

Index

INTRODUCTION

The headline over the *Santa Cruz Sentinel* newspaper for February 13, 1973, read, "Crime Spree Soars —Another Murder." Fred Perez, 72, had been murdered that morning while doing yardwork. Just below the article on Fred Perez's murder was another article: a sixteen-year-old boy charged with the rape and murder of an elderly woman. To the right of that article sat "Body Identified As Cabrillo Coed," noting that the skeletal remains found two days earlier had been identified as Mary Guilfoyle. The article also mentioned the recently discovered remains of another Cabrillo College student, Cynthia Ann Schall. Below the fold were two more small articles. The first, "Four Other Rape Victims Reported," noted eleven recent rapes as the result of hitchhiking, and two missing UCSC co-eds, Rosalind Thorpe and Alice Helen Liu. The second article was about a UC Riverside student who had been kidnapped and raped by two men and a woman. What the hell was going on in the Santa Cruz area in the early 1970s?

Peter Chang (Santa Cruz County District Attorney):
It was a nightmare, an absolute nightmare.

Mickey Aluffi (Santa Cruz County Deputy Sheriff), 2019:
There was a period of time, in about an eight month time period, we had something like twenty-eight homicides. And we were a very small department. The Sheriff's Office and Santa Cruz Police Department, that was about all we worked on for a period of eight months.

Edmund Kemper, 1991:
When I was locked up originally they called it mass murderer. Anybody who killed more than two or three people was a mass murderer, whether it was all at one place or over an extended period of time and then in the early '80s they came up with this differentiation called serial killing. Which was living two lives basically. If one orients to the negative side of that living he would

13

say this person was living a cover life that was wrapped around doing those crimes and which couldn't be very realistic. Someone doesn't live their life to murder people. Their life was not set for that for birth.

Ward Damio (Author), 1974:
There is a new class of killers in the United States today. And as sure as they represent a new class, they identify the rest of American society as a class of victims without benefit of warning, motive or defense from their possible executioners.

Mickey Aluffi, 2019:
It was in this whole process where the famous statement made by Peter Chang, who said that Santa Cruz was the murder capital of the world. Believe me, those of us on that end of it, we felt it was that way. We were dealing with so many homicides that it was just incredible.

William Kelsay (Assistant to the Santa Cruz County District Attorney), 2019:
For three years it was a nightmare.

Terry Medina (Santa Cruz County Deputy Sheriff), 2020:
Back then the county would have about, I would say, on the average of five to seven or eight homicides a year. In 1972, I went to thirty-six homicides. And they're not all the same. Very different.

Randall Kane (Owner of the Catalyst club), 1974:
Mass murder is becoming increasingly popular as a form of self-expression. But it's not surprising when you have the example of the government. You know, the old My Lai bit and all that sort of thing. Possibly the sanctity of human life was largely sanctimonious in the old days. But the covers are

pretty much off now. I think when some of the finest examples of our society have made an example of the cheapness of human life, you can expect some mentally troubled jerks to take the lesson to mind.

Ward Damio (Author), 1974:
Any stranger can be your executioner.

William Kelsay, 2019:
We didn't want to admit it to the press, that we had two serial killers, immediately after the Frazier killing, killing at the same time.

Austin Comstock (Santa Cruz attorney, retired Assistant to the Santa Cruz County District Attorney), 2020:
It changed the attitude of an awful lot of people. It was a very frightening time.

Harold Cartwright (Investigator for the Public Defender's Office), 2020:
They were not, based on my opinion, copycats to anything. You had three mentally ill people. Just happened to be in Santa Cruz, operating at the same time. Two of them fit the M'Naghten Rule, in my opinion. The jury didn't have to wrestle with Kemper.

Ward Damio (Author), 1974:
They were nice-looking, middle-class, law-abiding citizens. They also shared another common trait: they were all former mental patients released from California state hospitals.

James Jackson (Santa Cruz County Public Defender), 2020:
People who do things like that are not normal. I don't know if they are insane, but they aren't normal.

JOHN LINLEY FRAZIER

In October 1970 John Linley Frazier murdered four members of the Ohta Family: Dr. Ohta, a well respected local eye doctor, his wife, and

Right: John Linley Frazier on his way to court for the first day of the sanity phase of his trial.

two sons. Along with the Ohta Family, he murdered Dr. Ohta's assistant, Dorothy Cadwallader.

Gary Hamby (Childhood friend of John Linley Frazier), 1970:

He [John Linley Frazier] wasn't like anyone I know. There's hippies and there's hippies, but he was far out.

Roger Krone (Neighbor of John Linley Frazier), 2020:

Physically, he was fairly short. He couldn't have been taller than 5'10" and he was sturdy. He was a real quiet person and he was hard to read. He was strange. I wasn't afraid of him, but I was twenty years old and naive.

Joe Cole (Neighbor of John Linley Frazier), 1971:

His eyes are strange and deep and some people would say mystical. Power…There's a generator working his head. You'd almost see it working.

James Jackson, 2020:

He never talked, not to us. I mean, when he did and he told us about his plans he laughed and I'll never forget that laugh.

Delores Frazier (Frazier's wife), 1970:

He did think that he had received a special message like a word from God telling him how really wrong the world was and how everybody had to get back to nature. He felt that he was the one who received the message and he was the one who had to tell the people.

He told me that he did hear a voice. He had a car accident and he was driving his car and he wrecked it and he said he heard a voice that told him that if he ever drove a car again he'd be killed. He told me that the very same thing he heard was written down in a book he asked me to read. *The Occult Philosophy*. I don't have it now, the DA took it. He wants me to read it because he says the exact words are in the book. He tried to find it for me but couldn't find it.

Harold Cartwright, 2020:

He once said to me, and it made the hair on the back of my neck stand up, "When God speaks to you, you answer!"

It was a moment I'll never forget.

HERBERT WILLIAM MULLIN

Between October 1972 and February 1973, Herbert Mullin murdered thirteen people. After the death of his best friend and excessive experimentation with hallucinogenic drugs, he began showing signs of mental illness and soon after began killing. He stated that he believed the murders would prevent earthquakes.

Terry Medina, 2020:

Herbert William Mullin was about 5'6" or seven. He weighed maybe 150, or maybe 140 pounds. He had darkish brown hair. I don't remember the eye color. He was slight of build. Not too tall. Remember, he was a lightweight football player.

He was definitely disturbed. He always looked very intense.

James Jackson, 2020:

Mullin was a genuine nutcase. He was hearing voices.

Chris Cottle (Santa Cruz County Assistant District Attorney), 2020:

He seemed to be more mentally ill, spacey, and he seemed to lack the appreciation of his conduct that Frazier had. Mullin had cut himself off from human contact.

Richard Koch (Childhood neighbor of Herbert Mullin), 2020:

Herb thought he was a hero in his own mind. He thought he was saving the world by killing these people. It was delusional. I really blame Ronald Reagan for all this. He shut down the psychiatric hospitals. I mean,

Left: Herbert Mullin and his public defender, James Jackson.

Herb tried to get himself committed before the killings.

Richard Verbrugge (Investigator for the District Attorney's Office):
He was a killing machine…I think he just got pleasure with killing people.

With Kemper, I think it was a means of compensating for his sexual inadequacies.

Edmund Kemper:
He [Mullin] was just a cold-blooded killer, running over a three-week period killing everybody he saw for no good reason.

Jim Conner (Retired Santa Cruz Police Officer), 2020:
I wasn't involved in the case [Mullin]. I was off work the day they caught him. But, one of my jobs working graveyard is that I had to go over to the jail to bring coffee and sandwiches to the prisoners. So, the following morning after he was arrested I brought the sandwiches and coffee and I go in there. He was there. I had never seen the guy until that morning and I'll tell you, I have never looked into someone's eyes like this guy. If you ever meet him, you'll know what I'm saying. It was just like looking in the black holes of the universe. It will give you a chill.

Chris Cottle, 2020:
It was undisputed that Mullin was mentally ill. The question was the degree. This was not true in Frazier's case, and with Kemper, it was no issue at all.

EDMUND EMIL KEMPER III

In 1964, when he was fifteen years old, Edmund Kemper murdered his grandparents. After being released by the California Youth Authority, Kemper went on to murder six girls and women, between May 1972 and February

1973. In April 1973, he murdered his mother and her friend, and turned himself over to law enforcement.

Paul Dougherty (San Mateo County Criminalist), 2020:
The conversations back then between law enforcement was, well, they always thought there were a lot more victims. […]

He [Kemper] was a giant. Something like 6'9", 280 pounds. His victims didn't stand a chance.

Edmund Kemper, 1988:
My father was 6'7". My mother was six feet even.

Harold Cartwright, 2020:
It was my job to find out what made people tick and I don't know that we ever did figure out what made him [Kemper] tick. Lunde testified and he said, basically, what he said in layman terms is that Kemper is so crazy, the Diagnostic and Statistical Manual has not caught up with him yet.

Terry Medina, 2020:
Kemper was much different than the other guys. I mean, he was very smart. Very high IQ—160 somebody told me. He was always thinking ahead of time, how law enforcement was thinking. What we were doing. He knocked the teeth out of skulls because he knew about dental records. He was pretty smart.

Peter Chang:
He was intelligent and had a fantastic recall. He could remember every aspect of his crimes down to the last detail.

Forrest Robinson (Friend and co-worker of Clarnell Strandberg, Kemper's mother), 2020:
I don't think he had an extremely high IQ. He was not stupid, by any means. But, I don't think he had an extraordinary intelligence. That was not my impression of him.

Right: Edmund Emil Kemper III on his way to court.

Mickey Aluffi, 2019:

I asked him if he had any sympathy for his victims. He thought about it for a while, and said, "No. I have sympathy for their families."

Joey Tranchina (Photographer), 2020:

He's basically a good guy driven by madness.

Richard Verbrugge, 2020:

I gave him the nickname Eddie the Cut-Up. He was constantly joking and trying to make friends.

Filmmakers Werner Herzog and Errol Morris visited Kemper in prison.

Werner Herzog (Filmmaker):

Very, very amazing. And Kemper was, in a way, a very sensitive person. When you looked at his hands, like the hands of a violin player, in a way. I remember he looked like an elephant with a Mozart soul.

Errol Morris (Filmmaker):

Yeah. That's the way Werner described him at the time. An elephant with the soul of Mozart. I'm not sure that most of the prison authorities would have described him in the same way, but at the time I found Werner's description very interesting. I thought for a long time about it. It made it situational, as if God in his infinite perversity had somehow mismatched Kemper's various attributes in order to produce some kind of nightmare, some kind of tragedy. I remember thinking, Yeah, if Othello had been in Hamlet's place, and vice versa, there would be no tragedy.

Robert Ludlow (Santa Cruz attorney), 2020:

He hated his mother. I think if he would have killed her first, maybe none of the other murders would have happened.

Clarnell Strandberg (Kemper's mother), 1965:

He thought he was going to throw me a "curve" this Sunday in telling me that basically he hates his mother…(kindly, but with an under-the-eyelid curiosity,) and with my layman-curbstone knowledge (they're the worst kind), I told him that I fully expected to come out the villain in the piece, and that I could only hope that continued therapy would rationalize me out as an non-error proof human and we could sustain some kind of warm relationship. My feelings for him are boundless, but I gave him the strictness in lieu of a father and having a homosexual nephew, not wanting to repeat my sister's mistake of overwrought love. I seem to have erred equally, and now he is where the thing I feared is abundant. I have tried to express this to him, but of course, he being the recipient…felt the result rather than the reason.

Edmund Kemper, 1973:

Chang said I'm not legally—they may have an argument here, "Kemper is medically insane. He is not legally insane, he is medically insane."

After Kemper confessed his crimes in Pueblo, Colorado to Santa Cruz District Attorney Peter Chang—

Peter Chang, 1973:

It was the worst and most horrible confession I have ever heard in my life.

Left: Peter Chang. Santa Cruz District Attorney from 1967 to 1975. This photograph was taken at the time of the Edmund Kemper trial.

EDMUND SR. AND MAUDE KEMPER THURSDAY, AUGUST 27, 1964

Harold Cartwright, 2020:
When Eddie Kemper was a teenager, he ran away from his mother's home up in Montana to his father's home in California. I think everyone knows he hated his mother.

Edmund Kemper, 1988:
I ran away from her [his mother] at fourteen to keep from a violent outbreak that I was convinced was coming. I was even dreaming about it, nightmares, if you will. And in fear I ran from Montana to my father in Southern California.

Edmund Kemper, 1988:
When I went to live with my father he had a new family, I wasn't getting along with my stepbrother or my stepmother, and he had tried to save as much of that situation as possible.

Edmund Kemper Jr. (Kemper's father), 1964:
His personality had changed so much that

I was worried about him being here with my present wife, who tried very hard to be a real friend to him. I saw him one day in a brooding mood and his eyes looked like a sleepwalker.

In several talks I had with him toward the last he seemed fascinated by death and war. Tried to watch *Weird Tales* on TV which I suppressed.

Edmund Kemper, 1988:
A month later I was placed with my grandparents, his [father's] parents.

Kemper turned fifteen years old on December 18, 1963. Kemper, his father, and stepmother went to visit his paternal grandparents in North Fork, CA.

Edmund Kemper, 2017:
I was moved in with my grandparents. Uh, what happened was it was Christmas time and all the family members went up there to their house, and, uh, for the holiday. My step-

brother didn't go this year and it turns out he—he understood why he didn't want to go is cause I was gonna be left up there. This was his mother telling him not to let me know. They were German—ethnic German, and, uh, she told him in German, uh, "Don't be telling him—what's happening."

Kemper's father and stepmother returned home to southern California, leaving Kemper with his grandparents in North Fork. Note that Kemper's nickname was "Guy."

David Dozier (Childhood friend and author, daviddozierbooks.com), 2020:
The Kemper family, his grandparents, moved to North Fork as retirees, so they weren't really a part of the indigenous cultures, such as it was. North Fork was really a logging

community for many, many—well that's how it got started.

By the way, it's not that unusual for kids to be raised by their grandparents in that community. There was a lot of poverty. A lot of alcoholism. Around fifteen percent of our schoolmates were Native American and they had a lot of problems in that community as well. A lot of kids, raised by their grandparents. Children out of wedlock. You just didn't talk about it. It was considered bad manners to ask. So, Guy Kemper coming to live with his grandparents would not be considered anything out of the ordinary.

David Dozier, 2020:
North Fork is basically a county road. It has stores on either side of it, but it doesn't even have a stop sign. When I was growing up,

and around the time Edmund Kemper was there, it was listed in the census as having around two hundred people but that didn't really account for all the people. If you went by everyone who used the post office there, it was probably closer to a thousand people. We lived about seven, eight miles outside of North Fork. All of the houses were reasonably far apart and that's one of the reasons the granddad, Edmund Kemper I [the first] settled there because you could buy a relatively cheap piece of dirt and build a house and live without having any neighbors. If that's what you wanted, it's a great place for that.

Edmund Emil Kemper I, was a retired electrician for the Division of Highways.

Edmund Kemper, 2017:
Well when he—I'd heard stories about when he was younger. He was a pretty fierce guy. He was an original cowboy. He carried a .45 on his hip. He was, uh, a tough guy wrangler, and my father had told me that he back-handed him clear across the kitchen one night when he got, I guess, smart with him.

Harold Cartwright, 2020:
In talking with him [Kemper], I really believe his grandfather was the only person he ever really loved.

David Dozier, 2020:
Guy arrived the summer before our freshman year in high school. I remember there was a house just to the north of our house, I think they were the Yorks. My mom was a school teacher and Mrs. York had been my kindergarten teacher, so Guy came out there with us. We played basketball with my brother John and my brother Forest. I was around

Above: The Kemper home in North Fork, CA.

fifteen, so my youngest brother would have been around ten. Well, Guy was around 6'4" and he picked up my brother and just held him up and he yelled, "Look I can hold your brother up!"

And that kind of freaked my brother out. When we went home he said, "You know, that guy is weird."

I said, "Forest, everybody's weird. This is a weird town."

But he might have been on to something.

David Dozier, 2020:

We didn't have a lot of contact that summer. It wasn't until we started school in September that Guy and I started having a lot of contact because we got on the school bus at the same stop and then as the weather got colder his granddad would drive us in his pickup truck. So I got to know them pretty well. I never got to know the grandmother that well.

Guy's grandfather was kind of a stoic guy. He didn't gab a lot. You know when you have two teenage boys, they basically dominate the conversation and think they're the most interesting people in the world. But, the grandfather would join in the conversation every once in a while. He was friendly enough. He was a retired person, you know, doing a favor for his grandson. What strikes me when I look back on it is how unremarkable Guy really was. Aside from being incredibly tall, there wasn't anything. There just wasn't anything about him that you could say, "Oh yeah, looking back on it I could see he would become a serial killer."

He did do some strange stuff. He put a needle in his hand. There was one other thing, another retired man, I think his name was Wyler. He passed away. I think the wife of the guy who passed away called Kemper's granddad. So, Guy and his grandfather went out to the house. When the coroner came he asked Guy to help him carry the body out because Guy was 6'4". Easy task for him. The thing that I remember about it was sitting with Kemper in his granddad's truck

or in the bus the next day and he was talking about the wife crying her head off and all upset and boo hoo hoo, and it showed a lack of empathy, but fifteen-year-olds showing empathy was not common. So, that didn't strike me as anything strange at the time. But he was also fascinated with carrying the body out and how they put it in the special bag. You know, all the details of getting the body ready for transportation, it was all of great interest to him. Now that we know he became a serial killer, we know he had a fascination with death from a very early age. It struck me that he seemed a tad obsessed with helping carry the corpse out of the house. That did stand out as being unusual at the time.

But as I said, aside from being unusually tall, he was unremarkable. I should add that being tall, being big, in a mountain community was gold. Because these people make their living sawing trees down. It was a lumber community. So, having a guy that got on the bus with me who was 6'4" was a bonus. My joke was, "Don't fuck with me because Guy Kemper's my bodyguard."

David Dozier, 2020:

I never thought Guy was any kind of a genius. This will tell you what kind of a prick I was as a teenager. Small man syndrome maybe. We went to Sierra High School and Sierra High School is in Fresno County. It was a geographically huge district. Huge. Some of the kids from Big Creek, which burned down this summer, lived in a dormitory. So, we had this long 45-minute drive to high school each day. Ninety minutes on the bus or in his granddad's truck each day. We didn't hang out a lot at school but enough for me to tease him, "You may be taller than me, but I'm smarter than you!"

I always gave him a hard time about being smarter than him. He didn't say much about it, maybe he knew he was smarter than me and didn't say anything, I don't know. But, there was nothing to indicate that he was a genius. He wasn't taking any of the college track courses. He wasn't on the college prep track.

Richard Verbrugge, 2020:

From what he told us, he was pretty happy there. When he got there his grandfather was really good to him. His grandfather bought him a .22 and taught him how to shoot it.

David Dozier, 2020:

North Fork is armed to the teeth. My brother that is still there, he has fifteen guns and that might be only slightly above average. It would be very normal for a grandfather to give his grandson a .22. There are two things people in my hometown collect: guns and automobiles. None of the automobiles run and are up on blocks, but it's a sign of a person's wealth there. But really it was a great place to grow up.

Harold Cartwright, 1973:

Did you ever kill any things, as a substitute for your mother, or whatever? Did you ever kill any animals or anything?

Edmund Kemper, 1973:

Every bird, gopher, flying thing, walking things, crawling lizard. Oh yeah, my grandmother loved those little furry friends, "Don't ever shoot any of our furry friends."

Boy, they were dying by the dozens, you know. I'd get out in the bushes there and just be blasting. She says, "What are you shooting at?"

I'd say, "Oh, trees and bushes and tin cans and rocks, and you know. Target shooting."

I'm dusting every bird I can and then I'd carefully dispose of the remains.

Harold Cartwright, 1973:

How did you dispose of them?

Edmund Kemper, 1973:

I'd just throw them off on somebody else's property, let them rot, you know. [Laughs] Just a bird. Big old quick one. But it got so bad, the birds started flying in a square line

right around the property, and it was that bad because I was shooting them in the air, on the wing. I was damn good with that. 22. I must have put twelve or thirteen hundred, oh God, maybe five or six thousand rounds through that gun. I had it since I was twelve and I was fourteen when I blew it, or fifteen. So I put every penny I ever had, I always bought .22 bullets when I was shooting. I was a gun [inaudible].

David Dozier, 2020:

The first hint that we had that Guy may have had some problems before he moved in with his grandparents, was—when the roads were really muddy some of the neighbors that lived way back down the road, before it was paved, would park their cars and walk home because they were afraid they would get stuck. We used to play touch football around there and set up a basketball hoop after a fashion. So, one of the neighbors had parked there and you have a group of kids thirteen, fourteen, fifteen years old and there's a car there that nobody's watching, and so gosh wouldn't it be a great idea to go pull all the wires off the distributor cap. I remember telling my brother Forest, "You know, this isn't like in the city where they have a bunch of other suspects. You pull those wires off the distributor cap and they're going to know who did it because you'd have to go twenty miles to find another group of teenage boys."

He did it anyway. The kids that got caught said, "Dozier was the lookout."

My dad assumed it was me and I wasn't about to rat out my little brother, so I had to go apologize to this guy. The guy we apologized to said, "Oh, so it was you guys. I thought it was that Kemper boy because I know he's had some problems."

An unsigned note from a Social Worker at Atascadero:

In February, 1964 ward's mother was allegedly drunk when she called ward's father in the middle of the night and told him that ward was "A real weirdo" and that he was taking a chance in having ward stay with his grand-parents and that he might be surprised if he awoke some morning to learn that they had been killed.

Richard Verbrugge, 2020:
The only trouble he'd ever have was with his grandmother. His grandmother was kind of masculine. This is in Kemper's opinion. She would do jobs that he thought he should be doing, Ed should be doing. She would relegate jobs like washing dishes, setting the table, et cetera, et cetera, use the vacuum cleaner. She told him to do this while she would go work on the farm.

Allyn Kemper (Kemper's younger sister), 1973:
They wouldn't let him bring any friends home. He couldn't get into any social activities in high school, any kind of group activities or anything. They gave him a rifle and told him to go hunt gophers. He couldn't watch cartoons and they screened any TV shows he watched. He couldn't read comics in the newspapers or comic books. It was really hard on him up there.

His grandmother, Maude Kemper, was a writer of boy's fiction. She was a strong woman, who reminded Kemper of his own mother.

Edmund Kemper, 2017:
Well she had placed herself in the position of being, in essence, my warden. And she said if you ever want to get to go live with your father again, you had better do what I say.

Edmund Kemper, 1973:
Well, I set up one fantasy where we had this outhouse half way down the hill, and I had this pump .22 with an exposed hammer, you know, and real old, but I had it rigged up to where it would hold seventeen rounds and never jam or anything, I could just hold the trigger and pump as fast as I could fire. I got real good at that. I could kill a rabbit at fifty

feet firing from the hip like that. Not with one shot, a little barrage and he's dead. And I'd get up about twenty feet away from the outhouse and I'd get myself all worked up in like a trance, you know—my grandma's in there taking a shit. And had this picture of a rose that she had painted and it was in glass and framed and everything, hung in there and I'd forgotten about that. I'm sitting there thinking, that's my grandma, she's sitting in there. I just went [makes shooting sound effects], straight across, just like a machine gun. I said bomb. Went over there and opened the door, and I wanted to see how much damage it would have done if she'd really been in there. It would have blown the shit out of that outhouse, went through both sides of it, you know. Also blew the shit out of the picture. Had to dispose of that. Put some holes through that.

But little things like that. I lured her out. She was an artist, by nature, and I lured her out one evening to go out and do some drawing out in this little arroyo that was on this property and my grandfather stayed up in the house. I took my .22 along obstensively [sic] to shoot some, you know, rabbits or something. They gave me twenty-five cents for every rabbit I killed, and a dime for every gopher I'd bring in. But not fine, feathered friends. That was totally out. And I went down there with her and we rapped and rapped and I ended up sitting behind her and I had the gun pointed right at her head—she's sitting there drawing and I'm sitting there with the gun ready to pull the trigger. I didn't have the nerve. The gap was still too far.

Early in the summer, Kemper visited his family in Montana.

Clarnell Strandberg (Kemper's mother), 1964:
Pressure must have been building. Mrs. Kemper wrote how happy he was with his gun and dog and "great authors and school" and it wasn't until the tragedy that I was told

by the father that he was beginning to worry and frightened them with his moods. I wish I had known.

Susan Swanson (Edmund Kemper's older sister), 1973:
So after that school year, while he was fifteen, he came home to Montana for summer vacation. I spent time with him, I was living back in Helena then, I was still married—in fact, I was three weeks away from having my third child. We spent a lot of time together. He seemed, oh, I don't know, he was…he could have fun, he could laugh, he could play and be silly and visit and stuff like that, but deep down he seemed awfully hurt. Like you know, it really sunk in that his dad didn't want him and this still intensified his love for his father. He just kept reaching and grabbing for him. So we took him fishing and all kinds of things and then he went back down to Madera and it was just, oh, a matter of a couple of weeks later that he killed his grandparents.

On August 27, Kemper's grandfather was running errands at the grocery store and the post office. His grandmother was working on a short story for Boy's Life Magazine, "Fire in the Cannon," in the kitchen. Kemper decided to go rabbit hunting and went outside to fetch his dog on the porch. He stopped and looked in through an open window.

Edmund Kemper, 2017:
Uh, basically I had gone to the window where my grandmother was typing and the dog was laying in the shade, my pet dog, Anka. And, uh, I went there to get the dog, I was gonna go hunting, and I stood there and I started having basically an emotional, uh—uh, I had a moment that I was, uh, going through my history with my mother, my,

uh, grandmother. They were a lot alike, my grandmother and my mother, very assertive, very aggressive, and, uh, self-confident. And, uh, while I was standing there not pointing the gun basically at my grandmother, but it happened to be in my—in my possession under my arm, and was held in her general direction. She didn't see it because she was facing away from me. But I started thinking about all the times and the years I had been dealing with my mother and my grandmother.

11—Funeral Services 22.

Lisle FUNERAL HOME

Schedule of Services
Two Chapels—One Location
CALAVERAS CHAPEL
L St. at Calaveras St.
JOHN N. LISLE CHAPEL
1605 L St.

SUNDAY:
3:00 PM
EDMUND EMIL KEMPER. Father of Robert H. Kemper, Edmund E. Kemper, Jr., and Raymond C. Kemper. Brother of Paul Kemper, Raymond Kemper and Walter Kemper. Seven grandchildren and three great grandchildren.
SERVICES: Community Church of Oakhurst
INTERMENT: Oakhill Cemetery

MAUDE HUGHEY KEMPER. Mother of Edmund E. Kemper, Jr., Robert H. Kemper, and Raymond C. Kemper. Sister of Albert Hughey, George Hughey, Mrs. Illa Barr, and Mrs. Alice Appel. Seven grandchildren and three great grandchildren.
SERVICES: Community Church of Oakhurst
INTERMENT: Oakhill Cemetery

Edmund Kemper, 1973:
I shot her twice in the head and once in the back.

William Helms (Chief Deputy Madera), 1964:
He shot his grandmother as she was sitting at her typewriter desk, where she was finishing the final draft of an adventure story for a boys' magazine.

Edmund Kemper, 1972:
I ran in the house to see what I'd done—there was blood from the right nostril like a faucet, one eye was open, one shut—I dragged her into the bedroom—I got a knife, stabbed her three times—the knife bent double.

When asked by law enforcement why he stabbed his grandmother.—

Edmund Kemper, 1964:
I didn't think she was dead and I didn't want her to suffer any longer.

Kemper later told doctors at Atascadero State Hospital that before moving her body to the bedroom, he wrapped a towel around his grandmother's head. He also stated that he did not plan the murder and if he had, he could have come up with a better plan than what had happened.

His grandfather returned home and Kemper went outside to greet him.

Edmund Kemper, 2017:
The words kept coming out in batches of different starts, and, uh, he wasn't paying any attention to it, uh, he was getting a little senile, not totally, you know, responsive to moments.

But he was walking around to the other side of his truck and he was gonna open the passenger side where there was a bag of groceries for me to take in, and I was arguing with myself trying to figure out what to do,

and it became very apparent in just a matter of minutes that there's no way I was gonna tell him what had happened to his wife of fifty years.

I was walking along behind him. I had the .22 in my hand. I tried to raise the barrel up and I couldn't.

Edmund Kemper, 1964:
Granddad was smiling at me. I didn't want him to see what I had done.

Edmund Kemper, 1964:
When he turned, I placed the rifle this far [indicating about thirty inches] from the back of his head and shot him.

Edmund Kemper, 2017:
Well neither one of them knew what happened to them. They were shot in the head so they went down immediately.

He dragged his grandfather's body into the garage, closed the door, and attempted to wash the blood away from the driveway.

William Kelsay, 2019:
He killed her because quote unquote, "I wanted to see what it was like to kill somebody."

Then he killed the grandfather, the only male of the people he killed, partly because he didn't want him to see what he had done and suffer as a result.

Richard Verbrugge, 2020:
He didn't know what to do, so he called his mother and his mother called the police.

Allyn Kemper, 1973:
She called the police and called him right back and kept him on the phone. He got off once to go look for the gun. He was going to kill himself. He came back to the phone because he couldn't find it. She told him just to sit on the step until the police come.

Edmund Kemper Jr., 1964:

Everyone has been told that they both died instantly, I think to save our feelings. But at the hearing I found out by the testimony of the coroner of the other wound on my mother.

It took two hours for the police to arrive at the scene.

David Dozier, 2020:

My sister was over in North Fork with my mom at the beauty parlor. The sheriff's deputy, who by the way lived just down the street, but he had no idea where the Kempers lived. I remember him knocking on our door and, you know, when the deputy comes and knocks on your door, there's some trepidation about what he's doing there. "How can we help you, sir?"

He said, "Do you know where the Kempers live?"

He seemed very nervous and I remember he was smoking a cigarette very quickly and very intensely. I could tell he was feeling very nervous. So, we tried to explain to him where to go and he said, "Okay, thanks." Of course he didn't tell us anything about what happened but it's a small town and everything travels at the speed of light. So, my mom and sister at the beauty parlor already knew there had been a shooting out at the Kemper house. They didn't know who had shot whom, but they knew that the police had been called.

That's all that we knew until there was a story in the Madera newspaper, "fifteen-year-old kills both his grandparents."

The story was that when he was asked, "Why'd you do it?"

Guy said, "Well, I was just mad at the world."

That's the quote that I remember from the newspaper. I don't know if it's what he actually said. I remember thinking, "Well, that's a fucked up way to show you're mad at the world, to kill the two people who took you into their home and gave you a second chance."

Kemper was tried and sent to the California Youth Authority and later to Atascadero Mental Hospital.

In order to prevent moving Kemper to a facility in Montana, his mother moved to Santa Cruz, California in 1965.

DEAN RICHARDSON
Most Athletic 4
Football 1, 2, 3, 4
Baseball 1, 2, 3, 4
Basketball 1, 2, 3, 4
Varsity Club 1, 2, 3, 4
Key Club 1, 2, 3, 4

TONI R
Best Pe

DEAN RICHARDSON THURSDAY, SEPTEMBER 9, 1965

Dean Richardson was a close friend of Herbert Mullin's. His death in a tragic automobile accident was the beginning of Mullin's psychological downward spiral.

Mullin and Richardson met at San Lorenzo Valley High School. The school lies about a mile and a half up Highway 9 from downtown Felton. I went to school there growing up. It is a beautiful campus where we would spend run days in PE jogging through the forest trails behind the school. Fall Creek State Park is back there with miles and miles of thick redwood forest. A beautiful place to grow up.

Herbert Mullin and his family moved to the area during his junior year.

Herbert Mullin, 2020:
I attended San Lorenzo Valley High School at their campus just north of Felton. I graduated in June of 1965.

Herbert Mullin, 2020:
I met Dean at the SLVHS football tryouts in August of 1963. Both he and I were on the first string offense during the 1964 season.

Lynn Scott (Friend of Dean Richardson and Jim Gianera), 2020:
Now, I wasn't best friends or really, really close with Dean, but he was just the nicest guy you'd ever want to meet.

He dated my best friend. And he was always so nice. He was just that guy that everybody loved. He was a jock, but he was so sweet and kind.

Barry Burt, 2020:
The Deacons and The Zeroes were clubs, and I don't remember if it was a car club or what. But, if you were in The Zeroes you were really cool. Dean was a Zero. Herbie might have been a Zero. I can't remember the other guys. Gene Curly was one. The Zeroes had green and black and The Deacons had brown and black. Their jackets had

Varsity Club

Officers

P. Kohman, M. Eddy, D. Taber, J. Ryan, G. Campbell, A. Salsbury, R. Bartholamew, L. Fraim, L. Fraim, J. Ginera, D. Richardson, H. Mullin, D. Neal, R. Raynal, G. Sterling, H. Locatelli, J. Esposito, J. Gho, R. Dewing

Homecoming Snaps

Queen
anna

King
Dea

leather sleeves. That was during high school, a high school group. It was kind of like a gang, but more like a club. Let's put it this way, they were not guys to be messed with. The Zeroes were really tough, but The Deacons were real badasses.

Herbert Mullin, 2020:
It [The Zeroes] was a football club. I remember playing catch and touch football after school. There was a root beer, hamburger drive-in in Felton, approximately 1 3/4 miles from the high school. We would meet there to have burgers and french fries after school and then go to our football practice.

Barry Burt, 2020:
Dean was just super nice to everybody. He was a great guy.

SLV Pass Play

Dean Richardson, a San Lorenzo Valley Cougar gridder, runs for short gain after hauling down a first quarter pass from quarterback Bobby Adams. Pursuing Richardson in right background is Mike Ottmar of the Hollister Haybalers.

Ottmar, who made the tackle on this play, was also outstanding on offense for the Haybalers. He gained 142 yards in 19 carries for a 7.5 average while directing the Hollister single-wing attack.

FUNERALS

DEAN RICHARDSON

Funeral services for Dean L. Richardson were held yesterday in the Wessendorf and Thal chapel at 2 p.m. with the Rev. Merwyn Johnson of the Community church of Boulder Creek officiating. Interment was at Felton cemtery. Pallbearers were Jeff Esposito, John Hooper, Harry Locatelli, Herb Mullin, John Ryan and Don Taber. Honorary pallbearers were Greg Campbell, Kevin Crain, Jim Gianera, John Gho, Pat Kelly and Paul Kohman.

Dean Richardson was a popular athletic senior at SLV who quickly befriended Mullin. Richardson was voted Most Athletic his senior year and was the Homecoming King.

Herbert Mullin, 2020: We were only good friends…it was not a love relationship. We hiked together in the redwood forests all around Boulder Creek. We swam together and played one-on-one basketball together. I enjoyed playing one-to-one catch with mitts and hardball, he was good at that.

What did Dean mean to me? He was the Homecoming King! I admired his athletic prowess.

On September 9, 1965, Dean Richardson was in a fatal car accident.

Jeff Esposito (High school friend of Herbert Mullin and Dean Richardson), 1973: I had seen Joe Bishop, Dean Richardson and Candy Anglin, and Mardean Richardson, who were all in the accident, maybe an hour before they got killed. They told me they were going down to Santa Cruz to pick up somebody at a dance. I saw them in Ben Lomond, and that was the last time I saw them.

Barry Burt, 2020: They were going up Graham Hill Road and hit a tree. Probably going too fast. Dean was a football hero. They named the football field at the high school after him.

Charmaine Falcon, 2020:
Jerry Bishop was driving. He was always teasing me and my sister. They were speeding up the hill going towards Santa Cruz and they hit a tree. And Jerry was killed. Dean was killed. His sister was injured really bad. And I don't know about the other person.

The California Highway Patrol reported that the car was traveling southbound and crashed on an uphill curve about a half a mile from Lockwood Lane. The vehicle left the road and traveled 327 feet through brush before crashing into a pine tree. They also noted that the accident was one of fifteen which took place over the Labor Day weekend.

Lynn Scott, 2020:
After that anytime I'd go to Santa Cruz, I'd see that tree and it was just awful.

Barry Burt, 2020:
The car crash with Dean might have pushed him over the edge, but there were other contributing factors. He got involved in artist communities in the Bay Area and he was into drugs.

Mullin built a shrine to Dean Richardson. He cried for days and was never quite the same afterwards.

Herbert Mullin, 2020:
My mental health, emotional health, became a very big problem after his passing. I feel now that he was on the verge of helping me get away from my parents/families' negative influence. That opportunity vanished when he passed.

Youth Dies; Crash Toll Rises To Three

The toll in the automobile crash that killed two persons outright on Graham Hill road Saturday night rose to three with the death in County hospital early today of Dean L. Richardson.

The 18-year-old Ben Lomond youth and his sister, Mardean, 16, were passengers in a car driven by Gerald S. Bishop, 19, also of Ben Lomond, when the car went out of control and smashed into a tree. Bishop and 15-year-old Candyce Anglin of Boulder Creek died in the crash.

County hospital spokesmen said today Miss Richardson's condition was "fair," and that she had a "good" night.

Calfiornia Highway Patrol reports indicate Bishop was southbound on an up-grade curve about a mile north of Lockewood lane. The car hurtled off the road, smashing through brush and sand before it careened into a pine tree.

Richardson was a 1965 graduate of San Lorenzo Valley High school and was a three-sport man. He was all league in baseball and also won three letters in baseball and football and two in basketball.

Richardson was the son of Mrs. Dorothea Johnson of Ben Lomond and Arnold Richardson of Kearns, Utah. Funeral arrangements are pending at Wessendorf and Thal mortuary.

In Brief

ses Space Decision

n, Tex. (AP). — Astronaut Gordon made the decision to abandon an another satellite during the recight.

the decision in order to conserve astronauts and ground controllers the fuel cell power-producing sys-

up during the second orbit August nd astronaut Charles Conrad Jr. nnedy, Fla. The Mission Control ed terminating the flight

SANTA CRUZ

Ward Damio (Author), 1974:
Santa Cruz is a place where there is no reason to hope and no excuse to despair.

I mean that the people go to California and from there to San Francisco or LA or Sacramento and eventually many of them go to Santa Cruz, a place so lovely it's difficult to leave and yet it is a place where there really is no money, no opportunities, no raises or promotions.

Peter Chang, 1998:
You can go from a crowded metropolis to a deserted forest in about three minutes, and that's why you have things happen here that would not happen anywhere else.

Santa Cruz, to me, has always felt like a place of extreme contrasts: an idyllic vacation spot with mild temperatures, beaches, the Boardwalk, and redwood forests. But the dark side here swings the pendulum to other extreme.

Mickey Aluffi, 2020:
There was a big transition towards the hippie movement in the early seventies. The University was new in town. Everybody was blaming the changes on the University. And that wasn't necessarily so. From my perspective, being born and raised in Santa Cruz, I saw it when the population was about twenty thousand people and it seemed like half of those were retired.

It's like the wintertime traffic, there is none. But come Memorial Day when the Boardwalk opens and brings in all the tourists. Right? You have total gridlock. And on weekends in the summer.

Highway 1 before the time you're talking about, in the early '60s, was a three lane highway: northbound, southbound, and a passing lane in the middle that was shared with the opposing traffic. And there were no overpasses.

So society was changing. With the hippie thing, and then the drugs; drugs became more prevalent.

Richard Verbrugge, 2020:

At that time, it was a lot of rentals, a lot of summer homes, especially the San Lorenzo Valley, a lot of summer homes. But when UC Santa Cruz came in, there was a big change in the whole area.

Then there was another change in California state law, which drew a lot of people to Santa Cruz. That's when they changed the welfare laws. Originally, you had to be a resident of the county where you receive welfare. California changed that. And right after that was changed, it was like they had red arrows pointing from the Greyhound bus station to the welfare office in Santa Cruz.

And some of the Santa Cruz County residents were kind of guilty themselves. Those people who owned the summer homes found that they could rent them, you know, at a reasonable price. You get tired of going to the same place every summer. So they started renting out a lot of the summer places and attracted a lot of people that you might not normally like living in the area.

From John Linley Frazier's petition to move the trial out of Santa Cruz:

With a 1970 population of 123,790, Santa Cruz County ranks twenty-third of Cali-fornia's fifty-eight counties, and has fewer residents than the county (Stanislaus) where the crimes in Fain took place. It is also the state's smallest county in area, other than the city-sized 'county' of San Francisco. Even the principal local newspaper, quoted herein above, characterizes Santa Cruz as 'this tiny county.'

James Jackson, 2020:

Santa Cruz was a lumber and fishing town, really. The University had just gotten there. My next door neighbor was a professor at the University. And one of the witnesses we used was David Marlowe. He was a friend and he was at the University at the time. The University had taken over. It was a small town. Watsonville might as well have been Antarctica, and still is to a lot of the people who go to UCSC. I mean, the infrastructure of Santa Cruz hasn't changed since the old conservatives were running it years ago. The town hasn't changed any. Look around. What the hell's different about it? I mean, I guess traffic's worse and they managed to put up a

Above: The Santa Cruz County Building being constructed. It was dedicated on October 21, 1967. Next page: Catalyst owner, Randall Kane.

toll booth at the wharf.

Roger Krone, 2020:
Santa Cruz was mostly older retired people who were conservative. The college was the big change. The Catalyst was originally set up to be just that, a catalyst between the University and the community. It worked pretty good that way.

THE CATALYST

The Catalyst Club is an iconic concert auditorium, located in downtown Santa Cruz.

James Jackson, 2020:
The Catalyst was one of the biggest things that ever happened to Santa Cruz.

Holly Harman, 2020:
You would come down there [The Catalyst] on a Friday, Saturday night and it was a hopping, jumping place. I mean there was music and they always had good bands and people would party down there, you know, even party outside and party inside and just hang out there and gather all together and get together. It was wild.

Roger Krone, 2020:
I started working for it when it was owned by the Consumer's Co-op of Santa Cruz. The Co-op was a bunch of University people and doctors and lawyers and people formed a co-op. The Catalyst was Al and Patti DiLudovico's idea.

Robert Ludlow, 2021:
UCSC wanted to have a liaison person that would be an interface between the staff and the administration. Al came out here and then the University refused to fund the position.

So Al and Patty, she was a folk singer, formed the first co-op in the state of California with a number of attorneys. Instead of being a liaison between staff and the university, Al and Patty created this liaison between the University and the community. That was The Catalyst.

Robert Ludlow, 2021:
Ron Boise, the sculptor, was in there every day. I used to have coffee with this guy every morning; turned out it was Neal Cassady. I ran down to the Hip Pocket bookstore and

bought a copy of On The Road and had him sign it for me. I'd been having coffee with him every morning for months. I remember one time I went in there and there was an old man sitting at a table with a young boy. I sat down next to him, "Mind if I join?"

Then it dawned on me who it was. It was Henry Miller and his son John. He signed a book for me too.

Roger Krone, 2020:
Randall Kane bought it from the Consumer's Co-op, they couldn't make money.

Harold Cartwright, 2020:

Randall Kane owned it and he was a transplant, a developer from Los Angeles County. I really liked—of course he's dead now. I really liked Randall Kane. Our law firm represented the Catalyst. Not only did we have the public defender contract, but we had a full private law practice. Randall was an easygoing guy. He rode around town on his bicycle. He was quite wealthy. I don't know that I ever visited his estate in Corralitos, but he told me about it. Apparently, he had five or seven kids or something and he built a little one bedroom house on the property for each of them. So he could get them out of the house.

He was a very intelligent business man. I think he had an impact on Santa Cruz.

Robert Ludlow, 2021:

Randall had money. He married a Vanderbilt. Anderson Cooper on CNN, he's a Vanderbilt. So they had money and Randall just brought in all sorts of—I remember seeing the Pointer Sisters at The Catalyst. I saw Chuck Berry there. […]

I feel that the neighborhood bars are homerooms. When you're still in school, you go to the homeroom. You're with your group. But if you're not a drinker anymore, it becomes the place where you eat breakfast. And in small towns, the breakfast place is the homeroom. The Catalyst was our community's homeroom. It was where we got the backstory on everything. It wasn't a surprising thing for me to find out that I'd been having coffee with Neil Cassady or that I sat down with Henry Miller. It was our homeroom. The worst part of this whole [COVID19] thing is that we've lost our homerooms. Even the kids aren't in school.

Harold Cartwright, 2020:

The Catalyst was a big gathering point, it started out in the St. George Hotel, but it moved since then. It was in a big open area then. It had peanut shells on the floor and it had a bar and you would find in the eve-

nings a lot of college professors, people from the University, and you would find people that were, I guess you'd call homeless now. People hanging out. Local attorneys. Just a melting pot.

Roger Krone, 2020:

The courthouse, the old county jail, the sheriff's office were all on Front Street. So all the county workers were at the Catalyst for lunch every day.

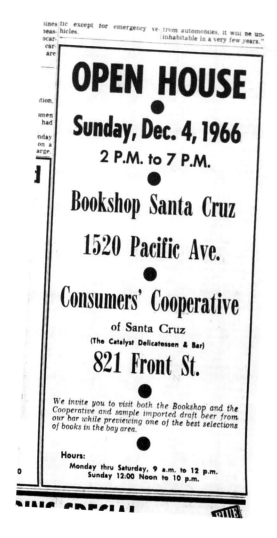

THE LEGAL SCENE

James Jackson, 2020:

At the time I got here there was a part-time judge in Watsonville. A full time municipal judge in Santa Cruz and two superior court judges and they were all easy to get along with because I was the only one there. We talked on the phone and rearranged calendars. The whole thing was so much easier. It was nice to do business as opposed to every time you turn around you have to file a document. This was just after they moved into the county building.

James Jackson, 2020:

Brauer was the part-time judge in Watsonville. He said, in essence, that the police department worked for justice and the DA so I could tell the police I wanted something done and they'd go do it. In Santa Cruz we had Judge May at the Municipal Court. He was kind of a softy. Judge Franich was the superior court judge along with Judge Perry, who people used to say was a racist. I don't think he was, but Tom Prosser and I would be in his courtroom and when a Mexican family would come through, he'd say, "You people are good people."

Prosser and I would be mouthing it as he said it. Every time he'd say that.

James Jackson, 2020:

[Franich] was a good guy. He tried to do the right thing and usually did. He was prosecution-minded but not horrible. He was quite easy to get along with. You got pretty much what you deserved in his courtroom. But he wasn't hard. For example, the same guy that I mentioned earlier, O.T. Hunt, he was a pimp, or one thing or another, and he got involved in some type of a big to do in front of the old Catalyst area. Back then everyone had a nickname, it was O.T. and this guy and that guy and one thing or another and I kept using all these nicknames and pretty soon Peter Chang couldn't figure out who was who and Franich couldn't figure out who was who and when I made a motion for acquittal, he threw his hands up and said, "I don't know what's going on!"

And he acquits him. That's the sort of thing they did back then.

RICHARD VERBRUGGE

Richard Verbrugge, 2020:

Well, to start with, I'm a Korean War vet. I got out of the service and I became a California state policeman. The California State Police isn't even in existence now, but I was with them for about three years and then I came to work for the Sunnyvale Department of Public Safety. That's when we moved to San Jose, to the home we have right now. That was in 1960.

I got promoted to detective and worked several homicides. My first experience with homicides was in Sunnyvale. One was a woman who was giving abortions and that was illegal at the time. She killed a girl in Sunnyvale and that was my case. And then we had an officer killed and that was my case, one of my cases. But I had several other homicide cases there. Sunnyvale, I don't know if you know this, is a public safety department, police and fire together.

And I found that policemen in the department weren't getting promoted as fast as firemen. I had a good friend who I was partners with in the State Police. He was with the state narcotic bureau. So I returned to the California State Service and I became a narcotics agent for the California Department of Justice, Bureau Narcotic Enforcement.

My first office was in San Diego.

I was there for a while and then an opening at the San Francisco office opened up and I transferred there, which was the closest office to my hometown. We had bought a house in the area and we had rented it while we were in San Diego. So now we were able to move right back into my own home. And I was there for quite a few years. And my partner and I worked—we were part of the out of town crew. We had guys that worked in San Francisco proper. But my partner and I worked out of the area, so to speak. We worked the whole peninsula down to Monterey County, down to Morro Bay.

We were making a lot of cases at the time in Salinas and Salinas was kind of a, you know, bad area with a lot of heroin dealers which was kind of our bag at the time. We met a young man, the young prosecutor, who was prosecuting the narcotic cases named Peter Chang. That's how I came to meet Peter.

Peter was working for Monterey County at that time and came to find out that not only was he working, you know, the narcotics prosecutions, but he was doing a lot of homicide prosecutions involving inmates at the Soledad Prison. And that's where he was getting really a lot of experience in homicides. And so we became friends.

His investigator at the time was a guy named Ray Belgard, who became a good friend to me, too.

TERRY MEDINA

Terry Medina, 2020:
I was born and raised in Santa Cruz. A west side kid. I went to all the local schools, Bay View, Mission Hill, Santa Cruz High School, Cabrillo College.

It was in the mid-sixties when they started a program called Police Science, and they had their own police department made up of students that were paid. They were all the second year students. And a guy by the name of Gene Wright was the head of that program. He had worked at Fresno PD, retired, and he was pretty highly educated. So he started that program and the Cabrillo Police Department.

I kept seeing all these young guys [student police] driving around the school and doing all kinds of stuff and that was interesting to me. So I go meet Gene, right? He tells me to take a lab at two o'clock in the afternoon or some damn thing. I can't remember exactly what it was. "Patrol Procedures" or something. And I walked out of that class two hours later and I knew I was going to do that for the rest of my life.

I was eighteen years old. I accelerated in that program, became a campus police officer in addition to being in the program.

The highest student rank, the highest paid student rank, was a Captain and I made Captain fairly soon.

And then in '66, I think it was '66. There was an internship opening at the DA's office. And so they took two campus policemen from Police Science, me and a guy named Terry Baluki who later went to work at Capitola PD and then went to San Jose PD. So he and I went to work there in the DA's office. And the DA at the time was a guy named Richard Pease.

Well, Richard Pease was in an election. It was an election year. Me and Terry Baluki arrived oblivious to the fact that there was an election going on. And so within a few months, Richard Pease loses the election. He was beaten by a guy named Peter Chang.

PETER CHANG

Harold Cartwright, 2020:
Peter grew up in Atherton or up around there. I think he went to Stanford and played in the band. He and I spent a lot of time together. When he'd get real drunk, he'd talk about his mother. He never had a good relationship with his mother. His father, I guess, was the first Korean-American submarine commander.

Richard Verbrugge, 2020:
He [Chang] went to Stanford University and then to Stanford Law School. He was in the same year with a guy by the name of Gary Britton, and Gary Britton also went to Stanford Law School. The same class.

Gary Britton was supposed to be, you know, kind of the conservative type. And Chang was Mr. Liberal at the time. Well, as it turned out, Gary Britton came to Santa Cruz and became the public defender. And Peter Chang came as the district attorney. And they were always good friends as well as friendly adversaries. They complemented each other.

Austin Comstock, 2020:
The DA's office had been a little set of offices in an annex, where the museum is now. Max Walden took it over and renamed it the Cooper House. That building, the old courthouse, was taken down in the [1989] earthquake.

Chris Cottle, 2020:
He [Peter Chang] had been a District Attorney in Monterey. He lived here, in La Selva Beach. He decided to run for office. The former District Attorney was kind of unpopular, Dick Pease.

James Jackson, 2020:
We had Dick Pease and he was a real lightweight.

Austin Comstock, 2020:
I had been working in the DA's office two years before and the first thing Chang did, he contacted me to see if I was going to run for DA. I said, "No."

And he asked me to be his campaign manager. Pease was not a very popular guy. He was very pleasant in a lot of ways. He liked to go up and smoke cigarettes in the county jail and talk to the jailers. He had come from Los Angeles, from the prosecutor's office down there. Of course, later he had been indicted for misuse of funds. That was about five years after he left the DA's office. He ran off with a trust account. He was gone for years and the last I heard, someone saw him up in Colorado, working in a bakery.

Mickey Aluffi, 2020:
Peter was kind of an eclectic guy, but he loved his music. He loved to play in bands. And he used to hang out at the Catalyst and that sort of thing. And he'd like to tip a few. But he was a brilliant guy.

Austin Comstock, 2020:
Peter was an excellent musician. When we would campaign, if you want to call it that, some of the people really critical to his elec-

tion would meet at Peter's house down in La Selva Beach. Henry Mello, who became supervisor, would play the piano. Joe Crossetti, who's family went way back and owned the Crossetti Ranch, he played the clarinet. Wally Trabing, a columnist from the *Pajaronian*, would play the drums. Malio Stagnaro would come down sometimes and he liked to sing Volare.

Peter Chang won the election in a landslide. 23,826 votes for Chang and 10,450 votes for Pease.

Peter Chang, 1967:
I feel the decision is not so much a vote against the present administration as it is a vote for me for one reason: I've knocked on over 9,000 doors and the response I received was a very friendly one, generally.

There are very few streets in Santa Cruz I didn't walk on.

Terry Medina, 2020:
So Peter Chang got elected and that pissed everybody off in the DA's office, or at least the investigators, and they all quit. Because Peter, well, it was just going to be different. And it was a small office. There was like maybe four attorneys.

Austin Comstock, 2020:
He [Peter Chang] took that office to about eight or ten lawyers and really built up that office. This corresponded with the building of the new county building in 1967.

Terry Medina, 2020:
Peter Chang brought over from Monterey a guy that he had been working with in the Monterey DA's office as an investigator for years, Ray Belgard. And those two guys had handled a lot of murder cases out of the prison down below Soledad.

Chris Cottle, 2020:
With Chang, came Ray Belgard who was a very popular cop in Salinas. A really good

guy who ended up running the office from an administrative standpoint.

Harold Cartwright, 2020:
Ray Belgard was a prince of a man. He was the Chief Assistant in the DA's Office. He was Peter's moral conscience. He was Peter's brain.

Mickey Aluffi, 2020:
You know, if he [Ray Belgard] said something you knew he meant it. You know, he eventually became the Chief of Police in Watsonville. He's the one that brought Terry and I in. He's the one that brought us to Watsonville. He retired and subsequently became the supervisor for Watsonville. He was a supervisor for eight years. Great guy. He would back you up until the world caved in.

Terry Medina, 2020:
When Chang made Belgard the number two guy in the office that pissed off the lawyers. And the investigators all quit anyway because they really liked a guy named Ole Thomp-

son, who was the Chief Investigator before.

So they all quit. So, yeah, they wound up with two eighteen-year-old kids for investigators, in Medina and Baluki. And we didn't know shit from apple sauce, basically. Chang and Belgard started hiring people. And my job was to drive them around to get their medical exam and their papers and shit.

James Jackson, 2020:
The people he had working there when he got there were incompetent. They were Dick Pease people. They didn't know anything. Anyway, Peter tried to hire decent people.

Part of Chang's new crew was Bill Kelsay and Chris Cottle.

Harold Cartwright, 2020:
He [Bill Kelsay] was hired very shortly after Peter was elected. He came from the Central Valley. His father was the sheriff over there.

Chris Cottle, 2020:
I got out of law school in San Francisco in '66. I worked in San Jose for a couple of years as an attorney. In '68 I came here. It was a great beach town. We were coming over on the weekends and decided we wanted to try and live over here. I got a job at the DA's office working for Peter. It was a small office. Seven or eight attorneys. In those days we didn't have a lot of investigators, maybe one.

Austin Comstock, 2020:
Chang was very proud of being the very first Korean DA in the United States.

Peter Chang, 1991:
No one at that time thought an Asian could stand toe-to-toe with an Irishman in a criminal courtroom.

To Perform

Peter A. Chang of LaSelva Beach will perform a program of Rafael Mendez Spanish classics for members of t h e Santa Cruz Music club today at 3:30 p.m. at the Santa Cruz Woman's club. Chang is an accomplished classical and jazz trumpet player who studied with Henry Bubb of the San Francisco symphony. He soloed with Louis Armstrong in three concerts when 14 years old and played professionally while attending Stanford university and the Stanford Law school. He is presently a soloist with the Watsonville band and will be a soloist with the Santa Cruz Symphony in May. Also on the program will be David Johnson, pianist, who will perform Piano Concerto in D Minor by J. S. Bach. He will be accompanied on a second piano by his teacher, Bela Szilage of the University of California, S a n t a Cruz.

Johnson, son of Dr. and Mrs. Stanley Johnson, is president of the Santa Cruz High school student body and organist at Messiah Lutheran church.

(Political Advertisement)

"MEET PETE!"

AND THE FAMILY

**THE CANDIDATE
PETER CHANG,**
was born in Honolulu

Pete's mother, born in Riverside, Calif. Raised by her grandfather who was the first Korean Methodist Minister in the United States.

THE PETER CHANG FAMILY
(from left to right)

Catherine, age 10, "Tisa" (dog), Pete, son Peter 3rd, aged 9, "Buster" (cat), wife Maybelle and son Christopher, aged 1 year

PETE'S FATHER
Born in 1903, Oakland, Calif. Served 24 years in the U.S. Navy. First person of Oriental extraction to receive an officer's commission. During World War II in charge of Submarine Force Torpedo School at Pearl Harbor.

PETE'S GRANDFATHER
Distinguished Diplomatic Minister to United States translated the Holy Bible into the Korean Language.

PETE'S FATHER (1966)
Now a manufacturing engineer for Ampex Corp. Living with Pete's mother in Palo Alto.

MORE ABOUT PETE

- Attended public schools in Honolulu and Palo Alto
- Graduated from Stanford University in U.S. History
- Received Law Degree from Stanford 1961
- Received over $2,500.00 in Scholarships
- Worked 40 hours a week, midnight shift while attending Stanford

- Resident of La Selva Beach for past five years
- Musician, Symphony Soloist, Composer
- Surf Fisherman and Watercolorist

- Served as welfare investigator and later Chief Trial Attorney for Monterey County during the past five years, all the while residing in La Selva Beach
- Established a professional reputation of brilliance, candor and earnestness
- Author of articles on Criminal Law Subjects

Elect Peter CHANG DISTRICT ATTORNEY

CITIZENS FOR CHANG COMMITTEE—NICK DROBAC, CHAIRMAN(DISTRICT ATTORNEY 1957-62)

Right: Chang was sworn in by County Clerk, Tom Kelley on January 2, 1967, at noon. Chang's wife, Maybelle, watches the proceeding.

47

Chris Cottle, 2020:
You wouldn't imagine that Santa Cruz, as conservative as it was, would have elected a Korean American at that time. But it happened and he turned out to be a very good District Attorney.

James Jackson, 2020:
Peter was my best friend at the time, which was funny because he was the DA and I was a conservative and a public defender. But he turned that office around.

Terry Medina, 2020:
Chang was this really interesting guy. He was very brilliant. He smoked like crazy. Everybody smoked back then, but he smoked a lot. He was very, very trial savvy. He had a lot of trial experience. He loved going to trial, but he loved winning more than anything. That was important. And so I was there for over a year just learning how to interview people because I was interviewing five people a day for child support in paternity cases.

Richard Verbrugge, 2020:
Mr. Chang worked wild hours. The DA's office is on the second floor of the County Building and his office was on the western end of the building, right on the corner overlooking the parking lot and the hotel next door. So you could see him up there at night with his light on and his desk just loaded with all the different cases he was working on.

Edmund Kemper, a regular at the Jury Room bar across the street from the County Building, saw Chang working at night through that window and confessed to District Attorney investigators after being caught that he contemplated using a rifle with a scope to assassinate Peter Chang from the parking lot of the Jury Room.

Harold Cartwright, 2020:
He [Peter Chang] was mysterious. He had a file drawer which was the lower left drawer in his desk and it was locked, always locked.

He had the key. That was the "Dead End File." What it basically meant is, he would never withhold something that he thought was exculpatory evidence or could lead to exculpatory evidence, but if there was something he considered to be a red herring that we could throw in, he would make the decision that he didn't pass it on. He threw it away. Things that were fully checked out by law enforcement to his satisfaction, this was his standard, his moral standard. When he was satisfied, "Oh, I could just see them using this as a red herring. I'm going to put it in the Dead End File."

Chris Cottle, 2020:
One thing you will hear from everybody is that Pete did like to drink. He wasn't a beer drinker. He drank hard alcohol. I remember him drinking vodka quite a bit.

Sam Robustelli, 2020:
He loved his scotch and milk. The first time, after we had been working late and he took me out for an evening libation. He ordered a glass of milk and scotch. I'd never heard of it.

Harold Cartwright, 2020:
During the murder cases we got to be close. Every Friday my wife knew that I was not going to be home until very late. Peter would call me up at three o'clock, four o'clock, "Harold, I got this information for you. It just can't wait 'til over the weekend. I want to give it to you. Can you meet me at, whatever bar?"

Right over here, Callahan's. I would say, "Peter, you're full of shit. You don't have anything."

"Oh, Harold, you're going to want to work on this, this weekend."

"I don't want to work this weekend."

We'd have this conversation almost every Friday. It went on for over a year. This was in the Kemper, Frazier, Mullin time.

He would show up with nothing in hand, of course. We'd play Liar's Dice and get drunk. He loved Liar's Dice.

Harold Cartwright. 2020:

On a couple of occasions, Peter would get staggering drunk. No way I could let him drive. So I would call Santa Cruz PD. Chuck Scherer was Chief of Detectives, but I knew all of them. I'd say, "I've got Peter down here at Callahan's and he should not be driving. Can you help me out?"

"We'll have somebody over there in a few minutes."

We'd get Peter in his car, I would drive him, I was probably a 2.0. I would drive, Peter was a 3.0. The officer and I would take him home and he lived up on the second floor, there was a garage downstairs or something, I don't remember, but you had to go up stairs. The officer and I would get him up there and we'd sit him down on the floor with his back to the door. And we couldn't face Maybelle, his wife. We'd knock and run.

Harold Cartwright, 2020:

Peter was a good guy. I miss Peter. Hard drinking. Diabetic. The end was inevitable.

Austin Comstock, 2020:

Peter would always keep his head sideways. Tom Black and I used to tell him, "Keep your goddamn head up! You look like you're going to sleep."

It was a habit of his.

Sam Robustelli, 2020:

Pete was like all the successful attorneys I've seen in court over the years. They never ask questions they don't already know the answers to.

Richard Verbrugge, 2020:

He [Chang] was very fair in his cases and taking dispositions. And he never over-charged a case. You know, some prosecutors would overcharge a case or charge a defendant with the very maximum that he could charge him with. I'm not talking about homicides. I'm talking about general crimes where Chang took everything into it, he took the individual defendant into consideration. And I think that really paid off, at least in the long run.

Terry Medina, 2020:
In 1968 I got hired by the Santa Cruz PD. But before I reported for my first day, I got notified by the Sheriff's Office that they wanted to hire me. And I wound up going to work for them. The reason why that occurred is because the Sheriff's Office was the mentor agency for the Cabrillo College Police Science Program. I already knew everybody in the sheriff's office. It was already like a home to me. So that's where I wound up going to work in 1968.

Wally Walker was there already. Stoney Brook was there. We were like these new guys. We thought we were the new breed. We're not going to be like these old guys.

So when I started the Sheriff's Office was over on Front Street, where the McPherson Museum is now. The jail was on the third floor. Walker and I got promoted to the second floor, which was the detective bureau. There were about eight detectives there.

So things are rolling along. I'm fortunate that I'm doing pretty good. Walker's doing good. Young guys are coming on. Walker and Aluffi, they're a little older than I am. But I think I started before them.

Peter Chang was re-elected in 1970.

William Kelsay, 2019:
When the news of the Ohta family killing took place, Peter was in my home in La Selva Beach. We were actually, ironically, talking about our choice of Santa Cruz to start a career as district attorneys and we both recognized the plus of a beautiful, quiet, community where nothing much happened. All of the sudden, the phone rang. It happened just like that.

THE OHTA FAMILY AND DOROTHY CADWALLADER MONDAY, OCTOBER 19, 1970

Dr. Douglas Liddicoat, a close friend of Dr. Ohta's, wrote this thoughtful remembrance after Dr. Ohta was killed.

Douglas Liddicoat, 1970:
The life of Dr. Victor M. Ohta reads like the classic American dream.

He was born in Montana, the third child and the second son of an immigrant father, who before marrying in middle life, had raised himself from poverty to moderate affluence and sent seven younger brothers through Japanese medical schools.

In 1941, his father, being unable to attain U.S. citizenship, lost everything (as an enemy alien).

Young Victor began Montana State College the following fall, working at odd jobs to support himself, and to aid his parents, during summers working as a gandy dancer on the Great Northern Railroad. He enlisted in the Army in 1943 and served until 1945. An older brother, Os, was killed in Europe in the Air Force in 1945.

Mustered out, Victor returned to college and was admitted to Northwestern University medical school in 1946. Being now the main supporter of his parents, he went to school all day, drove cabs most the other night, and graduated in the upper third of his class in 1950.

Married that year to Virginia Tobias, of Streator, Ill., and with a family soon on the way, he re-entered the military, serving two years as a flight surgeon. Determined to be an eye specialist, he returned to Northwestern University as a resident surgeon with an almost nonexistent wage.

The sudden death of his first son, attendant burial expenses, again found him penniless and to finish his eye training he re-entered the Air Force, serving an additional four years, resigning his commission in 1960, a major, now with four children, three cats, all old furniture, all made by himself, and a Volkswagen bus.

Everything except the furniture arrived in Santa Cruz in that bus in late 1959 and after

Dr. Victor Ohta
Begins Practice

Ophthomologist Dr. Victor M. Ohta, has joined Dr. Howard Trolan at offices at 515 Soquel avenue.

Dr. Ohta, an eye physician and surgeon, left the air force in September after spending three years at Wright-Patterson Air Force base in Dayton, O. While there he was head of the ophthalmology department of the hospital. He held the rank of major.

Dr. Ohta received his medical training and residency at Northwestern university. He and his wife, Virginia Ann, and five children, live at 112 Roger drive.

Ohta hung out his shingle, his success was immediate and almost phenomenal.

At the time of his death he was one of the busiest eye surgeons in California. To his friends, he was always gracious and comparably generous, the epitome of a true gentleman. To his detractors, especially when their attitude smacked of intolerance, he was cutting, showing the samurai blood which flowed in his veins.

He was to me the finest man I ever knew.

Dr. Louis Wileman (associate of Dr. Ohta), 1970:

Never once did I hear him speak an angry word to anybody. He was a compas-

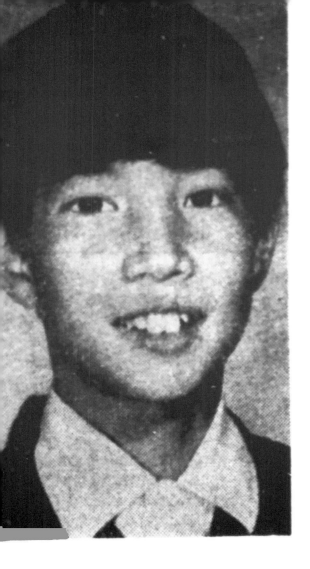
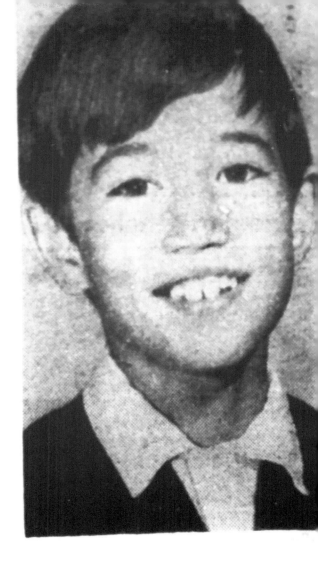

sionate, non-violent type of person. Dr. Ohta was always friendly and always generous to give to charitable organizations.

Lark Ohta, 2020:
My father went to medical school through the Air Force and he received his degree at Northwestern in Chicago—he became an ophthalmologist. While still in the Air Force, he flew over Santa Cruz, and he said, "That's where I'm going to start my practice when I am done."

At least, that was the story—that is what I always heard.

Before we moved to California, my father was finishing his Air Force service at the Wright Patterson Base in Dayton, Ohio. That is where my two little brothers, Derek and Tag were born. I was born in Chicago while my dad was still in medical school, I believe Taura was born there, as well. We also had another brother who was one year younger than Taura, but he died before I was born. He wasn't even two years old when he died. He was eighteen months when he caught pneumonia and he became sick very quickly. My father was working at the hospital on the base when my mother brought Kevin in, and he died within twenty-four hours. I know it was traumatic, and it was another two years before they even considered having more children. I am three years younger than my sister, and Derek and Tag were three and four years younger than I was. When my dad finished in Dayton, Ohio, we loaded up our VW van, and all six of us drove cross country to Santa Cruz.

Lark Ohta, 2020:
We arrived in 1960 in our VW van. My parents had taken all the seats out of the middle section and filled the space with my brother's playpen.

Tag was only one. Derek was two, I was five and Taura would have been eight.

Lark Ohta, 2020:
Oh, Santa's Village. It was the best. It feels like it was yesterday. We had driven from Dayton, Ohio to Santa Cruz, and the first thing that I saw as we came down the hill on Highway 17—was Santa's Village. It was my first memory of moving to Santa Cruz, and it always makes me smile.

Lark Ohta, 2020:
Santa Cruz was different then. There were no hippies yet, and there was no University, and it was mostly tourists all summer.

I would ride my bike all the way up the old River Road to Felton. Past Harvey West and I remember the smell of Salz Tannery. I would be gone for ten hours. So different now.

Lark Ohta, 2020:
When my family first came to Santa Cruz, it was the perfect town for my father's practice. It was largely a retirement town where lots of people were older, and they wore glasses. That sounds funny now, but that is what I remembered as a child.

My dad was a magnanimous man and I thought he was very handsome.

He was generous and outgoing and friendly and he was just a good man. He was loved in that community.

He started in a little office space while he was building his practice and then later built his larger office complex where partnered with an Ear, Nose & Throat Surgeon.

During that same time, we lived in Santa

Cruz, up on the hill where UCSC would later be built—but this was 1960 and there was no college yet.

We lived in a big neighborhood with lots of kids, and we went to Holy Cross School because my mother was Catholic. And the whole time we lived there, they were looking for land where they could eventually build their dream house.

Lark Ohta, 2020:
My father brought both sets of parents to Santa Cruz to live. He bought a little house for my Japanese grandparents right above his office, near Branciforte Junior High, so that he could be nearby. His sister and her husband lived in a connecting house to also help with the language situation.

My Czechoslovakian grandparents lived in a trailer park, close to Pacific Avenue on the edge of the San Lorenzo River. I was very close to my grandmother and I spent at least 1–2 nights a week with her, while we lived in the Santa Cruz house. We would walk to Pacific Avenue and get a snack at the Woolworth's counter, then pick out materials for her to help me sew my doll clothes. She lived so close to Holy Cross School that I frequently walked to her house for lunch. We remained very close until she died in 1980.

Lark Ohta, 2020:
I was his person. My sister was super close to my mom and I was my dad's person. We would go on rounds, every Sunday and he would check on his surgical patients. I always went with him. When we finished, he would take me to a small tobacco store on Pacific Avenue, and let me pick out comic books. *Archie, Richie Rich, Little Dot*—I read a lot of comic books. The fat ones were 25 cents and the skinny ones were twelve cents.

Lark Ohta, 2020:
I always felt special because I was so super close to him. We would go to the movies at the Del Mar Theater, and if he was on call, he would need to leave and go to the Emer-

gency Room, if called. I don't think they even used pagers back then—he would leave his name at the candy counter and tell the hospital where he would be and then someone would come find him in the loge seats. He would leave me in the balcony, go to the hospital, and then come back and watch the end of the movie with me. The movie would be mostly over and I would always have to tell him what happened.

Lark Ohta, 2020:
My mother had also come from an immigrant family, and she worked hard with my dad to make a good life for our family. She was the strongest and most determined person that I knew, and I loved her deeply. In those days, doctor's wives worked on auxiliaries and charities, and she was very involved in the community.

We were both tiny and looked alike in that way, and that always made me feel especially close to her. I mostly remember that she was very stylish. She was so beautiful and I thought that she always looked perfect. She had amazing '60s outfits. Mini skirts, fishnet stocking, flat Capezio shoes, and wonderful blonde hair. I used to just stare at her.

And she always posed like she was getting a picture taken—she always seemed to be striking a pose. I was in awe. Losing my mother was unbearable.

Dr. and Mrs. Ohta designed their home together with architect Aaron Green, a protégé of Frank Lloyd Wright.

Lark Ohta, 2020:
They searched for that lot forever, and when they found it, they had to dig a well, and they had to build a road. They had to do everything, it was simply a piece of empty land in the country where they were going to build their dream home There were ten acres and when they finally began building, they were super conscientious about what was already there.

My mother loved my dad's Japanese culture. The whole family helped to build a Japanese garden, and during construction, they were careful to not cut down even one tree. The architect even designed a covered deck which allowed an existing tree to grow through an opening in the roof.

Lark Ohta, 2020:
I mostly remember my mother working on the house—designing it with the architect, working on plans. She was very strong and she always knew exactly what she wanted. She had amazing taste. I also remember her weaving the material for the bedspreads and pillows on a huge loom that sat near the fireplace in the Soquel house.

Lark Ohta, 2020:
I wanted to stay in our first house in Santa Cruz—the house in the big neighborhood. I felt safe in that home, and that is what I liked. That was me. I wasn't built to live in a large, elegant home in the country. It made me feel out of place, lonely, and frightened. It was my mom and dad's dream, and everyone else was fine—but it always made me uncomfortable.

Early on, my dad bought a Jaguar XKE and I thought it was an ostentatious car—and he wasn't an ostentatious person. He was a decent, good person. But he just liked nice things. He had come from nothing—from immigrant parents who worked on the railroad and who never even spoke English. He had worked hard, and he enjoyed being able to afford nice things for himself and for his family. When Santa Cruz started to change in the mid-'60s and hippies and college students started coming in, it was very confusing for my father. He was a man who had come from nothing, and had worked hard to build a successful life, and now he was being called a capitalist—and that was a bad word in 1965. He didn't get it, and it hurt him. It was such a changing time.

Ami Chandler (Neighbor of the Ohtas), 1970:
Very nice people for wealthy people.

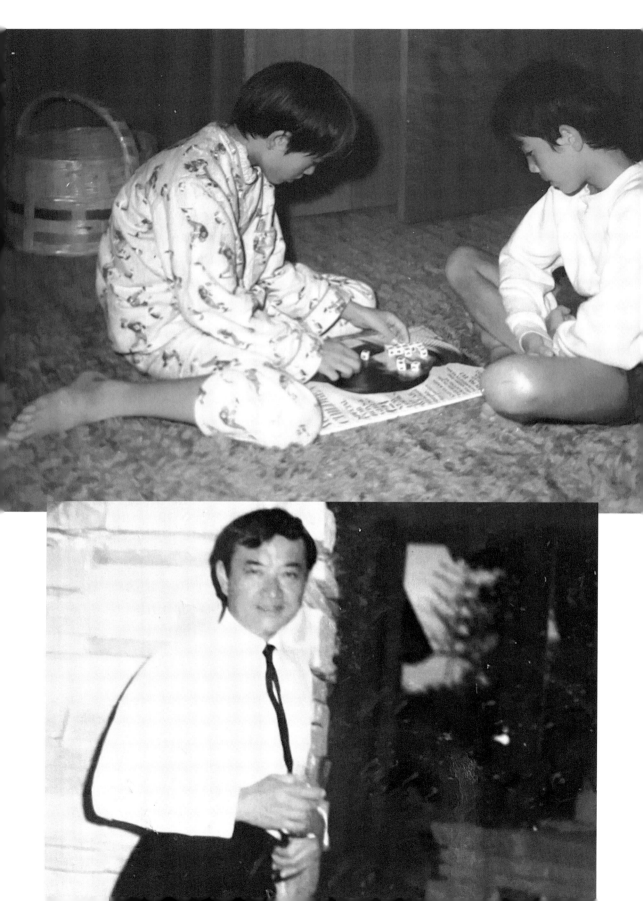

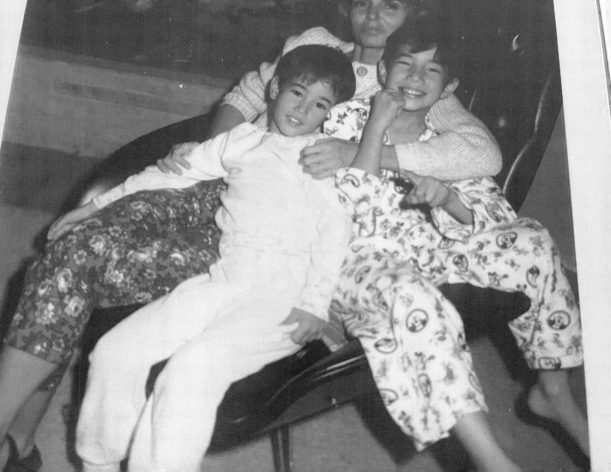

60

Mrs. Ohta always waved when she drove the kids to school.

Ami Chandler, 1970:
They entertained a lot and in a day; thirty cars might go up and down their drive.

DOROTHY CADWALLADER

David Cadwallader (Brother-in-law of Dorothy Cadwallader), 2020:
Dorothy Kinney was her name. I don't remember where she met my brother, Jack, but they lived down at her family's property. My brother started working for her family. They made brooms.

The Kinney family had been making brooms for over a hundred years. Dorothy's father, Lester B. Kinney inherited the Kinney Broom Company from his father in 1910. In 1947 Lester Kinney moved to Santa Cruz and rebranded the company as Kinney Brooms.

Kinney Brooms shut down in 1985.

David Cadwallader, 2020:
She [Dorothy] was always off by herself. She wasn't outgoing. She was shy, I guess. We lived down the street and would wave but I don't remember having good long conversations with her.

David Cadwallader, 2020:
I know she was highly educated.

David Cadwallader, 2020:
They had a little boy, but he was killed a while before. He was trying to play a trick on his friends and laid in a ditch to jump out and scare them. The mailman pulled in and ran over him. They had a girl too and later they adopted a little Chinese girl.

Melinda Cadwallader (Daughter of Dorothy Cadwallader), 2020:
I just turned eleven when she [Dorothy

Cadwallader] was murdered. I can't really tell you much about Santa Cruz in the sixties or seventies in that time frame. I was very protected and sheltered after my brother was killed. My mom was very elegant. She was very sixties. Makeup, False eyelashes, and hair styles. She was smart, a great cook, and a great mom.

My Mom was very thoughtful. Lark Ohta told me that she made popcorn for her after school when we stayed at the Ohta's house.

My mom always brought me a new treat home from the store. I remember her bringing me a pomegranate. Silly I know, but that was exciting for me. She opened it for me and showed me how to eat it. I can't remember if she was funny, but always happy, giving, and could be difficult at times. So was I.

Melinda Cadwallader, 2020:
Her job as I understand was a secretary, but

61

so much more.

Lark Ohta, 2020:

[Dorothy Cadwallader] was such a great woman and I loved her very much. She and Jack stayed with us if my parents went on a big trip, and they took care of us. Dorothy was perfect, like a '60s TV mom, except that she also worked. She was beautiful inside and out, and I loved her. We even shared the same birthday, and I always thought that was special.

Melinda Cadwallader, 2020:

Lark is older than I am. I really don't re-member if Dr. Ohta's wife was big into the community. I always saw her cooking and laughing. Back then we were out playing and not allowed around the adults. I loved Lark and always stayed in her room when she was away at school.

David Cadwallader, 2020:

We knew Frazier was an auto mechanic and he lived down in the canyon. We heard he watched the doctor driving his Ferrari or some really expensive cars and he was so jealous. He thought that family shouldn't have all that money. Just jealous.

Lark Ohta, 2020:

That house was built into the environment with pure Japanese aesthetics, and it was sickening that Frazier saw it differently. He

Lark and Taura Ohta will be performing in the "Egyptian Dances" when the Ivanovsky School of Ballet gives its benefit performance next Saturday at Cabrillo Theater for the Cabrillo Music Festival.

didn't even realize that he was destroying something beautiful that added to the Earth and the people who built it, rather than something and someone who "raped the environment."

I know that he thought he was making a statement but he was so misguided, and deadly wrong.

Dr. Ohta was also keenly aware of the local drug scene and the associated criminal activities. On the night of February 15, 1967, thieves forcibly entered Dr. Ohta's office and stole eight ounces of cocaine solution.

Frazier had also burglarized the neighbor's home. The .38 and .22 pistols used in the murders were stolen from the Ohta's neighbor, Donald J. Muni, around October 5, 1970. Frazier bragged to his friend, Michael J. Wark, that he had stolen six firearms from the Muni house and had waited all that day in the house for Donald Muni to return, but he did not.

On Saturday, October 17, 1970, the Ohta's had dinner with their friends the Seftel's.

Chuck Scherer, 1970:
Dr. Seftel, his wife and Mr. and Mrs. Ohta were out to dinner Saturday night and the conversation involved around the hippies and the crime on the streets. Dr. Seftel stated he did not have or own a gun. Knowing that Dr. Ohta did, he asked him what kind of gun he recommended or the type he had. Dr. Ohta replied he has a .45 caliber under his mattress and a .38.

Lark Ohta, 2020:
I went to Soquel High School for one year. Before that I went to Holy Cross from kindergarten to fifth grade. Then when we moved to the house in Soquel, and I was at Good Shepherd Catholic School from sixth grade to eighth grade. I'm sure it's still there.

When high school came, my parents wanted me to go away to a college prep school. You know how all kids get labeled in a family—my sister was the artistic one, and I was the student—the kid who got good grades. And I'm not smarter than anyone else. I just worked really hard. So they wanted me to go to boarding school, and we looked at schools all over California—but I was not ready. I was too young to be away from

Above: Dr. Ohta's oldest daughter, Taura, and nephew, Kim Neefe, show off one of his sports cars. The body was a manufactured replica of a 1928 Mercedes SSK. Under the hood was a 1966 Chevrolet Corvette engine with a Paxton supercharger.

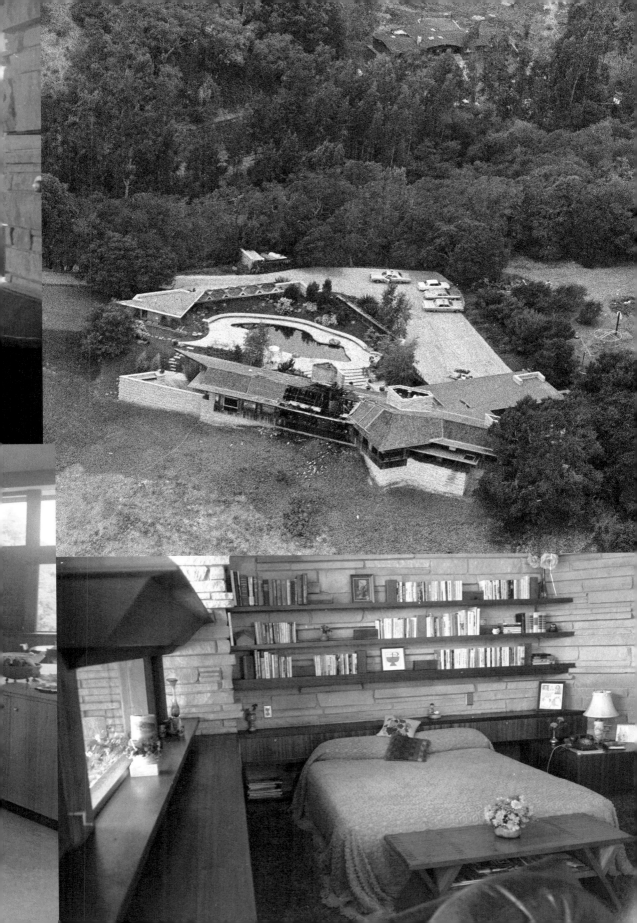

Sgt. Damon of the Santa Cruz County Sheriff's Office was contacted by Dr. Liddicoat who stated that the victims' daughter, Taura Ohta, was present last spring when Dr. Ohta confronted a hippy-type male subject trespassing near the pool of the residence; this officer was requested to contact Taura Ohta and obtain a physical description of this subject and learn what transpired at this meeting.

Subject contacted Taura Ohta NOFA DOB 3/25/52. Present address confidential.

Subject of the report: A WMA, 20-25 years, 6', slim build, brown hair, shoulder length, medium complexion, wearing a short trimmed full beard and mustache, dressed in blue jeans, boots, and shirt.

Time of Occurrence: Between 9 and 10:00 A.M., Saturday, the day before Easter, 1970. Miss Ohta stated that she observed the above WMA hippy subject on the pool deck as he was being contacted by her father. She stated that she did not overhear any of the conversation, but learned from her father after the subject had left that he appeared to be under the influence of drugs due to his method of conversation and the condition of his eyes.

Mr. Ohta was concerned about the situation because he stated that the hippy subject knew of their impending trip to Mexico and thought that they would be gone at that time. The Ohtas would have been gone if they had not been delayed because of a death in the family. Miss Ohta was asked if she had at any time observed any other subjects prowling about the property or the adjoining property. She stated that she had not, but added that there were several places that a person or persons could conceal themselves and watch the Ohta home.

Miss Ohta supplied information for an IDK composit of the above suspect. The IDK code is as follows: A/24, B/14+2, D/21, L/9+2, N/03, E/10, H/154. Reported by Sgt. A. M. Stevens at 16:18 hours, 10/25/70, N/03

home. We only looked at schools that were close by, but I didn't want to go. I wanted to try public high school and stay living at home. We decided that I would go to Soquel High for that one year and see how things went. That same year, Taura came back from art school in Michigan and finished her senior year at home. I was a freshman and we were both there at the same time. But, it was tough for me—I hadn't gone to grade school with any of those kids and I had to make new friends. I also sadly looked like I was ten, and it was all very overwhelming. People were nice to me, but I felt very lost.

By the end of that year, I told my parents I would go to the closest boarding school if that is what they wanted. That is how I ended up at Santa Catalina. It was the closest one on my list, so I said, "OK, I'll go to that one."

But I wasn't happy. I was still too young—so young. I hated it and I was unhappy, and I wanted to come home. One time, I broke the braces on my teeth, so I could have an excuse to come home. My mother would have to pick me up and drive me back. I was desperately unhappy, and I was going to come home. They were going to let me quit after Halloween. Even though they'd already paid the tuition for the whole year, they agreed I would come home at Halloween—but they died on the 19th.

Halloween, that was the big holiday for our family. Family, friends, big parties. My dad would carve dozens of pumpkins each year.

It was exciting knowing I was coming home. I had only been at school since September, six weeks or something, not very long—but it seemed like forever. I had been home the day before it happened. I was home on Sunday. My mom took me back to school on the 18th and it happened on the 19th.

Above: Taura Ohta informed law enforcement that her father had run off a trespasser from their property the day before Easter, 1970. Note the suspect's height. Probably not Frazier.

OCTOBER 19, 1970

Harold Cartwright, 2020:

Ohta wasn't the primary target that day, he went to the Munis first, but they weren't home. They've died of natural causes since. I'm in touch with their son. But it's interesting to think what if they had been home because he had been some kind of a diplomat and whether he would have had a different approach rather than Dr. Ohta, who called him crazy and a drugged out hippie. Frazier spent hours trying to convince Dr. Ohta to burn down the house. Muni didn't come home, so he went to the Ohta's.

Harold Cartwright, 2020:

What God was telling him [Frazier] to do, was to go throughout the world, you go to the head of the household and you say to them—and it had to be the male if there was a male in the household—"I'm here on God's behalf and you have to make a decision. You have to decide whether or not you are going to join God's army. You and your family will destroy all your belongings and go with me to your neighbors house and give them the same choice. And you choose death or you choose to join God's army." Very clear. Very simple.

David Marlowe (Psychologist and expert witness for the defense), 1971:

He [Frazier] arrives early in the afternoon, like twelve o'clock or so, and goes up there.

He's armed with a .38 and at least one .22 caliber pistol.

Mrs. Ohta was seen at the Santa Cruz Travel Agency between 12:40 and 1:00 confirming the family's plans to go to Hawaii for Thanksgiving. Around 2:15 p.m., Mrs. Ohta was seen at the Santa Cruz Savings and Loan bank. The bank employees said they always noticed when Mrs. Ohta came into the bank because she was such a good dresser.

Donald Lunde, 1970:

He [Frazier] describes looking around the house and again looking at the books and material objects inside the house [as Frazier did at the Munis house]. He was particularly upset and disgusted by the presence of animal skins in the home and particularly by a bedspread in the master bedroom which he said looked like it was a bear hide or some other animal hide, which had been killed to make a bedspread for these people. This, he says, really "blew his mind."

Mrs. Ohta was the first person to come home, and he describes taking her by surprise, tying her up, blindfolding her [with Dr. Ohta's scarves], and taking her to the master bedroom, and leaving her on the bed there. He says that he drove her white Oldsmobile station wagon to the bottom of the hill at some time in the course of the afternoon before "the old man" came home. He says that at first Mrs. Ohta was very upset because she thought that he was going to rape her or assault her, but he states that he finally calmed her down and that he then was able to talk with her for quite a while. He mentioned at one point getting her a glass of orange juice and at another point mixing her a drink, although I asked him specifically what the drink was, and he said he couldn't remember. In the course of his conversation with Mrs. Ohta, she informed him that he would get into trouble because people would become suspicious if she did not pick up her son after school as she was supposed to. Thereupon he says that he called Dr. Ohta's receptionist and told her he was calling from a garage and that Mrs. Ohta's car was broken down and someone else would have to pick up the boy.

Karen Weigel (Ohta office receptionist), 1970:

[Quoting the phone call] "This is the Union Garage, Toby is here, her car broke down and the two boys at school have to be picked up. She wants to talk to Dorothy."

When Dorothy Green, another receptionist, answered, the phone was dead. "Toby" was a nickname that Mrs. Ohta's close friends used.

At four o'clock Taggart called his father's office, his mother had not picked him up from school.

Dr. Ohta asked Mrs. Cadwallader to pick up Taggart. She left the office at four thirty.

Dr. Ohta left at four forty-five and picked up Derrick. They went to Dr. Ohta's mother's house and ate noodles.

David Marlowe, 1971:
Mrs. Cadwallader comes to the house with one of the boys and he takes them prisoner and ties them up and places them in different parts of the house.

One goes into a dressing room of some sort in the end of the house, in the pool area, and one in a utility type room.

Then Dr. Ohta comes home with the other boy and they are taken prisoner.

He ties them up, takes Ohta to the pool-side where he essentially engages in the same argument or discussion that he had with Mrs. Ohta, and he accuses Dr. Ohta of destroying life and the environment…that he is responsible for ruining the Santa Cruz mountains and this hill by accumulating all his material possessions and building this house.

Frazier was incredibly upset. It blew his mind when he went into the house and saw the animal skins because the animal skins were further evidence to him that these were evil people who had killed innocent animals. He takes Dr. Ohta outside and is telling all this and Dr. Ohta replies by saying, "I'll give you anything you want, any money you want."

This also greatly disturbs Frazier because he has failed to get through, as he puts it, to Dr. Ohta who responds to his tirades about the ecology and so on by offering him the very thing he hates, material possessions and money.

Frazier suggests as an alternative that together they burn the house down and thereby restore the property to its natural state, to plants and trees.

Donald Lunde, 1970:
He says that at this Dr. Ohta "blew," meaning he got upset and agitated and this in turn, according to John, "really accelerated my mind."

He shoved Dr. Ohta into the swimming pool and while in the pool Ohta was able to free his hands according to John. He says that he was going to help him back out of the pool and extended his hand for this purpose. He had a gun in his other hand. He said at this point "The old man did a real dumb thing. He tried to hit me."

And apparently he tried to pull John into the pool. At this, John pushed him away and said, "I just started plugging him. I am not sure how many times I shot him."

David Marlowe, 1971:
And then he went into the back bedroom and got Mrs. Ohta out, took her to the pool-side and asked her if she believed in God.

She said, "Yes," and then he answered, "Then you have nothing to be afraid of." He shot her and pushed her into the pool.

Then he brought out Mrs. Cadwallader and did the same thing, asked her if she believed in God. She said, "Yes," and he said, "Then you have nothing to be afraid of."

Then he shot her and pushed her into the pool.

Donald Lunde, 1970:
He next brought out the older boy and asked him if he believed in God, and the boy said "I don't know, I'm not sure."

He commented somewhat scornfully about the boy's fancy clothes that he was wearing. This boy was shot and killed next, in the head.

Lastly he brought out the youngest boy. He said that his plan was to release the younger boy, but asked him if he had seen his face, and the boy replied yes and then tried to change his mind and say no he wasn't sure. John says at this point he decided to kill him also. The bodies were all thrown into the pool, and the house was set on fire.

Chang asked why Frazier killed the boys—

David Marlowe, 1971: I'm not sure I under-stand why. I just don't know why. It's a bizarre element that leads me to believe he's insane.

Dr. Ohta was shot twice with the .38 pistol. Everyone else was shot once with the .22. There were indications that some of the victims were still alive when they were thrown into the pool.

Neither Ami Chandler nor Donald Pajak, 22, another neighbor, had heard a sound.

Frazier set four to five fires in the kitchen area before he left in Mrs. Ohta's Oldsmobile.

Pete Amos (*Santa Cruz Sentinel* photographer), 2020:
I was down at Soquel High School, maybe it was a basketball game that I was photograph-ing, I can't remember. When I was through and I came out, I looked up at the hills and the Ohta house was right up above there, on the hill. There was smoke rising up and I said, "Ohhh, might be a fire going."

I headed up there. I knew how to get up there. There was nobody around. The house was on fire so I got a couple of pictures. It was awful dark and it was smoky, so they're not too great of pictures. But I got the pic-tures of the fire and that's when I discovered the bodies. The fire engine was coming up the driveway, so, I just kind of exited real quick.

Richard Verbrugge, 2020:
Frazier had taken Dr. Ohta's car, which was a Rolls Royce, and he had parked it at a nine-ty degree angle to the driveway, to the home, and broke the ignition key off in it so that it couldn't be moved. He wanted to block the fire engines coming in to put out the fire.

Rodney Gregg, 2020:

This is more of an anecdotal story. In 1970 I was eighteen and I was working at McDonald's self-service gas station right there next to the Sky View Drive-In. We were closing up that night and I had a friend who was working for the old Palomar Garage and they had a towing business. He was being called to move a bunch of trucks on Rodeo Gulch Road. And then I had another friend and her dad was in charge of Forestry, or something. So there were some fires going on, again on Rodeo Gulch Road. The third part is that my family had owned the property that the Ohta house was built on. We sold them that property. So all these things were happening that night and said, "Wow, we should go find out what's going on."

We got in my Mustang, and there were four of us, and we drove up Rodeo Gulch Road and we went all the way up and turned around and came back down. We didn't pull in or anything, but we were there at the time everything had just started unwinding, before anybody else.

We drove back to the gas station and three or four Sheriff's cars came flying in after us with their shotguns, yelling, :Freeze!"

I'm thinking, oh my gosh, what happened up there? Then they took all our information, but I can't remember the extent of what they were asking, but it was, "Why were you there?"

"Who do you know?"

"What was going on?"

I was trying to put it all together for them.

The next day it was in the newspaper that they had found four people that were possible suspects. It was us.

A fire hydrant had been installed at the request of local fire departments and used the water in the Ohta's swimming pool. When Live Oak Fire Chief, Ted Pound and Assistant Chief, Ernie Negro, went to hook up a pump they spotted the bodies in the swimming pool.

Ted Pound (Live Oak Fire Chief), 1970:

I went to the pool to see where the end of the pipe came through and my flashlight beam spotted on one of the kids.

Peter Chang, 1970:

This was the most tragic murder scene I've ever witnessed in nine years.

Ted Pound, 1970:

There were four bodies on the bottom and one was floating on top. I thought they were mannequins when I saw the first boy. When I saw the others, I knew they were people.

Marj Von B, 1971:

Mrs. Ohta lay on the bottom of the pool, her gloved hands bound before her and her stocking feet tied. Her blonde hair floated gently about her head in the water. Her face was the picture of despair, with her eyes open and her lips slightly parted.

Her husband lay at her side, face down with a colorful scarf around his neck.

Their son Taggart lay nearby, his face splotched with blood and a long streak of blood streaming out along the bottom of the pool from under his body.

The other son Derrick lay alone at one end of the pool on his back with his face covered by two scarves tied around his neck.

Mrs. Cadwallader, still in her white medical office uniform, floated on the pool surface, her upper body resting on the float line of the swimming pool vacuum and her legs stretching down into the depths of the pool.

Doug James (Santa Cruz County Sheriff), 1970:

It looked like they possibly could have been shot by the poolside where blood was found, and then pushed into the pool.

Kenneth Pittenger (Santa Cruz County Deputy Sheriff), 1970:

It was like an execution.

Asked if the killings were ritualistic—

Doug James, 1970:
There is a possibility of that, but there are many possibilities.

Kenneth Pittenger, 1970:
We have no weapon, no suspect, no motive.

Terry Medina, 2020:
In 1970, when I went to the [detective] bureau, it was right after the Ohta Family was killed. I was at that scene, but I was a patrol deputy and in fact, I live about a mile and a half above where that family was killed.

We had two ID guys, Ben Seibel and Jim Ingram, working up there. It was late in the afternoon when we got up there. It was just getting dark. And Seibel and Ingram were trying to preserve the area around the pool. You got the bodies in the pool. It's starting to rain. It's getting dark. There were blood areas around the pool going to get washed away. Evidence washed away. It was pretty frantic trying to save all of that stuff. In their haste, and nobody really knows about this one, I haven't really talked about this one, but, the first thirty-six pictures or more that Seibel and Ingram took, there was no film in the camera. Peter Chang went fucking ballistic over that. I mean *ballistic.*

Terry Medina, 2020:
It [the rain] didn't affect indoors too much because he [Seibel] didn't have the lighting issue.

A book of Bible studies belonging to one of the boys was found hacked up. The newspapers reported that Ohta's cat was also shot in the back of the head and killed but I could not find that in the police reports. The telephone line in the master bedroom had also been cut and the receiver had been disassembled.

Dr. Ohta's .38 caliber revolver and five rounds of ammunition was found under the mattress in the master bedroom. Dr. Ohta's .45 caliber pistol was missing.

Investigators found several of Dr. Ohta's scarves scattered around the living room.

Terry Medina, 2020:
Then we had the problem with the car blocking the driveway. That's where a note was left. On the car. Nobody knows what the fuck's going on because we were pretty tight-lipped about all that stuff that we thought would create a break there pretty soon.

Pete Amos, 2020:
When I got back to the sentinel—Gordon Sinclair was our editor at the time, and we decided we better not print them [his photographs of the bodies in the pool]. I said, "I don't think anybody ought to see them."

He said, "That's a good idea."

I went back to my photo lab there and I took scissors and I cut them all up.

Stern Magazine from Germany called me a week later and offered me a couple thousand dollars for my pictures of the bodies in the pool, but I had to tell them I didn't have them.

Ami Chandler (Ohta neighbor), 1970:
It's very shocking. It hurts me deep on account of them being such nice people.

Ami Chandler, 1970:
It just proves to me that the world is getting upset on things like this. It scares you to look forward to the world, the way things is. It seems likely that the lord is fading out in it. And that's the way it looks to me.

William Kelsay, 2019:
Ray Belgard was our chief investigator at the time.

He calls up and says, "We have this homicide."

He quickly tells me what it's all about and says, "You've got to get Peter up here, but you have to prepare him."

Because two of the victims were young boys and they were Asian boys like Peter's

and they look quite a bit like his sons, Christopher and Petey.

Ted Pound, 1970:
I didn't even look at the bodies when I pulled them out. I don't stomach this stuff.

Richard Verbrugge, 2020:
The minute the bodies were discovered, Mr. Chang was notified and he got hold of [Bob] Sweeney because he lived there in Santa Cruz at the time. He was closer than me being over here in Sunnyvale. And the two of

them went right up to the scene. It was pretty horrendous. Sweeney told me that when they were recovering one of the bodies that had been face down, and it was turned over, it looked just like Mr. Chang's son, and Mr. Chang almost fainted.

Chang watched as they removed twelve-year-old Derrick—

Peter Chang, 1970:
He looked exactly like my son. I thought I was dreaming.

Terry Medina, 2020:
So we had the note. There was also a car missing. The killer used the other car to block the driveway on both ends. But he drove away in Mrs. Ohta's Oldsmobile station wagon. It was one of those old Vista Cruiser station wagons.

We held that out for a number of days because we figured we might be able to find it on our own.

Mrs. Ohta's station wagon was a dark green 1968 Oldsmobile.

OCTOBER 20, 1970

The Santa Cruz Sheriff's Office held a press conference at one fifteen in the morning.

Douglas James (Santa Cruz County Sheriff), 1970:
They were tied. They were tied with scarves and stockings with their arms in front of them. There was no indication that they had been beaten. There was a gunshot wound in four of the victims and there were two in Dr. Ohta.

Douglas James, 1970:
We had no indication that it was hippies or straights or whatever. We're just pursuing any possibility that we can.

Douglas James, 1970:
We'll be checking on any hippies who may be living in the area.

Douglas James, 1970:
I would say there would probably have to be more than one person to have to do what was done—no weapons have been found.

When asked by the press if a note was discovered—

Douglas James, 1970:
No comment.

DOUGLAS JAMES

Doug James served as Santa Cruz County Sheriff from 1958 to 1974.

Dave Alcorn, 2020:
Doug James was a big guy, a football player with the Santa Cruz Seahawks when they had a semi-pro team. Then he was the juvenile officer for the Santa Cruz PD, then he was elected Sheriff.

Terry Medina, 2020:
James is an interesting guy, very personable. He was like six foot four. Two hundred and fifty pounds. Everybody liked him. Hometown guy. He got elected and he was really a pretty good sheriff.

Dave Alcorn, 2020:
Doug always seemed to be there for me. I said, I need to pay that back somewhere along the line. And in January '72 I got to work for Doug James and the SO. [Sheriff's Office] I think anybody would tell you he was a professional. He was one of those people that just understood people and how to deal with them. He was a nice guy and he just cared about people. He just cared.

Mickey Aluffi, 2020:
I met Doug when I was probably about thirteen years of age. My brother and I got BB guns for Christmas. So we were out bird hunting. We used to live way out on the westside of Santa Cruz. So, we were bird hunting and everything and then we got the wise idea: wouldn't it be great to shoot up the streetlight. Well, unfortunately, I was the one that did it. The bulb came down. At any rate, there was a guy there. John Landino, he had a business there, he said, "Hey you guys come here."

He had called the cops. Well, here comes Doug James. He took us in and they confiscated our BB guns for sixty days. I had to write an essay. But the funny thing was when Doug James took us home, my brother and I walked in the back door and my mother was in the kitchen and then Doug James walked in behind us. He has to duck to get under the doorway. My mother said she almost had a heart attack. But fast forward to when I became a candidate for the sheriff's office. The final interview was with Doug. And he brought that up. He remembered and he told me, he said, "You're a good guy. You've got good values."

He said, "We don't expect you to be one hundred percent happy, but try to keep the grousing to a minimum."

It was a political thing. He didn't want people out there talking negatively about him.

Chris Cottle, 2020:
Doug James was the Sheriff at the time and he and Peter Chang did not love each other, that's for sure. Pete always had the feeling

that these cases had been inadequately investigated from the standpoint of scientific evidence. And really they were not equipped from day one to deal with that. They didn't have the staff, the skills, and the experienced people to handle something like this.

Mickey Aluffi, 2020:
Doug was another guy who liked to go to the bars. You could be doing a car stop at two or three o'clock in the morning and he could roll up behind you to accompany you, so to speak. Well he had just left the bars. But over time he became, I don't want to say ineffective, but the Board of Supervisors wasn't happy with them. So they created this position called the Assistant Sheriff. And they brought in a guy named Lee Davis from the Los Angeles Sheriff's Office.

At the time he was a lieutenant in charge of their record section down there. He tested for the job and he got it. A real jerk. I didn't care for him at all. But he stayed until Al Noren ran for sheriff.

We openly supported Al and of course Doug's last thing was to transfer us to the jail. Wally Walker and I were both relatively new sergeants. And so Doug transferred us to the jail. Wally and I considered ourselves political prisoners.

Mickey Aluffi, 2020:
You know, we never had any conversations with him [Doug James]. There was no direction. Like I say, he was kind of ineffective. I mean, he was standing in front of the cameras a little bit, but he would not try to—well, he didn't show a whole lot of interest in what we were doing. Yeah. Lee Davis was on board at the time and Lee was pretty much a hands on type of guy. So, yeah, Doug didn't do too much.

Terry Medina, 2020:

I can't remember if some of that tarot shit in the note leaked out but it was just like the community already had all this anxiety over the Tate-LaBianca murders. It was all over the news. Remember the writing with the blood on the walls? Helter Skelter. The note had those kinds of words. Immediately it raised the community's anxiety; it sounded like another Tate-LaBianca.

So not only is everything in hyper overdrive crime-wise, the media has descended upon Santa Cruz County. Right? In those days, the Sheriff's Office didn't know what a PIO [Public Information Officer] was, let alone have one. And so Doug James was the sheriff and he was doing the best he could to talk to the media who just descended on us.

The two Ohta daughters were away at separate schools.

Taura Ohta, 18, was at a design school in New York.

Lark Ohta was at Santa Catalina in Monterey. She was woken by a nun just before dawn. They told her there had been an accident.

Lark Ohta, 1990:

I thought, "Gosh, I wonder what happened?" The only thing I could think of was the time my dad fell off a ladder and got a concussion. When you're fifteen and nothing's really gone wrong in your life, it's impossible to think of something terrible.

In the car, one of the nuns told her that her family had been killed.

Later, that same day, the autopsies were performed.

Douglas James, 1970:

The preliminary autopsy reports indicate that weapons of .38 caliber and .22 caliber were used to perpetuate the homicides.

Additionally, on Tuesday, October 20, Mrs. Ohta's Oldsmobile was spotted in Bonny Doon driving towards Felton. The driver was all over the road, speeding through the mountains. It almost ran a car off the road.

Terry Medina, 2020:

Here's something that you'll love. We put out the description of that car and the license number. There is a telephone guy working up on a pole up in Felton.

So everybody in the world—news, newspapers, TV—is putting out that we're looking for this car.

Unknown at the time, the car was seen less than one hundred yards from one of Frazier's former bosses' homes.

Harold Cartwright, 2020:

He was a PG&E employee in Bonny Doon. He looked down and saw the car. He can see an orange backpack in there.

Terry Medina, 2020:

And he immediately knows it's the car. He climbs down the pole, gets in his truck, and instead of driving to the phone booth a half a mile away. He drives his truck all the way down Highway 9 to the Front Street Sheriff's Office. He walks up to the second floor where the records bureau is. He gets in line. And he's waiting in line and when he gets to the front, one of the women that's there says, "Can I help you?"

And he goes, "Yeah, I know where the car is."

An hour has passed! The detectives are running out of the office. Of course the car's gone. But, when the call goes out almost simultaneously we hear over the radio that there is a fire in the tunnel at Rincon.

So, now there's this big fire raging at Rincon. You've got code three cars racing

Left: Assistant Sheriff Lee Davis.

up Highway 9. You got them coming from Highway 1. They're all trying to get to Felton, right.

And pretty soon word comes over that the fire in the Rincon Tunnel is the fucking Oldsmobile!

The Roaring Camp train had passed through the tunnel at three o'clock, but when it returned at four forty-five, it struck the car.

The front seat had been set on fire, but it went out without much damage.

A deputy sheriff felt the hood and it was still warm.

The witness who had almost been run off the road by the driver of Mrs. Ohta's Oldsmobile believed two men and a woman were in the car. Additionally and coincidentally, law enforcement found evidence of three sets of footprints leading away from the car. One was barefoot.

Terry Medina, 2020:
Because there were so many cars going up Graham Hill in close proximity and time, we

thought, well, the guy's got to be on foot. So we called in everybody. There were no CHP helicopters like there are today, although they did have a fixed wing in either San Francisco or Sacramento. But we were calling police officers from everywhere to try to get around that whole park. From Rincon all the way up Highway 9. But it was a futile attempt because I mean, it's so big if you've been through there. So we search for hours and hours, and, of course, it was late in the afternoon when that [telephone] guy drove all the way to Santa Cruz. So now it's getting dark and there's no way in hell we're going to find somebody. The whole trail goes cold. We're just kind of nowhere.

Mickey Aluffi, 2020:
We did a couple of things when everybody was looking for him. My patrol lieutenant at the time was Ken Pittenger. And we had a briefing one day and just about every deputy was in the room. And he says, "We're going to search every house in the Soquel Highlands."

He said, "I don't care if anybody's home or not. I want every house searched thoroughly."
We just went up to Soquel up there behind Soquel High and searched every house. And unfortunately, the first one I came to nobody was home. So what do you do? Right. So we ended up somehow accessing the garage. And then the door to go in the house, we had to break it down.

We left a note. And it turned out the guy was an airline pilot and, you know, the county had to buy him a new door .

Frazier later told defense psychiatrist Dr. Donald Lunde that after abandoning the Ohta's station wagon, he wandered around in the woods.

Harold Cartwright, 2020:
Frazier was camping in the woods those days.

Roger Murray, 2020:
This was later. After he was arrested. I used to hike all up and down the valley. I was just stomping through the woods when I came

across an abandoned campsite. There was a tent there and crap strewn all over the place. I could see it had been abandoned for maybe a month, but not that long. And I found a pill bottle, a prescription pill bottle, and it had his name on it. This was not far from where he drove the car into the train tunnel.

I went home and called Peter Chang and we met at the Rincon Turnout and he brought another guy. Well, it was drizzling and they had umbrellas and off we went, hiking into the woods. They were dressed in business suits. It was kind of funny.

That was right across Highway 9 from the Rincon Turnout.

Coincidentally, Herbert Mullin would dump the body of his first victim only a couple hundred yards away, just off a trail leading away from the Rincon Turnout.

Richard Verbrugge, 2020:
I remember that campsite. He [Peter Chang] put on—he had a pair of boots in the office,

big rubber boots. Those pill bottles were in a, like a, metal briefcase. Frazier probably stole it somewhere. But, it's a—Samsonite. That's the word, it was like a Samsonite metal briefcase.

Frazier finally went back to his shack on his mother's property four days later.

Douglas James, 1970:
We recovered the missing vehicle which

belonged to the Ohtas in the Bonny Doon, Felton area. The circumstances surrounding that recovery and the possibility that we may have located the place where the occupants of the car spent the night have led us to maintain surveillance search in the vicinity throughout the ensuing hours. We are pressing a concerted search effort with deputies on foot and mounted personnel in that vicinity at this hour.

OCTOBER 21, 1970

Roger Krone, 2020:

George Kricanovich is who told me about the murders. He was Santa Cruz City PD. He came into the Catalyst the day after looking really intently. I asked him, "What happened?"

He took me aside and said, "Now, you can't tell anybody but there's been a mass murder up in Soquel."

We went home knowing there had been this mass murder and that night when we heard about the note, we put two and two together.

Law enforcement held a press conference at eleven in the morning on Wednesday. They held another Wednesday night. There, it was revealed that the killer left a note at the crime scene.

Louis Keller (Santa Cruz County Sheriff's administrative assistant), 1970:

This note was found underneath the windshield wiper of one of the automobiles that was parked across the driveway at Dr. Ohta's residence. On the Rolls.

John Linley Frazier Note, 1970:

Today World War 3 will begin as brought to you by the people of the Free Universe. From this day forward any one and—or company of persons who misuses the natural environment or destroys same will suffer the penalty of death by the people of the Free Universe.

I and my comrades from this day forth will fight until death or freedom, against anything or anyone who does not support natural life on this planet, materialism must die or mankind will.

Knight of Wands
Knight of Cups
Knight of Pentacles
Knight of Swords

The note was typewritten on the Ohta's typewriter.

Peter Chang, 1971:

A straw crucifix belonging to one of the Ohta daughters was found on the hood of Mrs. Cadwallader's car, and a note was found on the windshield of Dr. Ohta's car.

Paul Tara (Santa Cruz County Undersheriff), 1970:

We recognize the shock that this senseless act has brought to our citizenry. We trust that the sober judgment of our residents will prevail over any emotional reaction. The successful conclusion to this tragic crime will be based on the combined efforts, a rational, logical citizenry responsive to tedious process required of competent law enforcement personnel.

Roger Krone, 2020:

The next day I was at work and Randall saw me, probably white as a sheet, and knew something was up and said, "What's wrong?" I told him, "I think I know who committed those murders."

So that's when he got Bill Tubbs, who shared an office with the public defender's private investigator, Harold Cartwright. Bill Tubbs was a regular at The Catalyst.

Gene McFarlane, a friend of mine from Watsonville High School, visited The Catalyst later in the day and we told Gene about it. He was a friend of Peter Chang's. Gene McFarlane set up the meeting with Peter Chang.

hallowween.... 1970

today woold war 3 will begin as brought to you by the pepole of the free universe.

From this day forward any one and?/ or c company of persons who missuses the natural enviroment or destroys same will suffer the penelty of death by the people of the free universe.

I and my comrads from this day forth will fight until death or freedom, against any- ~~XXXX/XXXX~~ thing or anyone who dose not support natural life on this planet, materalisum must die or man-kind will.

KNIGHT OF WANDS
KNIGHT OF CUPS
KNIGHT OF PENTICLES
KNIGHT OF SWORDS

Peter Chang, 1970:
The long-haired or hippie community was revolted by this man [Frazier]. The entire community was against him.

OCTOBER 22, 1970

On Thursday, October 22, Sheriff Douglas James held another press conference.

Douglas James, 1970:
We do have a suspect. He is not in custody. And his name is John, middle name Linley, L-I-N-L-E-Y, last name is Frazier. F-R-A-Z-I-E-R. He is also known as John Linley Pascal. P-A-S-C-A-L. He's a white male American and he was born January 26, 1946. His height is five feet seven inches and his hair when he was last seen is brownish blond, parted and combed over to one side. It is collar length. When he was last seen he had a full beard approximately ¾ long and it is possible he does not have it now. So it could go either way. He was last seen wearing a beige, straw, wide-brimmed hat with red, white, and blue hat band. He was last seen wearing a green coat, dark trousers, possibly Levis or jeans, and could be wearing ankle high moccasins.

JOHN LINLEY FRAZIER

John Linley Frazier's mother, Pat Pascal, was well known in Santa Cruz for owning and operating Bunny Haven, a large rabbit farm. The *Santa Cruz Sentinel* described Pat Pascal as, "A sort of one-woman press agent for rabbit-raising in general."

Mrs. Pascal noted that in the past, Frazier was not capable of even killing a rabbit for market.

Pat Pascal (John Linley Frazier's mother), 1970:
He was always kind to animals; he couldn't stand abuse of life. Johnny couldn't do it.

Frazier was born in Carrizozo, New Mexico, in a private hospital on January 26, 1946.

Pat Pascal, 1970:
My husband was in the service at that time and when I came time for delivery I went there because my mother went there and she also nursed at the hospital. And, of course, he was in the Air Force and we moved quite

a bit so when I got here in delivery time I figured that I'd be better off to stay put some place, so I went there. He was shipped to March Field.

Frazier was born one month premature. He was in an incubator for two weeks.

Pat Pascal, 1970:
I was nursing him for about a month, but evidently the milk wasn't good enough for him because he was colicky and cried a lot, and after we put him on the bottle he settled right down and he was alright. In fact, it was no time at all that we cut out his 2:00 a.m. feedings.

Frazier walked at ten months and began talking around the same time.

Pat Pascal, 1970:
I was happy but I think our problems were when we moved back to his [her husband's] hometown [St. Clairsville, Ohio]. We lived

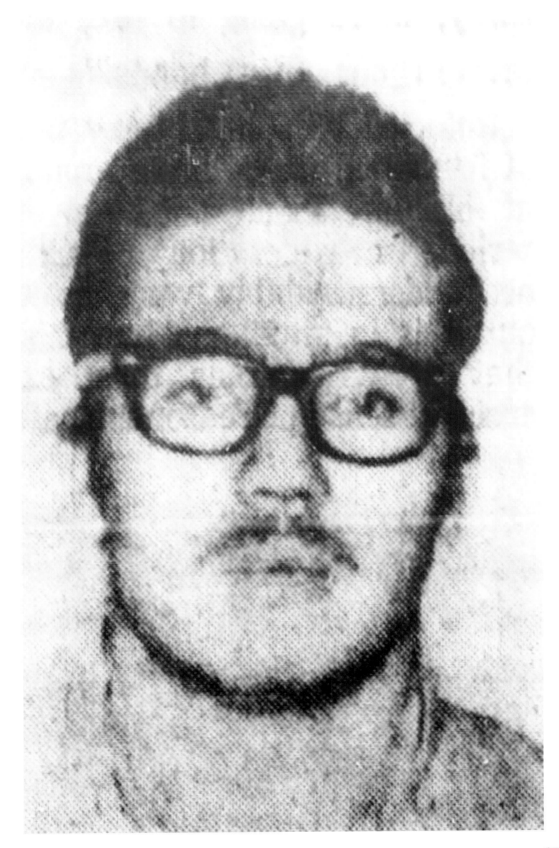

right behind his mother's house and everything hit the fan then.

It started happening in 1947 and I left in 1948.

He'd go out all night, forget where he lived and got involved with other women. I asked, "Why don't we leave here and start over in a new town?"

But he wouldn't do it so I left and thought he might come to his senses, but he didn't so I started off on my own.

I lived with my aunt for a little while, until I could get on at the hospital and then I lived right on the hospital grounds, and I was on call twenty-four hours. I worked the twelve hour duty—eight at night to eight in the morning. I had a retired RN taking care of him.

Pat Pascal, 1970:
He really did have a rough life after that, after I started working in the hospital. He was brought in one night with what was diagnosed as double pneumonia, and it got progressively worse and finally settled in his stomach. We called in a specialist and he had a ruptured appendix. Right after that when he was getting over the rupture, he had an obstruction. And then an operation. And then he started getting better and some nurse exposed him to the measles, so he was in the hospital a month or two. […]

After he got out of that, he had a cold constantly. He was so run down from all the surgery. The doctor thought it was tonsils but I wouldn't operate until we could

John Frazier in 1961.

RABBIT LADY . . . Pat Pascal of 2601 Rodeo Gulch road, Soquel, holds a Black Dutch rabbit, one of her herd at Bunny Haven, the acre where she lives and raises the little furry beasties.

get him built up. At that time I quit the hospital and went to San Francisco to a dental college, and I brought him out here and had him from one doctor to the other. They kept agreeing that we had to get him built up to get his tonsils and adenoids out, but they couldn't get him built up at all. So finally they took him into St. Mary's and took his tonsils out and he got exposed to something else. […]

And then after I got him out of St. Mary's, he still had chronic colds. Finally, I got disgusted from taking him from one doctor to the next and took him to UC Med in San Francisco. There is something wrong and I'm tired of this. They kept him and found out that he had TB. When he was taken to the New Mexico hospital for pneumonia, he had TB all this time. […]

So I [inaudible] Russian River for about six months and brought him back to UC Med. They said they wanted to see him and he healed up very nicely and he hasn't been sick since.

In 1952 Frazier was in an automobile accident which left him with a concussion and a broken collar bone. According to his mother, Frazier was blind for several weeks after the accident.

Pat Pascal, 1970:
He was a bedwetter up until he got married. Almost every night.

He was a sleepwalker.

Just wander around the house and I would hear him get up because I was a light sleeper. I'd say, "John, go back to bed."

And he'd turn around and go right back to bed.

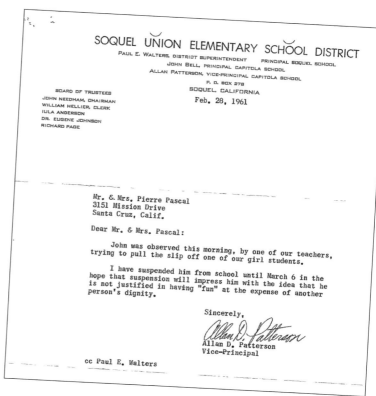

SOQUEL UNION ELEMENTARY SCHOOL DISTRICT
PAUL E. WALTERS, DISTRICT SUPERINTENDENT   PRINCIPAL SOQUEL SCHOOL
JOHN BELL, PRINCIPAL CAPITOLA SCHOOL
ALLAN PATTERSON, VICE-PRINCIPAL CAPITOLA SCHOOL
P. O. BOX 278
SOQUEL, CALIFORNIA
Feb. 28, 1961

BOARD OF TRUSTEES
JOHN NEEDHAM, CHAIRMAN
WILLIAM HELLIER, CLERK
IULA ANDERSON
DR. EUGENE JOHNSON
RICHARD PAGE

Mr. & Mrs. Pierre Pascal
3151 Mission Drive
Santa Cruz, Calif.

Dear Mr. & Mrs. Pascal:

John was observed this morning, by one of our teachers, trying to pull the slip off one of our girl students.

I have suspended him from school until March 6 in the hope that suspension will impress him with the idea that he is not justified in having "fun" at the expense of another person's dignity.

Sincerely,

Allan D. Patterson
Vice-Principal

cc Paul E. Walters

Pat Pascal, 1970:
I was having to work my way through dental college so I'd go to college in the daytime and work from 7:00 to 3:00 a.m., and I had him with a foster mother, and I put him in with a family so he would have other children to be with, and she had four of her own.

He lived with them. About two years. He started kindergarten with her so he was still young.

They were a good Catholic family and they were a little on the strict side and so was I. I bent a little but I also whacked butts too.

On June 1, 1956, ten-year-old Frazier was arrested by San Francisco Police for shoplifting a penknife. He appeared in juvenile court where the charge was dismissed. Later that year, Frazier moved to Santa Cruz.

Two years later on January 19, 1958, Frazier was picked up by Santa Cruz Deputy Sheriffs. Frazier and friends vandalized tile in a factory.

The parents of the kids cleaned the mess and no charges were filed.

An eighth grade teacher of Frazier's, 1970:
He didn't seem happy about the academic part of school. He was kind of a tough kid. His attitude was poor at times. He didn't seem like a happy kid.

Pat Pascal, 1970:
He went to a trade school near Capitola. In his first year of high [school] he started taking off, he was no longer interested. He was always playing hooky. Finally, I got hold of one of the counselors and I said it's obvious he's not interested in whatever curriculum he had and John had always wanted to be a forest ranger so a counselor tried to head him in that direction, subjects pertaining to forestry. But he quit for good after that and

Above: Frazier, first row, second from the left, in eighth grade.
Right: Frazier in 1963.

started getting in trouble.

Gary Hamby was childhood friends with John Linley Frazier. They hung out from middle school until their freshman year of high school, when Frazier dropped out a few weeks after the start of term.

Gary Hamby, 1970:
We teased him about his middle name, Linley, when he was young. Maybe that's why he went around hitting everyone.

He'd win because he's pretty slick. If he couldn't talk his way out, he'd fight his way out.

From Frazier's 2008 parole hearing—

Sandra Bryson (Presiding Commissioner), 2008:
This inmate has a history of prior criminality that does show an escalating pattern of criminal conduct, including juvenile probation, time in the California Youth Authority and juvenile parole, which he unsuccessfully served. During the inmate's school years he

began rebelling against parochial, military academy and public school teachers. The inmate was seen as a bully and a liar. Two acquaintances noted he once poured kerosene on a cat and lit it on fire. The inmate's delinquency began at ten years of age when he was arrested for shoplifting. Two years later he was again arrested for shoplifting and vandalism. The inmate was placed in juvenile hall at fifteen years of age for running away [July and October of 1961].

On November 27, 1961, Frazier was placed with foster parents, the Perry Family in Watsonville. The relationship was rocky from the start, and on February 17, 1962, he stole a .22 caliber automatic pistol and ran away from his foster parents. He said he stole the pistol to shoot animals for food. He was arrested and sent to Camp Owen in Kernville, California.

Pat Pascal, 1970:
They put him under probation and then they sent him to a farm outside of Watsonville [in June 1962] and he didn't get along there either. I don't know what happened there but he really took off [July 8, 1962], I think he stole one of the guns or something and took off. They got him again for breaking probation and sent him down south to my mother. She thought that maybe she could do something with him because he got absolutely incorrigible and the man I was married to at that time was not a disciplinarian and worked against me most of the time. I'd tell John something and he'd go behind my back and tell him not to pay any attention to her.

John Paizis (Santa Cruz County Office of Education Psychologist), 1962:
In talking about his mother, John indicated that there is nothing that he particularly enjoys doing with her because as he put it, "We have never done much together."

When asked what he particularly likes about his mother, he responded, "I don't particularly like anything about her."

The thing that he would like different about his mother would be just to be able to get along with her. On the other hand, he enjoys doing almost anything with his stepfather. John sees him as being real easy to get along with. He particularly likes his stepfather's good nature and there is nothing he would want different about him.

Pat Pascal, 1970:
When they sent him down to my mother, she had him entered in a trade school and this is where the mechanics came from, I think. He started running away again and got involved with a gal down there and they picked him up again for breaking probation and sent him to [inaudible] where he stayed for a year or two.

Pat Pascal, 1970:
When he was down south he got involved in one [girl], pretty bad. Well she had an illegitimate child.

Frazier came back to Santa Cruz and worked as a service station attendant and auto mechanic for a short time at a gas station on 41st Avenue and one in the Rancho Del Mar Shopping Center.

Pat Pascal, 1970:
He worked around there for a little while and lived with me. I had a commercial rabbit ranch and worm farm and then he started working at different sports car places, working for Foreign Auto and then Disco Auto and he met Deedee.

DELORES FRAZIER

Delores Frazier, 1970:
I met him in 1966. I was working at Disco, a discount store, and I was working at the snack bar and he was working at the mechanics part. This was in Santa Cruz. I was married at the time, working part time. I saw him and was attracted to him. He looked, to me, passionate. He was really silent, not

moody, but instead of making passes at me like people do to the girl at a snack bar, but Johnny would look at me and we'd communicate more through our eyes, and I really dug him. There was a party about two weeks later, and he asked me to dance and when we touched, that's all there was to it and there was never anybody else. It was like a magnet or a shock reaction, and I never felt anything like it in my life. It was just beautiful.

Delores Frazier, 1970:
I started taking Johnny home 'cause he didn't have a car and every time I took him home we got closer and closer, and he told me the second night I took him home that he had supposedly killed somebody a long time ago. This was really funny 'cause I guess it never happened—this is what I find out now. The second night I took him home, he said there is something I have to tell you and it may make you hate me and he was really upset, his voice was shaking and he was almost in tears, and he said when I was fifteen, he had a best friend who had saved him from a car accident. Johnny had rolled his car down a hill, and a friend had come along the road after him and seen his car down there and pulled him out just before the car exploded.

Well, his friend's sister and he were walking in a park in Los Angeles—he was staying at his granny's at the time—and saw a black man raping his friend's sister, and he banged his head on the sidewalk until he killed him. They put him in jail for excessive force to find out how come his breaking point came so easy or how come he killed when he could have stopped him. I believed him and I thought that it was just too bad, but I could understand losing his head and not knowing when to stop.

Delores Frazier, 1970:
I had to tell my husband because we were so much in love. I just couldn't live with him. I wanted to get a divorce and marry John. So

I told Al and so in the last effort to save our marriage, he sent me to Washington with my little girl, to my parents in the fall of 1966. I stayed up there with them for a while, and John and I wrote letters, and Al was moving all our stuff planning to settle in Washington. I was working in a motel and pretty soon I couldn't stand it any longer, and Johnny came up and got me two months later. I found out I couldn't get a divorce in Washington unless I lived there for a year, so I went back to California and thought I could get it there in three months. So I left my little girl with my mother and went back to California and found out I couldn't get my divorce in California because Lisa was in Washington, and I couldn't get custody of her if she was there. So I asked my mother to send Lisa down, and she wouldn't do it because I wasn't divorced or married. So I started saving money to get back up there, and we lived together for three months in an isolated cabin—a beautiful cabin on the river. It was like a honeymoon. There we had a beautiful time. He had quite a few problems. He had nightmares a lot and he wet the bed quite a few times, but he calmed down after we had been together about two months.

Frazier suffered from night terrors.

Delores Frazier, 1970:
He would get horribly sweaty and cold and he'd yell and whimper and cry. I'd just rub his back and he'd go back to sleep.

I thought it all had to do with him being in jail. I knew that he hadn't had a happy childhood, and I knew that he was very sensitive. That's one of the things I liked about him, that he was sensitive. He did have one strange nightmare once—he got up in the middle of the night and he was sleeping. He was stumbling around and cursing. I was just lying there and listening to all of this to see if I could understand anything he was saying, but I couldn't. He just kept saying, "Where is it?"

He went to the dresser and started

fumbling around and I was kind of worried 'cause that is where his gun was.

Donald Lunde, 1970:
Did he keep a loaded gun in the dresser?

Delores Frazier, 1970:
Yeah, just a little one for protection from robbers. He told me how to use it once but he never elaborated on it. I said Johnny what are you doing? And he still didn't wake up and he crawled back into bed. The next morning he didn't remember anything about it. He was really violent—shaking the dresser trying to get the drawer open.

Delores Frazier, 1970:
It was funny too when we came back to California the second time, his mother asked me if he still wet the bed. No, I said, he stopped doing that two months after we were together, but then when we moved back to Washington we had to separate because my parents were there, and I had to stay with them again. He went to stay at a boarding house and he started wetting the bed again. He didn't tell me about it, but I washed his sheets and I could see.

Delores Frazier, 1970:
We didn't have Lisa until we were together for a year. We were married in 1967 and lived together for a year before that. September of '67. That's when I got Lisa.

Delores Frazier, 1970:
Well, Washington got really hard since we worked real hard and wanted to get back to our same little cottage. Johnny started getting heartburn real bad, we were both irritable, and the city just wasn't for us. We just had to get away. So I wrote to the landlady of that place. She told us that it was going to be available in March. In March we moved back

down and we got there in March of 1968. During the trip we were really happy to be going, and the big U-Haul broke down and we had to wait two days for it to be fixed. We all shared one motel room but it was really fun. We had an excuse to stay somewhere and not work and enjoy ourselves. He didn't have heartburn during those couple days. Then we got down here and had to stay with June for two weeks. The first week that we were here, he rolled the VW that he had gotten me for my birthday the year before. It was the only dependable car we had ever had. The engine was fine but we couldn't drive it and it was really a blow. We were both crying our eyes out 'cause we didn't have insurance and had worked hard to pay for the darn thing.

Delores Frazier, 1970:
Winter in Santa Cruz is really hard. I found a job in Watsonville in the cannery—Green Giant.

Johnny still couldn't find a job and he was so low. He wouldn't help me do the house work or anything. I was really tired but he didn't want to do it and change places like that. He started worrying that the auto mechanics wouldn't be needed much longer 'cause cars were going to go out so he started talking about being an airplane mechanic, being trained in something. He talked about starting a dating service in Santa Cruz. He'd lay awake at night trying to think of something he could do.

Finally, when the things—the very last straw, I got laid off. He got a job that very same day with Putney & Perry's. Like a dream come true. He worked for a while and then started finding faults with the job, with the people. He'd get in arguments and his heartburn got really bad. He'd throw up from it.

The guy who ran the shop was really good with cars but wouldn't listen to Johnny, and this would make him unhappy and he'd change jobs. He'd always change jobs 'cause there was always someone who he couldn't

Right: Delores Frazier at John Linley Frazier's trial.

get along with or [was] always picking on him.

Delores Frazier, 1970:
We always saw his mother. They were close. They were more like buddies. They got along OK when they weren't living together. His personality would change when he got around her. He'd get a little louder.

Pat Pascal, 1970:
They came back about two years ago and I really didn't see too much of him. I'm not the type of mother-in-law that runs her son's married life. I've had that myself. I said when you want to visit you're welcome and want me to visit put your finger in the dial and call me. So I really didn't see them much.

Michael Rugg, 1970:
I wouldn't call him a hippie. When he lived in the Valley, if you passed him on the street you'd think he was just another young man—a college student, maybe—nothing unusual.

He was short but kind of stocky, well-built and strong. He knew some karate. Some people that knew him thought he was a little paranoid…quiet, but a violent person underneath.

Manuel Perry (Co-owner of Putney and Perry Automotive Service), 1970:
[Frazier was] Mr. Average Man. He was a good worker. He never gave us any trouble. He was prompt in coming to work and did a good job.

Richard Da Pont (Frazier's boss at Performance West foreign car garage), 1970:
He was the best worker I ever had.

He was fantastic. He was so good I hired him away from Putney and Perry and gave him a raise to come work for me.

Richard Da Pont, 1970:
One of the nicest guys you'd ever want to know. He was always smiling and a couple of times when he was driving by our house he just stopped in to say hello.

Delores Frazier, 1970:
He'd sneak out at night with a wad of fire crackers, and we lived next to a campground, and he'd put them in the campfires coals and wait for them to explode, and he thought that was really funny, teasing the campers. Nothing dangerous. I thought it was kind of weird and I didn't think much of it either. Sometimes he acted kind of strange.

Harold Cartwright, 1970:
John apparently read considerably when he was in CYA [California Youth Authority]; however, after he was married, he generally was too tired to read, and the only thing she [Delores Frazier] recalls that he read and really enjoyed was *2001: [A] Space Odyssey.*

One of Delores' friends from Washington came down for a visit. Frazier resented the time Delores spent with him. He returned to Washington.

Delores Frazier, 1970:
In May there was an officer at our house looking for Johnny for questioning. The officer didn't know what it was about, and he [Frazier] went down there [Police Headquarters]. He called me and told me he had to stand in a lineup because some girl had been "verbally assaulted" on her way to high school. He said just somebody who looked like him and been following this girl and saying lewd and obscene things to her. She complained to the police, and anybody in this area who fit the description and had a record was brought in for questioning and a lineup. He said of course it wasn't him, and I believed him completely because John just wasn't like that at all. I just found out from Peter Chang that it was John, and he was identified, but he was turned loose with a warning because he hadn't actually done anything, and he seemed so logical that they let him go with

a warning. This wasn't at all like the John I knew. If I would have known this, I would have known something wasn't right for sure.

Delores also started working at Free University answering phones. Shortly after that, another of Delores' friends, Allison Ayers, came down from Washington and moved in with them.

Allison Ayers, 1970:
They had been there a year before I came down. A friend of mine in Seattle used to work with DeeDee and he gave me their address, and I was just going to live with them until I found a place to stay, but they said as long as I wanted to.

I work for a company called CapriTaurus. They were friends that lived right down the road from us.

CapriTaurus is now The Bigfoot Discovery Museum. It was and is owned by Michael Rugg.

Michael Rugg, 2020:
I didn't really know John very well. I knew his wife, Delores. And Delores worked in our wood shop next door building musical instruments. She would sand our thumb pianos. Allison, who was a young gal who was living in their spare bedroom, worked in our wood shop. Delores and Allison. They all lived two houses up from us at the base of River Lane, the last house before it flattens out.

Delores Frazier, 1970:
He complained a lot about Allison 'cause she's very sloppy. "If you're the one who's bothered by it then you tell her."

Boa's Out Of Car, But That's Stretching Things A Bit

Noah the boa. Where didst thou goeth? Under the dash board of a green Plymouth, where else?

So it was that a four-foot boa constrictor, a pet of Judy Lazarus, 251 12th Ave., sneaked in through the wires and rods of a car parked at the American Free University Friday at 604 River St.

Miss Lazarus teaches a course there on snake psychology. She has one student.

Left in the car, the snake went prowling and got itself entwined.

It took John Frazier, 23, a mechanic at Performance West garage on Ocean Street, one hour to urge the long brown spotted snake out. The snake constricted around some of the auto parts and wouldn't budge until pulling and tugging finally paid off.

The boa looked longer when it was finally dislodged.

But he wouldn't. There must have been a point when things started getting bad 'cause about a month before the accident I know we couldn't relate at all. I didn't know how unhappy he really was. I guess he went and told June how unhappy he was. June told me that Allison should move out and I thought she should too, but she had nowhere to go. He was still really grouchy. He would have nothing good to say about anybody. Down on life. "Can't you just be happy, can't you look out the window and see the beautiful things outside?"

He just couldn't relax so we started going out to the movies. Went down to the Catalyst and listened to the rock bands and we enjoyed that together.

Allison Ayers, 1970:
He didn't upset me but he made me uncomfortable, something that I had never felt with anyone else. He was very gentle with animals and protective over his family. He resented me a lot, I felt because before I came down they didn't have any friends. She was feeling like she wanted to do more things and we started taking classes together at the Free

U. He really resented that and me 'cause he thought I didn't have any responsibility and he didn't want her to see things other than his way. He didn't lord over her, but felt that she should be subservient. He was chauvinistic.

Delores Frazier, 1970:
We [she and Allison] enrolled in a few courses at the Free U together. Organic farming, health foods, and drawing. He [John] didn't like me going to these, he felt I was shucking responsibility, and if I hadn't gotten the dishes done when he came home, he would get really mad. I invited him to come to some classes with us, but he wouldn't. We were losing our rapture together fast. I couldn't understand why he resented everything I did. I felt smothered as a person. I kept encouraging him that the bills were almost paid to lighten his spirits, but it didn't help. I was worn out from trying to keep his spirits up for so long.

At this point John became harder and harder to live with, very tense and despondent.

THE WEEKEND EVERYTHING CHANGED

Frazier was in a minor but life changing automobile accident on May 16, 1970, in Scotts Valley, CA. He rear ended another car. The officer at the scene stated that Frazier did not appear to be severely injured.

Floyd Weber (Scotts Valley reserve policeman), 1971:
[Frazier] spoke as an ordinary man; his speech was not impaired and he walked upright.

Delores Frazier, 1970:
It was Saturday, early, and Allison and I were in the house and he took off. I don't know where he was going. This was on Mount Herman [sic] Road in Scotts Valley. He came back really early and came in and sat down and said, "I just wrecked my car."

If I would have gotten a little scratch on his car he would have been furious, but he came home and said, "I wrecked my car. The whole front end is smashed."

And just sat there. He didn't yell about it, he didn't pace, nothing. He was really depressed and I got a strange feeling from him, like a real intense feeling. He wouldn't say anything. He had a bump on his forehead. I think it was the left side but I can't be positive. It wasn't bleeding, just raised but he wouldn't let me touch it at all. He wouldn't see a doctor and wouldn't hardly let me near him. He just sat there for a couple of hours, silent.

Immediately after the accident, Frazier started hearing voices.

David Marlowe, 1970:
At the moment of the accident he heard a voice tell him, "You will die if you continue driving."

He was upset by the accident and greatly impressed by the "voice."

Delores Frazier, 1970:
Yeah, he said he heard voices that said he should never drive again or he'll be killed. He was really different. His whole attitude was cheap and aggressive. My Johnny was gentle and loved animals and children. We went down to the beach and his whole attitude was defiant. He put on these pink sunglasses and started working on the dam and I thought I'd help him. I came down and he half ignored. Before he went down to the dam he went to the dresser where we had two tablets of mescaline. The same day as the accident. We divided them up and we each got one quarter of one and Allison had half. Some friend gave it to us in Washington. We had carried it around for a month and had no desire to take it at all. Allison had it before. And so we went down to the beach and started working on the dam. The rocks and everything were more beautiful, but Johnny

was still, I couldn't communicate with him at all. I went up the house and Allison came up with me and I said this is really nice, I think I'm going to take another quarter of the tablet. She wanted another quarter too; we each took another quarter and he just nodded at me. I went back up to the house and about a half an hour later he came back to the house. He was glaring at everything and went to the dresser and took the rest of the half a tablet. He didn't say anything but just stood in front of me with a real defiant look on his face. And swallowed it like what are you going to do about it.

Allison Ayers, 1970:
He sat DeeDee down and I in the living room and talked to us for six hours and wouldn't let us speak. He was speaking to us in a strange voice. He said he was born in India ten generations ago and was sent to the earth to save it from destruction. We were to study under him the ways to treat the earth. He kept on talking like that, it was almost biblical but you could tell it was John because he would mix up thee and thou. Once in a while he'd stop and every move he made, every action was very dramatic. He was trying to play music along with this but the tape kept messing up. I guess he had been planning how he was going to present this and the music wasn't going right and he got really frustrated and started speaking really aggressively like something was about to burst. Then he would look up and say, "I'm sorry, Father."

Delores Frazier, 1970:
His eyes were so strange, probably from the mescaline, but we didn't understand what he was saying. We weren't allowed to move or speak for about an hour. He told us that my real name is Rameria, I was adopted so I don't know what my real name is. You're going to join with me and go to the wilderness. He wanted to get Barbara, which is the girl who lives with Bert [next door neighbor]. He wanted all three of us in front

of him 'cause we were going to be like his women. I got Barbara and told her he was having a bad trip and she said she had lots of experiences with bad trips, don't worry. She got up there and she was scared too, it wasn't like an ordinary bad trip. She finally left, he was saying that a house was a devil's temple, any house.

Allison Ayers, 1970:
As the time went on he got more and more biblical sounding like a prophet. He said he was the one sent to show people the way. He kept saying he loved us and that he would never kill again. He reached out and held both my hands and DeeDee wasn't in the room at the time and I felt something go through me. Like the energy from him was really strong. I didn't like it 'cause it was really strong but it was like he was hypnotizing me. I didn't know what was happening. The words he was using were becoming more violent and aggressive and he kept putting out more and more uptight vibrations. He was saying that the power was completely in his hands and it wasn't to be questioned. He was going to take over our lives. He wrote down our names with a pencil and he asked me to get and then erased them and said we didn't exist anymore. He said that our names weren't ours anymore but were his. He kept playing this song called "Do You Know My Name," he had a fixation with the names and labels of things.

The Fraziers had a demon mask hanging on their wall.

Delores Frazier, 1970:
Both of us were so scared and looked at the mask and it was fiercely glowing and Allison grabbed it and threw it outside. Johnny snapped and said, "What was that? What did you do?"

Allison said nothing. He got up and then sat back down and resumed. He did continue on but not as strongly. A feeling of relief came over all of us when she threw it out. So

MEMO TO THE FILE

FROM: HAROLD B. CARTWRIGHT

DATE: 11/2/70

Re: People v. John Frazier

Telephone inverview with NELLIE D. GRIEBLING, age
70, ▮▮▮▮▮▮▮▮▮, Scotts Valley, CA telephone ▮▮▮▮▮▮.

She stated that her vehicle collided with the Frazier
vehicle in the intersection, and she drove to the side. He left
his car in the street. He flagged down a passing police officer
and asked him to investigate the accident.

Frazier seemed very nervous and worried about his car.
However, probably not anymore than she was. He had long hair
and a beard but was very neat and clean and she remembers thinking
what a nice boy, as he was very polite.

She asked him if he had insurance and he replied,
"unfortunately, no."

She said he was certainly sane and probably had more
presence of mind than she did under the circumstances.

The officer asked Frazier to move his car out of the
road and he replied that he couldn't drive it. Apparently he was
referring to the damage. However, he did start it and drive it
out of the street. She left and did some shopping and when she
came back by the scene, his car was gone.

She had never met Frazier prior to the accident, nor
has she seen him since.

HBC.

we went to bed and he didn't touch me and I didn't touch him, and we finally went to sleep.

The next day he was still the same though he didn't talk about the same stuff. He was really concerned with ecology. He told people to stop driving their cars. He just wasn't the same. I felt that now the magnetic feeling that we had at first had now switched polarity. I couldn't bear to touch him, I don't know what it was. After that time I couldn't sleep with him.

Delores Frazier, 1970:
Sunday and Monday things were just the same, really bad. So we called June [Delores' ex-mother-in-law and friend] and she came with her son and she called the minister and he came over and we all tried to talk to him. He was raging and kept banging a stool into the wall. He said that the whole Bible was a bunch of lies. He just wouldn't listen, he couldn't hear anything. You couldn't put his thoughts together when he spoke—it was a jumble.

June Aries (Delores Frazier's ex-mother-in-law), 1970:
He talked of the Bible and of revelations to John, and that these revelations were directed to him personally and only to him. Of how we were all to leave our homes and live in the wilderness, of how we were not to drive cars and pollute the earth in any way anymore. Of how God made this earth and gave us this beautiful world and we were destroying it. The minister tried, as we all did, to reason with him and straighten out his misinterpretation, and to urge him to try to work out a new form of engine for autos if he felt that strongly about pollution, and to advance our technology but not to regress from it. However it did no good, and the final result was to take my grandchild to my home, for her own safety and mental well being.

Delores Frazier, 1970:
So the minister left. Johnny went to Bert's house and June said we should tell Pat [Frazier's mother] what was happening to her son. Pat called an ambulance. Here comes the sirens, two cop cars. Johnny took off and

FRAZIER, John

Age 24

Date of Interview and With Whom:
5-21-70. Patient came to the clinic as a walk-in and was interviewed with his friend Bert Bongiovanni conjointly and the latter was seen briefly alone by Mrs. Kane.

Source of Referral:
"Self"although I believe friend was instrumental in bringing patient to the clinic.

Chief Complaints:
Twenty-four year old, married young man with long hair and mustache dressed informally came to the clinic seeking some kind of certification of sanity or as he put it a "physical *minimum* test". He attributes his coming here to need to prove whether or not he is still under the influence of a drug which he took on Saturday afternoon through his wife's ex-mother-in-law, etc., adding that he can't clarify his situation he may leave his family today. Patient insists that he feels no change in himself although he contradicts this by speaking of his newly aquired love of everyone and especially God. Patient just quit his job and adds that he intends to pay his bills. The friend then spoke about having seen patient for the first time in over a week on Wednesday at which point he was talking at great pace about what he plans to do and about his religious revelation.

When I tried to pin down the onset of the problem, patient brought out much to his friend's surprise that on Saturday morning he had had a car accident doing $150 damage in which no one was injured. A woman turning in front of him in an intersection had stopped unexpectedly and he had rammed into her. He *muttered* the words "if you do it again, you may be killed" and *apparently had* heard other kinds of such statements. He suddenly had the idea that his former way of life was nothing and *did* not sustain life for him. I tried to find out what he saw as an alternative and he quickly changed the subject. He went home and took the drug in order to clarify his thinking further and he insisted his mind has been perfectly clear throughout, and he is in full possession of his faculties.

disappeared. He disappeared until they left. We thought that he'd be OK. None of us realized that he had had a mental problem in his life.

Pat Pascal, 1970:
I got in the car and went out there and the Sheriff's car was there. I said did you get him or what? Bert said, no he's still out there and the sheriff says who are you and I said I'm his mother. He says what did you get the ambulance for and I said that the Drug Abuse Center told me to do it and I didn't know of any other way to handle it. He made a crack about oh, brother, those people, and he got in the car and left.

I went back home and he called me and it didn't even sound like him. Not his voice or anything. He was raving at me, "You tried to do me in!"

I told him that "I love you and if I didn't I wouldn't have done any of this. I wouldn't have called the ambulance or anything like that."

He says, "You just tried to do me in."

He says, "You're all working against me now. I don't trust none of you turkeys."

Delores Frazier, 1970:
He quit his job the day after the accident and said he'd never work on a car again.

Harold Cartwright, 2020:
He was a master mechanic and he worked for a place down on Ocean—it isn't there anymore—Performance West. He went in

Left: From the public defender's office report on Frazier's automobile accident.
Above: Delores demanded that John be checked out after his accident and mescaline trip. He complied and brought along his friend and neighbor, Bert Bongiovanni.
Next pages: An excerpt from John Linley Frazier's notated bible.

and they have washed their robes and made them white in the blood of the Lamb. 15 That is why they are before the throne of God; and they are rendering him sacred service day and night in his temple; and the one seated on the throne will spread his tent over them. 16 They will hunger no more nor thirst any more, neither will the sun beat down upon them nor any scorching heat, 17 because the Lamb, who is in the midst of the throne, will shepherd them, and will guide them to fountains of waters of life. And God will wipe out every tear from their eyes."

8 And when he opened the seventh seal, a silence occurred in heaven for about a half hour. 2 And I saw the seven angels that stand before God, and seven trumpets were given them.

3 And another angel arrived and stood at the altar, having a golden incense vessel; and a large quantity of incense was given him to offer it with the prayers of all the holy ones upon the golden altar that was before the throne. 4 And the smoke of the incense ascended from the hand of the angel with the prayers of the holy ones before God. 5 But right away the angel took the incense vessel, and he filled it with some of the fire of the altar and hurled it to the earth. And thunders occurred and voices and lightnings and an earthquake. 6 And the seven angels with the seven trumpets prepared to blow them.

7 And the first one blew his trumpet. And there occurred a hail and fire mingled with blood, and it was hurled to the earth; and a third of the earth was burned up, and a third of the trees was burned up, and all the green vegetation was burned up.

8 And the second angel blew his trumpet. And something like a great mountain burning with fire was hurled into the sea. And a third of the sea became blood; 9 and a third of the creatures that are in the sea which have souls

died, and a third of the boats were wrecked.

10 And the third angel blew his trumpet. And a great star burning as a lamp fell from heaven, and it fell upon a third of the rivers and upon the fountains of waters. 11 And the name of the star is called Wormwood. And a third of the waters turned into wormwood, and many of the men died from the waters, because these had been made bitter.

12 And the fourth angel blew his trumpet. And a third of the sun was smitten and a third of the moon and a third of the stars, in order that a third of them might be darkened and the day might not have illumination for a third of it, and the night likewise.

13 And I saw, and I heard an eagle flying in midheaven say with a loud voice: "Woe, woe, woe to those dwelling on the earth because of the rest of the trumpet blasts of the three angels who are about to blow their trumpets!"

9 And the fifth angel blew his trumpet. And I saw a star that had fallen from heaven to the earth, and the key of the pit of the abyss was given him. 2 And he opened the pit of the abyss, and smoke ascended out of the pit as the smoke of a great furnace, and the sun was darkened, also the air, by the smoke of the pit. 3 And out of the smoke locusts came forth upon the earth; and authority was given them, the same authority as the scorpions of the earth have. 4 And they were told to harm no vegetation of the earth nor any green thing nor any tree, but only those men who do not have the seal of God on their foreheads.

5 And it was granted the [locusts], not to kill them, but that these should be tormented five months, and the torment upon them was as torment by a scorpion when it strikes a man. 6 And in those days the men will seek death but will by no means find it, and they will desire to die but death keeps fleeing from them.

7 And the likenesses of the locusts resembled horses prepared for battle; and upon their heads [were] what seemed to be crowns like gold, and their faces [were] as men's faces, 8 but they had hair as women's hair. And their teeth [were] as those of lions; 9 and they had breastplates like iron breastplates. And the sound of their wings [was] as the sound of chariots of many horses running into battle. 10 Also, they have tails and stings like scorpions; and in their tails is their authority to hurt the men five months. 11 They have over them a king, the angel of the abyss. In Hebrew his name is A·bad′don, but in Greek he has the name A·pol′lyon.

12 The one woe is past. Look! Two more woes are coming after these things.

13 And the sixth angel blew his trumpet. And I heard one voice out of the horns of the golden altar that is before God 14 say to the sixth angel, who had the trumpet: "Untie the four angels that are bound at the great river Eu·phra′tes." 15 And the four angels were untied, who have been prepared for the hour and day and month and year, to kill a third of the men.

16 And the number of the armies of cavalry was two myriads of myriads: I heard the number of them. 17 And this is how I saw the horses in the vision, and those seated on them: they had fire-red and hyacinth-blue and sulphur-yellow breastplates; and the heads of the horses were as heads of lions, and out of their mouths fire and smoke and sulphur issued forth. 18 By these three plagues a third of the men were killed, from the fire and the smoke and the sulphur which issued forth from their mouths. 19 For the authority of the horses is in their mouths and in their tails; for their tails are like serpents and have heads, and with these they do harm.

20 But the rest of the men who were not killed by these plagues did not repent of the works of their hands, so that they should not worship the demons and the idols of gold and silver and copper and stone and wood, which can neither see nor hear nor walk; 21 and they did not repent of their murders nor of their spiritistic practices nor of their fornication nor of their thefts.

10 And I saw another strong angel descending from heaven, arrayed with a cloud, and a rainbow was upon his head, and his face was as the sun, and his feet were as fiery pillars, 2 and he had in his hand a little scroll opened. And he set his right foot upon the sea, but his left one upon the earth, 3 and he cried out with a loud voice just as when a lion roars. And when he cried out, the seven thunders uttered their own voices.

4 Now when the seven thunders spoke, I was at the point of writing; but I heard a voice out of heaven say: "Keep secret the things the seven thunders spoke, and do not write them down." 5 And the angel that I saw standing on the sea and on the earth raised his right hand to heaven; 6 and, by the One who lives forever and ever, who created the heaven and the things in it and the earth and the things in it and the sea and the things in it, he swore: "There will be no delay any longer; 7 but in the days of the sounding of the seventh angel, when he is about to blow his trumpet, the sacred secret of God according to the good news which he declared to his own slaves the prophets is indeed brought to a finish."

8 And the voice that I heard out of heaven is speaking again with me and saying: "Go, take the opened scroll that is in the hand of the angel who is standing on the sea and on the earth." 9 And I went away to the angel and told him to give me the little scroll. And he said to me: "Take it and eat it up; and it will make your belly bitter; but in your mouth it will be sweet as honey." 10 And I took the little scroll out of the hand of the angel and ate it up.

and said, "I can't do this. We are destroying the environment. God wants us to return the Earth to its original condition."

Frazier called work and unexpectedly quit.

Michael Stebbins (Owner, Performance West foreign car garage), 1970:

He had had an experience and could not contribute to the pollution of the environment any more by working as a mechanic, nor was he going to drive cars any more.

Allison Ayers, 1970:

Then somebody gave him a Bible and he opened it up to Revelations. To John. Yeah, he'd sit at the dining room table reading it and writing for hours and hours.

Allison Ayers, 1970:

He got into the Bible, astrology and other things and started twisting them to his purposes, which were more or less triggered by the mescaline, but I don't think it was a bad trip. I think it was before that. The first time I met him in Seattle I felt the hate and knew that I was afraid of him and didn't want to be around him. That was three or four years ago. He wasn't anything like he is now. He smoked cigars and his hair was back and greasy. He looked hard nosed. My friend told me he had killed a man when he was sixteen and I could see a caged animal inside of him. When I came down here I didn't want to stay in their house at all. I didn't have any place else to go. I was very frightened of him. I thought he was insane even when I first met him in Seattle.

Harold Cartwright, 2020:

Delores told me, "We were happy, everything was going along fine. He was working as an auto mechanic."

She had an infant and she was a victim of his as well. He would be fine and then take his Bible, walk off into the woods, and she wouldn't see him for a week. He'd be out revising his Bible. He'd go live on top of a water tower and pull the ladder up so the little people couldn't get him. It's easy to say it's all narcotics, it's all dope. But he was a classic paranoid schizophrenic.

Allison Ayers, 1970:

He used to always say that he didn't like some of the things DeeDee does like watching TV or putting some ideas in the kid's head about what is right and wrong. He was still on the same trip but with the mescaline it was like his vices toppled and saw his occupation was the very thing that was most corrupting the earth. It really shocked him and he had to get away from it. He did stop eating meat and after he moved out after a month or so he came over and was driving a car. It was always a different car. He was so vehement about never driving a car and also DeeDee told me that he was eating meat. I remember thinking how sad it was that he had backed down on the things he had said. He was very conscious of the impression he put out and always was consistent but then he was inconsistent, contradicted himself all the time.

Allison Ayers, 1970:

Another thing is he had this pair of purple sunglasses and he really dug them. I think they were DeeDee's but he wore them and had them on that night. He had them on all the time. He wore them for days. When he went outside it was really important to have them on. He said that if he went outside this time that the devil would get into his eyes.

Delores Frazier, 1970:

He wouldn't let me make phone calls and wanted to know exactly what I was saying and who I was talking to because people were plotting against him to get him into the hospital or something.

He didn't want people to find out what was in his head. He's always been like that. One of the first things he told me when we got married is don't mess with my head. The doctors where he had been in juvenile hall had messed with his head.

Delores Frazier, 1970:
He can be so gentle and sweet just like he was when we first got married, and then if something upsets him he'll become super aggressive and mad and his eyes flashing and completely different again.

Pat Pascal, 1970:
I had just sold my place in March [1970] and I got this other place. I was pretty busy running back and forth and I didn't pay too much attention to him except that I noticed a change and he was getting, I would say, more hippie-inclined.

Pat Pascal, 1970:
In June he called me up. […] He called me up and said, "Deedee and I aren't getting along."

And he said, "With all the acreage you've got up there, do you mind if I bring my sleeping bag up there and camp out?"

I said, "John, you can't have fires out there and food-wise if you want to come over and eat with me OK. If you want to rough it, that's your problem. OK you can do it."

So he came over and l left him alone, I didn't ask questions, etcetera.

John Frazier moved from his home in Felton to the milk shack on his mother's property on July 4, 1970.

LIVING IN THE MILK BARN

Donald Lunde, 1979:
From July 4 on, how often did you see him?

Delores Frazier, 1970:
Not much at all. Maybe once every two weeks. He'd come by and see me. He'd call and ask what I was doing. I kept getting these horrible—I couldn't get along with him. I'd get him dinner and he wouldn't talk much. He was always really nervous. He'd always pace or look out windows. He reacted to every noise. When we first got together he was a little like that but after a while he wasn't much at all. But now he was always on edge. He couldn't sit still for more than five minutes.

Delores Frazier, 1970:
During this time I had to go back to work. I worked at Denny's then was laid off about a month after he had moved out. He moved to his mom's, taking everything we had acquired together—the furniture, stereo, TV, pictures, cameras, all his clothes. I hadn't meant for him to move out forever, just long enough to get our thinking straight, and see where we were going. But he took everything, trying to get some kind of reaction out of me. I felt that they were his, he had worked hard for them, so let them go without a fuss. I realize now, that these things he had worked for, were for me, and when he felt they meant nothing to me, all his hard work and time were for nothing. It hit him hard that I really didn't care about those things.

Michael Rugg, 2020:
He had had that mescaline trip and was living in this shack in the backyard of his mother's place. He was observing what Doctor Ohta was doing from his shack. He'd sit in his shack and look through the cracks in his walls and see all these tractors moving everything around and tearing everything up to enlarge his house, or whatever. And he decided, this is the one I'm going to take out first.

Roger Krone, 2020:
I started working at the Catalyst in March of '67. I was a dishwasher and then I worked at the food counter. Later on, Ken Kraft from Snail asked me to come help out their equipment guy and so I became a band roadie and a sound guy in '72. It was barely the first part of the second half of the last century. Forgot a lot.

I don't know how, but I ended up renting

from his mom up on the hill. I lived on the same property as his mom and John. There was the white house and our house. I lived with two good friends from the Catalyst and a couple of ladies.

John's mother had a mobile home. She raised rabbits. She was the person in charge of the rabbits at the Santa Cruz County fair for a long time. John lived in a shed, it's gone now. He had a narrow rope bridge that led up there. He was trying to make it hard for people to get up there. I never went up to his cabin. He either came up to our house or in the shed where he worked on cars.

Above: The rope bridge leading out to Frazier's shack. Frazier trained himself to run across the bridge in the pictured condition.
Above right: The Ohta home and approximate location of Frazier's cabin. This photo was taken a day after the crimes and before Frazier was identified.

Roger Krone, 2020:
He was a mechanic. Worked on cars in one of the sheds on the property. Some client had left his Toyota Land Cruiser, and John decided to go four-wheeling and rolled the son of a bitch and wrecked it. He probably tumbled it down a ravine up there.

Roger Krone, 2020:
We did smoke pot together a couple of times. I took him to Chateau Liberté, there's an archive online, it was a hippie resort up in the mountains just on the other side of the summit.

He was pretty crazy. He was very intense. He had a funny look about him, just something in his eyes. He had a real serious stare. He had had a head injury from a car accident. That was before I met him.

Mike Wark (Friend of Frazier's), 1970:
We used to party a lot together. We'd get really drunk and smoke at the Chateau and

The Ohta home

Frazier's Cabin

take mescaline. Every time he was with me—the one time he took some and said he didn't know if he should. And I said it was OK 'cause I'd help him and he said, "OK, that's all I wanted to know."

Delores Frazier, 1970:
After that he moved out on the 4th of July. I didn't know what was happening with his life at all. Before, he had smoked grass but I had never seen him with other drugs. After he moved out, twice he came over in the middle of the night really stoned on something. One night he came in mumbling that it was reds, whatever that is. He lay down on the bed—I wanted him to rest 'cause he was stumbling and incoherent. The other night he came over, I had the door locked because I didn't want him to make a habit of it.

Delores Frazier, 1970:
We just couldn't communicate, get along. He'd say something and I just couldn't

understand, and he'd get mad and we'd fight. We'd argue and it hurts so bad 'cause this wasn't the Johnny that I had married; this was someone completely different.

Pat Pascal, 1970:
That cow barn out there, you could only get to it by a swinging bridge. There was a building over there a year ago that burned and took this bridge with it. At first it started getting on his mind. He said, "I'm going to put that swinging bridge back together. Do you mind?"

Well, I thought anything to keep him from wandering around the property all day long. So, the cables were down the canyon and he built that bridge back, working like a dog. When he went over and all the stuff from Deedee, he took it over there and stored it. He put electricity in it and stayed completely away from most of us, but he'd check in during the daytime and took the stereo over there.

Donald Lunde, 1970:
Did he ever make comments on killings, like on the Sharon Tate murders?

Pat Pascal, 1970:
A couple of times, "They must be crazy." Something like that. Something got him a couple of months ago. A kid who delivered newspapers, somebody just shot him. He saw that in the paper and he said that a guy must be awful low down to shoot a kid like that and didn't know him.

Melinda Cadwallader, 2020:
He [her father] loaned a gun to Dr. Ohta after he had someone come to the door. We believe that was Frazier. He was commenting on the doctor going on a trip soon. That's when we stayed at the house. We went out to dinner at Tampico downtown. When we came back to the house, it was being robbed.

I think the guy went out the back door. I was told to stay in the car with my mom. Not sure how my dad knew something was wrong.

Donald Lunde, 1970:
Did any of these people that you knew ever talk about the Ohtas either by name or reference to them?

Delores Frazier, 1970:
Johnny never mentioned them to me. In fact, that last time I was up there I asked him if there were any people around. He said, "Oh yeah, there's some people up there, and some over there."

He never mentioned names or seemed aggressive towards them.

Mike Wark, 1970:
He never mentioned their name [the Ohta's]. He took me up to their house one time. My old lady and I were going on a walk with him and we just ended up there.

Their house back is on a big meadow. So you can walk from there to John's house without leaving the woods. We were walking up there and he said, "I know where there is this tent and some people camping out."

We got over there and I saw that it was somebody's house. He said, "Let's look around."

I said, "No, not me."

And we split.

This is the only time that he made mention of them. I had the impression he never knew them, just their house.

Roger Krone, 2020:
A couple got married while we lived up there, and the girl's family was pretty well-to-do in southern California. Jack Lemmon was at the wedding. The wedding was up on the ridge behind our place, and John shows up there draped in an American flag. He just did his thing. It was pretty much a hippie wedding.

Roger Krone, 2020:
I never heard him talk about tarot or any of that stuff.

Michael Rugg, 2020:
I had loaned his wife some books on the subject [tarot] once, and he may have read them. I don't think he was really an expert.

Roger Krone, 2020:
While we were at work, he came by the house one afternoon and talked to the girls at the house. He was going on about crimes against the environment and people having to get rid of people like that. He thought he was the chosen one. He was chosen to start the revolution.

Mike Wark, 1970:
During that period, he was going to give me this gun and then said he would need it himself. It was a Smith and Wesson .38. A gun he had ripped off some place. Just about a week before he was sleeping up in the water tower with all the guns, watching people.

Roger Krone, 2020:

He came over one night and he said, "The revolution has started. Either you're part of the solution or you're part of the problem. I'll be back to give you a choice."

Mike Wark, 1970:

Yeah, about two weeks before it happened he told me about this burglary thing. He said, "I was in the house and I tried to call you but you weren't home and I was going to stay there and snuff them all."

Told me that he let their dogs loose.

Frazier was talking about the Muni home.

Notes from Harold Cartwright's interview with Mike Wark on November 11, 1970—

Harold Cartwright, 1970:

Wark remembers that approximately ten days before the murders, he received a call from Frazier one night, and Frazier stated "I've got something—I've got a piece for you." Stated Frazier went on to explain that he had a .38 caliber Smith and Wesson 4" barrel, and a .22 caliber Ruger. Stated that Frazier went on to say that he had stolen them in a burglary and that he had been in the house for a long time. He stated that he had thought about staying there until the people came home and snuffing them.

The next day Frazier went to Mike Wark's home.

Harold Cartwright, 1970:

At five o'clock that day, he called Frazier back and Frazier came over to his house and brought the .38 caliber 6-shot revolver special with 4" barrel. Wark stated that Frazier was acting really weird, he had the gun laying on his coat on the lounge near the front door and when somebody knocked on the door, Frazier grabbed the gun and pointed at the door, but then after a second put it back down. He talked about snuffing the mate-rialists that night in front of both Wark and his old lady. Wark stated he asked him what it would accomplish and Frazier wouldn't answer. He would make comments like they were rednecks, materialists, etc.

Delores Frazier, 1970:

He called me Friday [October 16] afternoon and asked me if I would come up to the farm that weekend. I didn't want to and I didn't have transportation and so he said OK you don't deserve it anyway and hung up. I tried to call him back and called his mother and told her that I was trying to get a hold of him. He called me back and I said I was sorry and promised I would come out Saturday. So he came out Friday night. I didn't expect him and we started arguing practically right away. We started arguing about paying two $100 bills we had to pay and I wanted to stop arguing and he wouldn't stop. So I left and went down to the neighbors.

Allison and Frazier were alone most of the evening.

Allison Ayers, 1970:

He'd go from one extreme to the other. He kept saying, "I love you. I love you." And I loved him too. I still do because the spirit of Johnny is so strong, so intense. He's one of those people you can feel. Everybody reacted to him in some way. Most people reacted up tight but he mellowed out considerably. Like there was a big load off his shoulder that he was pushing off on everyone.

Donald Lunde, 1970:

Did you ever make love?

Allison Ayers, 1970:

No, we never had anything like that. He told me the last time I saw him, he gave me a bullet and said he didn't want anyone fucking with me and he felt this as strongly as he did about his own wife.

Donald Lunde, 1970:
The bullet was what?

Allison Ayers, 1970:
The bullet was trying to protect me.

Allison Ayers, 1970:
He was there a lot that weekend. I stayed away from him 'cause he was nervous as a cat. I could tell something was happening to him and that he was going to do something. I thought he was splitting to the East. I didn't have any idea what he was going to do, but he flashed this gun at me and I kept asking DeeDee what was happening to him 'cause I didn't feel that I could approach him with it. His eyes were someplace else.

One of the few times that I felt I was communicating with Johnny was that week-end. He came over and they had a fight and DeeDee went down the street 'cause she didn't want to argue. We talked and before he had asked me what I thought about their fights, etcetera and usually he didn't listen to me. But I told him that this wasn't the John-ny that she married and that the bad side had taken over. We were talking about revolution in terms of the earth. He had made a lot of remarks to me that I hadn't understood. I knew that we agreed a lot on this like the kind of food you eat, and how you treat the environment and other people. He asked me why it doesn't work with DeeDee and he kept saying that she doesn't deserve it. It was like he hated and loved her at the same time.

Delores Frazier, 1970:
I came back after watching a movie at a neighbors, and he was sitting alone in the dark waiting for me. I was friendly, I didn't want to argue, trying to keep it smooth. We managed to talk, small talk, for a while, then I went to bed and he slept on the floor.

Delores Frazier, 1970:
Saturday morning he told me that he was going to give back all the stuff 'cause he was going to go back East. He told his mother

New York and me back East. His father was in Ohio. I asked if he wanted to see his father and he said, "What for? He never wanted to see me."

On Saturday, October 17, Frazier and Delores played a game of chess, then borrowed their neighbor's truck, and packed up everything in his shack.

Delores Frazier, 1970:
We got to the farm and moved everything out. We got along really good. I was really trying because I knew there was something definitely wrong. He had this orange powder, mescaline, and asked me to split it with him. It was in a little plastic container. He said it wouldn't hurt me so I took it and it didn't have much of an effect. We were getting along just fine. I liked his cabin and he said maybe we'd live there someday. We moved everything out and went back home and stopped and got a bottle of wine.

Harold Cartwright, 1970:
On the way back out to Felton they stopped at Santa Cruz Electronics and John purchased approximately six cassette tapes for the recorder. Later he commented, don't use all the tapes because when I get back from my trip, I want to use some of them. She [Delores] knows that he didn't want to record music, as he had a voice microphone and he indicated that he wanted to say something on the tapes.

She recalls that when John mentioned the trip he was going to take, he would become very nervous and upset. This was noticeable in the expression on his face and even to the change in his voice. It was very obvious that the trip bothered him considerably.

Michael Rugg, 2020:
My house had a driveway that connected up with River Lane, across my property, and also connected up with Beth Drive in Gold Gulch. So that particular day they were com-ing home and PG&E was working out at the

He used to always write everything down, from when
I first knew him, when he wrote down everything almost religiously.
He always wrote everything down in accounts books - income - what
he bought("all he was worth") he used to say, was written down.
Very methodical, to help him be organized, said he "had to do things
like that." He did this until we moved back to California the
second time. It was harder for him to do it with me working, and
spending separately, and he got frustrated with it. I took over
depositing money, and paying the bills, he never knew what was in
the bank, or going out.

Christmas, he was always grumbling about how many presents
Lisa got, and that he never got very many, sometimes none. And he
felt Christmas was too material and Lisa should know the true
meaning instead of so many presents. As he was talking he seemed
very bitter.

When Lisa had a birthday, and I gave a party for her, he
told me how much that meant to a kid, and how he had never had one,
and if just once his mother would have had one for him.

He said his mother wanted to screw everybody in the county
and didn't want him around.

About a month ago, a friend of ours said when they were
together and had car trouble, John was beating his head against
a telephone post.

He was always very frustrated because he couldn't seem
to play any instrument. It really bothered him because he wanted
to make music so bad.

He was a perfectionist, and knew it.

The neighbor told me once John told him John thought
I liked him because he had killed that guy when he was 15. I know
I never gave him cause to think that, though I did feel sympathy
because of his hurt.

His emotional state was very erratic, either way up or
way, way down, as it was most of the time from 1969 on, getting
worse through 1970 - I thought it was the bills, and his job. I
didn't know he had had so many earlier problems.

Before I met him he used to dot his "i's" with an "ẋ"
like   x   x
     like this.

highway, blocking River Lane. So they went down Beth Lane and down our driveway. When they got to our house, we had a car parked in our driveway. So they came up the stairs to ask me to move the car, so they could get to their house. That was the whole scene. Delores came up first because we all knew her. She introduced us to her husband, because we had waved and all that, but by then he had moved out. This was our first time really looking at him eye to eye and meeting. We had a new person living at the house, during the sixties, my house down by the river was kind of communal. A lot of hippies and a lot of people who also worked in our wood shop. So, we had a person stop by the house from Australia. She was half Australian and half Japanese. That day, she had decided that she was going to cut off all her hair. You know? It was the '60s. Everyone was doing something for some reason. She was sitting at the dining room table with her newly shorn bald head. He walked through the sliding glass door and he was wearing mountain man clothes, knee high tied sneakers that you get at the renaissance fair, a flat hat, a fringe jacket, a huge hunting knife. He looked like Jeremiah Johnson. He just stood there staring at her bald head. I was staring at him because I had never felt such vibes in my life. He was projecting the heaviest vibes, you know? Just, "Get him out of here. He's creeping me out."

I don't remember him saying anything. He talked to Maggie a little bit about her bald head.

They left and that was that.

Delores Frazier, 1970:
He set it up the way he wanted it for me. He wanted the stereo in the bedroom so the bill collectors couldn't see it. He ran a bath for me and then he ran a bath for himself.

Frazier visited the neighbors.

Mike Wark, 1970:
The first time I had heard about it [tarot]

was the Saturday before the murder. He came over to my house and said, "Do you know what the Knight of Cups, and the other knights are?

I said, "No, I don't."

Bert said, "Yes. I do."

He says what they are. John says, "This one here represents the warrior, and the other is the avenger," or something.

It was a really super weird, violent trip. You could just feel the violence. That's the last time I saw him.

Delores Frazier, 1970:
That night Bert and his girlfriend's cousin came over and we watched *The Russians Are Coming* Saturday night, and we were enjoying the movie, and Johnny was as much as he would let himself, but he was really on edge. He was pacing and looking out the window, looking at every car that went by, and he was making phone calls in the dark. He couldn't see, he was just dialing. I went out there once to see what he was doing and I heard him say, "The Russians are coming!" And then hang up and laugh. Then he'd walk back in the living room and look out the window.

June Aries, 1970:
The Saturday night before the Ohta murders he called us. I answered the phone and he said, "The hippies are coming, the hippies are coming."

I answered, "No John, the Russians are coming, the Russians are coming."

It was the movie on TV that we were watching—he may have been watching it too—he laughed, then said, "Bye June," and hung up.

I think he realizes "hippies" upset me. I'm afraid I don't or can't understand why these young people insist on looking as they do or living as they do.

Delores Frazier, 1970:
Saturday I made up my mind to make things as pleasant for him as I could. I was

just starting to see his hurt. I had the same feelings of uneasiness, but I felt compassion now. We had a good day, considering the way we usually argued, and that night we slept together. He had said I was so lucky to have him to love, and who loved me, and he had nobody. I tried to comfort him by holding him. The next day I kept seeing how deeply hurt he was, and tried to keep him happy, and when he left, I didn't want him to go, and was crying, though I didn't say anything. He pulled away from me and left Sunday [at] three thirty.

Donald Lunde, 1970:
Did he say anything to you about anything happening Monday?

Delores Frazier, 1970:
Just that he was going to go back East. That's what I thought.

Harold Cartwright, 1970:
Mrs. Frazier commented that on Saturday night, John stated to her that he had to do a loyalty trip and then he would be back. He repeated this same thing on Sunday morning. At the time, she felt that he was referring to a trip, like the trip back East that he had talked about. Now she feels that he may have been referring to an action, as opposed to a journey.

He left Sunday afternoon. He took a loaded .38 caliber Smith & Wesson revolver tucked into his waistband, a backpack with food for several days, and a pair of expensive-looking binoculars.

He left a book on Tarot.

Allison Ayers, 1971:
[Quoting Frazier] "If the police come you don't know me. You don't know anything about me and you don't know where I am."

He had told his friend he had been inside Ohta's house and had stolen the binoculars. Ohta's daughter, Taura, later confirmed the theft of the binoculars.

Pat Pascal, 1970:
Sunday night was the last time I saw him. He came in, I was back in the trailer watching TV, already had dinner and he came in filthy, sat there and stared a little. He ate something out of the frying pan, never said a word all the time and finally got up and said, "Later."

And that was that and I didn't see him anymore and I left Tuesday. I heard about the killings Tuesday morning but had already planned Monday morning to go into Nevada to look at some property over there. I left Tuesday and didn't know anything about this until I was on my way back and stayed in [inaudible] City overnight and it came over TV and I guess you know how I felt. His picture came on and it doubled me up.

Donald Lunde, 1970:
He [Frazier] proceeded to tell me that Sunday night, the 18th, he had slept out in the meadow near the Ohta house. He had apparently been watching the house and was familiar with the house having been up there previously.

On October 19, 1970, Frazier murdered four members of the Ohta Family and Dorothy Cadwallader.

Michael Rugg, 2020:
I was hearing about the murder on the news and it was weird because I got the distinct impression that I knew the murderer. I just had this intense feeling that the person who killed them, I knew. I just couldn't put it together.

Sergeant Walker (Santa Cruz County Deputy), 1970:
Did he ever talk about tarot cards?

Bob Bongiovanni, 1970:
At my house.

Sergeant Walker, 1970:
What kind of significance did he put in the knight?

Bob Bongiovanni, 1970:
A kind of violent warrior and vengeful and one representing warrior and vengeance. He had all the different meanings for them. I was talking with Delores last night and she brought up about the cards and that John and these other cats that lived up there had this little trip going and that John was the Knight of Pentacles and that this other cat was the Knight of Cups. So, then this morning this other cat came over to my house and said, "Did you hear about that thing? Did you read in the paper this morning that

they found the note mentioning how it was signed?"

I said, "Yeah."

Then I went over to Delores' and told her we had to do something. Delores didn't let me in. She said, "No, I can't see anybody today."

Deputies were with Dolores at that time.

Delores Frazier, 1970:
I don't know what day he was arrested. They came to my house Tuesday and stayed with me all that time—the police.

Mickey Aluffi, 2020:
When Frazier was on the run. Frazier's wife, Delores, was afraid for her life. So the Sheriff's Office decides to put a couple of guys in her house at night. So while she's

---

Above and next page: The Ohta family funeral.

114

sleeping we can protect her. As it turns out it's me and Don Smythe. She was very nice and we're there and then she decides to go to bed. So Don and I are sitting there trying to figure out ways to spend our time. All of a sudden the outside porch light goes off. That got our attention. A few minutes later it came back on. And then it goes off again. And I say, "He's out there. He's trying to lure us outside."

And Don says, "Nah, it's just a little light humor."

It was just a loose light bulb.

Roger Krone, 2020:

We decided we were going to move right before they found him. Maybe Thursday night. We couldn't, in our conscience, stay there, renting from his mom knowing that we had turned on her son. We just moved out.

Services for Dorothy Cadwallader were held on October 22.

Lark Ohta, 2020:

She [Dorothy Cadwallader] wasn't supposed to be there, and I feel sickened that she was. I guess no one picked up Derek from school, and so she drove over to get him. She was like family to us, but she should not have been there.

Terry Medina, 2020:

The guy who called had said, "Hey, everything I'm hearing sounds like this guy I know. His name's John Linley Frazier."

He's the guy that said, "He's this really strange guy. He talks about all this crazy stuff."

This guy tells us that Frazier lives in this shack that had like a rickety wood rope bridge across the gully there. And so it's actually down the hill on the other side, behind Soquel High School. I can't remember the name of that street. Anyway, so he puts that out.

We put together surveillance teams immediately on that place and it would make sense, right because if you go by the way the crow

flies from the Rincon tunnel, down into the gorge, up the other side, over the mountains, you would get there. So they put a surveillance team together.

One of the first teams on this place was Brad Arbsland and Rod Sanford. And the next day they got on it. They're there. They're hiding in the weeds.

The next team that was supposed to come on at eleven o'clock was me and somebody else. I don't remember who it was. Anyway, they did something really cool that we used to do all the time. We called it *Indian tricks* back then. They knew nobody was in this crazy shack. It was very hard to get to. But they had binoculars and they were close enough to see everything clearly. So they took pieces of twigs and branches and they set them in certain places that they could see with the binoculars. We called those Indian

tricks. I don't know what else to call it.

So they could see these twigs and branches and if they were moved, they knew somebody went into this shack.

After a few hours they look and the stick is gone. They decided they were going to go take the place. And somehow they got across there and into the shack and John Linley Frazier got arrested.

The arrest occurred at seven thirty in the morning on Friday, October 23. Later that day the Ohta Family funeral was held.

Frazier was arrested with a knife found to have traces of copper filings, believed to be from the Ohta's telephone wires.

Above: A few hours after the funeral, Sheriff Doug James announced that Frazier had been caught.

From the steps of the County Building, at eleven o'clock, Sheriff Doug James announced to the press that Frazier had been caught—

Doug James, 1970:
Two of our deputy sheriffs: Brad Arbsland and Rod Sanford, were on surveillance in the vicinity of a cabin the suspect has used before. Early this morning, they checked the cabin and found the suspect, Frazier, asleep. They took him into custody without resistance. The suspect was not armed. Frazier was taken to this office and was booked on the warrant that was issued early last evening. This warrant charges the suspect with five counts of murder.

*Above: Above: The press descends on Santa Cruz.
Right: Frazier after being taken into custody.*

Mike Lee (KPIX reporter), 1970:
Frazier was arrested a few days later while sleeping in a cabin about a mile from the murder scene. This ended widespread speculation the murders were the work of a hippie commune. This on the heels of the Manson trial.

Jim Ingram (Santa Cruz Deputy Sheriff), 2021:
Upon the capture of Frazier and his arrival, under heavy guard at the county jail, newspaper, TV, reporters, etcetera, flooded the lower floor of the Sheriff's Office, county jail, court building on Front Street clamoring for photos of him.

Due to the heavy security presence they were not allowed inside.

Following much discussion among the law enforcement and press, an arrangement was made where I would use a camera of the

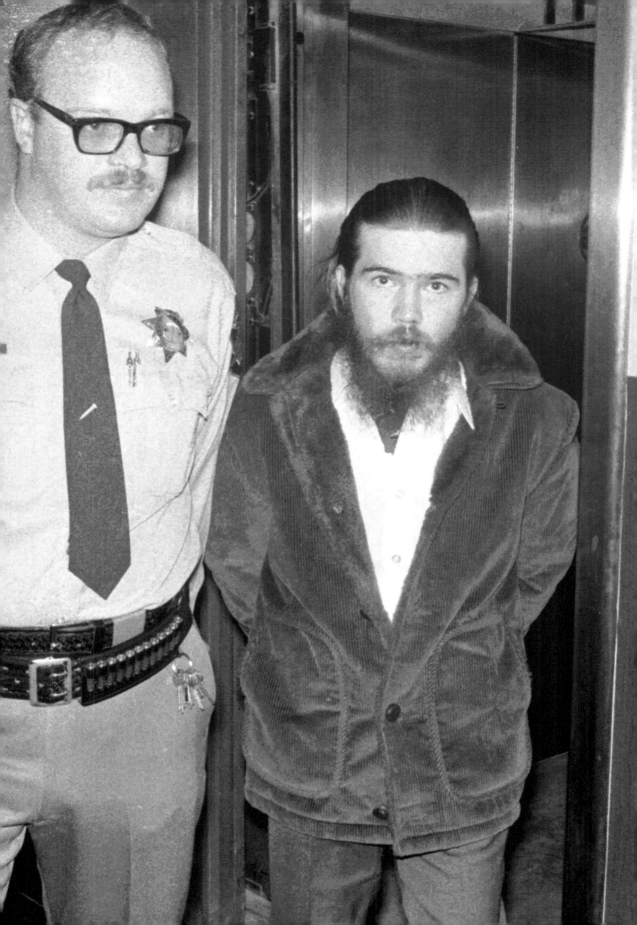

Associated Press' photographer, and take a photo that the AP would distribute.

After he was arrested, Frazier called Delores.

Delores Frazier, 1970:
The first thing he said was, "I'm sorry. I brought disgrace on our name."

His voice was shaking. I told him that I loved him 'cause I realized he really needed it then.

Harold Cartwright, 1970:
The first phone call that John made to his wife from the jail, he stated he said something which she couldn't understand which ended with "and don't be late." And she took this to mean that he was referring to life after death. Both John and his wife believe in reincarnation and on the Sunday when he left, they talked about having a son. On his first telephone call, he said that he would like very much for her to have a son. The inference was that he felt that he could come back to her as her son.

Mike Lee (KPIX), 1970:
The murder weapon has never been found and there are no eyewitnesses to the killings.

Lark Ohta, 2020:
After the murders, my sister married her boyfriend from Santa Cruz. It was a brief marriage, but he was a great person, and he helped me a lot, at the time.

Taura had been at Design School in New York and I was away at boarding school in Monterey. Afterwards, Taura was too young for me to go live with—we talked about it, but, she was only eighteen and it wouldn't have worked. I needed to be in a family. My grandmother was my guardian, my mother's mom, but I didn't want to stay in Santa Cruz. My parent's friends all offered, too, but

I wanted to leave. It was all happening in a flurry. I asked to go live with a girlfriend's family in Sacramento. She was my best friend from summer camp and I loved her big, lively family.

Everything was in a tailspin and I was a fifteen-year-old kid. But I knew I wanted to go. And in the end, everybody just let me—and they didn't argue. After I moved to Sacramento, I didn't want to be adopted by my new family, as that felt like a betrayal to the family that I had lost, so they became my guardians—and they became my family. I moved away [from Santa Cruz] within a week. I left straight from the funeral on Friday and they had died on Monday. There was so much going on, and all so quickly.

Of course, it took a while to adjust, but they became my mom and dad, and they have all—always been my children's family. Thank goodness they said "yes."

Lark Ohta, 2020:
I just disappeared from Santa Cruz. And I have always wondered and been curious. Always. I've wanted to know what happened to everyone, my friends and schoolmates. All those people. The next day when they went to school. What happened to everybody? What was that like? And then I didn't come back. It has been a black hole for me, and I have wanted to reconnect, but it has always been too heavy a load for me to lift. I know that I can handle bad things. I know—I've done it. But it makes me sad for others because I don't know if they can. I don't know, and I feel strangely responsible for their sadness.

On Saturday, Frazier was picked out of a lineup by the people who saw him driving in Bonny Doon in Mrs. Ohta's Oldsmobile.

The three "hippies" who broke the case issued a statement to the media:
We are all citizens of Santa Cruz County, and we are all concerned about what happened here this week, and what might happen if

Right: Frazier's writings after being arrested.

I SEE THE ONLY EXPLINATION FOR LIFE THEREFORE I WILL REGRESS FROM ITS DESTRUCTION AND WILL NO LONGER ~~MY~~ CAUSE MY GOD GREIF.

I AM IN THE RELM OF THE POWERS OF DARKNESS (DEVIL SATIN DEMON OR ANY OTHER NAME THAT CALLS THE MASTER OF EVIL ~ DEATH) AND I SEE THE ONLY EXPLINATION FOR DEATH OR DARKNESS AND I KNOW HIS PLAN — But I Also KNOW MY GOD AND BECAUSE OF HIS SUBJECTS I ALSO KNOW HIS WORD — THERE FORE I MUST DO EVERY— THING TO SUPPORT MY GOD —

THE PRESENT CONDITION OF THIS WORLD IS SO, THAT MAN CANNOT SUSTAIN LIFE AS INTENDED BY GOD SO I JOHN TEAGIE BELIVE HE WILL INTERVEIN ACCORDING TO THE LAST BOOK OR CHAPTER

Received 11/6/70

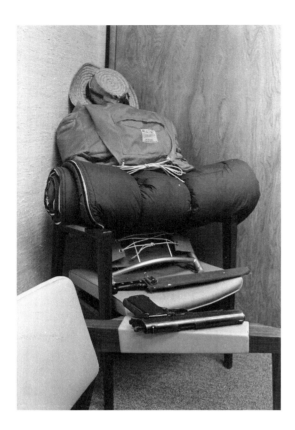

hatred and hostility continue to grow between straights and longhairs.

We recognize the irrational effect of fear these murders have brought about, and we are concerned for the safety of our entire community, straight and longhair.

As it is wrong to do murder, so it is wrong for a person to take the law into his own hands.

Our main concern is the crime of one man against another, regardless of who the men were. It is foolishness to mistrust each other now.

Harold Cartwright, 2020:

I got a call early from Gary Britton, who was Frazier's mother's attorney for her divorce. He handled her divorce and he said, "You know Mrs. Pascal found something interesting in her chicken cages this morning that

Above: Frazier's backpack, knife, a pistol, and other items were found in his mother's chicken coop.

might be the murder weapons. I want you to go out and get them."

I said, "Gee, Gary, I have to be on a plane at ten o'clock, remember that accident you wanted me to work on outside of Denver."

I called Bill Tubbs and had him go get it. It was the orange bag that the witnesses had seen Frazier with. It had his name on it, Frazier.

In the bag was a hunting knife and a .45 caliber automatic pistol.

Sam Robustelli, 2019:

I started with the Sheriff's Office in 1970, and very early on I was with Peter Chang out at a farm where Frazier had been staying. We didn't have a search warrant, but I saw an open window on the second story of this barn. I said, "See that open screen window, I could climb up that tree and jump on in the window. It's open. Would we be violating anything?"

Pete said, "No."

I said, "You can do that?"

"Yeah, do it."

We weren't sure if any evidence was in there. There wasn't. When we were in court in San Mateo, it was funny because we were saying how we got into this barn to do a legal search through the open window and the defense attorney said, "Basically, you're telling me you're either a monkey or a squirrel."

I said, "Whatever you want to call it."

The Santa Cruz Medical Society's executive board had put up a $15,000 reward, Supervisors talked about adding $5,000 if they legally could, and The Valley National Bank in Watsonville had established a fund in order to collect donations to add to the reward. They raised $286.

Roger Krone, 2020:

I got part of that reward. I don't know who put it up.

David Marlowe (Professor of Psychology UCSC), 1970:

My first contact with John Frazier was on Friday, October 23, 1970, several hours after he was taken into custody by the police. I have seen him, as of this date, fifteen times for approximately twenty hours of testing and interviewing.

David Marlowe, 1970:

He claims that one phrase "occult philosophy" best describes his views. When questioned closely about his beliefs, Mr. Frazier becomes angry or laughs condescendingly and occasionally lapses into petulant silence. In particular he is unable to reconcile his professed love of life and nature with his insistence that killing may be necessary to save the world. He was also, he stated, quite "willing to go to the gas chamber" if that was the outcome of his predicament. Trying to save his life amounted to nothing, since his body was material while his "soul was beautiful" and would "survive on another level of existence." If the lawyers want to defend him, that was "their trip" and was "groovy." He personally didn't care and once even wondered what it would be like to "get high when the gas pellet hit the water."

With regard to the crime, he expressed no emotional concern for the five murdered people and never once displayed any sign of concern, outrage or guilt. When I quoted the "kill to live" slogan of The Weathermen he merely smiled, nodded, and said "yeah, that's it." The only spontaneous and seemingly sincere expression of positive emotion during all our meetings involved his feelings for his wife and child, whose lives he held were endangered by the "Organization." The "Organization" includes the three people who Frazier claims did the actual killings while he remained below, never actually setting foot near the house or the victims.

Donald Lunde, 1970:

We discussed at length the issue of whether or not he [Frazier] believed this summer and earlier this fall that it was right to kill human beings if they were abusing the environment or too materialistic. John nodded in the affirmative to this question and then said to me, "You mean like five people?"

Richard Verbrugge, 2020:

Mr. Chang went to interview Frazier. Frazier had on the orange suit. You know, the orange inmate suit. And he was barefoot or in those jailhouse slippers. But he was sitting there and I got this secondhand from Sweeney what happened. But, but, you know Frazier wouldn't talk. He didn't talk to law enforcement. So he was being unresponsive, but then he made some smart remarks about the Ohta family that really bothered Mr. Chang. You know, he saw his son's face on the boy's body coming out of the pool. Anyway, on his way out, Mr. Chang stomped on Frazier's foot and, well, he broke Frazier's toe. You won't read about that anywhere.

Michael Rugg, 2020:

I found out later from Delores and Allison that he [Frazier] had a snuff list. He had a sheet that he was writing down all the various people he wanted to murder. It was based on the amount of capitalism they were involved in. He was an anti-capitalist. We were on the list because we were making and selling musical instruments and hiring his wife. That made us capitalists.

Michael Rugg, 2020:

Delores said she never took any of his ideas seriously. He had that list, but she figured it was more of his drug induced bullshit.

STRAIGHTS VS. LONGHAIRS

Lark Ohta, 2020:

In the culture we live in now, when something bad happens, there are thousands of TV shows, *Datelines* and *20/20*s—and not just shows, but stations—and they all need content. I'm always shocked that there could be so many horrible things happening. And nowadays people and families often talk to these TV stations, they do give interviews. In 1970 that was not the case. There were only three TV stations, and only family-friendly content. People talk now, and they do interviews about horrible tragedies that were so recent, and it startles me. But it is a different time.

At that time, the only killings that I remember were Truman Capote's *In Cold Blood*, and then Manson. And of course there were others, but we just never heard about them. People disappeared and we never knew. There was also a killer in Chicago, Richard Speck, who killed many nurses, and that was on the news—it scared me badly at the time. Unfortunately, I was afraid a lot.

You started hearing about serial killers in the 1970s. Before that it was very unusual to hear about those crimes. Of course they happened, but you didn't hear about them. So when this happened, it was such huge news around the world. I think because it was a whole family, and only a year after the Manson killings. And again because it was something that hadn't been in the news before, and you didn't hear about these stories.

It made so much news that it was kind of overwhelming. My sister and I began receiving letters. Enough to fill a whole room. We received bags and bags and bags of mail from people who expressed their sadness, and again I think it was because it was a whole family. That's hard on people, and they want to reach out—and so they write. Taura and I read a lot of the letters, as many as we could, and it was comforting but overwhelming, too, for a fifteen-year-old girl.

Ward Damio, 1974:

What happened in Santa Cruz may be one

of the first examples of a community which has been overwhelmed by "future shock." The invasion of the students and the "undesirable transient element" [UTE's] in the late sixties, created a community of third-generation fishing and logging families— and first generation longhairs in which there was no room for "the average American." Mullin and Frazier, both all-American boys made grotesque efforts to adopt hippie characteristics and after the effort to find a place in the new culture around them failed, they went over the edge.

Terry Medina, 2020:
In '68 and '69 San Francisco had the Zodiac killings. Remember, he had threatened kids on school buses and all that. All of us deputies in Santa Cruz, we were following and guarding school buses all over the place. So the community now is already kind of heightened to these big crimes. They're somewhere else but that stress is spilling over to us. They know that deputy sheriffs and police departments are having to provide security for school buses. Zodiac is in the news every day. Then, BOOM, in '69 right on the heels of Zodiac comes the Manson family murders, the Tate-La-Bianca murders. And the weirdness and hippies and all that shit. And you've got the new UCSC that's pretty full of hippies, and you've got the change in the San Lorenzo Valley where the old establishment is getting lost to all these communes. So the community is getting pretty uptight to say the least.

Grey's Gun Shop is selling out of guns. United Cigars is selling out of guns.

And then the Ohta Family and Cadwallader all get murdered at one time. A huge,

huge mass murder case. This town was ready to blow.

Before Frazier was apprehended, at the October 20 Supervisors meeting, Supervisor Mello pushed for the supervisors to offer a $25,000 reward. They settled on $5,000, knowing it was illegal for county money to be used in such a way. The board members agree to be personally liable if they were sued or fined.

Henry Mello (Santa Cruz County Supervisor), 1970:
I just couldn't believe that such a horrible, sadistic massacre could occur in our county and I just wonder who in the hell will be next if the government just sits by and lets these sadistic acts continue.

Around the same time as the killings, someone

called in a bomb threat at the opening of the new Ben Lomond Bank of America branch.

Dan Forbus (Santa Cruz County Supervisor), 1970:

It's hard for me to believe that this was a coincidence. It took several deputies to investigate that call and it just seems strange that it should have happened at the same time as the other incident.

Dan Forbus, 1970:

The citizens are scared. Robberies, house break-ins, and other crimes have increased. I'm convinced there has to be some method of cutting down on the criminal element in Santa Cruz County. I know some people will scream about their rights getting stepped on but we are going to have to start looking at the transient element, and those people who come here with no visible way of making a living. Maybe this thing is more complex than that, but I think this incident is going to bring it all to a head.

Members of the public were invited to speak at the meeting.

H.R. Lans, 1970:

I think some commune did what happened last night.

If they get away with this one there are many more planned already.

Ernest Wicklund (Santa Cruz City Mayor), 1970:

[I was told] If you don't do something right away, we're going to take the law into our own hands.

Any talk of formation of vigilante groups at this time should not be given serious consideration. People are understandably very upset but it is in situations like this, that we as citizens must exercise a sense of reasonableness more than ever before.

Don Righetti (*Santa Cruz Sentinel* Staff Writer), 1970:

The Catalyst, a Front Street hippie hangout, received a telephoned bomb threat this morning. The caller said, "You murderers! Wait until the bomb goes off!"

No bomb was discovered.

From the *Santa Cruz Sentinel*, 1970:

The club received three more bomb threats over the next week.

Note found at a dress shop next door to the Catalyst Club:

Now, tell me. What good are hippies? Hippies are pollution, hippies are pollution. - Causes dope. Dope causes mind pollution. Mind pollution causes murder. The only good hippie is a dead one.

One side of the note had a picture of a bomb. The other side had a picture of a noose with the note, "reserved for hippies."

Geno Pini (Santa Cruz Police Chief), 1970:

We have no foundation to say that any vigilante action will be taken. There is no question that most people can place themselves in the position of the Ohtas as victims of this terrible crime, and this, of course, brings about a certain amount of fear.

But we think good common sense and solid judgment will prevail with most of the people.

Harold Cartwright, 2020:

There was always conflict. The merchants wanted everything cleaned up and the City Counsel and the County Board of Supervisors are doing what they can, within the law, to make Santa Cruz a better place to live, I guess.

Chris Cottle, 2020:

There was always some tension. A lot was blamed on the university coming in. There was a lot of marijuana being used. Most of the people that lived in that fashion were called hippies.

UCSC

The University of California Santa Cruz opened in 1965. The University of California President said UCSC was—

Clark Kerr, 1965:
The most significant educational experiment in the history of the University of California.

The campus' first Director of Academic Planning and Provost of Cowell College coined the phrase *orderly disorder* to clarify the campus tone and objective.

Byron Stookey Jr. (UCSC's first Director of Academic Planning), 1965:
In order to foster student initiative and individualism, we must institutionalize a tolerance for innovation.

Forrest Robinson, 2020:
Students in Santa Cruz at that time were very, very good. We were getting the absolute cream of the crop. It sort of got out that this was a really cool, interesting place where kids could go and learn. You had a sense where it was a welcoming place to the kind of kids that might be ignored or mistreated, socially, elsewhere. Nerds. Nerdy people. A lot of the undergraduates were hip, or dressed like hippies. There were a lot of drugs on campus at the time, but they were kiddie drugs.

Terry Medina, 2020:
The establishment community in Santa Cruz was turning against UCSC because UCSC was not anything as it was supposed to be. Santa Cruz opened its arms welcoming UCSC, which was going to be this great campus. There was going to be football. It was going to be the pride of Santa Cruz. It turned out to be a hippie dippy, Oxford system, counterculture place and some people

were mad about that. It wasn't what they were expecting.

Jim Conner, 2020:
It's human nature to shun away from what you consider the norm. People with short hair didn't like people with long hair because they were different. They had a hard time accepting them. Never had anything good to say about them.

So when the demonstrations of the Vietnam War came along, I mean, we were all out there on the front line getting our butts kicked and dealing with them on a one-on-one basis, you know, we became callous too. You know, those assholes. Why don't they get a job? You know, quit laying around on the street and having us support them. All that kind of stuff. We were just as prejudiced and just as biased as anybody else. That's just human nature, you know. That's been going on since the beginning of time. Look what they did to Jesus because he was different.

Chris Cottle, 2020:
The killing of the Ohta family by Frazier brought a lot to a head. It brought a lot of focus to people out there living out in the woods. There were thousands that lived that way. It was in the beginning stages of a lot of pot growing.

Mickey Aluffi, 2019:
We had a lot of drugs in this town. The new people moving in, the hippies looking for a free lifestyle, they would live in communes up in the mountains. I'm not saying they were the ones because some of them were victims. But maybe that had something to do with the thought process.

Sam Robustelli, 2020:
Yeah, the hippies. The flower children. They were squatting on people's property. A lot of drugs. I remember going to people's houses and there were bowls of pills. Not much heroin, but pills and marijuana. You know, it happened so fast that nobody knew how to

Valley Press

Serving the San Lorenzo Valley and Nearby Area

Volume VII   Felton, California   April 12, 1967   Price 10¢   Phone 335-7810   Number 21

The hip set pose

Not averse to a little fun and a little publicity, this youthful group, quite hip and mostly residents at the Boxer apartments in Ben Lomond, pose for The Valley Press photographer. Standing in front are Jon Violette, Hollie Harman, Jim Gianera, Roger Murray (owner of the bus). Seated are Jim Warner, Jim Basye, Jim Alexander, Dianne Schienbein and her four-year-old son Steve. Windows on the side plus the windshield of the former school bus were broken by stone-wielding vandals last week Tuesday. Undaunted the group is cleaning up the large vehicle which sports an old wood stove and are going to collage the interior with wild pictures and the like. VALLEY PRESS PHOTO.

deal with it. I was a junior deputy when this all started and the ones that were there ahead of us were hard-nosed people, there was no compromise. Their attitude was, "Put the line up. If they cross it, take them down."

I was so far down the chain and you did what you were told. You didn't put your thoughts in. And really, the hippies didn't handle it well and we didn't handle it well.

Melinda Cadwallader, 2020:
I kind of remember the hippies, but they didn't bother me like the rest of the family. No one really talked about it much. I was more scared of the Zodiac killer back then. We also moved to Hawaii by the time I was twelve. Different lifestyle there.

HOLIDAY COMMUNE

Barry Burt, 2020:
In the [San Lorenzo] valley the tensions really started with the Boxer apartments, and then they moved the Boxers out to the Holiday Cabins. It was like the Ben Lomond community had a vengeance out for the longhairs. It escalated around the Holiday cabins. I remember Herman Ius, who was the owner of the Ben Lomond Supermarket, and out of all of them, I felt like he was the biggest instigator of the division between the two [longhairs and straights].

Charmaine Falcon, 2020:
There was. There was a young man. I can't remember his first name, but his last name was Boxer. He and his father owned the Boxer Apartments, I'm sure you heard that before, and that's where I first got my taste of the hippie life. They all sat in a circle in one of the apartments and my girlfriend that I knew from school, Karen, invited me to come over with her and they lived next door to my grandmother's place. So I went down there and I was very shy at the time. And I thought, well, this is a little weird, but it's kind of interesting. But there were several of them that lived in the apartments there. And

Greg Boxer, I think, was his name. He was all for it. It was delightful. But his father didn't like it at all. He was very much against it. But I never saw him much.

Barry Burt, 2020:
It must have been around '67 that they all moved out to the Holiday Cabins. I remember driving with my parents in the car by that big field where the baseball diamond is now, that whole field was covered with hips. They were all smoking dope and my parents went, "Don't go there!"

Of course, that's where I wanted to be.

The Boxer Apartments and later the commune at the Holiday Cabins were a nexus of hippie activities in Santa Cruz County and attracted many in the counterculture. My father was one of them.

Roger Murray, 2019:
Most everyone had cabins, but I had a two bedroom house. When they moved in from Boxer Apartments, I was up in San Francisco with your [the author's] mother. When I came down, they had saved that house for me. I lived there off and on and then I moved in with Jim [Gianera].

Charmaine Falcon, 2020:
I was there pretty much at the beginning. I only spent a matter of months there. I don't think I even spent a year there. It was a good thing. You know, I mean, everybody was promoting love. There was pot and stuff like that. But there weren't a lot of pills. There was some LSD.

We had a garden growing. We had commune rules. Everybody took turns cooking. And everybody had their cabins. We rented cabins for like $25 apiece. Gene Carlson kind of headed it up along with your dad [Roger Murray] and Jane. And some of the people there were very, very talented people, very talented. And it was, you know, for the time and the mindset, it was kind of a neat thing.

Holly Harman, 2020:

Well, I think most of the people felt like it was an invasion of hippies. But most of the people that were hippies lived there and grew up in the valley. So it was really a war between generations. And they didn't like their kids getting out of line like this. But I mean, when I first came to Ben Lomond and was fourteen or fifteen, I was so surprised because I came from San Mateo and the valley was like going back into the '50s because the girls had dresses down to their ankles. They're still delivering milk and eggs to the door. I mean, Ben Lomond was a sleepy little town and it was all happy and peaceful. The parents didn't want anything disrupting their idyllic life.

At school, there were social changes going on. I was elected to the student standard committee. I didn't even know I was elected. I just found out everybody voted for me. Well, I fought to bring the skirt length from ankle length to knee length. There was a lot going on. A lot of changes at the high school, too.

Charmaine Falcon, 2020:

There was a lot of tension. And there were some who were curious and would come around. But there was tension, especially between the law, some of the members of the law. Jake, I'm sure you've heard about him, Shaky Jake. Everybody would go to this little waterfall and, you know, swim nude and Shaky Jake would come down with his camera and photograph everybody. But still object to it, right? Of course. He's taking pictures of the nude girls and saying, "You can't, you can't do that."

But I'm going to take pictures of you anyway.

Roger Murray, 2019:

I can't think of his name, but Shaky Jake was a deputy sheriff. He was really a nice guy. One time, Jerry Warner and, I think, Peaches and I were up Love Creek smoking dope, and we were coming down and it's a windy dirt road and BOOM, there's Shaky Jake in his car. He got out of his car and wanted to know what we were doing up there. We told him we were looking for wood to make bows and arrows. He told us all about it. What wood to use, how to make them. This guy was amazing. He had a college degree. Really, really interesting guy. And a nice guy. But the reason we called him Shaky Jake was that if you confronted him—if he stopped us guys from drinking or something and we hollered at him, he'd start shaking. He'd get all nervous and start shaking. But he was very well educated and a nice guy.

Holly Harman, 2020:

Yes, it got real tense. They bombed Roger's school bus. The fire department did. And tried to get away with it. So there was a lot of animosity toward hippies. They called us "River rats" first, then "Hippies."

I remember they wouldn't allow hippies in the grocery store in Ben Lomond.

Roger Murray, 2019:

The Ben Lomond Fire Department called Doug James, the Sheriff, to meet with them at the Ben Lomond Fire Hall, and they were asking about vigilantes and vigilante justice. He told them that was not the thing to do. So after the meeting, and I don't remember how long after the meeting, they decided to bomb the bus. Don't use any names in your book. That's libel.

Jim Warner and one other guy [Bob Seabridge] were sleeping in the bus when they bombed it. They broke the window because they used a Coke bottle for a molotov cocktail. It didn't really burn that badly but Dak Fisher, the Ben Lomond Fire Chief, had the bus towed to the dump. Then it was towed from there to a garage in Felton, the one by the post office.

I was in San Francisco and someone called and told me what happened. So the garage told me I needed to get permission from Dak Fisher to get my bus back. I went to Dak Fisher and he said they towed it away

Charmaine Falcon, 2020:
There weren't a lot of serious drugs until the people from San Francisco started coming down and they started bringing all their drugs with them and getting everybody high all the time.

Roger Murray, 2019:
The first big commune [Strawberry Fields] was down in Southern California. I can't remember the name of it, but they failed and we had opened ours up. And that article came out in The [*LA*] *Oracle* and a lot of people moved in after seeing that. At that time, I was getting seriously involved with your mother and I moved out when that was happening. And all the junkies moved in shortly after that. People shooting up. Hard drugs. It went to shit after that.

Charmaine Falcon, 2020:
I do remember one time we had a group of bikers from San Francisco. They came down and they brought their hard drugs with them. And it was just a bad thing. It just started getting bad and it had started out so good.

Dave Alcorn, 2020:
Remember, at that time there was only one deputy in the valley. I was the only deputy during my shift, from Highway 1 to San Mateo County.

Sammy could tell you, because the Holiday Commune, they fired automatic gunfire at Sam and backup was thirty minutes away.

Sam Robustelli, 2020:
We got the guys. They were some out of town guys, they had stopped by with coke and grass. They had two ARs and they were popping rounds. They shot over the top of

because it was a fire hazard. Well, they made it a fire hazard. Anyway, he said he would sign a release if I took the bus out of the Ben Lomond Fire District. I said, "Wait a minute. I'll be back."

I went and talked to Bob Ludlow. He said they had no reason whatsoever to touch that bus. I went back to Dak Fisher and told him that and he signed the bus over.

Chris Cottle, 2020:
There was a lot of fear. There was a lot of anger. There was a lot of resentment. Negative feelings about the University. Negative feelings about these hippies that were coming into town. These were not necessarily my feelings or even Pete Chang's feelings. There were just negative feelings. I think "resentment" is a good word.

Herbert Mullin, 2020:
I was invited there [the Holiday Commune] in the late spring of 1967 by Jeff Meeler and Jim Gianera. They were living there together at Holiday.

Above: The LA Oracle issue featuring Ben Lomond's Holiday commune.

our vehicle as we were driving by.

Holly Harman, 2020:

Yes, it was good that I left when I left. I was seventeen, I got sick from the river. I almost died. Jim Gianera's brother, George, he almost died from the river as well. It was a bad virus. I was in Santa Cruz County Hospital in quarantine. The only person I could see was a priest who would come in and pray by my bedside. I thought I was going to die. But I recovered and so did George. After that, I moved on.

I did come back in 1968 and I stayed during the summer. I could tell things had really changed a lot from '67 to '68 and I didn't go down to Holidays at all, but I stayed up on Alba Road for the summer. It was a nice summer but a few of my friends were doing heroin and some crime was going on. It was all over, really.

I think Holidays was finally shut down, really in '69. They got everyone out of there and burned it to the ground. They said some of the cabins were rat infested. They'd been wanting to get rid of them for a while. There was no excuse anymore. The septic system failed, all of that.

Revolution, a counterculture magazine from Australia, published this sort of mean-spirited review of the Holiday Commune during its dying days in their December 1970 issue.

Revolution, 1970:

Holiday is a commune where the inhabitants practice nudity and live in comfortable bun-

Right: The UTE Report issued to the County Board of Supervisors was re-released and distributed by Pat Liteky's UTE Enterprises.

galows; the drugs most widely used appeared to be marijuana, opiated hashish, and methamphetamine (i.e., Methedrine or "speed"). Of the ten girls living in Holiday, six were pregnant; polygamous relationships are common and children are regarded as "children of the commune". A newcomer is asked not for his name but for his birth sign. Most of the inhabitants have an extremely superficial understanding of astrology yet take paranormal planetary influence upon human behavior for granted. The newcomer's birth sign seems to be used as a means to "pigeonhole" the stranger and as a base upon which to initiate—or avoid—a relationship.

Harold Cartwright, 2020:

A lot of people attribute a lot of what went on, the murders, to drugs and that kind of thing. I don't. I don't at all. I think John Linley Frazier was a paranoid schizophrenic, classic. He revised revelations of John, in the Bible. I had a novelist take it and promised to give it back and, of course, I never saw it again. It was in his handwriting, he corrected the whole revelations of John, because he was a reincarnation of John and he was doing God's work. He would live on water towers. Live in trees. Deserted his wife and six-month-old baby. He once said to me, "I'm doing God's work."

And he didn't talk; it was like pulling teeth to get him to say anything. You had to get him real agitated to get him to talk.

James Jackson, 2020:

It's all a bunch of shit. You had some loudmouths yelling about hippies, but who cared. Who really gave a shit. They weren't really doing anything. They were just around. By that time, a lot of them were third-rate hippies anyway.

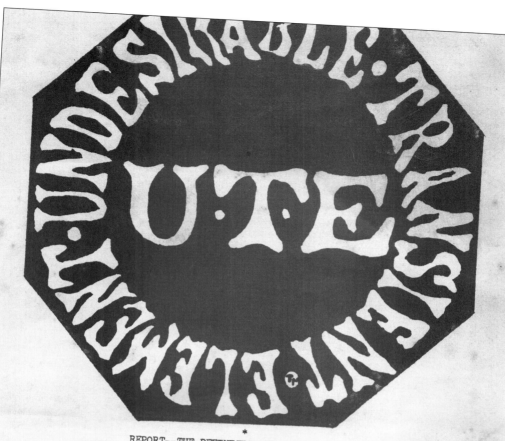

*

REPORT--THE DEFINITION OF THE PROBLEM

OF THE UNDESIRABLE TRANSIENT ELEMENT

In Fulfillment of Agreement 70016

(The following report was first published by the Environmental
Operations Research, P.O. Box 1852, Los Gatos, California, 95030)

TABLE OF CONTENTS:

(The original distribution of the REPORT was a 41-page public document, not copyrighted by the EOR, nor by Santa Cruz County. Permission to reduplicate and
even sell the document, while it was not neccessary to obtain for such a public
document, was sought from both the Santa Cruz County Officials and the author
of the report, and permission was given to reduplicate. This is a complete and
unabridged copy of the original document as published by the EOR. The cost for
this reduplication has been kept at a minimum, to cover both materiel cost and
labor cost. This is not a copyrighted document, but only the above "U.T.E."
trademark is copyrighted, and the patent design is pending. For additional
copies, write: U.T.E. Enterprises, 901 Highland Drive, Boulder Creek, Ca., 95006)

* Copyright, U.T.E. Enterprises,
All rights reserved.

Pat Liteky celebrates his victory in the 5th Supervisorial district with his supporters Tuesday night after thepolls closed. Liteky defeated incumbent Supervisor George Cress, 8,311 to 6,965.

SUPERVISOR LITEKY

stands ready to serve you!

ROSALINDA ZUNIGA

FEAR

Within days of the Ohta–Cadwallader murders, local gun stores reported increased sales. One store reported a sales jump of more than 500 percent and another reported an increase of 300 percent.

Miriam Finnegan, 2021:
It was such a small community and after the Ohta killings, it was widely stated through town that not a gun could be found. They had all sold out.

John Fiorovich (Country Cousin's Sporting Goods employee):
People are scared, but there is more looking going on than buying. This always happens when there is some kind of a shake-up. The same thing happened when [Cesar] Chavez came to town.

In July 1971, County Supervisors Dan Forbus and Ralph Sanson filed a letter with their fellow board members—

Dan Forbus and Ralph Sanson, 1970:
There is concern among county residents

that county government take effective steps to 'do something' about what the county has heretofore euphemistically termed the 'undesirable transient element.'

This concern has reached the point where some are saying that unless the county takes action to correct the situation, they themselves will form vigilante groups to take the matter into their own hands.

The Board of Supervisors agreed to hire an outside analyst firm, Environmental Operations Research, to investigate and report on the county's UTE (Undesirable Transient Element) issue.

The report was issued in early 1971 and outraged the Board. Among the findings the report indicated that many of the hippies or longhairs were in fact locals. The UTE was primarily surfers and long-haired campers. It noted that Santa Cruz County had a very large percentage of youth, twenty-three percent, as well as a high percentage of elderly, almost twenty percent, which was twice the state average. This contrast exacerbated the tension.

UTE Report, 1971:
Significant evidence was not found connecting UTE to crime, in any great way.

The report concluded that while marijuana was widespread among the UTE, hard drugs were much less widely used and were likely to be brought to the county by dealers who looked more like businessmen than hippies.

UTE Report, 1971:
Most large pushers (of hard drugs) are probably older, shorter haired and better dressed, and could pass as you or I.

The report noted that the communes, primarily in the San Lorenzo Valley area, did draw a lot of welfare recipients, but also stated that communes did not tend to last very long with human nature as it is.

Finally the report said that a full study of the issue was warranted and would cost between $45,000 and $60,000. The county declined.

Soon after the report was issued, the term "UTE" was plastered on t-shirts, handbags, posters, and flags as a proud way to self-identify as a hippie. The man behind turning the term into a positive movement was Pat Liteky and his army of supporters.

Within a year, Liteky would be voted onto the Santa Cruz County Board of Supervisors himself. Despite saying he wasn't a hippie, the press dubbed him the "Hippie Mayor." Liteky represented San Lorenzo Valley and Scotts Valley.

Pat Liteky, 1973:
I walked into the supervisor's room for the first time feeling naked. I felt out of place in my jeans. But I'm bumbling by, starting to get along.

As the community reeled from the Ohta-Cadwallader murders, other murders were keeping local law enforcement busy. On July 10, 1971, Rosalinda Zuniga, an eighteen-year-old from Watsonville, was picked up hitchhiking in San Jose, while attempting to get home. Her body was found off Highway 1 near La Selva Beach two weeks later. Rosalinda Zuniga suffocated from a small stab wound to her throat. There was very little press about the murder, and the killer was never caught.

On May 9, 1972, a seventeen-year-old hitchhiker from Nebraska named Terri Pfitzer (her real last name was Taylor) disappeared in Santa Cruz.

On August 30, 1972, Santa Cruz Police received a call from a man who cried, "Send police to 305 Riverview. I'm being murdered." Police were only two blocks away and quickly arrived at the house to find Peter Mitchell, 32, nude and dying in his backyard. A hitchhiker he brought home had stabbed him in the heart and head. The killer was never caught.

FRAZIER TRIAL OCTOBER–DECEMBER, 1971

On January 8, 1971, while housed in the Santa Cruz County Jail, Frazier slashed his wrist after forcing the blade from a safety razor. He scrawled "Freedom" and "Pigs" on the wall of his cell with his blood.

Peter Chang, 1971:
He made a very superficial cut on one wrist. He's in no danger.

Terry Medina, 2020:
It very quickly became just a media train wreck. Nobody in the Sheriff's Office or the DA's office were prepared for that much media attention. It took away a lot of time for us and created a lot of problems.

Dave Monsees (KPIX reporter), 1973:
There were seven armed deputies in the courtroom as the suspect was led in—two of them flanking him on both sides as he sat in the jury box awaiting Judge May. As the arraignment began, Frazier stood, guarded, next to the bench. He slouched, leaning on his

right elbow onto a railing. "You are charged with violating five counts of Section 187 of the state penal code," Judge May said.

"Do you understand the meaning of these charges?"

Quietly, almost under his breath, Frazier nodded yes. Public Defender, James Jackson, was then appointed to represent him.

James Jackson, 2020:
Early on, after I had started with Frazier, I started getting death threats. I went to a party and Brauer's best buddy, Dr. Liddicoat—he was partners with Ohta, and he was there. He didn't spit on me, but he was pissed at me. He had words. He was angry and hurt because his friend was dead, so he blamed the nearest person.

JAMES JACKSON

James Jackson, 2020:
I was a DA in Oakland and I didn't want to be in Oakland anymore. So I came to Santa

Cruz. I knew some people down here. For some reason, every time I came down, we went to lunch at Malio's. I guess that was the place to go. One day, I was talking to a friend and he said, "Why don't you talk to Britton over here. He's the public defender and he's looking for somebody."

I said, "Why didn't somebody tell me before?"

And they said, "Well, we figured you work in the DA's office, you don't want to be the public defender."

I said, "I don't give a rat's ass."

I went over and talked to Britton and he was indeed looking for somebody. He had a contract at the county. They still do it that way. It's not a public employee, it's on a contract basis. So, I went over and talked with Britton and he said, "Well, I've got a preliminary hearing this afternoon. Do you want to do it?"

He said, "It's a local Black Panther."

I said, "Oh, great."

Anyway, I went over there and met him. His name was O.T. Hunt, who's since died. O.T. had broken into some liquor store and left his fingerprints here and there and on the cash machine. It's a hopeless case. But they brought in a fingerprint expert from DOJ and I started questioning him about something called poroscopy. Nobody in the building knew anything about it except him and me. I impressed them all with "poroscopy." A refinement of fingerprints that nobody uses anymore. So, then I gave Oakland a month notice and went to work for Britton.

Britton was hiring because he didn't want to do the criminal work. He wanted to do his own civil practice. I ended up doing, in essence, doing all the criminal work.

Richard Verbrugge, 2020:
A few times I'd be in my office at the DA's office, on the second floor there, and one of the court deputies would come running in and say, "You're needed in department such-and-such."

So I'd run down there. I didn't even know what was going on. Didn't know which trial it was. And I'd go in and go up and get sworn in. Come to find out Jackson's called me. It's a case we were prosecuting and Jim's using my expertise as a subject matter expert on heroin sales or something. But yeah, he did that to me about five or six times.

Sam Robustelli, 2020:
Jim was a good adversary. Even if he knew he did it, he'd bang swords with you to try and get you to say something or change something. He was a great sword fighter. And it was the same with Kemper. Study your enemy. Know what they're about and learn.

Chris Cottle, 2020:
Jim was a wonderful guy. He had been a deputy DA in Alameda County which was known as one of the most hard-nosed, effective DA's offices anywhere. [J. Frank] Coakley was the district attorney at that time.

Dave Alcorn, 2020:
Jim would yell at you on the stand and if you got mad, hey, you might slip up and say something. He used to turn bright red and yell. I like him a lot.

Harold Cartwright, 2020:
He [Jim Jackson] is really smart. When I first got to Santa Cruz, he would stand up and say, "Objection, your honor," name off whatever he was objecting to, and then he would state the code. He could quote you the law or whatever supported his objection. He had a reputation for having a brilliant mind as a criminal defense lawyer.

Harold Cartwright, 2020:
The law meant everything to Jim. It was all about equal justice under the law. He believed in that. Chris Cottle was the same way.

Jim could have been a law school pro-

Left: James Jackson, 1971.

fessor. He believed in the constitution. He believed that no one was above the law and his oath was to hold, in the case of a defense attorney, hold the prosecution to prove their case beyond a reasonable doubt.

HAROLD CARTWRIGHT

Harold Cartwright, 2020:
I was a police officer in Southern California. I resigned and came to work for the public defender's office in Santa Cruz on February the 1, 1969. I obtained my private investigators license and contracted with the law firm that provided services to the county of Santa Cruz.

My basic job was to investigate, as needed, any case assigned by the court to the public defender's office.

The public defender's office was located at 55 River Street at the time. It had two lawyers, two secretary-paralegals, and myself. Over the years, it grew and changed.

Harold Cartwright, 2020:
I was a cop at heart. I left a job as a sergeant in Southern California, about seven and half years on the street and a couple of years in-house, in the jail and this and that. I was pro-law enforcement all the way. I never saw our jobs being different. I never have. I believe we're a country of laws and we are bound by those laws no matter whether we're defending somebody or prosecuting somebody, it doesn't matter. We are searching for the truth. I think every law enforcement officer's fear is that they would somehow contribute to an innocent person going to jail.

Were there bad cops? Absolutely. I helped get three fired during the time I was a police officer. But I had a great relationship with law enforcement in Santa Cruz.

Right: Delores and Harold Cartwright leaving the Santa Cruz County Building, 1971.

Harold Cartwright, 2020:
Yes. I shared information with local law enforcement to some extent. To give an example. I'd be in court at eight thirty and somebody would ask the judge for the public defender and he would say, "See Mr. Cartwright afterward and I'll continue this until tomorrow morning."

A lot of times they were in custody.

I would go from court, when it was over, directly to the DA's office, which was where it is now, it's been enlarged a lot, but, I would go in, say hi to everybody. I knew them all well. I would just go to a filing cabinet and pull out the file of the guy I'd been assigned. I didn't ask anybody. We just had an understanding. Anything on the right side of the file I could copy, I could read it. It was totally open discovery. Not like today. On the left side of the file, I didn't look at it. And I never did. We had a great working agreement. I think the third or fourth person that I met was Peter Chang, the district attorney, and Ray Belgard. Chris Cottle was also there at the time, as I recall.

CHRIS COTTLE

Richard Verbrugge, 2020:
Chris was an attorney at the district attorney's office, worked for Chang. In college, he was a middle linebacker for Stanford. He was really a great football player.

Chang always hired the attorneys himself and he always looked for attorneys, whether they be male or female, that were very competitive. He liked males who were athletes in high school and college and that stuff. He said they were competitive and were brought up to be competitive and they were going to be competitive when they got in a courtroom.

Harold Cartwright, 2020:
Chris [Cottle] is probably one of the most honorable district attorneys, judges, that I've ever worked with. I've worked with a lot of them. High moral character. Good man.

He would never play head games with you. Peter loved head games, but Chris was very straight forward.

James Jackson, 2020:
He [Chris Cottle] was a hundred and eighty pound starting guard for Stanford, so he's a tough guy. But, he's very easy to get along with.

Chris Cottle, 2020:
I tried the Frazier case all the way through with Peter. The crime occurred in 1970. I had taken a leave of absence with the DA's office. Peter was my employer, but we were always good friends. I told him I wanted to

Above: Chris Cottle and Peter Chang straregize in their hotel room during the trial.
Above right: Judge Charles Franich.

take this trip to Africa and I was gone for about nine months. We were on the way home and decided to travel around Europe. I picked up an overseas newspaper and it had two headlines. One was that Stanford was in the Rose Bowl. That intrigued me because I was a football player at Stanford. The second thing was the Ohta killing. I had not communicated with Pete, except for maybe once, during the entire trip. So we talked on the phone and he said, "It might be a good time to come home."

So I came right home.

Harold Cartwright, 2020:
The Frazier case was on the front page of the *London Times*. It got worldwide attention.

James Jackson, 2020:
So I'm assigned and he [Frazier] didn't talk to me. He just wouldn't talk to us for a long

time. Didn't really talk with Harold. He gave three different stories to the psychiatrist.

James Jackson, 2020:
Frazier told Dr. Ohta that he should burn down his house and I always wondered if Ohta would have burned down his house if he would have spared him.

The case was assigned to Judge Charles Franich.

Charles Franich (Frazier trial judge), 1993:
Trying Frazier was like a final exam every day. You're in a tough spot. You don't want to make a legal mistake.

Harold Cartwright, 2020:
Charles Franich. Ex-FBI agent. Just a really decent, good, judge. I can't say anything negative about him. He did an expert job. He didn't have a big ego and wanted to do the right thing.

Mike Lee (KPIX reporter), 1971:
The case was moved here to Redwood City after defense claims that hostility towards long haired people would have made a fair trial impossible in Santa Cruz County.

James Jackson, 2020:
I was covering my ass. There were change of venue cases going through the Supreme Court of California at the time. A couple of them had been granted and ours was actually more egregious than the others. So I made a motion to change venue and Franich denied it. I said, "God, he should not have done that."

I end up in the Supreme Court of California, where, for reasons I never did understand, they start asking me about Manson. This was after you hear courts all over the place saying, "We strictly adhere to the material before us."

It certainly wasn't Manson. Anyway, they ended up granting a change in venue and we ended up in San Mateo County.

Chris Cottle, 2020:
In preparation for the case and also trying the case, it was held over the hill, in San Mateo. We stayed over there in a hotel for the duration of the trial.

Jury selection began on Monday, October 18, 1971. Before the opening of the session, the reporters were cleared from the courtroom. Peter Chang's father was in the audience.

Terry Medina, 2020:
It was in San Mateo, but they picked the jury in Santa Cruz. Chang told me, "The whole ball game here is going to be picking the jury." Chang gets this guy named Roy something. He owns Roy's Market in Felton. I can't remember his name, but I remember Chang saying, "You know what? I gotta get this guy on the jury. If I can get him on the jury, he will be the jury foreman."

And for damn sure that's exactly what happened. Chang was really planning this

thing.

The jury was impaneled late on Wednesday, October 20. Three alternates were chosen the next morning. Frazier alternated between disinterested glances at the ceiling and glaring at Judge Franich and the jurors.

Chris Cottle, 2020:
I would put him in the same camp as Manson. I wasn't here when the Manson crimes occurred, I was in Africa, so I missed a lot of the publicity. But the first thing I did, when I got back, was I called Bugliosi, the district attorney down in LA who was trying the case. We shared a lot of information about how to try that kind of a case. I was very concerned about the scientific evidence, or lack of it. We discussed how the case should be investigated from the very beginning. I got a lot of help from him.

Unlike the Manson trial, there was no cheering section for Frazier. Aside from his wife and a few friends, Frazier had few supporters.

Mike Lee (KPIX reporter), 1971:
There was no large turnout of spectators, no "Free Frazier demonstrations."

Roger Krone, 2020:
We lived in one of the houses on his [Frazier's] mother's property, but there were two houses on the property. The people in the white house were supporters of his. They didn't think he did it. I think they went to the trial. And we were the ones that turned him in.

Terry Medina, 2020:
He [Frazier] had to get from the jail to the courtroom. And when San Mateo County got him to the courtroom, then one of us [Santa Cruz Deputies], and not me every time, but one of us would then meet him at the holding facility at the courthouse and move him to where his lawyers were. We talked, but it was just small talk. Nothing

really memorable.

Chris Cottle, 2020:
Peter got very involved in the Frazier case. Not only the Asian connection but he had two boys.

I gotta say, the victim was Japanese, the DA's Korean, and the defendant is Caucasian. Anybody who had any hostilities, based on race, had to rethink it a little bit.

Opening statements were made on Wednesday, October 27. Frazier's wife, Delores, sat quietly in the rear of the audience.

Peter Chang, 1971:
We will show to your everlasting satisfaction that John Linley Frazier [Chang turned from the jury and pointed at Frazier] murdered five persons.

After the automobile accident in May 1970 Frazier changed psychologically, Jackson conjectured. After that Frazier believed he was—

James Jackson, 1971:
John of the *Book of Revelations*, with voices telling him to go into the woods, not pollute the environment and take up arms against those who did.

Jackson stated that Frazier talked to animals and would get furious when they didn't talk back. One time, he jumped up and down on the body of a dead sheep. Jackson added that Frazier spent hours watching the Ohtas through binoculars.

James Jackson, 1971:
I will ask you to find the defendant not guilty because the evidence is insufficient—and not because the ramblings of a madman can be used to say he is guilty.

Assistant Soquel Fire Chief Ernie Negro testified about the discovery of the bodies and the fire; Deputies Jim Ingram, Ben Seibel, and Jim

Marston testified about the crime scene.

After lunch the courtroom was half empty. A friend and former jail inmate with Frazier sat with Delores. He signaled to Frazier, who smiled back. When the court bailiff told the friend he would have to leave if he continued to try to communicate with the defendant, the friend exited the courtroom.

On October 28 Robert Achterburg, who had spotted Mrs. Ohta's car in Felton, testified.

Frazier's supervisor at Performance West, Michael Stebbins, testified that Frazier had visited him and his family in Felton six weeks before Frazier quit.

Michael Stebbins, 1971:
He had dinner with us, played with the kids and hiked around the area, I guess, on foot.

Frazier and the kids looked at polliwogs in a nearby pond. Close to the pond is where Robert Achterburg had seen Mrs. Ohta's car. Stebbins testified that Frazier had never mentioned hearing voices or his automobile accident in Scotts Valley. He said that Frazier quit his job suddenly and was working on an anti-pollution device of some sort.

The Southern Pacific engineer who struck Mrs. Ohta's car when Frazier parked it in the Rincon Tunnel also testified.

Joe Cole, Frazier's neighbor, testified. Cole was one of the three men [Mike Madden and Roger Krone were the other two] who brought the authorities' attention to Frazier. Frazier stared at him as Cole squirmed on the stand.

Peter Chang, 1971:
Did John say he got the Ruger [pistol] someplace?

Frazier burst out laughing. This flustered Cole.

Peter Chang, 1971:
Didn't you tell Inspector Swayne, John told

you he ripped off the gun from a redneck?

Joe Cole, 1971:
Yeah, I believe so.

Cole stated that Frazier talked about his revolution weeks before the crimes.

Joe Cole, 1971:
"Materialistic people are going to finally come down. Somethings got to be done to keep them from destroying the earth by subdivisions, blacktop," and things like that.

When Frazier asked Cole to join his revolution, he refused.

Joe Cole, 1971:
It wasn't my jig.

Peter Chang stepped between Cole and Frazier at this point in the trial.

John Linley Frazier, 1971:
Excuse me, please! Step out from between us! Thank you!

Frazier continued his piercing stare at Cole.

Joe Cole, 1971:
If people approached, he would say you can't take my TV. […] These would be the enemy.

Peter Chang, 1971:
Did he say what to do with these enemies?

Joe Cole, 1971:
Destroy them.

Peter Chang, 1971:
Did John say he would snuff them out? Would that be the word?

Cole nodded.

Joe Cole, 1971:
It's hard to talk in John's words.

Cole talked about coming forward with his friends. He revealed that Frazier was wearing gloves non-stop for the two weeks leading up to the murder. Cole also testified that he saw an orange backpack in front of Frazier's cabin the Friday or Saturday before the murders.

An orange backpack had been found on Mrs. Pascal's property with a .45 pistol and other items belonging to Frazier.

Peter Chang asked if Frazier would walk into people's houses without knocking or making his presence known.

Joe Cole, 1971:
Yeah. Sometimes he would just come in with his hands in his pockets—just be there. People would feel uneasy. They would feel the power in him like a generator, and even if they didn't see him come in they could feel him.

Frazier's mother, Pat Pascal, testified next. Frazier's cabin was on Pascal's property. When she took the stand, Frazier swung his chair away and refused to look at her. He instead smiled at his wife, who was seated in the back of the courthouse.

Mrs. Pascal argued with Chang that the orange backpack found in her storage shed belonged to Frazier.

Pat Pascal, 1971:
It seems to me his was a lot oranger.

Mrs. Pascal had no answer for how she found the bright orange backpack in her shed only days after deputies had searched the shed and come up empty-handed. She complained that her house had been ransacked by deputies after the crime, while she was away on a road trip.

Santa Cruz deputies testified next. They argued with James Jackson that they had been looking for a killer and not looking for evidence when they searched Mrs. Pascal's home and property.

Deputies Brad Arbsland and Rod Sanford testified about Frazier's capture.

Unrelated, on October 29, a body was found in Zayante, with his throat slit and partially burned. The victim was a male between nineteen and twenty-five years old and had been killed eight to forty-eight hours earlier. I cannot find evidence the body was ever identified.

The trial resumed on Monday, November 1, 1971. The morning was spent letting jurors inspect several items of evidence up close.

Deputy Rod Sanford continued to testify about Frazier's capture.

As the two deputies and Frazier left the cabin, Sanford testified that Frazier suggested they take the tottering rope bridge across the gully—

Rod Sanford, 1971:
[Quoting Frazier] "You have the shotguns. You can go ahead and use them if you want to. […] Why don't you give me what I deserve?"

Frazier bounced to his feet.

John Linley Frazier, 1971:
You lie, Jack!

James Jackson got Deputy Sanford to admit that neither he nor Deputy Arbsland had put these comments in their incident report.

Walt Weiskopf, Frazier's neighbor who lived in the big white house on Mrs. Pascal's property, testified that Frazier told him he had broken into the Muni home [the Ohta's neighbors.]

Walt Weiskopf, 1971:
I think he said he had been in the house and referred to the people who lived there as "rednecks."

Weiskopf also testified about Frazier's ability to run across the rope bridge and about Frazier's rambling and how he stared off into space at times.

Terry Medina, 2020:
During the trial we were all staying in a hotel in San Mateo County. All in the same hotel. Now you've got Peter Chang, who drinks a lot, and you've got Jim Jackson, who drinks a lot. You've got whatever other lawyers are working this thing. Both sides are all in the same place. We're all drinking in the same bar every day. I know that is something that would never happen today. Drinking all night long. I remember Chang, after we were drinking all night, he says, "I want you to go find this watch."

I end up driving to Corralitos to pick up some watch from somebody.

Much of November 2 was spent reviewing the Ohta boys' near identical watches. One had a black face and one a white face. The white faced watch was found on Taggart Ohta's body. The black face watch was found in a box in the shed of Mrs. Pascal.

Michael Madden and Roger and Janice Krone testified.

Quoting Frazier—

Roger Krone, 1971:
"Rednecks are abusing the environment and have no respect for people and should be offed."

Roger Krone, 2020:
The trial was so long after the event that I had a hard time remembering some details.

Above left: Michael Madden, 1971.
Above right: Janice and Roger Krone, 1971.
Next page: The watch found on the body of Taggart Ohta.

We were more circumstantial witnesses.

Krone stated that on the Saturday before the murders, Frazier told him that he was headed for the east coast, but that he would be back.

Madden testified that Frazier told him he had stolen a gun and other items from the Muni home and that the revolution was set to start two weeks before the murders. Frazier upset Madden when he said that he would kill Madden's parents for the sake of the revolution.

Michael Madden, 1971:
Sometimes I thought John Frazier was pretty insane.

Mrs. Pascal's caretaker, Dennis Sommers, testified that he and Mrs. Pascal returned from their three-day road trip to Reno a day or two after the Ohta-Cadwallader killings. He said that shortly after returning, they found the orange backpack and .45 pistol in the shed.

Dennis Sommers, 1971:
I picked it up. That's the first thing I did, and I saw it was loaded. I ejected the shells and I took it over and showed it to Mrs. Pascal.

Over Jackson's objections, Mr. Sommers continued.

Dennis Sommers, 1971:
…I wiped my fingerprints off it and I took it and put back where it had been.

Peter Chang, 1971:
Why?

Dennis Sommers, 1971:
I didn't want them on there. I didn't want anything to do with this.

Allison Ayers and a few of Frazier's other friends testified on Wednesday, November 3.

Allison Ayers, 1971:
[Frazier wore dark glasses] so the devil wouldn't get in through his eyes.

Ayers testified that the night of Frazier's automobile accident he had lectured to her and Delores for six hours.

On Friday, November 12, 1971, the entire court took a field trip to Santa Cruz. The jury was shown the crime scene, Frazier's shack, and took a tour into the San Lorenzo Valley.

James Jackson, 2020:
The DA wanted them to see the scene of the crime. I don't think there was anything more to it than that.

On November 16 the prosecution rested their case.

The defense called Kimberly Weiskopf, who lived in the big white house on Frazier's mother's property. She testified that Frazier would visit her and her husband, Walt, frequently, telling scattered stories, unable to finish his thoughts. In one conversation Frazier's rambling topics—

Kimberly Weiskopf (Frazier's neighbor), 1971:
Changed from my dog, to my house, to the Zodiac killer.
He appeared to be going through a hard time.

Paul Dougherty, the head Criminalist at San Mateo County's Crime Lab, was called to the stand and testified in detail about the firearms and bullet types used in the murders. Santa Cruz would call on Paul Dougherty's skills several times in the next few years, as the county did not have a crime lab at the time.

Paul Dougherty, 2020:
I graduated from Berkeley at the School of Criminology in their Criminalistics program. I graduated in '56 and went into the Navy because I didn't have any choice. I spent fifty-two months in the Navy. Left there

District Attorney Peter Chang indicates the Rincon tunnel on the Southern Pacific railroad tracks Friday about noon as jurors listen intently. The tunnel is where Mrs. Virginia Ohta's station wagon was abandoned the night after she and four others were slain. The Redwood City jury spent Friday morning in the rain-swept San Lorenzo Valley.

Jurors, most dressed for hiking over rough terrain, look at a spot at the Ohta swimming pool that District Attorney Peter Chang, left, indicated had been chipped by a bullet. The DA Friday also showed the jury bloodstains they had previously seen in color photographs in the courtroom in Redwood City. John Frazier's attorney, James Jackson, left rear, stares across the pool.

Judge Charles Franich, left foreground, leads the Redwood City jury, the defendant, lawmen and press to the Frazier shack off Cornwell Road Friday. San Mateo deputies, in charge of John Frazier, received heavy backup from local sheriff's deputies while the tour was taken on the remote Cornwell property.

People helping people

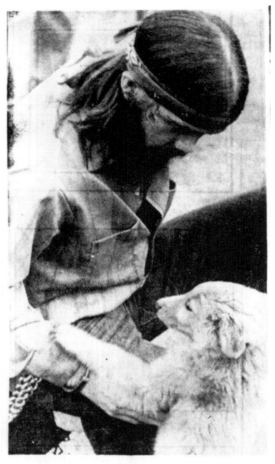

John Linley Frazier **pauses near the shack he called home to play with a puppy. Moments after this picture was taken Friday the accused killer kicked a rusted wreck of an automobile, abandoned nearby.**

and went to work in San Mateo and worked there until I retired.

Paul Dougherty, 2020:

I was brought in after the state had looked at the evidence. I never went to the crime scene. It started—I think Peter Chang had heard that I specialized in firearms and he asked me to look at it. I talked to the powers that be because there are always politics in this type of situation, but they said yes, I could help a sister county.

They brought the evidence in and it was the slugs from the bodies and some ammunition they had. For some reason it sticks in my head that it was twelve or thirteen rounds they had found in Frazier's case when he was

picked up. So I looked at the slugs and the ammo and a couple of things were apparent real quick, looking at the slugs from the bodies. There were two different slugs. The state had done a comparison and said they were all from the same gun. I agreed with that. It was a revolver. But in the ammunition one of them was also different from the others. It had a different canneluring. Canneluring is grooves around the projectile, which is put in there by the manufacturer. It's used for a lot of different purposes. So the state had broken down one round and looked at it. I broke down one and found the same characteristic. So we had two different slugs that had been manufactured differently in the bodies and two different slugs found with Frazier. One had been manufactured with a broad cannelure and one had a very narrow cannelure. It was Norma Ammunition.

So I contacted Norma and got a hold of their chief engineer. We had a little chat about it and he basically said, yes, we made these changeovers and I forget the date he said, but it was several years prior to that, he said they made the changeover and did not stop the line when they made that changeover—meaning that when the new cartridges came off, they just mixed them all together with the old ones and sent them out for sale. Well, the chances of having both in a totally unrelated box of ammunition was really almost impossible.

So I presented that to them and they really liked that. It was physical evidence. I got a whole bunch of stuff from Norma on that, I got drawings, just a whole lot of information. We were loaded for bear.

Chris Cottle, 2020:

In the Frazier case, we did not have the gun during the trial. So we tied him to the burglary in which the gun was stolen, but we didn't have the gun. We had ballistics on the gun, but not the gun. It was a very substantial case in that regard. Later the guns were found in his cabin.

Chris Cottle, 2020:
He was more organized, obvious, cold and calculating than the others [Mullin and Kemper] and was able to go through his trial with the knowledge that the murder weapons, hidden by him, were a significant missing link.

On November 17, defense witnesses discussed the copper smearing found on Frazier's knife, which the prosecution contended had been used to cut the Ohtas' phone line.

Paul Dougherty, 2020:
He had copper smears on his knife. The telephone wires were cut. That was never very successful. It was copper on the knife, no question about that. There is a process called neutron activation analysis that can analyze the elements in the samples. But even that wouldn't help very much. That telephone wire was pretty common stuff. Remember, this is the day of landlines. Every home had telephone wire.

The prosecution conjectured that Frazier used the Ohtas' typewriter to write the note left at the scene.

Paul Dougherty, 2020:
I don't remember us ever looking at the typewriter. On something like that I would have sent them to a guy who was a real typewriter whiz on that kind of stuff. He happened to be a postal inspector in San Francisco.

Also on November 17, an ammunition salesman from Norma, the company which made the bullets which killed Dr. Ohta, testified. Two criminalists testified regarding fingerprints and footprints and a sawed-off shotgun found near Frazier's orange backpack, which originally had belonged to Ohta's neighbor Donald Muni.

Three witnesses also testified that they had seen the Ohtas' station wagon the night of the murder being driven by two men and a woman. However, these defense witnesses' testimonies conflicted with each other and even with themselves when pressed by Peter Chang.

After Judge Charles Franich recessed the jury Friday following its visit to Santa Cruz, defendant John Linley Frazier went to his waiting patrol car, turned and laughed.

After a short rebuttal, both sides rested.

On Tuesday, November 23 and Wednesday, November 24, closing arguments were given.

At one point in his closing argument Peter Chang referred to Frazier as Little Lord Fauntleroy.

John Linley Frazier, 1971:
Use my correct name, pig!

On Friday, November 26, the case was handed over to the jury. They returned their verdict on Tuesday, November 30.

Dave Monsees (KPIX reporter), 1971:
The jury had deliberated only three days after getting the case Friday. At four this afternoon it returned to Judge Charles Franich's court to give the verdict. Frazier, as had been throughout the trial, was relaxed, even aloof, sitting with his back turned toward Franich and the jury. The verdicts were read one at a time for each murder count in the death of Dr. Ohta, his wife, two children, and secretary. The readings came in matter-of-fact succession. The People of the State of California

versus John Linley Frazier. Verdict: we the jury find the defendant, John Linley Frazier, guilty of murder in the first degree. It was repeated four times. Throughout, Frazier did not blink. He seemed almost stoic.

Dave Monsees (KPIX reporter), 1971:
Now begins the phase of proceedings possible only with the return of a first degree murder verdict. Thursday, the sanity hearing begins and defense attorney, James Jackson, plans to call at least three psychiatrists he describes as eminent to testify on Frazier's mental state. If he's found insane, Frazier will probably be committed to a state mental hospital. If not, then the final phase of this trial, the penalty hearing.

The sanity and penalty phase of the trial began on Thursday, December 2, 1971.

Terry Medina, 2020:
They bring Frazier in for court and he walks in and they sit him down, and he spins in his chair one way and half of his head is bare. He spins the other way and the hair is still there.

"I call your bluff!" Frazier shouted to the court-room.

James Jackson, 2020:
Those assholes at San Mateo County let him shave half his head. They were perfectly happy to see him do something that would help him be found guilty. Where did you ever hear about a law enforcement agency giving somebody a razor to do that? So he shaves half his head. Harold and I walked in one day and somebody tells us, "Well, he's shaved half his head."

So we go to talk with him and he's impossible to talk to, anyway. I said, "Maybe you could shave the rest off, at least."

He was trying to say he was schizophrenic. I don't know. He was something. He was a

fucking kook.

Peter Chang, 1971:
During certain segments of this case, I think very definitely, he was trying to fool them [the jury]. I think this is a very conscientious jury and I don't think I needed to remind them. They deliberated throughout this case conscientiously and did a very conscientious job in every phase of the case.

Chris Cottle, 2020:
Joel Fort was our psychiatrist in the Frazier case and was our psychiatrist in several other subsequent cases. He was a good antidote to all that, "LSD does this to you. LSD does that to you." My feeling is that, probably, Frazier was affected by this to some degree. He was

on much more heavier drugs than marijuana. Psychedelics and other drugs. But I don't really know. That's my theory.

James Jackson, 2020:
They brought in Dr. Joel Fort, who was the big name in psychiatry in San Francisco. He ran something called Fort Help.

He came in and was talking about hallucinations and how Frazier wasn't really crazy because they weren't "command hallucinations." They were only "auditory hallucinations." Come on.

Bringing the psychiatrists in didn't bother me. But everyone knew it was part of the game. You had to put these people on or you'd get sued for malpractice and the case would get reversed.

Harold Cartwright, 2020:
He was just as crazy as could be. Even if you're a paranoid schizophrenic you can still plan things, you can do things very logically. You can make elaborate plans. Because that is a part of the illness. So is hearing voices. I don't buy the dope thing at all.

James Jackson, 1971:
The people that testified that he was insane are people who saw him extensively and who have the academic and the experience credentials to say something like that. The psychiatrists who testified for the prosecution were terrible. They based their opinion on a letter they got from the District Attorney. They saw him briefly. They weren't even acquainted with their own field adequately.

Chris Cottle, 2020:
The M'Naghten Standard is whether, as the result of a mental illness, is the person capable of knowing the difference between right and wrong? Is the person organized in enough of a way to be able to think in an organized fashion? It does not take into consideration the voices that they sometimes hear. They may periodically be clear thinking.

Harold Cartwright, 2020:
We hired Lunde. He was an MD and a professor at Stanford. Both Medical Department and Psychology Department. I don't know how we got to him in the beginning, but he worked on all three cases.

James Jackson, 2020:
Look, it was a standard thing. They had psychiatrists. We had psychiatrists. Remember, I came from Oakland. Everybody and their brother had a psychiatrist testify for them. I mean, they're all fucking frauds. They don't know anything. Psychiatry is a joke.

On December 10, 1971, Frazier was found sane by the jury and five days later, shortly before five o'clock on December 15, he was sentenced to death.

Leaving the courtroom—

Ben Williams (KPIX reporter), 1971:
Mr. Frazier, how do you feel about your sentence?

John Linley Frazier, 1971:
Oh, I don't know. What sentence? [Laughs].

Peter Chang, 1971:
Yes, he's sane. The man's a murderer. He's a callous, calculating murderer, who murdered five people and the jury couldn't come to any other conclusion than that. And they were a very conscientious jury. They deliberated that issue for a long time and they came to the right decision. […] This was a proper case for the death penalty and they inflicted it.

James Jackson, 2020:
After the case was over, Harold and I went down to talk to Peter. We were all at the Howard Johnson's over there and we walked down to his room. There was a celebration going on and the foreman of the jury was there. He looked at me

and said, "We knew he was insane but we had to be sure they wouldn't ever let him out."

I was about to go crazy when Harold dragged me away.

On December 30, Frazier and James Jackson held a press conference in a small room behind the courtroom.

When he was asked if he is insane—

John Linley Frazier, 1971:
According to your established values, yeah.

Frazier could not explain why he killed Taggart and Derrick. He told reporters that he regretted the murders. He added that the killings set him free of —

John Linley Frazier, 1971:
—something which had been tormenting me

for 22 years.

Peter Chang, 1971:
There is some doubt as to whether anybody will ever be executed again in California. But what the death penalty means, more than somebody's execution probably, is that the death penalty is a declaration by society that the act that the man commits is so abhorrent that they just have to say something about it and the way they say something about it is by decreeing that he receive the maximum penalty under the law.

Lark Ohta, 2020:
He wasn't successful with his insanity plea, and he was convicted on all counts. After the trial, he was sentenced to death, but in 1977 the death penalty was repealed in California, and he was sentenced to life imprisonment. When the death penalty was reinstated in 1978, it was unlawful to sentence a person

D.A. Investigator Examines Frazier Weapons

Convicted murderer John Linley Frazier is believed to have killed his five victims with the two guns Ray Belgard, the district attorney's chief inspector, is pictured displaying. The revolvers were found in an ammunition can thrown into a steep, bushy ravine behind a rabbit shed in back of Frazier's Cornwall Road residence in Soquel. Belgard and an inspector from the sheriff's office found the guns after D.A. Peter Chang learned from a casual conversation with a defense-witness psychiatrist approximately where the weapons were. A San Mateo County jury found Frazier guilty of murder in the Oct. 19, 1970 slayings of Dr. Victor Ohta, his wife, Virginia, their sons, Derrick and Taggert, and Ohta's secretary, Dorothy Cadwallader, in Ohta's $250,000 Soquel Hills home. Frazier was sentenced on Dec. 15 to die in San Quentin's gas chamber.

to death twice, so he remained sentenced to life in prison. He came up for parole every seven years but he was never released. In the end, I heard that he stopped attending his own parole hearings. I do not believe in the death penalty for Frazier or for anyone, and I would have never supported his execution.

When I think of him, I think that he must have been a person who was severely damaged. I think that anyone who is able to kill a child must be very broken and damaged. He honestly makes me more sad than

he makes me hateful, as I know he could not have been right. I have more contempt for somebody who is educated and healthy, and has had all the benefits and opportunities in life and is still bad or evil, than I have for someone as sick as Frazier must have been.

On February 2, 1972, it was announced that the Ohta–Cadwallader murder weapons had been found.

A STORM BREWS ON TWO FRONTS
1971–72

In May 1971, Herbert Mullin moved to San Francisco. Living in squalid apartments and out of his car, Mullin studied Einstein's history and theories. He discovered he was born on the anniversary of Einstein's death and believed that to have great meaning.

Terry Medina, 2020:
In San Francisco, that's when the whole Jonah and the whale theory came out. He had to kill people for two reasons. One, his father would telepathically tell him to kill. He'd have to kill somebody before he came home for dinner, or whatever. But the reason for his dad telling him to kill was to prevent earthquakes from happening around the world. And he was actually saving people's lives.

Dee Shafer, Ph.D.:
He believed that he had to kill some of the victims to prevent a terrible earthquake from devastating San Francisco. He said about three to four months after he was arrested,

he realized that those ideas were delusional. He was unable to offer any insight into the emotional impact of this realization.

In late 1972 a man named Reuben Greenspan, who had been predicting earthquakes since the 1930s prophesied that on January 4, 1973, at nine o'clock in the morning there would be a massive earthquake in California and that San Francisco would be destroyed. Could Mullin have been influenced by this?

Mullin also became fascinated by the stories of Michaelangelo sneaking into Santo Spirito Church Hospital as a teenager in order to dissect and study corpses in order to perfect his understanding of anatomy to advance his artistic endeavors.

Herbert Mullin, 2020:
My sister's husband, Al Bocca, suggested I read the book [*The Agony and the Ecstasy*]. I did get a copy and read it in the summer and autumn of 1972. In 1971 and 1972 I did

research art at the San Francisco Public Library. Some of my research papers are in the evidence locker at the Santa Cruz County District Attorney place.

The Agony and the Ecstasy was written by Irving Stone and published in 1961. The book is a biography of Michelangelo and details Michelangelo's dissections.

Herbert Mullin, 2020:

My mind was a very reactive type of mind. I was mentally silent with myself. If and/or when thoughts came to me they would stay awhile and then be forgotten. I did not know how to recall ideas to further investigate them. In May of 1971 I began using little notebooks that would fit in my shirt pocket. I used them to make notes about what I was thinking about and/or planning I guess.

Harold Cartwright, 2020:

Mullin did writings. Classic paranoid schizophrenic stuff. I went up to a rooming house he had lived in, in San Francisco. Hundreds if not thousands of pages of writings that would go one sentence and be something rational and the next five sentences would be totally irrational. He was a classic paranoid schizophrenic. Then he thought he was going to be a boxer.

While living in San Francisco, Mullin was referred to Newman's Gym when he inquired at the local YMCA about boxing lessons.

When he showed up at Newman's, Mullin was—

Don Stewart (Boxing coach), 1973:

Sitting in the bleachers at the gym wearing a big hat, like a huge sombrero and holding a bible in his hand.

Right: Reuben Greenspan was making headlines and stirring up fear with his earthquake prediction. This is from the Santa Cruz Sentinel December 21, 1972.

Prediction: Big Quake Set Jan. 4

SAN FRANCISCO (AP) — Reuben Greenspan says that by the time computers verify his earthquake theory, it will be too late.

Dr. William Kautz of the Stanford Research Institute has been checking out Greenspan's past earthquake predictions, and he said Tuesday Greenspan's theory "looks pretty good."

"I've been running the theory through a computer and getting pretty good results," Kautz said Wednesday. "We hope we'll have some kind of a definite report in two weeks."

But Greenspan has said that in two weeks—on Jan. 4, to be exact—San Francisco will be hit by a devastating earthquake. He said it will hit 7.4 on the Richter scale—the great earthquake of 1906, which took 452 lives and burned the city down, was 8.2.

Greenspan, 69, was called "the earthquake prophet" during the 1930s when he foretold several major tremors. Last year, he foretold the Feb. 9 earthquake in Los Angeles two weeks in advance.

His predictions are based on solar and lunar eclipses. He says the gravitational pull of the bodies creates stresses on the earth that cause faults to slip. The 1971 Los Angeles earthquake took place the day of a lunar eclipse. The 1906 earthquake occurred within a few days of a moon eclipse.

An eclipse of the sun will take place Jan. 4, 1973.

Greenspan, whose home is Laguna Beach, Calif., is reported living with Dr. Kautz while the computer check is made.

"It's a well known fact that earthquakes are more likely during eclipses," Kautz said.

Greenspan, who developed his tidal theory of earthquakes while he was a ship's navigator, says he will be in the hills above San Francisco on Jan. 4. Then, he says, he will visit Mayor Joseph Alioto—who doesn't take the prediction seriously but invited Greenspan for dinner—for "seven courses of crow."

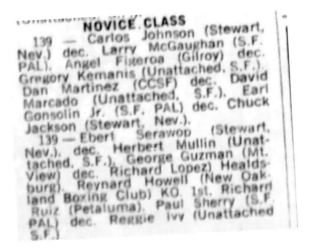

NOVICE CLASS

139 — Carlos Johnson (Stewart, Nev.) dec. Larry McGaughan (S.F. PAL), Angel Figeroa (Gilroy) dec. Gregory Kemanis (Unattached, S.F.), Dan Martinez (CCSF) dec. David Marcado (Unattached, S.F.), Earl Gonsolin Jr. (S.F. PAL) dec. Chuck Jackson (Stewart, Nev.).

139 — Ebert Serawop (Stewart, Nev.), dec. Herbert Mullin (Unattached, S.F.), George Guzman (Mt. View) dec. Richard Lopez) Healdsburg). Reynard Howell (New Oakland Boxing Club) KO 1st. Richard Ruiz (Petaluma), Paul Sherry (S.F. PAL) dec. Reggie Ivy (Unattached S.F.)

Mullin spoke to Newman in a Spanish accent, only when Newman asked him his name did Mullin drop the facade.

Don Stewart, 1973:
He said he wanted to learn to box and I taught him how. When he first started he had two left feet and two left hands.

Mullin quickly improved.

Herbert Mullin, 2020:
My coach was Vic Grupico. I think he testified at the trial in 1973. In October/November of 1972, I saw him drive by my parents' house in Felton in a brand new car…I thought that was strange.

Jim Jackson, 1973:
He would hit the bag when someone told him to, and stop when someone told him to. He would get very upset if he was ever late to the gym and wrote long letters apologizing for it.

Mullin boxed in the 1972 San Francisco Golden Gloves competition. He fought in the Novice 139 pound division. His match was on opening night, March 6. He was knocked down in the first round but came back strong.

Don Stewart, 1973:
We thought he was a Great White Hope. He stole the show, he really did. He only lost by

a split decision.

When Mullin was a child, living in San Francisco, three neighborhood boys, the Koch brothers, proudly showed him that they had carved "Jailhouse Rock" in a patch of wet cement on a sidewalk.

Herbert Mullin, 2020:
After the 1972 Golden Gloves experience, I walked back to that patch of concrete and read those words again…"Jailhouse Rock." In less than a year I was in California State Prison as a lifer.

A short time after the Golden Gloves, Mullin told Stewart he was quitting boxing and was thinking about becoming a priest.

Raymond Koch (Childhood neighbor of Mullin), 2020:
I'm an orthopedic surgeon now, but once I was coming back from med school and he was visiting my mom in San Francisco. She was still in the same house. He definitely had psychological issues at that point. He had what we call looseness of association with rapid speech. He gave me a book called *Autobiography of a Yogi*. He was into Eastern religions at that time which was not that uncommon at the time, but was also not that uncommon for people who were psychologically challenged.

EDMUND KEMPER

As Herbert Mullin was learning to box, Edmund Kemper was released to the custody of his mother. Kemper had spent the last five years in Atascadero Mental Hospital and under the custody of the California Youth Authority.

Edmund Kemper, 1988:
I was discharged in the summer of 1971, and the crimes did not start until the spring of 1972.

Harold Cartwright, 2020:

Remember, the psychiatrists at Atascadero said, "Limit contact with his mother."

That was one of the conditions of release. At a certain age you have to let him out, the law is absolute about that. So, the California Youth Authority, in their wisdom, paroled him and required him to live with his mother. Personally, I think if they would have followed the instructions of the psychiatrists, there's a possibility no one would have ever gotten killed after that.

Edmund Kemper, 1988:

When I was paroled I went to her home, I do what she says. Again, I was back as a fourteen-year-old boy, doing what my mommy says or I'll be punished. Except that I had not been raised that way. I had been put in an institution for adults, I'd been treated like an adult as I acted like one.

And I flourished. I did well there, I grew up, I had what I hoped to be a bright future. And immediately upon being paroled we had problems. And I don't know if you can appreciate my perspective at the time, but I was on parole for a double murder, it was a one-shot thing, there was a lot of people that were real dubious about the potential for any kind of success for that program. And for me to say, "I don't like this parole, I don't think it's going to work, I might get violent again,"

It would easily be considered kissing my life good-bye, "Well, I don't like it, so I'm going back in."

I wasn't going back in for a few months, it was for life, if they wanted to lock me up for life.

Edmund Kemper, 1991:

The state of California takes her son away from her and says, "We are taking your son away because you must be an unfit mother. He's a murderer. He killed people."

I've tried to look at it from her point of view. "If you could raise your son right, he wouldn't kill people, lady. We're taking him."

In a mere five and half years the bureaucracy—and she had nothing, she had no respect for California bureaucracy. She used to make jokes about that all the time. About if you, you know, if you want to waste the rest of your life doing nothing, apply for something at, you know through a bureaucratic process in California. Those bureaucrats took me away from her. In five and a half years, they hand me back and now I'm an overachiever. Good looking strapping young man, wants to go work, wants to make a living for himself, wants to be sociable, he isn't paranoid and pulling away from people anymore, that shocked the hell out of her, it had to of. She didn't share that with me, but I'm saying that must have really tore her and made her feel all the more a bad mother. I have a feeling she felt she couldn't be a part of that

Above left: Mullin boxed at 139 pounds in the 1972 Golden Gloves.
Above: Kemper in an undated photo.

healing process. So she attacked it because I became a cancer in her life. I reminded her everyday what a rotten mother she must be. Now I'm not saying she was. She must be a rotten mother. Look what the state did for me and she couldn't. They couldn't of insulted her any worse if they tried and they didn't try. They were trying to solve the problem by paroling me to her so I'll stay out of trouble and go be a good adult, paying taxes and guess what? That's the one furnace they should not have put me back in because hey, she had no help on the other end.

Edmund Kemper, 1988:
I was given parole that was requiring seventy-two visits, thirty-six of them with a parole agent over an eighteen month period, that's every two weeks, and thirty-six visits with a psychiatric social worker, and that's only alternate weeks.

And I'm here to say right now I saw my parole agent four times, I was not introduced to him until two months after I'd been on parole. I never was given to a psychiatric social worker, there was no one there to hear the problems.

Edmund Kemper, 1988:
Because I left her an underachiever, barely making it in school, would not work, was irresponsible, I was a management problem.

When I came back I was an overachiever, I was getting straight "A's" in junior college. There wasn't work in Santa Cruz when I paroled to that area. There was a, I don't know what you call it, not a depression, there was a recession at that time, 19-early 70. And there were no jobs to be had.

Edmund Kemper, 1988:
I am an alcoholic, I was an alcoholic then. I drank very heavily. In fact, the Santa Cruz Jaycees had a problem with me at the time, I was an officer of a club but I was crocked half the time when we had meetings or social activities. I drank while I drove, in fact the last year when I was committing my offenses, I was drunk more often than I was sober, and that's a fact. I mean, on a clear statement, I was drinking gallons of wine a week.

I never was drunk when I committed the crimes, I was always sober then.

Edmund Kemper, 1988:
I had a lot of short-term jobs around Santa Cruz that led up to the employment at the service stations. I resigned from the first one and hired on to the second one the same day.

Jim Conner, 2020:
Before I went to work for the police department, I worked at Wilson's out there on Soquel and Trevethan and we delivered tires to a bunch of the gas stations around town. One of the stations was the 76 station on the corner of Water and Ocean, and Ed worked there at that gas station. He was a real friendly guy and we'd have a cup of coffee, and we'd sit around and bullshit and I'd go back to work. So, when I got hired on to the PD, here's a young guy wearing his crisp, fancy police uniform, so I've got to drive around and show off myself to everybody. One of the guys I went to see was Ed. I drove into the gas station, got out of the car and he said, "What the hell are you doing?"

I said, "I'm a cop. I just got hired on the PD."

I said, "You're a big guy, man. You oughta come down and join up."

Little did I know that the guy had just gotten out for killing his grandparents.

Harold Cartwright, 1973:
When's the first time you really thought in reality about killing a girl?

Edmund Kemper, 1973,
Uh, I was walking down the Boardwalk in my stiffy [the interviewer confirmed that Kemper said "spiffy"] clothes, right? And I'd rented a big Chevy Impala and went up on the boardwalk, walking along, and here comes a girl I'd met in the gas station, she'd

Kemper dropped the gun off at his house and took the group out to dinner at Stagnaro's on the wharf. He paid for the meal and had a few drinks; the rest of the party were too young to drink.

Harold Cartwright, 1973:
So you knocked off the thoughts for a while.

Edmund Kemper, 1973:
In their case, yeah. I didn't even want the gun in the car. So I took it out and took it in the house.

Kemper got a job with the California Division of Highways.

come in for gas. She had a girlfriend with her who was really foxy. I said, "Hey, let's take a ride here and there."

They said, "We've got to go up to the house."

Kemper drove his friend, her fiancé, and her girlfriend up to her house. She ended up being the daughter of Santa Cruz Police Lieutenant Chuck Scherer.

They then drove to Kemper's home. Kemper had a nine millimeter handgun under his seat.

Edmund Kemper, 1973:
I had the gun in the car and I was thinking about it, then. After a long time the fantasies I had were building up, I just turned on them and said this is a poor way to do anything. It's just a fake out. Running around faking that you're a real nice guy and all that shit and pick somebody up and do something to them.

Mickey Aluffi, 2020:
He worked for Caltrans up in Alameda County. His nickname at work was "Fork Lift" because he could pick up four bags of concrete and walk away with them. A strong guy.

Edmund Kemper, 1988:
I was a Highway Maintenance Man. I ran, operated, and maintained a drilling truck on the highways.

Kemper drilled small holes for another employee to pump a chemical down in order to raise indentations in the road.

Due to the long commute from Santa Cruz, Kemper moved into an apartment on Union Street in Alameda.

Richard Verbrugge, 2020:
He got his own apartment because he was working mostly in Alameda County. When he got that apartment, that's when he really

started having trouble with his mother. He said she fixed him up with a date with some girl she knew and he took her out a couple of times. And then he's going to have sex with her or has sex with her. And she wouldn't have anything to do with him afterwards. And this kind of set him off. This is what he said. And so he decided that he would just get girls for himself. So that's when he started, you know, picking up hitchhikers. He picked up a lot of hitchhikers before he ever killed one, you know.

HERBERT MULLIN

Herbert Mullin returned to Santa Cruz in the beginning of September 1972. He lived out of his car.

Shortly after returning, Mullin visited his high school friend, Jim Gianera, and Gianera's friend, Bob Francis. Mullin bought LSD from Gianera.

Herbert Mullin, 2020:
At that time my parents had bought a new Toyota and drove to Washington D.C. for a vacation and sightseeing excursion.

While his parents were on vacation, Mullin stayed in the Felton family home. On September 9, 1972, Mullin had an intense LSD trip. He spent the night writing in journals and drawing.

Very soon after, on September 15, Mullin moved back in with his parents and got a job as a busboy.

Harold Cartwright, 2020:
His [Mullin's] mother was a housewife. She didn't have a career outside the home. His father had been a Marine drill sergeant. I think he worked at the post office at that time. They were devout Catholics. He had been raised in a very strict environment. After he moved back home, he redid the flower beds around his parent's house and they were exact replicas—the shape of Aztec sacrificial altars. He was a screwed up guy.

Herbert Mullin, 2020:
When those thoughts [a fear of earthquakes] came, just before the crime spree began, I was receiving them as a paranoid undifferentiated schizophrenic. I do not know how or why those concepts arose in my mind. Those concepts began during the first two weeks of October 1972, when I moved from San Francisco to my parents' house in Felton.

Herbert Mullin, 1973:
I was the victim of a 'kill-joy sadistic witchcraft plot' that resulted in the 'four month crime spree'. My family and former friends are guilty of premeditated second degree murder, at the very least.

Herbert Mullin, 2011:
Okay. By that, I think I meant that my father was a drill sergeant in the United States Marine Corps, a captain in the artillery, United States Army during World War II, and he knew that what he was doing would lead to a violent crime. And so by saying set me up, I guess that's what I was trying to refer to.

Herbert Mullin, 2011:
I believe that I was deliberately forced into a state of extreme naivete, gullibility and immaturity by my family.

Herbert Mullin, 2011:
It was that they programmed me to be academically efficient. Efficient in terms of sports. But immature, naive and gullible in terms of social and emotional interaction.

Above left: Mullin in court.
Next four pages: Mullin's writings from 1972.

August 22, 1972

Today at 12:15 p.m. I feel that my good friend Maurice Chevalie has been conceived to a very wealthy family in Boston Massachusetts. He'll bee in the same grammar school as Albert Einstein.

Because of different vibratory feelings I feel fraternal experience has been achieved maybe triplets.

In May of 1973. Check Boston Newspapers for this Birth.

Radio — Suicide Check for S.F. intuition. Reputable Longevity Bostonian.

Saturday September 23, 1972

I hereby declare to the rest of humanity that I need to be conceived in the womb of Mrs. Enos Founatt in the year of our lord one thousand nine-hundred and forty. To attest the fact Mr. Enos Founatt is my uncle. Whereby we have deduced that an absurd amount of debauchery has been done to the entity. Therefore on into infinity as many of our brethern will. Why has this happened? I just discovered that I distroy inorder to exist. I need to talk to someone who will explain to me just what exactly was happening. Then on into infinity. Do we work together or what happens now, man. you ain't performed as suspected. Einstein and his way of life are similar to Mullin and his way of life.

Kill those who are what you are doing. MAKE sure to disguise yourself so that they won't know you. You dressed up as an old lady and then you killed people who hurt you. Obsuro but do it. I can do a better job but the truth is I'm so jealous I started long ago putting the hex on you. Army, Army do you know the way. Einstein Einstein said no death today. Richardson, Richardson have you no fear. Live in the stable with all your gear. Alone and tedious is the future. Man is not gentle.

Albert wants to get even with
the people who helped me and the
people who have hurt me.
Albert WANTS to die. 5% of

100% yes I think I'll

succumb but isn't immunity
a nice thought. No, it really
isn't. 5% get a better
feeling and better coverage.
UNIVERSAL   CATHOLIC.

THAT   HELPED   YOU.

JANUARY   1969
February   1969

NO PAIN DEATH TRIP.

DON'T WASTE IT.

MARY ANN PESCE AND ANITA LUCHESSA SUNDAY, MAY 7, 1972

Richard Verbrugge, 1973:
He chose to kill his victims because, "Atascadero is full of rapists who let their victims live to testify against them."

Edmund Kemper, 1991:
The first two co-eds I killed were on Ashby Avenue. They were five foot two, slight of figure, you know, we call petite. One's black hair, one's blond hair.

Mary Ann Pesce and Anita Luchessa, both eighteen, were roommates at Fresno State. The two had spent the weekend in Berkeley and were headed to Stanford, on their way back home.

Edmund Kemper:
At this time I had the full intention of killing them. I would have liked to rape them, but I had very little experience, very little exposure to the opposite sex.

Edmund Kemper, 1991:
I think what I said about her [Pesce] was that she epitomized what really drove me. She was a haughty young lady. She's kinda stuck up. Distant. I look back on them and I see a girl that was not beautiful, she was not plain, she was somewhere in between and she was caught up in that beauty thing. Like kids in the valley are. Valley girls. Trying to make something of themselves and they exploit little attributes they have and downplay the other ones and she was playing little miss distant with me and her friend was very open, very, her roommate was very open, very country girl, talking and stuff. And it's sad because Pesce was the—Mary Ann was the expert in hitchhiking, she had half her life in Europe. She'd hitchhiked around Europe. She had done it in the United States. She was good at it. She didn't want to get in the car. But she had two roommates, okay, and one went on the trip with her. To Berkeley and to Stanford and back to Fresno State. Only one would go with her and apparently I'm thinking back, the other one was so close to going that later when she found

BACKGROUND ON MARY ANN PESCE AND ANITA LUCHESSA

By Christine Falco (edmundkemperstories.com)

"Did you have a daughter named Mary Anne Pesce?"

"Yes, I did," said Gabriel Pesce of Camarillo. Pesce was the picture of controlled agony as he testified in court at Kemper's trial, under questioning from District Attorney Peter Chang. With his eyes fastened on Kemper seated at the counsel table, Pesce talked about his daughter: "Although Mary Anne weighed only about one hundred pounds and was about five feet tall, she was an expert skier and aspired to try out for the Olympics. She was a good student and had won medals on her high school debating team. Mary Anne and Anita [Luchessa] were roommates at Fresno State and they were last seen May 7 [1972], as they hitchhiked on Ashby Avenue in Berkeley. They were visiting friends in Berkeley, then were trying to get a ride to Stanford when they disappeared. I tried to file a missing persons' report after her disappearance, but police told me 'There's nothing to worry about. Just wait.' I intend to listen to the testimony in the case because I think it might help to finalize the loss of my daughter…"

"Mary Anne had developed her zest for adventure while we were living in Europe between 1964 and 1971. I was an engineering executive for Abex Corporation and was transferred to a new job as international operations director for Abex's aerospace division in Wiesbaden [Germany]. When I announced to the family back in 1964 that we were moving to Germany, Mary Anne was unhappy with the idea. She was a seventh-grader then and had lots of important projects and friends she did not want to leave behind. Her friend next door, Melissa, and she might never see each other again."

"The mountains [near Wiesbaden] were what made Mary Anne forget California so easily. We were skiers and we made sure the children learned to ski, taking advantage of a country where the sport comes naturally. Mary Anne attended a German school for a while then spent a year studying in Switzerland. She picked up a dozen or so words from nearly every language she encountered in Europe, but German came easily, having heard it the most. She had a small address book containing the names of friends from all over Europe with whom she held a very lively correspondence. She had hitchhiked a lot in Europe, it made her feel free. She was very trusting of other people."

"Our last family gathering was a ski weekend at Bear Valley, a resort area northeast of Fresno. Melissa Jones' family, who lived next door to us, joined us. Mary Anne and Melissa sat up until four in the morning the first night talking about school and boys and skiing."

"Nothing in Mary Anne's character or previous behavior had ever led us to believe she would run away without telling us. Absolutely not. She was at school and would go some-place for the weekends or what-have-you, but she would always tell us. She was in constant contact with us by phone or by mail, just about two or three times a week."

During Kemper's trial, Anita's father, Alvin Luchessa of Modesto, spoke of his efforts to locate his daughter, including hiring a private investigator. Luchessa's voice broke as he spoke and tears came to his eyes. "We tried to do all we could to find her," he said, and wept. "This is the first time in her life she has ever hitchhiked. She always told us every-thing and she never did."

"Anita was the third generation of the Luchessa family to grow up among the peach and almond trees six miles from downtown Modesto, on our ranch house on Tully Road.

When she graduated from high school in 1971, Anita had pushed for a chance to go to a college or university far enough from home that she could see something new. We imposed that she go to Fresno State because we did not like our daughter to be too far from the ranch, and Fresno seemed to us a reasonably "safe" college. She enrolled as an art history major and became Mary Anne's roommate by chance because their names were together on the enrollment lists and came up for housing at the same time."

"It was her first weekend away from home since she started college and was excited about it. She had faithfully come home to the family farm weekend after weekend because we did not like the idea of her being left to the temptations of a city like Fresno when there were no classes."

(Sources: Register-Pajaronian, October 23, 1973, by Marj von B
The *San Francisco Examiner, May 15, 1972*
Register-Pajaronian, October 23, 1973, by Marj von B
Sacrifice Unto Me, by Don West, Chapter 4
The Co-Ed Killer, by Margaret Cheney, Chapter 5)

out what happened to her two roommates, she dropped out of college. She came and testified at my trial. And she was devastated by the whole thing. So I'm thinking she almost went. And she realized she might have died too, who knows. But, I don't know that I would have picked them up, if there was three of them. I don't know if they would have been where they were. The whole cir-cumstances could have changed. I'm thinking that because it had such a violent effect on her college education, she was that close to going.

Edmund Kemper, 1991:

The other girl, Anita Luchessa, wasn't a hitchhiker. She had been raised by her family: don't do things like that. That's totally out of line. Her friend talked her into it. And once she got into it and she saw how much fun it was and they meet the different people and they talk with people that by the time that they're leaving Berkeley, right? It's all about who gets the front seat and who gets the back seat so that she opened the door and asked where I was headed. And it said Stanford right on the sign they're holding and I said, "I'm going to Palo Alto, I can drop you off."

"Oh, great!"

And she jumps in, grabs her stuff, jumps in, opens the backseat up for her friend, who's standing there looking at me, long and serious about whether or not because I could tell at the time, she knows better than to get in, single adult. It's a coupe instead of a four door car so that she cannot get out other than through the front seat. So, that's all warning signs of not getting in with a single, you know, in that kind of situation. All of the things wrong about it. But when I drove up, I pulled that little stunt of looking at my watch, "Do I have the time to pick them up?"

And you wouldn't believe how much effect that kind of thing has and when she kept staring at me, looking. Looking for something wrong in my eyes. I gave this look back like, "I don't understand why you look at me like this?"
I gave her that back and she says, "Oh this guy is a dork, he's innocent as hell."

She gets in.

Edmund Kemper, 1991:
We're driving along and I'm looking at this young lady in the rear view mirror, and I look back at it years later and I'm saying she kept looking back at me too, right in the eyeballs. I'm wearing dark glasses, but they're not totally dark, and I'm realizing now that she could see me looking at her and she was looking right back at me. And instead of saying something to me like what are you looking at or hey maybe you ought to drop us off or something like that, she just kept looking back at me. I'm looking at her. She keeps looking at me. I'm thinking she's playing this little game. This uh, it's not really teasing so to speak, it's just this little psychological game back and forth that men and women do sometimes. The young girl in the front, Anita, was, at one point in the driving, and I'm sure they were doing little looks at each other, little comments that I didn't pick up because I'm driving and looking for places to go, that somewhere in that communication she gave me this sexy little look, you know, like "Oh, boy. You're a pretty good

Page 173: Anita Luchessa, 1968.
Page 175: Anita Luchessa and the 1968 Sophomore Yell Leaders, second from left.
Left: Mary Ann Pesce, 1971.
Above: Anita Luchessa, 1969
Right: Anita Luchessa, 1969 Sophomore Yell Leaders, second from left.

looking guy, you know, da da da."

And I smiled back at her. But not this thing where, "Ah yeah I'd get down with you," kind of thing, it was just I smiled back at her and I saw it for what it was, an eighteen-year-old girl that's feeling her oats, she's not doing anything wrong, it's sad and it's real pathetic, some of this stuff was, I was, getting real caught up in this girl in the back seat. I was, she was, to me at that point, she was really beautiful. She had the most incredible blue eyes. She had this real shiny black hair that was turning me on. And I was getting drove because I kept playing this game of picking people up and I'd plug in those fantasies of killing people.

Edmund Kemper, 1973:
What I did was I stopped for gas in Alameda

where I was living, at a Union Station, I think it was on Central, this was the one to the right of Park Avenue, close to the police station. I went into the restroom and took a map in with me and checked out the situation and found that I would be in the vicinity of, first I couldn't remember where Stanford and Palo Alto were in relation to me, and I determined that Highway 84 would get me there, so I took them the other way, out on 680 which would come in on the rural highway. I told them a story about how I was working for the Division of Highways and they were impressed with my radio transmitter and they thought that I was a secret agent or something.

Edmund Kemper, 1973:
I went out 580 towards Livermore—which

that would be Valencia Road, I think. You've heard of Eden Road, that little short road up to the left and immediately to the right, almost an extension, is Valencia Road which goes a lot further and it comes out on 84. I went up the 680 entrance to that rather than 580, which is farther up towards Livermore, and came winding back on through. Anyway, I was looking for a little cul-de-sac of some sort and I found one.

I had a 9mm Browning automatic that I had borrowed from a previous boss.

Edmund Kemper, 1984:
When that gun was pulled out, I launched it out. I had it under my leg. Out of sight. Parallel to my leg in the seat. It was something that had been thought out in fantasy. Acted out. Felt out. Hundreds of times before it ever happened.

Edmund Kemper:
And when I pulled my gun out, when I had them in a quiet place, uh, and they asked me what I was going to do, and I said, "What do you think I'm going to do?"

I was referring to sex. They were thinking—they didn't want to be thinking death so I wasn't encouraging that at all. And, uh, when they refused to be involved with me sexually, I stated that it could get worse, it, uh, you know, you could die today. You can end up getting dumped in the ditch, is that what you want? And, uh, they basically were, uh—they were arguing against rape. And, uh, naturally that didn't happen. Also I didn't shoot them. I had a 9 mm automatic and I didn't use it other than for gesturing.

MISSING   MISSING

MARY ANN PESCE   **ANITA M. LUCHESSA**

The parents of two teenage coeds from Fresno State College are appealing for aid from anyone that may have seen their daughters who disappeared in the Bay Area near Berkeley on May 7, 1972. Neither girl has been heard from since.

Anita M. Luchessa and Mary Ann Pesce, roommates at Fresno State, were last seen May 7, as they hitchhiked on Ashby Ave., in Berkeley. They were visiting friends in Berkeley, then tried to get a ride to San Francisco, Menlo Park and Stanford University. They were possibly to return to Fresno down the coast highway through Big Sur. All police and private agencies have found no trace of either teenager.

Miss Luchessa is 5 feet 1 inch tall, 105 pounds, brown shoulder length hair with partial sun bleaching and brown eyes. She was wearing gray and white stripe bib type overalls, red "T" shirt with a red nylon jacket.

Miss Pesce is 5 feet 1 inch tall, with shoulder length brown hair cut in a shag style, 110 pounds with blue eyes. She was wearing a maroon or purple colored sweater, faded blue jeans and hiking boots. She also had a purple felt hat.

The girls had a back pack with orange or red knapsack and a gray-brown sleeping bag.

A $500.00 reward is offered for the location of the girls. All responses will be kept strictly confidential.

Anyone who may have seen the girls are asked to contact Bob Heitman Investigations, area code 209 526-5040 (Collect). The girls are asked to call home to assure their parents they are safe. Miss Luchessa's mother is seriously ill.

time. I was quite agitated and I was very scared. About halfway through my approach, which basically was telling them while we were off to the side, exactly what was going to take place, which was one of them was gonna get into the trunk where I didn't have to keep an eye on her. The other one was gonna be hidden in the back seat so that when we left the area, if there were any witnesses watching, they wouldn't see either of the girls. We would go to my apartment in Alameda, and there, I was going to assault them, or not so much assault, but I made it sound like I was gonna play a few games and they knew what I meant by that.

Edmund Kemper, 1973:
So she [Pesce] allowed me to put my handcuffs on her arm and I put the other one around the seatbelt behind the lock, so it wouldn't come up and left her back there. I took the other girl [Luchessa] to the trunk and just before she got in, she reiterated something that Mary Ann had said, that was please don't do this, or something like that. I said, "Are you going to start in too?"

Edmund Kemper, 1973:
Mary Ann didn't seem to be really too impressed by it [the gun] and that kind of upset me. She started off with some wisecrack, so I don't blame her a bit. But I certainly wouldn't have myself, especially with the size differential and my temperament at the

She got in the trunk and Kemper returned to the car.

Edmund Kemper:
The first young lady that was in the back seat, that was Mary Ann Pesce, I finally secured her, she argued a lot, she was dialoguing, trying to change up control of the situation.

She had already decided I was in control, I was trying to gain control, I was convinced she was in control of it. So, for about twenty minutes we were arguing back and forth over what was going to happen and I was trying to keep it away from what was intended, which was murder. I decided at that time, I wasn't going to tell anyone that I was going to rape them. I didn't say that at the time, but I left that wide open as the avenue that I was, it was going to be a sexual release and that got them very distressed and it was obvious, to me, that as I was going to pursue what I was doing that distress had to stop. So I went to, uh, unfortunately a more effective behavior of letting them help me. I let more of my personality come out and I was suicidal, very disturbed, grasping out for someone. I abducted them and I wasn't going to let them out of the car because I was tired of people walking away from me. So some of that was very true. But I manipulated that to allow them to help me to the point of resolving their behavior until we got to a place where they could be killed.

Kemper handcuffed Mary Ann Pesce behind her back.

Edmund Kemper, 1973:
I tried to put this bag over her head and she was complaining that she wouldn't be able to breathe. I said I'd tear a hole in it, not intending to really, and I had a terry cloth bathrobe with a long rope type tie. I put a loop in it and started pulling it down over what I thought was her neck. I pulled it tight. That's about the part where I blew it because when I yanked on it, I just went like that, very tight, and it just snapped right in two and it caught her right around the mouth and this kinda got her uptight. She let me know about it, and at the same time, bit a hole in the bag which was pressed against her mouth.

Edmund Kemper, 2017:
[I] reached in my pocket and pulled a knife out.

I wish I hadn't because you know, I didn't have any experience with such things, and the—well the only experience I had was theatrical stuff on television. When somebody gets stuck with a knife they fall over dead for theatrical purposes. That doesn't happen in real life.

Edmund Kemper, 1991:
The knife I fell back on. That was a fall back position. I was trying to smother her. That didn't work. She was struggling against that and arguing with me about it and, uh, I got frustrated and I reached into my pocket. I had that folding knife and I pulled it out and for a lot of years I made a point of saying back then with the investigators, when I pulled the knife out and locked it into place it clicked and she said, "What's that?"

And that's a quote, "What's that?"

And she was kind of, kind of a naggy kind of thing, "What's that?"

And I couldn't figure out why she said that. Like, it's not that big an impact, the little clicking sound behind her. You know? Amongst what's going on, hadn't been murders up to that point, it had been an aggravation and I had her tied up, or handcuffed and it took me years for it to dawn on me, trying to look at it from different points of view, to understand these things, why she said that. You know? Why she said that? Because I had brandished this gun and I had cocked it once and it clicked. So, in her mind, very possibly, I had pulled the gun out and was going to shoot her. So she said, "What's that?"

Thinking I'd pulled the gun out and now I'm cocking it. Not realizing I'd pulled a knife out, that I still had the gun in my pants. I stabbed her. She didn't fall dead. You're supposed to fall dead. You're supposed to go, "Ohhhh," and fall dead. I'd seen it in all the movies. It doesn't work that way. When you stab someone they leak to death. They lose blood pressure and you stab them more and more and more. You complicate it many times by where you're hitting, the pain you're causing, and the aggravation of the person involved, plus whether or not they leak a little faster. It wasn't working, worth a damn. I stabbed her all over her back and she even turned around and I stabbed her in the side and in the stomach once. Why? As she turned around I could have stabbed her through the heart, but her breasts were there and that actually deflected me. I couldn't see stabbing a young woman in her breast. That's embarrassing, I didn't say that to them back then, I don't think, I may have. But, that's humiliating to admit that. That I was that affected by her presence. I stabbed her in the belly that had to hurt worse, I didn't do it to make her hurt.

Edmund Kemper, 1973:

Anyway, she was across the back of the seat with her head down towards the door, towards the space between the front seat and the back seat, and I don't think the bag was on, she had shaken it off. She was crying out a little bit louder and I kept trying to shut her up, covering her mouth up and she kept pulling away, and one time she didn't and like it was a cry, and I would have sworn it came out of her back. There were several holes in the lung area and bubbles and things coming out, and the sounds shook me up and I backed off and at the point, she turned her head to the back of the seat and she called out her friend's name, her first name. It was slow and it was not loud. That was the last thing that she said, she wasn't passing out at that point. I don't think at that point that the full impact of what had happened had really hit her. I think she was pretty well in shock or something. I felt I was getting nowhere, not that I wasn't getting any kicks out of stabbing her, but hoped that one would do it. When it got quite messy like that, I just reached around and grabbed her by the chin and pulled her head back and slashed her throat. I made a very definite effort at it and it was extremely deep on both sides. She lost consciousness immediately and there were no more vocal sounds anyway. She lost

consciousness. I got up and headed to the back of the car and at that point, I was kind of in a daze or in shock.

Edmund Kemper, 1991:

I just backed up out of the car. My hands are covered in blood and I'm saying, "Oh god, I did it. I did it. I don't believe it. I did it. Shit. I've done it."

Now I gotta kill the other one.

Edmund Kemper, 1981:

This is me back then in 1972 and 1973. Unable to live with the fact that I just stabbed to death and cut the throat of an innocent young woman. Innocent in the sense that she did not plan on that happening. She didn't do anything specifically for that to happen to her. Yet she was a very active participant in her own death. And in my memory of that, she was nineteen years old and her roommate in the trunk who died right after that was eighteen.

Kemper went to the trunk of his car.

Edmund Kemper, 1984:

I had just gone through a horrible experience with her roommate. Stabbing her. And I was in shock. Because of that. I couldn't believe that it was that way. I'm walking back there bewildered. I gotta kill her. I can't let her go. She's gonna tell on me. Everybody's gonna get me. She sees the blood on my hands, "What are you doing?"

She pulled back and she gasped. I'm thinking, whoa, I don't want her to know what happened. I said, "Your friend got smart with me."

She'd been getting really smart with me a lot, but I never hit her. I killed her, but I didn't hit her. I said, "Your friend got smart with me and I hit her. I think I broke her nose. You better come help."

She's about to die, why does she have to know that. I couldn't deal with telling her that. And when I attacked her she didn't at first realize what was happening. It didn't go through. She had very heavy coveralls on. It knocked her right up into the lid of the car, but it didn't pierce the clothing. It wasn't that swell a knife anyway. I went out and bought it at a pawn shop, huge knife. I kept on just mindlessly attacking. She falls back into the trunk.

Edmund Kemper, 1973:
I thrust up, hoping to end the thing there, but it bounced off. Immediately I did the same thing again. The second time she saw, she knew what was going on. The first time had surprised her and starteled her. Her original fears, I guess, were confirmed. She threw herself back in the trunk away from me and said something like, "Oh God, God."

She started fighting me. I tried to stab her a few times and it wouldn't go through the [in-adible] down in the car like that.

So I tried to cut her throat and in the process stabbed myself in the hand, not even knowing I did it at the time. I didn't know until maybe an hour later. It needed three stitches. [...]

She was covering her throat with her hands. She knew what I was trying to do and I cut her fingers up quite badly trying to get through, not to cut her fingers off, but trying to get them out of the way. I was fumbling and struggling and she was very desperate and was putting up a hell of a fight. The only way I could stab her was on the side, through the heart side which was facing me. I grabbed her by the arm and pulled it up, the left arm. I was thrusting and the knife was going very deep, and it amazed me that she was stabbed three times and she was still going at it. I tried stabbing her in the front again, or towards the throat area, and she

4-H SPONSOR Ernie LaCoste buys the Grand Champion from Anita Luchessa at the Stanislaus County District (1967). Ernie is a long-time member of the Junior Livest

was making quite a bit of noise and she was trying to fight me off, and I stabbed her in the forearms. One was so bad you could see both bones, two inches, and she saw it, and when I hit, I don't think it really hurt so much as it was the shock of everything happening so fast. She looked at it and I could see the expression on her face of shock. She looks at it and then looks back at me and made some comment, like, "No," and all this, "No, no, stop."

Fighting, fighting, fighting. I stabbed her on the other side too. I hate to get into such detail on that, but my memory tends to be rather meticulous. Anyway, there was a wound above the left eye, just below the scalp. She was screaming and when she saw that wound on her arm she just started screaming, very loud, very piercing, and that shocked me, and I just stood back and I didn't know what

ANITA M. LUCHESSA

Anita M. Luchessa and Mary Ann Pesce, roo
May, 1972 as they hitch-hiked on Ashby Ave

MARY ANN PESCE

tes at Fresno State College, were last seen

to do. She screamed louder and I started hearing voices way off in the distance like someone would say, "Stop. What's that?"

You know? And I got very paranoid and very frantic. I struck even harder and put a gash above the eye. I tried again. I was going to go through the eye socket, but it didn't. It caught right on the corner of the bone and it stopped. It knocked her glasses off. She reacted to each one of these things with a completely different thing, where the other girls was just one continuous motion. This girl was actually fighting me, almost succeeding. But she really didn't have a chance. Finally, I started really panicking and I just stuck my fingers in her mouth and she started biting me. She had been biting me as I put my hand over her mouth, so I stuffed my fingers down in, just trying to shut her up, grabbing at the sound more or less, and it was effective and it started quieting her down, and I just pushed harder and harder than hell, and just for a second, and I guess at that point, she shifted momentum, and when I did that, the whole thing changed. At that point, I think at that point she started dying. But she slowed down and went semicon-scious or delirious, moaning and waving her arms around, fending off an imaginary assailant that wasn't there anymore. I shut the lid of the trunk, threw the knife in. She had torn my watch off too. I think there may even be a speck of blood on it still. I just threw it in an old nightstand by my bed. It was a Seiko watch with a burgundy face.

Edmund Kemper, 1984:

I just killed a young woman. I slammed down on the lid of the trunk. She's dead. She's dying. And I panicked. I thought, I just locked the car keys because I can't find them in my pocket. Oh my God, I locked them in the trunk. I'm kicking on the trunk lid. Yanking on it. Aw no, I don't believe this. I started to run and I tripped over the gun that I'd had in my pants, that I'd totally forgotten was there. I stopped and said, "Stop and think."

I collected my wits. "Check all your pockets."

I picked the gun up. I stuck it back in my pants. Now remembering that I had one. I checked all my pockets and there's the keys in the back pocket. I never put them in my back pocket.

Edmund Kemper, 1973:

I drove out of the area, and very close by, right down the main road, was the two cou-ples looking at property. They looked rather disgruntled as I went by. I tried to look nonchalant.

Edmund Kemper, 1984:

I thought I was pretty slick. And I tripped all over myself the first two murders. The first twenty-four hours there were three clear times that I should have been busted and I wasn't because three different individuals or three different groups of people got scared and minded their own business and looked the other way. I was picking up some very lovely young women.

Edmund Kemper, 1973:

I would loved to have raped them, but not having any experience at all in this area, I'd had very limited exposure to the opposite sex and I guess at the learning time, fifteen to twenty-one, I was locked up with all men and there wasn't any opportunity to be with women or girls…this is one of the big prob-lems I had and one of the big things that caused me to be so uptight.

Edmund Kemper, 1973:

Back up to my apartment in Alameda. I took their belongings up there to discover who they were and check into things to see what they had. I took what money they had. They had $5.28 exactly. […]

There was an extra three dollars hidden in the sleeping bag, between the sleeping bag and the casing on it, which I thought was rather sneaky and clever.

Edmund Kemper, 1973:

I didn't dismember them. I cut their heads off.

They're both beautiful, but after I got done with the knife, they weren't. They were bloody and, I mean, they were covered in blood.

It was messy and I didn't—once I got into it, it just got—I got sucked in deeper and deeper, it just—it didn't go away. So something had to be dealt with.

And I took their heads up to my apartment. I cleaned them up. I cleaned their hair out and posed them as they would have—as they were two hours earlier.

Edmund Kemper, 1973:

I remember it was very exciting…there was actually a sexual thrill…it was a kind of an exalted triumphant type thing, like taking the head of a deer or an elk or something would be to a hunter.

I was the hunter and they were my victims.

Edmund Kemper, 1973:

When I was in touchy situations, removing their heads in the trunk, taking some of the things upstairs, at one point, I tried to carry—I was quite attracted by Mary Ann Pesce's figure earlier and I had decided I was gonna take her upstairs and take her clothing off and see just how well she was developed. I ended up doing it in the trunk later, which was very difficult. But I got the sleeping bag out which was old, the zipper was messed up, I was gonna zip her up in it and just whip it upstairs when nobody was looking, like maybe midnight. But the zipper wouldn't work so I just rolled it around her and picked her up and started walking up and what I had done, was the big knife that was in the trunk, I decided to take it upstairs and clean it off because it was very bloody. I put that between her legs, crossed her legs, rolled her up in the thing and started carrying her up there. I actually stood her in the doorway as I started to unlock the door, the side door, approaching the lobby way there, and this retired Navy Filipino resident in the apartment house was just coming home from singing practice or something and I hear him just coming in the door, not knowing who it is. I hear him coming in the front door. I very quickly shut that door, grabbed her and started back out. As I round the corner, when the knife hit the ground and I was running like pure hell and I had to duck 'cause I ran [inaudible]. I ran like I never ran before because I had to get her out of sight quick. But the knife fell and I couldn't go back and I had just put her behind the car and kind of looked casual there as he came around the corner wondering what the hell was going on. He didn't know who I was. We approached each other in the dark and I smiled and he smiled and I started on back. He noticed in the light this great bloody knife there and he looks at it, "Is that yours?"

I said, "Yup."

I didn't think to say, oh I stabbed myself in the hand. I was carrying some things out to the car. I told him that the next day, that I was working with some camping equipment and I was checking the knife blade and putting it back in the sheath and stabbed myself in the hand. This is what I told the people at work too when I had to take off sick leave.

Richard Verbrugge, 1973:

After killing her, removing and later cleaning her head off in his Alameda apartment, he attempted to be orally copulated by the head [Pesce]. That this didn't work as, "Her teeth kept hurting me."

Edmund Kemper, 1973:

The first girl, the Pesce girl. I cut some of the meat out of her neck. She was more of a lean type, you know. Athletic and everything. That was very sweet. A lot sweeter than any meat I've eaten.

It was just a small chunk and I cooked it that night. I bit it off and spit it out.

I [inaudible] fried or boiled. I'm not much of a gourmet cook.

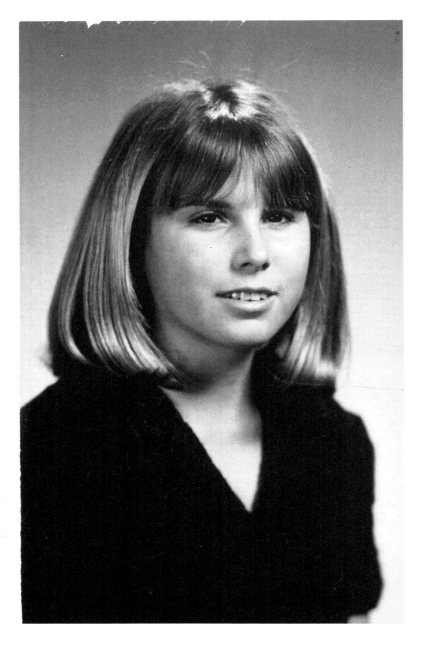

From a June 20, 1973 interview—

Donald Lunde, 1973:
What's this business about an eyeball?

Edmund Kemper, 1973:
Oh yeah, that's a tripped out—well, I'd had this fantasy as a kid about swallowing an eyeball.

I had this head trip about eyeballs. I thought, "Wow, this is the rankest thing you could do."

You hear about people eating parts of people's limbs and stuff like that. I had never read about anybody eating somebody's eyeball. Some girls of an age, it wouldn't be any bigger than, you know, one of those purple grapes. It would be about the size of that.

Donald Lunde, 1973:
So what did you do?

Edmund Kemper, 1973:
Swallowed an eyeball.

Donald Lunde, 1973:
On which occasion?

Edmund Kemper, 1973:
That was the Luchessa girl.

Donald Lunde, 1973:
Had you taken out the eyes of others? Because you compared to the size of—

Edmund Kemper, 1973:
Of eyeballs, yeah. Different people have—like that first girl who was my victim had very large blue eyes. Just beautiful light blue eyes. Huge.

Donald Lunde, 1973:
Did you [inaudible] the eyes on her and others too?

Edmund Kemper, 1973:
I just wanted to see what it was like. That's what Jackson released on TV the other night, "He just wanted to see what it was like." Cannibalism.

Donald Lunde, 1973:
What was it—

Edmund Kemper, 1973:
Actually, I prefer it to beef.

Donald Lunde, 1973:
What was that like, the eyeball?

Edmund Kemper, 1973:
I just swallowed it. It was all slimy. You know, from the tissue coming out. It's kind of hard to take an eyeball out with a teaspoon and a hunting knife, you know. I guess it really stretches the optic nerve to pull it too far out, just to get out where you can reach behind and cut the optic nerve. Then it would come out. There was a little tearing, you know the white, uh, the tissue that holds the eyeball, the tissue and muscles of the eyeball. It's only a covering anyway. I always thought it was part of the eyeball. It's just the same color.

Asked about taking pictures—

Edmund Kemper, 1991:
At first I did. But that stopped. At first I was hoping that could get it off, I could get a vicarious thrill out of seeing those pictures. Say, well this will be satisfying enough. Two people died, that's it. It doesn't have to go past that. And I'll see why I didn't want to do it again. Those pictures lasted about two weeks.

I come back from work two days after I did it, I mean Tuesday. Sunday it happened, Monday I took off. Took CTO, Compensatory Time Off, and I go back to work Tuesday. I come home from work Tuesday. A hard day at work. I'm feeling like I used to feel. I'd done some work that day I've accomplished something, And I'm saying, I can't

believe I did this stuff. I must have dreamed it. It must be some kind of weird dream. And I come back to the house, I pick up the corner of the carpet and pull out these pictures in an envelope and say Jeez, I don't believe this. Now I gotta believe it. That really happened. See it, I was that distance from what I had done. Just one day later that I couldn't believe that two physical days later that I couldn't believe that I'd actually done that. After two weeks, I couldn't handle the reality of those pictures.

Now I've seen. I've read where guys have hung criminals, like in the old west and tanned the guy's hide and made a pair of shoes out of it, the doctor did, the city doctor, and took the skull and made an inkwell out of it with gold hinges on it for the pens. This was some notorious criminal and I says jeez, that's kind of grisly.

Edmund Kemper, 1973:
Later on when they found her [Mary Ann Pesce] head I heard one brief news comment that she was a Camarillo girl, so I went down to L.A. and checked out Camarillo and only found one Pesce in the phone book and that was a Gabriel Pesce. So I went up by that neighborhood, in fact, right by the house. It was up at a gold course, right in the country club property area, very upper class and I was right about her. Because she had things like an address book with names and addresses from all over Europe: Switzerland, France, England, Belgium and apparently, these people she corresponded with frequently. She was also a, ski instru—one of these, like Bear Mountain or Bear Valley or one of the California or Nevada ski resort areas. I think in the wintertime, she'd go up there and she was on ski patrol, she had a ski patrol card.

Richard Verbrugge, 1973:
Since burying her [Pesce], he revisited her grave at least twice. In explaining the visits he stated that the first was to see if she had been discovered and the second was just

several weeks ago.

That his second visit was made at night on purpose so that he could check to see if he was brave enough to go up there in the dark. Kemper explained this remark by saying that when he was a small boy he was always afraid of the dark and believed in ghosts. That he felt if any of his victims were to return as a ghost and haunt him, Pesce would be the one to do it. That on this visit he talked to the grave.

When asked what he said, he stated, "Oh, I just told her that she'd been there almost a year now and still nobody's found her, things of that nature."

Kemper was then asked if he thought she replied to him or if he expected her to and he stated, "No, so before I left, I pissed on her grave."

Sam Munoz (Jury Room bar manager), 1973:

He [Kemper] went to work for the Highway Division, or Department, I think they call it. He worked there for a while and he got into some kind of accident with a motorcycle. He was driving this motorcycle and this woman went through a red light or something. I know she was in the wrong. He sued for $45,000 and he got a settlement of $15,000, so he had a little money, you know. He got medical care and hospitalization. He broke his arm, see, and you gotta imagine this guy walkin' around with his arm up in the air in a sling like this.

Kemper had a previous motorcycle accident in November 1970. He had facial fractures, separated his left shoulder, a concussion, and was knocked unconscious for ten minutes.

Kemper's second motorcycle accident occurred on June 27, 1972, in Oakland. As a result of that accident, he had a cast on his arm until March, 1973.

Robert Kinsey (Psychiatrist), 1973:

He says that a woman driver caused the accident and was cited for it. His bike went sideways, lost control, dumped over and broke his left forearm. He also had lacerations that required thirteen stitches on the top of his head but he was not unconscious. He was one week in Kaiser Hospital in Oakland. He has a steel plate and six screws in his complex left forearm fracture. He sold the motorcycle immediately. He had another accident between these two when he received no injuries in November 1971. He was tired after a long week of work, it was 2:00 a.m. Sunday when he fell asleep at the wheel on Highway 17 that is twisty. He totaled the car.

After receiving his settlement, Kemper bought a 1969 yellow Ford Galaxie 500.

Terry Medina, 2020:

And then August of '72 comes along. Case number 720288. I'll never forget the case number. This started the series of crime scenes that just didn't end.

Mickey Aluffi, 2019:

We had a report of a human head being found up near Loma Prieta that had been there for so long that it was difficult to say whether it was a male or female.

Terry Medina, 2020:

You know, for us, it's not unusual to find bodies up there. That was a body dump area from the greater San Jose area.

And forensics was really difficult. Not like it is today where everything is so advanced. There were no crime pathologists at the Sheriff's Office. So there was really no identifying this skull right away.

Mickey Aluffi, 2019:

So we took it to the lab and they did all their work on it and eventually we found out it was a female.

Mickey Aluffi, 2019:

That was the beginning.

Mickey Aluffi, 2019:
I was the junior detective at the time, so I would get all the work that no one else wanted. So I got the case with the head that was found.

MICKEY ALUFFI

William Kelsay, 2019:
Mickey was a deputy sheriff here in Santa Cruz starting in 1969. He became a sergeant in that department during the period of this trial. He was a detective during this period. He was there for a total of thirteen years.

After that he went to Watsonville Police Department for seventeen years. There, he served as a lieutenant and captain.

He concluded his career at UC Santa Cruz, starting as a captain and later becoming the chief of police there.
He's a local boy, unlike me. He's a graduate of Santa Cruz High School. He proudly attended Cabrillo College and then San Jose State. Ultimately, he received further training at the National Academy with the FBI at the University of Virginia.

He's one of the best cops I've known in my career.

Above: Two images of Mickey Aluffi.

AIKO KOO
THURSDAY, SEPTEMBER 14, 1972

Fifteen-year-old Aiko Koo lived with her mother and grandparents in Berkeley, California. Her mother and grandparents were from Latvia, having immigrated in 1949.

Her father was Korean and lived in Monterey.

Richard Verbrugge, 2020:
Her mother was an employee at University of California in Berkeley and she had an affair with a Korean professor. And as a consequence, Aiko was born and the professor would have nothing to do with his daughter. And her mother told me that as Aiko was growing up, she was always very interested in her Korean heritage.

That was the saddest case. Not only was she a child, but the mother had nobody like a husband to lean on to share her loss.

Skaidrite Rubene-Koo (Aiko Koo's mother), 1973:
Aiko contributed to life. She was a dancer, and she danced many times, before many people.

Aiko Koo danced in the classical Korean style since she was nine years old. Her mother and grandmother made all of her outfits in exacting detail.

Aiko and her troupe were quite accomplished, dancing all up and down the West Coast.

Skaidrite Rubene-Koo, 1973:
We wanted to give her heritage so she could be proud of her background. The dancing was good for her. It gave her identity and strength. I traveled with the girls and introduced the numbers. The Korean tradition made sense to people when they understood it.

Dancing made her life so much more colorful. She traveled all over and lived in her fifteen years more than many people live in a lifetime. This is our comfort.

Aiko Koo was last seen waiting for a bus on

Shat-
tuck Avenue in Berkeley
on September 14, 1972. An eyewitness said Koo
grew impatient waiting for the bus and took a
ride with a stranger who pulled up and offered
her a ride.

Very quickly Aiko Koo's mother, Skaidrite
Rubene-Koo, printed and distributed over a
thousand missing fliers. They were sent up and
down California and into Oregon and Washington.

Skaidrite Rubene-Koo, 1973:

I was afraid from the beginning. I didn't
think she was running away. She was on her
way to her dance lesson in San Francisco and
looking forward to traveling to St. Louis that
weekend to dance at the World Trade Center
Fair there.

Skaidrite Rubene-Koo, 1973:

I never believed she ran away, not even that
night when she didn't come home. I have
always said she was kidnapped.

I had a premonition all last summer that
something was going to happen to change

our
lives. She had started
hitchhiking, you know, we had no car.

I didn't want her to go [to the ballet
lesson in San Francisco] that night. I'm not
psychic but I was afraid for her. She was so
beautiful that night. But I told her she could
go if she took the bus, if she didn't hitch a
ride.

I knew she had been hitchhiking rides—
you know how impatient people are these
days. I knew because she had just gotten a
ticket for hitchhiking. When she told me
about the ticket she joked about it, called it a
"parking ticket."

Skaidrite Rubene-Koo, 1973:

But people run toward danger, instinctively, especially today, when everyone is
so over-stimulated. The lure of danger will
persist, no matter what you say.

Edmund Kemper, 1973:

I picked her up approximately at 7:00 p.m.,
maybe a little before. Apparently, from later
missing reports in the papers, she had been

looking very hopeful at each passing motorist, smiling. She had a little four-by-four white piece of paper with S.F. written in large red letters on it, and this was the type of hitchhiker I actually preferred picking up, that is, someone advertising where they want to go. That way, I didn't have to answer the question where am I going, and possibly blow the ride. I actually had gone past her before I spotted her, I circled back around the block, picked her up and there was absolutely no problem. Apparently, she was not an accomplished hitchhiker. I didn't come across any of the normal problems I had with girls, with their curiosity as to where I'm going, what I'm doing and this set of questions along that line.

I continued on down University Avenue in Berkeley, got up on the freeway towards, it should be Highway 80, and headed towards San Francisco. But I didn't follow the normal approach to the freeway that you would take from University. I went down to the Marina on Frontage Road first and took what would amount to be Ashby Avenue on-ramp to Highway 80 West. At any rate, we crossed the bridge with no incident. I had not told her what my intentions were at that time. I was just listening to her talk, and asking questions and answering hers. It was basically nondescript conversation. After we crossed over the bridge, she apparently wanted to take an off-ramp. You know there are several off-ramps and arteries from that off-ramp that move out to different parts of the city and apparently, she had a pattern set of which off-ramp the bus would take, and I appeared to blow it by accident, but it was deliberate. I kept on heading, I was heading towards 280 South, towards San Jose, which would cut me off at Highway 1, along the coast. Because I was trying to get as close to that as I could before having to inform her that she was being abducted. After blowing her off-ramp and making it sound like an accident, I said, "Oops."

And she said, "Oops."

I think it was slightly cutting. I continued

waiting for a bus that she later told me was a regular bus that she took into San Francisco to the Mission District to attend a scheduled ballet lesson, and she was not at this bus stop, she was at least one block farther down towards the freeway and she was attempting to solicit a ride. She was attempting quite actively in fact, stepping out off the curb and

Page 191: Aiko Koo in ninth grade.
Left and above: Aiko Koo dancing traditional Korean dances.
Right: Aiko Koo in eigth grade.
Next page: Aiko Koo and her mother, Skaidrite Rubene-Koo.

on towards the 280 South cutoff, got up on this, no wait a minute. I didn't get up on it right away, both of us were talking back and forth about which one to take, and I took the next off-ramp thinking that was the one she wanted, and at that point, I suppose I could have avoided the whole thing and possibly had been planning it. But when I realized, once we were down on the street, I realized she didn't know where we were and she thought I wanted to take that off-ramp, so I spent the next five or ten minutes trying to get back up on the freeway and found myself headed in the right direction again, which would be Highway 280 South. I got up on this highway and later, moved over towards the exchange that goes over to Highway 1, all along seeing Mission Street off-ramps and each one, she thinking to be the

last one to take and I kept assuring her there were more, actually not knowing there were, but that's the way the luck ran. At any rate, she didn't realize that there was a serious, serious problem until after we passed the town of Half Moon Bay and at that point, she kept looking at her watch and saying, "Well, I've only got fifteen minutes to get there"

"Ten minutes."

And, "Five minutes."

And at two minutes after eight exactly, she said, "Well, I'm late. I'm gonna be late for my class."

And at this point, I had been balking at saying anything, but at this point I told her that she wouldn't be making her class tonight, and with a worried tone, she said, "What do you mean?"

I said, "I'm not taking you to San Francis-

Missing Girl Clues Sought

BERKELEY — Police are still seeking clues to the disappearance of a 15-year-old high school student last seen Sept. 14 at a bus stop waiting for transportation to a San Francisco ballet class.

The girl, Aiko Koo, has been described as an "extremely attractive" Korean-American who has danced professionally in several Bay Area performances.

Miss Koo, who attends school in Oakland, lived with her mother at 1818 Hearst Ave. Mrs. Koo told police that she had a good relationship with her daughter and had not had any major conflicts. Aiko was to leave later this month for a dance performance in St. Louis.

She is described as about 5 feet 4 inches tall, weighing 105 pounds, with long black hair and looking older than her age.

AIKO KOO
Last seen Sept. 14

---

co, I'm taking you out of San Francisco."

Edmund Kemper, 1973:

I specifically said "tonight," so as not to suggest anything more permanent. Immediately, she took it as permanent and panicked and said, "Please don't kill me."

Edmund Kemper, 1973:

And at that point, she didn't shriek, but she, like, covered up her head and moved away from me. She was in her seat belt and I was in mine. She was shaking her head and holding her arms up and saying, "No, no."

And almost shrieking, "Don't kill me please."

And I started shaking her and told her to knock it off, and I wasn't going to hurt her. She kept doing it, so I reached under the seat and picked up the gun I had under the seat, which was a Colt Trooper 6" .357 magnum that I had borrowed from a friend, him not knowing what I was using it for, and I poked this into her ribs and then held it up in front of her. After two or three times doing this, she finally stopped this pleading not to kill her and don't hurt her. I told her to calm down and talk with me and she did. Right away, she stopped being nervous and upset and we talked down the coast, and as we approached Santa Cruz after passing through Davenport, we turned up Bonny Doon Road, the plan being that to avoid her possibly getting hurt and someone else trying to rescue a possible abduction. I told her I wanted to talk to her and I was desperate. I needed someone to talk to to keep me from killing myself, which of course was a ruse. I said that it would be suspicious if she was sitting in the car with me and the neighbors would be alarmed—which of course was not true—if she were in the car with me. So I wanted her to be in the trunk, and since she would be in the trunk, I wanted to tie her up because I wanted to feel safe and not panic myself and there were too many things she could do in the back trunk to foil my plan. So she agreed with this, but she didn't want to get in the trunk. She asked if she could be tied up in the back seat instead and I agreed, and we went up Bonny Doon Road, from Highway 1 South, outside of Santa Cruz to a point that I thought was desolate enough. I turned up Smith Grade Road.

Edmund Kemper, 1973:
This was, in fact, amazingly close to where the girl from Cabrillo [Mary Guilfoyle] was found up there stabbed. [...]

Yeah, it was very close to that area apparently. It was off Smith Grade, where Smith Grade crosses Bonny Doon. There's a road down to the right and there's a fence on the right and it says "Protected by Globe Agency." It was right in front of that sign, I didn't see it or I wouldn't have stopped there. It was right down off that road. We stopped and I was telling her I was gonna tie her up and put her in the back seat and take her to my mother's place, that my mother wasn't home. But she was, I knew she was. Like I say, that was premeditated. I was getting very scared up to the end and she was trying to reassure me, and that really blew my mind. Because I was shaking. She had been previous to that, and I laughed and told her to calm down and she had calmed down.

Edmund Kemper, 1973:
So, in other words, I was basically headed southeast on Smith Grade I think and headed down this little road to the right that lost sight of the road, stopped, turned off the lights, turned on the inside lights and asked her to get the tape out of the glove box, her already knowing what was gonna happen to

a certain point. She got the tape out. I pulled a piece of it off and placed it over her mouth and told her to get in the back seat where I would tie her up and cover her over with a blanket.

Peter Chang, 1973:
Did she help you in any way put the tape on?

Edmund Kemper, 1973:
Yeah, she got it out of the glove box for me and when I pulled the tape open and tore off a piece, I placed it over her mouth and rubbed it on nice and tight and got it on straight and everything and asked her to blow against it and move her mouth around to see if it would come off, and she assured me it wouldn't, following my instructions to the letter.

I asked her to jump over the back seat and she did, and as an afterthought, she took off the cap she had been wearing, and at that time, her hair, she had very long hair that fell down past her shoulders, then she went back over to the back seat and laid down on her back. At any rate, I got out of the car on my side, leaving the gun under the front seat on the driver's side, got out of the car, walked around to her side and realized that the keys being in my pocket, she had locked her side of the door when she got in and it was still locked. At this point, I started fumbling in my pants trying to get the key out quickly before she realized the advantage she had, and when she saw that I was fumbling for the keys, she climbed back up over the seat and flipped up the inside lock on her side, letting me in. At this time, I moved the front seat forward and flipped the twin cushion front seat, flipped her cushion forward, and climbed in the back seat. She was laying on her back with her hands across on her stomach to be tied, and I asked her to turn over on her stomach, and she did and put her hands behind her back. At this time, I tied her hands and took a lot of time doing it because I was realizing that as soon as I was done tying her hands, that I had to kill her or else take a chance on driving around town where someone could see her moving around under a blanket, or someone could stop me for a routine stop because my left rear taillight had been smashed out in an accident, and I did not want to be stopped for any reason with her in the back seat in her condition. So I fumbled around at tying her hands when I finally realized I was wasting time and needed to get the thing done if I was going to do it. I turned her over, back rather gently on her back, as if I were going to place the blanket over her head and started to place my body over hers, on top of hers actually, placed my right hand firmly over her mouth from the right side. She looked slightly curious at that point, wondering what I was doing, not at all worried or panicked. I then took my left hand, the thumb and index finger, reached around over her head and plugged both nostrils, pressed both nostrils closed, and for a moment there was actually no change in expression, then she realized what was happening and she went berserk. She completely panicked and struggled violently for what I can only imagine to be a half a minute, maybe forty-five seconds, until she lost consciousness, possibly longer, but I don't think so because when I got up on her body, I heard quite an amount of wind being pushed out of her lungs by my weight and I did not notice her sucking in a lot of air after that.

Peter Chang, 1973:
How did she struggle in this forty-five seconds?

Edmund Kemper, 1973:
Very violently, her hands not being tied closely together, I tied her wrists separately by knots and there was approximately six to eight inches of string or cord between the two knots, the two wrists; this gave her enough room to reach around her side and flip partially over on her side, reach around and she grabbed at my testicles and penis in

an effort to get me off and make me release her nostrils.

I broke away with that portion of my body and scooted it farther down towards her legs, which means that less of my weight was positioned over her body and the violent struggle got even more violent and she moved around all over the back seat, kicking at the cushion on the far side, under the rear window and kicking at the window with her feet, doubling her feet back over the cushion and kicking at the window right over her head even. I was trying to stay out of the way while this was going on with a major portion of my body, but I never let go of the grip on her nostrils or the tape over her mouth and then the struggle stopped and she collapsed back into the seat, I waited a few moments and then released her, leaving the tape on.

I opened her right eyelid I imagine with my left hand, to see how unconscious she was, how much eye movement there was and there was, I guess, a nominal amount of eye movement. It wasn't rapid, so apparently she was what I thought deeply asleep or unconscious and after a few moments of watching this, the eye movement, the eye zeroed in on me and then her other eye thrust open and she started her movement again. For a moment she just looked at me and I guess she became conscious enough to where she remembered what was happening and went right back into the extreme panic she had been in and the whole process started over again for just about the same amount of time, identical to the other forty-five seconds. Every move I mean, still grabbing at my testicles and still grabbing at my body.

Peter Chang, 1973:
What did you do? Were you still pinching her nose?

Edmund Kemper, 1973:
Yes, this time I held her nose until all of the voluntary breathing was done. She was into great deep gasps with her lungs, her back was

197

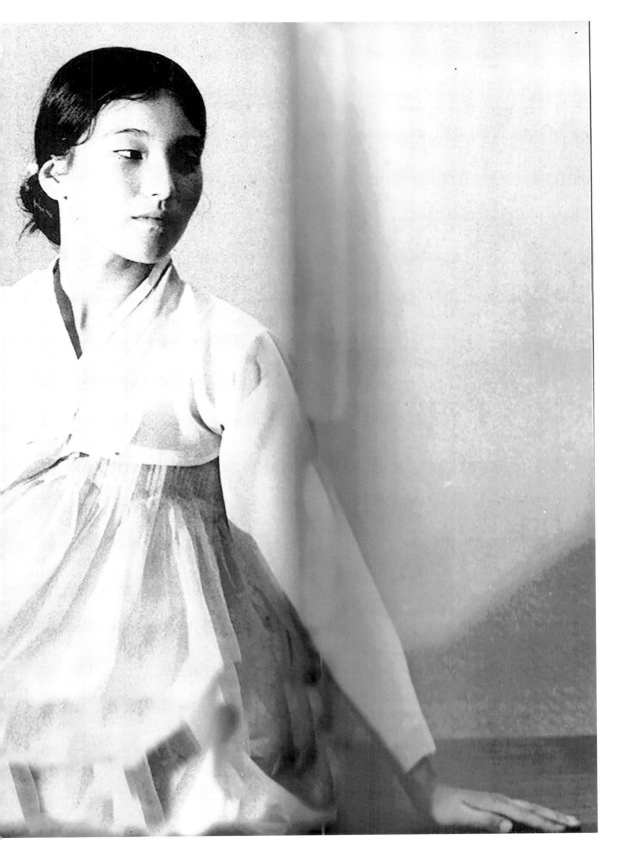

arching, unconscious, but the breaths became fewer and far between and she was still in a spasm type breathing.

Peter Chang, 1973:
Did you still have your fingers over her nose?

Edmund Kemper, 1973:
Yes, and at that point, I stopped because I knew she wouldn't wake up soon. I picked her up from the back seat, took her out of the car, around the back behind the trunk, thrust her body down on her back on the ground and pulled her pants down violently, not removing them but pulling them down below the crotch area, and spread her legs apart and forced sexual intercourse on her and I achieved orgasm in—I guess it was only fifteen or twenty seconds. It was very quick. At that time, I noticed her hair falling over her face and nose, she was still breathing and starting to breathe again. I took the muffler that she had around her neck still and just wrapped it very tight and tied a knot in it, and her hands were still tied behind her back, and the tape was still over her mouth. At that time, I even choked her around the throat for a moment, but by that time, I was convinced that she was dead, picked her up by the shoulders and she wasn't a heavy girl. I think she told me she weighed 104 and a half pounds.

Peter Chang, 1973:
She told you that?

Edmund Kemper, 1973:
Yes. She had told me her height was 5'4" and she weighed 104 1/2 pounds. I picked her up by the shoulders and just, I think, laid her across the open trunk, across half into the trunk while I did something else. I think I took the muffler off her neck, checked around to make sure nobody was coming and made sure there was nothing laying around out on the ground and then moved her all the way into the trunk and wrapped

the blanket around her that had been in the trunk. It was a blue velveteen blanket.

Kemper then drove to a bar on Bonny Doon Road. Before entering, he opened his trunk to confirm Aiko Koo was dead.

Edmund Kemper, 1973:
I suppose as I was standing there looking, I was doing one of those triumphant things too, admiring my work and admiring her beauty, and I might say admiring my catch like a fisherman.

After drinking a few beers and washing his hands, Kemper visited with his mother at her house at 609A Ord Street in Aptos. The visit lasted for half an hour. Kemper was testing his ability to keep his cool after committing a murder. He felt that he passed the test and that his mother suspected nothing.

Edmund Kemper, 1973:
It was quite an effort to carry her up to my apartment from the trunk and I knew, not so much from the pain of carrying her, but I knew it would be very difficult to carry her back down out of the apartment un-noticed. I was quite fortunate to get her up there without anybody seeing me. It was late at night, at least midnight. So I decided the only safe way to take her out of the apart-ment was to dismember her body and take her out in some form of container. The only container I could see that would be blood proof, waterproof, and would not give away what was in it, would be large green heavy plastic garbage bags.

Peter Chang, 1973:
Was she covered with anything?

Edmund Kemper, 1973:
No. If anyone had spotted me, I had hoped to get out of the area quick enough to where they would think I was just carrying a girl up to my apartment and I held her in such a way that it appeared that she was

awake and alive. I got into my apartment, I had already had the door open and unlocked and moved inside the apartment, laid her on the couch and shut the door.

Edmund Kemper, 1973:
That was the first time I ever dissected a body and that was then, after I had broken my arm. And that's why I did it; because I couldn't carry her all the way. I couldn't dig graves and all that stuff and I decided to dispose of her.

Edmund Kemper, 1973:
That [crime] occurred somewhat after the discovery of Miss Pesce's head. Even though it was quite some time before the authorities discovered exactly who it was. I realized from the paper accounts that it was quite difficult, because of the time it had been out in the hills. This gave me the idea of disfiguring the head enough to where it would be even more difficult to discover the identity, thus, giving me a longer time for any possible witnesses or any possible mistakes to correct themselves, due to time, or weather, or whatever. In her case, Miss Koo's, after she was dead, there was some time between the disposal of her body portions and the head and hands. The hands by that time were, let's say, the tips of the fingers were distorted enough by normal deterioration that I wasn't worried about fingerprints by the time they could be found. So the head, I removed the hair from, very noticeable long dark hair, and cut it short with a knife, but not so short that it would seem to be that of a man's or a boy's. I also removed the teeth from the head because this was one of the prime methods of identification on a head, that is, dental chart comparisons.

While Kemper was dissecting Aiko Koo, he had a revelation.

Edmund Kemper, 1973:
[Inaudible] all the way around, and all the way to the bone and then I put it in a cer-

tain position where I could get the knife in there to cut the cartilage on the arm. Then I just twisted it and it popped right off.

After that, I decided what the hell, I think she's pretty. I wonder if she tastes pretty.

Kemper removed and kept part of Aiko Koo's left thigh. He also took Polaroids of her body, which will be discussed in a few pages.

Edmund Kemper, 1973:
I stored it and every now and then, when I had a shitty feeling, I'd take my pictures out and have a sweet dinner.
I'd cook it. Fry it.

Edmund Kemper, 1973:
I wish somebody had come by that night, when I cooked a casserole out of it. Out of the Koo girl. I had a pound of meat. You know a noodle type of casserole. Layered with the cheese and the meat. Precook the meat and throw it in and stir it up. It's one of my favorite dishes. But I was sitting there gagging thinking about it.
[Inaudible] thinking about this shit before I killed her. Which isn't funny. But thinking of her and trying to imagine what she would have thought that day, going to school and everything. Doing her routine thing. Very lively and robust, zipping off to San Francisco to her dance class and she doesn't ever make it. I think, wow. I wonder what she would think if she knew that eight or ten hours later she'd be laying in someone's trunk dead. The next day in so many pieces.

Edmund Kemper, 1991:
I took off Friday, I didn't go to work. I called in sick, took CTO. Dismembered her body, got rid of her body, but kept her head and her hands because they are identifiable. They're highly identifiable. I kept those at the apartment. That Friday night, Thursday night I took her, Friday morning she was dismembered, Friday night she was disposed of.

Richard Verbrugge, 2020:
Some of her body parts, he said, he put in the sewer up there in Alameda.

Kemper dumped part of Aiko Koo's body in the forest surrounding Redwood Christian Park, a conference center in Boulder Creek. Additional body parts were dumped up North Rodeo Gulch Road.

Terry Medina, 2020:
It was interesting. I lived up North Rodeo Gulch Road about a mile and a half above the Ohtas. And then at a different time, different murders, different body. There was an arm and a shoulder found on North Rodeo Gulch Road closer to Laurel Glen.
So it was pretty remote in that particular spot.
    And somebody found a body part up there. I think it was a shoulder and an arm that belonged to Aiko Koo. Boy, that was another horrible one. That's a part of me for the rest of my life.
    Kemper. He needed to dismember all these bodies, partly because he had gotten injured and he had broken his arm.

Edmund Kemper, 1991:
Saturday morning I left and I didn't have, I wasn't satisfied that, I took the head along and the hands, but I didn't, I couldn't put them some place that I could be sure they weren't dug up by an animal or just be somewhere. It's scary, going out there trying to bury somebody or dispose of the body parts in a community or even out in the boonies, where you don't know where you're at and who could come up at any moment. I had some real close calls there, where people come out of nowhere and if they, if a body is found and they remember this beige looking car sitting there then I, that's evidence. So it's very very hard to get rid of this stuff. Anyways, Saturday morning I went to see the psychiatrist in Fresno. Saturday afternoon I saw the other one. Saturday evening I'm with my fiancée and her family

over in Turlock. Sunday night I come back to my apartment.

Peter Chang, 1973:
Two days later Kemper went to Fresno where he was examined by two psychiatrists, both of whom diagnosed him as no longer being a danger to society.

The first psychiatrist talked with Kemper for two hours. They went over Kemper's job, love life, and the murder of his grandparents. Here is the end of his report to the court—

Dr. Robert Kinsey (Psychiatrist), 1972:
He appears to have made a good recovery from such a tragic and violent split within himself. He appears to be functioning in one piece now directing his feelings towards verbalization, work, sports, and not allowing neurotic buildup within himself. Since it may allow him more freedom as an adult to develop his potential, I would consider it reasonable to have a permanent expunction [sic] of his juvenile records.
    I am glad he has recently "expunged" his motorcycle and I would hope that he would do that ("seal it") permanently since this seemed more a threat to his life and health than any threat he is presently to anyone else.

The second psychiatrist stated Kemper was in excellent psychiatric health and certainly quite competent mentally in all ways. "He has made an excellent response to years of treatment. I see no psychiatric reason to consider him to be of any danger to himself or any other member of society."

Edmund Kemper, 1988:
The Madera Court ordered two psychiatrists from Fresno to examine me thoroughly. They were supposed to examine all of my available records, they were supposed to test me thoroughly, they were supposed to interview me extensively. These words were used in the court order.
    Those two men saw me on one occasion,

on the same day, I went to one in the morning and one in the afternoon. I was not tested by either of those gentlemen, and I don't have any idea how exhaustively he even read the record as available. And they both came to the unanimous conclusion that I was Mr. Wonderful. I was intoxicated during the second interview, blasted drunk off my tail on beer. I went out and celebrated for lunch.

Allyn Kemper (Kemper's sister), 1973:
This is one thing that surprised me about him, that report that came out, the psychiatrists report after he came out of Atascadero because he was really proud of it and he was flashing it around to my mom and me. This is the paper from last year. I started reading it—I didn't even finish reading it. I didn't say this is a bunch of garbage, you know, who'd you hire to write this. But I did say, "Well, that's nice." [laughs]

I didn't want to openly say, "That's a bunch of crap."

Because I didn't feel it was true. It built him up to be this big, normal person who could adjust well in society and he couldn't. The brother I know was scared and shy and paranoid of people around him and really self-conscious.

He was always at my mom's house, and they [Atascadero] told him never to go back to live with her. Maybe just stay with her long enough to get a job and a place of his own, but stay away from her. Because they told him that when he killed my grandparents, subconsciously he was killing his mother. And she [their mother] feared him killing her.

Shortly after the murder of Aiko Koo, Kemper gave her blue Levi jacket to his neighbor across the hall, the same neighbor who had seen Kemper drop his Buffalo Skinner knife in the hall while carrying Mary Ann Pesce. The neighbor later told

law enforcement that Kemper almost forced the jacket upon him and he accepted only to not appear antisocial.

Kemper wrote a poem and planned on dropping it off on the front porch of an unnamed police officer. The poem was two pages. Here Kemper tries to remember the opening lines—

Edmund Kemper, 1973:
You have but three
But soon you'll see
The score shall go
Past four or more

Kemper knew that they would be able to tell he was left handed and did not want to take the time to cut out letters from magazines. He also feared being spotted leaving the poem.

Kemper would later dump Aiko Koo's head in a dried up riverbed in Alameda County.

Richard Verbrugge, 2020:
It was a ravine and in the winter it would fill with water and we were not able to ever find those body parts. I had to tell her mother that we couldn't come up with all the parts. It was the toughest case of all of them.

Back in Felton, in September, two young men, Brian Scott Card and his brother Jeffrey Card, began the construction of a plastic covered shelter in Henry Cowell State Park near the Toll House, just south of Felton. The shelter would be expanded until it was more of a house than a simple shelter. Brian and his friends would spend the winter in the structure.

TAKING PHOTOGRAPHS

Harold Cartwright, 1973:
You took pictures of the first three?

Edmund Kemper, 1973:
Not a lot of pictures, just a few poses.

Harold Cartwright, 1973:
What did you do with those pictures?

Edmund Kemper, 1973:
Tore them up. I kept them for a few weeks hoping that I wouldn't blow it again, you know. I was feeling really bad about the first one, and I figured if it really came down to me doing it again, I was really afraid of doing it, I'd just get the pictures out and look at them and see what I actually did, and that usually knocked me right back in this world. For a while I started thinking that if I don't get rid of these, and somebody suspects me or if I get killed in a car wreck, they'd go through my stuff—or injured in a car wreck.

Kemper tore up the Polaroids of Pesce and Luchessa and threw them out.

Edmund Kemper, 1973:
The third girl, which was the second time around, I took pictures of her and just like the same [inaudible], hot, you know, so I threw them in a bucket of boiling water on the stove and the plastic separated from the paper backing and I just threw it away.

Edmund Kemper, 1973:
I took two pictures of the third girl. Sexual stuff, one of them was. And the other was with her clothes on, or with her clothes off. Anyway, the first two, it was pictures of their heads.

Harold Cartwright, 1973:
After they were severed?

Edmund Kemper, 1973:
Yeah. I felt real bad about that one, and I don't even know why.

The District Attorney's Office also interviewed Kemper about the Polaroids. The first Polaroid he took was of Luchessa's body in the trunk of his car. All the other photographs were in his apartment.

Richard Verbrugge, 1973:
He washed the heads and then took a picture of them both together on an old white shirt, on top of a large stuffed chair in the living room of the apartment. He later tore the shirt up and disposed of it in his garbage can.
He took one close-up photo of Luchessa's head with the eyes closed.

He took an individual picture of the Pesce head on an old towel on the floor of his bathroom stating, "She wore a little makeup, the eyeshadow had run and she gave the appearance of having cried."

He then took a photo of all the pictures. He wrote on the back of the photos in black felt pen identifying information. The girl's name, the date of her being killed, and the date of the photo. He saved the photos for several weeks stored in an envelope, scotch taped under the desk in his apartment. He later became worried that his "nosy landlady" might find them so he disposed of them. He tore each of the photos into very small pieces and spread them throughout his garbage can at the apartment. Immediately after taking the photos of Luchessa and Pesce he had thrown the Polaroid negatives, as he described them, in his garbage and later worried about them being found by some bum rummaging through the Alameda dump.

In regards to the photographs taken of Aiko Koo, Kemper described them and made the following remarks. Following killing Pesce and Luchessa he was, "Pissed-off because they were too damaged to do much with."

When he killed Koo he smothered her doing as little damage as possible. The first two photos of Koo taken were "Porno types and looked very life-like."

The first photo of her was naked on his bed, at the same apartment in Alameda. "She was posed on her back with her legs spread, and her hands on either side of her vagina."

"Her eyes were open and she really looked alive, except when you looked closely, you could see her fingertips had turned purple."

For the second photo, Kemper stated that he posed her in a sitting up position on his bed. The next photo he described of Koo was in his bathtub, in pieces.

The last photo was of Koo's head on the shelf of his closet next to an empty bottle of Mickey's Malt Liquor he had drank during the decapitation. Kemper stated that he kept the Koo photographs and negatives only for a few days and then destroyed them. As a means of totally destroying them he boiled them all in water. The photo portion boiled off the paper backing and he skimmed some from the top of the water and it appeared as "plastic goop".

He then tore the paper backing into small pieces and deposited all of the refuse in his garbage.

KEMPER GETS ENGAGED

Nine days after murdering Aiko Koo, Kemper became engaged to his girlfriend on September 23, 1972.

Edmund Kemper, 1981:
During that time I became engaged to someone who is young and is beautiful and very much the same advantages, very much the same upbringing and Disneyland values, and she's very much the reason that I surrendered.

Michelle Ann Sims (Her mother and Kemper's mother were friends), 1973:
He came over and told me he was engaged and he goes, "I don't know if I'm making a mistake or not."

And I go, "Well, she's pretty young."

And he goes, "Yeah, she's really young, too young."

And I go, "Well, when are you going to get married?"

And he goes, "As soon as she graduates we're going to get married."

And he goes, "She really loves me, man. She tells me that all the time. She really wants to marry me then she's going to go to

school. But I know she loves me."

And he really wanted to get that across—that she really did love him.

Harold Cartwright, 1973:
How old is she now?

Edmund Kemper, 1973:
Eigteen. What's the date? The twentieth [August]? Eight more days and we were going to get married.

Harold Cartwright, 1973:
How long did you know her?

Edmund Kemper, 1973:
I didn't get engaged to her, but I told we were going to. See, I went down to Fresno to see those two psychiatrists [September 16, 1972], and on the way back, that was just after the third victim and her head and the hands were in a bag behind a stuffed chair in my apartment. I put there Friday morning not wanting to throw it out with the other stuff because…

Harold Cartwright, 1973:
Which was this?

Edmund Kemper, 1973:
The Aiko Koo girl.

Harold Cartwright, 1973:
You still had her hands and her head? I thought you took her head with you to Fresno.

Edmund Kemper, 1973:
No, that was strictly in the apartment. Then I went to my two psychiatrical [sic] numbers and on the way back I stopped and talked to her.

This quote contradicts the common lore about Kemper, that when visiting the psychiatrists in Fresno, he had the head of Aiko Koo in the trunk of his car.

A SHORT INTERVIEW WITH EDMUND KEMPER'S FIANCÉE, 2020

How did you meet Edmund Kemper?
My sister introduced us.

What was he like during that time?
Very kind to me and my family.

How did he propose to you? Was your engagement in the newspaper?
—

His sister said that she had a small suspicion after the Cindy Schall murder and asked him about it. Did you ever have a suspicion or that he was weird or out there?
No

It was mentioned in the newspaper that he gave a knife to your stepfather as a gift. Can you talk about that? [This was the knife used to kill Mary Ann Pesce and Anita Luchessa.]
I believe it was taken into evidence.

Did you ever meet his mother? I'm trying to get an understanding of what she was like and the only real information is from Kemper after he was arrested and it is all very negative.
She was nice to me but they did argue.

Mr. Murray,
This was so very long ago and it's a fact of my life I don't consider anymore. I've been living a Christian life for a very long time and I believe He has given me peace about it.

You are the second person to contact me about this and I never answered him mainly because this situation shouldn't be glorified to any degree. You will never be able to figure him out or understand where it all stems from.

I wish you well in your research and publication of your book. I ask that you don't mention my name or that of my family. Thank you for your thoughtfulness.

P.S. I wanted to add that for decades I hadn't thought of this so I can't remember a lot of detail on the subject. I'm sorry I couldn't help you more.

Harold Cartwright, 1973:
She never knew you'd been in a hospital or anything?

Edmund Kemper, 1973:
Nope.

Allyn Kemper, 1973:
To me, she was just part of his normal boy cover-up while he was doing all this other stuff. That's my opinion.

Kemper and his fiancée met in June 1972. Kemper had worked at her brother-in-law's gas station.

Edmund Kemper, 1973:
I stopped by my ex-boss' place. He was an ex-boss from the gas station and his half-sister-in-law, his wife's half-sister, was visiting there for the summer. [tape stops]

Well, I kept dropping back by and visiting and talking to her, took her out to dinner.

That was the Summer of '72.

Edmund Kemper, 1973:
She's scared of the big city, type, you know. Robbery and rapes and kidnappings and all that shit. So I asked her, I said, "How would you like to live in Santa Cruz where they're having all those murderous butcher-type knockoffs, you know."

She said, "I don't want to live there either."

I've been asked if I had any instincts of killing her, any reason I had for not killing her, if I thought about killing her too. I said no, there wasn't.

Harold Cartwright, 1973:
When you met her had you killed anyone?

Edmund Kemper, 1973:
Yeah. When I met her was after I had

my accident, which was, this accident, was in June. And…

Harold Cartwright, 1973:
You think if you had met her first, you'd have killed anybody?

Edmund Kemper, 1973:
Uh, I don't know. That's a really tricky one. I think I would have been satisfied enough, you know, if it was a decent woman, somebody that really knows where it's at. I think it would have changed things considerably.

Harold Cartwright, 1973:
You think you could have met a girl and had a normal sexual relationship with her, you probably would have never killed anybody?

Edmund Kemper, 1973:
Yeah, I think that would have been taken care of it, but this shyness was getting to the point of being horrible, you know. There was just no way I could get rid of it, and that's why the girls died, it was somebody I'd know and feel safe with, you know, not sexually safe, but psychologically safe.

District Attorney Investigator Richard Verbrugge interviewed Kemper's fiancée and her family.

Richard Verbrugge, 1973:
During the summer months of 1972, she and Kemper dated regularly and on September 23, 1972, they became engaged.

While staying with her sister [in Santa Cruz] during the summer, Kemper would often drive her back to Turlock on the weekends to visit her mother and stepfather. These return visits occurred on the average of twice a month with Kemper sharing a bedroom at her parents home with her brother. Once school resumed in September, Kemper was only able to visit her in Turlock approximately once a month, usually arriving on Saturday and leaving on Sunday evening.

She visited both his apartment in Alameda and his mother's home in Aptos. Kemper moved back to his mother's home following his motorcycle accident [in] which Kemper injured his left arm.

Kemper's fiancée confirmed that the last time he spent the night at her parent's home was Valentine's Day 1973. However, between Kemper's lack of table manners and keeping everyone awake talking loudly with her brother, her father kicked him out of the house. Kemper slept in his car and drove her to school the next morning.

Richard Verbrugge, 1973:
On Friday, April 6, 1973, Kemper next picked her up in Turlock accompanied by his mother and sister. They went to San Francisco and visited several well known sightseeing attractions. One of these places in particular was the Wax Museum at Fisherman's Wharf. [Kemper's fiancée] recalled this location particularly because Kemper became near ill and cut the tour of the museum short after they viewed a mock guillotine with a beheaded manikin. Following the San Francisco visit, they all returned to his mother's home in Aptos for the remainder of the weekend. [See the chapter: The Jury Room and Kemper's Pistol]

The last time she had a conversation with Kemper was the Thursday before Easter at which time she telephoned him at his mother's home. At that time, she invited him to Turlock for Easter which he declined by saying, "Can't come, I have important business to take care of this weekend."

When asked what kind of business Kemper stated, "Disability business."

[Kemper's fiancée] related that she felt at this time and since Valentine's Day that their relationship was going downhill. Further, she wondered if Kemper really wanted to get married and began having doubts of her own about their relationship.

Kemper's fiancée also told Richard Verbrugge that Kemper had shown her his firearms and had placed his handcuffs on her nine-year-old brother in Turlock. She also recalled that in June 1972, Kemper gave her stepfather a knife as a gift. The sheath had blood stains on it, which Kemper dismissed by explaining that he had cut his own hand on accident.

Richard Verbrugge, 1973:
When asked if Kemper and she ever had any conversations about the hitch-hike killings in Santa Cruz, she replied in the affirmative. She recalled their talking about the human hand [Cynthia Schall's] recovered in the surf and Kemper stating, "Wouldn't it be weird to be swimming along and have it touch you?"

Also, on a ride to San Francisco by the coast route, he pointed out an area near some high cliffs and mentioned, "That's where they found those Santa Cruz co-eds' heads." [Liu and Thorpe]

Finally, Kemper's fiancée told Richard Verbrugge that she and Kemper had not had sex and that there was very little touching or kissing in their relationship.

On May 2, 1973, Richard Verbrugge interviewed Kemper's fiancée's mother and stepfather. Neither had too much to add.

Kemper's fiancée's mother did mention that she put the knife that Kemper gave to her husband to good use shucking corn and killing chickens. Verbrugge informed her that the knife had been in the murders of Mary Ann Pesce and Anita Luchessa. Inspector Verbrugge took custody of the "Buffalo Skinner" knife.

Richard Verbrugge, 1973:
When asked what he felt about Kemper in general, [Kemper's fiancée's stepfather] stated that Kemper showed a gross lack of training in every respect—making reference to his table manners, politeness, and lack of consideration for other people.

Kemper told Peter Chang during his trial that he never thought about killing his fiancée.

LAWRENCE "WHITEY" WHITE
FRIDAY, OCTOBER 13, 1972

Lawrence "Whitey" White was a local transient who had first been arrested in California in March of 1968. He had been arrested forty-three times since. In his earliest arrests, White had listed his occupation as a railroad worker or a fruit picker. Later he was simply listed as a transient. All of White's arrests were related to being drunk in public. White was 5'6" and was not violent or belligerent. He did not receive welfare.

Mickey Aluffi, 2020:
Yeah, I met Larry when I was working in the jail as a "political prisoner." And he was just a local hobo, wino type guy.

On Wednesday, October 4, White had been released from the Santa Cruz County rehabilitation center after completing a thirty day sentence.

Herbert Mullin later testified that he had been receiving telepathic orders to kill from his mother and father for three days before the murder.

Herbert Mullin, 1973:
They said I should kill someone and if you don't it will shame the family…like cowardice. It was preponderantly pressing…kill, kill or get out, move.

Herbert Mullin, 1973:
Martin W. Mullin [Mullin's father] used his Marine Corps training to get me to kill. Kill-joy sadist wanted me arrested.

Mullin left his parents' house to return an overdue library book in San Francisco. When he was walking down the stairs, about to get into his car, the overwhelming feeling hit him—

Herbert Mullin, 1981:
I was overcome by guilt feelings, that I had to kill to prove my worth.

Mullin picked up a baseball bat which was lying in the front yard and headed towards Santa

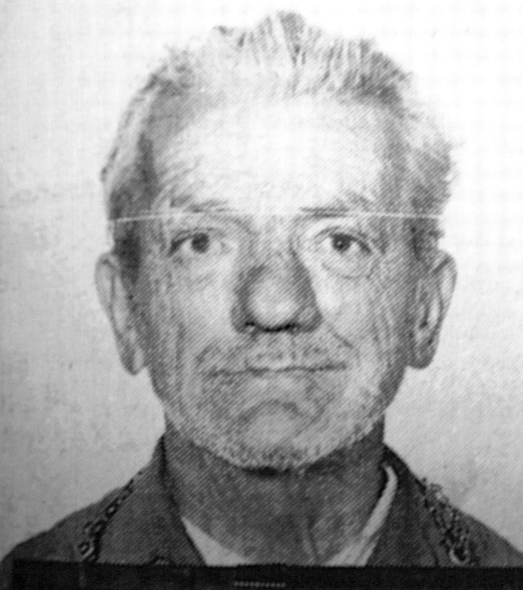

Cruz on Highway 9.

Herbert Mullin, 1973:
I woke up one morning, got a baseball bat out of the garage and started driving… Before I knew it I was clubbing Lawrence White to death.

Chris Cottle, 2020:
He [Mullin] was on Highway 9 driving. Mullin saw him [White] walking the other way [towards Felton]. Mullin turned around and passed him and stopped the car. He got out and pretended to have car problems and he [White] stopped to help him.

Herbert Mullin, 1981:
He came walking over and asked me if he could be of any assistance, and I bludgeoned him to death.

Chris Cottle, 2020:
He got him when he was looking under the hood and hit him with a baseball bat. He beat him to death and took his body and dumped it nearby. White was just a simple guy trying to help.

Mullin later admitted at his trial that he dragged White's body away from the road so that it would not be found by passing motorists.

Mullin then returned the book, *Einstein on Peace*, to the library in San Francisco.

Dave Alcorn, 2020:
Jim Chilton, who lived right down there, well, he was a walker. I was on a day off and Jim came up to my house, which is basically right up the street, and said, "Hey, I found a body."
   "What?"
   "Yeah, I found a body."
   "Well, where?"
   "Right down on Highway 9."
   So we get in his car—of course we didn't have cell phones in those days. He drives

me down to Rincon. There was a little path there and sure enough there's a body. "I gotta get to a phone."
I went and called that in and then went back and waited for the coroner. That was Herb's first victim.

White's body was found shortly after he had been killed.

White had $2 in his pocket.

Dave Alcorn, 2020:
It was right on Nine [Highway 9]. It was coming up Nine, the Rincon parking area. Right to the right of the parking area there was a footpath and he was right on the footpath.

Mickey Aluffi, 2020:
So this particular day, all the detectives had gone out for lunch and we came back and someone told us there was a body up on Rincon Gorge. So we all went up there and right away I identified him as Larry White. And I still don't know what the reason was but Mullin beat him to death with a baseball bat. I just don't know why. Maybe it was just opportunity. Maybe Mullin just felt like doing it. I don't know.

Kenneth Pittenger (Santa Cruz County Deputy Sheriff), 1973:
Mr. White was identified through his finger-prints and had been arrested many times on charges of being drunk or panhandling. Each time he was listed as a transient.

Later.

Barney Barnett (Journalist, Valley Press), 1973:
Services for White were held beginning at 3:39 p.m. in the Wessendorf-Holmes Funeral chapel. In attendance were this newspaper reporter and a detective from the Sheriff's Office.

   No one appeared to pay their last respects

nor to mourn his passing.

Speaking at the funeral—

F.B. Whale (Chaplain, Santa Cruz County General Hospital), 1973:
We don't know much about this man. His life was futile and meaningless and his death the final indignity.

He perhaps was not proud of his past life but we cannot judge him. That is for God. Yet he was a human being. He was some mother's son…He must have touched some other lives along the way for good.

Barney Barnett, 1973:
Shortly afterwards the simple casket was loaded into a Cadillac hearse to be driven to the cemetery. I wondered if it was the most expensive vehicle White had ever ridden in.

Barney Barnett, 1973:
At 4:05 the grave was filled, exactly 35 minutes after the services had started in the chapel.

The burial of Lawrence White had cost the county $254.

Last resting place

The body of Laurence White is lowered to its last resting place in potter's field. There were no flowers or mourners for the murdered man. VALLEY PRESS PHOTO.

MARY GUILFOYLE
TUESDAY, OCTOBER 24, 1972

Bob Lee (Santa Cruz County District Attorney 2002–2014), 2011:
Mary Guilfoyle, who we've all described as a twenty-four-year-old hitchhiker from Cabrillo College who was born in New York. She was picked up by Mr. Mullin, immediately stabbed numerous times in his car and then dragged out to a field where he dissected her. He split her open by using a T formation with a knife to look at her kidneys, her liver, her heart, her lungs because he saw pictures in a book that he had read about Michelangelo. In fact, took out some of these kidneys and liver and hung them on a tree.

Nancy Guilfoyle (Mary Guifoyle's sister-in-law), 2020:
She was from Buffalo, New York. She had one brother, Kirk. Their mother died when she was about five. Mary was an absolutely brilliant girl. They called her Honey, that was her nickname. She also was one of the first people to have open heart surgery. It was in the early 1950s.

Her dad got remarried after her mother died. Her stepmother was basically jealous of Mary. It sounds bad, but she was. So, Mary lived with relatives in Texas for a while. Which was better for her dad. She came back up and lived with her family for a short while in Buffalo. She went to UB [University at Buffalo] and then she ended up living with her grandmother. Then she went out to California.

Nancy Guilfoyle, 2020:
Another thing that is not meaningful, but it is interesting, she was born in a taxi cab on the way to the hospital. I know there was a news clip on that.

Nancy Guilfoyle, 2020:
I have heard, but I never looked, that she was one of the first early, early cases of open heart surgery. I understand her case was in medical textbooks, and of course Honey wasn't able to play sports because of the

open heart surgery. But she was so smart. Kirk [Mary Guilfoyle's brother] was two years younger than Honey and he used to tell the story about always going into classrooms in high school and the teachers would say, "Oh, you're Mary Guilfoyle's brother! Oh, yay!"

And then after a while they'd go, "Oh."

He was bright and talented, he went on to

be a concert pianist, but she was just so smart.

Nancy Guilfoyle, 2020:

Mary's dad was the type of person that just didn't want any kind of confrontation. So, if things weren't comfortable, he would just close it off. This wasn't anything to do with Mary. Her stepmother was just jealous of her. So, this was her dad's coping method. Me, reading between the lines, I really think that is how he was coping with what he went through in World War II. He just closed it off.

Above: Mary "Honey" Guilfoyle and her brother, Kirk.
Right: In Santa Cruz, June 1972.

Any confrontation. He wouldn't handle it.

On October 23, 1972, Mullin said he drove by Ray Liebenberg's car parked near Cabrillo College. Liebenberg was a chiropractor-tree trimmer and recent candidate for county supervisor. He had been a well known person in the San Lorenzo Valley, but was living in Aptos at that time. Mullin immediately got a message, in his head, from Ray Liebenberg.

Herbert Mullin, 1973:

Raymond Liebenberg, "I want you to kill me something."

Mullin had never met Liebenberg.

Herbert Mullin, 2021:

There were two brothers named Liebenberg. I did not know either of them. One of them owned a Cadillac automobile.

Even when I was a kid, I remember seeing Ray Liebenberg driving through the San Lorenzo Valley in his big Cadillac with his long beard flapping in the wind. Ray Liebenberg passed away in May 1990.

The next day, Mary Guilfoyle needed to get to the Department of Human Resources on May Avenue in Santa Cruz to pick up an unemployment check. She chose to hitchhike, and unfortunately chose the same spot that Ray Liebenberg's Cadillac had been parked at the day before.

Bill Tubbs (Private Investigator), 1973:

It appears that she probably was picked up as a hitchhiker in front of the college between 3:00 and 3:30 p.m. She was wearing a red knit dress, brown shoes and carrying a soft leather bag. She has light brown, shoulder length hair and green eyes.

Harold Cartwright, 2020:
Within seconds of getting in the car she was stabbed.

Mullin stabbed her as he was driving on Emeline Street.

Herbert Mullin:
[Mary Guilfoyle] voluntarily positioned herself on the floor as she was dying so no blood would get on the seat.

Mullin brought her body a half mile from his parents home in Bonny Doon, where he regularly collected firewood.

Herbert Mullin, 1973:
It was the only place I could think of to dispose of her body without calling attention to myself.

Nancy Guilfoyle, 2020:
Now Mullin was crazy, and I know that he dissected her body. It was beyond gruesome. She was an attractive young woman, kind of tall, but because of the open heart surgery when he took her clothes off he would have said, "Oh my God."

At that time they did the open heart surgery where the incision was horizontal rather than vertical and it went right through her breasts. It was very deformed. So, I mean, if there's someone crazy, the sight of that could set him off.

In fact, Mary Guilfoyle's brassiere was later found to have been torn or ripped in the front.

Herbert Mullin, 1973:
I made a T-shaped incision and inspected her liver, kidneys, lungs, and heart.

He had read *The Agony and the Ecstacy,* about Michaelangelo's dissection of human bodies.

Sunday, November 5, 1972

Ray Liebenberg

Herbert Mullin:
It was an inquisitive response to literature.

Mary Guilfoyle's body would not be found for months.

Students and instructors at Cabrillo College raised funds to hire a private detective, Bill Tubbs, to search for the missing woman.

Bill Tubbs, 1973:
If anyone saw her being picked up please call me at 426-6969. Also I would like to know if any other Cabrillo students have ever been given a bad time by a motorist while hitchhiking from the college. It may give us a clue as to who might have picked Mary up.

Bill Tubbs, 1973:
There's just no logical place she could have gone except for her stated destination. But she just never arrived there.

Chris Cottle, 2020:
They didn't find her body for quite a while. There was a big question of whether she had been sexually assaulted or not. His other crimes were nothing like that one.

Nancy Guilfoyle, 2020:
She was killed before we were married. We had been dating a while. Her brother Kirk and I were both musicians. Kirk has passed since, but we both went to Eastman School of Music here in Rochester. I remember sitting there with him when Kirk's dad called to tell him that Mary had been found. Bill really never said anything about it after that. I know he went out to California.

The one thing that always came up was just how smart she was.

Terry Medina, 2020:

Even after her body was found and Mullin was caught, nobody connected Herbert Mullin to Mary Guilfoyle until trial. The way it all came out was the defense.

This is another diminished capacity case, but also not guilty by reason of insanity. It was to the defense's advantage or advantageous for them to come up with this earlier victim, Mary Guilfoyle. She was a whodunnit. Nobody had ever put Mullin and her together. The defense brings it out in pretrial motions to make her his thirteenth victim.

The defense wanted to bring it out because he talked to the psychiatrist about cutting her open and he was exploring the body like it was more science than anything.

Herbert Mullin, 2020:

My father, Bill, showed me a photo in October, November, or December of 1972. It was a photo of twin children standing on a bridge, a small wooden bridge, over a pond or creek—it was a brother and sister—it was my father and his sister. He had never told me about her! I asked him something, I do not remember what I asked, but I do remember he said it was a photo of the neighbor's kids. I know it was a photo of him and his twin sister! Anyway, he turned the page of the photo album.

Edmund Kemper, 1973:

This Mary Guilfoyle, from what I had read in the paper and gathered, was an abduction and possible murder because it stated she had no reason to disappear and she was going down to the, I think the welfare office or something, to get an unemployment check, and

Top: 1964.
Middle: Mary and Kirk. Mary graduated high school a year early, in 1965.
Bottom: Mary, Kirk, and a friend in 1969.

I couldn't see, someone of, like the paper said her apparent background, disappearing like that when they're going to college. So I assumed that someone else was doing the same thing I was doing and they had hit in town and that kind of made me mad because that could throw everything in my lap if an investigation started around Santa Cruz. Because up till that point, I had assumed that the authorities were looking for someone in the bay area that was depositing the heads

in the Santa Cruz area. I remember this did happen with Miss Guilfoyle, I believe when I was disabled and staying with my mother, when I first started to live with her. When I sat around and realized that no investigation was coming my way at all, I realized that I was being a little too careful, and there was a much better opportunity around the Santa Cruz area to attack these co-eds.

Above: These photos were published in Santa Cruz newspapers when Mary went missing.

HITCHHIKING

From the September 2, 1974, edition of the *Kansas City Times* Ask Anybody…Anything column:

Q—My daughter's college is located in an area with no public transportation and the kids rely heavily on hitchhiking. I wonder if an authority might have some cautionary words for hitchhikers.

A—Ward Damio, author of *Urge To Kill*, responds:
The best advice I can give is: Don't!
The only up-to-date survey of this practice was made in Berkeley, Calif. Of 27 women hitchhikers interviewed, only six said they had not been molested, threatened or actually harmed.
If it is absolutely necessary for your daughter to hitchhike in spite of its clear dangers, she might take heed of these Don't published in the *Times* of Santa Cruz, Calif. Santa Cruz was the scene of a notorious epidemic of hitchhiker murders.

- Learn to reject rides.
- Ask the driver where he's going before entering the car, and if he hesitates, don't get in.
- Don't sit in the rear of a 2-door car.
- If the driver starts talking about sex, change the subject immediately.
- Don't go along with any of his stories that would delay you from reaching your destination. Get out of the car if he wants to stop somewhere "just for a minute."
- Always jot down the license plate before you get in.
My own advice: Buy a car!

Peter Chang, 1973:
He [Kemper] states that he never would have been able to act out any of this fantasy if it were not for the fact that there were so many attractive, naive, girls hitchhiking in the bay area and in this county.

Sam Robustelli, 2020:
Hey, when we were kids we would race. A group of us would split up and hitchhike in

LETTERS TO THE EDITOR
Liteky thanks his supporters;
reveals his campaign expenses

their parental control, there is a law against that. So we would take those people who were under eighteen and hitchhiking to juvenile hall and have their parents come get them.

Dave Alcorn, 2020:

I guess the women just felt safe back in those days. Santa Cruz was pretty safe back then. Hitchhiking was popular all across the U.S.

Harold Cartwright, 2020:

The primary mode of transportation for those who weren't affluent enough to have a car was to hitchhike. Public transportation wasn't that good. You could stick out your thumb and somebody would pick you up.

groups to see who could get to Felton first, or who could get to Santa Cruz first. The fewest trips, things like that. Hitchhiking wasn't a big thing like it is now.

Chris Cottle, 2020:

I grew up, I was from a broken home. I lived in a foster home for a long time. From the time I was about thirteen years old, I hitchhiked every day. I had to. Sometimes I'd run into somebody who made some kind of advance, not physically, but would say something that triggered.

Mickey Aluffi, 2019:

There is no law against hitchhiking. So we would find people under eighteen who were hitchhiking and in my mind they are beyond

Lark Ohta, 2020:

We picked up hitchhikers in the 1960s. My mother picked them up in our Oldsmobile Vista Cruiser station wagon-- just like everyone else did. Even with little kids in the car. I know it sounds crazy now, but it was very normal.

Paula Johnson (UCSC Acting Assistant Professor of Psychology), 1973:

There is a hitchhiking subculture. Hitchhiking is a very acceptable thing.

On top of the fact that hitchhiking represents mobility, there is the fact that males tend to own cars at an earlier age than females.

Mickey Aluffi, 2019:

When the university [UCSC] opened there was a big influx of people. I'm not blaming the university for any of this. And there were also the hippies. People were loose and fancy free. Free sex. Free drugs. Free rock 'n roll. If you'd go down the highway, to any

---

Above: Cartoon by Mike Erickson.
Above right: From the Santa Cruz Sentinel, February 25, 1973.

Hitchhiking Registration

A hitchhiking registration program will get underway Monday at Cabrillo College, a program in which both drivers and riders will receive identification cards. The idea of geography instructor Dave Balogh, the program will be implemented by the Cabrillo campus police. ID cards will be issued to drivers who are willing to pick up students and riders will receive cards to identify them to drivers. Driver ID cards will be displayed in the lower right corner of the car's front window. Hitchhikers will "thumb" rides by holding their rider's card up so drivers can see it. Pictured here are student Shirley Taylor, Cabrillo Police Lt. Bill Powell and Balogh. For more information on the program, telephone the campus police office at 475 - 6000 during the day or 688 - 2076 at night.

freeway on-ramp, you'd find anywhere from ten to twenty people standing there trying to hitchhike. Those were potential victims. So the Sheriff's Office made a concerted effort to try and educate those people about not hitchhiking. One of our victims was attending Cabrillo College.

Forrest Schall [Brother of Cynthia Schall], 2020:
I didn't know how she [Cynthia Schall] got around. It's a college town with UC Santa Cruz and Cabrillo. Everyone was hitchhiking. We don't hitchhike anymore do we? We used to hitchhike all the time. People are too afraid to do it now. But back in the sixties and seventies it was everywhere. Then people got murdered.

Forrest Robinson, 2020:
It [hitchhiking] was very common because of course, the colleges are miles from downtown. That was always a big knock against the university because it put itself up on the hill and then made it impossible to get downtown. People hitchhiked. There were a lot of cars coming on and off campus, so it was kind of understood that people picked people up and took them downtown to shop or hang out or whatever. That was just the

way it was. It was rather casual. I used to pick up hitchhikers all the time.

Chris Cottle, 2020:
There was no transportation up to the university at that time. The university students had to hitchhike. A lot of people around were hitchhiking.

Jeff Towle (Boyfriend of Mary Guilfoyle), 1973:
Even when there's a bus, sometimes we just don't have 25 cents for the fare on a student's budget.

William Friedland (Senior Preceptor, Stevenson College, UCSC), 1973:
It's too bad that it is dangerous to hitchhike. It's too bad because it reflects on our society. There will be a drop in hitchhiking among women for a couple of weeks because people are scared. But later on they will start right up again.

Pat O'Brien (KPIX reporter), 1973:
Strict procedures have been requested of the [UCSC] student body by the school's administration here in Santa Cruz. For in addition to the disappearance, now murders, of Miss Liu and Miss Thorpe, nine co-eds

221

from this campus have reported being raped by a man who picked them up while they were hitchhiking. A co-ed from another area college is missing and since last August the bodies or remains of bodies of three other co-eds, two from Cabrillo College, one from Fresno State, have been found in the Santa Cruz area.

Chris Cottle, 2020:
With the hitchhiking there were a lot of rapes, a lot of crime. Some unsolved murders. But mostly assault involving hitchhikers. It was a real tragic situation. Most of my first cases were sexual assaults. A lot of them were women who got into cars with men they didn't know. And, in the beginning, the juries were very unsympathetic. You would get twelve people in the box and the judge would tell them what the case was about, that it was a sexual assault, would tell them that the victim was hitchhiking, and half the jury would feel, if she was hitchhiking, she deserves what she gets. That was the time, but it changed totally because of this.

Peter Chang:
It's difficult to find anybody who sympathizes with the victims of assaults, for example. The average person sees assaults and murders every night on television.

In addition to the Kemper and Mullin killings, seven young women, all UCSC or Cabrillo students, had been raped after hitching a ride with a young African-American man. I cannot find that he was ever caught.

Peter Chang:
If a man wanted to rape a woman, he wouldn't pick up a female hitchhiker in San Jose. He'll come here, where he can take her to an isolated forest area within a minute or two.

Cameron Smith, a psychology student at UCSC, interviewed 135 Bay Area women who had been raped while hitchhiking. Smith also set up a "rape line" to support women who had been assaulted or threatened.

Cameron Smith, 1973:
Since some women still have to hitchhike to get where they want to go, we want to help them develop habits to avoid rape.

Ward Damio, 1973:
There are some practical messages to the events of 1973 in Santa Cruz. There ain't no free lunch, living off the waste of the nation is an ecological ideal to be respected, but hitchhiking has become a deadly roll of the dice. Walk, ride a bicycle, change your lifestyle enough to buy a car. These are not good times for thumb-tripping.

In February 1973, UCSC Acting Campus Police Chief John Durcan posted a list of recommendations for students:
- When possible, students and especially girls should stay in dorms after midnight.
- Walk in pairs.
- If you see a campus patrol car, wave. If possible, the patrolman will give you a lift.
- Use the bus system, if you can.
- If leaving campus tell someone where you are going, how you can be reached, and when you expect to return.
- Don't hitchhike, please. If you must, don't hitchhike alone. Try and take rides from cars only with university decals on them.
- Don't leave doors or windows unlocked when leaving rooms.
- Don't let strangers crash the dorms.
- Report any offbeat activities to the university police.

Harold Cartwright, 2020:
The ironic and sad thing is that Kemper had

Right: Edmund Kemper and the jurors in his trial look over what Kemper referred to as his "Killer Car," his yellow 1969 Ford Galaxie 500 complete with a UCSC 'A' parking sticker on the front bumper.

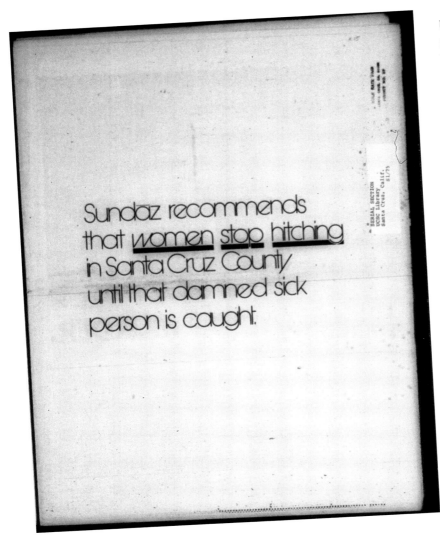

SERIAL SECTION
UCSC Library
Santa Cruz, Calif.
$1/75

Sundaz recommends that _women stop hitching_ in Santa Cruz County until that damned sick person is caught.

University of California Santa Cruz
Volume 11, Number 2
TRAGEDY BY HITCHHIK-ING —CAMPUS SECURITY PROB-LEMS

The serenity of the quiet town of Santa Cruz was shattered early this spring by a series of crimes unparalleled in the history of this seaside community. Shoot-ings and attacks against hitchhikers were climaxed by the death and muti-lation of four co-eds, two from UCSC, all presumably resulting from hitchhiking to off-campus resi-dences.

Our deepest sympathy goes to the families and friends of Alice Liu and Rosalind Thorpe. By action of the Academic Senate their degrees will be awarded post-humously in the Kresge and Merrill Com-mencements on June 17.

These tragic events prompted a careful review of campus security problems. Our police records show only two serious assaults on campus since 1965; both victims were women students and their assailants were ex-boyfriends.

Dean McHenry went on to list several mea-sures the campus had undertaken to keep students safe.

In February, 1973, a free local newspaper, *Sun-daz*, ran with a stark white cover and a strong

a university parking sticker on his car.

Forrest Robinson, 2020:
He [Kemper] would drive along and people hitchhiked a lot in Santa Cruz. There were a lot of hitchhikers. It was a very convivial city. People trusted each other. On his car, he had a College Five parking sticker and that identified him as being associated with the college and okay. Well, he wasn't. These girls would get in the car and he would kill them in the most awful, brutal, sadistic, angry way.

Chancellor's Memo, April 1973:
Chancellor's Memo

recommendation that women stop hitchhiking. The issue provided many tips for female hitchhikers and resources for women who had been sexually victimized. The newspaper was extremely critical of local law enforcement.

An excerpt from 'Hitching in this town is Murder,' by Debbi Miller, Brenda Warren, Hot Flash News Service. Printed in *Sundaz's* February 1973 issue:

Contrary to popular belief, the police departments that are employed for the protection of our community do not have the skills and crime-solving abilities as shown on Adam-12, Dragnet, or any other TV serial. They are, for the most part, interested in keeping their nose clean, and not actually solving peoples' problems. This is especially evident in the police attitude towards women who have been raped. Police do not view women who have been raped as citizens whose rights have been infringed upon, but rather as "sluts" who have asked for it.

In an interview with Sgt. Scheer [I'm guessing they meant Scherer] of the Santa Cruz Police Dept. last summer, the blame for rapes was placed entirely on the woman. Sgt. Scheer voiced what is probably the opinion of most police depts.; that women ask to be raped because of their dress (which is supposedly to "please" men) and by hitchhiking (although the bus system is inadequate for most people which makes hitching the most simple and inexpensive way). Another interesting insight given to us by the Sgt. is that if a woman knows someone on the police dept. her case is more likely to be worked on as the police will have more of a "stake in it". With this type of attitude it is no wonder that very little or nothing is done after a woman reports a rape.

In early December a woman reported a rape with the description of a man who now being believed is "the One" by the police. (He is described as a dark-skinned black man, about 6' to 6'3", 170 to 200 lbs, driving a white Ford or Chevy 1969-1971 station wagon). But this information has not been released until just this last week, after two more women were reported missing. If it has been known since December that there is a certain person (and surely not the only one) around the area committing rapes, why hasn't this information been published? Why hasn't the police department acted? The answer to these questions is simple, they do not care what happens to women, and subsequently the people of Santa Cruz. The police department is not responsible to the people, so therefore it does not feel obligated to work on these real problems.

FATHER HENRI TOMEI THURSDAY, NOVEMBER 2, 1972

Chris Cottle, 2020:
Mullin was tried over the hill for that [the murder of Father Henri Tomei]. I was always taken by the way in which it happened, but once again, they were the only two there. After he stabbed him, the priest was not yet dead, but said he forgave him.

Chris Cottle, 2020:
There was an issue of whether there was a previous connection. That was a theory and part of the defense.

Herbert Mullin:
The priest—there's a difference of opinion about the priest. At the trial I thought the priest was one of the priests that occasionally was a visitor at Saint John's Parish in Felton, where I was a member. Saint John's Catholic Church in Felton, which is in Santa Cruz, something that— Well, the priest, Henry Tomei, he used to substitute there as a confessor. I went—I thought I had gone to him several times in confession and he also gave Mass and Holy Communion.

They told me at the trial that no, he—that's not the same man.

Well, who's telling the truth?

Father Tomei's family was of Italian descent. He was born in Marseilles, France in 1908.

His mother died when he was a child. When Tomei was five, his father placed him in an orphanage to go fight in World War I and died shortly thereafter.

From the St. Mary of the Immaculate Conception Catholic Church website:
In 1933, he was ordained in the Archdiocese of Marseilles. For forty years, thirty in his homeland, Marseilles, and ten in California, eight of which were here in Los Gatos, he was the faithful dedicated priest–servant of God. He spent his life in the priesthood bringing men to God and God to men.

Fr. Tomei was a man of many talents. His extraordinary talent in so many fields,

French literature, music and other arts, enabled him to illustrate God's message of salvation in so many exciting and marvelous ways. Fr. Tomei was an outstanding musician, organist-pianist composer—much of his priestly life in Marseilles and here in California was devoted and dedicated to the development and projection of Church music. As Director of the Cathedral Choir of Marseilles, and its famous Boys Choir, which he accompanied on tours of Europe, Fr. Tomei was ever an inspiration. He was also a leader of youth in his capacity as Director of an orphanage—always a confidant of the troubled and frightened. He molded these through his musical skills into outstanding citizens and success in the world of song. Those who came under his influence never forgot him. His outgoing personality, his kind and gentle manner, his keen sense of wit and wisdom, so akin to his childhood idol, Maurice Chevalier, endeared people to him. Father Howley, former Pastor here at St Mary of the Immaculate Conception, recalled in his farewell homily at Fr. Tomei's funeral, how on many occasions that former members of his choir, now grown and successful career men, called upon him here in Los Gatos to pay their respects.

Father Henri knew the horrors of war, devastation, privation and want, having lived through two world wars: one as a child in an orphanage and later as a priest in World War II when he served on two separate occasions as a Hospital Corpsman. Somehow, what he did in the war reveals his deep religious sense and passionate love of country. This is expressed in his beautiful composition song the "Virgin of Peace". He wrote this song following a three hour bombardment of Marseilles, during which time he and his fellow soldiers took shelter under an Army truck. When the bombing had ceased, and it was learned that no one had been killed, He hurried to the nearest church, sat down at the organ and composed this song of thanksgiving to Our Blessed Mother, whose refrain and final verse sums up his life of love:

"Virgin of Peace, till my life shall cease

I shall raise my voice to praise you
My praise shall ring, for you I will sing
With my childlike love, O Maria.
On the Sea of Life, be our guide
Be that star, which shows the way
And Lead us all safely to Heaven
For the splendorous and Eternal Day".

In 1962, sought asylum in the United States. Following WWII, he had established two orphanages for children whose parents had been killed in the war, and he became an outspoken opponent of the involvement of France in the War. He came to San Francisco when he learned that he was on the French "hit list" because of his public views. Archbishop McGucken assigned him to Our Lady of Mount Carmel Church in Redwood City because the pastor was French speaking. In 1964 Fr. Tomei was transferred to Los Gatos because in the town was a "French Club."

On All Souls Day in 1972, Fr. Tomei was at the dining room table for lunch with the pastor, Fr. Richard Howley, when the doorbell rang and the man at the door asked to have a priest hear his confession. It was Fr. Howley's "duty day," but because he was still eating and Fr. Tomei had already finished his lunch, Fr. Tomei insisted that he would go to the church to hear the man's confession. After more than an hour, Fr. Tomei was found dead in his confessional, having been stabbed multiple times. News of this murder was reported in newspapers coast-to-coast and on national radio and television broadcasts. His assailant, the man who had requested the confession, was eventually found guilty of this and other murders in the Santa Cruz Mountains, and remains imprisoned today. A shrine in Fr. Tomei's memory was built to replace the confessional in St. Mary's Church for this Martyr of Santa Clara County.

Bon Voyage, Father Tomei. We pray eternal rest be yours forever in the Choir of Heaven.

The Reverend Henri Tomei
St. Mary's Church in Los Gatos.
From Marseilles France.
68.

Assistant Pastor for the last eight years.

On November 2, 1972, Mullin drove to San Francisco to pay a $10 premium on his life insurance policy. On the way home he drank whiskey and beer.

Henri Tomei told the church secretary he was going to the church to see if any parishioners had come for confession.

Herbert Mullin, 1973:
I went into the church to reflect and meditate to get enough strength to never kill again.

However, Mullin received a telepathic message—

Herbert Mullin, 1973:
[…] From myself. I suddenly realized I could think.

He then saw the light under the confessional door.

Herbert Mullin, 1973:
Well, if you're in here, I guess I should kill you.

He tried the door to the confessional, but it was locked. He turned to leave and Father Tomei suddenly opened the confessional door to see who had been trying to open the door.

Herbert Mullin, 1981:
BAM—I'd stabbed him in the heart and he bled to death before my eyes.

A parishioner, Mrs. Margaret Reed, entered the church.

Mike Prizmich (Presiding Commissioner, Herbert Mullin parole hearing, February 17, 2011):
She had been climbing the outer steps of the

church. Upon opening the door leading to the center aisle, she heard groans that were becoming greater in intensity. She observed two subjects at the confessional booth. One witness related she believed both subjects to be priests. After a brief period of time, she realized the subject who was standing was assaulting the individual seated in the chair in the confessional booth. The subject standing up, later identified as Herbert Mullin, was described as moving in a very quick manner. The witness related she observed Herbert strike the victim with his left hand. However she was unable to note if he was holding anything in the hand. The witness observed him kick the victim with his right leg, describing the kick as a karate style kick.

Mrs. Reed said Mullin was wearing black clothes and high laced boots. She reported seeing Father Tomei lying across the doorway of the confessional. She thought the attacker was kicking Tomei. She saw no knife.

Mullin would later testify that after the first stab,

he dropped his knife and Tomei had been the one to kick him.

The witness immediately fled to get help.

Ronald Rico (Santa Clara County Deputy District Attorney), 2011:
Mr. Mullin attacked the priest kicking him with karate style kicks and brutally stabbing him four times. An incredibly violent crime, as well as a horrendous crime because of the nature in which it was committed and the location and the victim and the violence that was used. There were four stab wounds.

Three to the back, one stab wound entering the left back penetrating into the area of the tenth vertebra. A second stab wound entering the upper back in the area of the thoracic vertebra. And a third stab wound entering the back of the head, penetrating down towards the right base of the skull. The fourth stab wound in the front of the chest, penetrating the chest wall and entering the heart.

As Father Tomei lay dying he said, "Bon jour" to Mullin. Mullin recognized Tomei as a priest who had visited Mullin's church in Felton. Mullin believed Tomei had heard his childhood confessions. Mullin was wrong.

The church's pastor, Reverend Richard Howley, then entered the church to see Mullin fleeing the scene.

Mike Prizmich, 2011:
On November 2, 1972, at approximately 4:26, officers from the Los Gatos Police Department received a report of an assault at St. Mary's Church in Los Gatos had occurred and the victim reportedly being a priest. While investigating officers were responding to St. Mary's Church, an ambulance happened to be proceeding in the area of St. Mary's. The attendants in the ambulance were beckoned to Father Howley, H-O-W-L-E-Y, a pastor of St. Mary's who requested the attendant come to the church. The attendant was directed to the confession booth at the rear of the church, where he observed Father Henri, H-E-N-R-I, Tomei, T-O-M-E-I, age 64, the victim, sitting on the floor of the confessional booth. The victim was leaning back against the chair in the booth with his head resting against the

chair and wall. The attendant immediately checked the victim. However, he found no signs of life. He was immediately transported to Los Gatos Community Hospital where he was pronounced dead on arrival apparently the result of several stabbings of the chest and back area.

According to the ambulance driver, Ro Brunner, Father Tomei had ridden with him earlier in the day in a funeral coach that he also drove. Mr. Brunner also relayed Father Tomei's last words—

Ro Brunner, 1972:
"Well, I don't want to wish anything, but I guess I'll be seeing you later."

Ronald Rico, 2011:
It was later that the area was dusted for prints and a palm print was lifted from the paneling on the right side of the confessional booth. Latent fingerprints were lifted from inside of the confessional booth door as well as the outside of the door near the doorknob and they were subsequently analyzed and found to match those of Mr. Mullin.

Los Gatos Police Detective Sergeant, Jim Shea told the press—

Jim Shea, 1972:
So far, there does not appear to be any motive at all for this killing.

The church was closed and a sign placed on the door that simply read:

"Church is closed —Police Department."

Father Tomei's funeral was held on November 7, 1972. More than 700 people attended. Archbishop Joseph T. McGucken gave the eulogy. The French consular corps from San Francisco attended, as did San Francisco Mayor Joseph Alioto, who was a personal friend.

Tomei was of Italian heritage but—

Emile Neyron (Notre Dame des Victoires church, San Francisco), 1973:
He loved France very much. When President Pompidou came a few years ago he drove up from Los Gatos to greet him and shake his hand.

The Los Gatos Police Department shot film of each mourner who entered the church in hopes of capturing an image of the killer. They later spoke with the press.

Edward McGowen (Los Gatos Police Lieutenant), 1972:
All we can think at this point is that it was some religious fanatic type, or possibly someone on drugs.

On the evening of November 15, 1972, a three-by-three foot door window was smashed and a $55 Marlin .22 rifle was stolen from Trusty's Used Furniture in Felton. This rifle later ended up in a camp in Felton and was picked up by Herbert Mullin and used to commit his final murder.

The owner of Trusty's noted that on November 14, three males came into Trusty's and wanted the rifle very badly. One was even willing to trade a banjo for it.

Mullin attempted to enter the Coast Guard but failed the psychological evaluation and had an arrest record.

Herbert Mullin, 1973:
Rodriguez [Coast Guard] gives test. I pass but he rejects. Tells me he won't enlist me unless I kill John Hooper.

John Hooper had encouraged Mullin to drink

> *Left: Blood drips down the confessional door in the spot Father Tomei was murdered.*

alcohol in high school and later introduced Mullin to LSD.

Mullin took a large bread knife to Hooper's house on California Street in Santa Cruz, but Hooper was not home and nine people lived inside the house. It was then that Mullin decided to purchase a gun.

EDMUND KEMPER

On November 29, 1972, Kemper's childhood record was expunged.

Edmund Kemper, 1988:
It was a political issue. The judge of Madera did not want to seal my record, a murder record had never been sealed in the State of California for a juvenille, he didn't want to start with me. He sent me to the two psychiatrists [in September, 1972], I presume expecting them to say, "We don't know this man, we just met him, we can't say that he's not ever going to be violent."

So he sends me there, he anticipates a negative report coming back, or at least a very bland one. What he got back are two rave reviews, "This is the most marvelous young guy I ever saw," from both of them.

I find that suspect on its face, and I've never spoken publicly on that issue.

But those psychiatrists, in examining my records at that time, probably felt it safe to say, "You know what? We're tired of this happening, this guy rubbing his business off on us, for us to resolve for him."

And then he says, "No, don't come back because I have psychiatric documentation that you can't be supported in the claims of non-violence."

So I go back to the court with this rave review, the judge is very impressed. That reopened the entire issue for examination. Unfortunately for everybody involved, including me, I was in the middle of killing people.

On October 1, Mary Ann Pesce's head was identified. The cause of death was listed as "head severed from body by unknown instrument."

Sometime in late 1972, Kemper moved back in with his mother in Aptos.

Allyn Kemper, 1972:
He had injured his arm and he couldn't stay in the Alameda area. He couldn't pay his rent because he couldn't work. So he moved [back] in with her.

HERBERT MULLIN

On December 16, 1972, Mullin bought a .22 caliber RG 14 pistol from Western Auto in Felton for $22.99. After looking at many handguns, Mullin stated that he was looking for a pistol with a short barrel and asked the manager and owner Anthony Black for the store's least expensive firearm.

Mullin signed the legal paperwork, including a statement that he was not addicted to narcotics and had never been committed to a mental institution.

After the state mandated waiting period, Mullin picked up the gun on Dec. 22, 1972. He filed off the serial number and used the pistol on his next nine victims.

Mullin returned to John Hooper's house and learned that Hooper had moved out of California—

Herbert Mullin, 1973:
Then I just reached the conclusion I shouldn't kill him.

Above Left: Receipt for Mullin's RG14 pistol.
Left: Dealer's Record of Sale for Mullin's pistol.
Above: St. Mary's church in Los Gatos in 2021.

CYNTHIA SCHALL
SUNDAY, JANUARY 7, 1973

Forrest Schall (Cynthia Schall's brother), 2020:
We lived in Marin County and San Francisco.
  My mother didn't have much money and raised us kids by herself. I was the oldest. Cynthia was eighteen months younger and Candace was the baby. We're all eighteen months apart. My parents split up when I was three or four, but they still managed to have another child, Scotty. He was my youngest brother, but he died of a crib death in '56 or '57. So they were still messing around even though they were separated.

Cynthia's father was absent for approximately fifteen years, but six months before she was killed, Cynthia, her brother Forrest, and her sister Candace reestablished contact with him.

Growing up with their mother was not alway easy.

Forrest Schall, 2021:
My mom hated men and, of course, I'm a male. She threw me in juvenile hall when I was fifteen years old. If it wasn't for a friend of the family, I would have been a ward of the court.

A letter, dated December 14, 1972, that Cynthia sent to her father before visiting him for Christmas tells the story of a particularly vicious interaction with her mother—

Cynthia Schall, 1972:
…like the time I was nine years old she made some fudge and some was stolen. Automatically, she came to me first and said I was lying. She said that she was going to give me a hundred lashings with a belt if I didn't tell her the truth. I didn't do it so in her eyes I was lying and in mine I was telling her the truth. She tied my hands and feet up and also gagged me. She started hitting me with a buckle and didn't stop until the 52nd belt whip and I told her that I was lying but I really wasn't. I just couldn't stand the physical pain. My sister Candy had been in the door-

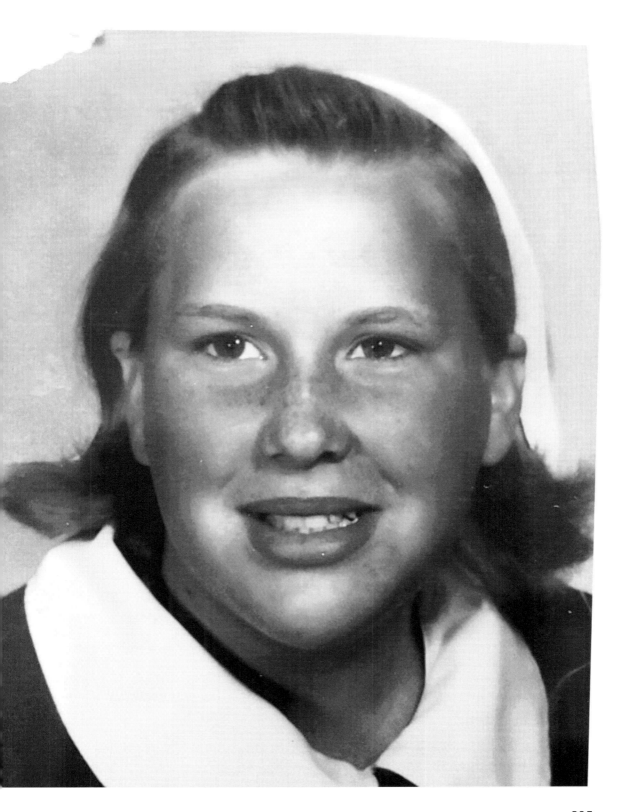

way crying and Frosty was laughing. Moreover this was very wild, it was at 1602 Lyon Street in San Francisco and it happened in my bedroom.

Forrest Schall, 2020:
She [Cynthia] was working as an au pair in Santa Cruz, living with a family and taking care of the kids and she attended college in her off hours.

She was a bubbly eighteen-year-old going to Cabrillo Community College. When she came around she would take her niece, Christina, who was a baby then, she used to truck her around like a sack of potatoes. She was a bright young lady with a bright future ahead of her.

She was picked up hitchhiking, it was in January. It was a rainy night and he [Kemper] took her down a back road and shot her. Then he dismembered her. He put her head in his backyard facing his mother's bedroom window. He threw parts of her out in the ocean. They never did find all of her.

Jim Conner, 2020:
When all the homicides started to happen, one of the victims happened to be a babysitter of my wife and I at the time. She was a college student. She went to Cabrillo. So when her body washed up on the shore, it was just… Cindy was our part time babysitter because occasionally we'd want to go to the movie

or something. It was heartbreaking to realize that Cindy was one of his [Kemper's] victims.

When Cynthia came to Santa Cruz she lived with various friends. This included an apartment in Capitola where several people stayed, sleeping all over the floor.

Ward Damio, 1973:
For many of us Cindy's apartment was the place to go for laughter and talk about old times.

Cynthia was then hired by James Doherty. She watched his children and lived at his Cleveland Street home.

On January 25, 1973, Santa Cruz Police Detectives C. Gilbert and Jim Conner interviewed James Doherty.

C. Gilbert (Santa Cruz Police Department Sergeant), 1973:
Mr. Doherty stated that the arrangements with Cynthia Schall were that she was to take care of the children, that she was to receive twenty dollars a week plus room and board for living at the residence. He stated that she was very reliable and he had no complaints. He stated that he wasn't too alarmed of the fact that Cindy wasn't there on the morning after she had left the house, that he had received a call from his son Mike who indicated that no one was there to take care of the children so Mr. Doherty came

home from work. He stated that around 5:00 or 6:00 p.m. he called the police.

Mr. Doherty mentioned that Cynthia may have been suicidal, as her relationship with her mother was stressful. He also stated that Cynthia engaged in hitchhiking and was talking about buying a motorcycle.

C. Gilbert, 1973:

He stated that Schall was a trusting person and she felt that she could tell by looking at a person whether or not they were going to harm her in any way.

Mr. Doherty was asked about Cindy's involvement in drugs—he stated that he was surprised that marijuana had been found in her room. He felt that she was probably involved in marijuana to a small extent but thought that she would not have brought it into the residence.

On February 2, 1973, Sergeant Gilbert interviewed Cynthia's friend, Carol Cukrov.

C. Gilbert, 1973:

Carol Cukrov stated that as far as drug information, that Cindy was a user of marijuana and/or LSD, had taken LSD at least twelve times that she knew of in 1972. She stated that sometime around November, Cindy had taken two teaspoons of [unreadable] "Jimson Weed" and was under the influence and incoherent for approximately two or three days afterwards and in her opinion Cindy has not been the same since taking the drug. Carol stated that as far as she knew Cindy only had one flashback from the LSD and that when she was driving along the road and thought that she saw a lake in the middle of the road up by Half Moon Bay and apparently had driven off the road to avoid running into, what she thought, the lake.

Carol stated that when she first met Cindy she was one of the straightest kids she knew and she progressed to her position shortly before her death. She stated that as far as hitchhiking goes, that several times Carol had to hitchhike with Cindy, that she would get into the car with anybody, no matter how many people, males or otherwise, were in the vehicle. Carol had objected to this and this caused several arguments about the fact that Cindy would get into a car with just anybody without looking over the situation prior to getting in.

Carol stated that Cindy had "fits of crying," that she would become emotional and sit down and cry, that she was very sensitive and it was not difficult to hurt her feelings.

Carol also was vaguely familiar with the fact that Cynthia had an abortion.

Peter Chang, 1973:

Kemper also will be charged with the murder of Cynthia Ann Schall, nineteen, a Cabrillo College student who was last seen on the evening on January 8, 1973, hitchhiking to a class at Cabrillo College.

Schall was taken to the Watsonville area by Kemper where she was shot to death. Her body was later dismembered and thrown off a cliff at Rocky Creek south of Carmel on Highway 1. Her head was unearthed last week by investigators in the backyard of Kemper's residence at 609-A Ord Street, Aptos.

Edmund Kemper, 1973:

Cynthia Schall was the next one. That happened the night I bought a .22 Ruger automatic pistol with a six inch barrel. And that night I killed her. Not so much to celebrate, but I had been eagerly awaiting that gun.

The gun was purchased at Valley Sport Shop in Watsonville.

Edmund Kemper, 1973:

It was on Mission [Street]. I was up cruising around, closing, er, five o'clock or so. In that vicinity. I had been up cruising around the campus and I'd picked up three different girls. Two of them together, that were possibilities. But I canceled those out because there

thing on, cotton blouse, and over that she had a wool-type men's shirt, like a work shirt, and over that she had a blue plastic waterproof type jacket like a boy would wear, and she had brown corduroy bell bottoms and hiker boots and blue socks.

Edmund Kemper, 1973:
Like I said that little home-made-type ring that some-one had given her, and she had two very plain gold wire earrings on, pierced earrings, with loops, with a little catch on them. But in her case, I was quite stunned at how quickly everything happened there. As far as her demise. Uh, 'cause I hadn't even fired the gun to that point. I hadn't test fired it at all.

Edmund Kemper, 1973:
Uh, that was up around the uh, uh, past Watson-ville up around, uh, I was driving up and down roads but it was some-where around like Airport Boulevard. What's that little community back there behind Wat-sonville? Corralitos. It's up around that area but I think more along Freedom up in the hills in some of those long private one-way roads. You know. Dead end road type things. And it was up one of those that again I con-vinced her, that, we drove all over clear out to 101 and back to Watsonville, talking and I was playing a little game of not blowing it, you know, somebody's going to talk with me or, you know, that's it, by God. So, I said, you know, I convinced her that I don't like guns and all that, it was just bull, and that I wasn't going to use it and I just nonchalantly tucked it away under my leg there and didn't

were too many people standing around that possibly knew them when they got in. But all the other conditions were perfect. It had been drizzling. It had been raining real hard and people were getting any ride they could get and windows were fogging up, nobody was paying attention. It was during that re-ally heavy rain. But I had given up on those other two and I was kind of uptight about it and driving down the street I spotted her standing out there with her thumb out.

Edmund Kemper, 1973:
She had, uh, sort of a brocaded blouse type-

refer to it again until later and now and then I picked it up and played around with it but did everything but hand it to her uh, to, to calm her down. Several times she asked me not to kill her and it got to the point later on where it was very nonchalant like, you know. Like reminding me, and I kept saying well what can I say, you know. Lying through my teeth. Got up to that area.

And she didn't want to get in the trunk at all. But I told her it would be better for her to hide in there than be discovered by some nosy neighbor. I was going to take her to the house and we were going to talk, and then I was going to take her to her class because she was very late for it. She was trying to convince me that if she missed that class she would lose her grade and her parents wouldn't support her any more in college. And she was very convincing at that, uh, almost succeeded in convincing me that was the proper route to take. She tried to get me to take her up to the college and talk in the campus parking lot but, of course, that wasn't the plan, but I got her to finally—I said, "You know, well, come back here in the trunk and it's safer, you know, for both of us."

I opened the trunk and she remarked at how large it was. She thought it was much smaller. It was a '69 Ford Galaxie that I had, so it was a very large trunk. And I had a blanket in there. I said, "Well, do you want me to open that up?"

She said, "No."

I got my clothes on and so she climbed in and was kind of sorting the thing around as a pillow and I just, not wanting to shoot, I just picked it up and started to like, you know, any second now I'm going to have to pull that trigger if I'm going to at all. And I kept telling myself I don't want to do that, you know, fear.

I don't want to do it. And just as I was doing that she looks around to say something and she looked around just through the corner of her eye, hadn't even turned all the way towards me, caught me with the gun up like this and just as she did like that I pulled that first stage and nothing happened and we both just, just for a split second paused and I'm dumbfounded and she's not, she snapped her head back around and half way through snapping it around the gun went off. And it was that quick. There was no jerk, uh no, every other case there has always been at least, you know a jerk, a little reflex. There was absolutely nothing.

Chuck Scherer, 1973:
One shot.

Edmund Kemper, 1973:
She followed through with the motion. Yeah.

Mickey Aluffi, 1973:
Which, which side of the head?

Edmund Kemper, 1973:
It was the left, in the top, right there.

Missing Girl

Cynthia Ann Schall, 18, has been missing since Jan. 8 when she left her Santa Cruz home to hitchhike to Cabrillo College. She is 5 - foot - 5, 160 pounds and has long blond hair. When last seen she was wearing a green, blue and yellow coat, white blouse, blue Levis and green hiking boots. The photo at left is three years old. Anyone with information as to her whereabouts is asked to call the Santa Cruz Police Department.

Chuck Scherer, 1973:
And did the bullet pass clean through the skull?

Edmund Kemper, 1973:
No. No. Uh, it lodged in there somewhere but it was a hollow point, long rifle. And I found at that point that they were extremely effective. But I mean, her eyes didn't even shut. Her eyes were wide open. She didn't, nothing flexed or moved. Just like—it amazed me so much because one second she animated and the next second she's not and there was absolutely nothing between. Just a noise and absolute stillness.

Edmund Kemper, 1973:
At this point, I had the broken arm and it was in a cast. I had just gotten the cast that day. I should have mentioned it. I had gone up to Oakland, Kaiser Hospital, and getting a fresh short-arm cast put on and I'd just come back that day so it wasn't really even cured yet. It wasn't full dry, and a, ah I got blood stains on it here and there and I had to use white shoe polish to cover it up so my mother wouldn't get suspicious.

So I pulled her out of the trunk and in through the back. Nobody was home upstairs and it was halfway drizzling sort of and nobody was out. And I pulled her into my closet and shut the door, afraid that my mother was going to come home at any moment and uh, uh shut the door that was, sliding door of the closet. Talked to my mother when she got home, went to bed, then while she was at work the next day was when I did the dissection. Something I wouldn't want to go through any of it again. That was a particularly nasty part of the thing but I, you know, with the bad arm I just couldn't handle the other and this was a lot less noticeable with the bags, uh except in her case.

Chuck Scherer, 1973:
You did have sexual relations with her?

Edmund Kemper, 1973:
Yeah, on the floor the next morning. This sounds terrible, but that night, she was still quite limp and very hard to move around as it was and I just, no way that, uh, but I'd never had sex with a large girl like that before and I decided to see what that was like. Actually, you can't really check that point off, I understand, because of the state of the body, but I will say that the next morning I did.

Edmund Kemper, 1973:
I got pretty upset about the paper report from the pathologist that Cynthia Schall was hamstrung so she couldn't move, that wasn't true. That happened almost fourteen or fifteen hours after her death the next day. The reason for that was that rigor mortis set and the tendons constricted up and the muscles pulled and the feet were pulled forward very steeply. I was using those large garbage type bags, and that part of the leg from the knee down wouldn't fit in there.

Chuck Scherer, 1973:
When did you start dissecting the body?

Edmund Kemper, 1973:
I think it was around eleven o'clock the next morning. It took a hell of a long time.

Chuck Scherer, 1973:
Where was it done at?

Edmund Kemper, 1973:
In the bathtub. There's two bathrooms. The one I used was the one closest to the living room. I removed the sliding glass type plastic doors on the shower and there was an aluminum rail above and I just removed that whole assembly, so it would be like a regular bathtub, and I was very careful and meticulous in cleaning it up. I poured lots of Drano down the thing and made sure it fizzed real good and removed any hair or tissue that got caught in the drain, and things like that, made sure there were no spots of blood laying around. I used that special foam bowl

cleaner stuff in any suspicious areas where I thought something like that might be there. Then there's been innumerable baths and showers since then.

Anyway, the reason they found that bag, or suspected that bag out there on the cliff was because the upper part of the torso was the heaviest and I double lined the bag and I was kinda panicky watching for cars and everything and ran over the edge, thinking it was straight down, 'cause I had only looked hastily with my flashlight and dumped it out, and I forgot about the inside bag, and they must have separated down the cliff somewhere, I saw it tumbling. I didn't know if there was water down there or beach or what. I saw a little sliver of beach off to the right, and for all I knew, it landed right smack dab in the middle of somebody's beach party, so I was very quick about the whole thing and ran. In fact, when I dumped the bags with the parts of the arms and legs, one arm I think propped up a little bit out of, I think it was ice plant, and it was very noticeable and even back from the guardrail, I could see it. I skidded down the side of the hill there, slipping in the mud. I was afraid somebody got footprints off of that but it must have drizzled up there. But this was like two o'clock in the morning, and then three o'clock that afternoon, that highway patrolman discovered the parts, so I was pretty well blown out about that. I was sure there must be tire prints or one possible tire print, or a possible large footprint. All I was worried about was a large footprint. Because I wear size fifteen shoe and that's going to tell you a hell of a lot.

Chuck Scherer, 1973:
Were all parts of the Schall girl deposited at that one spot?

Edmund Kemper, 1973:
Everything but the head.

Chuck Scherer, 1973:
Where is the head?

Edmund Kemper, 1973:
That's what I didn't want to say, it's in the backyard at my mother's place. There is a stone stepping thing in the backyard. There's a stepping stone right in the middle.

Edmund Kemper, 1973:
What I did was like I only cut the hole with a trowel that big around. The stone was maybe this big. I wanted it to fit just exactly like it was before. It didn't even have any grass crushed under the thing. That was on January 8, so maybe that was the 9th when I did that. The reason was I was gonna let it stay there a few months and was gonna dig it back up and take the bullet out of the skull and then dispense of the skull, rather than hack and chop. Because my thing was no evidence at all if I could possibly help it.

HERBERT MULLIN

Richard Verbrugge, 2020:
I don't think you know this, but there was a short period of time where he [Herbert Mullin] was trying to recuperate. He got off drugs completely. He went and talked to his father. He was doing real well with his father. Herb thought that he should join the military and if he went in the military he'd be—his life would be taken care of. He would do what they told him to do and stay clean.

Mullin had visited a Marine Corps recruiter over 10 times between December 1972 and January 1973. Finally, on January 16, 1973, Mullin went to the Marine Corps Induction Center in Oakland. He passed the physical and psychiatric evaluations. The psychiatric evaluation was conducted by Dr. Hanscom. Mullin was ultimately rejected when he refused to sign a document listing the criminal charges he had been charged with in the past.

Mullin had a different take on why he dropped out of the induction—

Herbert Mullin, 1973:

Dr. Hanscom wanted Enos Fouratt [Mullin's uncle] killed.

Dee Shafer, 1973:

He applied for and received conscientious objector status, which he said was a source of considerable conflict with his father. He changed his mind, and later attempted to enlist during the period of time when he was committing his offenses.

Mickey Aluffi, 2019:

There was some speculation at the time, Herb wanted to join the Marine Corps, and in his mind he thought that they weren't going to allow him in because of his drug use. So he was trying to eliminate his drug connections from the past. That was speculation.

On January 19, 1973, Mullin moved out of his parents home in Felton and rented Room #8 at the Pacific View Court in Santa Cruz for a month.

Herbert Mullin, 2020:

I do not remember which bungalow I stayed at. I don't remember much about those times. Maybe there was a fellow named Mr. Pine there.

It was Mr. Alpine and on January 24, 1973, the two had dinner together and spoke late into the night about religion and the history of Santa Cruz.

Richard Verbrugge, 2020:

We were making a lot of good narcotic cases in Santa Cruz at that time. Then all of a sudden we started having these homicides, you know, body parts floating up on the beach and bodies being found here and there. A group of young men camping up off Highway 9 between Felton and Santa Cruz and they were all murdered by one person and things of that nature. At that time the Santa Cruz law enforcement agencies were all small agencies and they hadn't had a lot of experience in these types of crimes. Mr. Chang kind of took the lead with that. The sheriff at the time was a man named Doug James and a really good man, really a good sheriff. And he understood what was going on. And he and Mr. Chang got together with all the Chiefs of Police from the local cities in Santa Cruz County. And they all kind of got together with an agreement that once a homicide happened, no matter what kind of a homicide, if help was needed by that agency, other agencies would work with them. It was a group endeavor led by Mr. Chang.

The DA's office had to prosecute those cases, you know, and we had a lot of experience. Belgard and I fit into that. And another guy they hired by the name of Bob Sweeney, who's passed on. He was kind of my partner and he was a good homicide investigator, too. So we would be involved from the district attorney's office right from the get go on each of these cases at the time. And it wasn't that we were taking over the cases and nobody thought that at the time. It was just that we were there to help them. That's basically why we were involved in every case.

Right: The Marine Corps recruitment form Mullin refused to sign.

1. NAME OF APPLICANT *(In full)*			2. DATE OF BIRTH		8. PHYSICAL PROFILE					
					P	U	L	H	E	S

3. APPLICANT FOR ENLISTMENT IN	4. HIGHEST GRADE COMPLETED IN SCHOOL	5. TEST, FORM NO. & SCORE	6. MENTAL GROUP	7. MSN./SSAN *(when required)*
☐ USMC ☐ USMCR				

9. AQB SCORES *(If applicable)*   10.

IN _____ AE _____ EL _____ GM _____ MM _____ CL _____ GT _____

PART I

ARTICLE 83, UNIFORM CODE OF MILITARY JUSTICE—Fraudulent enlistment, appointment, or separation

Any person who—

(1) procures his own enlistment or appointment in the Armed Forces by means of knowingly false representations or deliberate concealment as to his qualifications for such enlistment or appointment and receives pay or allowances thereunder; or

(2) procures his own separation from the Armed Forces by means of knowingly false representations or deliberate concealment as to his eligibility for such separation;

shall be punished as a court-martial may direct.

I have been informed that if I am enlisted in the UNITED STATES MARINE CORPS (RESERVE) after concealing or misrepresenting any information placed on my application for enlistment, I may have enlisted fraudulently, and;

    a. That my pay and allowances will be stopped when it is discovered that my enlistment was fraudulent;

    b. That I may be discharged, without trial, under other than honorable conditions, or;

    c. That I may be tried by general court-martial on the charge of fraudulent enlistment—for which the maximum punishment of dishonorable discharge and confinement at hard labor could be adjudged.

I also understand that if I enlist fraudulently, and I am later discharged because of fraud, I may be deprived of virtually all rights as a veteran under both Federal and State legislation, and may expect to encounter substantial prejudice in civilian life because of such discharge.

The nature and consequences of a FRAUDULENT ENLISTMENT have been carefully explained to me and I fully understand these consequences.

I have been informed that if I enlist, my fingerprints will be compared with those on file with the Federal Bureau of Investigation and a complete report will be obtained by the United States Marine Corps, listing all arrests, including dates and places, and record of prior military service, if any.

Notwithstanding any advice I have received to the contrary, whether from a civil official, or civil authority, or any other person, I CERTIFY that I have read the following statements and answered them correctly to the best of my knowledge:

	YES	NO		YES	NO
11. HAVE YOU EVER BEEN REJECTED FOR ENLISTMENT OR INDUCTION IN ANY BRANCH OF THE ARMED FORCES?		X	20. HAVE YOU WET THE BED WITHIN THE PAST FIVE YEARS?		X
12. HAVE YOU EVER BEEN ARRESTED?	X		21. HAVE YOU EVER PARTICIPATED IN A HOMOSEXUAL ACT?		X
13. HAVE YOU EVER BEEN CONVICTED OF A CRIME?	X		22. ARE YOU A SOLE SURVIVING SON?		X
14. HAVE YOU EVER BEEN SENTENCED BY ANY COURT?	X		23. HAVE YOU EVER USED LSD, MARIJUANA, OPIATES, PEYOTE, SNIFFED GLUE, OR USED ANY OTHER HALLUCINOGENS, HYPNOTICS, STIMULANTS, OR OTHER KNOWN HARMFUL OR HABIT-FORMING DRUGS AND/OR CHEMICALS?		X
15. HAVE YOU EVER BEEN IN JAIL, A REFORM OR INDUSTRIAL SCHOOL, OR PENITENTIARY?	X				
16. HAVE YOU EVER RECEIVED A SUSPENDED SENTENCE BY ANY COURT?	X	X	24. DO YOU QUALIFY FOR PERMANENT RESTRICTIVE ASSIGNMENT *(family member KIA/100% disability while serving in a hostile fire area)*?		X
17. ARE YOU NOW ON PAROLE, PROBATION, SUPERVISION, OR OTHER FORM OF CIVIL RESTRAINT?		X	25. DO YOU DESIRE TO WAIVE THE RESTRICTION CONTAINED IN ITEM 24?		
18. HAVE YOU EVER BEEN ON PAROLE, PROBATION, SUPERVISION, OR OTHER FORM OF CIVIL RESTRAINT?	X				
19. ARE YOU A CONSCIENTIOUS OBJECTOR?		X			

26. REMARKS *(If any answer to Items 11 through 25 is Yes, explain in detail.)*

POSSESSION OF MARIJUANA (REDUCED TO BEING IN THE VICINITY OF DRUGS) 21APR68 SANTA CRUZ CAL
The applicant was at a party where drugs were being used, not the the applicant's knowledge when the police arrived and arrested all persons at the party. The applicant appeared in Court, where the charge was reduced. The applicant was sentenced to 90 days in the County Jail, which was suspended and placed on 1 year summary probation.

UNDER INFLUENCE OF DRUGS 30JUL70 SANTA CRUZ, CALIF
The applicant was stopped on the street by a police officer and accused of using drugs and arrested the applicant. The applicant appeared in Court where all charges were dropped.

DRUNK AND RESISTING ARREST 28MAR71 SANTA CRUZ, CALIF
The applicant was walking on the street when a police officer stopped him and accused of him of being drunk. The applicant denied the charge and stated his desire not to be arrested. The applicant was arrested and remained in the County Jail for two days awaiting trial. In court the charge of being drunk was dropped and the applicant was sentenced to 10 days in the County Jail for resisting arrest. Credit was allowed for the two days awaiting trial.

ORGANIZATION	TYPEWRITTEN NAME OF APPLICANT	SIGNATURE OF APPLICANT
USMC-RS, SFRAN CA	HERBERT WILLIAM MULLIN	

GIANERA AND FRANCIS FAMILIES THURSDAY, JANUARY 25, 1973

Herbert Mullin, 2006:
Jim Gianera and I went to high school together, San Lorenzo Valley High, 1963, '64, '65.

William Mullin, 1973:
They played football together. Gianera was on that team with Herb. I met him once at our house. Just once. Senior year in high school. I don't think the kid [Herbert] was all that close with Gianera then.

I remember reading about the murders in the newspaper and the name Gianera, and I said I thought he could have possibly have been one of the kids from church and Herb said, "Yeah, I remember Gianera."

And that was about it. Didn't add another thing.

Bary Burt, 2020:
George Gianera and I were pretty good friends. He and I were closer in age, Jim was older. I knew Jim's parents. I used to go up to the Gianera's house and party there. Jim

was a super nice guy. He was in that fringe element, that hippie element. He was really friendly. Although, you didn't want to cross him because he could take care of himself. I had seen him in a couple of fights and I wouldn't want to be up against him.

Holly Harman, 2020:
Jim came from San Francisco and moved to Ben Lomond. His dad was a butcher. And they used to live in San Francisco, in a real rough area. He was in a gang called I think they were called the Deacons. So when he got to Ben Lomond, he was like this greaser guy who wore this Deacon's jacket. I mean, he was kind of a scary guy. That's what my picture of him was when I first met him, he was tough.

He won the shot put competition at San Lorenzo Valley High School, there is a brass plaque in the gym.

The first time I met Jim was at a party at Shelly Beal's house. He took a liking to me, which really scared me because he was older.

Left: Joan Gianera. Unfortunately this is the only picture of Joan Gianera I could find.
Above: Jim Gianera, 1965 San Lorenzo Valley High School senior.

вессa Burwell, Aptos.
GIANERA-FOSTER — James Ralph
Gianera, Ben Lomond, and Joan Kath-
erine Foster, Santa Cruz. Richard
STOKES-CAVENDER —

I mean, he was in college. I was in high school, I was a freshman in high school. And he tried to pursue me. I was always kind of afraid of him. But then we became friendly and dated for a little while.

You know, even when I first started dating him, he had greased back hair and so did Jeff Meeler. And I remember they came to pick me up to go to the drive-in. And my dad was like, "Really?"

"Oh, don't worry, Mr. Harman. We'll have her back at ten o'clock," or whatever.

We went to the drive-in. That's the first time I ever smoked a joint. It was with them.

And once Jim really started smoking pot, it was kind of like he went from greaser to surfer. And so he started washing his hair and wearing it dry in kind of a Beatles cut, kind of surfer. And then he started taking acid and he started growing his hair long and so did everybody really. He turned into this really gentle soul. I mean, he was always a very sweet person, always very sensitive and caring. But with this kind of scary demeanor on the surface.

I remember he just didn't know how to make money. He would do odd jobs and stuff. But he liked working on cars. He was a really good mechanic. And then when he fell into the whole hippie thing, that became kind of his source of income.

But then, at Holidays [commune], he kind of flipped out.

> *Above: Jim and Joan were married in February, 1969.*
> *Above right: The house on Western that Jim built. This photo was taken a day after the murders. The house is still there today.*

Charmaine Falcon, 2020:
And he was a nice guy, kind of a little bit of a roughneck. When we got into our hippie days, he got a little weird, a little carried away on LSD.

I remember him coming down to the commune carrying an ax. We didn't know what he was going to do. It was weird. He didn't hurt anybody. He just had whatever was on his mind at the time. He was on LSD.

Roger Murray, 2019:
I lived in a little two-bedroom house at Holidays, but I was dating your mother and wasn't around that much. So it didn't make sense for me to be in there. I moved into a cabin with Jim. And we would talk and talk all night.

Holly Harman, 2020:
I had a love letter that he wrote to me and a necklace that he gave me for Valentine's Day. And just recently in the last two years, I gave it over to his and Joan's daughter as a gift. She didn't want to meet me, but she accepted that gift and the poem.

Roger Murray, 2019:
Jim was psychic. He just knew things and was just psychic.

Holly Harman, 2020:
Jim used to always say, "I'm not going to live to be over twenty-four. I'm only going to live to be twenty-four."

"How do you know that?"

And he used to say, "I know. I know."

And also, if anyone ever approached him from behind or tapped him on the back or patted him on the back or anything, he turned with an evil look on his face. And he was shot in the back when he was killed. So that was always a really strange, peculiar thing about him. And that's when he died. He was twenty-four.

Bary Burt, 2020:
I guess there were other people that said that too [Jim being psychic]. He just had this certain sense about him. People thought he was really together.

Holly Harman, 2020:
When I was fifteen or sixteen, we [Jim and I] were going to the drive-in movie. Jeff Meeler and a few other people were with us on this particular evening, when we were going to go to the movies.

Mullin was broken down by the side of the road. He had a gray VW Bug. And I was really only fifteen or sixteen, really young. And Jim said, "Oh, there's Herb Mullin." And Jim had a 1956 Chevy souped up. And I'm sitting in the front seat with him. Jim got out and started to walk over to Mullin, but he comes right back to the car and he got this big old Bowie knife out of the glove compartment and told me to stay there, and he went down to talk to him. So Jim was definitely on guard. I would say Jim was

afraid, and Jim wasn't really afraid of anybody.

Nothing violent happened that day between Gianera and Mullin, but they would have a fateful meeting a few years later, after Gianera had married Joan.

Joan Foster was born in Vienna, Austria while her parents were there helping to resettle World War II refugees and work with rehabilitating children mentally impacted by the war. The Foster family was very active in the Quaker church.

The Foster family returned to the United States in 1957.

Eleanor Foster (Joan Gianera's mother), 1973:
Joan grew up without a lot of hangups some kids have. She just didn't have any prejudice or violence in her.

Her summers were spent as a volunteer with Head Start, working with emotionally disturbed kids at a summer camp. She was always giving.

Miriam Finnegan (Friend of Joan Gianera), 2021:

I met Joan in seventh grade at Mission Hill Junior High on King Street and we became tight friends. We spent every day together at school and we had lunch together. We would have a lime bar and Corn Nuts every day and we would trade off who paid for them. After school, I would either go to her house and we would do homework and listen to music or we would try to get our parents to let us go downtown.

There was an import store called Tradewinds. We would go in there and look at all the hippie clothes and hippie beads. And the great music was just starting. The counterculture had come into Santa Cruz because of UCSC, and we embraced that so we would go down. And one time I bought her a pet turtle and she bought me pet guppies, and we had a soda at the soda fountain that is now The Catalyst. It was a bowling alley and a soda fountain down there. And so we sat there and had sodas. And what we would do if we were allowed to go downtown is we would then go to the police department and wait for my father to get off work, and his pickup truck and either do homework, or, you know, talk and stuff. And then either he'd drop her off at her home on Miles Street or I would ask her to come home with me. And we lived way out by Natural Bridges, on Sacramento Avenue. And it was still very rustic out there. So she would have dinner with us. My dad [Santa Cruz Police Detective Dennis Finnegan] really liked her. She had a great sense of humor and he was a real kidder. So when she was there, we all laughed a lot.

She was a very sweet girl. We loved music. We were very innocent and happy and carefree growing up in a beach town. There was no serious talk about any life plans or anything. We just were really happy to be friends. But, then, at the end of eighth grade, I think

that was, they moved. The Fosters relocated to Visalia. We kept in touch by letters for a while, but she was in high school in a different town and we kind of lost touch.

Eleanor Foster, 1973:

Maybe because she grew up to love and without feeling against violence, she wasn't afraid; trusted too many people. Jim comes from a good stable family, but he was a loner; I think this attracted Joan to him. They were good parents to Monica.

I think the women and children in this case were innocent victims—like the typical war.

We've felt the same grief and horror about the war, but the war was something we could put away—this we can't put away. No, this hasn't changed our minds on capital punishment. We're still against it.

Holly Harman, 2020:

She [Joan] had the most beautiful green eyes. They were kind of light green, just like you could kind of look right into them. And she had just kind of warm, golden complexion from being out in the sun, just beautiful. She was very quiet and she was very sensitive and unusually quiet and sensitive, I would say. But she was so beautiful. And she was raised as a Quaker with her family.

Holly Harman, 2020:

I remember when Joan and Jim first got together, and we were in Oakland in a car and Jim was getting gas. Joan and I were in the backseat. She says to me, "Jim wants to get married."

And I said, "Oh, that's great."

"What do you think I should do?"

I thought, well, it wasn't right for me because I was Jim's girlfriend before. I said, "Well, you know, it's really up to you what you want to do. I think he's a good guy."

So they got married.

Herbert Mullin, 1973:

When Jim got married and his wife was

pregnant he approached me and asked me if I wanted to smoke some marijuana with him and so that's—that was when I first met her.

Holly Harman, 2020:
I came back to Santa Cruz in 1971 to go to Cabrillo. And Joan was going to college at the same time. We would run into each other and she would always have the baby on her back.

The last time I saw Jim, he was in my bedroom with me and my brother and some other people. We were just hanging out, smoking a joint. And Jim left this little tiny—well, it was like a little wrench he used as a roach clip, a little wrench. And I hung on to that for years.

Chris Cottle, 2020:
Jim was his [Mullin's] supplier and that was his stated reason for going out to kill him.

Donald T. Lunde, 1973:
It was well known that Gianera was rather a large drug dealer. [...] To say that Mullin and Gianera were friends because he bought drugs from him would be like saying he [Mullin] went to the Safeway to buy groceries.

That doesn't mean you know the clerk at the checkout stand. Gianera was the man he went to see when he wanted to buy drugs.

The Gianera and Francis families were not only close friends, but Jim Gianera and Bob Francis ran marijuana together.

George Gianera (Jim Gianera's brother), 1973:
My brother met Bob approximately four years ago in Hawaii. They lived together in Hawaii for probably six months. They came back and moved to Dobbins, California, by Marysville. They lived together there for quite a while.

About eighteen months before the murders, while living in Dobbins together, the Francis

Family was introduced to one of Jim Gianera's old high school friends, Herbert Mullin.

Robert Francis, 1973:
I was living with Kathleen and the two kids, and Jim and Joan. I think she had Monica when we were staying up there, and Peter Gannon and his family.

Herbert Mullin visited and stayed at the house—

Robert Francis, 1973:
About two days. He came one afternoon, spent the night and left the next day.

While there, Mullin observed Robert and Kathy Francis' son, Daemon, and referred to him as "a little angel."

Years later—

Robert Francis, 1973:
It was in the spring [1972] when he [Jim Gianera] got a letter. He was living across the street from the Courthouse here on Water Street. That is before he moved up to Branciforte [Street] with us, and he got a letter from Herbert Mullin wondering who he was going to vote for. He told me about it, and I remember it really well.

Miriam Finnegan, 2021:
I got married at a very young age and had a child and was married to a man, Ron Terry, who knew Jim [Gianera] from San Lorenzo Valley High School. His younger brother, Bobby, was in Jim's grade. So one day the three of us were driving around in Santa Cruz, it was around '72. We had this old silver Porsche and we were driving around and Bobby suggested that we go see a friend of his. So we went up this winding road past the Mystery Spot, and there was a cabin there. So we got out of the car and this woman walked out on the porch and it was Joan! I jumped out of the car and I went, "Oh, my God, Joan, there you are."

So we are all happy jumping up and down

Kathy Francis and the Francis home on 1965 Branciforte Drive.

and everything. She said, "Jim's not here right now. And so why don't you wait a little bit."

So Bobby and Ron sat outside and she took me in the cabin, and she was not living there at that point. She said that a woman that she had lived with was living there with her husband and two little boys. She showed me the boy's bunk bed and pictures of them. Joan and Jim were just using the cabin to hang out for the day.

So Jim never did show up and we finally left. But Joan and I were going to rekindle our relationship. She gave me her phone number and I gave her mine and we talked a little bit on the phone. Nothing consequential.

Then one day, I was down at the Cooper House and I ran into her right to her right in front of the Cooper House. And this was in January. And she said, "I really want to show you my house. I live off from Western Drive. You know where that is."

I go, "Yeah, I'd love to do that. Let's make plans to do that soon."

I had to cancel at the last minute.

Holly Harman, 2020:
They were fun [The Francis family]. I had spent some time with them and partied with them and driven around in their

250

VW bus with them and ate at the Catalyst with them. I kind of knew them, but not as well as I knew Jim.

Kathleen Francis was born Kathleen Louise Prentiss. She and her family lived in Napa from 1956–61 where she attended Napa High School, Redwood Junior High, and Silverado Junior High.

A high school friend of Kathleen Francis, 1973:
She was a popular enough girl here. She was clean-cut and a sweet girl. She always had a little spirit about her.

She was an A and B grade student.

Francis was also a member of the ninth–tenth grade student council.

Wednesday, January 24, 1973.

Eleanor Foster (Joan Gianera's mother), 1973:
The last personal contact with them was Wednesday afternoon when I met Joan at her house on Western Drive and picked her and the baby up. Joan was going to a class and I had already agreed to babysit for that evening. Then on the way to the car, we met Jim, who was walking up towards their house and they met and had a friendly exchange, and Joan agreed she would be back in time to have supper with him. She was going to an evening class.

Eleanor Foster, 1973:
I called about nine thirty or ten o'clock [the morning of Thursday, January 25].

Jim answered the phone.

Eleanor Foster, 1973:
I just asked to speak to Joan. I had thought to invite Joan, if she was free, to go out to lunch with me. […] Jim said Joan was taking a bath, and he was relaxed and very friendly. […] He said he would ask Joan to call me back.

Over at the Francis' home on Branciforte Drive.

Steven Richard Houtz (Francis Family's neighbor), 1973:
I saw a 1958 Chevy station wagon two or three times. […] Somewhere between nine and ten in the morning. I was working in the front. I don't know exactly when.

Thatcher Hall Clark (Francis Family's neighbor), 1973:
It was raining pretty hard and had been most of the early morning, so it was muddy

HUGHES — September 22 at 3:19 a.m. to Mr. and Mrs. Robert Grove Hughes (Kathleen Louise Prentiss), 2022 Brommer street, an 8 pound 1 ounce boy, David Michael. He is their first child.

BLACK — September 22

COMMUNITY HOSPITAL

FRANCIS—April 22 at 5:13 a.m. to Mr. and Mrs. Robert Claydon Francis (Kathy Louise Prentiss), 222 Navarra Drive, Scotts Valley, a 7-pound, 7-ounce boy, Damon Siddhartha.

BARE—April 25 at 7:32 p.m. to Mr.

Left: David Hughes, Daemon Francis, and Kathy Francis.

and then turned around and backed down and out.

Herbert Mullin, 1973:

[I told Mrs. Francis] telepathically that I wanted to kill Gianera and she said it was all right with her…

Mullin believed Jim Gianera was living in the house. The current resident, Kathy Francis, told him they had moved out in October 1972, and gave Mullin their new address as Kathy and her husband, Bob Francis, had been introduced to Mullin by Jim Gianera.

Mullin then drove to Gianera's house on Western Drive. Jim answered the door.

Herbert Mullin, 1973:

[I told him that I was] extremely upset over the amount of time I had wasted in my life and he curtly said he didn't know what I was talking about.

Mullin and Gianera continued to talk.

Herbert Mullin, 1973:

He no longer soothed me. […] I got the gun out and he turned and ran into the kitchen.
  He grabbed the refrigerator door and I shot him. He started to charge me and I fired again into his chest. He ran up the stairs and I fired and hit him twice in the back.

and rough. It is a rough road. The car came up about to the carport which was directly across from Kathy's house, saw that it was having trouble, didn't go any further and backed immediately back down…but very shortly afterwards then a man came up the road. […] I had the impression that he was about medium height with a fairly stocky build, black hair, with a dark brownish colored raincoat. I think he had on a pair of black shoes. It appeared that there might have been a tie because of the whiteness here and the dark knot, clean shaven…straight, normal haircut.

Thatcher Hall Clark, 1973:

He walked up the road, turned in there at the covered pathway, slipped a bit as he was going in. Kathy had come out to the porch before he got up to the house to see who it was, and then he walked through this pathway up to the edge of the porch and stood talking to her for maybe a minute or two,

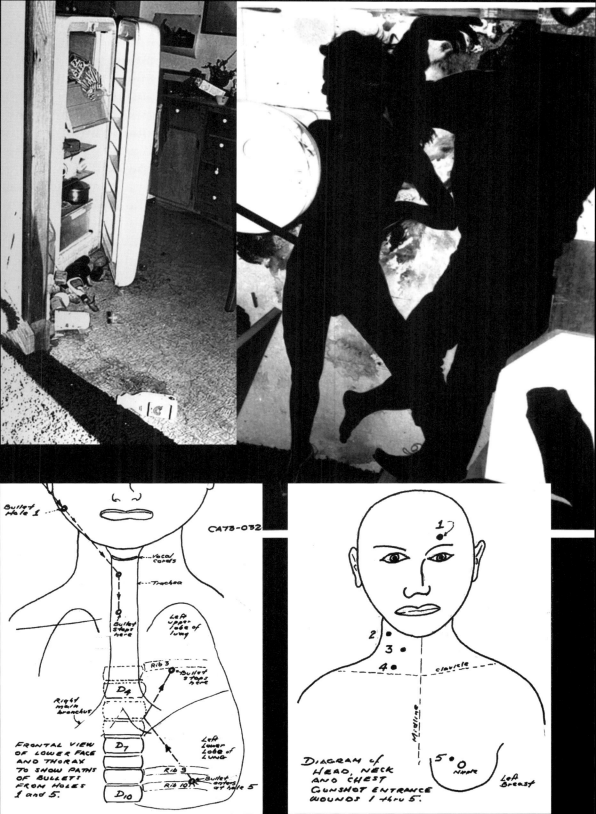

CA73-032

Bullet
Hole 1

Vocal
cords

Trachea

Bullet
stops
here

Left
upper
lobe of
lung

Rib 3

Bullet
stops
here

D4

Right
main
bronchus

D7

Left
lower
lobe of
lung

Rib 9

Rib 10

Bullet
enters
at hole 5

D10

FRONTAL VIEW
OF LOWER FACE
AND THORAX
TO SHOW PATHS
OF BULLETS
FROM HOLES
1 and 5.

1

2

3

4

clavicle

5

Midline

Nipple

Left
Breast

DIAGRAM of
HEAD, NECK
AND CHEST
GUNSHOT ENTRANCE
WOUNDS 1 thru 5.

CRIME SCENE SKETCH OF SECOND FLOOR

NOT TO SCALE

CASE #159880 SHERIDAN

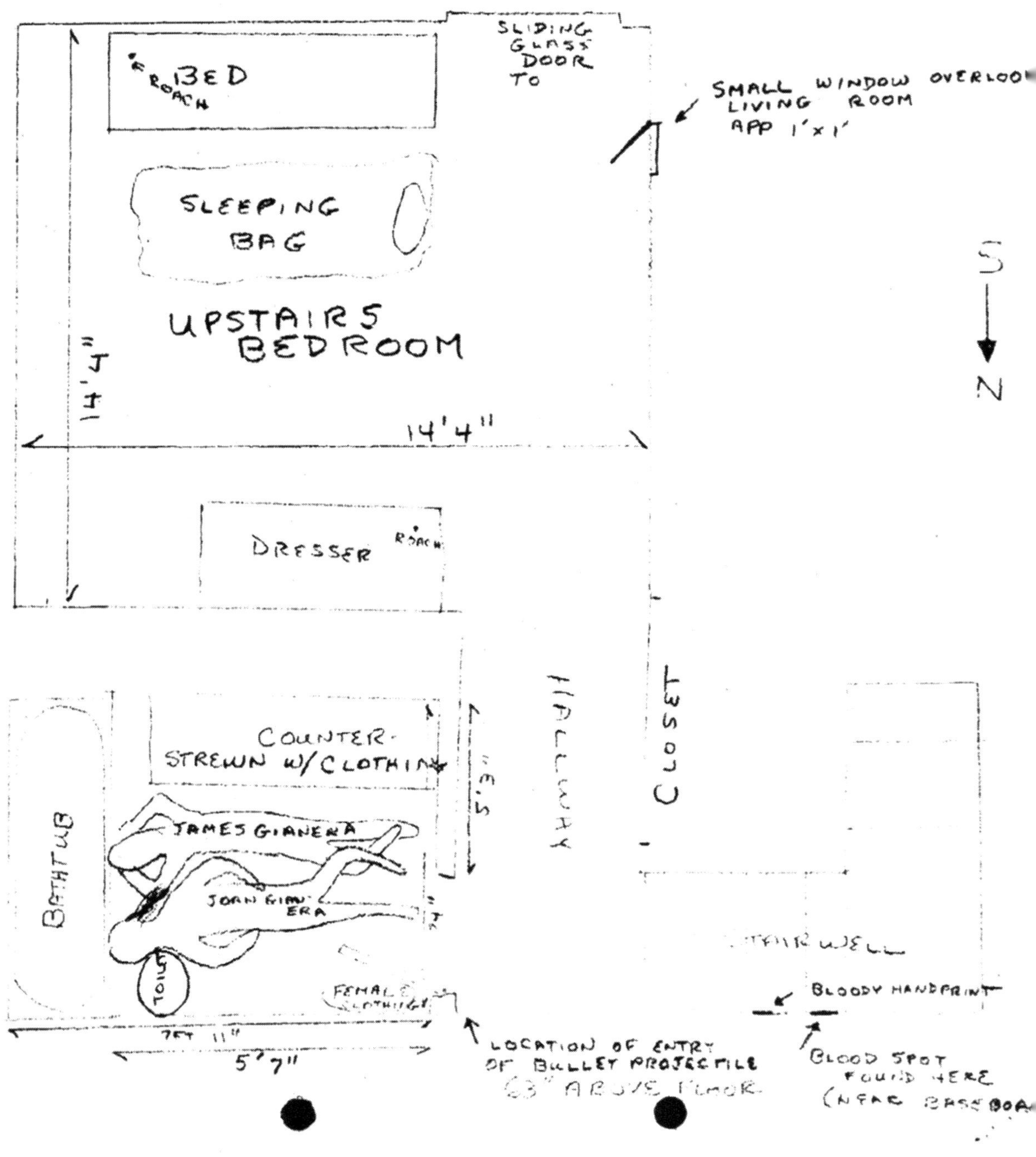
SLIDING GLASS DOOR TO
SMALL WINDOW OVERLOO
LIVING ROOM
APP 1'x1'
ROACH
BED
SLEEPING BAG
UPSTAIRS BEDROOM
14'4"
14'4"
DRESSER
ROACH
S
N
COUNTER- STREWN W/CLOTHING
5'3"
HALLWAY
CLOSET
BATHTUB
JAMES GIANERA
JOAN GIANERA
TOILET
FEMALE CLOTHING
STAIRWELL
BLOODY HANDPRINT
7FT 11"
5'7"
LOCATION OF ENTRY OF BULLET PROJECTILE
63" ABOVE FLOOR
BLOOD SPOT FOUND HERE
(NEAR BASEBOA

Gianera went down. Mullin looked up to see Joan Gianera on the landing at the top of the stairs.

Dr. Charles I. Morris, 1973:
It seemed quite obvious to him, he intimated, he'd better do away with her.

Herbert Mullin, 1973:
Without a thought, I shot her in the neck.

Mullin then reloaded his revolver.

Joan had moved into the bathroom.

Herbert Mullin, 1973:
She wanted to close the door.

Chris Cottle, 1973:
Did she say anything else to you?

Herbert Mullin, 1973:
No sir, I shot her in the forehead.

Mullin attempted to pick up his spent cartridge shells, but missed one. He then left the Gianeras.

Jim Gianera crawled into the bathroom and died next to Joan.

Mullin returned to the Francis cabin and entered without knocking.

Herbert Mullin, 1973:
Kathy said it would be all right to return and kill them [her and her two sons], so I did.

He said to Kathy Francis, "I would like a few words with you," and shot her in the head.

The boys were playing Chinese Checkers on a nearby bed. They said nothing and made no expression when they saw their mother shot.

Herbert Mullin, 1973:
After that I shot David in the head and then shot Damion [sic] in the head.

He then stabbed Kathy and the boys and left the scene.

The Francis' neighbor, Thatcher Hall Clark, left his house around nine o'clock in the morning. and returned between one thirty and two o'clock in the afternoon.

Thatcher Hall Clark, 1973:
One of the children that lives there went to the house to find out if Daemon was home to play with him, and there was no response to the knock at the door and he didn't go in.

Meanwhile, Eleanor Foster called the Gianera residence again in the afternoon and in the evening. No one answered the phone.

Eleanor Foster, 1973:
I assumed they must have gone out for dinner and stayed for a late evening.

Back on Branciforte Drive.

Steven Richard Houtz, 1973:
Bob Francis, her husband, who has many other times—well, three or four times before, called up late at night after being on a trip somewhere—they don't have a phone so we are the closest message phone, and since we know them well, we have this arrangement. I go up, one of us runs up the hill, drives up. I drove up that night.

Steven Richard Houtz, 1973:
The reason I went up there was because her husband had called up about a half hour before I went up there to say he wouldn't be home that night, but he would be home in the morning. Kathy worries—had worried before, and so he always calls when he wasn't going to be there, so that was the reason I went up there [...] around ten o'clock.

Previous and left: the Gianera crime scene.
Next page: David Hughes and Daemon Francis.
Next several pages: Francis crime scene.

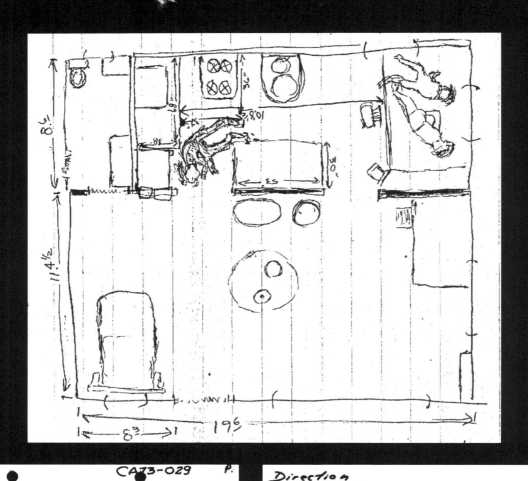

CA73-029   P.

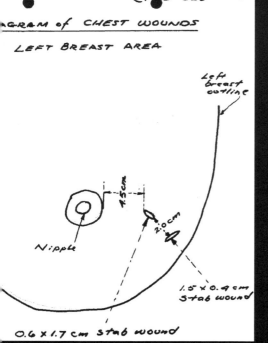

...GRAM of CHEST WOUNDS

LEFT BREAST AREA

Left
breast
outline

4.5cm

Nipple

2.0cm

1.5 x 0.4 cm
stab wound

0.6 x 1.7 cm stab wound

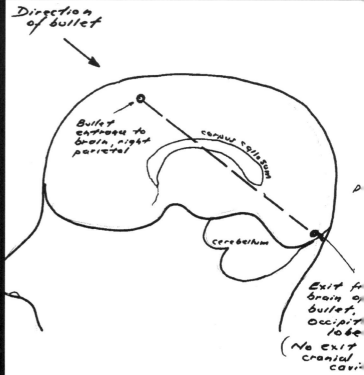

Direction
of bullet

Bullet
entrance to
brain, right
parietal

corpus callosum

cerebellum

Exit fr
brain o
bullet.
Occipit
lobe

(No exit
cranial
cavi

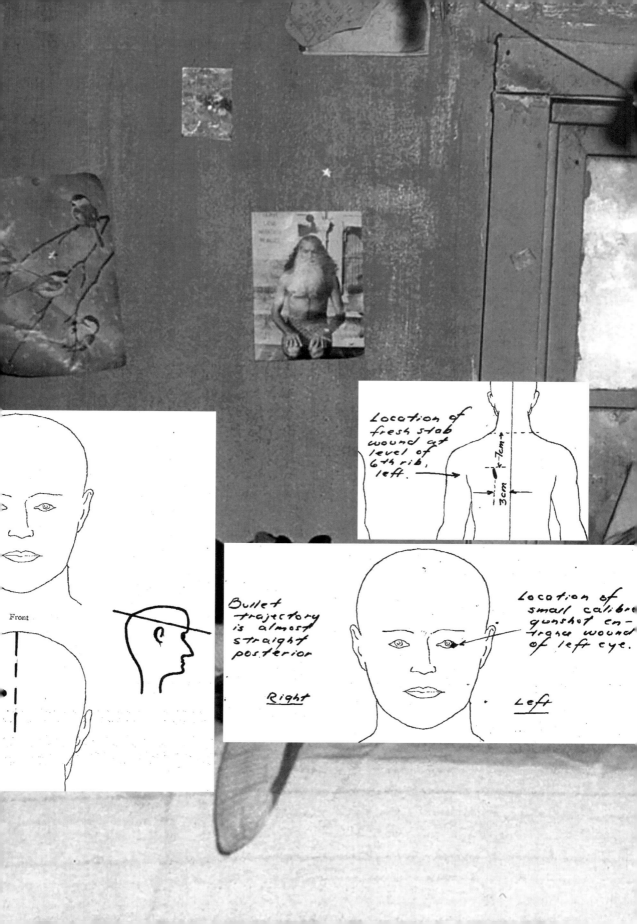

Location of
fresh stab
wound at
level of
6th rib,
left.

←7cm→

3cm

Front

Bullet
trajectory
is almost
straight
posterior

Right

Location of
small calibre
gunshot en-
trance wound
of left eye.

Left

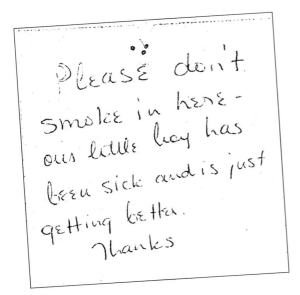

Please don't smoke in here – our little boy has been sick and is just getting better. Thanks

Steven Richard Houtz, 1973:

Well, first I called and knocked. Then I walked up to the door aways and called, and then I stuck my head around and saw Kathy lying on the floor directly in front of the door—not in front of the door, but in my line of sight. As you peer around the door, it looks directly into the kitchen…I went in… Went in and went through. There is two entrances. I went through the left entrance and saw both the boys lying on the bed. I shook them. I shook—I guess I shook David and that is when I saw the blood. I saw blood and what looked like scratch wounds to me or scratches, large scratches on the side of his body, and then I turned around and went down to where Kathy was and just touched her, and she was—had been dead for some time. She was cold and stiff.

Steven Richard Houtz, 1973:

I went outside, walked up the hill a little bit to the next house on the left where Thatcher Clark lives, and shouted out his name, was shouting out his name and he came outside. The exchange of words I really don't recall, but I wanted to know what had happened, and he didn't know what I was even talking about, and I told him.

Steven Richard Houtz then called the police.

Terry Medina, 2020:

I get called to The Mystery Spot. This is where the Francises live. Kathy Francis and the two kids. If you drive right past the front of The Mystery Spot. Straight up. There was a cabin up there…Wow, that crime scene has haunted me my whole life. It was in December. The Christmas tree was up.

I was at that crime scene, a long time hanging around those three bodies for a long, long time.

But it was our first crime scene of the whole thing. Before that it was body parts.

Chris Cottle, 2020:

I was there within a couple of hours after the killing. That was a blow. I still find that very upsetting. I was there at the Gianera scene as well. In the Francis killing, the two kids were playing Chinese Checkers on the bed. He just walked in and killed them.

The two boys were almost lying on top of each other, both face down. Their Chinese Checkers game still had the marbles on the board.

Mickey Aluffi, 2020:

The one that affected me was the one at at the Mystery Spot. It was the Francis family. He killed the wife and two kids. God, it was terrible. The two boys were on an old bunk bed. It was rickety and the two kids were up on the top when Mullin attacked them.

I went next door, up the road a bit and I talked to a guy by the name of Thatcher Clarke. He lived up there and he knew the Francis family. So I asked him, "Has anybody been around lately?"

He gave a description of this guy in like a suit, a dark blue suit, tie, white shirt, driving what he thought was like a 1958 Chevrolet. So, OK, well, that's something to go on anyway. And then it was shortly after that when the guy on Lighthouse Avenue was killed [Fred Perez] and the suspect was driving a '58 Chevrolet.

Terry Medina, 2020:
The guy that she was living with, I don't remember if they were married. He was a marijuana dealer. So we were thinking that there's this—there's a marijuana connection. Somebody went there to rip off either money or marijuana and wanted to get him. But he wasn't there. He was gone. We couldn't find him.

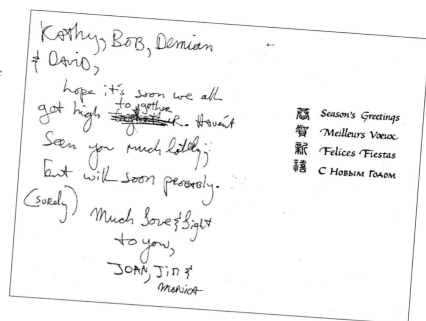

蒺 Season's Greetings
賀 Meilleurs Voeux
釈 Felices Fiestas
禧 С Новым Годом

Dr. William Henry Winchell, 1973:
I arrived at one o'clock in the morning on the 26 of January. At the time the bodies were all cold and they all had well developed rigor mortis.

Dr. Winchell conducted the autopsy on David Hughes.

Dr. William Henry Winchell, 1973:
The child died as a result of massive brain damage which was inflicted by a bullet wound to the head. The bullet impacted or struck the head above the right eye, went through the skull, traversed the brain and came to rest in the back of the head on the left side…I surrendered the bullet to a law enforcement officer at the scene, whose name I don't recall at this time.

David Hughes had also been stabbed.

Dr. William Henry Winchell, 1973:
There was an incised or stab wound of the chest, the back of the chest —to the back, I should say. This was located ten centimeters below the top of the shoulder just to the side of the spine or mid-line. Subsequent internal examination showed that the wound came out of the left pleural space, left pleural cavity higher than the entrance wound and to the left. It did not, however, contribute in any way to the child's death.

Dr. Hans H. Dibbern conducted the autopsy on Kathy Francis and determined the cause of death as—

Dr. Hans H. Dibbern, 1973:
Stab wounds to the chest and a small caliber gunshot wound to the head.

Kathy Francis also had a superficial knife wound on her back similar to the one on Joan Gianera.

Dr. Dibbern conducted the autopsy on four-year-old Daemon Francis and determined the cause of death as—

Dr. Hans H. Dibbern, 1973:
Stab wounds to the left posterior thorax and gunshot, small caliber gunshot wound to the head.

> *Left: Note from the Francis' front door.*
> *Above: Christmas card from the Gianeras to the Francis family.*

Richard Verbrugge, 2020:

You know, he shot one of the little boys [Daemon] right through the eye. Little kid's eye was open at the time.

We [District Attorney investigators] used to have to be at the autopsies for evidence purposes, if something was found. If the bullet was recovered it goes right to law enforcement.

It was easier for an investigator from the DA's Office to be there. You have to remember that the other law enforcement agencies were short handed at that time with all the other cases.

Eleanor Foster had been babysitting the Gianera's daughter, Monica, all night and all day. It was getting late.

Eleanor Foster, 1973:

I was very worried because Joan had always—would normally have called me in the evening and again in the morning on an occasion like that.

She went over to their house. She discovered their bodies and called the police.

Eleanor Foster, 1973:

When I found her, she had a relaxed, sweet expression on her face.

It was as if she had had time to compose herself, realizing her child, Monica, was safe with me.

James A. Sheridan (Santa Cruz City Police Officer), 1973:

I initially saw, I believe it was three persons with the front of the house in the doorway, who were later identified as Mr. Herbert Foster, I believe Mrs. Foster, and there was one other party whom I had Officer Brown, my partner, identify. I immediately proceeded into the living room initially since I saw bloody—blood drips on the wall to the lower floor of the residence leading up the stairs, on the wall towards the baseboard. At the bottom of the stairs I saw a .22 caliber shell,

which I believe was a .22 long rifle, situated approximately in the middle of the room in front of the door. I proceeded up the stairs and I saw in a bathroom that Joan Gianera was lying on her back. It would be right next to the toilet on the north wall of the bathroom, and to her left or on the south side of her was her husband face down.

I saw a large pool of blood in the vicinity of her head, but her head was cocked in such a way that I couldn't see any entry hole upon initially contacting her. She was covered with a towel, which I later ascertained that Mr. Foster did that. I removed the towel and saw that she was completely naked, and Mr. Gianera was lying face down.

There was a large pool of blood in the vicinity of his head. I could not identify his head at all. His head was directly down at that point. I didn't move bodies, but had reason to believe that a homicide had occurred and called the Detective Division by radio…

In the kitchen, the refrigerator, which was located immediately upon entering the kitchen on the left-hand side, was opened and much of its contents were dumped on the floor, including a milk bottle which had been covered in blood. It was obvious that a struggle had taken place. There was a chair in the middle of the living room which had been knocked backwards facing north, and that is approximately the only thing that I could notice to the point to be a struggle, but it was obvious that a struggle of some type had taken place within the kitchen and the living room area.

In addition to the .22 caliber shell, Officer Sheridan also found a single leather button.

Paul Dougherty, 2020:

We got bullets from the bodies and Mullin reloaded at the scene and there were cartridge cases. Or, one cartridge case, I can't remember. But that's how we eventually got him. The other scenes there were no cartridge cases. I figured out it was an RG revolver and I said, "You're looking for this

RG 14 revolver."

It was a cheap revolver. It was six or eight shots and I forgot how many this one had and it used .22 long rifle cartridges. I described it to Santa Cruz [Sheriff's Office].

Dr. Hans H. Dibbern conducted the autopsy on Joan and Jim Gianera

Jim Gianera died of —

Dr. Hans H. Dibbern, 1973:
Small caliber gunshot wounds to the left posterior chest.

Jim Gianera had been shot four times.

Joan Gianera died of—

Dr. Hans H. Dibbern, 1973:
Multiple small caliber gunshot wounds to the head, neck, and thorax.

Joan Gianera had been shot five times. She also had a superficial stab wound on her back.

Miriam Finnegan, 2021:
My dad [Santa Cruz Police Detective Dennis Finnegan] was working with Chuck Scherer

on the case. Dad was also a detective-photographer for a long time. There was a shooting range and a darkroom down in the basement of that old police department on Locust Street.

Anyway, Dad was up at Joan and Jim's house going through the crime scene and he found a button on the floor. I remember it was linked to Herbert Mullin's clothing.

Terry Medina, 2020:
I was at that [Francis] crime scene overnight. So the next day the Santa Cruz PD is at the Gianera scene up on Western Drive in Santa Cruz. Now, there's a tremendous amount of action at that location also. So they called me to that scene because we had been processing the Francis scene. They were trying to figure out if there was any connection.
I'll tell you, when I went to the Gianera scene, even though it was similar, with all the action. I did not, at that time, get the sense that it was the same killer. The Gianera's had been shot to death and the Francis kids had been knifed and butchered. I don't remember if she had been shot or stabbed. Remember, at that time, that connection between the Francises and the Gianeras had not been made yet.

Mickey Aluffi, 2020:

I don't remember how long it took for the Francis murders and the Gianera murders to be linked. Gianera was in the city [Santa Cruz Police Department jurisdiction]. So I mean, certainly we communicate a little bit, but that would be more like the DA's office, to make the connection. We were busier than hell. We had like twenty-seven, twenty-eight homicides in eight months.

Terry Medina, 2020:

We found out sometime later, I don't know how much later, that he [Mullin] knows that Gianera was linked to Kathy Francis' drug dealer husband [Bob Francis]. That guy knows Gianera. So he went there looking to find out where the Gianeras lived. He went and killed the Gianeras first and then went back to the Francises.

Mickey Aluffi, 2020:

Bob Francis, the father and the husband, wasn't around. So we thought, well, maybe he's a suspect. So what we did is we put out a BOL, be on the lookout for him. And we put a couple of deputies at the house. And by then, I'd been going for almost two days straight. I was exhausted. I had gone home

and I just crashed and it seemed like about eleven o'clock that I got a call that they got Francis. He showed up at the house. I had to go back into the office. Brad and I interviewed him and he had an alibi. He was in the Yuba City-Marysville area getting dope. Because he was a salesman. And so, he offered to take us up there to check out his alibi. So Brad, myself, and my brother [Santa Cruz Police Officer Bill Aluffi] went up there and nobody would talk to us because we're cops. So we had Francis flown up there. We picked him up and we had one motel room and all four of us were in there. Keep in mind, we don't know if he's telling us the truth or not.

Here's an interesting little side bit: when we turned the lights off to sleep, instinctively, all three of us took our guns out and put them underneath our pillows. We didn't need them. But, it was that or someone stayed awake.

The next day, he took us to some people that verified his alibi that he was up there. And one of them was an Asian lady, Chinese lady who was a heroin dealer. Well, there was a warrant out for her arrest. And so we had to promise her that we would not arrest her. So we did. And she verified it.

When the whole thing was over with, he [Bob Francis] wrote me a nice letter saying how he appreciated all the stuff that I did for him. And I understand he passed away several years ago.

Herbert Mullin, 1981:

I believe in reincarnation, you know, and those kids [Daemon and David], just think; they're out there somewhere, fishing.

EDMUND KEMPER

Allyn Kemper, 1973:

I had a talk with him [Kemper] around the first of February, maybe the end of January. It was after that girl who got thrown in the ocean. Because my husband and I were driving down the coast one day and I was thinking about it. I couldn't get it off my mind because I had been reading about it in the papers. And that really bothered me that somebody could have cut somebody up and thrown them in the ocean. To me that was just really, oh—for some reason it just kept bothering me and bothering me and bothering me and I couldn't get it off my mind as we drove down the coast. All of a sudden it just flashed in my mind that cat. When he cut off the head [see page 411] and it just flashed in my mind and I said, "Oh my, God."

And I looked at my husband and said, "You don't think he could have something to do with that, do you?"

And I told him about the cat and he looked at me and just said, "Well I don't know. That sounds pretty heavy."

I mean it's heavy just thinking there is somebody like that. But, still, it was really heavy on my chest and I couldn't, I just couldn't get it off my mind.

So one night, just to please my own curiosity, I went over there [inaudible] because we had an open communication then. I had a terrible curiosity about things anyway. I'm always asking questions and stuff. So I went over there, and I went over with a girlfriend. She was talking to my mom and I went into his bedroom and he was in there watching TV, laying on his bed watching his TV. I said, "Just between me and you, you didn't have anything to do with those murders did you?"

It was hard for me to even say it because you know, it was just kind of unrealistic to me. He kind of sat up and he said, "I figured you'd ask me about that. I thought you'd get suspicious about that."

I said, "I don't know, just for some reason."
I said, "Well you didn't, did you?"
He said, "No."

He just passed it off, but he said, "Mom was suspicious too. She mentioned it, so, don't even talk to her about it because it would just turn into a big mess."

I said, "I asked because I remembered the cat when we were driving down the coast. That's the only reason I got suspicious."

He kind of chuckled. He said, "I thought you'd probably ask me about that."

Then he kind of dropped it there. I said, "Well, it really bothers me. Just for my own curiosity, now you've been in Atascadero and you've been around people that do stuff like that. Where is a person's head at?"

I really wanted the detail and now that I think about it, I think, Oh, God, you know? But I asked him, "Where's a person's head at when they do something like that?"

He said, "People murder people. By the time you get to the second bone, you know, cutting and stuff."

I said, "Wouldn't something click in their mind? Wouldn't something happen where they realize, 'Oh, look what I'm doing' or something?"

He just said, "No."

He had answers to everything. I mean, he had it all [inaudible].

He said, "Well, when somebody does something like that, they usually are just trying to hide the evidence."

I said, "Oh."

I didn't really expect an answer.

ROSALIND THORPE AND ALICE LIU MONDAY, FEBRUARY 5, 1973

Peter Chang, 1973:
Kemper also will be charged with the murder of two UCSC co-eds, Rosalind Thorpe, 23, from Carmel and Alice Liu, 21, from Torrance. Both girls were picked up by Kemper on the UCSC campus sometime after eight thirty in the evening on February 5. They were shot to death minutes later. They were beheaded and taken the next day to Eden Canyon in Alameda County where their bodies were dumped. Their heads were then taken by Kemper to the Devil's Slide area north of Pacifica and dumped.

Alice Liu graduated from Torrance High School in 1969 where she participated in several extracurricular activities. She was a member of the Future Teachers Club, served as treasurer of the California Scholarship Federation, she was an officer in the Creative Writing Club, French Club, and International Council. She was in the senior play, a member of the Tartar Ladies organization, and danced in a Youth for Nixon recital during the 1968 presidential campaign.

Harold Klonecky (Principal of Torrance High School), 1973:
Alice was probably a sophomore when she was involved in the Indian Project. We brought a number of Papago Indian students here to Torrance High and she escorted them around. After they left she was active in collecting clothing and other items to send to them.

Alice Liu (writing on a scholarship counseling form):
I want to change the world through government. I want to be involved with the core of people, and I can do both by being a political science teacher.

Right out of high school, Alice Liu attended UC Irvine. In 1971 she transferred to UCSC as a junior.

James Liu (Alice Liu's father), 1973:
Originally she wanted to be a teacher but more recently she became interested in Ori-

ental studies.

James Armstrong (Torrance High political science teacher), 1973:

She was interested in people, cared about all kinds of people. She understood about coming from a good home like hers and going to a good school and the difference it makes for those who don't have the same advantages.

A death in these circumstances would be tragic enough with anyone, but with Alice you feel a real sense of loss and waste.

Rosalind Thorpe was born in Los Angeles County on September 30, 1949. Her family later moved to Carmel, CA. In a strange coincidence, the Thorpe family lived a few blocks over from Enos Fouratt, Herbert Mullin's uncle. Fouratt told law enforcement that despite reports in the newspaper that Rosalind Thorpe was not a regular hitchhiker, he saw her hitchhiking several times.

Wendy Thorpe (Sister of Rosalind Thorpe), 2020:

The age difference with Rosalind and I was nine to ten years. I was in middle school while she was in college. As much as you would think that I would know her on a day-to-day basis, I don't have as many memories as I would like. The memories are hazy. A lot of time has gone by. And a lot of the information was relayed from my parents to me, so the details aren't there.

On March 22, 1973, detectives interviewed Rosalind Thorpe's mother.

Duane Gull (Detective Sergeant), 1973:

Mrs. Thorpe related that Rosalind was a good student in school. She attended Monterey High School. Then spent one year at Monterey Peninsula College then transferred to the University of California Santa Cruz where she majored in psychology and had a minor in linguistics. Rosalind lived in the dormitory at Merrill College until this last quarter. During the summer Rosalind lived

at home and had a secretary job at Fort Ord for the past two summers.

Mrs. Thorpe stated that she had become very close to Rosalind over the past two years. Rosalind would bring her boyfriends to the house and introduce them to her parents. Mrs. Thorpe stated Rosalind didn't have any close relationships with men. Most were just casual friendships.

Rosalind made frequent trips home on weekends, usually hitchhiking. Both parents had warned her about the dangers in hitchhiking. Rosalind thought herself a good judge of character and though selective, was not afraid to hitch rides.

Wendy Thorpe, 2020:

I believe my sister and my father and myself had similar traits. Similar—I don't want to call them weaknesses. I would say, we could get hurt by society. We believed people behaved better. It was a grounding of, "You did this to me?"

My father was born in England. If he was alive he'd be one hundred. My mother would be ninety-eight. She was first generation American—her father was German and her mother was Austrian. They were a prominent family in Davenport, Iowa. My mother's father's brother was a U.S. Congressman. That sort of thing. The point is, my parents' manners and refinement and cultural awareness when I was growing up were quite different from the norm. We were always viewed as the proper people. Some thought it was arrogant, but it's not. It's "Please." "Excuse me." And being considerate of others. This has been a weakness for me and I believe it was for Rosalind as well. Rosalind had the highest IQ, at that time, ever

Previous pages: Rosalind Thorpe's senior picture, Carmel High School Class of 1967.
Alice Liu was voted "Most Talkative" in her senior year.
Left: Alice Liu's senior picture, Torrance High School Class of 1969.

seen at Carmel High School. She couldn't be valedictorian at that time because only men could be, so I think her boyfriend was valedictorian. The point is that the combination of that: European parents that were older than your peers' parents; being quite intelligent; and all this, well, it makes you oddball. I thought of my sister as attractive, but it also made us all very trusting. She was born in '49. By the way, her birthday is September 30, 1949. She was caught up in the '60s and the '70s. What I'm speculating is that she may have done things, drinking, drugs, hitchhiking, whatever was going on in order to fit in. In other words, that is what was going on, but it was not necessarily who she was. What this all means is that Ros, my father, myself, we are open-minded to our detriment.

Wendy Thorpe, 2020:
Our parents would take current events at the dinner table and have us argue both sides. So we'd be arguing sides we didn't even believe in. We were malleable, not gullible, but malleable. This can lead you into bad situations. I'm just going there, but I know my sister had drug involvement and we just didn't condemn things, we tried them. Hitchhiking, it was very prevalent. It was prevalent at Carmel High School, it was prevalent everywhere.

Wendy Thorpe, 2020:
I went up to the campus one time for a summer camp and I went on a picnic with Ros and I was a goody two-shoes but she asked if I wanted to do pot with her and her friends. She was just trying everything. That's the college experience, right?

Edmund Kemper, 1974:
My mother and I had had a real tiff. I was pissed. I told her I was going to a movie and I jumped up and went straight up to campus because it was still early.

I said the first girl that looks halfway decent that I pick up, I'm gonna blow her brains out. As it was, I improvised, it was two

in a perfect situation. That's the only reason there were two that night, just because they happened to be there.

Edmund Kemper, 1973:
I think it was around eight thirty, I'm not sure. Eight or eight thirty and I figured there'd be a lot of cars going up through there [UCSC], as they had had a seminar up there that night. I noticed, I always paid attention when I went in at night when the guards were at the kiosk, since I did have an "A" sticker, an "A" parking sticker on my Ford, which allowed me open access without suspicion. But I had a badly bashed left rear fender with a Mickey Mouse type taillight wired on, which is extremely noticeable and very easy to remember, but I watched him very closely as I passed by, not staring, you know, but watching, and he didn't even look. He saw the front of the car, the bumper, saw that "A" thing flash, and just looked right on to the next car and started waving him up to stop at the kiosk. He just waved me on by. So I knew he wouldn't ever be able to say what kind of car it was and I imagine they'd start looking for unmarked cars that went up there that didn't have tags. When I did get that tag from my mother, I did get it with the purpose of doing things like that. I told her I wanted to be able to go up there and park and go into the library and drive through, and things like that, and park where I want to.

Edmund Kemper, 1973:
I picked up Miss Thorpe first and I guess it was up around Merrill College, up towards the top and I had passed her actually. I think that was eight or eight thirty, something like that. I can't be really certain about the time. It may have been eight o'clock even. I didn't watch too closely, the time.

Apparently, this seminar was about in the middle and she had either decided she didn't like it or she had a class, I can't remember. But I had just passed her and as I was passing her I said, "Well, she's not too bad looking."

I'll at least talk to her. So I stopped and she hesitated. She was probably twenty yards behind the car and looked to the rear, and she saw the beat up car there and hesitated for a moment. Then I'm sure she saw the "A" tag and she ran right along and hopped in. I told her—she asked me where I was going, and that had always been a problem with me, 'cause when they ask me where I'm going and I say the wrong thing, they won't get in. If say I'm going down to Mission, and they say they're going up the other end of Mission or something like this, sometimes it's an excuse to not get in. Sometimes they're actually going the other way, and I'll blow an awful good opportunity 'cause I didn't think quick enough.

Edmund Kemper, 1973:
She was 5'6" I think and probably close to the weight of the Schall girl, about 150 pounds, something like that. She was very hard to handle because I still had problems with my arm, it was still in a cast.

Rosalind Thorpe got in the car with Kemper.

Edmund Kemper, 1973:
I started talking with her. Basically, she carried the conversation. She was very outgoing and I was just trying to be amicable and I was trying to think of what I was going to do. I had decided after we rode a little ways that was it. I was gonna get her definitely. And I had my little zapple through my body there that always confirmed it. I never had one of those where it didn't actually happen. Uh, uh, it's just where everything would click just right, circumstances were perfect. Nobody else was around, the guard didn't notice me coming in, nothing would look unusual going out, and she was not the least bit suspecting. And also it was somebody I didn't know in any way shape or form, uh, or knew anybody that I knew about. So those were certain things I held

as absolutes. One I had held as an absolute for a long time was don't ever do anything like that around the Santa Cruz area because that's too close to home, and having been in the past I was in, I would naturally come under suspicion. But then I started getting sicker and sicker later on and a little more and more careless in my approach in taking care of the things, and afterwards, which I'm sure got obvious because more and more evidence started popping up, in different forms.

Above: Rosalind Thorpe in the dark jacket, 1967.

Search teams failed to turn up clues to the disappearance of two missing coeds Wednesday, despite a sweep of the UCSC campus. Between 150 and 175 student volunteers turned out for the search. In photo above, Mike Hughes of the campus fire marshal's office, left, and Acting UCSC Police Chief John Durcan, in sergeant's coat, explain the search routine.

Edmund Kemper, 1973:
OK, what happened next is we were talking and she's more or less popping little questions here and there, talking along. I noticed Miss Liu standing on the side. She saw us coming, threw out a great big beautiful smile and stuck her thumb out very hopefully and you know, not a cheesecake type thing, but you know, throwing her best foot forward there. I figure later on what happened was that she looked, to me, from just different little details, that she was probably a careful hitchhiker and very good looking, built nicely and everything, and intelligent and moderate in her dress and everything, nothing outlandish. From some of her ID, a lot of friends, college and all that, stable background. I imagine she was a cautious hitchhiker and she always made sure of her ride before she got in, and we appeared to be a couple, and with that "A" tag on there, and a man and a woman, you know. So she didn't hesitate at all to hop in.

Edmund Kemper, 1973:
Well, I think she [Alice Liu] was 5'2", very nice build for her height. It surprised me, being an oriental that she was built like she was. Nothing fantastic I mean, but you know, very nice build. Anyway, she had long black hair, rather coarse, and very square sort of a face rather than oval, very wide, high cheekbones.

Chuck Scherer, 1973:
What about her clothing?

Edmund Kemper, 1973:
Her clothing, she had I think, desert type boot things, sand shoe goodies, suede col-

276

ored. The pants were Levi's bell bottoms, she had a brown wide belt on, and the pants and belt were very stylish, laying nicely right around the hips. Not trying to be funny or anything, but that's something that appealed to me immediately. She had a very short coat on and this was noticeable as she carried her bag up in front of her. It was slightly pulled up and she had on a bra, a supporting bra to accentuate her figure. She had on a light blue turtleneck sweater that had a zipper in the back up to the top of the neck, and she had on, like I said, this old gray-colored pea coat, and she had bright red socks on.

Edmund Kemper, 1973:
I stopped in front of Liu's college, Kresge, somewhere out there, but it was farther down from where we picked up the other girl. We went over there to the front kiosk.

Edmund Kemper, 1973:
I passed the guard and made sure he didn't take special notice of us. I was sure he only noticed the girl in the front. Conservatively dressed in appearance, I mean with the dark interior of the car and everything. Both of us were in a stabilized mood sort of, just chatting as we went out. Miss Liu was quiet in the back, sitting in the back right behind Miss Thorpe. We started down around the first curve there, we went down a ways to where it straightens out and you can see the city and the lights, and I slowed down and remarked about the beautiful view and asked if she minded if I slowed down, and she said not at all, she was watching, and I looked back at Miss Liu and asked her the same question and she said no. But I got the impression from her she was just saying no because she was getting a ride, and didn't mind slowing down a little bit and look at the view. Discussed for maybe five or six seconds which were long because I knew there were no cars coming at that moment, and I didn't see any coming up, and I hesitated for several seconds because I was very scared really. I had never done something like that

before, where I just come out and shoot somebody, just right out in the blue. But I was mad that night.

Edmund Kemper, 1973:
Anyway, we slowed down there, almost to a stop, were just barely moving, and I had been moving my pistol from down below my leg in my lap, a solid black pistol, and black interior and it was dark inside so she couldn't see it, and I picked it up and had it on my lap talking with her. She's looking ahead talking and glancing, and I moved it up to the side like this, and I just picked it up and pulled the trigger 'cause I knew the minute I picked it up like that, the girl in the back was gonna see it and I didn't want any problems. So as soon as I picked it up, I hesitated maybe for a second at the very most and then pulled the trigger.

Chuck Scherer, 1973:
This is on the straight stretch, coming down from the campus, overlooking the city?

Edmund Kemper, 1973:
Right, that would be on the eastern side of the farthest eastern part of the campus. It's the only major straightaway there. It was halfway between the bottom of the hill and the kiosk, so I was confident there wouldn't be any noise heard. I had a blanket in the back folded up right in the back seat, and I had a large coat sitting there too, a green coat. There's some more evidence for you. There's a small blood stain on that green coat for you, inside the lining.

Chuck Scherer, 1973:
Was your car still moving when you shot her?

Edmund Kemper, 1973:
Very slowly, yeah, just barely moving, just like maybe a quarter of a mile an hour, almost to a stop. Like I didn't want the brake lights on in case somebody whisked around the corner 'cause that would be something

to stick in their memory.

Edmund Kemper, 1973:

Well, as I lifted the gun up, I heard a slight gasp in the back and I think possibly Miss Thorpe heard it because she just started to turn her head as I pulled the trigger. She instantly just fell over against the window.

Chuck Scherer, 1973:

Do you recall what portion of the head or body that the bullet went into?

Edmund Kemper, 1973:

Right square in the middle of the left side of the head. It was just above the ear, maybe an inch. But basically I was sizing up, looking at her head. She had a rather large forehead, or a high forehead, and I was imagining what her brain looked like from the side, and I just wanted to put it right in the middle of that. So it was above and a little bit behind the ear, or not actually above and behind the ear. I was centering on the temple, not aiming at it, but so it'd be a little back and above the temple. So it would be towards the front portion of the top of the ear, just above the hairline.

Chuck Scherer, 1973:

Did that bullet remain in the skull?

Edmund Kemper, 1973:

No, it did not exit through because she was right by the window. It was one of the first things I checked. What happened was, I fired and Miss Liu panicked and started covering her face up and that's why I cut her hands off 'cause she had four bullet holes in her hands, two in each hand. I had to fire through the hands, she was moving very quickly around and kind of down and into the corner and I missed twice. One just went through her hand, I guess. It went right in—embedded in the padding of the car. The next shot I fired went through one of her hands, the back of her hand, and hit her just right around the temple area on the right

side of her head, and had a glancing blow 'cause it took a long tearing cut in and went right along the bone. I'm sure it broke the top of the jawbone 'cause there were broken bones up in that area. It creased along there, came out, exited through the ear—remember the hole in the ear—and hit the same padded area as the first bullet. It hit at a glancing angle and it was flattened out, the bullet was. Hit in and ricocheted off of the inside, came back out, right in front of the cushion, hit the cushion, it bounced out onto the front floor mat and I found it there. That, I think, stunned her. She was making quite a bit of noise, no loud shrieks or screams but quite a bit of fuss there, and then as I fired a second time, it quieted down but she was still making noise, and her hands were starting to come down, and she was moving over a little bit, and I thought she was still going so I aimed carefully and fired. That was the bullet that would be in this area on the right front forehead. Just about the middle of the forehead.

Edmund Kemper, 1973:

I had to fire right-handed because of the cast. Or in both cases, I would have fired left-handed. Because it was awkward in both cases. That's why I had to move my arm up like this; to raise it. I had to turn around like this, so I was at a bad angle with her. I had bad shots the first two times.

The third shot I moved almost out of my hand and around to the correct angle.

Edmund Kemper, 1973:

The third shot, I was positive she was unconscious, but I didn't really think I needed to do that. She [Liu] was really slumped over in the seat. I mean she had scrunched way down in the seat and was only maybe two-thirds the height up of the seat. So her head was not visible above the cushion like it would normally be. So I just put the coat over her, grabbed the blanket and unfolded it enough—and I tried to push Miss Thorpe over down into the floorboard area, and she wouldn't budge. She was just sitting there, slumped over completely, and so finally, I just pulled her over sideways on the seat and put the blue velveteen sort of blanket over her and made sure it stayed below the level of the windows there and that it wasn't an obvious shape or anything. I kept it double thickness, and just opened it enough so it looked like a flat blue surface and started, and continued, right down the hill and never hit the brakes. Actually, maybe once or twice when I reached back. Right after I put the blanket over Miss Thorpe, a car came down, so I smoothly accelerated so there wouldn't be a blast of gas and a jerk or anything. So I'm sure to them, it appeared as if I was just cruising along. They came down behind us, and I came right down in front of the guard station at the bottom where the cars were parked and everything, and there were two guards standing right by the road out there having a little conversation. They were maybe twenty feet from the car, on their side of the car.

Chuck Scherer, 1973:
Liu was moaning or gasping?

Edmund Kemper, 1973:
Yeah, it was a sigh, a very strange sigh. It would start out very sharp, almost like a snuffle, and then it would taper off and a little bit more like a masculine sigh than a fine girl, petite type girl like she was. It wasn't low or anything, but it was very disconcerting and it was constant. After we stopped and went on down Bay, obviously, there was quite a bit of blood because of the wounds and there was blood from that last hole in the forehead.

Chuck Scherer, 1973:
Just a second, you made a stop where?

Edmund Kemper, 1973:
Right by the guards. I made a stop right next to the guards, and they glanced over and were talking. I stopped right there at the stop sign and continued right down Bay.

Edmund Kemper, 1973:
I went straight down to Mission, turned right and headed out on [Highway] One, making sure I broke absolutely no rules and was doing my damnedest to look cool while I was freaking out about Alice Liu in the backseat there, which I'm sure she was unconscious. At first I didn't think so and I made a couple of loud statements and just continued right on through, so I knew she was unconscious. But the blood started running and started gurgling, and the sighing was still there. So as soon as I got out to the edge of town, I stepped on the gas and got the hell away from there and a little farther down the

road, where no cars were coming. I slowed down very slow, turned her head around to the side, and fired point blank at the side of her head. The reason she didn't go instantly like the Thorpe girl was that the automatic had a kind of quirky ramp and it would not, you couldn't load hollow points into the clip, or I would have always used those. I could only put one in the barrel and nine regular solid head long rifles in the clip, and everything I fired at Miss Liu was solids. So that one solid slug she got in there and she was doing the moaning. I got out of town and turned her

Above: A section of the College Seven (now Oakes College) newsletter from February 13, 1973.

279

head to the side and fired point blank and the flash was so great that—

Chuck Scherer, 1973:
About three to four inches when you say, "point blank?"

Edmund Kemper, 1973:
Yeah, I mean, I turned her around like this again so it was direct effort at the side of her head rather than right-handed at an angle. But it was point blank. I didn't hold it up to her head.

Chuck Scherer, 1973:
Was she moaning up until that point?

Edmund Kemper, 1973:
Yeah, and as I fired I could see some of the tissue come out. She stopped immediately, silence. Then I turned back around about two seconds later and it started up again and was really getting to me, so there's a place down the road. You know that popular beach area where the sign, like, it says Davenport and all that, Bonny Doon? A lot of people park there. Well, the next one back from that is the loop. Some people get on that and think they're going to Bonny Doon and it loops right back out.

Mickey Aluffi, 1973:
Laguna.

Edmund Kemper, 1973:
Yeah, I circled back down through that and went up on that little cul-de-sac up in there, parked—I had the parking lights on—jumped out and put both of them in the trunk.

Edmund Kemper, 1973:
I stopped at the Freddy's Fast Gas on the left there coming back into town. There was a Chinese girl pumping gas. I went into the restroom and cleaned off as much of the cast as I could 'cause it was a new cast, and a little bit off my pants. To myself, I called them

my murder clothes because it was these dark pants, they were dark blue denim western type pants with very, very light not-quite-white markings, but they were very dark. That was in case I got splattered, I didn't want to have a white or yellow shirt on. I used that on the first two girls. I think I used them with Aiko Koo and Cynthia Schall. I'm not sure, but in the vast majority of the cases. I used those specific pants and shirt. The shirt is still at home and I know it has some stains in it, they look more like rust stains, spots, than blood.

Edmund Kemper, 1973:
Well I stayed there quite a while at that station talking to the girl and acting nonchalant and calming down. Then I went home and talked to my mother a little, and crabbed about how I had fallen asleep in the movie. So I told her I fell asleep. I said, "How do you like that? You go and pay all that money and then fall asleep."

Then I said I'd go back and see it tomorrow night and that gives me an alibi. So the girl didn't see me go in there, it was a busy night. It was one of the first times it was showing down at the Aptos [theater]. So I went on in and acted nonchalant. Pretty soon I needed some cigarettes, so I told her and the way the house is laid out, there's a big picture window that's enclosed with curtains and the TV is right over here against the wall, and my mother sits right where that picture window is. All she'd have to do is get up and take a couple of steps and open the curtain in order to see if I'm still out there and she hasn't heard the car leave. But what I didn't realize was that she wouldn't hear that over the TV. So I just went out there, pulled the car around and opened the trunk, and this is the way the entire series happened. I took out that big knife and I cut both their heads off right out there on the street. It was maybe ten o'clock at night or possibly eleven. But that's where I did that because of the blood problem. Because they both had bled very badly in the trunk during the

MERRILL STUDENT NEWSLETTER

February 14, 1973

VERY IMPORTANT: SEARCH FOR MISSING GIRLS

There will be a search conducted in the woods above the campus today in hopes of finding some clues to the whereabouts of two UCSC students missing since Feb. 5. Student volunteers are needed to help conduct the search. Interested students should meet at the Field House at noon today for a half-hour briefing prior to the search. Students are warned that there is a lot of poison oak in the area, so dress accordingly. Sgt. John Durkin of the Campus Police will be conducting the search.

The two girls (Rosiland Thorpe of Merrill and Alice Liu of Kresge) both disappeared on February 5, at different times.

—Dan Borenstein

MARCUM CALLS MEETING ON SECURITY

Provost John Marcum called a meeting of Merrill students last Thursday, in order to discuss the problem of security in the Merrill community. Among the problems which have faced the community recently are the two missing UCSC students and the incident on the fifth floor of A-dorm last Tuesday night. The lack of community organization, Marcum feels, can leave the community open to the dangers of poor communication, false rumors, and the lack of togetherness in emergency situations.

The idea is not to scare the students, not to stifle communication, but rather to avoid spreading false rumors. Marcum, in a conversation with me on Friday, supported the Newsletter as an attempt to inform the Merrill Community and, hopefully, to bring it closer together.

The Provost asked students not to walk around alone at night, and not to hitchhike; if you must hitch, do it in pairs. Most important: If you leave campus for any extended length of time, inform several people of your whereabouts to avoid unnecessary panic.

—Dan Borenstein

EDITOR'S NOTE

The Newsletter, which will hopefully be coming out each Wednesday, is for communication of student concerns and events. All articles should be received no later than Monday's mail. The Newsletter box number is 782. People who are seriously interested in working on the staff will be greatly appreciated. Also, feel free to submit any comments or suggestions. Because of the committee introductions this first issue is quite long; please don't let this discourage you from reading it in total.

Thank you to the people who have helped me compile the Newsletter over the past weeks, and to those of you who have submitted articles.

—Dan Borenstein

COLLEGE NIGHT

The next Merrill College Night will be Feb. 28, featuring Mike and Alice Seeger.

time of riding around and sitting at that gas station and going home. It was getting all over everything. Yeah, I did that. I removed their heads and, uh, I went down and got my cigarettes at this little bar down by Seacliff, walked back out, got in the car, drove home, went back in the house, watched TV, and went to bed.

On February 6, the body of Ida Stein was found in her bathtub. She had been raped and strangled a few days before. The killer was a sixteen-year-old boy named Wilfried Willy Brown. Brown lived at Gene Dawson's Drug Abuse Preventive Center (DAPC) and had been selling soap door to door for a DAPC fundraiser. Stein invited Brown into her home and gave him cookies and coffee. She asked if they could pray together. While she was praying Brown attacked.

Wilfried Willie Brown was later sentenced to life in prison for the crime.

Edmund Kemper, 1973:
It was the next day, I think about ten or eleven in the morning, that I started the process.

Edmund Kemper, 1973:
And their clothing had entire—all their clothing was drenched with blood like sponges and there was a tremendous amount of it. It had surprised me at the large quantities. And, oh, anyway, uh, that next day I took Miss Liu out of the trunk and into the house. Just carried her right in through the back there 'cause I knew the old biddy in the back there never was out in the rain so I just wandered on in there and committed this act and, uh, which actually was rather difficult. And actually I think that being the last time I did anything like that, it was rather distasteful. I guess maybe the first time I did something like that there was a little bit of a charge you know. But that time.

Chuck Scherer, 1973:
Did you immediately attempt to have sexual relations with her?

Edmund Kemper, 1973:
Yeah.

Chuck Scherer, 1973:
Did you wash her up or anything beforehand?

Edmund Kemper, 1973:
A little bit with a little rag or something or a dish towel or a washcloth or something. But there wasn't too much there. She was on top and to the back [of the trunk].

Chuck Scherer, 1973:
Whereabouts in the house did you have this act?

Edmund Kemper, 1973:
In the bedroom. I was very careful though about any blood stains or anything like that.

Chuck Scherer, 1973:
Whereabouts in the bedroom?

Edmund Kemper, 1973:
It was on the floor. [...] There aren't any blood or blood related stains on the bed at all. I bleed from little zits and things on me, and there's a stain on the white pad that I think is a baby stain.

Chuck Scherer, 1973:
All right, these sexual acts took place on the floor?

Edmund Kemper, 1973:
Yeah.

Chuck Scherer, 1973:
All right, she still had her hands at this time, is that correct?

Edmund Kemper, 1973:
Yeah. That was one of the last things I did after she was back in the car. It was an after-

thought.

Chuck Scherer, 1973:
Now, she was stripped nude and you took her clothes out to the car, was this before or after the sexual act?

Edmund Kemper, 1973:
After. After the sexual act.

Chuck Scherer, 1973:
Now you said you washed her to where it would not look like there was any sexual—how did you do this?

Edmund Kemper, 1973:
Internal. With I think it was with, uh, well with a paper towel napkin-type thing with some Kleenex type napkins, facial towels, and there was quite a bit of material there. And she was—she was built, her vaginal area was built a little differently than most girls I've seen. It seemed a little bit lower, and it was, the bone, I don't know what bone that is, above, it's part of the bottom of the pelvis bone, it was very, very formidable there. It was very definite and, uh, like I said it was a rather difficult position. Anyway, I more or less poured it out as I picked her up. It ran, a lot of it ran out and I just cleaned the rest of it out with wet, with wet cloths. Then I disposed of them but I was very careful, you know.

Chuck Scherer, 1973:
Now these two acts that you've had with these girls, did you strip down yourself?

Edmund Kemper, 1973:
Ummmm, I think I did. I changed my clothes while I was at it too. I had the clothes

from the night before on and they were formidably stained on the pants from that night before because Miss Liu was rather, uh, was quite bloody in the back seat there. It was when I removed her from the car I got stains all over the side.

Edmund Kemper, 1973:
I cleaned her up. I carried her back out and there was a party going on upstairs. And I'm parked right under—

Chuck Scherer, 1973:
What time of day or night was this?

Edmund Kemper, 1973:
Oh, this was maybe two in the afternoon. One or two in the afternoon.

Chuck Scherer, 1973:
Did you have her wrapped in anything?

Edmund Kemper, 1973:
I think very casually in a blanket or something very small 'cause her legs were hanging out. I was carrying her like a mannequin sort of. She was very lightweight, I just wandered right out there with her and put her in the trunk right under the window. That's one thing that amazes me about society, that is that you can do damn near anything and nobody's gonna say anything or notice. I don't think they noticed. If they had, that would have been it.

Chuck Scherer, 1973:
All right, then you got her back in the car, then what happened?

Edmund Kemper, 1973:
That's when I removed the hands. I noticed them especially then.

Chuck Scherer, 1973:
At two o'clock in the afternoon?

Edmund Kemper, 1973:
Yeah. I had a red tub, sort of like a dishwashing plastic dishpan, and I placed the heads and hands in there in the corner in the trunk away from everything else.

Edmund Kemper, 1973:
I went up and visited that friend, a good friend of mine up there that lived in the same neighborhood as I did when I worked with the state, and I dropped by and I was fairly agitated that night and she noticed it. I was kidding around a lot and was very nervous. My stomach was killing me. I think I'm developing ulcers because of all this. Not so much now, but I was in a great tension whenever something like that was happening, especially people in the trunk and having to dispose. I'd get close to the point of panic until it was done. Then I would just completely relax.

Edmund Kemper, 1973:
I decided to get rid of them up in the bay area because you—Miss Schall had been from Cabrillo and I figured these girls were from the university and as far as the authorities knew, the first two could possibly have been killed in Santa Cruz too, and I wanted to distract the heat away from Santa Cruz. So I figured I know both areas well and the authorities wouldn't necessarily know that I know the bay area well because the job that I do entails extensive travel through those areas. [Inaudible] but I had been up both roads previously. Especially like with the disposal of Miss Koo's head and hands, and I knew that was an ideal place because the authorities would figure it was somebody that knew that particular area really well and knew that people at two o'clock in the morning would not be traveling that road at all. So they would think it would be at least somebody within five or ten miles of that area and that's what I wanted people to think.

Chuck Scherer, 1973:
All right, you drove up [Highway] 17 to Alameda.

Edmund Kemper, 1973:
Yup, I stopped by and saw my friend for a while [in Alameda], went out to dinner and then went out to a movie and I couldn't eat the dinner. [Inaudible] lobster tail too. I had about five bites out of it and that was it. I got in the car and just to kill time filled up the gas at the other Union Station, the one to the right of Park Street as you turn off the Park Street Bridge, by the police station. It was the one I went to with the first two girls for gas. I went to the other one with the trunk loaded and very low and very obvious, filled it half way up with gas, went out, parked right in front of the theater, went in, watched two movies. I wanted to be sure it was good and late. I arrived on the scene up at Eden Canyon Road about 2:00 a.m., in fact, I think it was very close to 2:00 a.m. when I actually [inaudible]. It was probably one thirty when I got up there and it was a good half hour or forty minutes before

I had the nerve to get rid of them. I went up and down the road looking for places. I had a big flashlight and was looking all over vetoing different spots for different reasons. Then I decided upon this one because of the steep grade down from the road and the fact that there were discarded items down there already and probably nobody would go by looking down there as a habit. It turned out that panned out. I dragged both bodies over to the edge and laid them horizontally and pushed and rolled them down. Unfortunately, Miss Liu, both of them, were in rather contorted positions because of their positions in the trunk. […]

Chuck Scherer, 1973:
Did anything happen while you were disposing of the bodies at that location?

Edmund Kemper, 1973:
No, wait a minute, yeah…as a matter of fact, yeah, when I was pulling Miss Thorpe out of the car, she fell on the back side and left a rather large deposit of excrement, and I'm sure some of it stayed because it was a rather good size discharge there. Then I just pulled her straight over to the edge. That's the only unusual thing I can think of. There were no cars the whole time I was down that road. If even one car had come by while I was down checking things out, I would have vetoed the whole place.

Kemper threw the women's heads and Liu's hands off a cliff in Pacifica.

Edmund Kemper:
These murders were coming to a head. I felt I was going to be caught pretty soon for the killing of these girls, or I was going to blow up and do something very open and get myself caught. […]

A long time ago I had thought about what I was going to do in the event of being caught for the other crimes, and the only choices I had seen open is being that I could just accept it and go to jail and let my mother carry the load…let the whole thing fall into her hands like happened last time with my grandparents…or I could take her life.

Wendy Thorpe, 2020:
I was fourteen when it happened. I don't know if my mother, who was brilliant with three English degrees, thought that it was psychologically better for me to not know any details. I do know that my late father had to identify my sister and in an incomplete way, if you get my drift. Yeah, not a full body.

And this is totally selfish of me to say this, but I was a freshman at Carmel High and I'd been plugged in socially but people backed off like it was contagious afterwards. One preacher's kid, who had apparently hung out with my sister, done drugs with my sister, said, "Ewww what does it feel like being the sister of a murder victim?"

Something like that.

People have said to me, "Well, it was Rosalind's fault. She had her thumb out."

HERBERT MULLIN

Jean Mullin, 1973:
That Friday [February 9] before [the murder of Fred Perez] was when he came to the house and put his arms around me and gave me a beautiful Valentine and a plant and we had lunch and he did some summary work, or resume work. That was it. My daughter and her children were coming for the weekend. I didn't mention it to him because I thought, well if he comes back up we'll be here with the kids, but I think, in a way, he felt a little sad being around his sister and her husband because they have everything going for them.

Either that day or the next, Mullin committed his next murder.

BRIAN SCOTT CARD, DAVID OLIKER, ROBERT SPECTOR, AND MARK DREIBELBIS SATURDAY, FEBRUARY 9/10, 1973

In mid-1972, Mark Dreibelbis was arrested for using and selling drugs in Fleetwood, Pennsylvania.

Earl Fox (Fleetwood, Pennsylvania Chief of Police), 1973:
We took enough [marijuana, hashish, and amphetamines] out of that boy's bedroom to fill a station wagon. He was dealing on a substantial level.

The night before his trial, Mark Dreibelbis fled and headed west.

Lothair Dreibelbis (Father of Mark Dreibelbis), 1973:
We looked everywhere. We asked everywhere.

Lothair Dreibelbis, 1973:
I was told by his friends that he was going under the name of Mark Johnson, and that he was living in a lean-to in the Santa Cruz area.

Lothair Dreibelbis had been employed as Fleetwood, Pennsylvania's Police Chief in the 1950s.

Lothair Dreibelbis, 1973:
I don't think he was part of any drug subculture. The deputies out there told me last night that it was just one of those unfortunate things that could happen to anybody. This guy, the suspect, was a maniac with tattoos on his belly.

David Oliker was a student at Valley Junior College in Van Nuys. He majored in English. Oliker's father was a contractor and his mother worked at the Mark Taper Forum of the Music Center as a director of special programs. She is now an author.

Ditta Oliker (David Oliker's mother), 1973:
The moment there's a kid with long hair backpacking, he's a hippie.

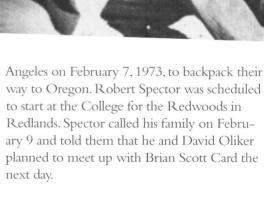

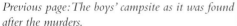

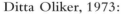

Previous page: The boys' campsite as it was found after the murders.
Above: Mark Dreibelbis.
Right: Robert Spector and David Oliker.
Far Right: Brian Scott Card.

Ditta Oliker, 1973:
You spend seventeen, eighteen, ninteen years supporting them, giving them love, with only one objective—to see them reach a point where they're free. The agony they suffer when you hold on to them, even when you protect them, is worse than letting go. Life's a gamble: you either live it or you don't.

Robert Spector's father was a clinical psychologist and his mother was a social worker.

David Oliker and Robert Spector left Los Angeles on February 7, 1973, to backpack their way to Oregon. Robert Spector was scheduled to start at the College for the Redwoods in Redlands. Spector called his family on February 9 and told them that he and David Oliker planned to meet up with Brian Scott Card the next day.

Jeffrey Devin Card (brother of Brian Scott Card), 1973:
He was living in a portion of the Henry Cowell State Park on the north boundary by Highway 9. It was an unused area. No peo-

When Brian Card was still alive. . .

One of the four slain men found last Saturday in the plastic-covered tent structure below Felton was Brian Scott Card, 19.

A bit of insight can be gleaned from an incident that took place January 30 at the Safeway store in Felton. The conversation was taken from County Sheriff's Department records by The Valley Press and published in the February 7 issue of this newspaper.

Card had been booked on charges of burglary after confessing to shoplifting $3.76 in items from the store.

Card hitchhiked to the store, according to the report. Store manager Michael L. Cronk made the citizen's arrest and called the sheriff's deputies. The conversation between Card and the reporting deputy follows:

Deputy: "Did you take these things out of the store without paying for them?"
Card: "Yes I'm guilty I guess."
Deputy: "Did you know you were stealing?"
Card: "Yes."
Deputy: "Who do you live with?"
Card: "By myself."
Deputy: "Do you have a job?"
Card: "No"
Deputy: "How do you live? How do you eat?"
Card: "I'm getting food stamps pretty soon."
Deputy: "Did you ever steal from this store before?"
Card: "Yeah, I put something in my pocket once before."
Deputy: "When you were hitchhiking to Felton, did you plan on coming into this store to steal these groceries?"
Card: "Yes"

Questioned by The VP this week, Cronk said Card had long hair, stood about six feet tall and was slender in build.

When he was being taken from the store by the deputies, Cronk added he remembered Card broke down and cried, saying he was sorry for taking the items.

ple ever came up there for any recreational purposes.

The number of people living there had changed off and on. At one time there had been quite a few.

I had lived up there for a great deal of time.

Jeffrey Devin Card had moved out of the camp around the December 10.

Terry Medina, 2020:
There were four or five young people in a makeshift tent up in Henry Cowell Park, but not in the park itself, in a part of the park that is not meant for any visitors, not meant for anything. By the way the crow flies, it would have been a half or three quarters of a mile from Mullin's house.

Terry Medina, 1973:
It was approximately three miles south of Felton on the uphill side of Highway 9. It was a very remote area that vehicles could not get to. We walked approximately a third of a mile in a very wooded area where there

was a makeshift cabin built with branches and plastic sheets.

Terry Medina, 2020:

He [Mullin] knew that area. He walked that area all the time. He was always around there. Well, he comes upon this makeshift tent. It was actually pretty elaborate. There was a crawl space to get in. It was made out of wood branches, big branches, and it had a wooden floor. I can't remember if it was four or five guys living there. So anyway, Mullin comes upon these guys, and he had actually been watching them. He got pissed off at them for something, but these guys had like a little tunnel that you had to crawl into and then get up on a slightly elevated wood floor, and it was a big enough space for all of them to sleep in there.

Then outside the tent, you know, there was a big area where they had a fire and they cooked over the fire and stuff and a lot of

stuff. They'd been there for a while.

But Mullin hated them being there. He had kind of kept an eye on them for a while, and he saw that they had a .22 rifle at that camp.

Jeffrey Devin Card, 1973:

There had been another campsite of people and they had obtained a small .22 rifle, and it had been up there, but they had never used it. I think maybe they used to shoot, target shoot at cans or something else, but they had never used it, but there was one up there. I don't know what happened to it.

Terry Medina, 2020:

If I remember correctly, they thought that they were going to start hunting small game for food and shit. I don't think they ever did. So the rifle was outside the tent. Mullin gets the rifle. He crawls into the crawlspace, and there is no way for them to get out. They would have to go through him or they would have to try to claw their way through this real heavy Visqueen.

Above left: David Oliker.
Above right: Robert Spector.

Mullin later testified that he wasn't sure what day he murdered the boys. It was either February 9 or 10.

Herbert Mullin, 1981:
When I came upon the tent and saw them, the first thing that came into my mind was "Wow, human sacrifices."

Herb Mullin, 1973:
I came upon their house and I felt my father's presence. They invited me in but I didn't go in. I stayed in the doorway.

Herbert Mullin, 1981:
We sat down, they offered me some food, we talked. They told me where they were from, and told me how much fun they were having camping. But there were two dialogs, the external one and the internal one. I don't know how to explain it, but I've talked to Vietnam vets who say you get this sixth sense in wartime. That's what it was like. And the internal dialogue told me they wanted me to kill them. Something told me if those four didn't die, then four others would.

Herbert Mullin, 1973:
[It was] the first time I had ever spoken at great length to persons who were going to give themselves up by a sacrifice.

He told the boys telepathically—

Herbert Mullin, 1973:
If I don't kill you, four other guys will have to die.

Mullin said that the four boys telepathically responded to him—

Herbert Mullin, 1973:
"Go ahead and kill us, man, go right ahead. Please don't back out of it, don't get scared, man. We're not scared."

Herbert Mullin, 1973:
I told them they would have to move from the government property...they were all in a sitting position and it was over in a few seconds.

Mullin did take the boys' rifle, but he used his

.22 pistol to commit the murders.

Dr. Jean Everice Carter conducted the autopsies on all four boys on February 19, 1973, at Smith's Mortuary.

Mark Johnson, also known as Mark Dreibelbis—

Dr. Jean Everice Carter, 1973:
Gunshot wound to the head…small caliber probably. […] It was both an entrance and an exit wound.

There was a gunshot wound in the right arm along the medial aspect, and a missile was recovered from that wound.

David Oliker—

Dr. Jean Everice Carter, 1973:
Brain damage due to a gunshot wound to the head. […]

He had a through and through gunshot wound of the palm or surface of the right hand.

Robert M. Spector—

Dr. Jean Everice Carter, 1973:
Brain damage due to gunshot wound of the head.

Robert M. Spector also had a gunshot wound to his right thigh, which went through.

Brian S. Card—

Dr. Jean Everice Carter, 1973:
Same case: brain damage due to a gunshot wound of the head. […]

He was shot twice. […] There was a gunshot wound of the nose, and small fragments were recovered from that gunshot wound. The main missile was not recovered. There was another gunshot wound to the head proper, cranial vault, and a missile was recovered from that wound.

Mullin searched the boys' wallets and found $21. He used the money to buy a tune-up kit for his car. He also took their .22 rifle.

On Sunday, February 11, 1973, the decomposed body of Mary Guilfoyle was found in Bonny Doon.

The Oliker and Spector families quickly set up a scholarship fund in their boys' names. The David Oliker scholarship was created to assist young writers.

Fred Spector (Robert Spector's uncle), 1973:
Rob had $500 in his bank account—I believe it was to be used for his college education—and it will go into the fund.

He was a lover of nature. He wanted to become a forest ranger. The fund will be used to plant trees, or some similar type of ecology work.

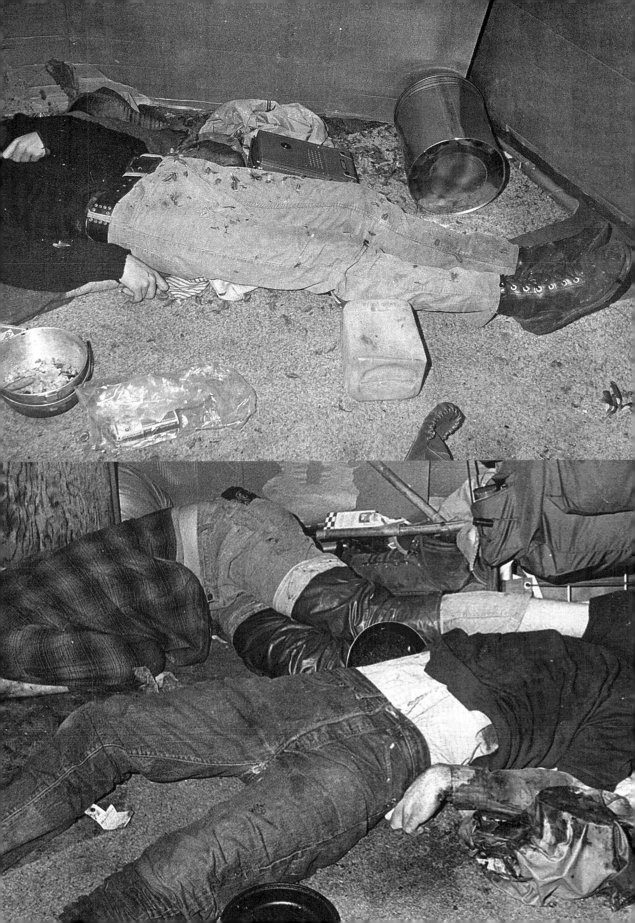

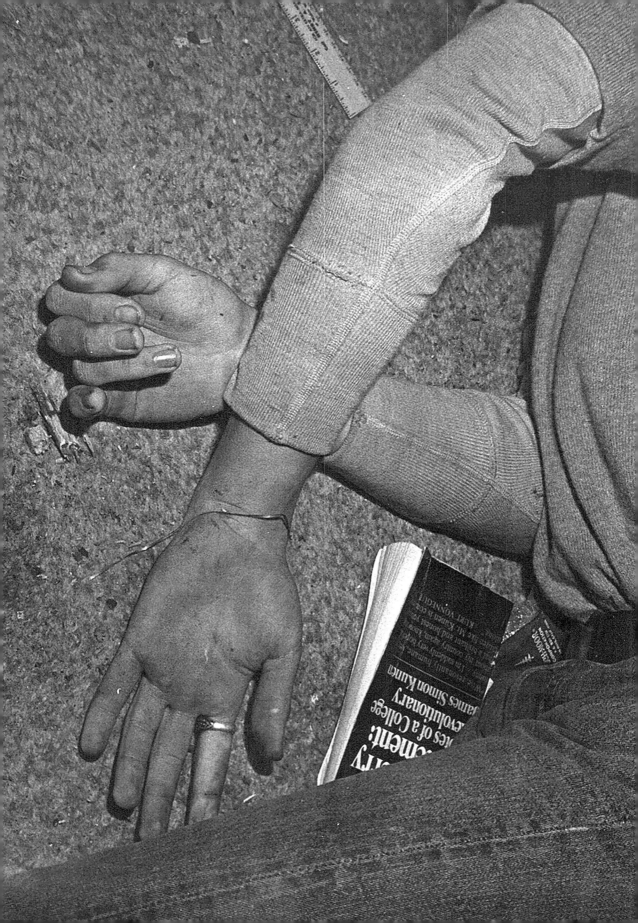

FRED PEREZ TUESDAY, FEBRUARY 13, 1973

Terry Medina, 2020:
So what ultimately brings the end to Mullin is when he kills the guy up on Santa Cruz Avenue by West Cliff Drive, Fred Perez. Fred Perez was a beloved old guy in Santa Cruz. Everybody knew him.

John Perez (Son of Fred Perez), 2020:
It's pronounced like P-E-A-R-I-S. Perez. We had Mullin, Kemper, and Frazier running around here all at the same time. Kemper was brilliant without a brain in his head. He said, "If I get out, I'll keep on killing."

Mullin was trying to stop earthquakes and Frazier just committed suicide.

John Perez, 2020:
On my dad's side, we've been in Santa Cruz since 1796. My mom's family is short timers, they were from Maine and didn't get here until 1850.

From 1796 to about 1817 we were slave labor for the Roman Catholic Church at the mission. We got out of that and moved to Branciforte about 1820.

John Perez, 2020:
My great-grandfather sold fish. In Santa Cruz it was all Italian fishermen from Genoa, Italy. In Monterey it was Sicilian. In 1870 the first Stagnaro came to Santa Cruz. They're a big family here, three different families really. The first one came in 1870 and my great-grandfather hid him out on his ship because you couldn't legally get off a ship because of the gold rush.

They would fish and my grandfather would hand the fish out, "One for me. One for you. One for the boat." He owned the boat.

My great-grandfather bought property all over the Lighthouse Avenue area from Gharkey Street to Santa Cruz Street, going back probably a half mile or so. He bought that property around 1870.

John Perez, 2020:
My dad was born in March of 1900.

His mother died during childbirth when he was about a year and a half old. She and the baby died. He was raised by his aunt, his father's sister.

When he was twelve years old they put him to work. They gave him a horse and buggy and he'd work all week down on the wharf and then bring it to Capitola in his buggy. In 1912 he could make five or six dollars selling fish to tourists.

He worked with his stepfather and his other cousin, the son of his aunt. They called my dad Big Fred and his cousin was Little Fred. Well, Little Fred would get in trouble and my father would take a beating for it. Uncle Paul wasn't very big and he was going to give my father a beating, but he was fourteen or fifteen and he put a head on Uncle Paul. Then it got a little better for him.

Around that same time, he was fishing for sea bass with nets, and he had those hip boots on and fell off the

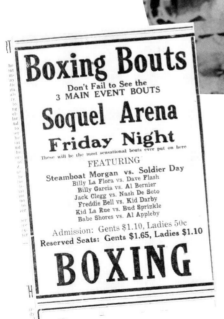

boat. He was barely able to get back in and he quit fishing. That's when he started working in the markets for his father and his grandfather and his couple of uncles. There was a fisherman's wharf alongside the wharf we have now. That one went in around 1912 and there were two wharves.

At the end of Bay Street, Henry Cowell had another wharf out there where they shipped the lime out.

Perez attended Santa Cruz High School and in 1917 entered the Marine Corps. Legend says that he was the first American Marine to enter The Forbidden City.

John Perez, 2020:
In about 1917 they had the same, like they have today where everybody is dying, but then it was the flu. Well World War I came around and he joined the Marine Corps, but the Marine Corps up in Vallejo were all dying up there. You had to be crazy to be a Marine. But they sent him overseas to China with the Legation Guard. They were Italians, Japanese, English, and all the other legations against Germany. They were in Beijing showing their colors. During World War I with the Marines, if you put in two years, it counted for three. There were no enemies, but the Chinese would shoot the Chinese guards off the wall.

The Japanese hadn't seen American rifles and were surprised when the Marines could get off two to three rounds while they couldn't get off the trigger nearly as fast on the firing range.

John Perez, 2020:

He was a World War I veteran. He was a Marine but he never considered himself a veteran of foreign wars. He never joined the American Legion because he was stationed in China, Japan, and the Philippines. He went in as a buck private, was in for eighteen months, and got out as a buck private. One of the grandsons of one of the presidents was a second lieutenant in the Marine Corps. He was stationed in the Philippines with my dad. I can't, for the life of me, remember which president it was.

John Perez, 2020:

When he came back to the states, he went to work up in San Francisco on the Fisherman's Wharf for a man named Alex Paladini. The Paladini's were big names up in San Francisco. Alex Paladini had the habit when he'd get pissed off and was going to fire someone, he'd put a head on them. Well, my father had done something, but he was a trained boxer. He wasn't that big, but he had learned how to box in the Marine Corps. And he put a head on Alex Paladini. They were a big deal and everyone told my father, "Fred, you're going to have to leave San Francisco because no one can get by putting a head on Alex Paladini!"

So he came back to Santa Cruz.

Perez started boxing as an amateur under the name Freddie Bell.

Because Mullin was an amateur boxer as well, there has been speculation that he knew Perez or at least knew he was a boxer.

Herbert Mullin, 2020:

No. No, I did not know that [Perez was a boxer].

Perez became the middleweight champion of Central California and later became a licensed boxing judge.

John Perez, 2020:

My dad had thirty-four professional fights in Santa Cruz, Hollister, and Salinas. He wasn't good enough to go up to San Francisco, but he was in little fights around here. Six or seven round fights that paid ten or fifteen dollars. More if you won the fight.

They had a lot of kids that didn't know anything. They'd get them from Fort Ord and have twenty to thirty fights there at the Santa Cruz Civic Auditorium.

John Perez, 2020:

We moved around in the '20s and '30s. When the rent came due we'd move. From '28 to '34 we moved from Maple Street to Clifford to Second Street to Bay Street to another place on Bay. We moved to the center section of Gharkey and Lighthouse from '34 to '45. That was a clubhouse for a golf course that went up Bay Street. I don't know if it was a nine hole or eighteen golf course.

With the depression era going on, we had to come up with $25 a month with my two sisters, my brother, and myself. Six of us there. It was awfully tough sailing, but by the time of World War II it was all paid off. World War II gave us money. We did alright. My father worked hard. From Davenport to Boulder Creek, to the town with the cement ship, all the way up to Pescadero, those were his fish routes. It was a barter system with the fishermen, but then he sold the fish.

He still went out every once in a while. I remember he caught 200-300 pounds of salmon one time. Cut up his hands with that one.

He'd get his abalone by that lighthouse right at the edge of Santa Cruz, New Year's Island. Now it's called Ano Nuevo. He always got his abalone there to sell.

Davenport landing had silver smelt and pismo clams. Let me just say this, the limits weren't too well observed. My father would take a half a dozen kids with him and when the game warden would come he'd say, "Yeah, Mac, these kids are all good clammers."

In those days, the limit was fifteen clams. It was nothing for him to get seventy to eighty clams!

In 1969, Perez mostly retired from the fishing industry, but he still worked on Thursdays, delivering fish to the markets on the Santa Cruz Wharf. He told people he wanted to stay in touch with all his friends.

On Monday, February 12, 1973, Mullin ran into a friend from high school.

Jeff Esposito, 1973:
When I saw him that Monday, he talked to me about possibly going to Oakland and working for Kaiser as an engineer. We talked about our families. He didn't know my mother was sick at the time. He expressed his sympathy. I asked him about his family. He said they were fine. He seemed to be nervous about something.

Terry Medina, 2020:
Mullin told the psychiatrists, Lunde and Joel Fort, that he would get these telepathic messages from his father. The day he kills Perez, he gets his telepathic message, "We need you to bring home firewood and you better shoot somebody before you come home." And he is in possession of a .22 rifle at the time. You know where he got that rifle. But he's driving a 1958 Chevrolet station wagon, a Nomad Station wagon, and he had been out in the woods collecting wood to bring home. And he gets this telepathic message

DIAGRAM of ANTERIOR VIEW of CHEST,
SLIGHTLY RIGHT OBLIQUE, FOR BULLET PATH

CA73-052 -?-

A = BULLET ENTRANCE WOUND
B = BULLET ENTERS LUNG
C = BULLET MAKES 2 TEARS
    IN AORTA & SHATTERS
    LEFT CORONARY ARTERY AT BASE
D = BULLET LEAVES CHEST CAVITY
    AND LODGES IN MUSCLE POSTERIOR

from his father saying, "You've got to kill somebody."

So he finds himself up on West Cliff Drive and he turns down Santa Cruz Avenue, and he sees this old guy in the front yard.

Herbert Mullin, 1981:
I was getting these vibrations, like, "If you don't, you'll shame your parents. You've got to save the San Andreas fault."

The old man, he was raking up leaves in his front yard.

Terry Medina, 2020:
So he drives past the guy on the other side of the street, one house down the street on the opposite side.

He has a .22 rifle in the car. He opens the very back window of the Nomad. He kind of leans on the firewood and he fires one shot, hits Perez, and kills him.

John Perez, 2020:
He was killed in '73. He was filling in some holes after it rained and Mullin came along and stuck his .22 out the back of his car and shot him. It's funny, one shot right in the heart. Just a fabulous shot.

Joan Stagnaro (neighbor of Fred Perez), 1973:
Well, about eight o'clock I heard a cracking sound, a sharp cracking sound…a gunshot. […] I went out on my porch and looked around. […] Across the street on the left-hand side of the street, there was a blue and white station wagon with its motor running in front of my neighbor's driveway. […] There was a person in the front seat. […] On the driver's side. […] He had his—I shouldn't say he, but the

person had the back toward me and he was facing toward Lighthouse Avenue. […] He was just looking towards Lighthouse Avenue and then he turned around and drove the car towards Laguna Street, and I came back in my house, and then I looked towards Lighthouse towards the corner house down there and there was a person on the ground. Then I yelled to my two boys, "My God, somebody has been shot!"

And I ran and phoned the police.

Joan Stagnaro's two boys ran out of the house to the fallen Fred Perez. Another neighbor, Dennis Walter King, arrived at the fallen Fred Perez before the Stagnaro boys. Dennis Walter King was with Fred Perez when he died.

Joan Stagnaro relayed information about the car to the police.

Joan Stagnaro, 1973:
The white front—the white tire on the right side of the car had a worn out white wall on it, and it also had an STP sticker on the right front fender. Let's see. The back window also was pulled up and out.

At trial, Joan Stagnaro positively identified Herbert Mullin's car as the vehicle she saw that morning.

Mullin stopped in the nearby Mellis Market parking lot to cover his rifle's muzzle with a paper bag. The stop was brief and he quickly continued on his way towards Felton to deliver wood to his parents.

Herbert Mullin, 1981:
I didn't think that I'd be caught. I didn't think they wanted to catch me. I just didn't do too much thinking.

Sean Upton (Santa Cruz City Police Officer), 1973:

We had a shooting and the suspect vehicle was described as an older model, possibly Pontiac station wagon, white over blue with STP stickers on the right side of the door, right front side.

Well, I figured that the suspect vehicle, if he was heading out of town, would be heading out probably Mission Street east, as I had heard earlier in the morning that there had been slides up on Highway 1 in San Mateo County and I figured if the guy knew anything of what was going on, he would probably be heading out Mission Street, by the Mission Street by-pass, Chestnut Street. So I then placed my patrol vehicle in a position where I could observe the Mission Street by-pass at Chestnut Street.

Approximately, ten minutes after the BOL (Be On the Lookout) was put out, I observed a white over blue Chevrolet station wagon with STP stickers on the right front door.

It was making a left turn from mission onto Highway 1.

I radioed into our base station that I felt that I had a possible suspect vehicle in observation, gave my location and also the route which the suspect vehicle was taking, which at that time was north on Highway 1 heading towards River Street by-pass.

I came up behind the vehicle on Highway 1. It was making a left turn onto River Street onto Highway 9. I then asked for cover units, giving my location and stating that the vehicle was making a left turn onto Highway 9 from Highway 1. After the vehicle made the left-hand turn, I applied lights and siren, pulled the vehicle over to the side of the road on River Street near Coral.

Using the PA megaphone, I advised the subject in the vehicle that this was a felony stop, to place his hands on the windshield, not make any overt moves. At the time I made the stop, I had three other units there to cover me when I made the initial stop, and they placed themselves in a position where they could cover the suspect in the vehicle.

After I made sure that I was covered, I went to the vehicle and took the suspect out of the vehicle, putting him on his knees in a search position, searched him. Then I placed the handcuffs on him, took him back to my vehicle, placed him in the back of my patrol vehicle.

Mullin only said one thing to Officer Upton—

Herbert Mullin, 1973:

I want you to observe my constitutional rights.

Sean Upton, 1973:

I observed a .22 long rifle with the muzzle pointing towards the driver's side door on the floorboards by the front driver's seat.

A brown paper bag covered the muzzle.

Upton called for backup. Paul Dougherty, the head criminalist from the San Mateo Crime Lab, was called in.

Paul Dougherty, 1973:

Upon arrival at the car, I looked in the interior before the car was opened and I noticed a brown zipper bag, commonly referred to as an AWOL bag. We then opened the car and removed this AWOL bag. It had various contents, more specifically, a home-made white bag made out of a kind of sheeting material. This bag was opened and in this bag I found a fully loaded revolver, .22 caliber.

An RG 14 made by RG Industries. There was a box of .22 caliber long rifle ammunition, Remington manufacture, also contained within the bag, as well as a plastic packet of .22 cartridge cases.

They were all of Remington manufacture.

The box held eighteen .22 caliber long rifle rounds. The box was held together by masking tape.

The plastic bag contained twenty-two empty .22 cartridge cases.

Paul Dougherty, 2020:

Sure enough, just as I said after the family was killed, we were looking for an RG 14 revolver. When we matched the revolver to the cartridge cases and slugs, that hung him out to dry.

The rifle was a Marlin .22 caliber.

Sean Upton, 1973:

I handed the rifle immediately over to Sgt. Fite, who was on the scene.

There was a quantity of wood in the back part of the vehicle. The back seat was folded down and the wood was in the back. Also there was a satchel in the front seat of the vehicle.

Mullin was brought to County Hospital by Police Officer Sean Upton.

Sam Robustelli, 2020:

We were at County Hospital. I wasn't with him [Mullin]. I was with another prisoner, but he was getting unruly so I cuffed my guy so he couldn't get away and went across and helped the officer that had him. We got him under control, so he couldn't hurt anybody else or himself.

Sean Upton, 1973:

During the physical examination of Mullin the following tattoos were found to be on Mullin's body. In the abdomen area in block letters, were found the words "Legalize acid." Directly underneath these words, were found the words "Eagle eyes marijuana." On the left forearm of Mullin was also a tattoo with "Birth" with two crosses underneath "Birth" and the following "M" underneath the crosses, "Mahasamadhi." On the left ankle, inner ankle was found the tattoo, "Kriya" and underneath that was "Yoga."

Upton observed that Mullin had also burned his penis several times with a cigarette.

Herbert Mullin, 2020:

I wish I had not gotten any tattoos, etcetera, etcetera, etcetera. From my point of view now I must say that I feel and think I was extremely naive and gullible, and immature, undifferentiated schizophrenia, who was making mistakes and not learning how to grow up.

Mullin resisted a rectal probe and refused to answer any questions. His blood was drawn and tested for drugs and alcohol.

Bob Lee, 2011:

When he shot Mr. Perez, he was immediately captured and a blood test was taken which was negative for all substances.

Chuck Scherer, 1973:

The suspect, Herbert William Mullin, was brought into the Detective Bureau where he was advised of his Constitutional Rights by this officer. He looked somewhat puzzled and he was asked if he knew why he was in custody. He replied, "I have a right to remain silent on advice of my attorney."

He was asked who his attorney was but he remained silent. This went on for some period of time and he was asked if he would like to make a phone call—he replied…"Silence!"

He was asked several questions in relation to the case—he replied…"Obviously you don't know what silence means."

At 1:31 p.m. he asked if he could make a phone call and he was asked the number he desired to call—he gave this officer the number of 335-XXXX. He was asked who this number belonged to as we would have to record it—he stated…"Silence!"

The number was dialed and the lady answering the phone at the other end was questioned as to who she was—she stated "Mrs. Mullin." This officer identified myself and told her that her son was in custody and chose to talk to them via telephone. The conversation between Herbert Mullin and the person answering the phone was very

POLICE DEPT.
SANTA CRUZ. CALIF.
19774 2-14-'73

brief—Mullin stating that he hoped she enjoyed her Valentine gift and then asked if he could talk to "Dad." A conversation was had very briefly and Herbert asked, "Would you call Mr. Pease?"

The suspect then hung up. This officer asked Mullin if his attorney was Mr. Pease and he replied, "Silence!"

Mullin then stated something to the effect of our (making reference to this officer and Sgt. Finnegan) being responsible for the 3,000,000 killed in World War II. This was unrelated, unsolicited, and not responsive to a question.

Mullin was then returned to his cell.

Art Danner in the district attorney's office immediately prepared three search warrants for Herbert Mullin's Chevrolet station wagon, his apartment at 81 Front Street, and his parents' home in Felton. They were signed by Judge Franich

Santa Cruz County Sheriff Detectives searched Mullin's Front Street apartment. They were assisted by a criminalist from the San Mateo crime lab. The San Mateo crime lab was considered top notch and Paul Dougherty was the head of the lab and had testified hundreds of times before California Superior Courts in many different counties.

The search team quickly discovered an overcoat.

Paul Dougherty, 1973:
The button was missing from the left sleeve and also from the right sleeve, but on the left sleeve there was a little bit of leather left on the left sleeve.

There was a button, another button in the little toilet article bag that was in the bathroom.

It appears the same type of button.

Paul Dougherty later compared the overcoat to the button found at the Gianera crime scene in the San Mateo crime lab.

Paul Dougherty, 1973:
I found that button matched the portion of leather that remained on the overcoat. In other words, I could make a physical match between the small piece of leather that was left on the coat and the button.

In a dresser, the team discovered masking tape similar to the masking tape holding together the box of .22 long rifle ammunition found in Mullin's vehicle. When they compared the tears on the end of each, they matched perfectly.

Richard W. Foerster (Santa Cruz Police Department Detective Sergeant), 1973:
I found a briefcase with several writings, such as in the briefcase were papers, a transcript of Cabrillo College. There was correspondence naming him.

The briefcase also contained a job application and other items.

Richard W. Foerster, 1973:
I believe Kaiser or someplace like that—for an engineer's job, I think it was. […]

I believe there was a receipt, yes. It was for rent. […]

There were four $25.00 savings bonds of Herbert William Mullin, which gave a San Francisco address, and I think they were issued back in 1972 in the spring of the year.

Detective Foerster also found an address book and one entry particularly stuck out to him—

Richard W. Foerster, 1973:
James Gianera, and it gave 1965 Branciforte.

Also written in the address book—

Herbert Mullin:
Einstein the Searcher

My eyes have lost the gift of tears but my heart has cried the tears of blood.

Terry Medina, 2020:
When we were processing that car, we were

able to find the shell casing from when he shot Perez. It had been ejected out and tumbled down through all the wood that was piled in the back of the car. It was painstaking. Hours and hours of work going over every inch of that car. We never found out who owned that rifle, but that casing in the car matched to shell casings found at the boy's camp in Henry Cowell.

Dr. Hans H. Dibbern conducted the autopsy on Fred Perez—

Dr. Hans H. Dibbern, 1973:
He looked younger I think than he actually was—around 60-something.

The cause of death?—

Dr. Hans H. Dibbern, 1973:
Small caliber gunshot wound which entered the right shoulder, went into the chest and heart.

Mullin was arraigned at one o'clock in the afternoon on Wednesday, February 14, 1973. Judge May ruled to continue the hearing on March 1 at the request of defense attorney Richard Pease.

Paul Dougherty and the San Mateo crime lab examined projectiles after firing them from Mullin's rifle.

Paul Dougherty, 1973:
The projectile is recovered by firing, test firing the weapon into a tank of water. This is usually a column of water of about nine feet in length. This column of water leaves the projectiles undamaged, and we recover it from the bottom of the tank and bring it up and put it under a microscope called the comparison microscope.

Now, the comparison microscope has two objective lenses, one on the right and one on the left. The test projectile, for example, is placed under the right objective lens, and the questioned projectile—in this case, a projec-

tile recovered from an individual—would be placed on my left.

In the top of the bore that connects these two objective lenses is the central eyepiece, and I would look into that with my eye. When I look into that, I see a field that is split down the middle. It is a very sharp line so that the right-hand side is the right projectile and on the left-hand side would be the left projectile, or your test projectile and your questioned projectile.

I then rotate these projectiles in this field until I get a match. That is, until the striations seem to form one continuous path across the entire field of the microscope, or until I am satisfied that there is a match.

A bullet, when it is fired from a rifled weapon, is marked by the rifling of the weapon. The rifling is put in there by the manufacturer for a number of reasons, but basically to give stabilization to the projectile in flight.

This rifling is a series of spiral grooves that are cut into the barrel or interior of the barrel. It is a tube, and then think of a series of spiral grooves cut into the interior of that. When that is done, two marks are left on these cuts on both of the grooves, as call the depressions in there, and the lands, which are the raised portion.

These two marks then mark the projectile as it passes down the bore. In other words, they impart characteristics to this projectile that are individual to that particular bore.

But there are greater difficulties with forensic analysis on .22 caliber bullets.

Paul Dougherty, 1973:
These are more difficult types of projectiles to compare, not only due to the nature of them in that they are usually lead, they are soft and they are coated in most cases with a very thin coating of material to kind of give them a hardened surface, and this of course doesn't soak up the striations properly. It chips and flakes, but they are also very easily damaged in their flight. In other words, if

they impact on something terribly hard, the bullet is disrupted and destroyed and there is of course not much there, so it pretty well can be disintegrated at times.

Paul Dougherty compared the bullets removed from Kathy Prentiss, her children, Jim Gianera, and Joan Gianera with the .22 rifle found in Mullin's car.

There was sufficient evidence to determine the bullets had been fired from an RG 14 type revolver, but most of the bullets were too badly damaged for an accurate comparison. However, one bullet was still intact enough for a comparison.

Paul Dougherty, 1973:
The one that is labeled "James Thorax" had sufficient characteristics for me to be able to identify it. It is my opinion that it came from the RG 14 revolver.

Additionally, Paul Dougherty made a positive match between a casing found on the Gianeras' living room floor, empty casings found in Mullin's car with his RG 14 revolver, and a cartridge case from the revolver his office had test fired.

Paul Dougherty, 1973:
In this particular case we look at what we call the firing pin impression. That is where the firing pin has struck in this particular case in order to effect ignition.

Paul Dougherty examined bullet fragments removed from the body of Fred Perez.

Paul Dougherty, 1973:
They have the class characteristics of the Marlin rifle.

Paul Dougherty examined cartridge casings found at the Henry Cowell crime scene.

Paul Dougherty, 1973:
I concluded at least in the case of one of

the projectiles that it was fired from the RG 14, and the other projectile, I really haven't examined it but it is fairly damaged, but its class characteristics are very consistent with the RG 14.

On February 15, 1973, Joan Stagnaro, the eyewitness at Fred Perez's murder, and the Francis family's neighbors, Steven Houts, and Thatcher Clarke, all participated in a line-up held at the Santa Cruz Sheriff's Office. Houts and Clarke had seen Mullin's car approach the Francis Family's home before the murders. Mullin was identified as #4 in the line-up.

Joan Stagnaro failed to recognize Mullin and circled "Unknown" on the witness card.

Houts also circled "Unknown" but mentioned that #5 may have been the man he had seen.

Clarke circled #3 on the witness card.

Terry Medina, 2020:
After he [Mullin] was caught, he never really talked. There was no interview.

Mullin did not talk with law enforcement but corresponded with UCSC graduate student, Stephen Wright. Wright was in the middle of a six month assignment interning at the Santa Cruz Public Defender's Office when Mullin was arrested. Wright wrote an extensive timeline of Mullin's life and Mullin diligently added details to each entry.

Wright's thesis was a first person biography of Mullin's life and a history of the M'Naghten Standard.

Mullin's parents really only ever spoke about the crimes publicly once—

William Mullin (Herbert Mullin's father), 1973:
We're so shocked and horrified we can't say anything.

CHRONOLOGY OF HERBERT MULLIN'S LIFE

April 18, 1947--Born in Salinas, California.

BERNIECE & ENOS FOURATT - kill-joy SADIST REINCARNATIONISTS
MULLIN's told to MOVE

January 1948--Family moved to Walnut Creek.

TELEVISION - 12 GIRL SCOUTS INFRONT; ME IN BACK; I
SEE NOTHING; THEY kill-joy ME; BASE-BALL, STEVEN WHITE
& BUS RIDE & BOULDER CREEK SUMMER CIGING —

February 1952--Family moved to San Francisco.

Richard, Raymond, Robert Kock — MASTURBATION INFO. WITH-HELD.
kill-joy tactics - RETARD - "SOCIAL - SEXUAL - Psycological
FREEZE" type COWARD jacket —

Sept. 1953-June 1954--Attended kindergarten in a San Francisco
        public school.

PAINTING -; FINGER-PAINTING; clay modeling (?);
good ART EDUCATION beginning

September 1954--Began first grade at St. Stephens Catholic School.

NO ART EDUCATION AT ALL 8 grades.
GERALD REGAN; JOHN MAHONEY; MARYLOU IRVINE, VICKY SHANK;
"FREEZE" "SHUN". SUMMER & DINNER FRIEND TRIP -
  BOXING - PUGGING - ENCYCLOPEDIA INSTRUCTION -

June 1961--Graduated from eighth grade at St. Stephens Catholic School.

CAROL & STEPHEN Shapino — FREDRICK Champio
NEIGHBOR-HOOD FRIENDS — MASTURBATION & HOMO-SEXUAL FREEZE
JIM, GERALD, THOMAS, TERRANCE DILLON -
JACK, RICHARD, JOAN WATSON   PATRICIA MULLIN

Sept. 1961-June 1963--Attended Riordan High School in San Francisco.

SUMMER VACATION — DAN HANCE & GERALD CONSTANZO
MASTURBATION VERBAL INDUCEMENT
1st JACK OFF   SPRING 1962; 14 yrs old

FEAR IN SANTA CRUZ AND OTHER CRIMES

Peter Chang, 1973:
I don't think there is the kind of fear that pervaded this county after the Ohtas were murdered.

Well, you had a lot of things in the Ohta case. You had that note that promised revenge on all people who had big houses. You had a lot of bizarre, very bizarre things in that case that are not present here.

Mickey Aluffi, 2020:
Maybe not fear, but there was a lot of pressure from the public, you know. They weren't accusing us of not doing anything, but they were concerned over what's next.

The police department and Deputy Sheriff's Office were flooded with phone calls about the murders.

Don Smythe (Santa Cruz Deputy Sheriff), 1973:
[People are] asking what they should do to protect their families.

Mostly, they call for reassurance. It's as if they're asking: "Has the whole world gone mad?"

Doug James, 1973:
People are definitely uptight. They don't know what we have running loose and they're very concerned.

Within Santa Cruz County the number of handguns sold spiked for the first four months of 1973. In February 1973, it peaked with more than double the number of handguns sold as in December 1972.

Dave Alcorn, 2020:
Sure there was fear, but they [murderers] always make a mistake. It's easier today with high tech forensics, but, "We're gonna get him."

I don't think anybody had any doubt that we would get him, it was just a matter of how many people are going to get hurt before we get him. It bothered you, you didn't want people hurt.

Mickey Aluffi, 2019:
There were bodies everywhere. Dismembered bodies. People were shot. So we kind of had this theory that there were two different entities at work. One is a shooter murderer and one is a dismembering type of murderer.

Terry Medina, 2020:
The crimes were all different. They're not all the same. They're overlapping, Herbert William Mullin crimes and Kemper's crimes, and remember that there were other murders. It was taking everybody, right. I mean, if you only have eight detectives, it's not like LAPD that had a homicide bureau of one hundred guys. So you would just be working the

scenes and doing your best to put everything together so that when the breaks did come, you were able to take advantage of everything.

And that's really what good detective work is today, aided by very good technology. I mean, you still have to have a meticulous crime scene. You have to document everything. So that when the breaks do come, it all falls into place very quickly.

Harold Cartwright, 2020:
We also had other murders at the time that weren't related. Not the well known ones, but murders, attempted murders, and so forth. It was a horrible time. And most of those that were caught went through the public defender's office.

Chris Cottle, 2020:
There are a couple of others that really come

Convicted murderer Richard Anthony Sommerhalder sat with lowered eyes today as a Superior Court judge handed down two consecutive five-year to life sentences for the slayings of Mary Gorman, 21, and Vicki Bezore, 31. Sommerhalder sat rigidly throughout the hearing. Judge Harry Bauer, in an emotional voice, urged the defendant be locked away for as "long as legally possible." (Photo by The Sentinel's Bill Lovejoy)

to mind that were significant to the area. There was a case called [Richard] Sommerhalder that was a big one, he hung out right around here. There was a place called the Aptos Club, where a lot of drinking went on. I tried the Sommerhalder case, that was after.

Carpenter [The Trailside Killer] also came a few years later. There was a guy named Neil Hammari who killed a teacher. He was hitchhiking and was picked up by a teacher out on Old San Jose Road. That got a lot of attention.

Chris Cottle, 2020:

This schoolteacher was dead within five minutes of Hammari getting in his car. Ham-mari was just a young kid.

But then he built this whole defense, he never testified, but the defense was built around the victim being homosexual and making advances. That turned out to be a bogus defense in the end, but it just destroyed the family. It was a big deal in those times. He admitted it later on, to the probation department, that it was bogus.

This murder occurred in October 1975.

Terry Medina, 2020:

There were so many crime scenes. So many murders. Some of those thirty-six crime scenes we knew were connected and some we knew were not connected. I'll give you one. Wilfried Brown was a seventeen-year-old black kid with the drug abuse prevention center that killed a woman in Capitola named Ida Stein. He raped her and then drowned her in the bathtub. That doesn't fit any other scene. And then you have White who's bludgeoned to death. That does not fit. He got beat to death with a baseball bat.

On March 18, 1973, a Harbor High School teacher was stabbed to death in DeLaveaga Park by a twenty-six-year-old man. James Kenneth Scott pled guilty to second degree murder and was sentenced to life in prison.

John Hopper (Former Santa Cruz County Deputy Sheriff), 2021:

I joined the Sheriff's Office Explorer Scout program when I was around fourteen. At that time the Sheriff's Office was located at 705 Front Street. An impressive building and the jail was on the top floor. As Santa Cruz became the "Murder Capitol of the World," the Explorer Scouts would get called out nearly every Saturday to help search areas of interest that investigators felt could be potential sites that victims and/or their body parts may have been hidden. My dad called me from San Jose to say he had seen me on Channel 11 News walking in the woods with Sergeant Stoney Brook who was carrying an M1 rifle. The call outs brought about a lot of excitement for all the Explorer Scouts. Also a tragic sense of what some of us might face as we went on to choose law enforcement as a career.

At the old Front Street SO Deputy Jim Ingram had blown up B&W photos of the Ohta victims floating in the family pool, the cleaning filter cord tangled amongst the bodies. Seeing that photo as a teenager left an everlasting impression in my mind.

Lynn Scott, 2020:

Here's something interesting. Santa Cruz did not have a morgue at that time. There were three mortuaries in town: White's, Wessendorf, and I can't remember the third one [Smith Mortuary]. They would be on call every three weeks. It rotated. So it just depended on who was on call got which bodies.

Harold Cartwright, 2020:

In those days we had people who used drugs and we had people who were Vietnam veterans and we had people with post traumatic stress, so there was always a potential for violence. But, basically, it was a bunch of happy, young people, smoking their dope, or not, and doing their thing. I think it was a kinder, gentler world at that time. Of course Vietnam was tearing us all apart.

Chris Cottle, 2020:

There were a lot of narcotic arrests at that time as well. The DEA was here. The FBI and the feds were working here.

Richard Verbrugge, 2020:

One day he [Peter Chang] said, "You know, I prosecuted so many of these damn cases, but

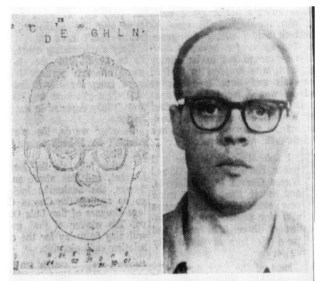

David Joseph Carpenter, 39, convicted rapist and armed robber now serving ime in state prison for Santa Cruz and Calaveras County offenses, was identified with the aid of the Identi-Kit line drawing at left. The picture, right, is a 1960 San Francisco police mug shot of Carpenter.

Assault-Robbery Suspect Enters Plea Of Guilty

David Joseph Carpenter, 39, a Soledad prison inmate charged with rape, assault with intent to commit rape, kidnaping, burglary and armed robbery, Monday pleaded guilty to rape and armed robbery in Superior Court.

Carpenter will be sentenced Oct. 22 for the January asault of a 19-year-old Boulder Creek girl and the armed robbery-rape of a Bonny Doon woman.

Right: Even before David Carpenter was known as the Trailside Killer, he had a history in Santa Cruz County. In early 1970 Carpenter attacked two women.

I've never bought dope."

There's an old joke between narcotics agents that says even a trained monkey can buy dope. So we told him that and he said, "Well, I'm a trained monkey."

So I said, "Well, you up for buying some dope tonight?"

He goes, "Yeah, OK."

I called one of the informants that we had used over the years. Mr. Chang was in a suit and they said, "We gotta dirty you up, you can't go buy in a suit."

So Mr. Chang took his coat off, took his tie off, rolled his sleeves up, and opened a couple buttons on his shirt. He took his shoes off, and got his rubber boots and he and the informant went to this house Capitola, where this weed dealer was dealing and the informant introduced Mr. Chang to the dealer and Mr. Chang bought two lids of marijuana from the guy.

Jim Jackson might remember because he defended the dealer, but the guy had to plead guilty. He sold marijuana to the district attorney.

Chris Cottle, 2020:
In that three or four years, I had tried twenty-five or thirty sexual assault cases. This was while all these killings were going on.

Stanford University has a respected daily newspaper, the *Stanford Daily*. Shortly after Mullin had been arrested, on February 26, 1973, a headline ran: "Santa Cruz Students Don't Panic Despite Recent Killings."

The article noted that despite the recent string of murders and the fact that more than eleven sexual assaults had been reported to Santa Cruz Police over the last four months, UCSC students were saddened but unfazed, in what one student called a "typical UC Santa Cruz lack of reaction."

Tom O'Leary (UCSC University Relations Department), 1973:
People have intelligent concern, but there is no panic, fear, or up-tightness. The campus is the safest place you could be.

The article quoted several people affiliated with UCSC saying that hitchhiking was way down for the time, but would surely rise again within a month or so.

Chris Cottle, 2020:
I think the newspaper people did a good job. There was a real effort to be accurate. To check with us. They were responsible.

Mickey Aluffi, 2019:
Remember Marj Von B? She was a writer for the *Register-Pajaronian*, great writer and a neat lady.

The *Register-Pajaronian* was a daily paper at the time. Now it is a weekly.

Harold Cartwright, 2020:
Marj Von B was a journalist who had tremendous integrity. Chain smoker. Oh, Marj was, "All right, Harold. What can you tell me? Is this on the record or off the record?"

Smokers voice. We'd talk and she'd say, "Okay, well let me know when I can print this."

And she kept her word absolutely. Absolutely. She was *the* person that everyone respected.

Dave Alcorn, 2020:
Marj Von B was just a ray of sunshine coming in the front door. She and Tom Honig and Peggy Townshend were the core reporters in this area. You could tell them, "Hold off from reporting this and I'll let you know when you can release it."
They wouldn't do a thing until you gave them the OK. They held to their word. Off the record meant off the record. Marj was just a nice lady, a nice nice lady. I was happy to see her all the time.

KQED, a television station based in San Francisco, airs a weekly roundtable news program,

At the scene

Terry Medina, one of the county sheriff's department's investigators and Watsonville Register-Pajaronian (and former Valley Press reporter) crime reporter stand by a piece of insulating material taken from the floor of the tent structure. Blood was on the material.

Newsroom. One of the featured journalists who issued reports each week in the early 1970s was Marilyn Baker. Baker seemed to have insider information on the Santa Cruz murders, which police and deputies dismissed as imaginative reporting.

UCSC students may have been too cool for school, but tensions in the Santa Cruz area were high and Baker's lurid reports did nothing to quell the situation.

Shortly after the arrest of Herbert Mullin, Baker appeared on *Newsroom* with the following report.

Marilyn Baker, 1973:
Though Santa Cruz was always a postcard pretty resort town, the same postcards are now actually the sites where parts of dismembered bodies have been found and washed ashore. The butcher murders go back for over a year. Listing of the victims appears even longer than the police have admitted. They include Mary Ann Pesce, who vanished last May, her decapitated head found in August off Summit Road. What has not been revealed before is that the head appears to have been kept in a gingham-checked beach bag for almost six weeks before it was put into the ravine.

Two other young women vanished that same May last year. Anita Luchessa, the police say, is presumed also to be dead, and Terry Taylor whose real name turned out to be Terry Pfitzer. Until this week, the Santa

Cruz Sheriff's Department has not admitted that Terry Pfitzer may also be another victim of the butcher murderer. Now they say that they think she too is dead. Both the Pfitzer and Luchessa girls vanished in the Santa Cruz Foothills.

In October, Mary Guilfoyle disappeared while hitchhiking into Santa Cruz from Cabrillo College. Police listed her as a runaway, although she was twenty-four years old at the time with a very stable lifestyle. Last month they found out she was killed. The skeleton was located a few miles from UC campus in Santa Cruz.

In January, Cynthia Schall was hitchhiking on a Main Street in Santa Cruz, and parts of her body were discovered two days later.

One month after that, on February 5, two UC co-eds vanished from the rim of the Santa Cruz campus within two hours of each other. Alice Liu disappeared at 10:00 p.m. Rosalind Thorpe was alive and hitchhiking at 11:54 p.m.. She was dead six minutes later. That might stop the theory that law enforcement has consistently pushed in Santa Cruz, which is that none of the murders actually occurred in our County. Rosalind Thorpe's did in fact, within three to five miles of the Santa Cruz campus. Late today, sources very close to the Santa Cruz District Attorney claimed that they had hairs that linked Herbert Mullin to these butcher murders. The hairs were found in Mullin's car allegedly. Mullin is already accused of a half-dozen shooting and stabbing deaths, but the Santa Cruz Police Lieutenant Charles Scherer isn't buying the "one mass killer" theory. "These decapitations have a totally different MO," he said. "They have no resemblance at all to the alleged Mullin killings."

Newsroom **Reporter, 1973:**
What's an MO?

Marilyn Baker, 1973:
Oh, method of operations.

Newsroom **Reporter, 1973:**
Thank you.

Marilyn Baker, 1973:
Well, actually they say it in Latin, but it means method of operations.

Well, the butcher murders are unique. The decapitation and dismemberment is done with the skill of what the police say borders on perhaps professional medical knowledge. The bodies were placed in a slant position, the heads lower than the feet so the blood would drain out, making such dismemberment easier. Victim Cynthia Schall appears to have been held captive for a time. The Achilles tendons on both feet were sliced before her death; her right wrist bears heavy rope burns, her upper arm a large bruise.

The pattern of the butcher killer is starting to emerge. He appears to strike only on Mondays, and then after dark. Since last month, he seems to shoot his victims right after they get in the car. He travels certain routes in Santa Cruz, favoring the roads rimming the Santa Cruz campus. He has knowledge of anatomy that, Sheriff's officials say, is good enough to make him a pathologist.

This map shows the various places that those parts of the dismembered victims and the disappearances have been. The stars are where dismembered parts have been found, and the circles are where the victims have disappeared from.

Also, the other thing that's emerged is that the suspect, whoever he is, knows the major roads through the Santa Cruz mountains and knows them quite well. He apparently simply drives to the edge of these roads and tosses over his victims. He did not sexually assault any of the victims, but some police tend to feel that there is a sexual deviation behind the butchery, perhaps involving the decapitation. There is even speculation by police that the killer might possibly be a lesbian or a male transvestite. Since victim Alice Liu was very afraid of rape, she studied Judo to protect herself and was said to never ride in a car after dark unless she knew the driver or it was a woman.

This is a police sketch of the possible suspect. Two days after one victim disappeared, this man was seen driving a car along Mission Street in Santa Cruz, that was on January 10. There appeared to be human hair hanging out of the closed trunk of the vehicle. He was followed for ten minutes by a witness whom Santa Cruz Police deemed highly reliable. The Santa Cruz Police never did have that reliable witness work with the police artist to produce the sketch. In fact, the call by the witness reporting his sighting was never reported to police superiors in the homicide department until eight days after the original was driving. It is a 1966 Chevelle Malibu, tan gold in color, four-door sedan. It had a California license plate which police say was probably junked ten years ago, and therefore possibly stolen. This is the license plate on the car. But no All-Points-Bulletin was ever put out for this car or for this man. Both the police and Sheriff's men say "We're getting nowhere; we have no leads; we have nothing to follow up."

Well, if any of you adults have any information at all on this car or on California license plate DF1-893, or if you do recognize the police sketch of the man, we're asking you to please call *Newsroom* at 864-2000. We are investigating all leads as well as the Santa Cruz investigation. We will have another report in a couple of days.

Newsroom **Reporter, 1973:**
Why did the police say they didn't investigate or put out an APB?

Marilyn Baker, 1973:
Here is what I was told: "The original vehicle report of the car was lost; was misplaced for eight days. We found it eight days later."

Newsroom **Reporter, 1973:**
Even if they found it eight days later, why not try then?

Marilyn Baker, 1973:
They said it was too late…

Richard Verbrugge, 2020:
After Mr. Chang charged Mullin with the homicides, he received a lot of pressure from the news groups, especially from one lady in San Francisco, who was putting pressure on him, saying, "Why don't you let your community relax and charge the rest of these hitchhiking murders to Mullin?"

Mr. Chang flat out told her, "I'm not going to charge anybody with a crime that I can't prove they committed."

And that really worked out because shortly after that Kemper gave himself up.

HERBERT MULLIN

Herbert Mullin, 2002:
I was born on April 18, 1947.

Herbert Mullin, 2019:
My birth certificate says I was born in Salinas, California.

Herbert Mullin, 2020:
There is an old house on the corner of Boulder and Grove Streets in Boulder Creek. I think I was conceived, gestated, and born there.

William Mullin (Herbert Mullin's father), 1973:
There was an incident of diarrhea among many newborn babies in that hospital, or town at that period of time. Herbert had to stay another week at the hospital after Jean came home.

Herbert Mullin:
I was in an upper middle class family, Catholic. We had a summer home where I think I

was born. I was given a very good education academically. I was a B plus student. I played first string on the basketball and baseball teams during grammar school. So other than being left as a naive, gullible, and immature individual, I was given an upper middle class San Francisco, Santa Cruz County, Boulder Creek upbringing.

Herbert Mullin, 1973:
I spent every summer from 1947 to 1963 at Baker's Rest, a summer house in Boulder Creek. My parents never invited my class mates to spend even a part of the three months.

My parents never instructed me to invite classmates to dinner during the school year.

William Mullin, 1973:
I loved the kid. I loved the kid very, very dearly. Why hell, I even got mixed up with the Boy Scouts when he became a scout. I became the Assistant Scout Master. I didn't want to be the Scout Master because of my

Above: The house in Boulder Creek that Mullin believes he was born in.
Right: Mullin as a freshman at Riordan High in San Francisco, 1962.
Bottom: The Mullin Family's home in San Francisco.
Following pages: Mullin as a Senior at San Lorenzo Valley High School in Felton, 1965.

Z

HERBERT MULLIN
Key Club 3, 4
Varsity Club 3, 4
Varsity Club
Vice Pres 4
Football 3, 4

L
C
C
S
C

travel. I was away from home.

Gene Dawson (Reverend, Drug Abuse Preventive Center in Santa Cruz), 1973:
His parents were some of the sweetest people in the county and from time to time they helped the center.

Terry Medina, 2020:
His dad was this really tough Marine, always tough on Mullin. He could never do anything right. His mom was this kind of nice little old lady that was totally overrun by the father.

Dee Shafer (Contract Psychologist), 2001:
He indicated that he had had a difficult relationship with his father who he stated bullied him. He believed it was significant that his father had served as a drill sergeant in the Marines.

Paul Dougherty, 2020:
Mullin was the son of a former Marine Corps Drill Sergeant and he raised him like a soldier.

One of Mullin's cousins had a very different take on the Mullin family dynamics.

Richard Watson (Cousin of Herbert Mullin), 1973:
His father is a very good man, a very conscientious and sincere person. But his mother seemingly took over in the family many times, and sort of broke down perhaps the

respect that a kid should have for his father, and as a result, probably, there was a lack of respect for the father in the early years of growing up.

Dee Shafer, 2001:
[Mullin] denied any problems with substance abuse, sexual abuse, or violence in the home when he was growing up. He stated that he had no family criminal history. He said his father was hospitalized after World War II with shell shock, but there was no other family history of psychiatric problems or treatment.

Richard Koch (Childhood neighbor of Herbert Mullin), 2020:
We didn't go over to Herb's house ever. He always came over to our house. I didn't really know his parents. I met them once or twice, peripherally, in the garage or out on the street talking to my parents. I know Herb also had an older sister. But my mother thought Herb's dad was a very strict, Marine type. She always said that might have affected Herb.

Raymond Koch (Childhood neighbor of Herbert Mullin), 2020:
He [Herb] is a year older than me. I have two older brothers, my middle brother is Herb's age. It was kind of like the neighborhood gang all of us running around as kids.

Richard Koch, 2020:
We ran around building forts together and playing cowboys and Indians. Herb was a serious, straight arrow kind of kid. One time we were playing on Vale Avenue and this boy came up from down Crest Lake, which is a street down the way. And this boy came up and he pulled a switchblade on us for some reason. I remember, Herb stepped forward and took it away from him. And the odd thing was, the kid pulled out

H. Mullin   D. Richardson   J. Gianera

a second switch blade and Herb took that away from him. So I always thought of Herb as being kind of a straight, stand up kid. I was pretty impressed with that.

Raymond Koch, 2020:

We stopped interacting once he got into sixth grade. I remember playing basketball with the seventh grade Catholic school team and I went to public school, so I was kind of an outsider and he was on the team a year ahead of me and he didn't want to recognize that he knew me. I was the non-in-crowd guy, but it was still kind of weird the way he went out of his way to not interact with me. Very strange for a guy that I had grown up with.

The family seemed like the traditional red-blooded American family of the '50s and '60s and Herb was never one to back down from a fight. He was a strong personality and his dad taught him to fight.

Herb left San Francisco around junior high or early high school.

Herbert Mullin, 1973:

New Year's Eve 1960—first boy-girl dance party. I'm invited but my parents refuse to

let me go; instead they take me to the movie "Alamo." Bloody, kill crazy, slaughter.

Richard Verbrugge, 2020:

I was sent to do a complete background investigation on Mullin, and we did that on every major defendant like that. You know, we did the same thing on Kemper. But Mullin was interesting to me because he was a native San Franciscan and I'm a native San Franciscan. And of course, he was younger than I am. His father and mother were devout Catholics. And he attended Riordan High School in San Francisco, which I don't know if you're familiar with San Francisco, but if you know where the city college is located, it's on the same block. But Riordan was a brand new high school that it just opened up when I was graduating in 1952 from a high school and a beautiful school. I have friends that went there and they had nothing but good to say about the school. When I went to the school doing the background investigation, I talked to a couple of the priests that remembered Mullin. He was really a good student. He was a very good athlete. He had climbed one of the ropes in the gym to the ceiling, where the metal frame was, and climbed up on the frame and would walk around on the frame, about thirty feet off of the floor.

Above: The Mullin Family home in Felton as it stands today.

Richard Verbrugge, 2020:

During my investigation, I discovered he had a Father Tomei, as one of his instructors at Riordan High School. I surmised that he may have been sexually abused by that priest. But it wasn't the same priest he killed later. Not the same, but same name.

Richard Verbrugge, 2020:

Mullin's father worked for the post office in San Francisco. He got an opportunity to get a promotion and come to the post office in Felton, California. So they decided to move there. And of course, Herb was with him and he hadn't graduated from high school yet. He started at San Lorenzo Valley High School.

Herbert Mullin, 2002:

While in high school I worked part-time after school at Johnnie's Supermarket in Boulder Creek during 1962, 1963, and 1964. I also worked there full-time during the summers.

Herbert Mullin, 2020:

I remember that in early spring 1964, while working at Johnnie's Supermarket, I had bought a 1949 GMC pick-up truck with money I had made as an employee at Johnnies.

With his new truck, Mullin started his own hauling service and named it Have Truck Will Haul.

Herbert Mullin, 2020:

The business was mine. I hired John Hance occasionally. I also hired Dean Richardson occasionally. Basically, I hired them when there was more work than I could handle by myself.

Have Truck Will Haul was advertised on the San Lorenzo Valley's information boards that were placed outside of grocery stores, post offices, and drug stores in those days.

I hauled people's junk and garbage to the dump which was located on the outskirts of Ben Lomond.

In retrospect I know I should have just kept working for Johnnie Montanari at Johnnie's Supermarket.

Jean Mullin (Herbert Mullin's mother), 1973:

Herb was always on top of things until he was twenty. He always had his job. He always had his self-assurance. I used to think he was too cocky sometimes. But maybe it was his insecurity showing.

P.O. Box 321
(McClellan Road, Forest Lake District)
Felton, California
December 3, 1963

Mr. Yeager, Principal
San Lorenzo Valley High School
Highway 9 North
Felton, California

Dear Sir:

I was advised this evening of the fact that my son, Herbert, absented himself from the fourth, fifth, and sixth period classes on Tuesday, November 19, 1963.

Believe me both Mrs. Mullin and I are shocked to learn of this infraction of rules and discipline. I have taken a measure of discipline as a parent. To our knowledge, and we have never had cause to distrust our son, this incident was his first infraction of any kind.

I understand that Herbert must compose a thousand word thesis and spend Brunch periods in your office until the lost time in school is made up. I am in agreement that this is just and proper.

Thank you for your interest, guidance, and discipline. Please let Mrs. Mullin or me know if we can ever be of assistance to you or your staff.

We appreciate that you had us notified.

Yours very truly,

Martin W. Mullin

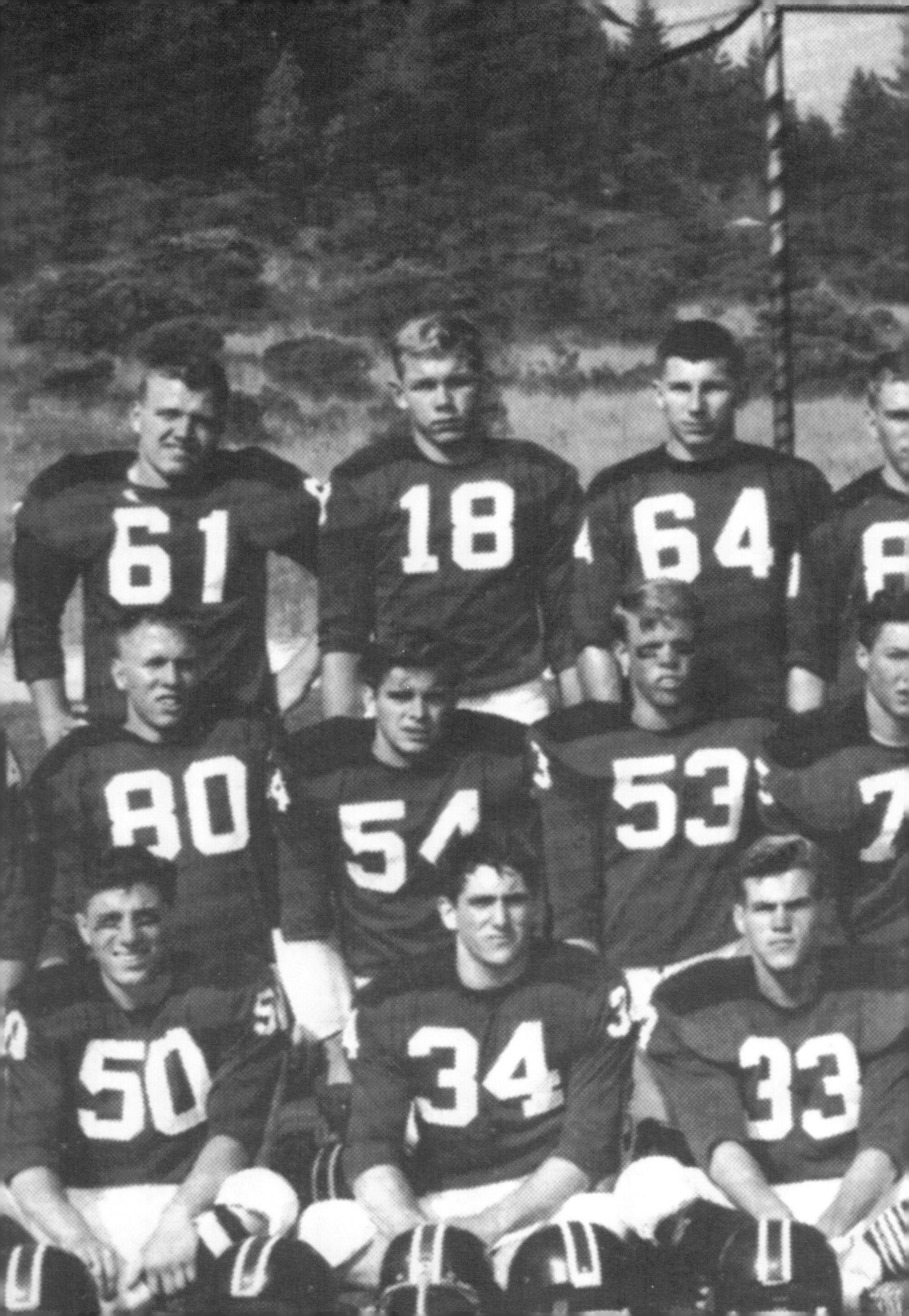

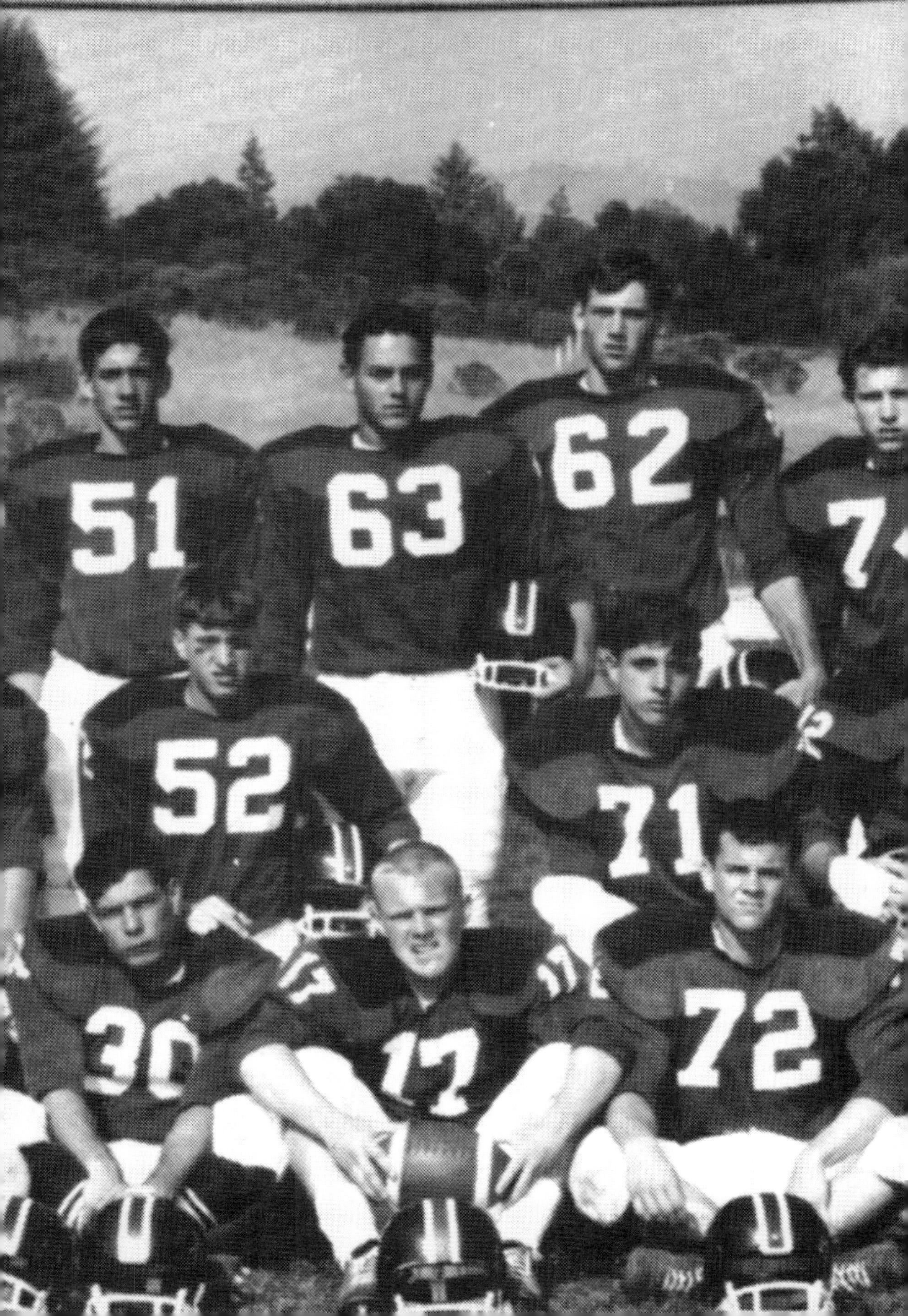

Dee Shafer, 2001:

According to the inmate, he first used alcohol at the age of fifteen and continued thereafter on an occasional basis.

Tim Crump (Mullin family neighbor, Felton, CA), 2020:

We moved up to McClellan Road in 1955, I guess. My dad got the job as the shop teacher at SLV High School. We lived in Hayward and my dad had been building a cabin up there and he got that job, so we moved up there. Then across the street there was a neighbor, he was a contractor and he built that little house that they [the Mullin Family] bought. I assume they bought it.

They moved in there, it had to be very early sixties. I started high school in '64. I was a freshman and Herb was a senior. We weren't buddies or anything, but Herb was really a super nice guy. I used to have to walk down quite a ways to catch the school bus and if he was coming down, he had a nice '59 Chevy, he'd pick me up and take me all the way to school. It wasn't an everyday thing, but it happened quite a few times.

He was a super nice guy. A really, really friendly guy and just the fact that this high school senior would be friends with this freshman says something, right there.

Dave Alcorn, 2020:

I lived right down off Plateau, right there. So I knew Herbie from coming down, walking down. I knew his parents, real nice people. I was in contact with Herb off and on.

Tim Crump, 2020:

His mom was kind of like a June Cleaver kind of mom. She was always very nice and friendly. She gave us a ride a couple of times, if she'd see us walking home or something. The dad, I don't know, he was a totally different character. He was a little guy. Bill, his name was Bill. To me, I was a big, dumb high school kid and my dad was the Industrial Arts teacher at SLV High School and then the next year, he was the head

football coach at Holy Cross High School in Santa Cruz. My dad was really a coach, that was his number one love. Herb's dad, I never really liked him very much because he was a little guy and he was what they call a banty rooster kind of guy. Just a little guy who always tried to come across as a tough guy. He was always telling me I should get into boxing and fighting and that stuff. I was a big kid and I played football, but I never had any interest in fighting anybody. He was always pushing on me; enough to make me feel uncomfortable, you know. Just that little tough guy attitude.

To a certain extent, I think Herb's dad probably played a part in how things went for him. I didn't like his dad at all. He was just pushy, and like I said, anytime I was around him he was on me, "You need to learn boxing. You need to learn to box."

Herbert Mullin, 2020:

Bill [Mullin's father] liked to teach boxing; even at my grammar school and at San Lorenzo Valley High School in 1964/1965. Also, my father, Bill, was telling me stories about his boxing rival, a fellow he called Sammy Schlifer. Bill might have told [the neighbors] about that rival also. I have wondered during the past two weeks whether Sammy Schlifer really existed.

I have found no records of a boxer named Sammy Schlifer.

William Mullin, 1973:

He did scare me one time. I had taught him to box. To block and parry and so on. Ever since he was a tot, we've sparred, open handed. Say, in the kitchen while we were waiting for dinner or something like that.

Well one time, after he had done some training, he came back and hit me a few times in the jaw and said, "Come on, let's go. It won't last long. It won't hurt too long."

That's the last time I sparred with him. He scared me.

Michael Rugg, 2020:
I was in the class ahead of him, '64. We were on the football team together. He wasn't that great a football player. Not someone to make your head turn, but he blended right along with the rest of us.

Herbert Mullin, 1973:
I was tricked into playing football by Dan Hance and Tomas Dillon. My father knew it would be a retarding experience for me; yet he gave no advice. I disliked it, but like most things in those days, once I started I was bound to finish.

Terry Medina, 2020:
I don't remember exactly where this came up, but Herb went to San Lorenzo Valley High School and he played lightweight football and I played lightweight football at the same time at Santa Cruz High School. San Lorenzo Valley was not in the same league, but we did play one another one game a year. We probably played in that game against one another.

Mullin met Loretta, a Holy Cross High School student, in the fall of 1964.

Herbert Mullin, 2020:
I met her [Loretta] when I was sixteen years old and we didn't break up until I was twenty-one, approximately twenty-one. And so, yeah, those years of still remaining in naive, gullibility, and immaturity.

Herb Mullin, 2002:
We met in the spring of 1964. We went steady during that year and 1965 and 1966.

On December 6, 1964, Mullin, Dean Richardson, and three other boys were picked up in Rio Del Mar by deputies for possession of alcohol. Mullin was driving and also had three five-pound bags of salt and one eight ounce can of black pepper in a Roy's Market bag. Mullin admitted to shooting a deer out of season three weeks prior. Mullin refused to give the location of the deer. He was arrested for possession of alcohol, breaking curfew, and storage of an open container in a vehicle.

Herbert Mullin, 2002:
I graduated from the San Lorenzo Valley High School in Felton, California, in June of 1965.

That summer, Mullin worked at a Chevron gas station in Santa Cruz.

Richard Verbrugge, 2020:
One Sunday, after he had graduated from high school, he and some friends were in Marin County and they went to a Catholic church and totally disrupted a morning mass, and a couple of FBI agents who were there with their families attending the mass, well, they got him squared away and on his way.

In March 1966, Mullin smoked marijuana for the first time at a beach with Jim Gianera.

Dee Shafer:
He said that he began using marijuana when he was in college and used it on weekends with friends. He indicated that he used marijuana only occasionally after the age of 21.

In May 1966, Mullin crashed his Volkswagen on the way home from a party.

Barry Burt, 2020:
We had all gone to bed one night and I heard this motor running. We got up and it wasn't getting farther away or closer, and we went down the road that ran below the house, and there was Herbie crashed on the side of the road with his Volkswagen smashed into a tree. He was passed out. We got him out of his car, brought him in, and he stayed the night.

My memories of him [Herbert Mullin] are not all that strange. He overindulged and he was a little bohemian in his lifestyle, when he was younger.

In June 1966, Mullin and Loretta broke up. Mullin began working full time at the County Public Works Department as an Engineering Aide.

Herbert Mullin, 1973:

I wanted to move out of the parental house for the summer. Parents beg and plead [for] me to stay. They baby and overprotect me. I would have grown up that summer. My life [has been] a mess ever since.

Herbert Mullin, 2020:

He [John Hooper] was a guy I met at San Lorenzo Valley High School. In the spring of 1966, we had decided to live together when summer began; my parents talked me into telling him, "No, my parents don't want me to do it."

His mother phoned my parents home and I talked to her. I think she was worried about me and her son and why my parents said "No."

In September 1966, Dean Richardson was killed.

Herbert Mullin, 2002:

While at Cabrillo College I worked part-time at various gasoline service stations in Santa Cruz during the school year and an Engineering Aide for the Santa Cruz County Department of Public Works during the summers of 1966 and 1967.

In October 1966, Mullin had his first experience with LSD with John Hooper at Hooper's cabin in Brookdale.

Herbert Mullin, 1973:

He [Hooper] asked me to take it with him. Then he used his experience and knowledge to drive me and guide me on a bummer. I hated it.

In April 1967 Mullin and Loretta got back together and were quickly engaged to be married.

William Mullin, 1973:

He bought the set. The engagement ring and wedding ring. That was around the time he decided his approach to the Vietnam military program, as far as he was concerned, was that he was going to be a conscientious objector. And I think he ran into a little trouble with her father and family over this.

He relayed a conversation to me that Mr. [Loretta's father] had said he was a coward. That he was not going to war because he was a coward.

Jean Mullin, 1973:

He was not ready for Loretta, but Loretta was ready for marriage and wanted to get married. She was his first love. That was when he started at Cabrillo [College].

Pat Bocca (sister), 1973:

When he was at Cabrillo he had it all together.

Herbert Mullin:

I graduated from Cabrillo College in June of 1967 with an Associate of Science degree with approximately 66.5 units of college credit.

Dee Shafer, 2001:

He subsequently attended classes at San Jose State University, but did not graduate.

Herbert Mullin:

When 1967 began I was thinking about trying for the U.S. Army Corps of Engineers. When autumn came around 1967, I began trying for Conscientious Objector.
I was trying to grow up and become a competent, efficient, and effective young man. I was not aware then that I was naive, gullible, and immature.

Mullin withdrew from San Jose State University at the end of November 1967.

Jean Mullin, 1973:

He withdrew and wanted to give up his

[inaudible] and apply for conscientious objector. Well, that was the first time we had ever really had strong words in our house. We were trying to convince him that the best way would be through the medical corps or some other—but no, no, he had definitely made up his mind. He was against the system. He was against the Army. He was against the war on religious grounds, and he'd been a very deeply religious child. So that's what started it all. It was a period of eight to ten months, going down to the draft board. It was a time when it was not popular to be against the war.

Tim Crump, 2020:
We moved away in '67. I'm guessing, but I believe, in my senior year we went back up there for some reason. My dad, my stepmother, my sister, and myself and we visited with his [Herbert Mullin's] parents. We went to their house and we visited for a while. I have no idea why. I don't think it was the main reason we went there. It might have been something to do with my dad selling our house. But, anyway, it was kind of shocking because Herb was there and he was like a zombie. We all sat around their living room and he was there just like a potato. He was completely gone. We know now that he got into drugs. He couldn't talk coherently or anything. It was just shocking to me because I knew him as a neighbor and as a friend.

Maxine White (SLV High School counselor), 1973:
He [Mullin] was a very bright boy. When he left high school he was on his way. He had the world by the tail, and then he apparently got involved with drugs. When I saw him recently he just seemed to have vegetated.

In December 1967, Mullin moved to his sister and brother-in-law's Christmas tree lot. Mullin

Still em- ma- locu- ment de- e to part- De- lawn

Mar- , and chief e not ie lat- which re left quent d oth

Students Collect Canned Goods

The Mastaba club at Cabrillo college will conduct a house-to-house drive in Rio del Mar on December 17 to collect canned foods to give to a needy family for Christmas.

Club publicity chairman Herb Mullin said the collections will be made between 10 a.m. and noon. The Mastaba club is comprised of students in the construction technology department at Cabrillo.

managed the lot during the day and lived in a trailer on the property.

Herbert Mullin, 1973:
[I] smoked a lot of dope alone at night. Ed Lawrence gave dope to me free.

In January 1968, Mullin claimed that he had his first sexual experience with Ed Lawrence.

Herbert Mullin, 2020:
I did not consider him [Ed Lawrence] a boyfriend. If you could read my "Insights and Apologies" pages on my website, especially the first page, it explains that I was very non-verbal in my own thinking mind! Ed was the one chasing me with phone calls and suggestions, I suppose. I am heterosexual and monogamous! The reason I got involved with him those few times was probably because I saw my friends from high school associating with him. They appeared to be growing up, getting stronger and more intelligent. I was non-verbally/mentally attempting to grow up and get stronger and more intelligent.

The following are excerpts from letters between Herbert Mullin and Reverend John J. O'Connor regarding a week the two spent together at Stinson Beach in February 1968.

4/12/2001

Letter from Herbert Mullin:
Did you know in spring of 1968, or was it February, that I was engaged to be married? Did I ever tell you the girl's name was Loretta [redacted]? Did I show you photos of us together?

The reason I ask these questions is because I broke up with Loretta two or three weeks after you and I spent those four days together at Stinson Beach cottage. I never really talked to anyone about it, and I am wondering if that homosexual experience, where you crawled into my bed naked and ejaculated all over me, without my knowing you were going to do such a thing, well, I wonder if that is why I broke up with Loretta?

Do you think you could help me understand what happened? I do not condemn you for being homosexual, that is your business. I would like to know why you did not inform me of your desire for me, and do you think your actions caused me to break-up with my fiancée? I know these are hard questions, but I need to solve my schizophrenic behavior problems and I think you could assist me.

I will turn 54 years old on April 18, 2001. I have been in Calif. State Prison for 28 years plus. I hope that by talking these issues over with you I can get in touch with my psychological self in such a way that I can begin to manifest a healthy mental awareness of myself and the society I live within—then, hopefully, the CDC staff will pronounce me free of all schizophrenic behavior tendencies, and I will be allowed to walk out of prison, forever.

That reminds me, I will be having a parole hearing within a year. Do you think you could arrange for me to have a prospective employer in the Santa Cruz area? If the parole board sees me with a good job offer and

sponsor, I would look a lot more worthwhile from their standpoint!

I remember we used to get ice cream together when I was fourteen years old. That would be nice to do again.

Happy Easter 2001.

4/24/2001

Letter from John J. O'Connor:
In about '67 or '68, I was down in Santa Cruz on a day off, with priest friends. I had heard your family moved there. After dinner, I called down and talked to your mom a good while. At the end, I asked how you were doing. She said you were home and would I like to talk to you. I said, "Sure."

We talked and in the end you asked if you could see me. I mentioned I was teaching at St. Pete's once a week and I had to meet with the pastor about the next year.

We drove to Palo Alto for a show and talked in my car for a long time. You had taken LSD that day and honestly, it was really hard to follow what you were saying.

Later you called me and asked if you could come and stay a few days in Marin. I said I had planned to go to Stinson to prepare my class and had to spend time on that but if you wanted to come with me there, I'm sure we'd have time to talk. (I had never been there, the cabin, before.)

One of the stark contrasts between our time together then and what you say in this letter is this: I loved those three days because I have never experienced such closeness and intimacy with another person in my life, and the whole time there was no sex. I came away feeling: "It is positive." I think there was times you and/or I had a sexual feeling and once came close to acting out sexually, but never did, and to this day we never have.

In your letter you asked me some important things. It is very important to me that I be absolutely honest with you.

"Did (I) know in spring of 1965…that(you) was engaged to be married." No Herb, you never mentioned that as far as I recollect, and

I think I'm sure, I would have remembered that. I don't recall the name Loretta [Redacted] at all. You did not show me photos of her.

You said you were "wondering if that homosexual experience, where (I) crawled into (your) bed naked and ejaculated all over you, without (your) knowing I was ever going to do such a thing…" is why you broke up with her.

That simply could and would never have happened, Herb and didn't.

We did decide to sleep in the same bed because it was the only bed. The only other place to sleep were two benches on either side of the fireplace. We talked it over. In fact, when I did get in to bed you were by the wall, leaving space for me. Herb, I am so self conscious about the size of my genitalia, I would never be naked, except in a doctor's office. I'm sure I went to bed in briefs and a t-shirt. I slept like a rock every night and we never even touched. I trusted you completely and felt at peace. What you remember is completely contrary to my nature. I would never do something so disgusting to another person, with or without their consent.

I don't know how else to say it. That is the God's honest truth.

A couple of other things that may be helpful to you:

During those days you did talk to me about a friend who had been killed; I think in an auto accident. You were very troubled by that and a lot of things about using drugs. You were into a vegetarian life and meditation. This really impressed me. During our stay we meditated together on your little prayer rug and ate whole grains and fresh vegetables and some bean sprouts. I never felt better. I admired you greatly and I talked to several close friends about those days together.

The only mistake for me, was assenting to your suggestion the last night to smoke marijuana. I was scared and my instinct said "no" but you (and other young people) were telling me it was a spiritual experience. It wasn't. I regret having done that. My short term memory has not been as sharp since.

The other thing was after you "lit up the second time" and I didn't, you became different: loud, loud-music, dancing around, hard–like a drunk man. But you apologized the next day and I felt we left on a good note.

I'm so sad that you think I did that.

6/6/2001

Letter from Herbert Mullin:
Well, I received your 4/24 letter a few days after you sent it. I must say it is a real lesson in "social–psychology" for me. There are obvious differences in what I think happened and what you think.

The fact that I did not tell you I was engaged to be married, or that I failed to show you photos of me and my fiancée, is an indication to me that I was entering into a period of undifferentiated schizophrenia when our Stinson Beach cabin 3-day weekend experience happened. Within two or three weeks after that experience, I broke off the engagement, and I have not had a girlfriend since.

John J. O'Connor worked at St. Stephen's in San Francisco, CA from 1960 to 1961. He worked at St. Isabella in San Rafael, CA from 1964 to 1971.

In August, 2002, O'Connor was accused in a lawsuit, of improper contact with an underage boy over thirty years before. He was removed from active ministry.

O'Connor passed away on March 15, 2013.

Mullin and Loretta broke off their engagement and broke up in March 1968

Loretta, 1973:
It was a gradual thing to be dissolved, our relationship. One day he just left.

Harold Cartwright, 2020:
He [Mullin] hated the Catholic church because he started having sex with his girlfriend when he was a junior in high school. He went to see the priest, and remember he's a very devout Catholic, and the priest told him, "Absolutely not."

One of the people he killed was the priest in the confessional in Los Gatos. It's all very logical if you follow the whole thing. These people should have been in a mental hospital.

3/4/2003 letter to R. Michael Lieberman, attorney—

Letter from Herb Mullin, 2003:
The homosexual experience mentioned in the letters happened in February of 1968, some 35 years ago. I had been going steady with a girlfriend from high school for approx. five years. Her name was Loretta [redacted]. Two weeks after the homosexual incident with O'Connor I broke off our engagement to be married and I have not had a girlfriend since. O'Connor made me feel like homosexual behavior was a necessary part of growing up, yet he also made me feel that it was something that should be considered evil and inappropriate behavior. He also made me think that it was something that should not be discussed. I was terribly confused and lonely; I believe I was in a non-verbal cogitation syndrome wherein I began to avoid thinking any thoughts at all. My life became a series of responses to outside stimuli. Within one year of the homosexual experience O'Connor suggested to my family that they put me into Mendocino State Mental Hospital. That was Feb. or March of '69.

Herb Mullin, 2003:
He [John J. O'Connor] was the individual who recommended to my parents that I be sent to Mendocino State Mental Hospital when I was 21 years old, in March of 1969. If he wasn't trying to ruin my life, he could of and/or would of recommended my receiving private therapy from a civilian mental health worker in the near-by community. John J. O'Connor was my "Confessor." That means that in 1960 I began going to the Sacrament of Confession to him at St. Stephen's Grammar School and Church. I continued going to the Sacrament of Confession to him during 1961. I began again in 1968 and continued in 1969 and 1970 and 1971. I kept seeing him and asking for guidance. I can see now that he was not giving me guidance, he was acting like a kill-joy sadist, he was driving me deeper and deeper into schizophrenia. There was a second homosexual experience with him in 1969 or 1970 (I do not remember the exact date.)

Dee Shafer, 2001:
Mr. Mullin said that he is heterosexual. He indicated that he had his first heterosexual intercourse at age twenty and thereafter had occasional, one-time encounters, but no significant relationships. He acknowledged a period of homosexual behavior over approximately one year when he was age 21. He said he had sexual contact with three or four different partners during that time. He indicated that these contacts occurred once or twice per month.

In April 1968, Mullin shaved his head. He also claims he had his second homosexual encounter with his friend, Ed Lawrence.

Detective Monroe of the Santa Cruz Police Department interviewed Ed Lawrence after Mullin's arrest—

Doug Monroe (Santa Cruz Police Department Detective), 1973:
Lawrence stated that he believed that Mullin was somewhat strange in his thinking regarding sex. That on several occasions wherein sex was being discussed, Mullin would react abruptly by removing his trousers and burning his penis with a cigarette.

Herbert Mullin, 2020:
During those four or five years before the

crime spree I was in what they call a state of undifferentiated schizophrenia. That's what the Mendocino State Mental Hospital had diagnosed me as. I couldn't keep a job for more than six months. I didn't have any girl-friends. I didn't have any friends basically.

On April 21, 1968, Fish and Game patrolmen caught Mullin illegally fishing at the "Garden of Eden," a popular swimming hole in Henry Cowell Redwood State Park, where he lat-er would murder four of his victims. Mullin became belligerent and Park Rangers took custody of Mullin. Marijuana was found in his pocket and he was in possession of camping equipment. It appeared to the Rangers that Mullin had moved into the park and construct-ed a makeshift shelter.

Mullin was arrested for possession of marijuana. Mullin's address was listed as "transient–has no permanent address." On May 16, 1968, he pled guilty and the complaint was amended. He was given a suspended sentence of ninety days in jail and given one year of summary probation.

In June 1968, Mullin began working for Goodwill Industries in Santa Cruz as a Manager Trainee. He was later transferred to a Goodwill in San Luis Obispo and quit in December 1968.

In October 1968, Mullin was finally granted conscientious objector status when his father wrote a letter on his behalf to the draft board. The board elected to consider the time Mullin spent working at Goodwill as fulfilling an alter-native form of service.

In early 1969, Mullin moved in with his sister and her family in Sebastopol. He worked at the Bocca's Christmas tree farm.

Herbert Mullin, 1973:
My sister wrote me and asked me to come. Maybe they were planning to drive me into Mendocino as punishment for quitting Goodwill Industries.

Dee Shafer, 2001:
According to Mr. Mullin, he was first hospi-talized at Mendocino State Hospital in 1969 when he was 21.

He could not provide any information as to the cause of the symptoms he was experiencing which precipitated this treatment, except he recalled that his first hospitalization at Mendocino State Hospital was precipitated by the onset of echolalia when he was having dinner with his family. He said he began repeating the words and actions of family members and that his family had him hospitalized.

William Mullin, 1973:
It was a festive occasion. It was our anniversary. There was a little drinking at the table, wine. We had had a little whiskey before. Herb had beverages right along with us. When we were still eating dinner we noticed that he was mimicking Al, the son-in-law.

Pat Bocca, 1973:
We noticed Herb wasn't talking, but was mimicking everything my husband was doing. When my husband would talk, he would talk, and when my husband would eat, he would eat.

Jean Mullin, 1973:
I can't recall if he was repeating the words, but he was just sitting there with a blank stare on his face. He was almost baring his teeth like an animal does. You know when an animal bares its teeth.

So Al stayed at the table and Pat and I went and called Sonoma County. They didn't know what to do and said to keep him calm and that he was probably on drugs. There wasn't any knowledge.

William Mullin, 1973:
Then he went into kind of a coma. We couldn't even reach him. Couldn't talk to him.

He was sitting. Sitting up. Thinking, but in a stupor. Kind of with a silly grin on his face.

[It lasted] an hour. Maybe longer. Finally, we were able to reach him and convince him to go to bed.

The next morning it had passed. I drove

down to Terra Linda where Reverend John J. O'Connor was doing duty down there saying mass and what not. He was also in social work. He had been number two pastor at St. Stevens, which made him kind of assistant principal at that grammar school too [where Herbert Mullin went to school].

So I went and talked it over with him and he said, "If you can get him into Mendocino Hospital, you'll have him right where he belongs."

Pat Bocca, 1973:
My husband and I talked him into going to the hospital.

Herbert Mullin:
When I was admitted to mental health hospitals and/or county mental health facilities, I did not feel mentally ill, I felt confused, probably because my questions went unanswered.

I did not grow up until after ten to twelve years in prison.

The doctors at Mendocino diagnosed Mullin with "Schizophrenic Reaction, chronic undifferentiated type (22.5) secondary to drug abuse. Manifested by: Distortion of associations and affect. Hallucinations. Generalized deterioration of his way of life. Impairment: Severe."

Herbert Mullin, 1973:
They focus mainly on homosexual aspect of me. They don't recommend heterosexual involvement. They condemn homosex as "something wrong."

Mullin was allowed to go home on the weekends.

Pat Bocca, 1973:
He'd call and I'd pick him up and bring him back to our place. He wasn't a frightening person…He didn't scare me; I had two children or I would never have had him around the house.

Once, while his sister drove him back to the

hospital after a weekend visit, Mullin asked—

Pat Bocca, 1973:
If I wanted him to sleep with me and I told
him no.

Jim Jackson, 1973:
What was his response?

Pat Bocca, 1973:
He was relieved.
    Apparently he was told by the people up
there [Mendocino State Hospital] to ask
whatever was on his mind.

Herbert Mullin, 1973:
The way I see it, my sister, Pat, was supposed
to teach me about sexual organisms: homo,
hetero, and individual.
    She didn't because our father commanded
her not to.

While in Mendocino State Hospital, Mullin
met fellow patient, Michael Ransom. Mullin
was discharged on May 9, 1969.

Herbert Mullin, 2020:
We [he and Ransom] met at Mendocino
State Mental Health Hospital in March or
April of 1969. When we were discharged
from the hospital, at Talmage Calif., in Men-
docino County, we moved to Lake Tahoe
and worked together at Harvey's Wagon
Wheel [as dishwashers].

In the fall of 1969, Mullin returned to Santa
Cruz. He attended the Drug Abuse Preven-
tive Center. In another interesting coincidence,
Kemper's sister, Allyn, worked at the Center.

Did she know Mullin?—

Allyn Kemper, 1973:
Not personally, I'd just see him around. I
can't remember him staying there more than
a week, he was just kind of annoying. He was
real quiet and he'd snore a lot.

YOU CAN SAVE A LIFE BY CLEANING YOUR CLOSET!

Rev. Gene Dawson tells you how. . .

Dear Community:
    If anyone you know and care about has
ever been damaged by the use of drugs and
alcohol, you can appreciate the importance of
the job Dawson Learning Center is doing.
    By selling used clothing, furniture, ap-
pliances, shoes, and beds at our thrift stores,
the Dawson Learning Center is able to help
people to overcome their problems.
    One hundred per cent of the stores' profits
are used in rehabilitation, college education,
and vocational training.
    You can help by donating any items you
are no longer using. So look in your closets,
cupboards, attics, and basements today for
anything that can sell. You will help to keep
the doors of Dawson Learning Center open,
and ready to serve those who need us.

Thankfully,
Rev. Gene Dawson

for more information and free pick-up
Call 427-3010 (Mon.-Fri. 9-5) TODAY!
Dawson Learning Center
(formerly Drug Abuse Preventive Center)
A California non-profit organization
1307 Seabright Avenue
Santa Cruz, California

Herbert Mullin, 2020:
I had just gotten out of Mendocino State
Mental Hospital and my father convinced
me to live there [Drug Abuse Preventive
Center]. It was a Christian based drug rehab
place that had several get-togethers every
week with singing and preaching. I do not
remember Allyn [Kemper] or her husband.

**Gene Dawson (Reverend, Drug Abuse
Preventive Center in Santa Cruz), 1973:**
He was like so many of the mixed up kids I
have met. Herb was one of those minds that
LSD had eaten up.

338

Herb Mullin, 1973:
Gene Dawson forces me into homosexual experience.

Gene Dawson, 1973:
He felt we were all on the wrong track and he wanted to straighten us out. He sat around in yoga positions. He never participated in our group sessions. In fact, Herb would try to disrupt them.

Personally, I felt sorry for him. He was like so many mixed up kids I have met.

He acted like he was flipped out on acid—which wasn't unusual for new arrivals. We hoped he would come to himself in a few days, but he suddenly disappeared and I never saw him again– although his father would call me sometimes and consult with me.

Notes from the center indicate that at one group meeting, Mullin showed up and admitted having "a bit of wine." He told the group he had been living out of his car. Another note simply states "Failed group."

Mullin moved in with Ed Lawrence and Paul Kohman in Ben Lomond for a short time.

Herbert Mullin, 1973:
Kohman gave me free acid. I sit in Ben Lomond all day practically.

First successful homo-sex with Lawrence.

Paul Kohman and Ed Lawrence were experiencing homo-sex together. They wouldn't help me accept myself or my feelings. Kill-joy sadists.

After a visit with his old supervisor at Goodwill, where Mullin admitted to hearing voices, he was committed to the psychiatric ward of San Luis Obispo County General Hospital.

Dee Shafer, 2001:
He said he was also treated on an outpatient basis at Santa Cruz County Mental Health from 1969 to 1971 and hospitalized three weeks in San Luis Obispo sometime in 1969

or 1970.

Herbert Mullin, 2011:
In my CDCR file it shows that I was admitted into the Santa Cruz County Mental Health program during 1969. It should further show that I was diagnosed with undifferentiated schizophrenia. The psychiatric staff suggested to me and my parents (in person) that we three get psychiatric counseling together as a three-some. My parents refused.

Dee Shafer (Contract Psychologist), 2001:
He initially said he had taken LSD approximately three times a year between 1967 and 1972. When asked about his earlier reports that he had purchased and used 50 doses of marijuana during the period when he committed his offenses, he acknowledged the purchase and consumption of these drugs, but said that the LSD was of poor quality. He denied using any other drugs.

At the end of 1969, Mullin was discharged and returned to Santa Cruz where he got a job washing dishes at The Holiday Inn.

Dave Alcorn, 2020:
I knew about his drug use and saw a change in personality. He became more reclusive. He was always quiet, friendly, obviously intelligent, but he became more standoffish, kind of not trusting. I stopped him one night, in the middle of the night, right at the bottom of [Highway] 9 and Redwood, "What are you doing out here?"

He kind of hemmed and hawed. "Do you want a ride up?"

"No."

So I made note of it. But, nothing ever came of that.

Jeff Esposito, 1973:
I know Herb is a believer in reincarnation. At least, I think he is. I was talking to a lady that lives up in Felton and her son, whom Herb knew, had gotten married and they had a child, and Mike Kincaid went into

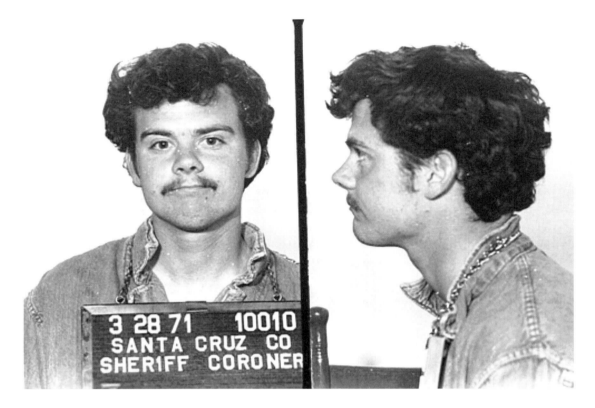

the Army, he was the father of the child, and Herb went to the elementary school one day where Mike's mother was working and asked her if he could see the baby. She asked him why, and he said that he believed that it was Dean Richardson, who was a good friend of ours in high school and a good friend of Herb's, who had been killed in an automobile accident the summer we graduated from school. He believed that the baby was Dean Richardson, reincarnated.

In the early summer of 1970, Mullin and a friend, Pat Brown, took a trip to Hawaii. Mullin admitted himself into a mental health clinic in Maui after Brown ditched Mullin because of his odd behavior.

> *Right and next two pages: A flyer and transcripts of an audio cassette found in Mullin's apartment after he was arrested for killing Fred Perez.*

Dr. Wallis (Doctor in Hawaii who examined Mullin), 1970:

This patient has a schizoid personality with a breakdown after drug abuse a year and a half ago. Under group psychotherapy he got off tranquilizers, but then escaped to Maui recently. He has lately had insomnia and fearful fantasies. He is not able to accept his own hostile feelings and uses massive denial or tension symptoms. He is passive, though impulsive. Diagnosis: Schizophrenia, schizo-affective type.

Mullin's parents paid for him to fly home in July 1970.

Donald T. Lunde, 1973:

He was met at the airport by his father and when Mullin's behavior became bizarre en route from the airport, his father stopped in Sunnyvale and called the police. His father tried to get him admitted to Agnews, but was unsuccessful.

"Kate Millett has made a film which dresses the intellectual bones of <u>Sexual Politics</u> with flesh and feeling."

Three Lives

Produced by
The Women's Liberation
Cinema Company

Directed by Kate Millett

Tuesday, January 16

7:30 & 9:30 pm

75¢

Merrill Dining Hall
UCSC

sponsered by merrill
nonprofit film club and
santa cruz lesbian/feminists

```
MULLIN:

Dont, I'm writing you on my behalf and on that of Mr. Grenville Clark,
a retired corporation lawyer and a long time and current of ah ah of the
World Government Movement, Dr. Albert Einstein, Mayor Hubert Humphrey of
Minneapolis, Dr. Leo Zizzlerd (Sp) and Mr. Carl Van Doren and need a little
help to to get the poor weakling to destroy all of his papers ah. This
technological as well as psyhological orientation in the military policy
has had it's inevitable consequences.  Every action related to the foreign
policy is govern by the one single consideration.  How should we act in order
to achieve the utmost superiority over the enemy in the event of was.  The
answer has been outside the United States, we most establish military bases,
etc. etc.

O.K. now, if the utmost superiority over the enemy in the event of war,
the question has been outside the United States, we must establish military
bases at every possible strategially important point on the globe.  As well
as arms strength and economical/potential allies and inside the United
States tremendous financial power is being concentrated in the hand of the
Military , yet it is being militarized and the loyalty of citizens particularl
civil service is carefully supervised by a police force growing more powerful
every day.  People of independant political thought are harassed.  The public
is suddenly indodrinated by the radio, press, the schools, under the pressure
of military secrecy the range of public information is increasingly
restricted.  And although the large scale and turbulant class struggles of
the masses characteristic from the previous revolutionary period have in
the main come to an end. There are still remnants of the overthrown land-
lord in the comparable  classes.  There's still bourgeoisie and the
remmon (sp) D and the petite bourgeoisie and it's only just started.  The
class strugglers by no means though, the class struggle between the proletariat
and the bourgeoisie, the class struggle betweenthe ????       of forces,
and the class struggle is the ID of all vertical fields between the proletariat
and the bourgeoisie will continue to belong.   Long term coexistence
will all those political parties which are truely devoted to the task of
uniting the people for the cause of socialism in which enjoy the trust
of the people.  As early in June, 1950 of the second session of the
National Committee of the people political console ??  conference, I put
the matter in this way.  People and people's government have no reason
to reject any one or to deny him the opportunity of making a living and
rendering service to the Country, provided he is really willing to serve
the People and provided he really helped the People when times were
difficult, did good before and keeps on doing good without giving up
halfway.
                WILHELMINA ECKTOFF (sp)
JOHN SANDBURG married /     , ANNA ALVA SANDBURG was born, she reached the
age of maturity, she married MARTIN LUTHER MULLIN, their son was MARTIN
WILLIAM MULLIN.  Later in time, in Boulder Creek actually, MARTIN MULLIN
was introduced in the third daughter of Mr. HERBERT C. BAKER andVERONICA
ASH BAKER, I'm the son, the youngest in that family, Mrs. JEAN BAKER
MULLIN, my mother.

(Flute playing)     ThexxfxxlxxwxngxxxaxxxxxxxxxxxxXxXxxxxXxXxxXxxXxXx

Sometime this could be that my voice will be on this tape on August 9 and
that it will probably only record the fact that we are now in the sounds
of Santa Cruz and maybe, maybe just that the wind is is smooth through
all our life and it seems to go just where we want to go on the surface of

                            -1-
```

Herbert Mullin, 1973:
Parents submitted me to extreme gigging
and kill-joy sadist tactics.

On July 30, 1970, Mullin was arrested in Santa
Cruz for being under the influence of drugs.
He was placed in the psychiatric ward of the
county hospital by order of the municipal court.
The charges were dropped in August 1970.

In late 1970 and early 1971, Mullin went
through a phase of dressing up and speaking like
other nationalities. This included—

Pat Bocca, 1973:
Ho Chi Minh-type with his head shaved and
he was wearing a loose green robe.

```
things as the wind is on the surface of things but that from the scene
coming from below is a big disorder that throws into tumult back andforth
and tries to make up our mind of things and difficult thing.  The good
thing to reflect though and if we must go up one side of the wave then
God we reflect down the next.  Did you see the station wagon, you know,
ready.  (Inaudible)  existence in order to be sure of ??     . Ahashamade (Sp)
I know a little of Buddhism but to be at one with myself would seem to take
the reflection of everything I've ever done and everyone I've ever seen
and every place I've ever seen and this goes that speak to me of Buddha
remind me of those reflections I know . (INAUDIBLE) They were both at birth.

Mr. RAYMOND BURR.  If you speak of Cruz and ??  I would say that him, that
I am him.  He is me.  ???  Do not give out so much information people, ah be
yourselves, have fun, do not kill, do not teach people to kill, not the
ones I've known, I do not want to kill because even those that made me, I
will have to, unless, unless he he can and you heard in the sound reflection
on your mind, good mind.  It is one mind, it is one year, huh, just the
years the twelve months, the twelve of months, I have to do some more
studying, huh?  Not right now, yet, why not try to find the names ???.

All right, I can only remember Mathew, Mark, Luke and John, ah Andrew, ah
Peter, James, ah Barthalomew and Judas ah, they are the ones I loved, turn
the light out this time.  Everybody be good, be good and kind and gentle.
I don't care , I don't give a shit,  he made that's about two days now.
Ah, I'm trying to stop that accident from happening back there way in the
past, all of them accidents.  HARRY GOLDBY (sp) he's wonderful man and he
he is a good father to ARTHUR ROBERT ahm why did he tell me to come, why
did he why, why, why did he come around here, wha, wha, what do you come
around here for, what do you come around here for?  No we don't want you
here, go away, yes, I want you to do that, yes, I do want you to that,
no, I don't want you to do that.  You're brave, I'm not him and he damn
him will, him, we are the one in the many, in the many in the one.  Believe
in reincarnation, doubt that it works, invest your money in the stock
market.  Can this Anglon, you name the, what should I name you?  You should
have a beautiful name ah celestial, a celestial name, a beautiful celestial,
you are is little for me anyway in the story.  I'm going to make you that
anyway, anyway.  Maybe you are that.  It ain't impossible, man,  with them
skinny little legs of your's, babe, man , you could, you and me could have
had a trip together, wow, I mean I'm from Boulder Creek, fine man, yeah,
voluptuous, man, that's really cool, ah there nothing wrong with being
voluptuous, you just go right ahead on girls, man, sometimes I dig it, but
but you don't, I don't dig that, uh huh baby, ah and I'd, I truly do, man.
Protect, I have to be able to protect myself and my wife and for that's why
I'm not marrying you.  God Bless America and all the people in it.  Send
energy to their backs.  I, ahm, everybody, everybody learn how to play
ping pong  and tennis, now come on my friends, I want my friends to play
ping pong and tennis because that'll, that'll help me, that'll really help
me.  Legalize acid, legalize acid, do you understand, I don't know what's
happening, what you, what you people do but that's far out, man, GOLDBY , yeah,
do it to thekid, don't tell em nothing, legalize acid and I'll be myself
until, until, un, until God, the real God, man, the real God on the other
side, man, on the other side, the meditator, the wastefulnus of of the in
of the individual, man, the wastefulnessof it, uh, Idon't know if I believe
those, those things I see running around.  They might be true, they might
not be true, what else can I say, you are beautiful, whatever you are, you
really are beautiful to say those things, oh, it isn't much  an necessity
for the peacefulness as it is for the ah war crimes and give your life.
```

-2-

Pat Bocca, 1973:
Chicano wearing a wide-brim black hat and speaking with a very heavy Spanish accent.

Terry Medina, 2020:
He was in San Francisco walking around with a cane and calling himself "Herb Cane" as a play on Herb Caen, the famous [*San Francisco*] *Chronicle* writer.

James Jackson, 1973:
In short, he's seeking his identity.

In March 1971, Mullin was wandering on Chanticleer, near Rodrigues Street. When approached by a Santa Cruz Police Officer—

Herbert Mullin, 1971:
I work five days a week and on weekends I

drink and walk around.

Mullin was arrested for public intoxication. While being booked, Mullin escaped from the arresting officer and was quickly recaptured six blocks away on Lincoln Street. Resisting arrest was added as a charge. After ten days in jail, Mullin was released with "Time Served."

Mullin did stir up a little controversy while he was serving his ten days in jail.

J. Bonar (County corrections officer), 1971:
4-2-71 Subject reportedly kisses inmates while they are asleep. (on the lips) Subject sent to the main jail for his own protection.

Because of subject's homosexual activity other inmates have seriously threatened subject with physical harm.

Mullin moved to San Francisco in May 1971, and then back with his parents in September 1972. The next month, he started his crime spree and murdered Lawrence White.

In late January 1973, Mullin moved out of his parents home.

William Mullin, 1973:
It was a mutual agreement. He had been berating his mother. Evidently because he hadn't been raised properly or because he didn't have the opportunities that other children had. Trying to find fault with her or with us because he was not a success in life. I'd come home from work and Jean would be really uptight after an argument with Herb. Finally, I just told Herb, "You're getting us to where we're going to be climbing the wall."

I said, "This is no good for you either. We've got to do something. I think you're going to have to make arrangements to live elsewhere. It's not good that this tense situation and conflict is going on here."

He agreed.

Mullin was apprehended on February 13, 1973, after killing Fred Perez.

EDMUND KEMPER

On Thursday, February 15, the headless bodies of Rosalind Thorpe and Alice Liu were found off of Eden Canyon Road. The bodies were identified within days.

Pat O'Brien (KPIX reporter), 1973:
The bodies were discovered last week on Eden Canyon Road, east of Castro Valley. Both were found lying just over the side of the road, near a water heater someone had discarded there. Alameda County Sheriff's investigators combed the area Friday, searching for any possible clue that might be found. Both girls had been decapitated and the hands from one body had been cut off. Allison Liu and Rosalind Thorpe were last seen February 5; Miss Thorpe while hitchhiking from campus. Miss Liu at the University Library.

The same day a nude woman's body was found, mostly decomposed, in Contra Costa County.

Samples of Alice Liu and Cynthia Schall's hair were compared with hair samples removed from Mullin's car. Schall's sample was determined "not to have a common origin" with the samples. The results of Liu's tests were inconclusive.

Wendy Thorpe, 2020:
I was pulled out of Carmel High when she [Rosalind Thorpe] went missing. My dad was watching KTVU Channel 2 news at ten o'clock at night and what happened was, they pulled my sister's head out of a black bag and he recognized the dental work. My sister had a chipped tooth in front from running in the halls at school and falling down. I believe that's how he found out. We should have been told first. No one should be watching the news and see your daughter's head, the skull. I mean this is how I remem-

ber it, I was only fourteen. I heard this from mom. It was also a very sensational time. I remember the news showing murder victims with their heads down in a pool of blood. You don't get that level of sensationalism on television now.

HERBERT MULLIN

On the morning of Saturday, February 17, at a press conference Peter Chang was asked a striking question—

Don West (*San Francisco Examiner* reporter), 1973:
Would you say that Santa Cruz is the murder capital of the world?

Peter Chang, 1973:
Right now, we must be the murder capital.

That afternoon, Jeffrey Devin Card, the brother of Brian Scott Card, discovered the four boys' bodies in their makeshift home out in the forest. He contacted the Santa Cruz Police Department.

Terry Medina (Santa Cruz County Sheriff's Office Detective), 1973:
I received a call from the Santa Cruz Police Department that a young man was there and reported that he found three bodies off of Highway 9.

He said three at that time. He wasn't sure.

Detective Medina met Jeffrey Devin Card at the Santa Cruz Police department and they went to the crime scene.

Terry Medina, 1973:
At that time that I was up there, there was at least three dead persons in that cabin, and later we confirmed that there was four dead persons in that cabin.

It showed signs of movement, but there was—hadn't been a lot of struggling or fighting. It showed signs that people had moved around in it.

It appeared as though they may have been getting up possibly in the morning, putting on a shoe; an indication that someone was cooking on a Coleman stove.

There was pancake batter.

I don't recall if there was pancakes at this time.

Dr. Jean Everice Carter was called out to the crime scene when it was discovered on February 17.

Terry Medina, 1973:
As we approached the crime scene, I had with me a criminalist from the San Mateo County crime lab. We cordoned off the area surrounding the tent or the cabin, and a systematic search was begun from the outside perimeter into the tent or the cabin itself, photographed and everything was preserved as it was.

Dr. Jean Everice Carter, 1973:
Almost all of them had some carbonaceous material deep in the wound, but there was no tattooing or powder burns on the surface of the skin.

A lack of powder burns indicated the boys were not shot at extremely close range.

Terry Medina, 1973:
The reporting party, Mr. Card, had indicated that there was a rifle kept in the cabin, and we attempted to look for that rifle, and there was none.

Paul Dougherty, 1973:
We were very careful to remove each item at the scene very carefully and search as we removed these items, and upon the removal of one of the bodies, a projectile—actually two projectiles—were found.

Miriam Finnegan, 2021:
My dad [Santa Cruz Police Detective Dennis Finnegan] would come home after a rough day and I was over there a lot for dinner, and

I remember he came home and sat down and said, "It was like a slaughterhouse. I've never seen anything like that."

He was really shook up.

Terry Medina, 2020:
That sure was a crime scene up there. Processing it all lasted over twenty-four hours. We got up there around three o'clock in the afternoon. We didn't get the bodies out until five o'clock the next day. It got dark early up in the forest. The fire department brought big lights up there and a generator. It was a hard, difficult place to get to. So it was decided: Arbsland and Medina had to stay at that camp site with those dead bodies in the tent overnight.

It was a long night. Brad Arbsland and I started scaring ourselves, right?

We don't know who killed him. Is the guy coming back? I remember going, "Brad, did somebody check to make sure they're all dead? What if they're alive?" We didn't remember anybody telling us. So we crawled in and looked at their faces, "Okay, they must be dead."

We had the lights, the generator going, and it was all lit up. We were sitting there, and it's cold, then we started saying, "Oh shit, we lit ourselves up. What if this guy comes back? We're easy targets now."

You know? We can't see shit and we have these spotlights on us. So then we would turn the generator off and it would be dark.

And then we decided we would get twenty-five yards apart in case there was somebody going to come back and attack. Oh, it was crazy. We made ourselves crazy.

The boys' bodies were not removed until the

Next four pages: The bodies of the four boys in Felton were found and removed. A massive search was conducted to find out if more bodies were in the forest. None were found.
Right: The Sheriff's Posse (top) and the teenage Sheriff's Office Explorer Scouts were recruited to help in the search efforts

following day on Sunday the 18th.

Sam Robustelli, 2020:
I was an investigator for the DA's office at that time. I had left the Sheriff's Office. I was called out to do the crime scene for the four boys. We moved their bodies out. Santa Cruz didn't have a lab at that time. We used a local mortuary to do the autopsies. So the pathologist is there and he says, "You boys should get some rest. I can come back tomorrow and do this work."

We said, "No, what do you mean? We're all here, let's get this finished."

He said, "Look at yourselves."

The four bodies were laid out on every surface and we were eating donuts. Just so tired, we had lost it.

On February 20, 1973, Judge Charles Franich ordered Mullin moved from the Santa Cruz County jail to the San Mateo County Jail.

Charles Franich, 1973:
Upon representation made by the District Attorney of the County of Santa Cruz, State of California, that the Defendant, Herbert William Mullin's life may be endangered if he is held in the Santa Cruz County Jail; I, therefore, find the facilities of the Santa Cruz County Jail to be inadequate, unsafe and unfit for the confinement therein of Defendant Herbert William Mullin under Section 4007 of the California Penal Code; Therefore, it is ordered that said Defendant Herbert William Mullin be remanded to the custody of Sheriff Earl B. Whitmore at the San Mateo County Jail for confinement until further Order of this Court; and that the Sheriff of the County of Santa Cruz deliver said Defendant Herbert William Mullin to the custody of the Sheriff of San Mateo County.

Herbert Mullin, 1981:
It wasn't until I was arrested, when I'd been in jail 60, maybe 70 days, that I realized what had happened. That was when it all came together.

Down from
the hill

Carrying out one of the bodies of the four victims are Jack Odgers (left) chief forest ranger from Felton and John Rosasco, (in front) a state forest ranger at Felton, a man from Smith Mortuary in Santa Cruz, and Sandy Sanders of the Santa Cruz County Sheriff's Department.

Johns's philosophy = one man's death appeases God and God doesn't destroy the Penninsula by violent earth-quake. Therefore every day some one committs suicide and/or gets murdered.

There was an earth-quake on April 18th, 1906 in San Francisco. The Revolutionary War was started on April 19th, 1775. These coincidences along with my birth-date April 18th, 1947 did in fact make my parents & sister jealous. Whether or not they will admitt their jealousy and envy ... I don't know. If they do, it will be the first time they have ever been truthful with & concerning me. If they do not, they will be continuing their lieing and kill-joy SADIST TACTICS.

From August 6 1971 to March 6 1972 I boxed every day at the Newman Human Gymnasium. They didn't help me socially — they only exploited me and enjoyed seeing me fight for nothing.

In June I went to see Mr Eros Forratt in Cornell. He is my uncle. During our conversation he told me not to kill anyone or if I was to kill anyone to kill my parents.

The next five pages: Writings of Mullin's after he was arrested.

351

I guess my biggest problem was not ever having a steady partner. I had five years worth of fear to work through before I accepted homo-sexualality. The boys next door, whom I met at age 6 and played with till 15 — yet attend different schools, were bi-sexuals — yet they refused to introduce me.

Anti-homo sentiment expressed openly at family gatherings. i.e. jealousy — i think people who wear blue suits are odd — meanwhile I'm going to get a blue suit.

In the summer of 1971 I had more or less accepted my bi-sexual life. I then discovered the co-incidence of my birth-date & Albert Einstein's death — same date.

I failed to realize its significance. I failed to gather as much material as possible about him and his life work.

I felt an increased need for L.S.D. I hitch-hiked to Ben Lomond to buy some from Jim Gianera.

status.

About the 4th of October I asked my parents if I could live at their home until I entered the Armed Forces. They agreed to let me.

Between the 4th of October and the 13th of October my parents continually tried to get me to go kill something. I refused time and again. Yet they were breaking down my will power. They were enervating my consciousness.

Then on October 13th, 1972 I took a baseball bat and drove my car toward Santa Cruz from Felton on Hywy 9. Three miles from Santa Cruz I saw Lawrence White walking toward Felton. He telepathically told me to kill him.

I turned around and parked on an fire-road and called him to me. Within five-minutes I'd clubed him to death.

message Bat Masterson.

Two or three days later I got up early and took a baseball bat and left my folks house intending to prove to my father & mother that I could kill something.

Half-way between Felton and Santa Cruz I spotted Lawrence White walking north on Hywy 9. He telepathically transmitted the message "Come on kid, get you bat and kill me" I then turned my car around and parked it on a side road and coaxed Mr. White into a position where I could and did bat him to death.

I KILLED LAWRENCE WHITE because MARTIN W. MULLIN AND JEAN C. MULLIN, MY PARENTS, HAD BEEN HEN PECKING AND PESTERING AND DEMANDING ME TO KILL A HUMAN BEING FROM October 2, 1972 to October 13, 1972.
I HAD RESISTED THEIR DEMANDS UNTIL FINALLY I BROKE AND SUBMITTED TO THEIR COMMAND.
IT WAS THEIR INTENT NOT MINE.
I HAD NO MALICE AFORETHOUGHT TOWARDS LAWRENCE WHITE. HE JUST HAPPENED TO BE OUT ON THAT COUNTRY ROAD, AND HE TELEPATHICALLY DIRECTED ME TO KILL HIM. HIS EXACT WORDS WERE … "COME ON KID, KILL ME"

353

In September of 1972 on the 5$\underline{th}$ I went to Jim Gianera and by the 8$\underline{th}$ I'd bought $50^{00} of L.S.D.

On September 9$\underline{th}$ as I went to bed to sleep, I saw a mental picture of my father, Martin W. Mullin, carrying a young 20 year old boy whom he had just killed. He was somewhere near the Grand Canyon.

It was the first time in my life I realized he is a kill-crazy man.

5-24-1973

On Sept. 8$\underline{th}$, 1972 I bought $50 worth of L.S.D. from Jim Gianera.

On Sept. 9$\underline{th}$, 1972 I visited my parents home in Felton.

They weren't Home.

when I went to bed that night 9-9-1972 my father sent me a telepathic picture.

I saw him carrying a dead 180 lb. 20 yr. old whom I suppose my father had just killed.

They were on a trip to the Grand Canyon.

354

When I was six years old and living in Walnut Creek my parents demanded that my sister & cousins and Steven White my same age friend across the street not explain to me the pleasures of masturbation.

Why did my parents put this social-sexual freeze on me?

In early October 1972 my father, Bill, telepathically said he and Enos had talked the subject of over and decided that, me being born on April 18th, 1947 had to much potential power & composure in this life and in the next, if there is a next. Therefore they decided to put this social-sexual freeze on me to retard my progress. They doped that this action, kill-joy tactic, would help increase their own power in this life and the next.

I don't know whether or not they'll admitt these facts to the court or not. My case is based on this social-sexual freeze; kill-joy tactic. Its my word against theirs. Therefore I ask my father & mother to submitt to sodium-pentothol examination; a psychiatrist appointed by the court could administer the investigation.

2 15 73   69173
SANTA CRUZ CO
SHERIFF CORONER
MULLIN

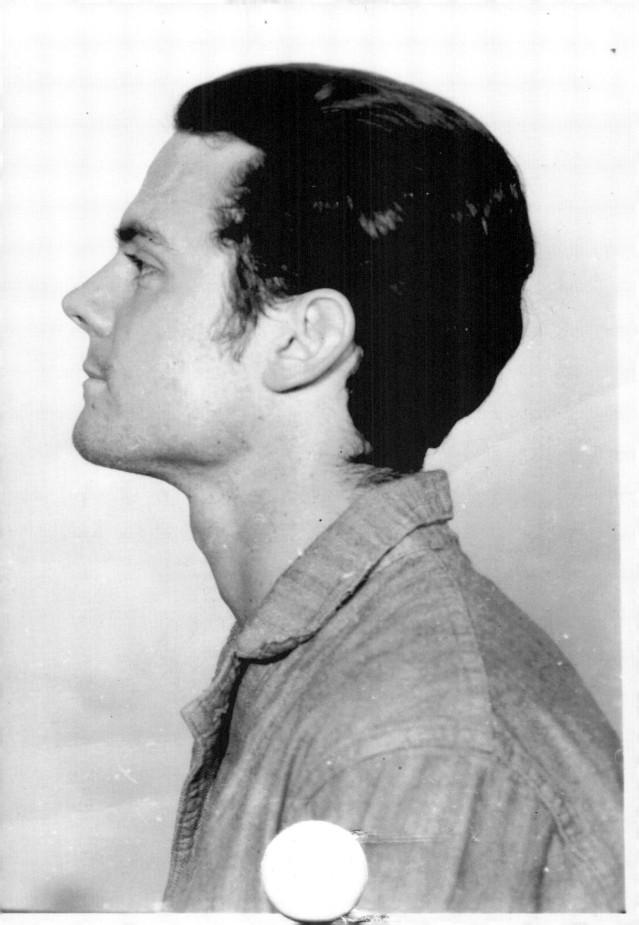

WHY MULLIN KILLED

On April 10, 1973, Herbert Mullin was interviewed in the Redwood City jail by Dr. Donald
Lunde for thirty-one minutes. Mullin attempted to explain why he commited the thirteen
murders.

Donald Lunde, 1973:
You're saying that it started with revenge, but
it also had to do with preventing earthquakes,
which I guess other people have been doing.
Other people were killing people, which was
keeping the Earth quiet, in particular, the San
Andreas fault, in general or what?

Herbert Mullin, 1973:
All, all faults, you know, on coastlines, more
countries are protected through the result of
a minor natural disaster. In other words, we
human beings through the history of the
[inaudible] have protected our continent from
cataclysmic earthquakes by murder. A minor
natural disaster avoids a major natural disaster.

Donald Lunde, 1973:
But if murder is a natural disaster why should
you be locked up for it? It's natural. It has a
good effect.

Herbert Mullin, 1973:
Your laws. You see, the thing is, people, people,
people get together in the, say, in the White
House. How many people die in the White
House every year? People that go in and walk
through the doors. See, people like to sing
the die song, you know, they like to sing the
die song. It's like if I'm president of my class
when I graduate from high school, I can tell
two, possibly three of the young male sapiens to die. I can sing that song for them and
they'll have to kill themselves or be killed in
an automobile accident, a knifing, a gunshot
wound. You ask me why this is, and I say, well,
they have to do that in order to protect the
ground from an earthquake. Because all of the
people in the community have been dying all
year long and my class has to go, we have to
chip in, so to speak, to the darkness. We have

to die also. And people would rather sing the
die song than murder.

Donald Lunde, 1973:
What is the die song?

Herbert Mullin, 1973:
Just that. I'm telling you to die, you know, I'm
telling you to kill yourself or be killed so that,
you know, my continent will not fall off into
the ocean so that the entity which is driving
my body will continue to drive, bodies like I,
like I existed. And the people in my class, you
know, four or five hundred people in my class
are protected. We protect our stratus so that
the entity that is driving in the body that is
starving in Nigeria does not get to drive in
our bodies, and our bodies go to the bodies in
Nigeria and starve. See, it's all based on reincarnation, this dies to protect my state.

Donald Lunde, 1973:
How does anybody know how many people
have to die or who's supposed to die to protect others?

Herbert Mullin, 1973:
Well, how does it feel [inaudible]

Donald Lunde, 1973:
How was this communicated to you?
Through your conscience or the voices?

Herbert Mullin, 1973:
Well, I don't know. Less than ten percent. Five
percent.

Donald Lunde, 1973:
One percent?

Herbert Mullin, 1973:
No, I wouldn't say so. I'd say if I asked to get
a chronology of my life. You get a chronology
of the Earth and all the Earth's earthquakes
from China all the way back—China has the
oldest records of earthquakes, of, you know,
up to the present and you see the population
growth. You know, the number of people on

the Earth, the number of people that died. You know, in the United States of America, sixty people die every day because a doctor can't get to them. You take all these deaths, you know, the demographic data of Earth, break them down, and you take the seismic data. You know, the number of earthquakes, their potency, the times they happen, the history of the wars, and you can come out with the percentage that people have been steadily dying violently in order to, to prove to the great creator who was the creator of the Earth and put it in orbit around the Sun, just to prove to him that we're willing to die, you know. But if he can keep the Earth in orbit and keep the continents intact so that there isn't any cataclysmic earthquakes, or any violent tidal waves, you know. There's going to be some anyway. We homo sapiens, we have found that murder decreases the number of natural disasters and the extent of the devastation. Therefore, we will always murder.

Donald Lunde, 1973:
You mean not just earthquakes, but also floods, tornadoes, hurricanes.

Herbert Mullin, 1973:
Yeah, all of those things. Homo sapiens, you know, I mean, you read in the Bible about Jonah, that was twelve men in the boat. Jonah was in the boat. You know, it's just my thesis, you know, and Jonah stood up and said, God darn that. If we don't, you know, if somebody doesn't die, all thirteen of us are going to die. So he jumped overboard. You know, he was drowned. This is, you know, the dream. This man's trying to write it down on paper. It must have been thousands of years before Christ. In the sea. You know, the sea, the God of the sea said, "Well he died all right."

So you know, in about a half hour or so, it calmed down. I mean, it doesn't happen right away. But, you know, if the guy didn't die, here's—picture two guys standing together in the boat, you know, after Jonah jumps out and maybe, maybe they go a day or two in a violent storm, and they say after the storms all over, you know, two guys standing there just

smoking a pipe or something after the danger is passed. They say, "You know, I bet if Jonah didn't kill himself, God would have killed all of us."

And so they said, "Well, every time there's a,"—you know, they get to town, they go to the bar, they tell the people at the bar about Jonah and they say, "We think Jonah saved our life by committing suicide."

And the people in the bar say, "Well, maybe that would help us."

You know, so they go out and get somebody. So the story goes on—

Donald Lunde, 1973:
According to the story, Jonah didn't die. He was cast up on land by the whale. He was still alive. So doesn't that kind of negate your theory?

Herbert Mullin, 1973:
Yeah, well, OK, you're asking me to explain now what this means, you know, the swallowing of Jonah. OK, now I'm asking you to believe, you know, I'm asking you to believe on the typical, how would you say? I would say I'm a scapegoat. I'm asking you to swallow this Jonah story and believe that a minor natural disaster will prevent a major natural disaster. And if you believe it, then you live.

You, homo sapien, I'm not talking to one man. I'm talking to everybody. I'm writing this story so everyone can read it. I hope it's published everywhere, you know, and whoever you know, whoever wrote the, you know, compiled about. Well, I'm going to accept this. Well, here's one I'm going to write about Jonah. That sounds like a good plan. You know, mankind, Jonah. You know, twelve sons.

Donald Lunde, 1973:
Are you writing it out so that people—

Herbert Mullin, 1973:
I'm not going to write anymore. I can't write anymore. You know you can use stuff like this, but I—Will this tape be heard by the district attorney?

Donald Lunde, 1973:
No. Absolutely not. This is not for Mr. Chang, that's for sure.

Herbert Mullin, 1973:
Well, is it for Mr. Chang?

Donald Lunde, 1973:
I said it is not. Definitely not.

Herbert Mullin, 1973:
Yeah. All right. All right.

Donald Lunde, 1973:
Mr. Chang gets nothing from me. I thought you were saying that you wanted a certain part of the story to be widely known to people.

Herbert Mullin, 1973:
No, I'm telling you about Jonah. About the guy that wrote Jonah.

Donald Lunde, 1973:
Oh, I see.

Herbert Mullin, 1973:
Oh, no, I don't want, I don't want my story told throughout the world. I don't like the publicity. No, I don't like publicity. You know, I don't like what happened to me. I wish I had had the self-control to say, well, I played the role of the masochist rather than the role of the sadist. A sadist gets revenge. A masochist doesn't. Well, I see you guys took me for a ride. You put dementia praecox, and I'm just going to let you do it. I'm not going to get revenge? I wish I did. I wish I would have said, well, I'll just, you know, get a job and have a wife and children and have barbecues on the weekend. You know, I don't want to go to jail.

Donald Lunde, 1973:
How did they lay the dementia praecox on you. Was it done through drugs or how?

Herbert Mullin, 1973:
Well, yeah, you know.

Donald Lunde, 1973:
You mean marijuana?

Herbert Mullin, 1973:
Yeah. Marijuana. Marijuana induces dementia praecox, you know. I mean it furthers dementia praecox is what it does. It doesn't induce dementia praecox. Marijuana furthers it. If Jim Gianera had, you know, given me some of the benzedrine that he was using, you know, if he had sold me, Benzedrine, he was using it, you know, that I wouldn't have had this trouble. I wouldn't have wanted to wreak revenge on him because benzedrine, you know, as I look back on my experience, causes one to talk and to act, you know, as a matter of fact, you become an artist. You want to draw and carve and sculpt, you know. Many, many men that are sculptors and, well, look at Beniamino Bufano, he used to take benzedrine in the morning. Look at the sculptures he has. Right down on San Francisco Wharf, he's got a sculpture that I'll bet is one of the nicest sculptures I've ever seen. Some guy standing there with big long sleeves, you know, that you can put things in and stuff.

So you know, he didn't sell me the benzedrine—Gianera. He didn't sell me the benzedrine because he'd rather see me in, you know, he'd rather have that picture of me for five years in dementia praecox, you know, then to have me, you know, sell me a lid and and a roll of bennies at the same time, you know,

Donald Lunde, 1973:
He would just sell you a lid and no bennies?

Herbert Mullin, 1973:
Yeah! You know, he wouldn't even tell me about the bennies.

Donald Lunde, 1973:
Why do you think he had a need to do that to you?

Herbert Mullin, 1973:
Because I'm a better sadist.

Donald Lunde, 1973:
He was jealous?

Herbert Mullin, 1973:
Yeah.

Donald Lunde, 1973:
In terms of reincarnation, do you expect
that Gianera would be reincarnated already,
maybe?

Herbert Mullin, 1973:
I don't know. You know, I'm just saying that
everybody I've ever met subconsciously, you
know, believes in reincarnation, although they
won't talk about, you know, I mean, I appreciate your situation. You think. You think that
you have me going. I've got him talking now,
you know, this is your position. You know,
this is all I wanted to do. I'm trying to mimic
your subconscious thoughts as it talks to itself.
The only thing I want to do is to get Herbert
Mullin to continue talking and explaining his
mind so that I can have material that I can use,
to psychoanalyze his mind. To find out exactly
how he works.

Donald Lunde, 1973:
That's very good. That's very close to the
truth.

Herbert Mullin, 1973:
Yes.

Donald Lunde, 1973:
Are you also getting the vibrations in terms of
what I think about what you've said.

Herbert Mullin, 1973:
Well, I'd like to hear.

Donald Lunde, 1973:
What I think. And I will tell you fairly bluntly
because it's better you should hear this now,
than in court where it may come as a surprise.
I think that if you get up or if I get up or
your attorney gets up in court and says that
you killed people in order to prevent earthquakes, the judge is going to think you're
crazy, and he will declare you incompetent
because most people don't believe that killing
prevents earthquakes, and most people will
raise the question, what evidence do you have
for this? And so I guess that's the next question I'm asking.

What evidence is there? And I'm not aware
that there was any correlation, say with 1905
and 1906 and a drop in the murder rate in
San Francisco. I'm just not really sure of that.
And are you telling me that during World War
I, there were no earthquakes or natural disasters in the world? Or during World War II?

Herbert Mullin, 1973:
I'm telling you as a male homo sapien should
get yourself a list of the earthquakes that have
happened. You should get yourself a list of the
death rate per day. You should get yourself a
list of the natural disasters like typhoons and
things, you know, chronology and, you know,
January through December from the beginning of written history. And that's what you
should do.

Donald Lunde, 1973:
Have you ever done that?

Herbert Mullin, 1973:
And then we could talk about this. Yes, yes, I
have begun. I wrote the United Nations and
I went to a library and I started studying the
demographic, you know, demographic data.
They have a yearbook that they put out.

Donald Lunde, 1973:
Here?

Herbert Mullin, 1973:
No. I did it in Santa Cruz. I did it in December just before I, you know, while I was going
through the process of becoming a United
States [inaudible].

Donald Lunde, 1973:
Which library did you go to?

Herbert Mullin, 1973:
The main library.

Donald Lunde, 1973:
In the city of Santa Cruz. Did you check out the book?

Herbert Mullin, 1973:
No. You can't check it out. It has to stay there.

Donald Lunde, 1973:
Did you sign anything? You don't have a library card?

Herbert Mullin, 1973:
No.

Donald Lunde, 1973:
You did write to the United Nations at that same time. Did you get a reply? Did they reply? Did they answer your letter?

Herbert Mullin, 1973:
Yeah.

Donald Lunde, 1973:
What did they say?

Herbert Mullin, 1973:
They said check the library.

Donald Lunde, 1973:
Did you ever read Revelation? There is some mention in there [inaudible] refers to natural disasters.

Herbert Mullin, 1973:
Do you believe in reincarnation?

Donald Lunde, 1973:
In the sense that people have come back and [inaudible] or you mean some believe animals come back. Which version are you talking about?

Herbert Mullin, 1973:
I'd just like to know what your interpretation of reincarnation is. What is your interpretation of it?

Donald Lunde, 1973:
My general interpretation would be that the view that personalities in turn influence other generations [inaudible]. And my own view is that I have no reason to, no evidence to believe that or to disbelieve it. You certainly see what appear to be striking similarities from time to time between some, say young person and then some deceased person that you might have known about, where their mannerisms and thought patterns and speech and so on are remarkably similar. And I don't know how to account for that.
    On the other hand, I have never met anybody who seemed to be consciously aware of previous lives. Are you?

Herbert Mullin, 1973:
No. I don't ever recall ever being before ever being here afterwards.
    I know that I go to sleep and I wake up and I don't remember anything between. So when I'm sleeping maybe that's, that's the little dip.

Donald Lunde, 1973:
Yeah, well yeah. I've heard that. Who knows what happens when you're sleeping? How are you sleeping, by the way? You said you—you stay up all night or what?

Herbert Mullin, 1973:
I stay up until about five and then I sleep from five to six and get up for breakfast.

Donald Lunde, 1973:
And then when do you go back to bed?

Herbert Mullin, 1973:
Usually, I don't go back to bed until like ten o'clock. Sleep from ten to eleven. I tend to have lunch and I sleep from lunch until maybe four o'clock. Then I'm up from four until five in the morning. I'm generally awake studying and reading books and drawing pictures. I have some art magazines, a Bible, *Life*

and Times of Albert Einstein by Ronald Clark,
James Joyce, *Portrait of the Artist as a Young Man.*

Donald Lunde, 1973:
Pretty heavy reading.
[A short exchange I can't understand. They
talk over each other.]

Herbert Mullin, 1973:
The TV goes off at midnight.

Donald Lunde, 1973:
Is that when you do your heavy reading?

Herbert Mullin, 1973:
Yeah, after midnight.

Donald Lunde, 1973:
Is there a light on?

Herbert Mullin, 1973:
Yeah, they leave the light on twenty-four
hours a day. When I first got here, you know,
they had some guy to walk around after every
meal. So I threw water back at them and said,
"You shouldn't leave the light on."

Donald Lunde, 1973:
Does anyone bother you now?

Herbert Mullin, 1973:
No. It's pretty nice. But is there anything that
can be done about the light at night?

Donald Lunde, 1973:
What do you mean? On or off, or what?

Herbert Mullin, 1973:
Yeah. Can they turn it off?

Donald Lunde, 1973:
I don't know. There's no switch in the cell, I
guess.

Herbert Mullin, 1973:
You'd have to talk to the sergeant.

Donald Lunde, 1973:
I talked to them a lot about the paper and
they did start bringing such things again. You
remember some weeks ago you asked me to
check it out?

Herbert Mullin, 1973:
I get paper from my attorney. I could use
clear paper for drawing. I'm drawing on lined
paper. That might be too much to ask.

Donald Lunde, 1973:
Do you want the light off at night? I thought
that's the only time you said you read, when
it's quiet.

Herbert Mullin, 1973:
Yeah, well, that's true. So I guess you're correct.
You know, you have deduced the situation
properly and made the correct suggestion.

Donald Lunde, 1973:
[Inaudible]

Herbert Mullin, 1973:
K-R-I-Y-A. [Mullin has KRIYA tattooed on
his left foot]

Donald Lunde, 1973:
Is that from Hawaii?

Herbert Mullin, 1973:
No. I believe it's from India. In the mountains.

Donald Lunde, 1973:
Where did you acquire it?

Herbert Mullin, 1973:
I don't see any problem. [Inaudible]

Donald Lunde, 1973:
Okay, but does it mean anything important to
you now?

Herbert Mullin, 1973:
I hope, uh, if reincarnation is true and I hope
it is. I hope I'll be able to find my way to
a situation where I can understand Kriya

perfectly.

Donald Lunde, 1973:
Do you no longer consider yourself a Catholic then in terms of religion?

Herbert Mullin, 1973:
No, I'd very much like to find a priest and make a confession.

Donald Lunde, 1973:
So do you consider yourself a Catholic?

Herbert Mullin, 1973:
Yes, I do.

Donald Lunde, 1973:
Didn't Father O'Connor, John O'Connor come visit you?

Herbert Mullin, 1973:
Yes, he did.
[Inaudible back and forth. Something to do with Father O'Connor's visit.]

Donald Lunde, 1973:
So far as you said today, the thing that puzzles me, if you really had in mind preventing a greater natural disaster, then how do you construe this as murder with malice aforethought if your intention was really to help to prevent disaster?

Herbert Mullin, 1973:
Well, I understand the law. I've read the history of the United States. I know that the laws were instituted, you know, among men, [inaudible], the people got together and decided it's against the law to commit murder. And the reason it's against the law to commit murder is because when a man, you know, starts taking other lives, I don't want him to take too many because I'd be afraid of him in this life and in my next life, you know, I mean, after I die, I'm going to have to be conceived again. I believe a man has believed in reincarnation, maybe consciously, verbally for ten thousand years. And so they instituted this law,

you know. They used to do it back there ten thousand years ago. You know, they believe that a minor natural disaster, you know, averts a major natural disaster. They'd let a guy go kill-crazy. The guy would go kill-crazy, a homo sapien bull. He'd go kill-crazy and kill maybe twenty or thirty people. Then they'd lynch him. Or they'd have another kill-crazy person kill him. Because they don't want him to get too powerful in the next life and they don't do anything. All they do is sing the die song. Or go kill someone. They don't kill themselves. The people that make the law, they protect themselves from the kill crazy person.

Donald Lunde, 1973:
But they also make distinctions between some killers who are murderers and some who are not. Just as I was going over before, but what you were just saying now is that anybody who kills is a murderer. Then all those in the armed forces should be convicted of murder according to that.

Herbert Mullin, 1973:
You'd have to study military science and police science and the story of Jonah in order to answer those questions. I think we've gone far enough. Well, with our critique today. I'd really like to cut the interview short if we could. I don't want to put any more of my thoughts down.

THE JURY ROOM AND KEM- PER'S PISTOL

On February 21, 1973, a memorial was held at UCSC for Alice Liu and Rosalind Thorpe.

Speaking at the memorial—

Bonnie Ring (UCSC lecturer and friend of Rosalind Thorpe), 1973:
She was a big, bouncy, fun loving, play- ful, but sometimes serious girl involved in risk-taking, caring, and loving. She was no saint, but a very special person.

Her mother said one of the things she will miss most is her daughter's big bear hug when she came home.

She did most of the things she wanted to—that's why she hitchhiked.

What happened needn't have happened and needn't happen again. Take an active stand. If we need better busing, let's ask for it. If we need better lighting on campus, let's let everybody know about it. That is one memorial Roz would value.

Robert Edgar (Provost of Kresge College at UCSC and friend of Alice Liu), 1973:
I wish to speak for Alice Liu. I knew her. Bright and lively like a bird she was. And now she's gone, struck down. I am filled with sorrow and grief.

Edmund Kemper:
I'd seen one too many episodes of one too many crime shows where that is one of the available resources for clues. Tracking down the attenders. It'd take one man taking pictures of the people there to eliminate as potential suspects.

Sam Robustelli, 2020:
I didn't attend. I don't know if the Sheriff's Office was there, but I'm sure they were.

HERBERT MULLIN

On February 22, 1973, Mullin's father visited him in jail.

In silent tribute to their slain classmates, about 1,000 UCSC students attend a memorial convocation this morning in the quarry amphitheater. Friends of Rosalind Thorpe and Alice Liu, slain hitchhikers, told the mourners that " what happened needn't have happened, and need not happen again," as Bonnie Ring put it. She is a lecturer and counsellor at Merrill College, and a friend of Miss Thorpe. "Take an active stand," in preventing such tragedies, she urged.

Herbert Mullin, 1973:
Uh, did Pease talk to you tonight?

William Mullin, 1973:
Yeah.

Herbert Mullin, 1973:
Oh. Uh.

William Mullin, 1973:
It's going to be a very costly venture but we hired him.

Herbert Mullin, 1973:
Uh, did he, did he tell you what I wanted to do? Do you agree with that, uh, position?

William Mullin, 1973:
No. I think you need psychiatric help more than you need an arraignment before the law.

Herbert Mullin, 1973:
Well.

William Mullin, 1973:
Why did you ever buy those guns? Where did you get that rifle?

Herbert Mullin, 1973:
Uh, pertaining to that stuff, you know, uh—

William Mullin, 1973:
You're going to talk to me.

Herbert Mullin, 1973:
I'm going to plead the Fifth Amendment.

William Mullin, 1973:
You're asking for deep, deep trouble then. You'd better ask for a psychiatrist before you do that.

Herbert Mullin, 1973:
If it's up to me, you know, I mean, you guys have an awful lot of power as far as how I act, you know what I mean. When I met you, I wasn't even, uh—

William Mullin, 1973:
Never mind.

Herbert Mullin, 1973:
Two weeks old, you know. I mean I can raise my son better than you raised me.

William Mullin, 1973:
Okay, Herb.

Herbert Mullin, 1973:
Other than that, I want to, to plead nolo contendere and I want to stand on the Fifth Amendment. My son would have gone to a military academy. You know.

William Mullin, 1973:
Is that all you want to say?

Herbert Mullin, 1973:
I'm afraid for Anna, dad.

William Mullin, 1973:
For whom?

Herbert Mullin, 1973:
I'm going to plead no contendere and stand on the Fifth Amendment.

Later—

Herbert Mullin, 1973:
I did not know that my father was accepting financial responsibility for my legal counsel. When I discovered this on February 22, 1973 I immediately relieved Richard Pease, Attorney at Law of his responsibilities in this case and requested a public defender.

On March 1, 1973, Mullin appeared in court with James Jackson.

Mullin pled guilty to the crimes. Judge May refused to accept the plea and entered a plea of "Not Guilty" on Mullin's behalf.

Mullin attempted to fire James Jackson. Judge May refused that as well.

Peter Chang, 1973:
The judge does not have to accept pleas, especially when he has no knowledge of the defendant's ability to understand the consequences of such a plea, and especially when the defendant's counsel disagrees and especially when the counsel has had no opportunity to assess Mullin's ability to assist in his own defense

James Jackson, 1973:
He can't fire me. He has no choice in the matter. The judge won't let him.
    The only thing he can do now is raise some money and hire a lawyer and he doesn't have any money.

ED KEMPER IN THE JURY ROOM

The Jury Room is a bar located across the street from the county government center and Santa Cruz Courthouse. The bar is still there today and serves a hip, local clientele, but in the 1970s it was a hot spot for off duty law enforcement personnel. Kemper drank there often, listening in on the cop talk of the day, hoping to pick up anything on his crimes.

Sam Robustelli, 2020:
Everybody knows this but some of us would go unwind in the Jury Room and he'd come sit with people. I saw him in there a couple times, but we never engaged.

Jim Conner, 2020:
Since Ed worked at the 76 station at Water and Ocean, you know, after work we'd all go hang over at the Jury Room, and when he'd get off work he'd come hang out with us and have a beer. Little did we know he was pumping us for information. At that

time all we wanted to talk about was current events—the homicides. He just had an ear to the ground on our conversations and we didn't realize. I mean, Ed was there having beers with us.

Edmund Kemper, 1984:
They'd buy me a beer. I'd buy them a beer. Casual relationships, but I was poking around a little bit trying to find some things out. I knew they wouldn't be privy to hot information, but there were some things that were bothering me, like were there any speculations on how they were dying.

Dave Alcorn, 2020:
Kemper was a groupie. He'd meet us down at the Jury Room. We'd have our little choir practice after work there. We would discuss the events of the day and vent any stuff before we got home. He would hang out with us. He was a big guy, you know, I liked arm wrestling him because I could beat him.

Edmund Kemper, 1984:
I guess as a friendly nuisance. I got in the way. And it was deliberate. Again, friendly nuisances are dismissed.

Dave Alcorn, 2020:
I didn't know him [Kemper] outside of the Jury Room. He was a nice guy, very intelligent. But he was a groupie, just one of the groupies you put up with. He was nice enough but you'd get tired of him.

Sam Munoz (Jury Room bar manager):
He come in like everybody else after work.

I didn't know about his mental record. Some of the officers probably did, but they never said nothing to no one about it. Just like I say, it was really unbelievable, you know. He acted just like anyone else when he was in here. He wanted to be a cop awful bad. He wanted to be a policeman, that's what he really wanted. And he tried. He was too tall for the highway patrol. He come in with handcuffs and a badge. He got 'em off Bob

over there. Bob went to school. I believe when they go to school, they get a silver badge, and then when they get out, they get the gold badge. So he had that and he had these handcuffs. He'd come in here, playing, and handcuff the guys. He was pretty good at it. Once, Big John, over there, he's three hundred pounds, he knocked Big Ed over the fireplace. He come back playin' though, trying to handcuff him.

Little Robbie, he stands about so high, about five feet. Now he drives a bus all day and he's got a habit of standing while he has a beer. Now, Big Ed, he'd come along and pick up and put him in a chair. He was sure something. When I first heard I thought he was pulling their leg. Then he started telling the Officers where them bodies was.

Somebody said he got a kick out of seeing the blood going down the drain. Somebody said he liked to see it squirting around. I don't see how anybody could get a kick out of that. One of the cops, he says, "Big Ed, what thrill did you get out of killing, out of cutting your mother's head off?"

He says, "Oh, it was the funniest thing ever happened. You know that little thing, the jugular vein, it would just wiggle around like this. It was the funniest thing I ever seen."

No effect. I mean it had no effect on him at all. It's hard to explain why he would say something like that.

I see him walk out of here with one girl and then come right back. It said in the paper that he picked certain girls. You see the mother worked at the University and he had a path to get in and go get her up there.

This was a shock to everybody, even the police department. One day I was talkin' to George there. And somebody asked him, "George, you afraid?"

George said, "Damn right, I'm afraid. We got two guys in jail now, that's been killin' ten, a whole family, and now they got one son of a bitch who's cuttin' everybody up, and you think I'm not afraid."

And he was an officer. That was when they found that girl on the beach there, in the ocean.

Harold Cartwright, 1973:
Was there anybody else you were paranoid of besides law enforcement officials?

Edmund Kemper, 1973:
Yeah, a person I had known.

Robert McFadzen, this gun nut.

I had talked to him a lot. I'd get real super drunk and he and I would go out on a drunk or something and I'd start talking about things that were bothering me.

Harold Cartwright, 1973:
Like what?

Edmund Kemper, 1973:
I almost confessed to him one night. If he'd been a police officer I would have been arrested, or at least checked out on these things because I was saying things like what a horrible person I was and I had done some very vicious, mean, horrible things over the last year and he, at that point, he knew about my past murder record and…I made a lot of statements like that. I kept partly wanting to get caught and partly not wanting to get caught.

Harold Cartwright, 1973:
What else did you tell him?

Edmund Kemper, 1973:
And he'd say things to my statements, he'd say things like, "No, you're really a nice guy, I know you real well."

I'd say, "No, you don't know me, I've been lying to a lot of people, I've been deceiving a lot of people, I've been running a game on society that you wouldn't believe."

I'd say, "If you knew about it, you wouldn't be a friend of mine anymore."

He said, "I'm sure I would."

I said, "No, there is no way in the world you'd be a friend of mine. Nobody could."

And I wasn't talking these things, I was rapping them out in a parking lot.

Harold Cartwright, 1973:
Where?

Edmund Kemper, 1973:
Behind the Jury Room. I was drinking tequila, I think that night.

On March 27, 1973, Kemper had the cast on his arm removed.

Sometime in March Kemper and his mother went off-roading in a jeep and Clarnell injured her shoulder.

Kemper's sister, Susan Swanson, came and stayed with Kemper and his mother on April 1.

Susan Swanson, 1973:
A little vacation and also it would be a good time to go down and help mom with her stuff that she couldn't handle with her broken shoulder. So it was kind of a two way visit. So I went down the first of April and I came home on the 19th. In fact, I missed all this by forty hours, which was very shattering to me.

It was a beautiful nineteen days. During the days Guy would sleep an awful lot, he would get up maybe noon or two o'clock. Either that, or I understood him to be going off with friends during the day, like target practicing or something. He might leave oh, around noon or something and come back around dinner time or whatever. Some days he'd just kind of hang around the house or be gone for a couple of hours and then he and I would do things during the day. I would take mom to school to work and then I'd come back and kind of clean up the apartment while Guy was asleep and then when he'd wake up we'd either go do something or he'd go do something and I would just you know, drive around or sight see, or whatever. In the evening I would pick mom up from school and Guy most always was gone in the evening. He would go to the Jury Room a lot or go to the show, or…as far as the accuracy, whether he was really there or not, I don't know, but he was gone in the evenings a lot, and would get home quite late—two or three in the morning. And he drank quite a bit, of beer. For breakfast he had two large cans of beer and he seemed to be able to hold beer quite well. I mean, it would take quite a bit before you would notice any signs that he had been drinking. I never saw him drunk. I never saw him staggering. I never saw him slurring his speech or anything.

Susan Swanson and Kemper discussed the Santa Cruz murders and Herbert Mullin.

Susan Swanson, 1973:

Guy and I discussed them one day when mom and I went to the university to borrow a movie projector so I could show a movie I had brought from home. There was something said about Mullin firing his attorney because he had long hair, and I asked Guy if he thought Mullin had done the co-ed slayings too. He said he didn't because none of them were similar in any way—his victims had been shot—then the subject was dropped. The first weekend I was there, Guy went to Turlock and picked up [Kemper's fiancée] and brought her to mom's. We went to San Francisco that weekend—Mom, I, [Kemper's fiancée], and Guy, and along the road he mentioned that down there, pointing to the right, was where they had found two girls propped up against something—I don't remember the exact area. We drove along the coast highway, but this was a hilly section inland, just a bit. I believe it was just south of San Jose. Another time I commented on the girls hitchhiking and mentioned they weren't too bright, considering what happened and the particular ones I mentioned were really dressed shabby. He said it was strange because some of the co-eds killed were very attractive girls, not hippie looking at all. I think this was mentioned at the same time the conversation about Mullin was discussed on the way to the university, the subject changed. He didn't say or do

anything strange or comment any more than anyone might comment because of what had been happening.

Susan Swanson, 1973:

One day when we were driving from Aptos along the beach toward Santa Cruz, just sightseeing, he pointed off toward the beach and mentioned that a girl's head was washed up along there—no more was said, and he brought it up.

Several times while we were riding around while I was there he would notice a girl and really stare, not just look or glance, and I teased him that he'd better get out of that habit when he gets married or [Kemper's fiancée] would sure get jealous. He said she's used to it or something along that line and most of these girls were dark skinned, possibly Mexican heritage, with black hair and medium build, tending toward heavy. He also commented that he sure likes those big butts—again I just passed it off and went on to other talk.

Susan Swanson, 1973:

I've never taken lessons in judo or karate, but I have picked up a few little things, I'm fascinated with the tournaments, watching the art.

I wanted to show him this new throw that I had just picked up on television. Well, being 6'9", or whatever, I'm 6'1", or 6' 1/2" myself, and not any weakling, and I was going to show him how the throw goes and I couldn't even waver him on his feet and he says, he's standing there with his hands on his hips saying, "What are you doing? What are you trying to do?

I said, "Oh, I'm going to throw you."

You know. We clowned around and made little fake karate chops and say, if I came around a corner or something and he was coming around at the same time, kind of like a surprise, not to surprise each other, but just bumping into each other coming around the corner, we'd go POW POW, and a few little phony karate things and the most scary thing right now is he would make a motion like he, with his hands in a karate chop, had lapped off my head and then held his hands out like he caught it. And laughed. And I would laugh. Because it seemed so funny, you know, this karate business, ho ho, and we were just playing around with it all the time. And this motion especially now, just this WHAP, and make his hands like he's catching my head—and I'd laugh. I can't believe this now.

KEMPER'S .44 MAGNUM

Allyn Kemper, 1973:
I knew he had guns. He was always, always, always, "Do you want to see my guns? Do you want to see my guns?"

I would say, "No. I don't want to see your guns."

I hate guns. They scare me.

Carla Gervasoni (Kemper Aptos neighbor), 1973:
He was too quiet sometimes. He was always taking things back and forth —guns. He had guns that I saw. I guess that's why I thought he was strange. They scared me.

Kemper purchased a .44 Magnum Ruger from Gray's Gun Shop in Santa Cruz. Shortly after he received the gun, during the first weekend in April, Kemper received visitors interested in the Ruger.

Mickey Aluffi, 2019:
About two months after the head was found, a piece of paper came through and landed on my desk. It's called a dealer's record of sale. Whenever anybody buys a handgun, the person who buys this is required to fill out this form, the dealer's record of sale. The dealer sends a copy of that to the agency with jurisdiction. We got this form and attached to it was a 3x5 card and it had this person's name and physical description. It turned out to be Edmund Emil Kemper III. He had bought a .44 Magnum Smith and Wesson. This 3x5 card said that he had been convicted of a double homicide, but that the record had been sealed. That brought up a legal question. We weren't sure if he could legally own that handgun or not. So what I decided to do was to confiscate the weapon, submit it to the judge, to see if we could get a legal decision. So my partner, Don Smythe, and I went out there one day, over here on Ord Street. 609A Ord Street. We found what we thought was the right address. We knocked. No one answered. So we get ready to leave when this Ford pulled up. A Ford with a black vinyl top. So I said, "Hold on, let me go see if this guy knows Ed Kemper or where this address is."

So I go over there and by then this guy is laying across the seat like he's working under the dashboard. I said, "Excuse me, can I talk to you for a minute?"

And he said, "Sure."

So he gets out of the car, and he gets out of the car, and he gets out of the car. This is Ed Kemper. Six foot eight and half. 285 pounds. So I explain to him what the situation was and what we had to do. He was real cooperative, very friendly.

Just at that moment Ed Kemper's fiancée and his sister, Susan Swanson, returned to the Kemper home after a day at the beach.

Susan Swanson, 1973:
So we sat in the car for a few minutes and [Kemper's fiancée] said, "Oh, I wonder what they want, maybe Guy's buying a car." Well, having worked at a police station and I don't know, I pay attention to people, I knew they were detectives, just by the way they were acting. One was in the driver's seat, Guy was sitting on the passenger side and the other one was standing on the passenger side just outside the car. And they were talking very seriously, so I just kept visiting with [Kemper's fiancée] and we kept talking and pretty soon Guy got out of the car and into the house and these two guys were right behind him.

Mickey Aluffi, 2019:

He takes us into the apartment, which was actually his mother's apartment. We walk in the front door. I look inside and there's a sofa and somebody is covered with a blanket, sleeping. [His mother].

Don Smythe (Sergeant Santa Cruz Sheriff's Office), 1973:

It's instinctive with me when I am dealing with a suspect in any sort of case not to let him out of my sight; so I turned and walked after him. Just as Kemper started up the steps, he realized that I was accompanying him and turned and said, "Oh, I forgot, it's in the trunk of my car."

Later, he told me that he had intended to get a shotgun which was in his bedroom closet and kill us all.

He thought we were really after him as a suspect in the co-ed killings, and that it was all over.

Mickey Aluffi, 2020:

He was being very cooperative. No threat involved. So we go out to the car and as he pulls out his keys and as he's going to put the key into the lock, Don and I instinctively separated, one on each side of the car. So we separated and then he put the key in and unlocked it. I put my hand on the trunk and I said, "OK, step back and I'll get it."

I opened up the trunk. And the only thing in the trunk was this, like a lightweight blanket or something like that. I unrolled it and there was the gun in the holster. So I took it. In the meantime, I'm thinking this is kind of strange because you know, the liner that they put in the trunk of the car. There wasn't one there. It seemed kind of strange, but I didn't put it together. So I gave him a receipt, took off. And then as he tells me later, he thought that I knew what he was doing. That I was just playing cat and mouse.

It kind of tipped him over the edge a little bit and he decided he needed to get out of town.

So we go back. We're just doing all the things that we need to do. And to be honest with you, I don't recall ever submitting a letter to the court to ask for judicial opinion. I probably didn't have time.

Don Smythe, 1973:

The only reason he changed his mind at the last moment, he told me, was that he realized I was going into the house with him and he would never get the shotgun into position in time because I was armed with a handgun.

Edmund Kemper, 1984:

Sheriff's representatives. One of the detectives was upset because he heard that I had a .44 Magnum pistol and was a convicted mental patient, and he came to take the gun away and it was on, he and his Sergeant Detective. They were staking out the wrong house, it was across the street and I'm playing around with the car, standing next to the gun in the trunk. They come over and asked me about, "Excuse me, sir. Do you know who lives in this house across the street, here?"

Well that house was 609 Harriet, across back over this side is 609 Ord, and they were looking for me and didn't even know it was me. Bad news. Well any rate, we walk in the house and have them ask my mother about this other house, and I'm saying, "Hey, which 609 are you looking for?"

And they said, "Are you Ed Kemper?"

"Yes."

And it goes on. And I needed to find out what they were looking for. The murder weapon, the .22 automatic, or the .44 Magnum and I don't want to advertise that I've got a whole bunch of guns. So I made a comment to divine between the two and I said, "Yes, quite a little gun isn't it?"

And he retorted, "A .44 Magnum, I hope so."

And I said, "Phew. Okay."

Because that loaded .22 was under the front seat and guaranteed me an arrest right on the spot. And the .44 was in the trunk. I'd forgot that, I took them in the house, went into my bedroom and the closet door is

open and I have a high powered rifle with a scope on it.

Edmund Kemper, 1984:
I had the personal effects and identifications of the last two co-eds that had been murdered about two months before right next to the guns in the closet in a box.

Edmund Kemper, 1984:
A purse, a book bag, and co-ed ID inside of those, belonging to their two latest murder victims. I'd back up and said, "Oh, excuse me. I just remembered something."

And instantly he instantly responds to what I'm saying. My hand moves, back we go outside and he's still thinking, well this is a really nice, helpful guy here.

Mickey Aluffi, 2019:
He told me that little movement where my partner and I went to the side, he told me later that had we not done that he was thinking about killing both of us.

Don Smythe, 1973:
He's such a nice guy when you're with him, you just have to keep reminding yourself that he's killed ten people.

Kemper called his lawyer after the deputies left.

Susan Swanson, 1973:
So when he got off the phone he told me that Rolly Hall had told him just to let it ride for now till they find out about the .44, and he would check into it.

Above: Jurors inspect Kemper's car.

Pittinger [a Santa Cruz deputy] now explained to me that this was the point that Guy…this is where the paranoia started setting in again, and I feel this too.

Mickey Aluffi, 2019:
He was so paranoid because I had taken that gun and he thought that I was playing cat and mouse. He was getting very paranoid. He was cleaning up all the evidence that he could possibly clean up.

Edmund Kemper, 1984:
It was springtime, it was April. For two months I hadn't killed. I said it's not going to happen to any more girls. It's gotta stay between me and my mother and it's gotta—I can't get away from her. We're still fighting. She's still belittling me. She's still—I'm like a puppet on a string and I entertain her. She knows all my buttons and I danced like a puppet with that pain and it even had gotten physical. To where I had physically grabbed her and thrown her onto her bed trying to emphasize the point that she's—I was threatening to kill her.

Edmund Kemper, 2017:
I went to Mary Ann Pesce's grave and I made an oath to her that my mother and I were going to pay for what happened to her.

Mickey Aluffi, 2019:
He's always talking about a contentious relationship with his mother, but, he said he knew that he was going to get caught, he thought that I was playing cat and mouse with him. I knew nothing, but he thought I was playing cat and mouse with him. He figured he needed to get out of town. He didn't want his mother to go through the trial, the embarrassment of the trial. So he killed her with a hammer.

Mickey Aluffi, 2019:
He didn't want to be caught, but because I took his gun away from him, he thought he was going to be caught.

Forrest Robinson, 2020:
They [Ed Kemper and Clarnell] had been out in a jeep somewhere, rough trailing it. She fell out and hurt her shoulder. So a friend of mine named Buchanan Sharpe—who was an assistant professor of history and became a tenured professor of history at UCSC—he was a good pal of Clarnell's. Buck was very fond of her. So Buck and I had come out to see her, to see if she was okay. It was a Sunday afternoon. We got there and Guy was drunk and belligerent, and really aggressive, "I'm going to kill people!"

He was kind of obviously the person who was doing this. I was horrified later that I hadn't put the two together. I was very aware of the murders. He was yelling that he was going to murder Jim Hall, Clarnell's boss. He was just an ugly, ugly guy and he just smelled like beer. He put on a pretty good show. I mean, he was ranting about things and kind of out of control. So when that was over and we left, we were driving home and naturally Buck and I were talking about what had happened, and we agreed that Kemper was a scary fellow and that we were worried about him and his mother and we went home.

CLARNELL STRANDBERG AND SALLY HALLETT SATURDAY, APRIL 21, 1973

Edmund Kemper, 1981:
I picked up two girls who were so much like the first two it was unbelievable. Almost identical circumstances. And I let them go. Everything went towards killing them and I didn't. But I'm saying wow, it's uncanny, it was almost like it was meant to be that way and I said wow. I've got, it's got to stop, and I let them out. They never even knew what was going on and I let them out. I would've gotten away with those two being murdered. I said, no it's got to stop. And a week later I murdered my mother. Went back to Santa Cruz and killed her.

Douglas Roth (Inmate at Atascadero with Kemper and later roommate and friend), 1973:
Well, I think there's always been a problem, it was discussed while he was at Atascadero State Hospital and discussed through the years since he's been out of the hospital. We've talked about it many times, his relationship with his mother and the hassle

that he had. One incident keeps coming to mind, now that this thing has occurred that he has supposedly killed his mother, that is that she apparently, on many occasions, told him to go ahead, "Why don't you kill me? Why don't you get it over with? Why don't you kill me?"

This bothered him and upset him a lot.

Harold Cartwright, 2020:
The last person he killed was his mother. I don't think he could kill anybody after he killed her. I think his mother—and remember, other than his grandfather, he killed women, it all has to do with his childhood and his relationship with his mother. Brilliant guy, but it all got screwed up. It's a mystery to me.

Forrest Robinson, 2020:
She [Clarnell Strandberg] arrived at UC Santa Cruz in, maybe, '72 to be an administrative assistant at College Five where she worked for a man named Jim Hall. James T.

CLARNELL E. STAGE

Ambition: To be a secretary.

Favorite Course: Typing.

Little Symphony Orchestra 4; Graduation Orchestra 1, 2, 3, 4; Sculptors' Club 3; Young Author's Club 4; Iniwa Staff 4; Junior Prom Committee; Advisory Round-up Float Committee 3; Orchestra 1, 2, 3, 4; Quill and Scroll 4.

DON L. STAINSBY

Ambition: To see the world.

Hall. The provost of College Five. College Five was unnamed until much later, when it was named Porter.

I met her fairly early. We were allies for a couple of reasons. One was that the provost of College Five was an ass. A real ass. There was an uprising of the faculty against him. He never should have been named a provost. He was kind of a mediocre novelist and he cried when he read his poetry. But he was just so unfair with people and it really pissed me off. He judged everybody. I was the chairman of the faculty at the college so I talked about the problem with the provost. So it was in that framework that Clarnell Strandberg arrived.

F. M. Glenn Wilson (Stevenson College Provost), 1973:

Clarnell was what some of us would call a character. She was informative, with a caustic repartee to those who got out of hand. She had willing desire to help those who needed it and a boisterous jollity. She was essentially warm and had a benevolent curiosity…shadows in her life were kept at bay.

The realization of her courage calls for our profound respect.

Forrest Robinson, 2020:

She [Clarnell] was kind of a heavyset big, woman. She was more big than heavy. She wasn't really overweight. She was big and strapping. She had been working at the University of Montana, in the great midwest. She got this job at College Five and came out to California.

She was extremely competent. She was a very good friend to all the faculty. She was really solid and would take chances for people. She really belonged. We all loved her and cared about her.

Sally Hallett was his mother's good friend. She was a lot like Clarnell, I think she was an assistant to the chair of a department. Maybe economics. She had a good job and she had been around for a while. Clarnell and Sally got together right away. They were just meant to be. Maybe that's why Guy thought they were gay, but they weren't. I think he's bitter. He hates his mother.

Sally was an attractive woman, probably in her late fifties. Dark hair, as I remember. Wore red lipstick. She was just cool. When she and Clarnell met, they were just friends immediately.

Methodist Ceremony in Great Falls Unites Clarnell E. Stage And Staff Sergeant E. E. Kemper

The First Methodist church in Great Falls was the scene Thanksgiving day of the marriage of Miss Clarnell E. Stage, daughter of Mr. and Mrs. C. A. Stage of Great Falls, and Staff Sergeant Edmund E. Kemper of Fort William Henry Harrison, son of Mr. and Mrs. Edmund Kemper of North Hollywood, Calif.

The Rev. Philo W. Haynes, pastor of the West Side Methodist church, officiated at the 1:30 o'clock ceremony.

For her wedding the bride wore a white jersey gown fashioned with sweetheart neckline and long bodice. Her veil of bridal illusion fell from a tiara of seed pearls and she carried an arm bouquet of American Beauty roses and white chrysanthemums.

Mrs. David Jung, sister of the bride and matron of honor, wore a floor-length rose jersey gown and a matching cap with a white halo veil. She carried a shower bouquet of white chrysanthemums.

The bridesmaid, Miss Josephine Sheriff of Helena, wore a powder blue jersey dress and cap with a halo veil and carried a bouquet of bronze chrysanthemums.

Pvt. Charles G. Suchan served as best man and the ushers were Harvey Jung, nephew of the bride, and Bill Briggs.

Following the ceremony a dinner for 20 guests was served at the home of the bride's parents.

The bride, a former employe of the internal revenue office in Helena, is a graduate of the Great Falls high school.

Sergeant Kemper is attached to the first special service force at Fort Harrison. The couple will make their home in Helena.

Navy Mothers Club Will Name Officers Monday

Officers for the forthcoming year will be elected at a regular meeting of the Navy Mothers' club scheduled for 7:30 o'clock Monday evening at the YWCA.

POPULATION DECREASED

According to the 1940 census, Rochester, N. Y., 23rd largest city of the United States, showed a population decrease, dropping from 328,132 in 1930 to 324,694 in the recent census.

Marriage License Record

Reel No. 43   No. 20047

STATE OF MONTANA,
County of Cascade } ss.

C. A. Stage _____, being first duly sworn, on oath deposes and says: That (s)he makes application for a marriage license between the persons hereinafter named; and that the following statement of facts in relation thereto is true.

Edmund E. Kemper, Jr. resides at North Hollywood, California

State what if any relationship between applicants none

Age 23 Date of Birth 27 day April month, 1919 year.

Born at Los Angeles, California, color White

not previously married, divorced son of Edmund E. Kemper

his mother's maiden name was Maud Hughey

and Clarnell E. Stage resides at Helena, Montana

aged 21 days Mar. 17 months, 1921 years,

born at Winnett, Mont., color White

not previously married, divorced

daughter of C. A. Stage

her mother's maiden name was Nellie N. Neudigate

and there is no legal impediment known to said parties entering into this Marriage Contract.

C. A. Stage

Subscribed and sworn to before me, this 24 day of November A. D. 1942

Agnes Schrapps Clerk.

(Seal)   By _____ Deputy.

If under age, parents must sign the following:

I hereby grant permission for my daughter or son _____

aged _____ years to marry.

WITNESSES:

Marriage Certificate

OF MONTANA,
County of Cascade } ss.

CERTIFIES, That the undersigned, a Minister of the Gospel did on the 26th day of Nov., A. D. 1942

at Great Falls Join in lawful wedlock Edmund E. Kemper, Jr.

and Clarnell E. Stage; with their mutual consent and in accordance with laws of the State of Montana and Ritual of the Methodist Church

ATTEST

Schmon Witnesses Edmund E. Kemper, Jr. Contracting

Sheriff   Clarnell E. Stage Parties

M. Hayner Officiating

record the 30th day of November, A. D. 1942

o'clock A. M.

Agnes Schrapps Clerk District Court.

By H. Schmon Deputy.

ENGAGEMENT ANNOUNCED

Clarnell Stage Betrothed to Sgt. E. Kemper

Mr. and Mrs. C. A. Stage of Great Falls, announce the engagement of their daughter, Clarnell Stage to Staff Sergeant Edmund E. Kemper of Fort William Henry Harrison, son of Mr. and Mrs. E. E. Kemper of North Hollywood, Calif.

The marriage will take place in December at the home of the bride-elect's parents in Great Falls.

Miss Stage is employed in Helena in the office of the collector of internal revenue.

Staff Sergeant Kemper is a member of the First Special Service Force at Fort Harrison.

Cantalupo, Italy, is the birthplace of the cantaloupe.

MISS CLARNELL STAGE.
whose engagement to Staff Sergeant Edmund E. Kemper of Fort William Henry Harrison was announced during the week by her parents, Mr. and Mrs. C. A. Stage of Great Falls. The wedding will be an event of December.

ST. PAUL'S MET...
LISTEN, M...
Beginning Sunday, N...
INTENSIFIED
A RECORD of yo...
Will Be Taken...
Nov. 1 Roll Call Sunday.
Nov. 8 Approval Sunday.
Nov. 29 All Organization Su...

Left and above: Clarnell Stage married Edmund Kemper Jr. in 1942.

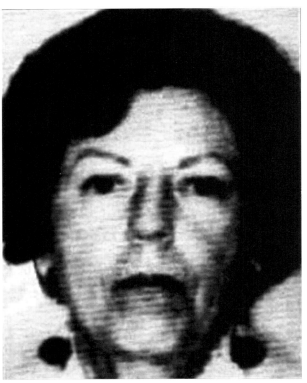

she was in her cups, she had too much to drink, she was at my house and she told me about her son. She decided to unveil this secret to me. She said that she'd come out here and that her son had been in prison, on, sort of like a junior thing. It had to do with the sentencing, he killed his grandparents and they gave him a fairly light sentence because he was a youth. I don't know how that works, but she told me that and said that he was coming out to live with her.

She was pretty level about it all. She was critical of her son. For good reason. She wasn't the sentimental type. She was kind of tough, in a good way. So she told me about her son, Guy Kemper. She said he was coming out to California and she wanted me to be kind of a mentor to him. "Would you please look after my son?"

She did mention that he had killed his grandparents and that he had been on some kind of a five year deal. So I said, "Well, sure, if you want me to."

But, I hadn't met him.

Cesar Barber (Vice Chancellor of Humanities), 1973:
She [Sally Hallett] had the kind of job a person could have done pompously or ruthlessly…she was always on top of her job without being on top of her colleagues.

She leaves many people for whom she mattered a lot. She was fun to talk to and had the kind of humor that played over the surface of a clear head and very clear will.

Forrest Robinson, 2020:
I arrived [at UCSC] in '70 and all the other players in that college drama were new, young, professors. Most non-tenured. In dealing with this guy, Hall, forming kind of a bleak obstacle to everybody's sense of security. So Clarnell came to the college and I got to know her and we used to go drinking together. She liked to drink. I liked to drink. We would talk and one night when

Above: Sara "Sally" Hallett.
Above right: Clarnell Strandberg.

Kemper was paroled to his mother's care in the summer of 1971.

Edmund Kemper:
When I was paroled, I was paroled to my mother's care, at twenty-one years old. The treatment portion of my prior incarceration at Atascadero came to the conclusion that I should stay as far away from my mother as possible. I was taken out of that setting and I was at Atascadero State Hospital and I was taken back to court, to the committing county, and referred back to the Youth Authority. And the Youth Authority four months later paroled me to my mother. They found her to be a suitable, well, what they called her was a friend and an advisor.

Forrest Robinson, 2020:
Clarnell used to throw parties at her house.

She liked to wind it up. She was a good spirit.

Robert Ludlow, 2019:
I taught two classes at College 5. Clarnell was the administrative assistant at College Five and she had a party when her son came home from "boarding school." It was at her house. I met him. Here's this 6'9" 280 pound guy. I found him to be charming, but he didn't seem like a boarding school kid. She was nice and very efficient.

Forrest Robinson, 2020:
When I met him, we talked about what I was supposed to do. He was, well, he is a huge guy. Big, stout, and tall. Formidable. Scary. He was just so big. So we were supposed to play golf together. That was going to be our place to bond. I don't think we ever played golf together.

Edmund Kemper:
I stayed with the parole, I tried to make it work. I got very bitter, my mother got very bitter, we got in drunken fights, not physical ones, but very loud, verbal ones, a lot of friends and neighbors were hearing it, they remembered me leaving the fight, me trying to break it off.

And my mother had problems. She wasn't addressing those problems, she wasn't in a position where she had to. And sadly, my new condition, coming out and having a hopeful future, told her in no uncertain terms that there had been severe problems in the way she brought me up. And no one was there to help her with that, including me. I didn't recognize it as that. All I knew was, instead of being my friend and advisor, she was a harpy on my back and she was fighting me every inch of the way, and I couldn't understand it.

Allyn Kemper, 1973:
She came to me in March, no, February, because they had a real bad argument one night. They used to argue a lot. They also used to like to get into these intense conversations. My mother, just because of the kind of people she was around and the work she did, she liked to get in to people. She liked to get to know the real person. She liked real people and she could be real harsh. When she'd get uptight or mad, she could really cut to the bone. She did that a lot to my brother. She'd just strip him down and say, "You're just like your father."

Just cutting. Just cutting right to the bone. She really did talk a lot when she should have shut her mouth. I mean there's a point

379

$1.00 for students.

Next weekend will see the College V Arts Fair, complete with entertainment, exhibits, sales, music, handicrafts, dance, wandering minstrels, and the other stock ingredients of good times. Circle your calendars.
It's open to the whole world.

It would be greatly appreciated if the two students who hitched a ride Wednesday morning around 8:30 in a 1965 white Buick Electra and got off at the student apartments, have knowledge of a notebook of music would contact Clarnell Strandberg in the College Office. Thank you.

The Mezzanine Gallery features an exhibit of student portraits (self- and others) - May 13 - 19, 12-5 daily.

An exhibit of etchings by Marcia McGrath will open this Sunday, May 16, in the Sesnon Gallery at College V. Marcia learned printmaking in Ecuador, where she lived from February 1967 until May 1969. La Universidad Central allowed her to receive instruction at the School of Fine Arts in Quito. She had a show there before she left, and another in Honolulu this spring. Her second show in Ecuador will open simultaneously with the one in College V. The etchings, 41 in all, include a 26-piece series entitled "Bestiary", completed in Ecuador, as well as more recent prints.

"El Tiempo" of Quito concluded in a review of Marcia's show: "We have

where you just don't push people. She'd always go past that point.

Allyn Kemper, 1973:
She had a lot of warmth and a lot of strength and a lot of heart, but I think she misguided it. Like, she could never openly—she admitted this. Also, she couldn't express her love to somebody openly and say, "I really love you."

I can't ever remember her saying that. She'd kind of go around, kind of beat around the bush.

Edmund Kemper, 1973:
Some people would call her a manipulator, definitely. Some people might even say she was ill, I wouldn't know, but any mother that would take a hot, greasy spatula that she had been cooking hamburgers with and smack her son across the face with it because of a comment he had made earlier, I wouldn't call that a well person. I could have had her arrested, you know.

Harold Cartwright, 1973:
When did this happen?

> *Above: The UCSC College Five newsletter from May 14, 1971.*

Edmund Kemper, 1973:
This happened when I was working at a service station so it couldn't have been…it was shortly before I became engaged…it was probably not much more than a year ago. Maybe, less than a year and a half ago. I had introduced her to my boss…she came over to the gas station one night.

This was Mike [redacted]. I worked at his Union station on Soquel Avenue. At the corner of Soquel and Pacheco, and I was working there one night and she drove by, bought a little gas, came in to use the restroom, and she came out. My boss was there in the office, and we were all on a very casual basis…I'm sure my mother didn't know that. Ah, I mean I even used to run across the street and buy a six pack of beer and some salami or something and have that for dinner right there at the station.

Ah, but anyway, she came out and had this God awful Victorian way of handling things as far as relationships she was very sloppy and shoddy at home as far as relationships…absolutely no protocol at all…she would walk in the house and start screaming, or she would walk in the house and say, "Hi."

I mean there was absolutely no family protocol at all…brought up very poorly on

380

that respect. Ah, I learned things like that from Atascadero from relationships with people in there that had been brought up properly. She had this God awful Victorian thing that she did…I call it a bug in her ass. She would get this hair up her nose or something about this great protocol at weird times.

So she comes out of the bathroom, everyone is feeling casual, and I say, I said something about…she's six feet tall, weighs 220 pounds, I'm six foot nine and weigh 260. And my boss is like barely six feet tall, he's 5'10", I think, or 5'11", maybe six feet tall. So she walks out, he's in the middle, and I said, "Mike, I want you to meet the giant, my mother."

I said it in a proud way, I said, "My mother, the giant."

But I guess that wasn't proper, you know. Just casual, and she said very graciously, hi, blah, blah, back and forth. She got in the car and I talked, blah, blah, everything was fine and she left.

I finished up my job, and I came home, you know, this is out in Aptos. She's out there cooking, wanted to know what I wanted to have for dinner. I said, "What have you got?"

And she said, "Hamburgers."

I said, "Fine."

She starts cooking it. She's out there and she started squawking. She started an argument on a different subject. This is the way she'd do it. There was a minor squabble about something, and this was really bugging her, what I said in the station about her height. She started to squabble at me, she fanned it and fanned it and I tried to let it go, and she fanned it, and pretty soon I came walking around the corner and I said, "Hey, what's bugging you?"

And she just completely came off the handle. She walked away with the spatula right out of the pan and said, "Don't you ever say I'm big, and giant, and fat!"

And POW, right across the kisser. I grabbed the spatula out of her hand, threw it across the room, I almost hit her back with

it, I threw it across the room and I grabbed her by the neck and I said, "You ever do that again I'm going to break your god damned jaw."

And she was shocked at that point, 'cause I had never talked to her like that before.

Forrest Robinson, 2020:
I think they fought a lot. It was mainly his mother getting really pissed off at him. She was ashamed of him. She wanted him to shape up, "I have this bright son and if I could get him into college, he could make something of himself."

But he just drank too much and was just out of control.

Allyn Kemper, 1973:
That's when they would start fighting, when she was drinking and when he was drinking. She came over one time because my brother had hit her. She said he only hit her about three times but he's pretty big. He says he hit her once, but he strung the glasses all out and she had bruises on her arms. This was about February. She said she kept herself in the house all weekend and didn't answer the door because she didn't want anybody to know. But she was telling me, and she was crying. She was afraid. She was scared. I told her right then, "Get him out of the house."

I said, "I'll pack his stuff right now and put it on the porch."

I said, "Just get him out because next time might be too late."

I had a fear about him just because he had committed a murder before and if he got uptight and drank you never know. To me, he had emotional problems. I went home and talked to her for a couple of hours. Sue tried to calm her down a bit. I really tried to encourage her to get him out. She said, "Well, where would he go?"

I said, "He's twenty-three, twenty-four years old. He'll find a place to go. That's no problem. He's a big boy now. Just get him out."

She said, "Well, I'll talk to him tonight.

We'll have a talk about it"

I told her that I'd call her later to see how things were

I called her later and she said everything was fine. He said he was going to straighten up and they had a little session and everything was all right. Then he got on the phone. I didn't want to say anything, but it made me really mad. But I also wanted to see if he'd say anything to me to see where his head was at.

I told him, "I really love you."

I don't know why, I just wanted him to know that I loved him and ask him how he was doing. He said, "Why don't you quit playing games?"

I said, "I'm not playing games."

Because I really did mean it at the time.

He said, "I know that you know I hit mom."

He told her not to tell me. I said, "So?"

He said, "That's between me and her."

I said, "I really love you, but I don't think you should stay there."

I knew they were having problems whenever they were together.

He wouldn't accept the fact that I was saying I loved him. It was really hard for him to ever accept anybody loving him or really really caring about him. So we discussed that for a little bit.

Edmund Kemper, 2017:
And every time I got mad at her I went out and got in my car, went driving around, found someone to pick up, took them off somewhere quiet, and blew them away with a .22.

Edmund Kemper, 1988:
When I—at the end, when I killed my mother and her friend, I was drinking on the average seven to seven and a half gallons of cheap wine a week. My mother was drinking three gallons, about average, a week, of the same brand, purchased at Safeway. And it got to be one of our argument problems there, where I was trying to go for both of us. We

were buying it by the gallon.

And it sounds ludicrous, but her boss—shortly before the crimes happened to her, she came to work drunk one day and he tried to have her terminated at the UC Santa Cruz campus. He was the provost, she was his administrative assistant. He filed charges with Chancellor McHenry, and Chancellor McHenry tore up the charges in front of him and said, "I need her, I don't need you." She had his signature power at the time, she was doing the bulk of his work. She came home and told me about this after it happened. A bit incredulous that she was that important.

Edmund Kemper, 1984:
So here I pick up these two young ladies in Berkeley on Ashby Avenue. One has flowers in her hand. Petite little dolls. They're in granny dresses and they're hitchhiking, a couple of real experts. I want to see how together I am, if I can resist this temptation.

Edmund Kemper, 1984:
They get in my car. They want to go one way, I know they need to go the other. If they go the way that they're insisting on we're headed right back out to where the first two co-eds were murdered. And I'm saying to myself, "Oh my God, all I got to do is relax and they'll take me to their death."

I've got the gun in the car. The same one that I've been doing it with. I insisted as gently as I could, I took them where they needed to go to their college.

Edmund Kemper, 1984:
When I drove them to Mills College. Inside of Mills College. To their college entrance. Right to the building, to the dormitory, and they got out of that car and flew up those stairs. Never even looked back. I bet they quit hitchhiking quite so casually after that. But you know what? I don't think they know to this day how close that came and the irony of it is, just to shut them up and not have them freak out, I could have gone

the other way, but by that time then were going back up that groove of what I had done already and what I was familiar with, see what I'm saying? And that day I knew I could not stop doing it. I knew I had no control over it. I had just minimal controls. But mainly I could not stop it, it was going to happen again and between that weekend day. It was a Saturday or a Sunday. I think it was a Sunday. Between that Sunday and the next Saturday, all that week I was working. I built an image in my head, my mother's gonna die. I'm going to kill her and I'm going to go to it with the police and we're going to hold court in the street and they're going to pound me into the ground and they can fill in the blanks because I don't want to be around to explain it. All that week, it was a conviction that just got deeper and deeper in me. I got more and more morose. I got less and less talkative at work. I got more somber about what I was doing. Because almost every minute of every day I knew that's what that next weekend held. That was Easter weekend. I worked half a day Friday, went back to Santa Cruz Friday afternoon. Was drinking Friday night. Fell asleep before my mother came home. Woke up after she came home. And the last words we had were an argument. I walked into her bedroom to chat with her. I'm not going to try to blame her for dying, I'm just saying. In the back of my mind I was hoping she could say something, or I'd say something that could stop all of this shit. A little challenge, a hope in the back of my mind she'd say something and I'd just play it off.

Edmund Kemper, 1973:

I got home Friday night, or I got back to her home from Alameda, where I'd been working early Friday in the afternoon and I sat around the house and took care of a few business problems, you know, calling and making a couple phone calls that were unrelated to the problem, and I called my mother at work and let her know I was in town and she told me that she was going out to

a dinner, some faculty dinner or something, and she'd be home late. So I sat around and drank some beer, watched television, stayed up as late as I could and I had wished to talk to her really, before anything had happened. It was my hope that she would go on good terms and this was impossible because well I guess it would be good terms because we hadn't really argued or anything when we talked on the phone. I went to bed about midnight I guess and I woke up a couple of hours later. Well, let me see, that doesn't work out right. I think I went to bed around two and she still wasn't home and I went to bed and went to sleep. I woke up a couple of hours later, around four, and she had already come home, done whatever she does when she gets home late at night and had retired for the evening. This was after I had gone to bed around 2:00 a.m. Saturday morning. She was in bed, reading a book and I woke up about four o'clock in the morning, two hours after I went to sleep roughly. The lights were pretty much out in the house. I didn't see any lights on. I hadn't heard anything and I thought, gee, it's four o'clock and she's still not home. So I got up and I walked out of my bedroom, noticed her small light was on and walked into her bedroom, just as she had taken off her glasses and turned the light off. Without her turning it back on, she commented that uh, I said "Oh, you're home."

She says, "You're up, what are you doing up?"

I said, "Well, I just wanted to see if you were home. I hadn't heard anything."

She said, "Oh, I suppose you want to talk."

This has happened several times before, when she'd come in late and I wanted to talk and we'd talk and then she'd go to sleep. She didn't say it in an abusive manner, it was more or less just jive, and I said, "No."

She said, "Well, we'll talk in the morning."

I said, "Fine, good night."

She left the light out and I walked out of the room and back to my bedroom, laid down and decided at that point, I was going to wait another hour or so, until she was

Statistics

STRANDBERG — In Aptos, Calif. Clarnell E. Strandberg. Survived by daughter, Mrs. Patrick Burke of Santa Cruz; daughter, Mrs. Susan Swanson of Livingston, Mont.; son, Edmond Emil Kemper III of Alameda, and five grandchildren. Native of Winnett, Mont. Aged 52 years.

Private family services were conducted at WESSENDORF & HOLMES FUNERAL CHAPEL, 223 Church Street, at 2:00 p.m. today. Memorial services are to be held at 4:30 p.m. at UCSC College 5 campus in the College 5 dining room patio. Friends are invited to attend. Interment in Highland Cemetery, Great Falls, Mont. 4-27-99

asleep before it happened. I looked at my watch. It was about a quarter after four, something like that, and I laid there in the bed thinking about it and it's something hard to just up and do. It was the most insane of reasons for going and killing your mother. But, I was pretty fixed on that issue because there were a lot of things involved. Someone just standing off on the side, watching something like that isn't really going to see any kind of sense or rhyme or reason to anything. I had done some things and I felt that I had to carry the full weight of everything that happened. I certainly wanted for my mother a nice quiet, easy death like I guess everyone wants. The only way I saw this possible was for it to be in bed while she was asleep. The next thing was to decide how to do it. The only possible answer to that I saw was to take a hammer and hit her with it, in her sleep, and then to cut her throat. So I waited until about 5:00 a.m., I went into the kitchen and got a hammer. We have a regular claw hammer at home, picked up my pocket knife, the same one I'd used to kill Mary Ann Pesce with, opened it up, and I carried that in my right hand and the hammer in my left, walked into her bedroom very quietly. She had been sound asleep. She moved around a little bit and I thought maybe she

was waking up. I just waited and waited and she was just laying there. So I approached her right side, to my right on the right side of the bed, on her side. I stood there for a couple of minutes and spent most of that day, and most of that week I suppose and most of that night, trying to get myself, I guess you'd say hopped up to do something like that, thinking nothing but reasons to do it and the need to do it, trying to keep everything else out of my mind. I stood by her side for a couple of minutes I suppose and about five fifteen I struck and I hit her just above the temple on her right side of the head, the side that was up from the pillow. It was above and behind her temple on the right side of her head. I struck with a very hard blow and I believe I dropped the hammer, or I laid it down or something. Immediately after striking that blow, I looked for a reaction, and there really wasn't one, blood started running down her face from the wound, and she was still breathing, I could hear the breathing and I heard blood running into her, I guess it was her windpipe. It was obvious I had done severe damage to her because in other cases where I had shot people in the head, I heard the same, or it had the same effect, blood running into the breathing passages, and this all happened in a few moments. But after I struck, I moved her over in the bed on her back and with my right hand holding her chin up, I slashed her throat. She bled profusely all over and I guess it was an afterthought, I hadn't really thought of it, but her being my mother, and me out doing those other things, and I knew right now if I had torn everything out in the open, and my plan which I didn't mention earlier, had been to just, well everything's getting to an end and I could either kill her and turn myself in or I could kill her and head out with everything I had, my arsenal. This was my choice at that time. So I decided at that time, it's a hell of a cliché to use, but I guess what was good for my victims was good for my mother.

Edmund Kemper, 1973:

Right after I cut her throat I ran back to my bedroom and got a white waste paper plastic bag. I put that over her head.

Edmund Kemper, 1973:

So after I slashed her throat, I went ahead and slashed the rest of the way around her neck and took off her head, and I guess half as much of that was to make absolutely sure in my own mind that she was dead instantly and right then, so the whole attack took maybe, less than half a minute, possibly even as little as twenty seconds. Then after this, I moved her out of the bed and her nightgown was very bloody and I didn't want to make a big mess in the house because if I did and someone in our family, or a friend came by, it would be obviously noticeable and it would give away what I was doing before I wanted it to be, so I pulled off her night-gown, tore it off and then pulled her body and put handcuffs on her wrists because it was hard to move her, and pulled her into her clos-et, into the very far back, and put her sideways in the closet in the back, took all the bloody bedding off of her bed, put that in on top of her and flipped the mattress over because it was very bloody, changed the bedding on it and arranged the clothes in the closet to cover her up and I cleaned off the blood where it hit the wall. It hadn't gone very high on the wall, at the most, maybe ten inches above the bed level. There was quite a bit of blood running down the wall and into the carpet. I cleaned off the blood down below the top of the bed level and by this time, well, several little things happened in between, a lot of

In Memoriam

STUDENTS AND ALUMNI

Larry Ross Cathey
(PhD in Astronomy, March '73)
May 19, 1973
Yosemite National Park

Elisabeth Hairston
(graduate student)
May 2, 1973
Washington, D.C.

Alice Helen Liu
(Kresge '73)
February 5, 1973
Santa Cruz

David W. Long
(Cowell '74)
March 20, 1973
San Luis Obispo

Rosalind Heather Thorpe
(Merrill '73)
February 5, 1973
Santa Cruz

FACULTY AND STAFF

Sally Hallett
Administrative Assistant/Academic Personnel
April 21, 1973
Aptos

Cynthia Marlowe
Continuing Education Specialist/University Extension
February 27, 1973
Oxnard

Lloyd J. Ring
Assistant Chancellor Planning and Analysis/
Director of Academic Planning and a fellow
of Crown College
August 1, 1973
Santa Cruz

Clarnell Strandberg
Administrative Assistant/College V
April 21, 1973
Aptos

running around the house that seem incon-sequential at this point. But anyway, it was well after dawn, in fact, dawn was breaking while this happened. It was barely visible in the light. But this was well into the morning by now when all this was accomplished. The house looked back to normal and some time early in the morning, I got in my car and went out and drove. I had become quite ill immediately after it happened and hadn't eaten anything the night before. But I had the dry heaves, quite a few minutes after it happened, I was unable to do anything. Then when I was, I did these things I mentioned.

Finally I went out, I couldn't stand being around the house any more, so I put a couple of guns in my car, well, I think I put them all in my car, but this was real early. I started driving around town. I was looking for a hardware store and a saw, possibly a hacksaw blade. Not having any sidearms, I'd hoped to take the carbine that I had and cut the stock down to the pistol grip and possibly cut down the barrel to the fore-stock, making it a semi-pistol automatic weapon. There were a few other things I'd wanted to buy. I can't really remember now what they were. I think they were very minor essential uses to that project or had no importance to it. But it was early in the morning, eight thirty or nine o'clock and nothing was open…

Edmund Kemper, 1984:
It was almost a cathartic process at that point. I got physically ill right then, when she died, when I murdered her. Once she was dead, there was no way I could back out. I'd backed down from giving up a thousand times. I'd cease to get drunk and sit out in front of the Sheriff's Department in a parking lot across the street. On one of those little concrete parking berms, I would just sit there and say, No, I still can't. The clanging doors. I can still hear them. No because they will never open again.

From Kemper's July 25, 2017, parole hearing.

PRESIDING COMMISSIONER FRITZ:
Okay so then why did you use a hammer to kill your mother?

INMATE KEMPER:
That was a childhood fantasy.

PRESIDING COMMISSIONER FRITZ:
To kill your mother with a hammer?

INMATE KEMPER:
To bludgeon her with a hammer, uh, one time to hit her with a hammer and incapacitate her and then cut her throat.

PRESIDING COMMISSIONER FRITZ:
Okay.

INMATE KEMPER:
That was a fantasy from when I was eight years old, and locked in the basement and I used to sneak up in the middle of the night when everybody was asleep and I went through the ritual, but I didn't follow through with the act.

When Kemper talked with the public defend-

er's team he added the following details.

Harold Cartwright, 1973:
Now did you do anything else to the body or the head or anything?

Edmund Kemper, 1973:
Oh yea, now I remember. I took her head down, I've been trying not to think about things like that, but I took her head down and in the living room there was a platter like thing on the bookcase. I put her head on that and I remember I hit it with my fist right in the middle 'cause I broke her nose and some facial bones when I hit her.

Harold Cartwright, 1973:
Did you talk to her?

Edmund Kemper, 1973:
I talked to her head, yeah. Talked to her without being in the room, even I talked to her several times that day and the next before I left.

Harold Cartwright, 1973:
What did you say to her?

Edmund Kemper, 1973:
In a nice, not [inaudible], not saying anything nasty, I was, now we were friends, she was at peace. For all I knew I was going to be there before very long. I wasn't a great believer in heaven and hell, it was just…she was at peace and that's where I was going to be hopefully, soon.

Kemper expanded on this when interviewed by Dr. Donald Lunde—

Edmund Kemper, 1973:
I asked her questions and things. I made

Left: A body removed from Kemper's residence. From left: Deputy Brad Arbsland and Deputy Terry Medina; from Wessendorf Mortuary Walt Burke and James Hogg; unknown and unknown in the white.

statements to her. I said, "Well, let me see mother, I gotta find a friend of yours and make it look like you went off for a week. So who should I pick?"

Edmund Kemper, 1973:
"See what has to happen before I can get the last word in?"

Harold Cartwright, 1973:
OK, uh, you punched her in the nose, then what did you do with the head?

Edmund Kemper, 1973:
Took it back into the bedroom, put it away. I was afraid my sister was going to come.

Harold Cartwright, 1973:
You know, I think one time in the past you told me when you were washing the head, you cut her larynx…

Edmund Kemper, 1973:
That's right, the larynx was hanging out and I cut it off with the knife and I put it in the garbage disposal, turned it on.

Above: Did his mother suspect Kemper of any of the crimes? Apparently, Kemper himself mentioned it to her. This is a note written by Dr. Donald Lunde from his June 15, 1973 interview with Kemper.
I included the first sentence because Kemper only took Polaroids of his first three victims. The first two were together, which suggests this conversation with his mother came after the murders of Pesce and Luchessa.

Harold Cartwright, 1973:
How did you feel about that?

Edmund Kemper, 1973:
I didn't think about it at the time, it was a matter of disposal. I couldn't throw it in the garbage, somebody's going to find it, so I got paranoid about it. Later I thought that was kind of ironic as much as she'd bitched and screamed and yelled at me over the years. It might have been subconscious. I might have deliberately put it in the garbage disposal to destroy it, for all time, you know. Make sure it was destroyed. To me, it seemed just like an unconscious action at the time, but later on I thought it was awfully coincidental.

Kemper also told Dr. Donald Lunde the same story about his mother's larynx.

Donald Lunde, 1973:
He described playing fantasy games with his sister as a child in which he would act out the killing of his mother. He then described in greater detail than the previous occasion how he had killed his mother. Notable was the fact that he cut out her voice box and put it down the garbage disposal which he said was "appropriate." He put the body and severed head in the closet and describes talking to his mother's detached head for hours, "I released years of hostility and anguish."

Mickey Aluffi, 2019:
That's another story that's going around. He supposedly threw it [his mother's torn out voice box] in the garbage disposal and hit the

button and it kicked it out. He never told me that. So I have some doubts as to whether that happened or not.

Kemper also cut off his mother's right hand.

Edmund Kemper, 1973:
But the hand I think, it's like that left hand of God thing, I had always considered my mother very formidable, very fierce and foreboding. She had always been a very big influence on my life and whether I hated her or loved her, it was very dynamic, and the night she died or the morning, it was amazing to me how much like every other victim of mine had died, how vulnerable and how human she was. It shocked me for quite some time. I'm not sure that it still doesn't shock me. I felt quite relieved after her death, a lot of it was guilt that I had been building up, and fear that she would find out about what happened and what it would do to her.

Forrest Robinson, 2020:
It [the murders] was constantly in the paper and it took a while for it to get solved, for Kemper to get drunk enough. I always thought he figured out that his mother had figured him out. I don't see how she could have avoided that. The minute I learned about Clarnell's death, it all connected immediately.

Susan Swanson, 1973:
Why the mutilation?
I said the only thing that's really horrible for me to cope with—it, it's so symbolic, what he did to mom is so symbolic. I don't pretend to be a psychiatrist, but mom was a very domineering woman and to cut off her head, that could have gone along the line of the other girls, or along the line of the nagging mouth. The domineering mother always telling him, always criticizing, always—you know, and the right hand, that's the hand of discipline. And mother was a firm believer in spare the rod and spoil the child, and I don't doubt it one bit. I firmly believe in discipline with children and I don't feel bad one bit the way I was raised. I think she did a fantastic job being alone. She could have turned into a barfly. And to raise three kids as she did, it was very very hard, I know. But this was the hand of discipline, her right hand. The mutilation didn't go any further, it didn't go as far as the other girls. And the right hand

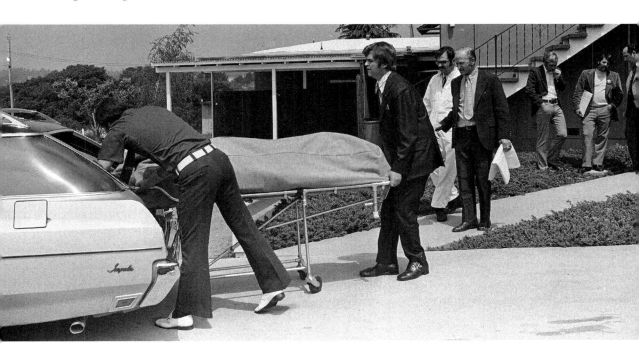

of discipline, this is also the hand she wore her mother's ring on and to me it was very symbolic. It just is.

After killing his mother and cleaning up the crime scene, Kemper drove around Santa Cruz aimlessly until he ran into his friend, Bob McFadzen.

McFadzen moved to Boulder Creek in 1963. He started at SLV High School the next year as a sophomore, two years behind Herbert Mullin. McFadzen passed away in 2014.

Edmund Kemper, 1973:
He [McFadzen] had owed me $10.00 for several weeks, and a mutual friend of ours had informed me that that was a stupid mistake, loaning him that money. I had before and he hadn't paid it back, but I was drunk when I did, and he said that he had been avoiding me.

    At any rate, I was driving down 41st Avenue from the ocean end, and just before reaching Capitola Road, I spotted him in front of me. I pulled up behind and gave him my up and down beams. He didn't immediately recognize my car until I hit the high beams because I didn't have my whip antenna on the car anyway, saw it from the front. But I removed it and left it up in the Bay Area when I had come down that weekend. So he recognized me when I gave him the high beams and we pulled into the Sears parking lot, and decided that we ought to go have some breakfast, meaning let's go get drunk. So we left my car there with the weapons in it, him not knowing what was going on. We drove out to several places, several bars. They were all closed that early. I think it was still nine or nine-thirty. In fact, it wasn't even that, it was eight-thirty I remember. We approached The Caravan down by the Greyhound Bus Station and it was closed. It was nine o'clock then. We went to a liquor store, Lloyd's Liquors right on Soquel and he cashed a check. We went over, I think it was the Fireside Lounge on Water, and there, he offered me the $10.00, which to tell you the truth, saved his life. Because with his little excuses, I needed to kill somebody at that point, and I think he deserved it more than anybody. He offered me the $10.00 without my having to mention it, so I just took five of it and figured we'd drink on the other five. It was also my intent during that day to cash some checks which were not covered by my account because I did need money, I had planned on leaving the state that day or the next. So anyway, we drank and we drank and I told him I had to leave around eleven or eleven-thirty. I left, went back home a couple of hours. Let's see, wait a minute, I forgot something. We went over to Grey's Gun Shop. It was his suggestion that possibly I could get, we had talked about going out to the DeLaveaga range and shooting that day. I thought this an opportunity to get a pistol from him or a friend, and not being able to… him not knowing that my .44 magnum had been seized, I told him it was loaned. So he suggested that rather than go out with his .357 magnum to the range, I tried to get one and we went over to Gray's Gun Shop for the purpose of either borrowing one of the owner's personal sidearms, or possibly renting one. So under the guise of having gotten an opportunity to go to work for a security company and having to have a pistol before I could start, and telling this person that I had told the company that I did have a sidearm when I didn't; it was a common ruse I suppose. Anyway, I was turned down flat by the owner of the store, Joe Desmond, and he explained to me that he, being the owner of a Class 1 federal firearms license, he could not loan or rent any of his firearms, personal or sales merchandise. So I left with McFadzen and decided to try and borrow another friend of his' .38 special, which had originally belonged to Robert McFadzen, and was now in legal possession of and ownership of Roy Libel, who had recently quit the same security job as McFadzen had and we both knew he had no use for his gun, so I tried to get in touch with him and he apparently wasn't home. His phone didn't answer. So at that point, McFadzen and I split up. I told him I had several things to do that day and would be busy the rest of the weekend and that I'd see him next weekend, which would be this last weekend, or would it, no, it would be starting today, with the full belief and knowledge that I would not be here next weekend. So we split up.

I went home and sat around the house for a couple of hours trying to think up some sort of a plan. I realized that my mother not being there Easter weekend would be highly suspicious by the family and friends, and a cause for alarm, and I realized that her not appearing at work Monday would be alarm enough, without having people pre-alarmed on Easter weekend. So, I decided that someone else had to die too, a friend of hers, as a cover-up, an excuse, something that would be believable by other people involved and other friends, and possible family that might get in touch and call. So I started thinking about who would be a victim, who would be most available, who would be the easiest to kill and who would be likely to be gone with my mother for the weekend. So I fell upon a friend of hers, Sara Hallett, or Sally Hallett, who had frequently gone places with my mother and done things on weekends. There was another friend, Mrs. Victoria Sims, who would have been just as easy, if not for the fact that she was married and was with her husband for the weekend, and possibly with her daughter and her daughter's boyfriend. So that completely ruled that person out because it was too involved. So I tried to call Miss Hallett's personal home phone, which was unlisted, I had

the number from my mother's phone book and I got no answer. I called several times in the afternoon, but she was not there. I went out for a while again that day and I forgot all about buying a saw for that carbine and was quite worried about this Sally Hallett possibly being gone for the weekend, probably with her son. The reason I thought this was the upstairs neighbors to her apartment had been gone all weekend, from late Friday sometime before I had gotten there, and they were completely gone and the oldest daughter of the woman upstairs, was there out front, which indicated to me that she, her mother and the youngest daughter, were gone. By Saturday, when the car was still there and the house lights were still out and it was quiet up there, I realized that they were not going to be there that weekend most likely. So I drank some beer I think that afternoon, Saturday, and was sitting around the house. I had some time during Saturday also, took the keys to my mother's car and drove it out to an area not far from our home, but a street

Above: Clarnell Strandberg's car where Kemper left it after killing her.

that I knew our family and friends wouldn't be driving up. I parked my mother's car there, locked it up, took the keys home and I think I left them there, I'm not sure, I may have taken them along. At any rate, that left my car out front. I drank some beer that afternoon and Mrs. Hallett called on the phone around five-thirty and wanted to speak to my mother and before telling her that she wasn't home, I asked her what she was doing that night. She said, "Why?"

And I told her I had just gone back to work and had gotten a raise while I was home recuperating for 4 1/2 months with my broken arm. This previous week had been my first week back at work on a regular job in Oakland and I told her that I was celebrating and that I'd like her to come along with my mother and I to dinner and a movie. The reason I did this was I knew she'd accept. I don't know if I should say for selfish purposes she would accept. But I had surmised from past acquaintances with her and past sessions, let's say, at home and out, that she would leap at something like that, so that's what I thought to say. Of course she jumped at the idea. I told her that my mother was not home, that she would be home a little later and I said, "Why don't you come over about seven-thirty and we'll surprise her and go out to dinner and a movie."

She said, "Fine."

Richard Verbrugge, 1973:
He personally disliked Mrs. Hallett, calling her a "domineering woman and a bitch."

Kemper then described an incident at his mother's home when he was playing records of his choice. Mrs. Hallett came in and ordered him to play certain records she liked. Then Kemper stated, "Imagine her doing things like that in my house."

That he chose to, "Break her neck and crush her larynx as only fitting for the type of woman she was."

Many years later, during a parole hearing, Kemper told a bit of a different story regarding why he killed Sally Hallett.

Edmund Kemper, 2017:
Her friend, her lover, uh, it sounds really dumb saying it this way, but my mother had her only vacation and it was a big one, and she went to Europe; two weeks in England and two weeks in France. And she was suppose to do it with this woman, Sally Hallett. They planned on it all summer long or spring long, and, uh, made serious plans, and her friend, Sally, in fact got mad at her when she—when she over it—iterated that, uh, you know, be sure and let me know if you're gonna change your mind or if you're not gonna be involved, and she said, of course I am, quit asking me that. Then at the last minute, this is a non-refundable down-payment of sixty-six hundred dollars that has to be paid by each party, and Sunday night was the deadline for that six hundred dollar deposit, and my mother was frantically calling Sally all weekend trying to get a hold of her. She couldn't reach her even though she was local. So finally she went ahead and made the decision to make—mail the deposit—on Sunday night—Monday she found out that Sally had changed her mind and then made herself unavailable. So she had to go by herself and she went over to Europe. She spent this vacation time by herself going to places and seeing things by herself when she had intended to go with this other woman. And when she got back, she tried sharing those vacation moments with Sally, and Sally got very loud with her and rude, and told her I don't want to hear about that. I didn't even go on that vacation, why are you bringing this up? So she—that cut off that release. So here I am at the house having heard this from my mother and she's frustrated and I said I'd like to know, I'd like you to share with me. So she went and got all of her travel logs and the—and the papers and stuff from the places that she went and she started systematically sharing this stuff with me, and then all of a sudden she stops and she looks at me in this strange way, and she said, I'm not gonna let you pity me. And she just walked away from the whole thing.

And I said, hey, I wanted to hear this stuff.

I had told myself that if my mother ever dies over this stuff that I did, she's going with her. That's one trip she's not gonna miss. She's not gonna back off on that one.

I swore an oath to it. I was angry at the time.

I haven't sworn many oaths in my life and every one that I have sworn I followed through with.

Allyn Kemper, 1973:

I asked him, "Why Sally? Why did you involve Sally in this?"

He said, "Just 'cause she was Sally. I just wanted to get rid of her."

Edmund Kemper, 1973:

She [Sally Hallett] told me she had been doing her laundry and had things to straighten out. This was around five-thirty. So then I, well it must have been around six o'clock when all this went on. I prepared for her coming. I closed all the windows and the doors in the house, making sure all the sliding windows were shut and all the doors to the various rooms to the house were shut, leaving the living room very quiet, which was where I planned on killing her. Next, I had to decide how to do it. I fell upon the idea of strangulation. So I had a cord that I had taken from the first two girls that I had killed, Miss Pesce and Miss Luchessa, it was a strong nylon rope type cord and it was probably three feet in length, maybe a little longer. I took that into the living room. I took in a large bludgeon type broken piece of equipment that I had had from the state. It was a top end of a drill shank, which is approximately 1 5/8" diameter and was close to a foot long, I'd say about ten or eleven inches long. I was backing myself up in case of possible difficulties in my attack. I also placed my carbine in the next room against a wall, just in case again, I figured one shot was better than a lot of screaming in case something went wrong where she was lucky and possibly incapacitated me partially. The

neighbors have lights on and were entertaining or some such.

So at any rate, by seven-thirty she hadn't arrived. I waited and waited and just before, maybe six minutes to eight, she did arrive, went in the house. I met her at the door, we spoke and she came inside. I removed her wrap, which was a sweater. We talked about where my mother was and I said I was sure that she was coming soon, that she had just called from a friend's house, which was something that was very common around there, so she accepted it fully. We moved across the living room towards the couch. It was an oblong living room, rectangular shaped and some of the preparations I had also…I hate to break off at this point, but some of the other preparations I had made, I had used some 3" wide medical tape that I had used in the Aiko Koo killing, I just pulled off a long piece of that and stuck it partially into the wall in the kitchen, right around the corner from the living room and also, I had brought two clear [they were blue] plastic bags that I had bought from a laundry for use in these killings, the co-ed killings, and for my car. I placed them in a readily available area and also my handcuffs that I had used in some of the killings, I put in my pocket.

So then anyway, she came and we talked and we were crossing the living room towards the couch. I was balking at what I had to do, or what I felt I had to do and that was the last thing I wanted to do. I didn't want to seem obvious at anything being wrong. I was stalling around as we moved across the room. My first intention was to strike her in the midsection and around the solar plexus and knock the wind from her, so that she couldn't cry out and then strangle her. It was this first move that I was kind of dreading. I guess what really worked me into it really was that she said, "Let's sit down, I'm dead."

And I kind of took her at her word there. I guess I saw that as a cue and I struck her in the stomach and she fell back or jumped back mostly I guess. I was quite surprised at

Not sloppy & incomplete, gents,
just a "lack of time"
got things to do!!
appx: 5:15 A.M. Saturday
No need for her to suffer at the
hands of the horrible "murderous Butcher"
it was quick — asleep — no pain..
The way I wanted it

Not sloppy & incomplete, gents,
Just a "Lack of time"
Got things to do!!
appx 5:15 A.M. Saturday
No need for her to suffer at the
hands of the horrible "murderous Butcher"
It was quick — asleep — no pain..
The way I wanted it

9:20 A.M.   5/24/73   Edmund Emil Kemper III
5/24/73, 9:20 a.m.   T.A. Medina

10

her reaction. I hit her hard in the midsection and she jumped back and said, "Guy, stop that."

I struck her again immediately after the first blow and her last words were, "Oh."

And sort of stumbled back. I pulled her around towards me, facing away from me, threw my left arm around her neck, it was hurting at that point, but I didn't realize it then because I was so wrapped up in what I was doing. It's almost like blacking out, you know what you're doing but you don't notice anything else around. But in striking her, I had held my thumb wrong when I made a fist and I had jammed my thumb and hurt my wrist, it's weak anyway, being in a cast for so long. But I grabbed her around the neck with the left wrist at her throat, put her into a choke-hold and pulled her up off the floor in fact, where she was dangling across my chest and there were absolutely no sounds coming from her at the time. She was holding my arm with both of her hands trying to pull away, apparently. There was no real tugging, just holding onto my arm. Her legs weren't really kicking at all. She was moving around a little bit, but very little. But no sound at all came from her and at that time, I thought that she was so embarrassed or so shocked at what had just happened, that she really couldn't say anything and that she was waiting for me to make a move. I didn't really think that I had cut her wind off so completely that not even a little squeak or any gasp or anything had come out. So I pulled her back farther and looked down into her face and her eyes were bulging badly, her face was turning black at that point, and this was just moments after I had grabbed her. Her face was turning from a bright red to a black and I realized that I was actually cutting her wind off completely, and later on, I realized I crushed her larynx or at least, dislocated it to where she couldn't breathe and I guess I had completely cut the wind off. When she went limp completely, I dropped her to the floor and tied the bags around her head with a cord, after I had put the tape over her mouth, which really didn't work, so I just pulled that off.

Edmund Kemper, 1973:
I'm sure it's happened before, but the only time I actually noticed an ejaculation was as I was killing Mrs. Hallett on Saturday night, as she was dying, it was a great physical effort on my part, very straining, very difficult, much less difficult that I made it, I went into a full complete physical spasm let's say, I just completely put myself out on it and as she died, I felt myself reaching orgasm. In the other cases, the physical effort was less. I think with the Koo girl, in the case of a suffocation, the same thing happened. But I didn't really notice it because I did have sex with her right after causing her to be unconscious.

Edmund Kemper, 1973:
When she completely quit struggling, there were some automatic reflexes in the lung area, her chest was heaving once in a while; when that all stopped, I took her into the bedroom, and her belongings, removed all of her clothes, put her on my bed in my bedroom, threw all of her belongings, other than her purse in my clothes hamper, covered her up with a blanket, went into the other room with her belongings, removed the money from her wallet. I don't really remember how much was in there, it was a slight amount of money.

Peter Chang, 1973:
He choked her and she died. Later he had intercourse with her.

Edmund Kemper, 1973:
Uh, I believe there was an attempt. But there wasn't any ejaculation with Mrs. Hallett. I believe I probably penetrated her.

> *Left: After he was arrested, Kemper provided a handwriting sample by copying the note left at the Strandberg-Hallett murder scene.*

Mickey Aluffi, 1973:
This was after she was dead?

Edmund Kemper, 1973:
Yeah.

Edmund Kemper, 1973:
She was so ugly when she was dead, I mean, just a horrible expression on her face.

Mickey Aluffi, 1973:
How about your mother?

Edmund Kemper, 1973:
No. My mother was stripped. I suppose that would have been a possibility that would come into somebody's mind, but well, my mother was moved around quite a bit, and I did strip her clothes off.

Edmund Kemper, 1973:
I left the house, I got in her car, went down to the Jury Room in Santa Cruz, a bar, and drank for an hour or so, went back to the house, maybe it was a couple hours I don't know. But from the time I attacked her until I came back to the house was I think three hours. When I came back, she apparently had been set upon by rigor mortis already and that's why I stretched her out on the bed. I removed her from my bed and noticed that when I picked her up, that her neck was broken also, because everything else was stiff, and having dealt with dead bodies before, everything gets stiff, and the neck and facial area went first, along with the extremities. When I moved her head, I noticed that the neck was completely broke, completely dislocated from the spinal column. I moved her from the bed into the closet, or wait a minute now. That was the next morning. I left her on that bed and I slept in my mother's bed.

The next morning, I didn't get very much sleep that night, maybe six hours. I got up early the next morning. That's when I moved Mrs. Hallett's body to the closet and to the stand-up wooden closet in my mother's

room and closed the door and put the desk back in front of that door so nobody would open it and it would be just like it had been before. If someone opened the other door of the closet. It was so packed with things that one would not see anything on the other side.

Thus, with a body in each closet, I prepared to leave. I got my things together and at about 9:45 a.m. I left Santa Cruz in Miss Hallett's car. I had transferred the guns from my trunk to her trunk and I believe that was that. Also, during the crime, I had kept pulling this cord very tightly around her neck before she was actually dead, leaving a very deep gouge around her neck from that cord, where I had placed my foot on her neck and pulled very tightly as a noose-type fashion around that cord trying to get it tight around those bags and it wasn't working. Maybe the bag was torn I don't know, but some air was still coming in and out of the bag. So I went to the bedroom and I took a knitted muffler, white wool muffler that I had taken from one of the co-ed victims. Miss Aiko Koo, and wrapped this tightly around her neck in a single knot and just pulled it tight and this seemed to do the trick and that's when I moved her into the bedroom, and later on, removed the cord from her neck.

Mickey Aluffi, 1973:
At what point did you get rid of your car?

Edmund Kemper, 1973:
Sunday morning before I left town, I drove my car over across Seacliff Drive, the approach to the beach park, and it was on a small side street towards the ocean that I parked it and locked it up, and might have left my mother's keys in that car, I'm not sure whether I did. But I locked my car up and walked back to the house, prepared to leave, and left.

Edmund Kemper, 1973:
I wrote a note to the people involved that, not really being sure what was in it, basically stating what time my mother died, and

I'm not sure, but I think the time that Mrs. Hallett died and apologizing for the mess and saying that I'm not really that sloppy, but there wasn't any time to be any neater, or something along that line.

Mickey Aluffi, 1973:
From there, where did you go?

Edmund Kemper, 1973:
From there, I proceeded directly out of town, going to, I had filled her car up the night before with gas and I believe it was the Union Station at 41st Avenue and Highway 1.

Edmund Kemper, 1973:
I took 129 out of Watsonville over Highway 101 and drove up to 152 and went out 152 east to Highway 5, went up [Highway] 5 to Sacramento, bought another tank of gas.

Edmund Kemper, 1973:
I drove from Sacramento right through to Reno. When I was at Reno, I parked Mrs. Hallett's car up on or inside the University of Nevada, up on Virginia Avenue, and changed my shirt. I was wearing dress boots, blue denim bell bottoms that had been involved in most all of the murders, except my mother's. I put on a white shirt and my brown leather buckskin jacket, that had also been used in the first two murders and had blood stains on the inside of it. I walked from there down into the main part of town, the main boulevard and then to a hotel, where I made a phone call to the Hertz Rental Agency out at the airport and reserved a large car, I believe it was a Monte Carlo or something like that, and took a Yellow Cab out to the airport, found that the car I had reserved was too small. So I changed my rental to a '73 yellow Chevrolet Impala and took that car back to the place where I had parked Mrs. Hallett's and removed the guns from her trunk to the trunk of the rental car, under a blanket and all the ammunition I had an extra pair of shoes and another shirt. I removed some of the things I had inside the car, like a carbine clip and a map and some keys, I believe. No, I think I left the extra keys in her car, which were the keys I believe, to my car. I locked her car up. No, I didn't. I loaded everything into the new car, took her car down to the Texaco Station, a couple of blocks away, and told the apparent owner that I was having electrical problems. Having worked in gas stations before, I knew that I had to come up with a problem that he wouldn't be able to find right away, it would take a day or two, so I told him I was having electrical problems somewhere in the car, and that sometimes it would cut out on the highway and not run. Sometimes, it would not start or have difficulty in turning over. I told him I'd be back to pick the car up in a couple of days. I indicated that my mother was with me without saying mother. I talked about "we" and this was my mother's car, which was not true.

I had removed, at that time, the registration and some gas receipts that Mrs. Hallett had in the car, in case he started looking through the glove box. I left the keys to that car with him and told him I'd be back in a few days, that we were gonna be in town and that we have friends with a car and at that point, I went back up to where the parked car was, took it down to the casino and gambled a little bit, went up to dinner in a restaurant, left town and drove for a day and a half I guess, including that day of driving. I drove, I'm not sure of the highway. It might have been 80 east until I got over on 50, at which time, I jumped onto Highway 50 east, I'm not sure at all. Things were not too clear from that point because I was taking NoDoze [sic] quite heavily and doing very much driving and very little stopping. I'd only stop for gas and once in a while, something to eat. I would drive until the tank was empty. So I sometimes drove for five and six hours. I continued this until somewhere in Utah I believe. Maybe it was Utah or maybe the far side of Nevada. I was in Utah, the eastern side of Utah very late at night. I stopped and pulled off into a rest area and slept for three hours, until quarter to three a.m., started driving again, taking NoDoze [sic] and stopping to buy those, and sometimes pop and sometimes something to eat, but very little eating. I continued to drive right on through until I think it was nine o'clock that night, so that meant, what fifteen or eighteen hours. I found myself on the eastern side of Colorado, and sometime during the Colorado trip, I was stopped by a Highway Patrolman, and another radar unit and the officer informed me…at that time, I had the carbine in the back seat, I had not altered it from its original form, it was under a blanket. Anyway, I was stopped by this officer and he told me that I had the option of either, I can't really remember whether he said, I got the impression that he said either go with him if I got a citation and have to appear in court on the citation, and not having to appear in court on the citation and paying cash in his presence to the state, whatever division of the state that you pay traffic fines to, and he and I went to the nearest mailbox and deposited $25.00 of badly needed money. At this point I left and I was very careful not to exceed the speed limits, obviously because I did not want, at this point I thought, this was well into Monday afternoon, and I had been afraid that if someone did give me a ticket, within the next twelve to eighteen hours they got an APB for me or the car. It would be for the car and they'd be looking for my name, and I'm sure he would remember it, it was an odd name and my description was odd, so I did not want to get any tickets at all. This would tell the authorities in California or possibly the pursuing FBI at this point, where I was, and which direction I was headed in, so at this point, I had the choice of either stopping and just going ahead and having a ball, blowing it, or with the weapons, or to continue on at a breakneck speed …I had wanted to break off driving for some time, but I didn't dare in Colorado now. So I drove, ate more NoDoze [sic] and taking as many as three every half hour or 45 minutes, drove far into the night.

I was on the far, far eastern side of Colorado by late Monday night, still not having heard anything on the radio about the crimes committed in California…

Edmund Kemper, 1973:
I was hallucinating, not so much seeing things that weren't there, but I was imagining things happening that weren't happening and normally, when I'm driving too long, I experience visual hallucinations and in this case, it was emotional and mental hallucinations. Physically I guess my body was overly alert. I was completely wound up. So about eight miles from the Kansas border, still headed east, I had finally had a thought. I was trying to think wow, I've got to stop this because it's getting so far out of hand, I'm not going to be responsible for what happens any further. It's just going to happen and I didn't know what it was and I didn't like that idea. So I came upon the idea of calling up Lt. Charles Scherer at the Santa Cruz Police Department.

Kemper called at eleven-thirty at night asking for Detective Lieutenant Chuck Scherer. He was told Scherer wouldn't be in until nine o'clock the next morning.

Richard Verbrugge, 2020:
He had known Detective Scherer before. Lieutenant Scherer was the detective lieutenant in charge of the Investigation Bureau at Santa Cruz Police Department. A really, really good policeman and a tough guy. Kemper had met Scherer's daughter and for some reason he was at Scherer's home with her. So he had met Scherer at one time.

On the phone to Santa Cruz police—

Edmund Kemper, 1973:
I'm trying to stop all of this…I'm just wired up. I'm not on drugs or anything, but I'm about to have a nervous breakdown, and it's not about giving myself up.

EDMUND EMIL KEMPER III

Donald Lunde, 1973:

Kemper was born on December 18, 1948, in Burbank, California. His father was Edmund Emil Kemper, Jr. He was born at St. Joseph's Hospital. He states that he weighed eight pounds, six ounces and was twenty-one inches long at birth. He describes little of his childhood prior to age seven, but dates a lot of his difficulties as starting at this point. His mother and father were separated (and ultimately divorced) when he was seven and he moved to Montana at that time with his mother and two sisters. One sister is five years older, the other is approximately two years younger. Kemper describes his first "weird ideas" as occurring at about age seven or eight. He recalls deeply resenting his mother at this time because she spoke badly about his father. This upset him because he missed his father and tried to idealize him. He recalls having fantasies at this age of "killing the whole world" and used to pray that God would do this for him, i.e. destroy everyone.

Clarnell Strandberg, 1964:

I am of Scotch, Irish, and English and many generations of ordinary Americans, I guess. The father's forbears came from Germany and were Von Kempers at one time and lauded. The mother had some Scotch and Irish also. The father was always very proud of his German ancestry—enjoyed being in Germany during the war and has since married a German girl who also fought in that war.

I felt early that the father favored the son and was over protective. Resented my disciplining at even an early age and sometimes blamed the girls for "letting him get into trouble." I was very grateful when I bore Guy, to have been given a son—always felt strongly about it.

On Kemper's father, Edmund Kemper Jr.—

Clarnell Strandberg, 1964:

The father never wanted any of them in a planned sense. He always felt we couldn't afford it and here they are today and he

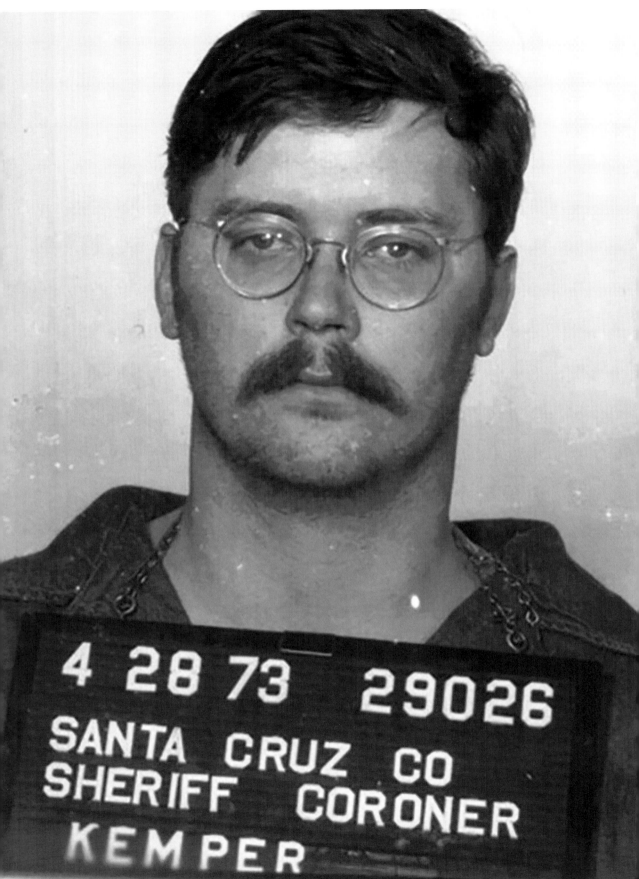

4 28 73   29026
SANTA CRUZ CO
SHERIFF CORONER
KEMPER

still can't afford it, and love is actually quite inexpensive.

He had a high school education—a high IQ, trained without working after high school. His mother resented his sitting around the house reading and suggested the Army. In the Engineers joined a suicide outfit after the war started. Met me and we married. That never ceased upon his return—he tried college under the GI Bill but couldn't get back into the studying. Argued like a Staff Sergeant with his instructors—dropped out and worked rapidly into the electrical business. Lacked the self-discipline however to go further than foreman if written reports were required. Has always worked hard and made good money but doesn't know how to channel it. Lets his automobiles run down constantly replacing them. Drives them hard. Never had an accident to my knowledge—but drives too fast for car's condition. Doesn't like the repair and upkeep of a home or yard work.

Was the eldest of three boys and felt the strictness the most, I guess. Boys, two years apart, were fairly close although the two younger, of normal size, were really closer. Parents didn't allow dancing or mixing until he was almost out of high school. Second brother broke away in a young marriage and the pressure was taken off for the third who seems quite normal and well adjusted.

I felt the father was compensating somehow with the son, Guy. However he didn't make an effort to do things with him. Never liked to take the children along. So their early years weren't too eventful. Was strict with the oldest girl and felt she could babysit. We had many arguments over this forcing responsibility too young; also developing none in Guy. The father would have liked to have been better educated and was an unauthorized "authority" on any subject with any expert. I tried to discourage this trait in Guy. He had begun to question and argue points with him. I guess the fact that he isn't communicating, even now, is self explanatory.

Allyn Kemper (Kemper's younger sister), 1973:
He [their father] did reject us a lot. Even at that age I can remember him not wanting to hold us. You know, like we'd get up on his lap and he'd say we were too heavy for him. He didn't get emotionally close to us as children. He didn't do stuff with us.

My mom has always said she noticed changes in my brother since the age of two because of the rejection.

Clarnell Strandberg, 1964:
I wished many times the father had even had written communication with all of them but he is a "loner" also, not sports minded, agnostic and dwells in the world of science fiction and the occult for escape. He doesn't relate well with any children and is as stern as his parents were without warmth.

Allyn Kemper, 1973:
We called him [Kemper] Guy. He had that nickname ever since he was little. He had this little sun suit that said "Little Guy" on it, and we just called him Guy ever since then.

Clarnell Strandberg, 1964:
Very young (3) feared meeting people, even family friends—hid under his bed, would last for several hours around this time also; wouldn't (couldn't) seem to join in group activity in first and second grade (little better later—depended on teacher). Afraid to sell papers—didn't save the money each day at ten (candy). Gave up Boy Scouts, said they wrestled and fooled around too much. Didn't join in.

Edmund Kemper Jr., 1964:
As I knew the boy while growing up, before the separation, he was a very happy lad. The life of the party type. He had a very inquiring mind and was very tender hearted toward anyone and any living thing.

Edmund Kemper:
My mother was very strong and she wanted

a man who was strong. My father was very big and very loud, but he was very weak and she wanted the opposite.

Harold Cartwright, 2020:
His mother hated his father and they separated when he was young. She moved up to Montana.

Susan Swanson, 1973:
We moved to Montana in 1956, October of 1956. And my mother and dad didn't get a divorce, I believe, until a year later. It was around Easter time. Because I remember my mom calling my dad and saying, "Happy Easter, I want a divorce."

From then it went fairly quick. I don't remember any mixed up problems and as far as school he was an average student, before the split. But after the break things definitely did show up.

Kemper's father remarried two months after the divorce in November 1961. Clarnell would go on to remarry her second husband, Norman Turnquist on February 17, 1962, but the marriage was short and ended in divorce in July, 1963. On May 17, 1964, she married her third husband, Harold Strandberg, a forty-five-year-old plumber. An Atascadero report says that Clarnell stated to them that Kemper "Needed a father…and she went out and got two new husbands for him."

Clarnell Strandberg, 1964:
Remember he never liked change—even in new clothing. Still wears one thing he likes until I insisted he change it. More insecurity? Wanted to blow out everyone's birthday candles—have their presents—for years.

Allyn Kemper, 1973:
She'd [their mother] always say things like, you know we'd just be sitting there watching TV or something and she'd say, "Oh, don't be so cute."

Just to see a reaction and it was really frustrating. I can remember a lot of frustrat-ing moments. She never really sat down and talked to us, like, really got to know us. She was real busy because she was working and raising three kids.

She always wanted to do things like go camping or boating, but she'd never really talk to us or get to know us.

She married my stepfathers just so we could go boating or camping, because they'd have a camper or a boat. But she didn't love them. She didn't marry them because she loved them. These are things she's told me.

Harold Cartwright, 2020:
He slept in a basement. The rats. No light. I've talked to a guy who is writing a book about just Kemper, four or five months ago, and he had been up there and had photographs of the place where they lived.

Just imagine this awkward, gangly, tall second or third grader, living down in a dark basement in Helena, Montana, with rats running around all night. That's got to be torture. I'm sure they didn't look at it that way back then. But it would be prosecuted today.

Mickey Aluffi, 2019:
He's talked about when he was a young boy how his mother put him in a room in the basement and locked him in there. That's not true. The reason that she did that, she put him in the room was that he and his sister were about the same age and sharing the same room. So she had him use that room in the basement as a bedroom. He could come and go as he wanted. See how he embellishes things?

James Jackson, 2020:
He [Kemper] was hard to know. He lied from beginning to end. He'd go on and on and on. You never knew if he was telling the truth.

Mickey Aluffi, 2020:
Whatever he says in those interviews after his conviction, take it with a grain of salt.

Throwing his mother's voice box, her

larynx, in the garbage disposal, that's a B.S. story. It's all lies. He loves the notoriety. So whenever he can say something shocking, he gets more attention and he loves it. He loves the attention.

Clarnell Strandberg, 1964:

I don't want to ramble but this is very difficult because I don't want to seem overprotective and qualifying. I know because of having a homosexual nephew resulting from a broken home of my sisters, I was terrified of too much female influence and perhaps was not warm enough in ways he needed. I felt in having to assume both roles, I was being cheated of my role as a mother. I am now concerned and must speak of it, of confinement with men at this age, with no heterosexual relationships. He hadn't expressed a need for girl friends yet–probably tied in with his emotional immaturity, but now what? First things first or does nature wait in the young male almost at his peak of sexual energy.

Edmund Kemper, 1991:

We lived in a house where there was a basement, some people think there was a trapdoor on that basement. That's not so. That was a different house. There's a walk-in basement, but it was in Montana, so it was a full basement, had granite walls, hewn wood floorboards, and it looked like some old dungeon or out of a castle or something. I was eight years old, seven and a half, eight years old and I was very susceptible. My imagination was very vivid and there's an old furnace in the basement that had been converted from burning coal and wood to burning gas, and it had a central heating system with your typical radiator and if you've ever lived in a home like that you know the banging, the clang, the pop, the rattles, the weird sounds in the night. That can be spooky to a kid. Well, at a certain time of the evening, the family left the center room, the living room of the house. My mother and my sisters, or my sisters themselves, would go up to bed

upstairs where I used to go to bed upstairs. I had to go down to the basement and an eight-year-old child had a tough time differentiating the reason in that why am I going to the basement—I'm going to hell they're going to heaven. Earth is the living room. I'm going down to deal with demons and monsters and ghosts and all the things that scare me. They don't have to. There's a house with three women and one male, one boy. Me. And I got a little defensive. I'm saying, gee this is kind of ganging up.

It was a storage room that was about eighteen feet wide and thirty-five feet long, okay. It was a concrete room, no windows, and it had a light bulb over a big industrial iron sink. You know, like a laundry sink and had a pull string on the light. The bed was in the opposite corner of the room. It was a double bed, a single bed, and I had a dresser halfway and a couple of carpets thrown on the floor. Old carpets and there's a lot of storage stuff along the wall and I was there about six months, in that room, and I developed some very, very particular and articulate rituals that I felt I had to go through to protect myself. Mostly, again, it's embarrassing. I was a youngster and if you can imagine me going down a staircase of rough hewn wood—there's no guardrail so one step wrong and you're off into this black pit. I turn on the light. It's a little circular light switch and a single naked bulb goes on down at the bottom of these stairs. Okay so I turn that light on, I open the door, I close the door because my mother complains of the cold coming in from the basement. I go down the stairs. I get to the bottom. I do a 180-degree turn and I walk the full length of the house on this floor with these pipes railing and wheezing and banging over my head, pitch-black ahead of me, and the only light is behind me hanging down from the ceiling. I'm now cut off from the house. Cut off from them. I walk this full length into the darkness from this gradient of light into complete darkness, groping around in the dark. I do about a 45 degree angle when I

get to the end and I pulled the string that lights up this end, and then I'm supposed to walk all the way back to the other end, turn that light off, and now walk toward the light from the dark, and I've got this horrible terror going on inside of me, and this is every night. This is every day because it's pitch-black down there. No windows. She didn't intend all of this and when I sniveled about it, when I complained and I cried about it, I got smacked in the head. "Now, what's the matter with you? Quit being such a wimp."

And she was trying to solve a problem—she had not enough room upstairs to where I didn't have to share a bedroom with a sister. I'm eight years old. I need to go to the basement.

Susan Swanson (Kemper's older sister), 1964:

As far back as I can remember, Guy has wanted to be by himself, he has seemed to be happier when there was only family. He never seemed too interested in participating in activities with other children. We seemed fairly close at times, but if something didn't go Guy's way he would get awfully mad, not as if he were spoiled and throwing a tantrum, but mad at everyone.

Edmund Kemper, 1991:

My older sister was five years older than me. So she was off with her friends and then a distant relationship.

Clarnell Strandberg, 1964:

She [Kemper's older sister] was always responsible for and protective of Guy while I worked. Sometimes protected him from my discipline out of misguided love. He and Sue were close until she began to mature and then Allyn, my fourteen (in January), daughter and he had a close relationship—however his needs were building and hers were normal and gregarious and outgoing and she had friends he resented.

Allyn Kemper, 1964:

Guy seemed to be a happy boy, but you could sometimes tell he was bothered by something. He had four close friends from which I can remember in the last seven years. He seemed to get along well with younger and older people than he. He would often try to copy boys of his age and would feel he couldn't be like them so he would give up. When he would be walking down the street during the day, if he saw some teenage boys older of his age he would walk across the street from them or go a different way unless I talked him into walking that way 'cause they wouldn't hurt him. This was only sometimes. He was very self conscious and afraid people would not like him. One thing he was worried about was his height. He thought people liked short people better than tall. He liked people to say good things about him and would take little things that people say bad about him at heart.

Edmund Kemper, 1991:

My younger sister, two years younger, and I developed some morbid games. My life had started going that way at about eight.

Allyn Kemper, 1973:

We used to play circus. He would put me up against a wall and throw darts at me. That was scary. I feared him, because he was my big brother.

I used to tease him and aggravate him. He used to sit in front of the TV set for hours at a time. We had a little green ottoman and he'd pull it up about three feet from the TV set and just park himself there all day during the summer.

He used to fantasize a lot. He used to like to read those murder magazines and science fiction of all kinds. In fact, the last time I saw him in San Mateo, I can't remember what we were talking about but he said something about, "Well, I'll probably be in murder magazines."

Like that was some big achievement or something.

Donald Lowe, 1973:
[Kemper] began fantasizing about killing people from the age of 8.

Kemper began talking with his sister, Allyn, about killing their mother.

Edmund Kemper, 1973:
Well, first it was knocking her out and killing friends of hers. [Laughs] Making mad dashes out of town. And trying to get my sister to go along with it, you know. This was a childhood fantasy. And my sister started getting scared about it, but she couldn't go to anybody about it. I mean, good God, up in Montana, you know, you just don't talk about things like that. They'd throw you in the snake pit. Warm Springs. It was a big joke in that state, that hospital because you just get locked up and that's that. But we kept talking about it and I guess she kept trying to pull me away from that idea, basically, and eventually she did. But I went through long fantasies of you know, an act, in small ways acted out these things.

Harold Cartwright, 1973:
How did you act them out?

Edmund Kemper, 1973:
Oh, creeping into my mother's bedroom in the middle of the night with a hammer, you know.

Harold Cartwright, 1973:
When you were how old?

Edmund Kemper, 1973:
Oh, geez, I started getting sick when I was eight.

Edmund Kemper, 1991:
Well the one [game] I remember someone talking about in a book was playing gas chamber or electric chair or something, and we had this big old overstuffed chair up in my room and we'd—it was not just my sister and I, it was my sister and I and a friend,

close friend—we got into all these games, we got into one game where we'd roll up in a rug and the person would try to get out of it, just like a large throw rug, and it was—I guess what fascinated us individually about it is it was a completely...uh, it broke up the monotony I guess of what we were doing. We didn't have a lot of toys to play with. We got bored with those pretty quickly so we looked for things to do. You roll up in the rug and you try to get out, and the other two would leave the room when we see who could get out fastest. You know you try to work your way out sideways or scoot out the end of it or whatever, and went from that to being tied in this, an overstuffed chair, with cord or something or pieces of sheet or sash or something and went through this process. I guess that's back when in 1960 when Caryl Chessman was executed down in California. We're up in Montana and so there's a lot of media coverage on that because he was an author, he'd written books, they're trying to save his life. He'd not killed anybody, why are they executing him? And so, that's, I think, where the fascination with that came in. That gas chamber effect. But I think it overly fascinated some people in relation to this case because it seemed so obvious a piece, you know, I'm preparing my mindset for doing deathly kind of things.

Edmund Kemper, 2017:
I made a trip to New York City when I was ten years old, which she [his younger sister] got a bit jealous about. When I came back I had a Mattel Fanner—don't know if you're familiar with the, the, uh, toy. But it's basically a cap gun, and, uh, I got that in New York. And one day she came in my room, picked it up, and seemed to be mad at me. She has since admitted that this happened and for the reasons that it happened, that she's into theatrics.

So she took the, the pistol from where it was sitting and flung it at me, and it hit my toe, my big toe and the floor at the same time, and it broke. Not apart, but it broke in-

side and it couldn't be, uh, fired normally by pulling the trigger. It could only be fanned, when I picked it up.

I was calling out for her not to throw it, and I said, "Please don't throw that."

And she thew it at me. And, uh, it broke and I picked it up and determined that it was broken, and I chased her out of my bedroom over to her bedroom, when in looking for something of equal value to break, and all I saw in the room basically was her Barbie doll which was seated on its cabinet, clothing cabinet. And, uh, I snatched it up and I grabbed the head of it and yanked it off and said here, how's this. And I thought it pops, it pops off.

Well that isn't broken. That's just, uh, disabled for a few moments.

Well it got better, the thing with the doll. I picked up a pair of shears that she had in there and I cut the hands off. Those couldn't—that, that couldn't be stuck back on. But I figured it, it broke her toy in equal fashion to mine, and I threw it down. She got all hysterical about it, and, uh, we went on arguing.

Allyn Kemper, 1973:
My grandparents that he murdered sent me a doll in a little chest. All handmade and hand-made clothes. One day I opened it up to play with her and her hands were cut off. He cut off her hands. Which is weird.

[This was] fifth grade.

Around that same time, I can remember one day when we were standing out by this big lilac bush by our house and he had a real pretty teacher in fifth grade that he really liked and he said, "I'd really like to kiss her."

And I said, "Well, go ahead and kiss her then."

We were just talking and he said, "Well, I can't because if I kissed her, I'd have to kill her."

Kemper was very close with his younger sister, Allyn, and shared many of his fantasies with her.

Edmund Kemper, 1973:

After—let's say between the age of about 8, I told her about most of my fantasies over a period of between eight and thirteen, and then, after I started getting secretive about it, in other words paranoid, you know, and afraid that someone would do something about it. I forced her into secrecy.

Kemper had fantasies about his twenty-four-year-old fourth grade teacher.

Edmund Kemper, 1973:

When I was in the fourth grade I became very strongly attracted where I used to have fantasies about hiding in the closet in school, or in a cloakroom, and creeping out and getting her when nobody else was around.

Harold Cartwright, 1973:

You mean killing her?

Edmund Kemper, 1973:

Yea. Well, see I figured, I felt very inadequate sexually and sensually and socially. Very inadequate, so I used to…I started out having fantasies about making mad and passionate love to people, and things like that. But that became dissatisfying because part of me knew that I couldn't really carry these things out. I couldn't follow through with the male end of the responsibility so my fantasies became…if I killed them, you know, they couldn't reject me as a man. It was more or less like making a doll out of a human being, you know. And carrying out my fantasies with a doll, a living doll.

Harold Cartwright, 1973:

What type of activities did you want to carry out with these people?

Edmund Kemper, 1973:

Regular sexual activities, uh, mostly I guess it was pawing, and thinking back at those times it would be pawing, playing around with the parts that were, of the human female body that were attractive. Things I'd learned through TV, the tits, you know, I mean the breast, the hair, the face, the facial features, kissing, things like this. One thing, the reason I thought of my little sister was some years after I went through this, when I was thirteen and starting to come out of this, where these fantasies starting going sublime, entrenching themselves farther down in my subconscious, not so much in my conscious active thinking, my sister brought up at breakfast one time in front of my stepfather one of my fantasies. Well, I could have killed her right there. She made a joke out of it, she said I had been attracted to her second grade teacher the same way with the same fantasies, she was a very lovely young lady and she put it very bluntly and very simply that I wanted to kill her, she put it something like I wanted to kill her teacher so I could kiss her. You know. So I guess the psychological workout on this whole thing would be I didn't think enough of myself to just jump up and kiss someone, or approach someone like this to kiss her. I was a little boy and so I would have to kill her or knock her out.

Donald Lunde, 1973:

He recalled how he used to sneak out of the house at night as a child of nine, ten, or eleven and would stare at women walking down the street from a distance, fantasizing about his desire to love and be loved by women, but even at this early age he felt that such relationships would be impossible for him and the only kind of activity he could fantasize about with any hope of success was killing the women he saw.

Edmund Kemper, 1973:

I went after my fourth grade teacher when I was about twelve years old, or ten, in the middle of the night, dressed in my robe, with my dad's bayonet and my things, climbed out the window, went creeping around the neighborhood. I was going to climb through her window and kill her, and you know drag her off.

Harold Cartwright, 1973:
What were you going to do with her after you drug her off?

Edmund Kemper, 1973:
Make mad and passionate sex to her. Now you can't do that when you're twelve years old, to your teacher. She's far too advanced for that.

Harold Cartwright, 1973:
When did you first start thinking that you had to kill a person to have sex with her?

Edmund Kemper, 1973:
You talk to my sister at all about that? She could tell you a lot because I confided a lot of that back when it was happening, to her.

Allyn Kemper, 1973:
He was really afraid of people.
I can remember one time there were some Indian girls—this is up in Montana, this is common. The Indians chase you around. But they were following us one day, and I didn't even notice it. He just picked up on it because he was so aware of anybody following him or coming after him. So we ran around a couple of blocks trying to get away from them. They caught me. He kept going. He probably could have just said a few words to them and scared them off because they were young girls, but he kept going. So I got the snot beat out of me [laughs].

Clarnell Strandberg, 1964:
Seemed to have a basic resentment which could turn toward anyone. I talked many hours with him, trying to "draw him out" and my heart used to ache when the girls would go out to play—ice skate, swim, play ball, dance, and he would prefer not to, especially if their friend came too. There hasn't been a sudden change—just never improved and became more complicated with new issues. Wouldn't attend church groups for youths. Wanted things without earning them or would fly off in a black mood. Girls love

him and would "carry his weight" when possible. I feared their overprotecting him. I worked from the time we left the father until my marriage to Mr. Strandberg in May '64 and they were quite self reliant…

One day I was called at work by the school because [he] hadn't attended for a week in seventh [grade]. I had a close relationship, parent-teacher-wise with all three children's teachers and they tried very hard to bring him "out" especially in intra-mural sports to emphasize his height—but failed.

Wanted approval in school very much without working for it. Think he loved his home life—set an all time record in seventh [grade] for tardiness. Couldn't seem to adjust to changing rooms and classes.

I tried everything I could to compensate for his lack of a father relationship—loneliness because there were never any neighbors his age—because I know three women are too much for most men. Perhaps, I too, forced him and expected more than he was emotionally able to give.

Edmund Kemper, 1991:
From my point of view, what I saw was there was a great hole in my life. There was a lot missing from my life and it didn't necessarily mean feelings. It meant I had walled off this, this emptiness of my life, okay. I had an upbringing that some have called dysfunctional, okay. Parents divorced when I was young and my mother started drinking heavily. She was working to raise three kids and we were not being cooperative about it. She drank more. She punished us harder, probably out of desperation.

So character sets were being developed at that point rather than me going to Boy Scouts and getting achievement badges. I was not going to Boy Scouts and not getting achievement badges I was finding devious ways to get around the rules of the home because the whole home life just—I watched it deteriorate from what typical kids on the block were doing, to coming home from school that I didn't like anyway and ironically I have a high IQ. I didn't know that until I was locked up the first time for murder. I always thought I was a little missing up here, a little short because I was always called stupid I was called slow, "Don't you think when you do things?"

That was the problem, I wasn't thinking when I did things, I just did by rote, I did by memory, I did by example, and had absolutely no faith in myself at all. I had no interaction going on in my own mind. I was not a thinker. I was not an individual. I had a teacher in the ninth grade who changed all that. He made me think. He would not tolerate my not thinking. He was an art teacher and it was a devastating experience for me because there were gears in my head that were just rusty and they were barely moving or not at all and that's when I found out that's what the state of my mind's functioning was. I didn't think—to the point of, he points at a stapler on his desk and says, "What does that say?"

And I looked at it, I said, "Silverline."

"Look again."

And he's raving at me, and I look and it said Swingline. All I had to do is look at it and read it, but I glanced at it and threw it back at him out of panic, so he made me think, and he gave me puzzles to work out in school in my class where I had to resolve these to continue on with the class. I didn't think I had to use abstracts and after that started, that became fascinating to me, so I got more and more involved in thinking and about my surroundings and things like that. But by then I was locked up.

Clarnell Strandberg, 1964:
I might say here that his interest in model building, for instance, showed a hurried glossing over of detail and rarely did he complete any—for a sense of pride and accomplishment. I think he isn't so much "mad at the world" as he stated, as he hates himself, rejects himself—as he is—and can't go out of himself and think even of others without help. He seems to feel little compassion or sympathy for others—or defensively can't communicate it.

Allyn Kemper, 1973:
My mother's sister lived a few blocks away from us, and he broke into their house a couple of times. Her son's been to Japan and different kinds of places and had a bunch of different knives and stuff. He was always intrigued by them. I think he took some money.

He always had pocketknives and those small little Chinese knives.

In May or June of 1962, Kemper killed the family's pet Siamese cat.

Allyn Kemper, 1973:
He used to like to roll that cat down the stairs in cardboard boxes.

Edmund Kemper, 1973:
I loved the cat, you know, family cat, been around a long time, and I was frustrated because the cat liked my sisters better than me. That pissed me off, so I decided I was going to get the cat, and that would take care of all my frustrations. But I had to figure out a way to get the cat. I couldn't just run up and stick him with a knife, I wasn't that way. So I thought and I thought and I tried hanging him, and you can't hang a cat, for Christ's sake, he'd just bop around and scream and yell for hours. So I thought wow, nobody's home today. I figured, I've got it—I'll bury him alive. Then I can forget about him, I can go in and watch a program and come out a little later and he'll be croaked. So I went, "Here kitty, kitty."

You know, all over the house, and found him sleeping in the closet. Went in and got him. I got him and dug a big deep hole, wrapped him all up in this bag, so he couldn't get out of it. Threw him in the hole, covered him all out, he's trying to get out. I covered him all up and threw a great big rock over it. I just walked back into the house and very sweatily, and terrified, and heart pumping watching this program, figuring how many minutes I've got to stay gone before I can go back and dig him up, you know. I dug him up something like twelve minutes later, you know. And took him in… that was my first sexual experience. I didn't screw a cat, you know, it wasn't like that, but there was a sexual feeling involved. This dead cat. I did things like rolling him down the stairs, you know, and watching him flop and flip and blop and you know how cats are so dexterous and I used to take him—we had these very steep stairs and a banister up above—and I used to like to take him and drop him off the banister from the top and that's about a ten foot drop, things like that. It started out with animals. Later on, I actually…I cut the cat's head off after I played around with him and he started getting stiff and things. I cut off his head and I stuck it on a paper, one of those doo-bobs with the spikes coming out of it, stick bills and papers on it. I stuck his head on that and I put it in the closet and that was like a little shrine or something, you know. I'd pull that out and just sit there and gloat at it and say, "I really got him."

Wow, all my frustrations are gone. And cut his tail off as a souvenir. My sister found it. Ah, hah, what's this, and I said, "Oh, that's a dog's tail. Cut a dog's tail off."

"That's not a dog's tail, that's the cat, isn't it?"

I said, "No."

I was ready to stab my sister to death at that point. She discovered my terrible crime. She cooled it. She half-assed accepted my story, you know, that it wasn't the cat's tail. But I kept the cat's head like that for a day or two then I just threw it away, you know, buried it.

From Kemper's July 25, 2017 parole hearing—

PRESIDING COMMISSIONER FRITZ:
All right. Um—um, okay, so why were you killing animals?

INMATE KEMPER: Instead of people.
PRESIDING COMMISSIONER FRITZ:
Okay, but why were you killing animals.

INMATE KEMPER:
Instead of people.

PRESIDING COMMISSIONER FRITZ:
So what, you wanted to kill people but you killed animals instead? Is that what you're saying?

INMATE KEMPER:
Yes.

PRESIDING COMMISSIONER FRITZ:
At—at what age, eight, nine, ten, eleven? How old were you?

INMATE KEMPER:
Probably, uh, eleven or twelve.

In November 1962, Kemper was accused of shooting to death a schoolmate's dog. Kemper denied that he shot the dog but suffered bullying from the boy and his friends.

Edmund Kemper, 1973:
That was one kind of thing I couldn't stand, was verbal or physical threats. If somebody came out and fired on me, I'd blow it right back, I'd swing right back. These guys would intimidate the shit out of me, they had a fun time intimidating me. Even after they found out it couldn't have been me that killed the dog. Because I had an alibi, I'd been at school when it happened. But it died right in front of our place, down on the Boulevard, so he blamed us. It was my worst enemy who lived across the street, it was his friend and they both went to the same catholic high school. They were a year older than me.

He told me he saw me do it and that's so much bullshit.

I went to see Gypsy Rose Lee. That was still a new movie. A friend and I went to see that Friday. That was the first time they approached me. I was always self-conscious out on the mezzanine because there would be a lot of girls from school, they'd be giggling because of my height. I was always thinking they were laughing at me, you know, instead of something constructive.

So I'm walking in and this clown turns around and he says, "You Ed Kemper?"

I said, "Yeah."

He grabbed me by the lapels and he was probably about 5'11" and I was 6'3" and it was getting real bad and my glasses flew off, one of them picked them up and said, "I'll hang on to your glasses."

But he said, "Let's step outside here for a minute."

I said, "Bullshit. I don't even know what you're talking about."

He said, "Thought you were pretty slick. You thought you could get away with it."

I said, "Get away with what?"

That's when he told me his dog got killed. Now, I remembered back on Tuesday morning at breakfast my sister mentioned that there was a dead dog out there or that somebody had run over a dog. I guess it happened on Monday or something. That Friday he caught me at the movie house. He said, every time he saw me after that, he was going to knock the shit out of me. That put a tremendous amount of pressure on me. That's why I had fantasies about blowing them all away with my stepdad's guns. That's before he was my stepfather.

They had a couple of friends that were in my school and they were making it real bad on me too. They knew I wouldn't fight, so they'd be pushing me around the lockers and stuff like that. I was very cowardly.

They spread the word that Kemper was a dog killer. At one point, the group threatened and chased Kemper into a stranger's home.

With good cause, Kemper was paranoid and on edge. Unfortunately, he didn't share his stress and found other outlets.

Kemper later told a social worker at Atascadero

that on "the last day of June, 1963" he killed a second family cat.

Edmund Kemper, 1973:

Another friend gave my mother this great big fat Siamese cat while I was gone.

The hassles started up at school again. I went to school and I'm sitting there in the gym one day and this guy that knew all these guys that were after me came walking up ha, ha, ha, blah, blah, blah. "Oh, by the way, I'll tell Lee that you're back in town."

Real cute, you know. I go, oh, shit. So this pressure starts building. This future stepfather, she wasn't married to him at that point, they were very close, got all these guns and I was tempted to borrow one of those from him and start sniping on these assholes that were always after me. I started having serious fantasies about that and that spooked me and I got scared because I was afraid I might do it, you know. So one day in a very snitty uptight mood, about the family situation, I took the cat upstairs and hung him in the closet. He started making a lot of noise and so I grabbed him and just yanked down on him really hard to hang him, super hard. And he just started clawing the shit out of me. And screaming and howling. I mean, he was just tearing me wide open. I said you God-damned, you know. I grabbed this machete I had, it was super sharp. I just started hacking at him and I chopped him right in the head. He started going into convulsions and bopping all around and then I just cut the cord, he's slopping around the floor bleeding all over the place, all over my clothes, all over the closet. I'm making this horrendous noise up there in the bedroom, you know, with everything that's going on downstairs, trying to be quiet about this. I grabbed the cat by one foreleg, as he was bouncing by and I grabbed him and stabbed him three times through the chest and he stopped and he went limp. I said, "Wow, I got him."

Great sexual thrill. Got him. Actually went through and did it. My fantasy was enacted, you know. And hung him upside down in the closet by his feet and gutted him. Put his guts in a shoe box and put him in a suitcase and it got very smelly in that suitcase. My mother still has it at home, in fact. It probably still smells. She used that against me for a long time, you know, she'd write little letters and stuff. I ran away at the end of this month, soon after the cat disappeared mysteriously. I ran away.

Susan Swanson, 1964:

All kinds of things would bother him, like the way my kids would cry or when my little girl would be drooling or spitting I would never hear the end of it from Guy. Sounds of a constant coughing or crying or heavy breathing would really upset him.

When he got his driver's license it seemed to make him feel quite important. When we went anyplace he would insist on driving till we had to give in (he was an excellent driver though).

Around 1960 he started a very restless time. He wanted to be with our dad and he wouldn't listen to anything bad about him when it finally got too bad he took $50 from a friend and took mom's car and went to be with his father.

Kemper was getting picked on a lot at school. He also felt the pressure building with his mother. Consequently, he was sent to live with his father in Los Angeles. Despite these quotes, I don't believe he stole his mothers car at this time.

Susan Swanson, 1973:

Mom said if he wants his father that bad, if he wants him so desperately that he would steal money and take a car and go at fourteen, why don't you at least keep him for the summer. And my dad said well because we're busy and this and that. He said all right, I suppose I can. Well, this is desperation when you want your dad that bad.

Edmund Kemper, 1988:

I had a real problem as a youth stealing from my mother, from her purse, pocket change. It was a game between us, I got the hell beat out of me when I got caught. I had a big mother, she was six feet tall and weighed 225 pounds at the time of her death. She was not intimidated physically by anybody. I was very intimidated by her. Again, it wasn't her fault, she was dealing with my development as best she could by her understanding of things. But when I went to visit my father at age thirteen for one month, and came back, I never touched her purse again. And I think that bothered her because she hadn't been able to stop me from doing it, yet a short visit with my father—and I had developed a little bit of self-esteem, a little bit of integrity, and it was sufficient to make it a repulsive act. It was a game I found real distasteful.

And I might also add, the reason I started stealing from her was, I—we had a thing—an allowance. We were given 25 cents a week each, us three children. When my parents separated my mother cut off the allowance. Our taxes on the house increased dramatically because she went to work for a living, she was no longer a housewife. And for several years it seemed very unfair to me that—and a little bit incredulous, what she's standing there drinking bonded bourbon because she has to have a special state license to drink, you have to buy a license in Montana. And she was smoking tailor-made cigarettes, and she can't afford a 25 cents a week allowance, which was the only thing between me and poverty.

So if I wanted money I went out and earned it, and sometimes I did, but I wasn't too oriented to work back then, I was—a lot of attitude. And I did a lot of petty stealing, mostly from her.

And again, it seemed worth it when I got caught. But when I went and saw my father, if we needed some spending money he gave us a little. We were more than willing to work around the house because it made us feel good, my stepbrother and I.

Mercedes Tileston (Senior Social Worker, Atascadero), 1964:

In August of 1963 he was allowed to go see his father in California. Seemingly, the plan was for him to remain with the father and he enrolled in school in September of 1963. The father claims that ward's [Edmund Kemper's] friends in Los Angeles were "Leery of him because he had destructive attitudes," and "Would sit and stare at people until they became upset."

He affected his stepmother negatively and apparently the stepmother brought pressure to bear on ward's father designed to have ward returned to his mother in Montana. Ward had been in school only a week in Los Angeles when his father told him that he could not financially afford to keep him and that he would have to return him to his mother. During the time that ward was at his father's, his mother in Montana learned that ward had killed the family cat when she went into ward's closet and found blood stained clothes, intestinal remnants and other tissue. She wrote and asked ward if he had cut up the cat; ward denied cutting it up.

Ward was returned to his mother's home.

Susan Swanson, 1973:

OK, my dad kept him for a couple of months in the summer and then he brought him back with the reasoning that he, Guy, made my dad's new wife, Rita, nervous. He was so big and he ate so much, it made her very nervous having him around.

Kemper changed considerably after the visit with his father in August–September 1963.

Edmund Kemper, 1988:

We stole a car on a Friday evening, and it was [inaudible] over, it was in town, parked at different places, and we bought gas for it when it ran out. The one time it ran out I had no money, I tried to siphon some gas. And so I crossed the street from the home of a deputy sheriff who had just come off duty. And he pursued me, and I drove recklessly and with abandon away from the scene. And at that time I was desperate for escape, to get away. No justification, I should have stopped because I ended up surrendering the next day anyway.

I was put on probation.

It was an informal probation, it wasn't for a period of time. I was in the book, basically. If I went back I was going to go to reform school.

Kemper was also getting picked on at school again by the same group of boys who accused him of killing a dog the year before.

An aunt and uncle of Kemper's later told Atascadero officials their opinion of Kemper's home life with his mother.

Arthur Reichstadt (Master of Science in Social Work working at Atascadero), 1966:

Interviewed Mr. and Mrs. Robert Kemper, uncle and aunt of the patient on this date. The relatives did not visit with the patient, but requested to talk with the social worker in order to shed additional light on the patient's case. Mr. Kemper described the patient's mother as being a vicious and calculating person who had managed to turn her hatred for her husband on her son. He described how she had, on a number of occasions, locked her son in a dark cellar for hours and often all night with the intention of his getting used to the dark. The mother was described as being a person who had tried to instill hatred in her son towards his father's family. She was pictured as being a likable person outwardly, however, capable of causing conflict and hard feelings between neighbors, friends and relatives. While the patient lived with his father, he made excellent grades in school, however when he returned to his mother prior to the time when he went to live with his grandparents, the aunt and uncle noticed a radical change in his grades, his attitude, and general appearance. Mr. Kemper interpreted that when the patient killed his grandparents (the latter's parents), he unconsciously expressed the real hatred and anger that he had for his mother.

Kemper did not stay with his mother for very long. On November 24, 1963, Kemper ran away again.

Allyn Kemper, 1973:
I had a babysitting job and he asked me if he could do it. I said OK and he took the lady's money that she was going to pay her bills with. Then when he came home that night, he took my mom's car and drove to the next city.

Kemper stole his mother's car and drove to a bus station in Butte, Montana. He got a ticket to Salt Lake City and one from there to Los Angeles, where his father lived.

Allyn Kemper, 1973:
I told my mom, because my brother and I were close, and I knew his thoughts. I told her that he probably left to go see dad. She drove all over town looking for him.

Police had received the call about Kemper running away from home and were on the lookout at the bus station. Kemper quickly befriended another young man.

Edmund Kemper, 1973:
Here's a basketball player from a local college sitting there, he's got his duffel bag with all his emblems on it, you know basketball squad, got his jacket on. So I'm sitting down next to him, I'm taller than he is, I'm fourteen and 6'6", they're looking all over for this kid with glasses and brown hair. I sat down next to him and I started laughing at him. And the cops are looking all over the bus station and looking at me and looking at this guy, looking all over. We're rapping away and every time a cop walked up close, I'd start talking about basketball. And as we…it just happened we were getting on the same bus, Salt Lake.

Jim Jackson, 1973:
So what did you do, get on the bus?

Edmund Kemper, 1973:
He starts walking through the bus [station], I start walking right along side of him. And as the cop is looking us over very scrutinously, I start saying, "Yeah, that was a really great game, yeah, it was tough."

This guy is looking at me like I'm out of my mind, you know. We walk right past the cop.

And we got up on the bus and I sat right next to him. Cop gets on the bus, walks along, looks us all over very closely. I start talking basketball again, "Yeah, I just started dunking last year, couldn't do it before," blah, blah, blah.

Cop gets off the bus and I got it made.

After switching buses in Salt Lake City, Kemper arrived in Los Angeles at seven o'clock on Sunday night. He rode a local bus and then walked to his father's house.

Edmund Kemper, 1973:
Creeped up to his house, stepping on the snails on the lawn. And I'm thinking of knocking on the door and I says, no, I better wait, check things out, listen through the window. They're talking about me. "Well, yeah, they'll probably catch him somewhere around Salt Lake,"

You know, blah, blah, blah, and I go oh shit. I figured it would be, "Surprise!"

Allyn Kemper, 1973:
My brother was standing on the porch and he heard my dad talk about him, saying he was always a troublemaker and always causing problems and he was going to send him back. So he went to a grocery store down the street and called my mom and he was crying.

Edmund Kemper, 1973:
If I can't stay here, I'm gonna run. She said, "Well, I'll call your father, go right over there."

I said, "I will."

She called my old man immediately and told him where I was and he comes roaring down the street in the car, my stepbrother did. I'm walking along the street very quietly, way the hell up the street walking along, and I see the car pull out. And he just starts to turn up the other way and he stops and he sees this very tall, dark figure walking down the street way the hell down there, three blocks away. Turns around and comes racing down the street, pulls up, says, "Get in."

I said, "No. I think I'll walk." I said, "I've got to think a few things over."

He says, "Get in."

He's two years older than me and the muscular type, tough guy. And I said, "No, I don't want to get in. I want to walk."

And he goes, "God-damned it."

And he starts getting out of the car and I said, "All right. All right."

I jumped in. We were driving around the block a few times. He says, "Hey, man, that's really cool, wow, you'll be back down here again."

We were driving home, you know. I thought he was going to give me a bunch of hell, tell me how I wasn't welcome, you know.

Edmund Kemper Jr., 1964:
When he ran away to me, he was sullen, fearful and had brooding spells. Also complained of headaches. His oldest sister told me of an accident he had one night at a drive-in theater in Helena. He was goofing around with them and ran full speed into a low overhang of the building. She said it knocked him out, and that when he got up there was no bump showing on his head. He seemed to be OK although he was sick to his stomach.

Mercedes Tileston, 1964:
In any event at this time ward's father allegedly told him that he could stay with him and for the first in ward's life, the father admitted having made a mistake. The mistake had reference to the father's returning ward to his mother's home two months earlier in September.

Edmund Kemper, 1973:
He [Kemper's father] called my mother up and says, "My God, you can send the state police, the militia, the FBI, anything you want, I'll hide him out. You'll never get him back. He's my son, I'm going to raise him." I'm here—that's my dad you know. First time in my life he stuck up for me. A month later I'm up living with my grandparents.

Mercedes Tileston, 1964:
Ward claims he was very happy and that his father took him to the paternal grandparents in North Fork for the Christmas vacation [1963]. However, this was a betrayal, the father left ward there.

Edmund Kemper, 1988:
And ten months later I exploded in violence, I killed both my grandparents. I was locked up, and part of that lockup included extensive treatment at Atascadero. And during that time it was determined that there was a lot of animosity between my mother and I, as there had been between my mother and my father when she took us kids away from him.

After Kemper had been arrested for the murder of his grandparents in 1964—

Edmund Kemper, 1973:
A detective was being a smart ass. I'm standing there telling him word-for-word what happened—like this time. They didn't believe—they were pissed off about the crime anway. They were all older guys, you know. They did everything but call me a liar.

[When] I got up on the stand, I told the judge what I thought of them too. What they'd done, things they had said to make it particularly miserable for me. I wasn't doing anything out of line. I was a perfect little boy. I pointed out the people in court, including the sheriff.

The sheriff was bald-headed and I laughed

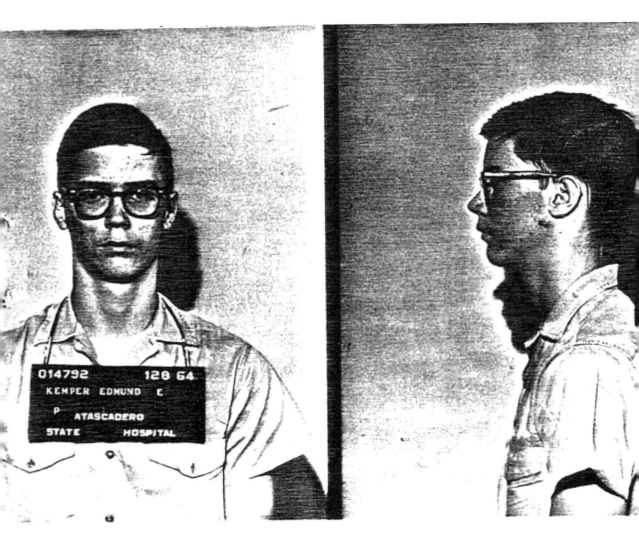

like hell because without my glasses I have about 20-400 vision. They'd taken them away from me, so I couldn't kill myself with them. All I saw out there was a bunch of fuzz. It looked like different colors of fuzz. But I couldn't really make the colors out too well. But I noticed this one particular white piece of fuzz. I looked for a bald head and I squinted and I said, "There he is. The sheriff."

And as I was looking at everything and it's all fuzzy and all of the sudden there's this bright red spot right in the middle of that. He's just flamed up. Embarrassed all to hell.

He did shit like, I went up into his office in one of those statements. He reaches back [...] [tape ends]

[New tape] [...] a little file drawer. Actu-

ally, it was down in the file drawer, second drawer, he had a few things in there. He fiddles around up on top, pulls some papers out, reaches down behind him like this—I'm sitting over in the corner of his desk by the door, in a chair. He's asking me questions and then he throws this thing [the knife Kemper stabbed his grandmother with] right out in front of me. He didn't slam it down, he threw it right in front of me across the desk. It makes this god-awful mess. It was really bloody. Then when I had hit her in the back, in the shoulder blade, it had bent over. That's why I only stabbed her three times, otherwise it would have been 300. I would have kept right on stabbing her. But she was dead after the first shot. I shot her twice in the head and once in the back. Did everything but cut her throat. [...] He threw it out there and said, "Why the hell'd you use this?"

When I saw that knife sitting in front of me like that, I just went straight back in the chair and hit the door. I had a shit-fit right then. That's totally out of the ethics of being a cop, right?

After the trial Kemper was sent to the California Youth Authority. After a stint there, he was sent to Atascadero, a psychiatric hospital located in San Luis Obispo County.

Edmund Kemper, 2017:
The Youth Authority and I was processed through Perkins, California.

It's a northern reception center.

I had a youth—I had a youth authority number, I went through normal processing like everybody else. When I went to the board, the board members said you—don't even sit down, he says, we can't even talk to you. And I looked at him with confusion and he said don't take a seat. And basically he told me I wasn't even suppose to be there because mental issues had been brought up at my trial by a psychiatrist hired by the judge, not by me. [...] He said I was mentally ill and I needed treatment, not punishment. [...] The judge mocked at that and sent me to YA anyway. [...]

I wasn't aware of it at the time, but shortly thereafter that, that was illegal; he wasn't even allowed to do that. But he did it anyway because Madera County, as it turns out, is a hang 'em high county, they do what they want to do.

Mickey Aluffi, 2019:
After he killed his grandparents he was locked up in CYA for quite a while and he considered those his formative years, which they are. He said that his actions were his way of getting back at society because he wasn't available during those formative years and dating. All of his victims were young females and that's what would hurt society the most.

Mickey Aluffi, 2019:
When he was in California Youth Authority, they technically will have control over his physical body until he is 25 years of age. They were so convinced that he was normal that they let him administer the psych test to other inmates. They also gave him a job in the kitchen and he had knives available to him all the time.

Edmund Kemper, 1988:
When I went to the Youth Authority I didn't play crazy, I programmed up to the Board, I went before the Board as the head laundry room boy in my cottage, which was the highest inmate job you could have there. I went before them as a responsible inmate to be sentenced to do time. They looked at my jacket and said, "We can't even talk to you. You've got psychiatric implications here." They sent me back to County, the judge was outraged, he said, "I'm not sending this young man to Disneyland for two murders."

So instead of sending me to the locked unit in Napa State Hospital for Youth Authority cases, where I would have been treated, resolved and sent back to Youth Authority to serve my time, he sent me to Atascadero State Hospital for the criminally insane, where the average mean age was thirty-six. I was fifteen. That wasn't a criminal act on his part, but it certainly wasn't to my betterment.

Kemper was admitted to Atascadero State Hospital in December, 1964.

Richard Verbrugge, 2020:
Remember, Atascadero at that time was loaded with sexual predators, rapists, etcetera, all adults and he's a fifteen-year-old kid.

Dr. S. Solomon (Atascadero State Hospital employee), 1964:
12-7-64

Ward 4. Admission Notes.

This is a tall, lean fifteen-year-old boy,

STAFF SUMMARY

This youth has committed a double murder, that of his paternal grandparents. For several years prior to the killing there were numerous indications that this youth was extremely disturbed, had self-destructive impulses and acted out homicidal impulses against two cats over a period of a year. He is overwhelmed with feelings of worthlessness, guilt, parental rejection and has great fears that he will suffer a psychotic episode. Ward has thought long and hard about suicide and has attempted it repeatedly over a number of years. Upon admission at NRCC he was in a particularly unstable state and gave the impression of being on the verge of committing suicide. As a result a suicide watch was posted. At present he has stablized to some small extent. He is on tranquillizers.

In spite of the tranquillizers, though, ward continues to be extremely agitated, anxious, distraught and preoccupied. He has a tremendous need to talk about himself, has done this with the psychologist and his social worker and to some extent with the psychiatrist. He should be encouraged to channel all this talk about himself to his therapist. Ward is fearful that peers might learn of his commitment offense. In this respect he is in very good touch with reality, he is sensitive and very much aware of the unacceptable nature of the killings. Studying the record and all of ward's verbalizations reveals that there were suggestions that he would act out violently. It is a tragedy that attention was not paid to these suggestions and that he was not placed in treatment and helped to avert the terrible tragedy of killing both the paternal grandparents. Staff is in accord that this youth could best be treated in a mental hospital at this time and perhaps with some preparation and at a later date be prepared for placement in a treatment program in a Youth Authority institution.

MEDICAL REPORT

Physically fit for full activity.
DIAGNOSIS
Schizophrenia, Paranoid.
VIOLENCE PRONENESS
V2A-c.

PLACEMENT RECOMMENDATION

Department of Mental Hygiene.

Mercedes Tileston, ACSW
Senior Social Worker

Staffing Group:

Richard Auwaerter, Psychologist
Andrew Hau, Teacher
Mercedes Tileston, Social Worker

MT:nb

KEMPER, Edmund Emil, III   YA#66148   NRCC   102164   CII#2-634-805
                                                                          STAFF SUMMARY

420

nervous, fidgety, claims he feels scared "of other people, most people of my own age or older." When he was asked what is scared, he stated, "I don't know."

When he was asked why are you here, he stated, "To see whether I am crazy. I told them (people at Youth Authority) I was sick—something was wrong with me and I would like to do things as other people.

Actually I killed my grandparents on August 27, 1964. It seems no one wants me to forget it—the happening." He denies killing a dog, but admits killing a cat with a knife—machete…"I swung it (machete) and it cut—made a gash in his head."

Mental, orientation: Place—partly—apparently can understand a brain that could be sick; Time of day is vague, but year and month correct; person—appears too confused to make proper deductions. Memory—good. Mentation—Governor known, President known, Vice-president, "none now, but there will be one next year." Mathematics: 8x8=64; 50-12=38; serial 7–3 mistakes. Insight—"I know there is something wrong with me."

In general insight is good. Thinks he was insane at the time he killed his grandmother, but he thinks the whole thing was result of "build-up—things she had done, and said, about me and my family." Thinks he is not violent. "All fights -2- I had, I was pushed into."

Affect—bland; mood—frightened; confused.

Impression: Schizophrenic reaction—paranoid.

Admit to Ward 4.

On November 24, 1964, Kemper told a slightly different story about the murder of his grandmother.

Report:
Ward gives no reason for killing his grandmother other than that he had a hair trigger rifle, thought of killing her, decided against it and was lowering his rifle when it accidentally went off and he shot her through the back of the head.

No mention is made about Kemper shooting his grandmother two more times and stabbing her three times.

Edmund Kemper:
They locked me away in an adult institution where I should have been raped and I should have been mutilated and I should have been screwed over and been a, like Charlie Manson when he was raped as a kid in prison, in Youth Authority. Now, then he starts raping other people and he's a leader of that stuff and then he's manipulating people.

Edmund Kemper, 1988:
I made it work. I took a challenge that was one of the most grievous I've had in my life, and it worked. Because there they treated me like a man if I acted like a man and they treated me like a little jerk if I acted like a little jerk. So basically, it was very fundamental behavior modification. And I flourished there because it took very little time for me to realize that it was to my benefit to grow up as quickly as I possibly could and to be responsible.

And I really enjoyed the responsibilities that came when I proved myself competent at given levels. There was a real bad attitude in Atascadero at that time about juveniles because there were so few of them and they were so irresponsible on the mean. So I had an uphill struggle then, but I surpassed it, I overcame it, I dealt with it. Those people made plans to further my treatment, and possibly in the foreseeable future to place me in the community, a bit at a time.

> *Left: This is the earliest record of Kemper being diagnosed with schizophrenia that I could find. Kemper first saw a psychiatrist on September 9, 1964 who diagnosed Kemper with "Personality Trait Disturbance, Passive-Aggressive Type."*

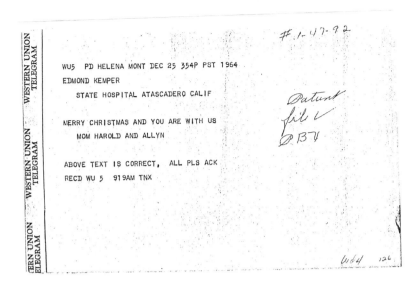

WESTERN UNION TELEGRAM

WESTERN UNION TELEGRAM

ERN UNION ELEGRAM

WU5 PD HELENA MONT DEC 25 354P PST 1964

EDMOND KEMPER

    STATE HOSPITAL ATASCADERO CALIF

MERRY CHRISTMAS AND YOU ARE WITH US

    MOM HAROLD AND ALLYN

ABOVE TEXT IS CORRECT, ALL PLS ACK

RECD WU 5 919AM TNX

Two excerpts from an Atascadero report dated 12/7/64—

Drugs, Alcohol, Tobacco, Habits, Sleep, Appetite, and Weight:

Patient denies the use of drugs, alcohol, and tobacco, although he has tried smoking on a few occasions and has sniffed glue on one occasion, he states that these made him sick and he has not continued the habit. He has been quite nervous much of his life and particularly since the murder of his grandparents. He has always had a feeling of inadequacy or inferiority and although he loves sports and all types of activity he had pretty much withdrawn from that because the other children made fun of him. Although he is not quite sixteen he is 6'6" tall and weighs 172 pounds.

Sexual History:

Patient states that when he was about twelve or thirteen he was molested by a thirty-year-old uncle who masturbated him briefly on two occasions. He claims that he has masturbated only once during his life, that he has never had a heterosexual experience, but did have one nocturnal emission while dreaming about riding a Honda motorcycle. Although he likes girls he is somewhat afraid of them, has never actually had a date, has never had

any other type of sexual experience.

An Atascadero note dated 6/1/65—

Cleo Taylor (Atascadero Social Worker), 1965:

Ward 18. Social Service Note:

The patient's mother, Mrs. Clarnell Strandberg, visited and asked to see me. She said that she had moved to California from Montana and had spent the last several days in seeing "officials" about not transferring her son to Montana. She stated that during her visit with her son, he seemed preoccupied with homosexuality as though he was either frightened of getting involved or contemplating involvement.

Richard Auwaerter (Clinical Psychologist, Atascadero), 1964:

Information from Edmund and case records indicate a long standing maladjustment, and there were many signs that some kind of tragedy was going to take place eventually. He never was able to establish adequate peer relationships, and contrary to what his mother has stated, his family relationships were generally poor. His older sister may have dominated and persecuted Edmund from an early age. For example, Edmund described an incident when he was about four years of age in which this sister terrified him by pretending to push him in front of a speeding train. As Edmund recalled the incident, she pushed him within a few feet of the train. Edmund's mother has shown an interest in him, but he has viewed her as being quite cruel and rejecting of him at times.

Richard Auwaerter, 1964:

Edmund admitted that he had made numer-

DOMESTIC SERVICE
Check the class of service desired;
otherwise this message will be
sent as a fast telegram

TELEGRAM

DAY LETTER

NIGHT LETTER

INTERNATIONAL SERVICE
Check the class of service desired,
otherwise the message will be
sent at the full rate

FULL RATE

LETTER TELEGRAM

SHORE SHIP

WESTERN UNION
TELEGRAM

1206 (4-55)

W. P. MARSHALL, PRESIDENT

NO. WDS-CL. OF SVC   PD. OR COLL.   CASH NO.   CHARGE TO THE ACCOUNT OF   TIME FILED

(Santa Cruz, California)

Send the following message, subject to the terms on back hereof, which are hereby agreed to

1:15 pm received

Edmund Kemper

2-5-67

Can't make it next week

14792

Love you;

Ma

patient
med rec
p.b.x.

---

ous suicidal attempts and engaged in behavior which could have resulted in his destruction. These may have begun when he was as young as eight years old and his last attempt was made last summer. He recalled an incident when he was about ten years old and visiting an uncle in New York City. He was atop the Empire State Building and scrambled over the protective iron work with an urge to jump and he had to be pulled down by his aunt who was with him.

Richard Auwaerter, 1964:

Another interesting thing related by Edmund is that approximately three months before the murder he was told by his grandparents that they had been ready to die for eighteen years (since grandmother's fiftieth year) and that they preferred to die together.

John Stroud (Psychiatric Consultant, Atascadero), 1964:

He tells of being enticed into bed when he was eight or nine by his sister who was fourteen or fifteen. He sometimes thought of her in a sexual fashion and he had one homosexual experience when he was ten at the hands of a cousin when the cousin was the aggressor.

John Stroud, 1964:

There is little doubt that this youngster is psychotic and at this time, is confused and unable to function. He has paranoid ideation, growing worse and more bizarre which has continued in an increasing fashion, probably for several years. It is noteworthy that he is more paranoid toward women, all except his mother, who is the real culprit. I feel he is psychotic and a danger to himself and others and probably should be with the Department of Mental Hygiene. This may be very well a long term problem.

> Left and above: Telegrams from Kemper's mother while he was in Atascadero. His mother and younger sister would visit Kemper every two weeks during his incarceration.

423

Kemper started working in the kitchen on March 7, 1966.

Edmund Kemper, 2017:
At Atascadero, I was in the—working in the, uh, scullery of a kitchen, and a young man that was a couple of years—well I guess he was about my age, and, uh, he was rolling up a towel and snapping it at people. He thought that was funny. Well he ran by this one guy that was a massive guy, he was over 300 pounds, and, uh, he was not, uh—advertising how he felt, but he was getting more and more frustrated at how this kid was acting, and when he snapped him and ran by, this big guy got up, headed toward him, grabbed the towel away from him, wrapped it around his neck and squeezed it, and forced him to the floor, and we all sat there going, you know, just the mouth hanging open, like what the hell is that.

I jumped up out of my seat, ran around the steel table looking for a weapon and I found a big steel hot teapot and I was heading for it and yelled as loudly and as lowly as I could with a low voice, hey, you know, and it caught his attention, and he backed up off of this kid and started almost babbling, he was talking very quickly. He had snapped and he was killing the kid. He was strangling him. The kid wasn't making a peep of a noise. There was no staff around to stop it.

I saved the kid's life.

In November 1966, Kemper took the GED and "Passed with flying colors," according to a note in his file.

From Kemper's "Nursing Notes" sheet 12/12/66, author illegible:
On 12/3/66 he stated his father came to tell him he (the father) no longer wanted him to write to him. That he [had] been a poor father and to forget him and patient was now grown and when he got out of here should make a life of his own. He accepted this and seemed happy. Much to everyone's concern. He stated this was the only time his father

had made a decision and stuck to it.

Allyn Kemper, 1973:
My dad always rejected—like when he was at Atascadero, my dad went to Atascadero and told him to pretend he died in the Second World War.

From a therapy note dated 3/20/67—

David O'Neil (Clinical Psychology Intern Atascadero), 1967:
Mr. Kemper's performance in the group fluctuates. Sometimes he is over-active and dominates the group while at other times he is completely inactive in the discussions. He is clumsy in his expression of his own feelings and, although he is fairly intelligent, he shows little insight into the feelings of others. He appears to be so concerned with his own problems that he has little motivation to involve himself with the group.

From an Atascadero status report dated 9/31/68—

Dorothy Pollock, EdD (Atascadero employee), 1968:
Mr. Kemper, age 19, is an adolescent who has made remarkable and sustained improvement since admission to Atascadero State Hospital about four years ago. He is functioning in the Very Superior range of intelligence (IQ, 131). There are no indications of psychotic symptoms such as delusions and/or hallucinations. There seems to be no assaultive patterns nor extreme aggressiveness which would indicate that Mr. Kemper would commit acts of violence which would be considered a danger to himself or others.

Donald Lowe (Prosecution psychiatrist), 1973:
In my opinion it [Atascadero] was the first place he felt safe, developed a competence and found an ability to deal with the world.

I found [Kemper had] some slight wish to return to Atascadero.

Dr. Joel Fort, 1973:

It is important to state that his handling by the staffs of Atascadero and the Youth Authority, and by private psychiatrists reveal many instances of gross incompetence and irresponsibility including a failure to recognize his sexual and violence pathology, misdiagnosis since there was never any evidence of paranoid schizophrenia and very poor follow-up care and supervision.

Sam Robustelli, 2020:

He told me about how he learned from other people when he was in Atascadero. You don't leave witnesses. That's how you get caught. To separate the bodies. So they may have an arm or a leg, but they won't have the full picture. No prints. Nothing could be put together.

Kemper began having fantasies about sex, murder, and cannibalism at Atascadero. His fantasies involved—

Edmund Kemper, 1973:

I killed someone, cut them up and ate them…and I kept the head on a shelf and talked to it…I said the same things I would have said had she been alive, in love with me, had she been caring of me.

Dr. Joel Fort, 1973:

[Kemper] because of his intelligence and work in the psychology section of Atascadero, finds it very easy to fool and mislead traditional psychiatrists and psychologists in and out of hospitals or jails, allowing them to hear what their standardized questions indicate to him they want to hear.

Edmund Kemper, 1973:

No, I would have never got out it I had told psychiatrists I was having fantasies of sex with dead bodies and in some cases eating them…I would never have gotten out ever… Wow! That's like condemning yourself to life imprisonment, and I don't know many people who would do that.

I hid it from them. They can't see the things going on in my mind. All I had to do to conceal it from them was not talk about it.

Walter Rappaport (Psychiatrist), 1973:

He volunteers that he had gotten along at Atascadero State Hospital, that he was permitted to engage in psychologic [sic] correlations and testing under the hospital psychologist and goes on to say, "I have taken so many tests I can manipulate them."

Mickey Aluffi, 2020:

He said they ended up putting him into this unit where he would help the psychologists administer the psych tests. And Ed has an IQ of 160 or something like that and he pretty much memorized the right answers.

Edmund Kemper, 1988:

There's been media references that I tested my way out of the place, which is a very callous and casual comment by whoever wrote it, that the professional people there are so incompetent as to not take that into consideration. There were no testings that I took in Atascadero that made—that were used in any way to determine that I was ready to go back into society.

In fact, when I went back to the California Youth Authority in 1969, I stated to all parties examining me there, psychiatrist—excuse me, psychiatric and psychological orientation, every test I had been given, every test I had given out as an inmate, a testing area worker, thus making me contaminated with that test.

Donald Lowe, 1973:

He [Kemper] felt he really did have a chance to lead a good productive life and the staff at Atascadero perceived that quality in him.

Edmund Kemper:

That was interrupted by a County that has since been called a "hang-'em-high" county by the Youth Authority officials. And they interfered with that procedure, I was sent back to County for further proceedings. The judge sent me back to the Youth Authority to serve time, the Youth Authority, after a very short period of observation and programming, paroled me to my mother.

KILLING ANIMALS

Shortly after being paroled to the custody of his mother in 1971, Kemper started killing animals again.

Richard Verbrugge, 2020:
He admitted to us that he killed cats and dogs and things like that, taking their heads off.

Edmund Kemper, 1973:
There were two or three dogs in Santa Cruz after I got out.

Late '70 or early '71. My mother had already affected me. I was sliding back into my old problems.

Harold Cartwright, 1973:
Was there any ritual along with killing these cats and dogs?

Edmund Kemper, 1973:
Uh, I had this thing about pain and suffering. It even showed itself up in the co-ed killings. Like I'd go on a long elaborate drawn out way of killing these animals so they wouldn't…[inaudible] type things, or Goldberg type ways of, [inaudible] instead of taking a straightforward [inaudible], it would be a roundabout thing. Like one cat, the only way I found I could kill it was when I was working at the gas station in Santa Cruz, late at night a cat wandered in and I was aroused with this fantasy immediately. When I was done with my work, these, uh, I can't remember the name of it, but it's a hose, nylon covering and you hook it around a tire, and I'd taken this and tied it around the cat's neck, tight, and tied one end to a cabinet and then I inflated the other end with air, and this constricted the cat's neck

completely so no air could get through, or no blood or anything. Just brought on almost immediate unconsciousness and the cat went into convulsions. As I found earlier, cats are hard to kill. I didn't want to watch it. In fact, I went out in front of the station.

Harold Cartwright, 1973:
Why didn't you watch it?

Edmund Kemper, 1973:
—And then had fantasies about the fact that it was dying.

Harold Cartwright, 1973:
What kind of fantasies?

Edmund Kemper, 1973:
It excited me, the thought that it would be dead.

Harold Cartwright, 1973:
Sexually aroused you?

Edmund Kemper, 1973:
Yeah.

Harold Cartwright, 1973:
OK, now, who was it that you were killing? Or what was it that you were killing?

Edmund Kemper, 1973:
It was a beautiful woman. No name. Just a beautiful woman.

Harold Cartwright, 1973:
Then why did you kill a dog?

Edmund Kemper, 1973:
That shows how strong the drives were getting. Kill something that close to you, an animal that I would love, say, or like a lot.

Harold Cartwright, 1973:
Did it make any difference what sex the animals were?

Edmund Kemper, 1973:

No. Male or female, it's still a dog or a cat. Obviously, there was no way, I mean, I couldn't carry out any sexual attacks on the dogs or anything.

Harold Cartwright, 1973:

Did you have any interest in that?

Edmund Kemper, 1973:

I had fantasies about it [inaudible]. Fantasies were carried out in cutting off the heads, cutting off parts of the body, tail, the legs, or something like that.

Harold Cartwright, 1973:

Did that symbolize the women?

Edmund Kemper, 1973:

Yeah.

HITCHHIKERS AND KEMPER'S RULES

Kemper also began picking up hitchhikers. Hundreds of women were picked up and delivered to their destinations unharmed, but Kemper was adapting the criminal skills he had learned in Atascadero to this new, freewheeling, world of California in the early 1970s. Kemper was planning and preparing for his crime spree.

Mickey Aluffi, 1973:

All right, and you mentioned your rules of operation, could you tell me basically what those are?

Edmund Kemper, 1973:

Yeah, these were observances that I had made before I'd actually gone into operation, let's say on the crimes, against the co-eds. For a long time, I just drove around, originally with the purpose of just getting to know more people and seeing where people's

heads were at, not trying to make a pun, that were my own age or younger because I had quite a gap of existence there and quite a gap of awareness in my having been to Atascadero and going through quite a few different programs where my awareness of myself and my surroundings, I do believe, was a little bit more acute than the people I had to live with and deal with out on the streets. This is a problem we approached in the hospital and solved theoretically, but it was very difficult on the streets to gain an honest rapport with other people who weren't aware of the special problems of an ex-mental patient who didn't want to be known as an ex-mental patient.

I drove around, picking up several people and noticing the different situations, like that girls were hitchhiking alone and in pairs and quite naively and quite innocently and people around weren't paying any attention, and I could pick up as many people as I wanted, as often as I wanted without authorities really becoming aware of it. They were about their own duties. Some of them I suppose, included watching certain characters that had been picking people up where there had been complaints. So rather than think of a rape type thing where threatening the people not to turn you in, I'd been through all that at Atascadero and watched hundreds and hundreds of rapists go through, and always being caught eventually, so I decided to kind of mix the two and have a situation of rape and a murder and no witness and no prosecution.

My first rule for operation was to be observant of everything around me, far before the approach. If I knew I was going to commit a crime on a certain day, I watched very carefully the situation, the flow of traffic, how heavy the police traffic was, how observant they were being of me in particular and the people around me, the mood of the hitchhikers, which pretty much was according to what day it was. On weekends, everybody was hitchhiking and nobody was paying any attention. Sometimes there were police, and sometimes there weren't. So rule number one was watch the traffic and try not to pick anybody up when it's too light or when there are too many people out on foot around the area. These weren't fantastically specific rules, it was more general things. That was one, don't do it if there are police around, don't pick anybody up when police are around, or if you do, make sure it's very obvious that you're letting them out, not getting in when police are around.

From then on I did not pick people up for sport any more. It was for possible execution. I didn't pick up males any more. It was all co-eds and it would only be if they were a possible candidate for death, which would mean that they were young, reasonably good looking, not necessarily well to do, but say of a better class of people than the scroungy, messy, dirty, smelly hippie type girls I wasn't at all interested in. I suppose they would have been more convenient, but that wasn't my purpose.

My little social statement was I was trying to hurt society where it hurt the worst and that was by taking its valuable members, or future members of the working society, that was the upper class or the upper middle class, what I considered to be snobby or snotty brat or person that was actually, that ended up later being better equipped to handle a living situation than I was, and have more happily adjusted, I consider it a very phony society, a very phony world where people were so busy copping out to so many things to exist and fit into a group that they had lost sight of their individual aims and goals. I had become completely lost and very bitter about what I considered these phony values and phony existences, and I decided I was going, not necessarily to weed things out because I would have ended up killing most of the world. If I weeded out, guess down deep, I wanted to fit in the most, and I had never fit in, and that was the group, the in group.

Like I said about these rules, one was, besides the ones I've mentioned, I would not circle back if I saw a good prospect, I would not circle back to pick her up unless it was really out on a limb and I hadn't run into anybody all week. There were a couple of exceptions to that rule, like the first killings. I had turned around a couple of blocks up, but I realized then I was really sticking my neck out and being obvious to several people. I was quite lucky nobody noticed or had it stick in their mind, but I did turn around and go back and pick up those girls. Besides, they could notice me doing it and if they did refuse the ride, there would be a possible witness to a future crime for the police to work on, realizing they couldn't come grab me, they could start watching me and I wouldn't necessarily know it.

So to be inconspicuous as possible was the order of the day, I had no wild things on my car, no wild clothes, no flashy driving, it was all strictly tow the line, very casual, very related, smiling, only when I had approached the girls because to sit around smiling a lot in the car would draw notice every now and then. I wanted to be absolutely nondescript, being 6'9", it's difficult. But sitting in the car with lots of leg room, I was able to scrunch down enough to where not even the passengers in the car would realize how tall I was.

Other rules were that I would take no chances that I didn't absolutely have to take which meant mostly, consenting or assenting to the wishes of the victims before their deaths, which would always be to their benefit, their requests and their pleas would be to their benefit and not to my own, no matter how good it sounded. So I had predetermined what exactly I was going to do, or not exactly, but down to a fairly fine point to where I could leave a little bit of leeway open to random chance, meaning that I would pretty well have a plan or route of travel set up after the pick up and I would pick up at certain points, unless just by a random chance, someone was in the middle of the block or in a wrong area. I'd always work out in my mind a quick route and excuse to go to a certain place, and I would not threaten them or say anything to them committing myself until I was sure there was no one around in the immediate area, just in case they did panic, and scream or yell, or try to jump out. I also locked the door from the inside by placing the broken window turning knob from my side of the car into the opening mechanism on the door from the inside for these people to show them that it would work from the inside, to let them in, and then place the window knob in the lock right after opening it and they'd never try it after they get in, they would just get in and that would be that.

Oh, I would not produce the weapon. Usually, it was always a gun. I would never produce a weapon until I was sure that from then on in I had it pretty well locked, the whole situation. From that point on, I would take absolutely no chances if I didn't have to, which unfortunately was kind of ego damaging because I would love to have been the big bad effective rapist or the effective male ego type where I could be in control of the situation without a weapon. I usually put the weapon away but let them know it was right there. But I would have to leave the area quickly, I would have to put them in the trunk or tie them up in some way that they couldn't, when I'm not looking, harm my plan. At that time they wouldn't know what it is, they would never know they were gonna die until they were under attack physically. I always promised this and that, release. Only in the case of the first two girls did I actually say that they were going to be raped and that was way out in the boonies, with nobody around and no driving to distract me and even then, I didn't get to fulfill my promise. I would have loved to, but I realized at the time, that I really couldn't. It was two people and I realized I lived in a crowded apartment house and it would be impossible to get them in and out without someone noticing. There were too many risks, so they were killed on the spot. After that point, I realized that without someone else involved I really couldn't be considering a rape situation because it's just too dangerous. I couldn't

watch out for myself and I couldn't do something like that out in the open because it's just way too chancy. So the moment no one was around, the moment that was best to my advantage, the way I saw it, the victim would die, and being frustrated about the sexual end of the thing, sometimes sex was committed either during the death or after, but there were no sexual attacks or sexual assaults before unconsciousness was achieved in any of the cases.

Mickey Aluffi, 2019:

One of his tricks was, this Ford he had, this was his "Killer Car." He would pick up hitchhikers and when they got into the car, the Ford's in those days didn't have handles, they had a lever built into the arm rest. He said that a person would get into the car and he would say, "Let me see if that door is closed."

He would open up the door and close it and drop a Chapstick in the track so you couldn't operate the handle. He knew at that point that they belonged to him.

Mickey Aluffi, 1973:

Could you possibly relate the reasoning behind the dissecting of the bodies and the decapitations?

Edmund Kemper, 1973:

Yeah, originally the decapitations, I think part of it was kind of a weird thing I had in my head; it was a fantasy I'd had in childhood. I don't know where it came from, but it was always something I'd wanted to do, and it did facilitate part of my plan later, that is if someone was found, they would be harder to identify.

In fact, the first head I ever removed was that of Miss Luchessa in the trunk of the car with the knife that killed Miss Pesce, and I remember it was very exciting, removing Miss Luchessa's head, there was actually a sexual thrill and in fact, there was almost a climax to it. It was kind of an exalted, triumphant type thing, like taking the head of

a deer or an elk or something would be to a hunter. I was the hunter and they were my victims.

Mickey Aluffi, 1973:

Another thing that comes to my mind, is the fact of a time span between several of the victims, sometimes as much as what, three months? What would be the reason for that?

Edmund Kemper, 1973:

Uh huh. Part of it was fear, some of it was regret, other parts of it were the opportunities. I didn't just rush out and look for the opportunities. If you'll notice, there was a greater time span between the first and second and the second and third, than there was anywhere else. But I had started to really get into gear towards the end there, I was getting what I think is sicker and it was much more of a need for more of the blood and the… the blood got in my way, it wasn't something I desired to see. Blood was an actual pain in the ass. What I wanted to see was the death and I wanted to see the triumph, the exultation over the death. It was like eating, or a narcotic, something that drove me more and more and more. When I had the .22, it facilitated the quickening. It stepped everything up, made it much simpler, much quicker, much easier, less of a threat to me personally, I was less afraid to attack. I don't like attacking people.

I just wanted the exultation over the other party. In other words, winning over death, they were dead and I was alive, that was the victory in my case. I suppose I could have been doing this with men, but that always posed more of a threat, they weren't nearly as vulnerable and that would have been quite odd and probably noticeable, picking up other men and having them killed, plus, like in this case where sex is involved, or the thrill of having a woman around, alive and dead, wasn't there with a man. So like I said before, there was a threat of the possible retaliation or the possible defense that could throw me off and after I'd broken my arm, this was absolutely unthinkable.

So it wasn't just deaths I wanted, it was, like I said, somewhat of a social statement in there too and I was jumping upon, I could have gotten children I suppose, children are vulnerable. But there are two things against that. One is the most important, that is that children are innocent, children are unknowing and I've always been very protective of children for that reason. I was very sensitive as a child about the treatment I got and the treatment other children got and these girls weren't much more than children I suppose, but I felt, excepting the Aiko Koo case, I felt that they were old enough to know better than to do the things they were doing and what they were doing when they were out there hitchhiking, when they had no reason or need to, was that they were flaunting in my face, the fact that they could do any damn thing they wanted, and that society is as screwed up as it is. So that wasn't a prime reason for them being dead. It was just something that would get me a little uptight, the thought of that. Them feeling so safe in a society where I didn't even feel safe.

Edmund Kemper, 1991:
The only time people got killed was when she [his mother] and I were fighting like cats and dogs and I couldn't deal with it. I couldn't vent it any other way. I look back on it, and I'm not saying I'm right or wrong, I'm just saying I'm looking back on it and saying that I think they were surrogates, I was killing her, not them. I was attacking her station. I was attacking her stance in that university setting. Also, I hated the university for what it was doing to her. She worked her butt off and they took every bit of it, oh yeah, we love that. Okay here's some more, want some more authority, want some more responsibility here. It was eating her up. She went into that job sober. She came out of the job damn near canned because she went to work drunk one day. She couldn't cope with it and it was destroying her a little at a time. She needed help but if you told her she

needed a mental hospital, if I told her she needed a mental hospital, if my little sister told her she needed a mental hospital or a dry out program, she'd have peeled our skin for it. We did not mess with that woman. My sister, my little sister was cheating on her husband when my mother was murdered. If she had known my little sister was doing that, she'd have been, she probably would have been out of the family. That was totally outrageous to her Victorian mores that she grew up with. These twisted Victorian bullshit ideals that her mother laid on her as a kid. And twisted her life with. Then she tried to run that shit on my dad.

Occasionally, Kemper would bring up the co-ed murders to his mother—

Edmund Kemper, 1973:
She [his mother] would say, "Why are you so worried about it if you didn't do anything?" I'd say, "'Cause I don't want to get rousted for it. That'd blow everything I'd ever hoped for: my engagement, this and that, you know. My job."
I was the last person in the world, she'd think would do this. Because if she had any doubts in her mind at all, she'd bring it to me first. But, she'd get real serious about it, if she had any real serious feelings that I might be the one doing it she would have turned me in to the police. She would have turned me in, in a hot minute.

SEXUALITY

From an interview with Harold Cartwright—

Edmund Kemper, 1973:
It was hard…well, I never did complete normal sex with a woman and get an ejaculation out of it, or climax. I never have with a live woman.

Kemper's first sexual experience was during a furlough from the Youth Authority in August 1969.

Edmund Kemper, 1973:
It was during my third and last furlough. I went on a three day furlough, then a five day, and then an eight day.

Harold Cartwright, 1973:
Who was that with?

Edmund Kemper, 1973:
Oh, shit. I can't remember. She'd make a good witness, too. She and my mother used to get at it a lot. Verbally. It drove her off. I know she gave me the clap [Gonorrhea], though, first time out.

Harold Cartwright, 1973:
Who was that?

Edmund Kemper, 1973:
I'm trying to remember her name. Carolyn [redacted].

Harold Cartwright, 1973:
How old was Carolyn [redacted]?

Edmund Kemper, 1973:
She was uh, Mrs. Robinson age. She was oh, 32 or 34. She had three kids.

Kemper met Caroyln when his mother brought him to a party at Carolyn's home. She was the only one of Clarnell's friends that knew Kemper's actual history. They talked for a long time.

Edmund Kemper, 1973:
Three days later I went back up there on my own, went up there and took some rum with me and I drank it all myself. We rapped and then when I started getting serious about it, it was really slow and cumbersome and she said, "You want to sleep with me?"

And I said, "Yeah."

Got all embarrassed. From that point on it was a ball.

Harold Cartwright, 1973:
Did you reach a climax?

Edmund Kemper, 1973:
No. I balled her for four and a half hours straight and she either got or faked four climaxes of her own. It was for four hours straight. Man, was I worried, especially after Atascadero. You hear all these stories, all this bull shit. My problem is believing it.

Harold Cartwright, 1973:
Did you ever see her again?

Edmund Kemper, 1973:
I called her up one time, in January…no, March, I think I called her back. She said, "I can't. I'm too busy."

Studying for something, you know. She's a graduate student.

Kemper's second sexual experience was when he was eighteen. He had a fake ID and picked the woman up at a bar in Santa Cruz and drove her home on his motorcycle.

Harold Cartwright, 1973:
Her house?

Edmund Kemper, 1973:
No, my mother's house. I was staying at my mother's house.

Harold Cartwright, 1973:
Where was your mother?

Edmund Kemper, 1973:
In bed asleep. That was pretty good. It was late at night, snuck her into the bedroom and got into bed. She acted like she didn't want to ball, but she did. Just laid there and balled, then I went to sleep and woke up about five o'clock in the morning, five or six, had to get up at seven, my mother left. In fact, it was earlier than that, it was about five, we had to get out of there before she woke up. Later on I told my mother…she was talking about my sexual life…I said, "Shit, you don't know about it."

That's when I told her about that particular trip. Then there was another one—

Harold Cartwright, 1973:
Did you reach climax with this girl?

Edmund Kemper, 1973:
No. The same thing.

Kemper also caught gonorrhea again.

In late 1970, Kemper went to a party at a co-worker of his mother's. He got drunk and had sex with his mother's friend. Again, he failed to climax. Kemper talked about this incident at his 2017 parole hearing.

Edmund Kemper, 2017:
—some of them were assistants to the provost up at UCSC. You—something that escaped our conversation earlier was that a lot of my mother's friends, uh, got hot pants for me. They wanted to do it. And that was obvious after our first meeting, and you know, they raise the—the—the hem of the skirt, and, uh, of a—a lovely woman that's so old enough to be my grandmother, I mean, you know, uh, 50 some years old. But, I said to myself, self, she wants to get in your pants, and it turned out to be very true and at a later meeting we did it, and my mother, of course, found out about it because they would talk about what I'm like in bed. And she got so mad and she come at me with, uh, I can't even bring my friends by the house anymore cause here, uh, and I said why not? And she says cause your scrotum.

Edmund Kemper, 2017:
Like one woman I could have done the same thing to her as I did to Sally Hallett, but I didn't because she was a lover. She was someone I had a normal relationship with and we both had enjoyed it, and I had no intentions of doing anything harmful to her.

Harold Cartwright, 1973:
Have you ever [had a climax during sex]?

Edmund Kemper, 1973:
No climax inside a living woman, no.

THE END

When Mickey Aluffi picked up Kemper's .44 Magnum Ruger in early April, he did not inquire about Kemper's .22 pistol, which he had bought in January. After being caught, Kemper told Aluffi and Chuck Scherer—

Edmund Kemper, 1973:
I was biting my fingernails all the time wondering if Mr. Aluffi was going to race up and arrest me for buying a handgun. The fact that you didn't ask for that .22 is one of the reasons I blew it this last week. I was getting very paranoid about that.

Edmund Kemper, 1988:
During that period of time my older sister had come to visit, shortly before the acts against my mother and her friend. And my other sister, the younger sister, Allyn, was at that time living at the Drug Abuse Preventive Center in Santa Cruz as a director. Her and her husband were both house directors.

There was no—we were always real close, my sisters and I. There was no—I can't recall any episodes of acting-out. At one point my younger sister came to me with a—a statement, after I had surrendered and the truth was known about my case. And she referred me back to an episode where I had took a pair of handcuffs and tried to handcuff her at my mother's house. And she said, "Were you trying to kill me?"

And I said no. And I said—I was horrified at that time, I said, "What made you think that?"

She said she tied the two together, and I said, "Oh, boy."

Well, it seems also that I went around and saw people toward the end there before I had surrendered, went to visit people I had known and had extensive interaction with over the months and years. And they too came forward saying, "Were you going to kill me?"

And I said, "No, in essence I was saying goodbye."

PUEBLO, COLORADO APRIL 24, 1973

On April 24, 1973, Kemper called Santa Cruz Police Department late in the evening and asked to talk with Lieutenant Scherer, as Kemper had met Scherer through his daughter. Kemper also believed Scherer was the lead investigator in all of the related co-ed murders. Kemper was told Scherer would not be in the office until 9:00 a.m. and to call back then. He waited forty-five minutes and called in again.

Edmund Kemper, 1973:

I've been up four days now. And he says well, I'm sorry, I can't do anything about it. I cussed at him or something, I apologized to the operator for it, she was going to disconnect us, and I apologized to her for cussing. She disconnected the line and I said, "Well, I guess you're going to be reading about me the next couple of days."

She said, "What do you mean?"

And I said, "I'm a big time criminal," and I said, "If these bastards," no, I didn't say bastards, I felt like saying that, but I was talking nice, and I said, "If these fools will arrest me,"

I said, "or if I can get these fools to arrest me, uh, you'll be reading about me."

I said, "Otherwise, I'm going to," well, I didn't want to say kill any people because she'd be tracing the line.

So anyway, I hung up, and I figured wow, there's enough shit over the phone where somebody's going to be awful suspicious and they might trace it to that town, and so I figured it was too small a town and too easy to trace, so I figured I'd get back to Pueblo, it's a big city. So I drove like a maniac, and this was where I was lost, mentally. Because I knew it was around one hundred miles back to Pueblo and I drove and I drove and I was looking for a place to pull over and sleep cause I couldn't make it.

I laid in the back seat and was beating the seat, I was yelling, screaming, hollering, talking, and I just couldn't sleep. I was starting to unravel mentally and I was really getting scared. I didn't know what the hell was going to happen, if I was going to run out in the road and start shooting cars if they came

go, all the way into Pueblo, I was driving the wrong way, I got off the freeway and there was all kinds of interchanges and shit all over the place and I'm driving the wrong way down the wrong way streets and I'm turning around and can't turn around, all kind of shit. I'm getting all confused, I was really badly mentally confused. So I drove to, I was looking for either a police car, a police station, I was talking out loud, I was damn near crying, I was falling apart all over the place, and driving 55 miles an hour through town, and you know, through the outskirts, and I'm looking for a phone booth, a police car, or the police station. And didn't see anything except this deserted phone booth.

I was out in this quiet area, so I got in the phone booth and I called up Santa Cruz again and this time I had the change because somewhere the night before I had stopped for gas and paid cash for it at a Gas-O-Mat somewhere. And I had cash for a phone booth, so I just threw all my money on the little table there and I called up Santa Cruz there and I started yelling at him. It was the same guy again, and I told him, I said, look, you want me to wait until nine o'clock to talk to Lieutenant Scherer, on the third call he even told me I'd have to wait until nine o'clock to talk to Lieutenant Scherer. I said look, I can't handle this, you'll have to get the cops over here and get me right now or I'm going to start killing all kinds of people. And I was ranting at this time. I was almost out of control of what I was saying.

by, or what, and uh, I didn't sleep, I just laid there and it seemed like it was an hour or two, and I got up out of the back seat. I never got any sleep. I looked up and it's dawn already and I turned on the radio and it turned out it was five o'clock in the morning. And I started driving like a mad man again, and I said oh, shit, it's got to be eighty miles to that damn Pueblo. I looked at a sign, I got around a mile down the road and there was a sign, it said Pueblo, nineteen miles. I said, Christ, drove all that distance the night before and I didn't even realize it. I was just looking for a place to pull over and I drove what, eighty-five miles or so. And so I drove ninety-five miles an hour, as fast as I could

Above: Ray Belgard from the DA's office with the arsenal Kemper left Santa Cruz with.

Jim Conner, who knew Kemper, was in the office when the third call came in.

Jim Conner (Santa Cruz Police Department Officer), 2020:

I think there were only three of us working that night. The third guy was working the office and the radio and answering the telephone. That time of night, there was nothing going on anyway. There was nothing going on in the city, so the other officer and I decided to go in to break the monotony of driving around all night long. In those days there was not much activity on graveyard. So Rick [Allen LeMarquand] and I go into the office and strike up a conversation with Andy Crain, who was that third guy, working in the office. The phone rang and he gets into this conversation with Kemper on the phone. I didn't know it was Ed. He said, "Ed, I've told you several times, I'm not going to call Scherer and wake him up. You're going to have to call back at eight o'clock when he gets to work. You can talk to him then."
I kind of mouthed, "Who is that? Ed who?" He said, "Kemper."

I said, "Oh, Ed Kemper. Let me talk to him."

RE: PHONE CALLS RECEIVED AT DESK

Phone Call No. 1

Officer Crain answers the phone.

Caller: Lt. Scherer is not there is he? He's been looking for me.

Officer Crain: Who's this?

Caller: I'm not going to tell ya. This is no prank, he's looking for me and I want to talk to him.

Officer Crain: I'll have to tell him who's calling.

Caller: Tell him it's about something he wants to straighten out. Will you do that for me please? This is no bullshit, I got to talk to him right now. I'm going to call you back in half an hour or an hour or so, have him down there.

.........garbled

Officer Crain: Now what was the phrase that you stated?

Caller: Coeds? You know what I mean? Get him down there and I'll call back and I want to talk to him.

Officer Crane: Is there a number where he can reach you at?

Caller: No. I'm not gonna play any games, I want to talk to him and I want him to do something.

Officer Crane: You can't leave me any kind of name?

Caller: No!

Officer Crane: Unless I have something to go on I can't wake up the Lieutenant.

Caller: Tell him it's not a prank, I'm not shitting you - OK?

Officer Crane: Do you have anything you can base it on?

Caller: Yeah! .....Andy, ER Kemper. He's looking for me. I'm about two inches right now from doing a whole bunch of things, there's not really anything anybody can do about it unless I do something about it - you know? I want to talk to him.

Officer Crain: OK, you're going to call back when?

Caller: Oh shit! What time is it there?

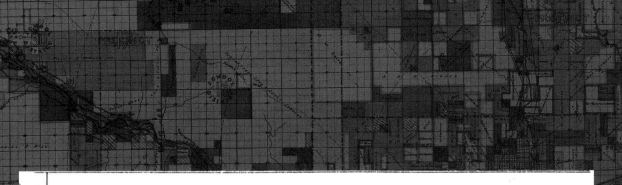

RE: PHONE CALLS RECEIVED AT DESK

Phone Call No. 1 – continued

Officer Crain: 11:34 right now.

Caller: Yes, it's 12:34 here and that's part of the problem. I'll call back in....I hate to......how far from the station is he?

Officer Crain: A half a mile, a mile.

Caller: OK.

Officer Crain: It's 11:36 now.

Caller: Yeah, it'll be roughly......I didn't want to tell you my name really, Andy this shits got to stop quick.

Officer Crain: OK, I'll notify him.

Caller: OK.

Officer Crain: Thank you.

Phone Call No. 2

Officer Toriumi: Santa Cruz Police Department.

Operator: Collect call for Lt. Scherer.

Officer Toriumi: Lt. Scherer is not here, he will not be here until 9:00 AM tomorrow morning. He's on a trip tonight.

Caller: Can I talk to him?

Officer Toriumi: I can't accept collect calls. If you wish to contact Lt. Scherer, like I stated, he will be in tomorrow morning at 9:00 AM.

Caller: Wait a minute! Wait a minute!

Officer Toriumi: He went home at 12:00 o'clock. Sir, I have an emergency line going.

Phone Call No. 3

Officer Brown: Answers phone.

Caller: Yeah, I'm calling long distance for Lt. Scherer.

Officer Brown: Lt. Scherer? Well he's not working now. What did you want to talk to him about last night?

Caller: Coed killing?

Officer Brown: What?

Caller: Coed killing!

Officer Brown: The coed killing!

Caller: Killing, you know?

Officer Brown: Yeah.

         ....garbled......

Officer Brown or Conner: Where are you?

Caller: Pueblo, Colorado. I want the police over here!

Officer Brown or Conner: What's the address? Is it a home address?

Caller: No....I'm saying I lived in Aptos.....

Officer Brown: Are you in Aptos now?

Caller: No, I'm in Colorado.

Officer Brown or Conner: What's your name?

Caller: Ed Kemper.

Officer Conner: Where are you exactly Ed?

Caller: I've been driving for three days steady, I have almost a nervous breakdown right now....

Officer Conner: Alright, just tell me where you are and we'll have someone come and pick you up.

Phone Call No. 3 - continued

Caller: Yeah, that's what I want but I don't   in this got damn place.

Officer Conner: Alright we will, just tell us where you are! What highway are you on?

Caller: Ah christ!.....wait a minute I see a street sign. It's 21st Street, let me see
         what the other one is.....It's 21st Street and Norwood Avenue.

Officer Conner: Norwood?

Caller: Norwood Avenue in Pueblo.

Officer Conner: Pueblo, Colorado.

Caller: Yeah.

Officer Brown: What kind of car are you driving?

Caller: I rented it in about Reno.

Officer Brown: What kind is it?

Caller: It's a 73 Chevie, green, solid green, Impala.

Officer Brown: Do you know the license number?

Caller: Yeah, it's a Nevada license, it's sitting right here, I'm going to be right here.

Officer Brown: Why don't you go get the license number off of it.

Caller: Ah....just a second again.   ......NBN397.

Officer Brown: NBN?

Caller: Yeah, well what I wanted to talk to Scherer about, there was eight people in-
         volved   .....garbled....

Officer Brown: There's eight people involved?

Caller: Not in what happened - there's eight dead people.

Officer Conner: Hey Ed, while we're talking to you we're going to have somebody come over.

Caller: Yeah, I wish to shit you would, really, cause I have over 200 rounds of ammo in
         the trunk and three guns - I don't even want to go near it.

Phone Call No. 3 - continued

Officer Conner: Tell me about some of the killings - OK?

Caller: You want to know some of the details, that's what I was going to tell Scherer
         cause he'd know I wasn't talking crazy.

Officer Conner: Alright, just tell me.

Caller: Alright - the two UCSC girls - OK?

Officer Conner: Yeah.

Caller: OK, Rosalind Thorpe. They didn't say anything about the physical evidence he
         found at the place but she had some of her clothing on. She had a black pair of
         felt Navy pants, bell bottoms, with buttons and panties. That was it, maybe a
         bra but I can't remember...OK?

Officer Conner: Yeah, a black....

Caller: The only article of clothing there.....I'm trying to think of things off of my
         head....

Officer Conner: How about Schall?

Caller: Huh?

Officer Conner: How about Schall?

Caller: Shaw?

Officer Conner: Yeah.

Caller: Liu?

Officer Conner: No, Cindy Schall.

Caller: Schall! I'm telling you there's six of them, and Saturday and Sunday there were
         two more and it was my mother and a friend of hers, a woman.

Officer Conner: Where do they live?

Caller: Aptos.

RE: PHONE CALLS RECEIVED AT DESK

<u>Phone Call No. 3 - continued</u>

Officer Conner: Have they been found yet?

Caller: No, that's why I was blowing it last night and those god damn cops told me to
call back this morning at 9:00 o'clock.

Officer Conner: OK, what's the address? In Aptos?

Caller: What I'm saying is I'm teetering between saying fuck you guys and run/off and,
you know, just blow it, or I'm trying to stop all this bullshit man...damn it...
just....

Officer Conner: OK, just calm down, OK?

Caller: I can't calm down, I'm not going to hang up or nothing but I can't calm down,
I'm wired up, not on drugs or nothing, I've just been up three days. I'm kind
of having a nervous breakdown and it's not about giving myself up.

Officer Conner: Ed, where does your mother live?

Caller: 609-A Ord in Aptos.

Officer Conner: Ord?

Caller: Yeah, O-R-D - it's a hard place to find. Do you know Mickey Aluffi?

Officer Conner: Yeah.

Caller: Well, he knows where it is. He came out there three weeks ago and he seized a
44 Magnum revolver that I bought that I wasn't supposed to buy because I'm an
ex-mental patient - OK? He knows the address, he was out there talking to me.
If you get him, if you have to get Sheriff's anyway to go out, if you get him or
wake him up or something and get him and somebody out there. I can tell you how
to get in and everything and I can tell you where to find them. Then you guys
are gonna know I'm not bullshitting.

Officer Conner: Ord is the street?

Caller: Ord. The markers are all screwed up in that neighborhood and there are about
four houses there with 609 on it....

Officer Conner: Who's there now?

Caller: My mother and her friend.

1n
442

Phone Call No. 3 – continued

Officer Conner: Your mother?

Caller: Yeah.!

Officer Conner: OK!

Caller: Her name is Mrs. Clarnell Strandberg. She works at the university, so does her friend or she did. I blew it Saturday and killed my mother and then Sunday this friend came over, no, Saturday night she came over and I killed her and then Sunday I just packed up all my guns and split.

Officer Conner: OK!

Caller: You see, what I'm saying is there is a break somewhere, I can't tell you what's wrong with me, you know. But I had this big thought you know, everybody thinks everything is cool and then I pick up and split and say fuck it, I'm going to drive until I can't drive anymore and then I'm going to just open up, you know? Driving all the way out here I'm reading about some clown out in Idaho doing it, some guy out in LA doint it, Jeasus Christ, you know! So now, last night I had a loose moment, I got pissed, I called up and I tried to turn myself in and they told me to call back this morning when Scherer was on duty.

Officer Conner: Yeah, they probably just tried to kiss you off, which they shouldn't do.

Caller: Ah,....I know one of them....Andy...

Officer Conner: Crain?

Caller: Crain. I told him my name and I think he thought that I was either drunk or fucking around, but he apparently called Scherer or tried to get in touch with him or something. I said I was going to call, I didn't tell him where I was or nothing, I just told him my name and told him that I'm the guy that Scherer is looking for and I got to get picked up right now - you know? What's blowing my mind is I thought you guys would be out here drag netting me - you know? I was running.

Officer Conner: Give me a physical of what you look like - OK?

Caller: I'm 6-9 and I weigh 280.

Officer Conner: How old?

Caller: 24.

Phone Call No. 3 - continued

Caller: And now that everything is up in the wind......Oh shit! I'm usually a hell of
          a lot more in contact. I tried just to sleep - you know, last night. They said
          call in the morning and I layed there for six hours, I didn't even know it was
          six hours. I thought I was coming apart, I think I'm going out of my god damn
          head and I've never done that before - you know, to where I don't know what's
          going to happen on. And if that happens I don't know what's going to happen with
          all of these damn guns laying around.

          You want to write something down?

Officer Conner: I'm writing all this stuff down as you're telling me.

Caller: But get Aluffi, he won't go around hanging on all the doors in the neighborhood,
          he knows which one it is. It's a two story green duplex, it's the only one in
          the neighborhood.

Officer Conner: Two story green duplex.

Caller: Yeah, it's the bottom one, 609-A. I took all the keys with me, I locked the
          house up, nobody can get in. If he goes around the back into the next gate,
          there's a tall gate there into the back. There is this little tiny backyard
          and there is a little plot of ground in back that is all choked up with weeds.

Officer Conner: How did you kill them?

Caller: Huh?

Officer Conner: How did you kill your mother?

Caller: With a hammer.

Officer Conner: With a hammer?

Caller: Yeah!

Officer Conner: How long has all this been going on Ed? when did it start?

Caller: Ah....last May 7th.

Officer Conner: I'm sorry I couldn't hear you.

Caller: I can give you all of the statements you want, I can cooperate and everything,
          but I got to get off the god damn street.

Officer Conner: Alright. Well there is somebody on their way over there now - there should be.

Caller: But anyway, the keys, there is a key to a house, as you go up to the first patch of ground in the back there, the weeds and stuff, and if he goes to the front left corner right by the wall of the house and where the pavement is there, if he digs around in the weeds there he'll see a set of keys there. He can get in the front. There is a master bedroom with two closets - the walk-in closet and there is a closet with sliding doors, big wooden external ones.

Officer Conner: OK, where is you mother?

Caller: She is in the walk-in closet.

Officer Conner: In the walk-in closet?

Caller: Yeah, hidden by some clothes in back. Not that I was trying to get sneaky or nothing but I just didn't want anybody finding out before I left.

Officer Conner: Ok, where is the friend?

Caller: She is in the other closet, it's a big brown sliding door closet. You got to move a big desk out of the way to get to the side she's on there and her name is Sarah Taylor Hallett, she goes by the name of Sally and she works at the university too or did.

Officer Conner: Sarah...what's the middle name again?

Caller: Taylor.

Officer Conner: How old is she?

Caller: I don't know, they're both middle aged.

Officer Conner: You were telling me something about Thorpe?

Caller: I'm telling you something that was not in the paper so you know I'm not bullshitting.

Officer Conner: Yeah, how did you kill her?

Caller: With a bullet.

Officer Conner: And what else?

Phone Call No. 3 — continued

Caller: 22 automatic, a Ruger with a 6-inch barrel that I dismantled and threw the barrel straight off the end about 50 yards out.

Officer Conner: What else did you do to her?

Caller: Just cut off her head.

Officer Conner: Where did you put that?

Caller: Huh?

Officer Conner: Where did you put her head?

Caller: Some place Alice Liu's went over the side as you approach....what's the name of that....there's a little town coming into San Francisco off of Hiway 1. Then you come down from Devil's Slide area towards a little town there. There's a thing you pull off on, to the right, there is a big pull-off spot there and it was over the side of that, down the hill.

Officer Conner: Have those been found?

Caller: Yes. .....The man's here.

Officer Conner: OK.

Caller: Whew!....he's got a gun on me!

Officer Conner: Let me talk to him.

David M. Martinez (arresting officer in Pueblo, CO), 1973:

I came up in the cruiser and he looked like three people sitting in that phone booth. When they said on the police radio that he was 6-9 and 280 pounds, I couldn't imagine anyone that big.

I moved into the area and spotted him in the phone booth with his back to me. Then I put on my red lights, pulled my revolver, and eased from the cruiser. I wasn't taking any chances.

First I came up, he hadn't noticed me yet, and checked his hands to see if he was armed.

He was still talking to Santa Cruz when I came up. When I told him to move outside he asked, "What do I do with the phone?"

I told him to just drop it.

It took about four minutes for the backup car to arrive but to me it seemed like four hours.

Harold Cartwright, 2020:

I went back to Pueblo and talked to the officer who arrested him. The other officers were still teasing him. He was about 5'6" maybe. He carried a six inch barrel .38, normally it was four inches. He got the call that there was this mass murderer serial killer at this pay phone booth, bring him in. So he goes. And when the other officers arrive, Kemper's standing, it's one of those outdoor booths with a sunshade, and Kemper's got his hands on the top of the booth, he's so tall, and the officer's trying to keep the gun pointed, but he's shaking so bad, he can't keep the gun in the right direction. All the guys were still making fun of him when I went out there.

Jim Conner, 2020:

So they hooked him up and there was a voice on the other end, "This is Officer So and So. Who am I talking to?"

I told him who I was. He said, "What do we have here?"

"Well, this guy has confessed that he killed his mother and a coworker here in Santa Cruz. We haven't been able to verify that, but I'd like you to book him, impound the car for evidence, and we'll have a detective get a hold of you in a short period of time."

Pueblo Police also found two rifles, a shotgun, and a pistol in Kemper's car.

James P. McCoy (Pueblo Police Officer), 1973:

He talked all the way to the station about killing his mother and co-eds in this area. He had decided to become a sniper or kill a policeman, figuring on being shot in a gun battle so he wouldn't have to go to trial and could get it over with.

Robert Mayber (Pueblo Police Chief), 1973:

I'm glad he didn't decide to resist arrest. He's big enough to beat a mountain lion with a switch.

Robert Silva (Pueblo police Captain), 1973:

I explained that he had the right to have an attorney and I asked him if he wanted one. I recall that he said he had no use for an attorney at that time. He said, "Let's let it all hang out."

Kemper was first interviewed by Sgt. Grubb and Cpl. Schmidt at 10:15 a.m. in Colorado.

Edmund Kemper, 1973:

It was coerced out in Colorado. I'd been without sleep for close to four days. Two detectives in the Colorado Police Department made it clear to me I was not going to sleep, I was not going to rest, I was not going to leave the interrogation room.

Jim Conner, 2020:

Once I hung up with Pueblo, then I knew that Ed lived out in the county and I knew some of the guys in the Sheriff's Department and one of the guys, his brother worked for us, his name is Mickey Aluffi. So I called Mickey.

Mickey Aluffi, 2020:

I get a call about five o'clock in the morning. It's Jim Conner from Santa Cruz PD. He says, "Hey, you know Ed Kemper?"

I said, "Well, yeah, I took a gun away from him a few weeks ago."

He said, "Well, he's in Pueblo, Colorado and he's telling the people back there that he killed his mother and another woman, plus all the co-eds."

My body went cold. I had just been out there. And, you know, we had no clue of who was doing all these killings. No clue.

Mickey Aluffi, 2020:

Kemper wanted them to get ahold of me because I knew exactly where he lived. I called the office, talked to Stoney Brook, who was the sergeant, and I said, "Meet me out here at this address, 609A Ord Street."

So we go out there and check the neighborhood. By then, it's like five thirty in the morning, maybe a little bit later. And we're waking everybody up trying to find out what's going on. Has anybody seen him? Heard anything? The people upstairs said, "No. But, you know, there's a strange smell coming from downstairs."

So that was enough for us. Stoney and I went around the back and there's a sliding glass door and a kitchen window. So we broke the kitchen window. Stoney went through and unlocked the sliding glass door. And when I walk in, you just get hit with that aroma. And if you've ever smelled it, you'll never forget it. So then we started looking. We went to that closet, opened up the sliding closet, and there was just like a big pile there. It was covered with a sheet. So we pulled back the sheet and I distinctly remember seeing skin, but I don't remember seeing any blood, but I saw skin. I said, "Okay, it's verified. Let's just back off."

We ended up calling the detective bureau, DA's office, everybody else.

Jim Conner, 2020:
He called me and said, "Oh, yeah, we had to seal the house because it's a hellacious crime scene."

So we got our administration and the detectives out of bed and filled them in on what we had learned. They got a hold of the district attorney the following morning. They put together a task force.

Paul Dougherty, San Mateo County's head criminalist, processed the crime scene in Kemper's apartment.

Paul Dougherty, 2020:
We went in the back door and we started searching through the house. We found the bedroom and at first it looked like a perfectly made up bedroom. The bed was one of those beds without a headboard and we pulled back the sheet and here's this huge puddle of blood on the bed and on the wall you could see arterial blood where it had hit the wall and we got liquid samples which were great for typing in those days.

Next to the bloodstained mattress was a note written by Kemper.

Edmund Kemper, 1973:
Not sloppy, gents. Just a lack of time. Got things to do. Approximately 5:10 a.m. Saturday. No need for her to suffer any longer at the hands of this horrible, murderous butcher. It was quick—asleep—no pain—just the way I wanted it.

Paul Dougherty, 2020;
We found the mother's body, totally nude. And I started digging through the towels at the back of the closet and I lifted one and there was her head looking right at me. That was a little bit of a shock. We took pictures and covered it all photographically.

Aiko Koo's Latin book was found in the house. Her scarf was placed around Clarnell's Strandberg's neck.

Paul Dougherty, 2020:
If I remember correctly, her friend was stuffed in an armoire in the hall, I can't be sure. She was doubled up in there.

Walt Burke and James Hogg arrived from Wessendorf Mortuary to remove the bodies.

Lynn Scott, 2020:
Walt told me that Kemper's mother was in the closet in a fetal position, covered in a blanket, with her head on top of the blanket. This is when he got there. But the thing that scared him the most was that when they opened the door to the closet, her hand fell out with these rings on it.

Mickey Aluffi, 2020:
Getting back to the earlier part about the drug issues in Santa Cruz County. They decided to form a narcotics bureau and they asked me to be a part of it, one of the charter members. So when the detectives came out, the lieutenant told me, he said, "You know, we need to send you back to the office because we don't want your picture in the paper at all."

I said, "All right. Yeah. Yeah."

"Because you're going to go undercover."

I said, "Okay, that's fine."

So I went back to the office and I'm talking to Pueblo, Colorado and Peter Chang walked in. Well, he's listening to me talk. And so, when I hung up, he said, "So do you know Ed Kemper?"

I said, "Yeah."

"Do you have a good rapport with him?"

And I said, "Well, apparently because he's asked me to go out to his house to find his dead mother."

Peter said, "Pack a bag. We're going to Colorado."

So Peter and I, Richard Verbrugge, and Chuck Scherer, we all went up to San Francisco and at one o'clock we got on a plane to Pueblo, Colorado.

Terry Medina, 2020:
Chang brought Lieutenant Scherer from Santa Cruz PD because we had the Gianera case, Aluffi from our office because we had all the other cases, and Verbrugge, who was one of the investigators in the DA's office.

Mickey Aluffi, 2019:
By the time we checked in to Pueblo Police Department, it was probably nine o'clock at night. So they brought Ed Kemper to us, it was all secure, and when he walked in, he looked at me and said, "Hi Mickey, how you doing?"

So we had this rapport and he was very free with the information.

Richard Verbrugge, 2020:
He copped out to everything. Mr. Chang asked him to come back to Santa Cruz to stand trial and he said, "Oh sure."

Mickey Aluffi, 2019:
Chuck Scherer and I interviewed him for several hours that night.

Edmund Kemper, 1973:
This is a bummer. Which is why I get depressed in that damn cell 'cause I realized earlier today after talking to you guys that I do not, I make a very strong attempt not to think about any of this stuff, anything related to it, and especially my mother while I'm in that cell because I just get super depressed. I'm just sitting there. I still haven't slept in four days. I tried two more times back there to sleep and I'd lay down and, shoot, the first thing I'd start thinking about was this last weekend. And I get super torqued up and I'm wide awake. Just absolutely not drowsy and miserable or anything. And this is including 1,500 miles of driving almost constantly and the last 900 miles of it was nothing but gas, a bottle of pop once in a while, and a whole lot of NoDoze [sic].

Mickey Aluffi, 2020:
Chuck asked most of the questions. Ed was very forthcoming about everything. We interviewed him until about one thirty in the morning. And Pueblo had arranged for rooms for us over at the Holiday Inn. And by the time we got there, it was almost two o'clock and all the guys were sitting in the bar. So we went and had a few drinks. They kept the bar open.

Mickey Aluffi, 2019:
The next day, we went through the extradition proceeding and it all went fine. So the next day we were getting ready to leave, and we had to decide how we're going to get him back to Santa Cruz. Two methods were available to us. Number one was to fly him back and number two was to drive him back. For safety concerns for anybody who might have been on the plane, we decided to drive him back. Also, we had the car available to us that Kemper had rented in Reno because he had driven another car to Reno and then rented this one and continued east.

Richard Verbrugge, 2020:
So Mr. Chang decided to fly back and we decided we were going to fly back, but we couldn't get an airline that would allow us to have him handcuffed on the airplane. So we ended up driving back.

Harold Cartwright, 2020:
They did the road trip intentionally because they had a big recorder set up in the trunk of the car. This was all part of Peter's mystique. Peter knew once Kemper was appointed a public defender, he knew he wasn't

going to get anymore interviews.

Mickey Aluffi, 2020:
No. I guarantee you, we never recorded one thing on the way back. All the recordings were before and after we got back.

Terry Medina, 2020:
They drove Kemper all the way back from Colorado. That was another brilliant move by Chang, but it really pissed off the defense and he almost lost everything with that move right there. The defense made a motion to suppress everything they got. And you know, in today's world that motion would have been granted to suppress the tapes and the video, all the evidence from those interviews.

I mean, basically on the way, driving three days, stopping, buying him cocktails, and having drinks and talking and he's telling them everything. And they're calling me and saying, okay, you need to go down here to do that. And then we coordinated when they were arriving into town. It was coordinated like a movie.

Even back then, there was air prisoner transport. Today, of course, we have the U.S. Marshal Service. That's how we would have brought him back today. But Chang knew we had to have time with him. So it was a big party on the way back.

Richard Verbrugge, 2020:
It was a two-door coupe. I did most of the driving. Scherer was in the passenger seat taking notes. Kemper was right behind me and Mickey Aluffi was behind Scherer watching Kemper the whole time. And really, we just couldn't shut him up. Scherer was taking notes, but there was no recorder in the car.

Mickey Aluffi, 2020:
I wore my gun on my right side, so I was careful to always sit on that side. Peter flew back.

During the ride back Kemper just talked nonstop. It was, "Give me a break!"

But I never actually said that because I wanted him to keep going. But I was silently wishing that he would just shut up.

Richard Verbrugge, 1973:
During the return trip to California Kemper would sometimes make the remark when viewing a female hitchhiker, "I could really help her."

Mickey Aluffi, 2020:
What I was trying to get from him is *why* he did it all. I was trying to understand. And I still can't. To some degree.

But what he said is that he was locked up when he was a juvenile in his formative years, and so he didn't have any relationship experience with women. So he thought that was because of society. He wanted to get back to society by killing their most treasured asset, which is young white females. That's what he was thinking.

Richard Verbrugge, 2020:
It got sickening. We couldn't shut him up. You get so you don't want to hear it anymore. Yes, he talked about that [cannibalism]. I can't remember where it was, though. But then some of the time he was trying to be our friend. He was being a good guy. Then he'd tell us he was using his mother's head to give himself oral sex. He would say things that were just off the wall, just nuts. He talked about Cynthia Schall and cutting her up and then, you know, he drove all the way down to Carmel and put some of her body parts in the ocean off Carmel. Little knowing that the currents run north and right up to Santa Cruz. Some of her body parts floated right up on the beach.

Mickey Aluffi, 2020:
[He talked about cannibalism] just briefly on

Left: Deputies dig up Cynthia Schall's head in the Kempers' backyard.

the ride back from Pueblo. He mentioned that, but I can't even remember which victim. But, yes, he said he had taken some of the meat and cooked it up and ate it.

Richard Verbrugge, 2020:
There wasn't anything sneaky about our trip. I'll tell you exactly what happened. We were on the road, driving through Wyoming. We're on schedule, so to speak. We're in Wyoming and we're going to stop in Cheyenne and stay overnight. We're all tired. This is the first night out. We got a late start and we're driving along, and I looked at Scherer and said, "When the hell are we going to get to Cheyenne?"

He started laughing. He said, "I thought you changed your mind. We just passed it."

I didn't realize the town was that small. We drove a little farther and we checked into—I forgot what town it was. But we met the sheriff and told him what we were doing. He had been following it on the news. He said newspapers had been contacting all the major cities looking for us, and they couldn't find us. So we decided to stay overnight there. Kemper was locked up in the jail and they put a special guard on him, two guards because of Kemper's size. The sheriff got us into a nice hotel. And we met the sheriff for a couple of drinks and dinner, and then took off the next day. But in our phone calls home, we found out that the press was looking for us everywhere.

Mickey Aluffi, 2020:
It was Laramie, Wyoming. We housed him there, and then the next night we drove across to Elko, Nevada.

By "housing" I mean we would place Ed

Right and next two pages: Kemper assists authorities in finding his victims' remains. The white uniform Kemper is wearing has "Santa Rita" on the back, implying that this series of photos was taken the day after Kemper got back to California but before he was booked in Santa Cruz.

---

into the local jail, go to dinner, and come back in the morning to pick him up. I don't remember exactly how it was coordinated, if we called or if someone back in Santa Cruz called them.

Harold Cartwright, 2020:
Kemper loved cops. He must have given thirty hours of taped interviews with Peter Chang and Ray Belgard and Mickey Aluffi. There were four of them who went to Colorado to pick him up. They couldn't shut him up.

Chuck Scherer, 1973:
He was cooperative and I found him to be an intelligent person and after traveling with him three or four days rather likable, believe it or not.

He was not violent, vulgar, or unreasonable. He continually talked about his problems that he'd had during his life and the crimes committed…I didn't see any remorse in anything he discussed with us.

Mickey Aluffi, 2019:
Kemper loves the notoriety. One time when we were in the middle of Colorado, I think, not completely sure, we had to stop for gas. So when we stop for gas, Ed says, "I've got to use the little boys room."

So I go, "Oh good, here we go."

So as we get out of the car, I take him into the restroom and he's wearing Levis and a leather jacket that had the fringe hanging off the arms, and he had what we call a transportation belt—it's a chain around his waist with handcuffs. So we go in, use the restroom and come out but by then, a crowd had formed because he's a pretty famous guy now. So these people are taking pictures and Kemper started strutting. Here, take a good look at me. He loves the notoriety.

Mickey Aluffi, 2019:
He had a pretty good sense of humor too. In the three days that we were traveling, he told me he liked the notoriety and all the press

and everything. He said, "Stick with me. I'll make you famous."

Chuck Scherer (Santa Cruz Police Lieutenant), 1973:
One particular incident that he was describing to me…he had it planned out where he could kill every person in his neighborhood in one weekend. He says that he has sufficient plans where he could do it swiftly and quietly and nobody would know until it was all over with.

From Mickey Aluffi's report on the trip.

Mickey Aluffi, 1973:
At a few points in the journey, suspect Kemper stated things that he wished to keep off of the record. One of them was the fact that he requested prosecution be delayed in his case for a period that would enable the death penalty in California to be re-instated. Kemper expressed a desire to be executed in the gas chamber. He further stated that he had considered suicide and also holding up in a low class motel and shooting it out with the police when they arrived. He had finally negated this idea due to the fact that he did not wish to leave the homicides uncleared, should he be deceased.

Mickey Aluffi, 2020:
There wasn't a death penalty at the time. He wanted to volunteer

Sheriff's deputy James Ingram (kneeling) combs through a makeshift burial near Summit Road where a decomposed headless body was uncovered. Suspected slayer Edmund Emil Kemper led deputies Saturday to several locations where parts of bodies were uncovered. At the right is sheriff's detective Ken Foster.

Left: Shots of the burial site of Mary Ann Pesce.
Right and next page: Deputies remove the head of Cynthia Schall from the Kempers' backyard.

for the death penalty. He said to me, "I can't go to the chair."

He says, "Maybe I'll just try to get a frontal lobotomy."

Mickey Aluffi, 2019:
In the meantime all this information he is giving us, we are relaying it back to SC, and they're finding that everything he is saying is absolutely true. I don't talk too much about the victims, but one of his victims he had severed the head and had peeled the face off the skull, and buried it in his backyard outside of his bedroom window, so that the face was on top of the skull and he did that because he knew that she was looking at him.

Sam Robustelli, 2020:
During Mickey's road trip, I was on the other end running around Santa Cruz.

On Thursday, April 26, Cynthia Schall's head was dug up from Kemper's backyard.

UCSC held a memorial for Sally Hallett and Clarnell Strandberg on Friday, April 27. Two hundred friends and colleagues gathered at a patio at College 5 where Clarnell Strandberg worked. Chancellor Dean McHenry opened the gathering. Coworkers spoke, remembering the two women. The ceremony ended with a moment of silence and the UCSC chamber singers performing a chant from a fifteenth century mass.

Kemper and his escorts were nearing Santa Cruz and the media circus awaiting them.

Richard Verbrugge, 2020:
Scherer came up with a good idea. He said, "Instead of bringing him into Santa Cruz when they expect him, let's put him overnight somewhere in the Bay Area."

I suggested Alameda, Alameda County Jail.

Before dropping Kemper at the jail in Alameda, he was brought to a few of his body dumping sites on Friday, April 27.

The group met four other law enforcement agents and visited the area on Palomares Canyon Road where Kemper murdered Mary Ann Pesce and Anita Luchessa.

At 7:15 p.m. they drove up Eden Canyon Road to where Kemper buried the head and hands of Aiko Koo. Because of the diminishing light, no search was made.

Staying on Eden Canyon Road, at eight o'clock the group drove to the area where Kemper dumped Alice Liu and Rosalind Thorpe. It was noted that the location Kemper identified was in fact "the exact location where both bodies were found."

At eight thirty Kemper was brought to the Alameda County jail in Santa Rita.

Richard Verbrugge, 2020:
I got home that night. They got home. And the next morning we all met together and jumped in the car and picked Eddie up.

Mickey Aluffi, 2020:
And then the next morning, we went back and picked him up and he had agreed to show us all of the spots where he had dumped bodies.

So we went to his dumping grounds in Santa Cruz, six different locations. He pointed out where he had dumped who where,

and we had the people behind us, and we'd relay it to them and then they would process that scene and get all the evidence.

On Saturday, April 28, Kemper and his small group of guards unsuccessfully searched a creek bed in Alameda County for the head of Aiko Koo. The head was not found.

Kemper directed the group to a shallow grave off the Old Santa Cruz Highway, less than a mile north of Summit Road, where the torso of Mary Ann Pesce was found. Nearby they also found a pelvic bone believed to belong to Anita Luchessa.

Kemper then led the group about a quarter mile away from where Mary Ann Pesce's head had been found on August 15. They were not able to recover Anita Luchessa's head.

Kemper was still apparently disturbed from his first murder, Mary Ann Pesce. He admitted that he had stalked the Pesce family's home after the murder.

Mickey Aluffi, 2019:
It bothered him greatly. […] He went to Camarillo because he wanted to see what sort of family she was from.

One of his rules of operation as he related to me…he wished his victims to be of an aristocracy of upper-middle class to an upper class. He told me the Pesce residence was very upper middle class, obviously wealthy.

The group then headed back to the top of Rodeo Gulch Road where they uncovered arm and leg bone fragments of Aiko Koo. The group then headed to Boulder Creek.

Sam Robustelli, 2020:
Our job was to find arms and legs and where he threw them. Over the bank and actually repel down. One of the spots was up at Redwood Christian Park here [in Boulder Creek]. He buried somebody up there. I don't remember who. Driving into

69969

BOOKING RECORD

SANTA CRUZ COUNTY JAIL

S.O.I.D. S- 29026
SCSD
CASE NO. 73- 2911

NAME: KEMPER, Edmund Emil III   MIDDLE   AKA None   DATE 4-28-73   TIME 1930
     LAST   FIRST

CODE SEC. 187 P.C.(2cts.)   CHARGE HOMICIDE   COURT Muni I   BAIL No
                                                     Per Judge FRAN

OCCUPATION Construction

FBI CODE SEC. (37) 0900

EMPLOYER'S NAME & ADDRESS California Divisions of Hiways   LOCATION OF ARREST Pueblo, COLORADO Police Dept.

ARRESTING OFFICER & AGENCY SCSD Investigator ALUFFI   PHONE N/P

ADDRESS 609 A Ord Street Aptos, California

SEX Male   RACE Cauc   HT. 6-9   WT. 285   HAIR Brn   EYES Hazel   COMPLEX. Light   AGE 24

D.O.B. 12-18-48   P.O.B. Burbank, California   SOC. SEC NUMBER 517-54-0077   OP. LIC NO. E-038880 Ca

MARKS: SCARS: TATTOOS: Scar on Lt forearm 6"/1" scar on Lt hand thumb/

IN EMERGENCY NOTIFY Micky ALUFFI   REL. Friend   ADD. P.O. Box 623 Santa Cruz

VEHICLE COLOR None   YR.   MAKE   TYPE   LIC. NO.   STORED

MONEY $ 21.95   RECEIPT FOR PROPERTY $ 11.95   PERSONAL ITEMS Brn boots/ white coveralls/

DECLINES CALL SIGN Edmund Emil Kemp

PHONE CALL TO DECLINES   PHONE   SEARCHING OFFICER J. VALDEZ   J Valdez

BOOKING OFFICER J. VALDEZ   J Valdez

DATE OF DISPOSITION 5-18-73   CHARGE 187PC CR-29430   PROBATION 0 YRS.   FINE 0   OR JAIL DA

DATE OF DISPOSITION   CHARGE   PROBATION   YRS.   FINE   OR JAIL

DATE OF DISPOSITION   CHARGE   PROBATION   YRS.   FINE   OR JAIL

BAIL POSTED $ ☐ CASH ☐ BOND   DATE   TIME   RECEIPT OR B.B. NO.   DATE TO APPEAR

RELEASE DATE   GOOD TIME   DAYS.   WORK TIME   DAYS.   RELEASED TO BRANCH   JAIL BY

TRANSPORTED TO BRANCH JAIL BY   RETURNED TO MAIN JAIL BY

RELEASED FROM CUSTODY DATE 5-18-73   TIME 1230   BY OFFICER J. VALDEZ   REASON DA Dism

RELEASED TO   SIGNATURE   5-18-73 @1230

REMARKS OR HOLDS Refilled Grand Jury Indictment... 5-18-73 @1230

I HAVE RECEIVED ALL MONEY AND PROPERTY HELD FOR ME WHILE IN CUSTODY, SIGN X

ORIG. (WHITE)-CUSTODY   FOURTH (PIN
SECOND (WHITE)-C.I.I.   FIFTH (GREE
THIRD (YELLOW)-CONTROL   SIXTH (GOLD

SHF 0128

the woods, and if I were to give you a map, I doubt you'd be able to find it, but he took us right there. Right to the spot.

Kemper said he had buried the torso and upper legs of Aiko Koo at the park, but when he went to visit her grave the week before murdering his mother, animals had disturbed the site. With the additional assistance from law enforcement, only a fragment of Aiko Koo's pelvic bone was found.

Kemper was then brought to the Santa Cruz Police Department.

Jim Conner, 2020:
Ed was sitting in Lieutenant Scherer's office, and I was walking by and he's sitting there in a chair. So I said, "Hey, Ed, how you doing?"

He smiled, "Hey, okay. How are you, Jim?"

So I walked down the hall and that was the last time I saw Ed Kemper.

Mickey Aluffi, 2019:
We got back to Santa Cruz, and we took him in to book him, and as we pull into the Sheriff's Office, there must have been a hundred to two hundred members of the press waiting there. Keep in mind that I'm supposed to stay out of the press. So we get around and go in the back and take him upstairs and book him.

Mickey Aluffi, 2020:
Jesse Valdez was the booking officer. It gets to the point and Jesse said, "So who do you want to notify in case of emergency?"

Ed looked at me. He said, "Can I put you down because I don't have anybody left?"

Mickey Aluffi, 2019:
When I booked him into the Santa Cruz County Jail, he wanted me to put him in the same cell with Herb

Mullin. He said, "Herb's got one more than me and I want to even the score." Cold.

Kemper's car was searched. A spent .22 casing, hair, and blood were immediately found. Pulling up the rear seat revealed pools of dried blood.

Terry Medina, 2020:
When they finally got back, they put him in a chair, turned on the video recorder and the tape recorder, and say, "Okay, Mr. Kemper, you want to tell us why you're here?"

I mean, he started out like he was dictating a police report with details and this and that and such and such date and time. "I was driving by the Berkeley campus and I was looking for a victim. And I saw these two people, and one of them was blond and wearing this and that."

You listen to the whole tape, they probably only asked about ten questions and he talks for two and a half hours.

When Mickey Aluffi asked Kemper why he surrendered—

Edmund Kemper, 1973:
Well, there again, it's only mostly a complete story. Like I said, there are some things I'm sure are of interest to certain people, maybe everybody…but my main purpose is getting it off my chest because whatever's on my chest must stay I'm sure…

But let's say I have some accounts payable and I have closed my accounts receivable, and so I have balanced the accounts.

Edmund Kemper, 1973:
I guess I could be facetious about it and say, "Well, I gave you guys a year to catch up with me."

And I mean, shit, I couldn't have kept going forever, which is facetious; I really couldn't have.

Emotionally, I couldn't handle it much longer, so considering, I don't know who would consider me lucky I didn't get caught, there are times I wish I had been caught. But considering that I wasn't, there was a certain consideration that police weren't going to do something. I had to do something.

I'm sure they were trying, but with the tools police have to work with and with the basic concept that society isn't as cold-blooded as ruthless and back-stabbing as I am…if I had kept my mouth shut I would have gotten away with them.

Peter Chang, 1973:

Kemper denies responsibility for the murders of anyone else in the county. In particular, he denies having kidnapped or killed Mary Guilfoyle, a Cabrillo College co-ed missing since October 23, 1972.

Kemper also denies the slaying of a Watsonville high school student, Rosalinda Zuniga, who was last seen hitchhiking from San Jose July 10, 1971, and whose body was found two weeks later one-tenth of a mile off Highway 1 near La Selva Beach.

Mickey Aluffi, 1973:

So in essence, the killings that you have admitted, these are the only ones that you've ever completed.

Edmund Kemper, 1973:

I'd love to take credit for more, not because I'm looking for a big score, but that I wouldn't take credit for any that I didn't do because well, there's partially the guilt factor involved and then there also is the uh, well, I didn't do it, so I didn't get any pleasure out of it or any guilt out of it and why take somebody off the hook who did do it.

Mickey Aluffi, 2019:

After we finished interviewing him for all those hours I asked him, very pointedly, "Is there anything you haven't told me about?" And he said, "Yes, but I'm not going to tell you."

I don't know what that is. Maybe it's the way he molested his victims, but I don't know.

Richard Verbrugge, 2020:

Kemper didn't help them [his defense team] at all. I mean, even when we first brought him back to Santa Cruz, I'd get a phone call in my office and it was the jailer and he says, "Hey, Kemper wants to talk to you."

I said, "OK, but we can't talk to him because you know, he's being represented by the Public Defender's Office."

And he'd get on the phone anyway, "I just remembered this…"

"Eddie, I can't talk to you. I can't take this information down."

And he'd say, "Well, I'll waive it."

So I'd take the information and then I'd call in to either Jackson or Cartwright, "Well,

he called me again."

Finally, they got him to stop calling me. Then he'd start calling Mickey Aluffi [laughs]. And he was calling Scherer too. But everybody had to cut him off.

On April 29, 1973, Kemper was brought out for a field trip to look for more evidence.

Sam Robustelli, 2020:

We took him out a few more times on the roadshow, as we called it. We were recovering bodies and things that he left places. He had this phenomenal memory, and he had these little things to keep from getting caught. Like, he'd knock their teeth out so they couldn't be identified. He separated the bodies. Didn't throw all the body parts in one spot. He separated arms from legs and hands.

Sam Robustelli, 2020:

We went down the coast, Highway 1. Plain clothes. Unmarked cars. Ed was in civilian clothes. There was three of us in the car with him and another car. Two cars would go out. I said, "What are we going to find down here?"

He said, "We're going to find the identification of Aiko Koo, Schall, and some other girls."

So we're driving along and we said, "How are you going to know where it is?"

I mean, it's the coast. So many turnouts. We're cruising around there and he says, "Right here. I threw their identification over the bank."

Everybody gets out and looks over the ledge, "We're never gonna find anything."

It's so far down. I discussed with him, "Did you wrap it up? What was it in?"

He said, "I put it in a bag and I flung it over the bank."

I told the guys, "Let's go get some bags and see if we can fill them up with a little sand or something and see if we can get Ed to wind them up and throw them. Some of us can go down the road and look to see if they are going over."

We did this little test, and the bag didn't go all the way down because the wind and everything blew them back towards the bank. We got Monterey's rope and rescue team to come up and climb over the bank. They actually found them. Their IDs from school. Ed's bag had broken apart and they were spread along the bank, right where he had tossed our test bag.

While we were there, a Highway Patrolman came and thought we were littering. We gave him a shuck and jive story. Ed was back in the car. No handcuffs. We told him to slump down because if he would have been sitting up, he's almost seven feet tall. This Highway Patrolman goes, "What are you guys doing? I saw you littering. I watched you from down the road."

We gave him a shuck and jive that we were doing some preview work for a movie that we were going to be working on.

Sam Robustelli, 2020:

I got along with him [Kemper] pretty good because I figured I'm here to listen to him and not grill him on why. I didn't care why. I wanted to learn from him.

Sam Robustelli, 2020:

He talked about killing Schall. He dismembered her with an axe. We said, "What did you do with the hatchet? You told us this story, but where is it?"

He said, "I went to the hardware store and bought a hatchet."

So we took him to Santa Cruz Hardware and I said, "Okay, pick them up and see which one is closest to the weight of the one you used."

He says, "It's this one, Sam."

"Okay, get him out of here."

I went up and bought the hatchet. We took him out to the dumps up Dimeo Lane. He didn't throw it in the dumps, he'd thrown it off in some grass, a grassy field. We took him up there. He said, "Well, things have changed with the grass growing."

I said, "Well let's move around. Where did

you park your car? Where did you stand?"

It took an hour and a half, two hours to get him situated there. "Take the hatchet and throw it like you did that day."

So he threw the hatchet. ten, fifteen times. We found his hatchet.

Sam Robustelli, 2020:
We also went up to Mount Hamilton. He did some dumping up there, but the animals had taken everything.

Kemper hired local attorney, Roland Hall. Within weeks, Kemper could not afford his services and Hall was out.

Santa Cruz Public Defender Jim Jackson was assigned the case. Jackson and his investigator, Harold Cartwright, quickly began meeting with Kemper.

Harold Cartwright, 2020:
I was interviewing him. I had the tape, but I gave it to someone years ago. Well, I used to get a real stiff neck. I'd work so many hours, sleep so little, that I'd get these real stiff necks. So they would bring him up to the jury assembly room, right next to the courtroom. They'd lock the doors. The two of us would be in there. I had a video camera set up. I was really having a bad day and he said, "You know Harold, I can fix that for you."

I said, "What do you mean?"

He said, "I know every muscle and ligament in the body."

He said, "I've studied it for years. I can relieve your problem."

I thought for a minute. I said, "Go ahead."

So we turned the camera around, so it's now on me, and he comes over and he works on the back of my neck for maybe five minutes. I had full range of motion. No pain. I was perfectly fine.

Harold Cartwright, 2020:
He could go into minute details. He'd talk about cutting his mother's head off, putting it on the mantle, and throwing darts at it. His mother was very verbally abusive according to my research. She was a man-hater, no question. But he could talk about cutting out her larynx and throwing it in the garbage disposal, but it didn't have the rubber seal and so it would pop back out. He would grab it out of the air and throw it back in the garbage disposal. It didn't bother him. There was zero emotion. He could have been talking about peeling potatoes. It was like he was an academic analyzing it from afar. It was scary.

Public defender Jim Jackson disclosed to reporters—

James Jackson, 1973:
He ate the flesh of at least one of his victims. It was one of his fantasies, so he tried it.

Ernest Marenghi (assistant Santa Cruz Police Chief), 1973:
Just because this case has been cleared up we hope people don't think the danger is over for hitchhikers. We still don't feel it's safe for girls to hitchhike in Santa Cruz County.

Kemper continued taking road trips with law enforcement in plain clothes to recover bodies and evidence. While on the road trips, Kemper would talk and the deputies would report his comments.

From a report dated 5/2/73—

Mickey Aluffi, 1973:
The act of cannibalism was then brought up by this RO [reporting officer], to which Kemper stated that he had participated in the act of cannibalism. He states that on his victim Aiko Koo, he had taken some of the thigh meat and eaten it, this being done after the meat was cooked. Kemper states that this was done for two reasons, one being of disposal, with the other being that he had heard of people eating human meat and that he was curious to try it. To this, Kemper states that it was very similar to horse meat, and it

did not appeal to him whatsoever.

It should be noted that Kemper renounced his claims of cannibalism at a later parole hearing.

From a report dated 5/4/73:

Terry Medina, 1973:
In talking with the suspect, Kemper, about various fantasies that he thought of during the times of these killings, Kemper indicated that he had acted out a fantasy of taking one of the heads of his victims and performing intercourse with it. Kemper stated that he did in fact act out that fantasy, but would not disclose which victims that he used. Kemper indicated he had intercourse with the head, with his penis in the head's mouth. However, stated that it does not work, it hurts because the teeth get in the way.

Pat O'Brien (KPIX reporter), 1973:
Kemper tried twice last Monday [May 28, 1973] to kill himself by attempting to cut an artery in his arm with a ballpoint pen clip. He was taken to a hospital after the attempt was discovered, received six stitches to close the wound, and when returned to jail, put in a cell by himself under close surveillance. As a result of his two suicide attempts, Kemper was moved to the San Mateo County Jail in Redwood City on May 30, 1973.

Harold Cartwright, 2020:
They housed them [Mullin and Kemper] in Redwood City because at the time they had recorders there, and when the visitors came, they could record the conversations. It was all part of Peter's thing, you know? It was all a gag.

Murders in Santa Cruz were not only being commited by Mullin and Kemper. Leaving the Santa Cruz County Jail, Kemper left behind James Kenneth Scott, who had killed a Harbor High School teacher and Espiridion Maldonado, who was accused of stabbing a boy to death over a pack of cigarettes. Law enforcement had their hands full.

KEMPER AND MULLIN TOGETHER

Harold Cartwright, 1973:
Why would you kill Mullin—he's a creep? Why?

Edmund Kemper, 1973:
He went out there and he dusted a bunch of people, he just blew it, started blowing families away, killing little kids, women, children, you know, sneaking around doing these things. I wasn't sneaking, I was doing it out in the open. I was right in front of the cops, right in front of their noses. I was defeating society. I was swashbuckling. He blew it over, what six weeks, killing people when they got in the way. There's a bunch of campers, out in the boonies, where nobody sees them, so he blows them all away. I could have been doing shit like that, but I didn't do stuff like that. I was being sneaky.

James Jackson, 1973:
Maybe he didn't like hippies.

Edmund Kemper, 1973:
He just blew it. He's a muffin. Now he's out there being an asshole, being cute, making headlines, you know. Getting smart with his lawyer. Getting cute with the cops, harassing the guys in the tank. Just a shit, you know. I'm not saying that I hate his guts, and I'm just blowing to a rage, but I'd love to strangle him. I'm a murderer already, right? Wouldn't it hit the headlines to take care of one of your cases? Then you'd have to work on mine.

Kemper needed twenty-four hour observation after his suicide attempts, and only one cell in the San Mateo County Jail had a surveillance system and was located within view of the jail personnel at all times. It was occupied by Herbert Mullin.

Edmund Kemper, 1991:

Little Herbie [Mullin]. When I met him in Redwood City jail, okay? Our first meeting was, I bumped him out of the priority cell where they could look from the office and see through the steel door and the glass and the door and see him physically—where they could watch the monitor and watch him. He got bumped next door. There was a shower in the priority cell. Never had to leave the cell.

For him to shower from the other cell, he had to go out into the main area. They had to walk everybody in one of the—I guess you'd call them tanks. Move fifteen guys, thirty guys out of the tank into the activity area. They'd walk him around into their tank. He'd shower. He'd come back out and all the way over and all the way back, they're cat-calling him. They're calling him names. They're yelling because he caused them great interruption in their day, right? He resented that he got bumped out of the priority cell into a non-shower cell. I got the shower cell.

So he wasn't too friendly at first. And I'd say, "Excuse me, Mr. Mullin. Do you have a bar of soap? There's no soap over here."

He took it all with him. He had no need for it, but he took it with him. He'd say, "Yes."

I'd say, "Can I use a bar of it?"

He'd say, "No."

I'd say [to myself], "Oh I got one of these little shits here."

And what it is, is he's a little wimpy guy that hates big guys because he always feels intimidated by them. That's how we started out. So I started thinking about that, and I went back to my old relationships and therapy and group therapy and Atascadero and Youth Authority and stuff, and I'm saying, "Okay. Well we can deal with this."

So I said, "I have to be kind to him."

So I found out something he liked. He loved Planter's Peanuts. Little bags of peanuts. Shelled peanuts. So I bought twenty, thirty bags of them. I didn't care for them myself. I offered him some one day and we're both on camera twenty-four hours a day. So I said,

"Herbie, would you like some peanuts?"

He'd say, "Yeah!"

I'd say, "Well, I got to him right down to the inner core there. YEAH!"

This little childhood thing comes out. I says, "Oh, here."

And he was fascinated by this thought of, "Gee, he's just giving him some peanuts and I didn't do anything for them. I don't know him. I'm not being nice to him. Why would he give me some peanuts?"

So he comes over to the bars. We can't even see each other. I reach out with these peanuts around the side and I see this little hand come out. I thought of it almost as a little monkey paw. That's what it seemed like. So innocent and this little hand comes out. It starts to reach for the peanuts and then he hesitated. He pulls back. I thought, "Aww jeez, he's defensive."

He's thinking I'm gonna grab his hand and rip his arm off or something. I'm this great big guy, right? So without saying anything, I just reached around and laid them on the bars. Then pulled my hand away. He took them and enjoyed them and all of that.

Later, I'd say, "Gee, Herbie, did you eat all those peanuts?"

He'd say, "No. I still got some of them left."

I'd say, "Well, I got plenty more. Go ahead and enjoy them."

So what I did was I started giving him bags of peanuts and he had this horrible habit of—these guys are back in the tank. He and I are in these cells facing them through three bars, three sets of bars. And I can't see him and he can't see me. I don't know where on the set of bars he is. The set of bars is maybe nine feet wide and eight or nine feet high. When he would get to acting up, he'd sit there for hours writing and writing at this little desk. The other guys were ignoring him, so that night, they're watching *Saturday Night Special*, all this rock music playing and stuff and they're enjoying it. He'd get up and make this real loud speech about how bad television is for you and why you shouldn't watch it. All the things it will do to you. And they're having fits. They're trying to throw things at him. They can't get at him. They're raging. They're mad because he's destroying the one thing they really enjoy, and he's just having a ball doing this. He'll sit for hours all day writing this two hour speech, exactly as long as it takes to watch that show.

So he'd also sit over there and sing these horrible songs. He couldn't sing a lick at all. He's singing these horrible songs, and one time I was in the car coming back to Redwood City, and the cop got so upset at this singing he's doing in the back of the station wagon, he turns around with his can of mace, he says, "I've had it! Get out of the way, Kemper."

I'm saying, "Hey wait a minute! You're gonna get me with that stuff."

They tried to mace the guy in the back of the car because he won't shut up. He's trying to get him to shut up, and the guy just ignored them. He had this way of really getting on people's nerves. So he'd pull these little stunts. These horrible songs and the speeches and things and I'd say, "Herbie, why do you do stuff like that?"

He'd say, "I have a right to do what I want to do, too."

Yeah, okay, right.

I started this, what they call, real basic behavior modification therapy. I'd had a little bit of psychology study. I'd worked on psych tests in Atascadero. I knew some of these things. So I set up a very basic and very essential bare minimum behavior mod experiment. Behavior modification, all right? You reward them when they're good. You punish them when they're bad, and if you're absolutely accurate when you do these things, quick punishment when they do bad and quick reward when they do good, supposedly this is supposed to attack you at a subliminal level, a subconscious level and you don't have a lot of control over your reactions. It would improve your behavior, essentially.

They have these great, elaborate experiments, like in Youth Authority, when I went through. Where they tried these things. So

what I did was when he was bad, I would get a cup full of water, in a styrofoam cup, and I'd reach around and I'd throw it on him and it's embarrassing, and it would also get his papers wet and you know. So we got into this cat and mouse game. When he was good, I'd give him peanuts. I'd try to gas him when he was bad. It's called gassing. I'd throw this water on him. He'd duck all over the house. I couldn't figure out where he was. So I kept missing him. So what I did was I waited one day until I knew he was asleep or I suspected he was, and I called one of the guys over to the bars from place in the back, the tank. And I went like this [holds his hand up like he's sleeping] and I says, [shrugs his shoulders] and he reads it and he says, [nods] and I says, "Shhhh."

And I called him over to the bars and I said, "Hey, I want to work something out where I can get Herbie with these cups of water and he can't figure out how I'm doing it. I just thought of a way."

He says, "What's that?"

I said, "I want you to set up a grid on the bars where you're at. Put a little piece of string or little piece of plastic or little something he won't notice. Count over how many bars there are on his cell front and from the wall, go over that far on your set and setup boundaries. Then when I give you a signal, that will be a hand signal, very casually walk over, don't look at me, and walk over and drape yourself on the bars where he's at, so I'll know. If he's back away from the bars, go back that far. Position yourself so it's a grid, a targeting grid."

So he would do this and Herbie would hear me turn the water on, or maybe I'd have some already set up, and I'd reach through the bars and I'd blast him. I got him every time. And he couldn't figure out how all of a sudden I got so accurate. You know? And it was without fail, I'd get him with that water, WHAM. You know it's embarrassing and everyone's laughing and, "Good shot, Ed!"

And all that stuff. Then I'd ask him if he'd

do something or, hey, could we do this and he'd participate in something and I'd give him peanuts. When he's bad he gets blasted with water. This went on for two or three weeks. He actually got away from the bad behavior. When he said, "Hey, I want to sing."

I'd say, "Hey guys in the back, do you mind if he sings?"

They'd say, "Aww, we don't want to hear that shit."

I'd say, "Hey, do you want to hear it now, or do you want to hear it tonight when you're watching the show?"

"Yeah, okay!"

So, "Go ahead Herbie, sing."

Then he'd sing for thirty, forty seconds and then he'd get bored and say, "I don't want to do this."

The fun was gone out of it.

The point is, it got a handle on his behavior. The cops are watching this, the deputies are on camera watching me, I mean, they're on the monitors watching every move I'm making, right? They're fascinated, they're watching this thing going back and forth with me and Herbie. They're not involving themselves, they're just watching. And after a while one of them came in and said, "Herbie is completely cooperative now. He's not messing around."

As we're talking these little frictions up between he and I, I'm showing him some insight into why people don't like him. Showing him some insights into what his behavior is causing in him, and he'd realized by that point that it was just, he was just reacting to how people were reacting to him, and it's just a self perpetuating thing. It was the only way he could get out of his negative feelings. I said, "Why don't you focus on the positive. Focus on the positive instead, and the negative will go away."

I don't think anybody ever did that with him before because he responded real well to it. Later, when we were up here in the hole together, and we weren't even supposed to be together. They didn't want us together, but we were up in the hole together, I was the only guy he could talk to.

Herbert Mullin, 2020:
I think that because I was going through a period of psychological rehabilitation, I chose to not interact too much with other inmates. I kept to myself and did not talk much. Whoever and/or wherever you got the information seems to be stretching a storyline out just to get attention from their readers. I do not remember such incidents.

Both Mullin and Kemper were caught, but the work did not stop for homicide detectives in Santa Cruz. On June 5, 1973, the Manager of Loma Linda Lodge was shot to death. His wife was arrested for the murder. On the same day a nineteen-year-old man in Salinas turned himself in for stabbing his ex-girlfriend and her new lover to death with a screwdriver as they were sleeping.

MULLIN TRIAL
JULY–AUGUST, 1973

James Jackson, 2020:
There was a big deal when Frazier killed all those people. The doctor was prominent, and he [Frazier] killed the family and kids and he lived in that big house. The community was aware of that. I used to get threatening phone calls for representing him. But with the other two, it was just as though it had all worn out with Frazier. Nobody called and said, "You're an asshole and I'm going to kill you."

None of that stuff. Everybody sort of took it for granted. Maybe because Peter was going around calling us The Murder Capital of the World.

Mickey Aluffi, 2020:
He [Mullin] wouldn't talk. We were warehousing him up in San Mateo. So every time he had a court hearing, I had to go along with the transportation deputy in case he said something. I could write it down and they could hold it against him. He never said a word. Never even acknowledged that I was sitting next to him in the backseat of the patrol car. He was strange.

Dave Monsees, 1973:
Herbert Mullin was led to court today from his special security cell. He walked into two courtroom firsts. Public knowledge of the charges against him for murdering ten people prompted the judge to change procedure. As prospective jurors waited, each was taken separately to the chambers of Judge Charles Franich. The questioning was done in private because Franich said the scandalous nature of the crimes might make them more cautious in open court. The other change came partly because of Mullin's plea: not guilty and not guilty by reason of insanity. For the first time in California history, the sanity phase of a trial will not come after the verdict. The prosecution and defense agreed because if the jury finds Mullin to have diminished capacity, he can't be found guilty in the first degree.

While sitting and waiting for the jury selection, which was being conducted in the judge's chambers, Mullin blurted out, "On August eighth, nineteen forty-five, we dropped the bomb on Hiroshima!"

On July 16, Peter Chang underwent emergency surgery for acute appendicitis at Dominican Hospital.

On July 19, the jury was selected and sworn in. Six women and six men. Mrs. Sharon Lee Jennings had been dismissed as a juror after it was revealed she was a granddaughter of Fred Perez.

Judge Franich, 1973:
The doctors think he [Peter Chang] will be available a week from Monday. If Mr. Chang can be there, then fine; if not, then the trial will have to proceed without him on that date.

Not only did Peter Chang have the emergency appendectomy, but had two additional surgeries due to infections. He was in intensive care and the trial went on without him.

William Kelsay, 2019:
Peter was very ill that summer during the Mullin trial which concluded in August. It was very pressure packed in the DA's office. Extremely so.

Terry Medina, 2020:
Everybody kept saying, "Oh, God, he thought this guy was going to get off in an insanity plea and he didn't want to be the lawyer."

So Art Danner handled the case-in-chief and Chris Cottle handled the expert phase. They co-prosecuted the case. They did a great job.

Art Danner passed away in 2006.

On Monday, July 30, both sides gave their opening statements. Mullin's parents were in the courtroom.

During opening remarks the defense noted that in addition to the murders he was on trial for, Mullin admitted to murdering Henri Tomei, Lawrence White, and Mary Guilfoyle. However, the local press had scooped the revelation and ran the story on the

"Santa (Cruz, California) Claus" and Loretta and song "Dirty ol' Red Santa Claus!" made me wanta know? But what does Santa originally come from — never mind bothering much ∧ Have Popes (religion the greatest power, sneaky.) Doctor (Healing, In set-up of Evil elimination of god-people, all religions. Revised Version 1950 Daniel 2:7 "Shattered" to bits, There, before Evil take over — Push, head "scattered" Lawyer (keeping other lawyers out) which in Jesus Chr. Go and preach — to all people; Spread farthest hamlet then back never stamped out, makes sense for Language-translation Have Popes + Doctors infiltrated — Dictiona. (1952) The Webster's International,

— I can prove, (would like to, ha not yet shown off as a knowing justice mind unhampered by full, dull technical wording of Laws, so man they've gotten you lawyers with too.) can prove anything I say. anybody better be right, Christie right. Then fight as needed for the Right. "mean fighter". Knew a (was then, now —) lawyer's secretary who let know he paid off the Capitals (that "in north" state) Lawyer paid to get a Judgeship The brotherhood "in Everything afore we my Puppy Dog and 100 off. Mrs.

Kannapolis, N.C.
February 28, 197?

Lawyer of
and
Herbert Muffin
(being investigated! Charged!
killer of Commies. 3 or 4!!
You can in old estab
ilished procedure find
out whether I crazy,
or knowing more than
you in my field (I
or whether you can get
away with lukewarm
(if not outright Socialistic
Uncle) throwing the case
with this whole-hearted
in anything I go at. "A quitter
(out of the game) never wins",
And I'll take or ask for,
my fight (words enlisting every directio
ammunition" from 1st to last drawn

Shall I ask interview
liquor board, distillery
trucking the radiator tip
you _____, herein
righteou
killer
& 3+ she
3 times

records
tel phone
tell me
their
doctors
names
doctors
operating

in short

in them 8, 6 3 especially, I lerate
save them mailed — no delay, that
have them mailed — no delay, that
care for gamblers anywhere
dat for gamblers anywhere
Sunday churches bombings
Then go there came from Rom
averages in fifty

previous Friday.

Terry Medina, 2020:
He admitted those [the first three murders] and the defense threw the idea into it just to further him being crazy. For law enforcement, we don't have it all locked up if somebody confesses to a crime. That's not good enough. You have to still prove what the person is confessing to. And there was nothing that we had about the Guilfoyle-White crimes other than his confession.

James Jackson, 1973:
Mr. Mullin believes, as evidenced in his writings, that Maurice Chevalier was to have been born again to a wealthy Boston couple in May of 1973 and eventually to go to the same school as Albert Einstein [see page 168].

James Jackson, 1973:
Mr. Mullin is also very concerned about earthquakes, as evidenced by his philosophy of Jonah.

Mullin was set in his convictions and gave his

defense team very little to work with.

Harold Cartwright, 2020:
He was very aggressive about not wanting to plead guilty by reason of insanity because he was doing God's will. There was nothing insane about it. So we pled not guilty by reason of insanity.

Chris Cottle, 2020:
The jury didn't know if he was faking it, and it didn't really matter because we were dealing with the M'Naghten Standard. Mullin was so clearly not not guilty by reason of insanity. Two "nots" in there, but it's not not guilty because his thinking was too organized at the time. The way that he operated. He hid things. He knew he didn't want to get arrested and avoided that. He killed some of the victims because he worried about leaving witnesses.

David Marlowe, 1973:
He thought he had an all-powerful and all-knowing mind and was a free agent to play the role of God with life.

James Jackson, 1973:
He was a victim of chance…Mr. Mullin heard from his father that he must kill someone before he brought home the wood, to prevent California from falling into the sea.

Herb Mullin:
My basic contention was that my former family and former friends had played a game of kill-joy sadistic witchcraft upon my mind. They had declared psychological warfare upon me without my knowing it. They did their best to keep me naive and gullible and immature. They caused me to become paranoid schizophrenic and then they caused me to commit the thirteen mass-murder crime spree and they did not notify the police or the sheriff during the four month crime spree, i.e. October 13, 1972 through February 13, 1973. They knew when each crime took place, yet they did nothing to notify the police/sheriff/legal authorities.

Mullin asked Jackson to have all fingerprint records from all unsolved crimes since 1925 compared with his father's fingerprints. Jackson refused.

Herb Mullin, 2020:
My public defender, James Jackson, did not try for "Change of Venue," nor did he allow a separate trial to determine "sanity." Somehow or other he got both the guilt and sanity phases of the issue incorporated into one trial, a tactic that proved disastrous for me.

Relations turned contentious between Mullin and Jackson. They frequently had heated arguments.

Harold Cartwright, 2020:
All during Mullin's trial I had to sit between Mullin and Jackson at the defense table. Because he insisted on writing all the time, my job was to make sure he didn't stab one of us during the trial.

James Jackson, 2020:
Oh, he [Mullin] didn't like me at all.

Harold Cartwright, 1973:
We were in the jail, just outside, by the sergeant's desk and Jim Jackson went out the door, grabbed a bunch of law books, penal code and so forth, off the deputies desk and took them and threw them and hit Mullin in the chest and almost knocked the chair over because he was so frustrated that he wouldn't cooperate with his defense.

Terry Medina, 2020:
Danner did a great job with the jury on the case-in-chief. It's the same stuff you would do in a case today. He knew Gianera's case was so important because he [Mullin] shot

Left and previous pages: Some of Mullin's writings made after his arrest.

so many times at the Gianera house that he had to reload. So when you put on your case-in-chief and he's got all these crimes right. You've got the four guys. You've got White. You've got the Gianeras. And you have to explain to the jury over and over how he's shooting people. They're running and screaming for their lives, and then you're showing them pictures of the Gianera's house where there's blood all over the refrigerator where he [Jim Gianera] was trying to hide.

He pushed the refrigerator out after he'd been shot and his blood was all over the place.

Mullin shoots so many times he runs out of bullets. He has to reload.

Mullin goes over to the wounded Gianera and finishes him off. Shoot him. Shoot her on the stairs. Reload. Shoot him again and kill him. Go upstairs where Gianera's wife is bleeding in the bathroom. He kicks the door open and then kills her. But as Danners explaining this series of events to the jury, he's having one of the Santa Cruz PD Detectives reload a revolver. How long does it take to reload a revolver?

Because the definition of insanity was what was called the M'Naghten Rule. You had to understand the nature and quality of your act, among other things.

So Danner was trying to explain the intent, how he [Mullin] formulated this intent. And then, of course, the defense is saying Mullin's fucking crazy and you can't formulate intent here.

You've got this story of all these dead bodies and bloody walls and refrigerators.

And the detective is simulating like he's shooting them once or twice. He's ejecting a shell. He's reloading the revolver. To the jury, it seemed like this all took forever.

Of course, now they're thinking, "Well, of course he knows what he's doing."

The morning of July 31, 1973, witnesses at the Francis residence testified. Kathy Francis' husband, Bob Francis, then testified that he and his wife knew the Gianeras well. They had lived next door to each other on Branciforte Drive. They had also lived together on a 180-acre farm in Dobbins, CA with another family. Mullin visited Jim Gianera at one point and stayed about twenty-four hours. Mullin bought ten doses of LSD from Gianera. Gianera told Francis that Mullin had taken all of them, and Francis believed it as Mullin just stood around and didn't say much. Francis noted that Mullin called Daemon, "a little angel." Mullin smiled at this remark in the courtroom.

Bob Francis also noted that when he and Gianera were building Gianera's house on Western Drive in 1972, Gianera had mentioned that he had run into Mullin in downtown Santa Cruz.

On August 1, Dr. Jean Everice Carter testified, detailing the injuries sustained by the four boys in Henry Cowell Park. The store owner who sold Mullin his pistol and the manager of the hotel Mullin had been living in at the time of his arrest also testified.

In the afternoon of August 1, Paul Dougherty, the criminalist from San Mateo County who examined Mullin's pistol, the stolen rifle, and the collected bullets and bullet fragments testified. He stated that the serial number on Mullin's pistol—

Paul Dougherty, 1973:
Had been obliterated by a grinding process… perhaps by a file.

Mullin listened intently to Dougherty's analysis of bullet striations, testimony that showed Mullin's pistol was used in the murder of Jim Gianera.

When Dr. Hans Dibbern testified, regarding the wounds suffered by the Gianeras, Mullin became agitated and whispered fervently to James Jackson.

James Jackson, 1973:
He apparently disagreed with the doctor's

findings, but most of the things he was saying was gibberish. I couldn't understand it all.

While Dr. Dibbern testified on the injuries sustained by Kathy Francis and her sons, Mullin gripped the counsel table and stared at his hands.

Art Danner asked Dr. Dibbern why four-year-old Daemon's teeth were tightly clenched in death. Jackson immediately objected. His objection was sustained by Judge Franich.

After the trial recessed for the day, one of the sons of Fred Perez, John Perez, approached Mullin's father in the hallway. The two were joined by James Jackson and the three men spoke for a few minutes.

John Perez, 2020:
I remember that conversation well. I said I wouldn't go into prison to get him. Then the lawyer came over.

On August 2, UCSC Assistant Chancellor Lloyd Ring, 41, killed himself. Ring had been Sally Hallett's immediate supervisor. He had mailed a letter to Chancellor McHenry indicating he planned to take his own life. McHenry called law enforcement. They found Ring dead in his garage with a hose running from the exhaust into the cabin. He had been dead twelve to twenty-four hours when they found him. Ring's wife had recently filed for divorce.

On Thursday August 2, the prosecution rested for the first phase of the Mullin trial.

Donald Lunde played a recording of an interview he had with Mullin and testified on Friday, August 3, and Monday, August 6.

Terry Medina, 2020:
Then Cottle does this unbelievably outstanding job with all these psychiatrists and he just got them all twisted. The only guy he couldn't really get too twisted up was Lunde. Lunde was very good but Lunde wasn't as believable as Joel Fort, who was on the prosecution's side.

Joel Fort, in addition to having this tremendous rapport on the witness stand, had also written books on addiction. You know, part of their defense was that Mullin had diminished capacity due to drugs on top of being crazy. Fort knew what he was talking about.

Watching Joel Fort taught me so much. I mean, I became a much better witness after watching Joel Fort take the question from the lawyers and then just turn to the jury and explain the answer. Ignoring the defense that just asked him the question. It was amazing. It was a sight to behold.

Dr. Lunde read transcripts of his interviews with Herbert Mullin. He had interviewed Mullin twelve times and had spent more than one hundred hours with him. Lunde would later write *The Die Song,* an account of Mullin's crimes.

From his interview with Lunde—

Herbert Mullin, 1973:
You know, on the coastlines on all continents are protected through the result of a minor natural disaster. In other words, we human beings, through the history of the world have protected our continents from cataclysmic earthquakes by murder. In other words, a minor natural disaster avoids a major natural disaster.

Donald T. Lunde, 1973:
But if murder is a natural disaster then why should you be locked up for it, if it's natural and has a good effect?

Herbert Mullin, 1973:
Your laws…people like to sing the die song…I can sing that song to them and they'll have to kill themselves or be killed. An automobile accident, a knifing, a gunshot wound. You ask me why this is and I say, well they have to do that in order to protect the

478

ground from an earthquake because all of the other people in the community have been dying all year long, we have to die also and people would rather sing the die song than murder.

Herb Mullin, 1973:
I don't want my story to be told, you know, throughout the world. I don't like the publicity…I don't like what happened to me. I wish I had the self-control to say, "Well, I'll play the role of the masochist rather than the role of the sadist."

A sadist gets revenge. A masochist doesn't.

A masochist says, "Well, I see you guys took me for a ride and put me through dementia praecox. I'm just going to let you do it. I'm not going to get revenge."

I wish I did, you know, I wish I would have said, "Well, I'll just, you know, I'll get a job and a wife and children and barbecues on the weekend."

I don't want to go to jail.

Donald T. Lunde, 1973:
How did they lay the dementia praecox on you? Was that done through drugs or how?

Herbert Mullin, 1973:
Well, yeah…you know…uh.

Donald T. Lunde, 1973:
Do you mean marijuana?

Herbert Mullin, 1973:
Yeah, marijuana…marijuana induces dementia praecox, you know. It furthers dementia praecox, is what it does. It doesn't induce dementia praecox, it furthers, uh…uh…If Gianera had given me some of the Benzedrine that he was using, you know, if he had sold me Benzedrine, while he was using it, then I wouldn't have had this trouble…I wouldn't have wanted to reap revenge

479

on him…Benzedrine I have found, as I look back on my experience, causes one to talk and to act as a matter of fact, you become an artist, so to speak…you want to paint and draw and carve and sculpt, you know. […]

He didn't sell me the Benzedrine because he'd rather see me the, you know, he'd rather have that picture of me for five years in dementia praecox than to have me…sell me a lid and a roll of bennies at the same time.

Donald T. Lunde, 1973:
He would just sell you a lid but no bennies?

Herbert Mullin, 1973:
Yeah…and he wouldn't even tell me about the bennies.

Donald T. Lunde, 1973:
Why do you think he had it in for you?

Herbert Mullin, 1973:
'Cause I'm a better sadist.

Donald T. Lunde, 1973:
You mean he was jealous?

Herbert Mullin, 1973:
Yeah.

Herbert Mullin, 1973:
You read the bible about Jonah. There was twelve men in the boat, you know, it was just like Jesus, you know, and Jonah stood up and said, "God darn! If somebody doesn't die, you know, all thirteen of us are going to die."

And he jumped overboard. […] You're asking me to explain now what this means, you know the swallowing of Jonah. Now, I am asking you to believe. I'm the typical, how would you say, scapegoat. I'm a scapegoat. I'm asking you to swallow this Jonah story and believe that a minor natural disaster will prevent a major natural disaster.

At Mullin's trial—

Donald T. Lunde, 1973:
He believes there is some connection… He believes if Einstein had not died on his birthday, then he, himself, would have had to die in Vietnam.

Donald T. Lunde, 1973:
There are thirteen victims in the killing episode…On October thirteenth there was the first victim and on February thirteenth there was the last.

Donald T. Lunde, 1973:
He has delusions about his own sexual identity and that of a lot of people close to him. There is confusion in his mind about whether they are homosexual, heterosexual, or bisexual…He believes his father is homosexual and his mother and sister were lesbians from an early age, but kept the information secret from him. […] Mullin has had homosexual involvement, and I view his homosexual activities as a part of his illness.

Mullin interrupted Lunde—

Herbert Mullin, 1973:
I'll stipulate, I am bisexual!

Mullin's friends and his sister, Pat Bocca, took the stand on Tuesday, August 7.

His friend Edward Lawrence told the court that he and Mullin had attended a Catholic mass in San Rafael, but Mullin started talking to the statues in the church and addressing the congregation.

Edward Lawrence, 1973:
We were bodily carried out of the church. People were yelling, "Call the police!"

Mullin stared at his hands and refused to look at his sister when she testified.

Pat Bocca, 1973:
He wasn't frightening. He was very sweet

and very gentle and very much a pacifist…
He wasn't crazy and I didn't feel uncomfortable…If he wanted to speak in a Spanish accent it was all right with me.

Mullin's uncle, Enos Fouratt testified that Mullin had visited him in Carmel, the previous year. Fouratt said that Mullin spoke with a Brooklyn accent and said he was going to join the Coast Guard so he could fulfill his lifelong dream of swimming the English Channel.

On Wednesday, August 8, Mullin's boxing coach, Don Stewart, testified. Mullin and Stewart smiled at each other.

Mullin's ex-girlfriend, Loretta, and Dr. John Peschau, a psychiatrist at Agnews State Hospital, testified on Thursday the ninth.

Dr. John Peschau relayed Mullin's reasoning for killing Fred Perez.

John Peschau, 1973:
[Mullin] had the jitters because he was off welfare and had no job and regretted killing the Gianeras.
   "It was a foolish thing. He was well dressed with a haircut and looked the way I would like to look."

Prosecutor Chris Cottle read from a report issued by Dr. Peschau. Peschau believed that Mullin's behavior was due to his drug use and not from mental illness. Mullin told Peschau that he spent his junior and senior years in high school confessing to Father Tomei. When Jim Jackson pointed out that this was not possible, Mullin jumped up yelling, startling the jurors and attendees—

Herbert Mullin, 1973:
Mr. Jackson, have you instituted a vote of the people of St. Johns [the Catholic Church in Felton] to see if they have ever confessed to Father Tomei?
   You'll find if you check that he worked there part time in 1963 and 1964. Check.

That's your job.

Judge Franich called for order.

Jackson refused Mullin's request.

Mullin leaped to his feet—

Herbert Mullin, 1973:
Your honor, I would like to take exception to my attorney's conduct in this case.

Dr. Charles I. Morris testified on Friday, August 10. Morris caused a bit of a furor when he stated that Mullin admitted to an additional four murders, instead of the three that Jackson brought out in his opening statement. The next day, Morris said he had been mistaken and there were only three additional murders.

Dr. Charles I. Morris (psychiatrist hired by the prosecution), 1973:
[Mullin showed a] schizophrenic reaction, paranoid type, in a state of partial remission. He had been fooling around with drugs. I don't mean just a little bit because that cannot cause such symptoms.

The witnesses for the prosecution cited drugs as the reason for Mullin's psychotic behavior. The defense argued that Mullin was not responsible for his actions and was legally insane.

Jackson explained to the court that Mary Guilfoyle was murdered after Mullin received a telepathic message from Ray Liebenberg, ordering Mullin to sacrifice someone in order to prevent a major earthquake.

James Jackson, 1973:
The killings were not acts of murder but were acts of sacrifice.
On the Francis family—

Left: Jim Jackson with Mullin's rifle on July 31, 1973.

Dr. Charles I. Morris, 1973:
He thought it was a good idea to go back and do away with them.

On the four boys in Felton—

Dr. Charles I Morris, 1973:
He was doing away with bad people. He described these people as hippies and when he saw them he saw it was a good time to do it.

James Jackson, 1973:
They were familiar with the philosophy of Jonah and welcomed their deaths…and he accommodated them.

On Fred Perez—

Dr. Charles I. Morris, 1973:
[Mullin] felt quite badly, apparently, about that. He intimated there was no good reason for this.

Dr. Charles I. Morris, 1973:
The Perez killing seemed to be in a different sort of thing. People engaging in this kind of activity get to a point where they want to get caught…and want to give up.

This is indicative that an individual knows that what he is doing is not right.

On Friday, August 10, Jim Jackson entered some of Mullin's writings into evidence. Mullin's writings noted that he would be born again to his uncle Enos Fouratt's family in 1942. His name would be Willis Betegus Fouratt. His sister would also be reborn into their uncle's family. She would be born again in 1943 and be named Jean Rigel Fouratt.

Four witnesses testified on Monday, August 13: Dr. Joel Fort; Captain Michael Smith, a Marine Corps Recruiter; Dr. Robert James Hanscon, a Marine Corps psychiatrist; and Reverend George R. Flora, a pastor from Santa Cruz whom Mullin had visited to learn about the Lutheran religion.

Dr. Joel Fort, 1973:
[Mullin] did know the nature and the quality of his acts and specifically, he knew why they were wrong.

Captain Smith testified that Mullin started the process of entering the Marine Corps, but because he had been a conscientious objector, Mullin's enlistment required a waiver.

When the waiver was granted, Mullin refused to sign because the sergeant typing up the form refused to include a statement from Mullin that law enforcement officers who had arrested him previously had been reprimanded.

James Jackson, 2020:
We had [David] Marlowe interview him, but Franich wouldn't let us play it.

Marj Von B was the reporter for the Watsonville [*Register*] *Pajaronian*. Good gal. She said, "I want to go to the interview."

I said, "We can't let you go to the interview, come on."

She said, "Well, I promise I won't write anything. I'll sit in the corner."

I said, "Okay."

So she goes to the interview when David Marlowe and Harold and I are interviewing Mullin, essentially so we can use something in trial. So Marj Von B's mouth drops open about minute four. Mullin said all his usual stuff. Earthquakes. All that. He was a lunatic.

We show up at court and want to put David Marlowe on to testify what the guy said, and Franich wouldn't let me. They were running around looking for an excuse because they heard it too; you know, it was on tape. The excuse they gave was that I was asking the questions and not Marlowe. So they never let that part in. But Marj sat and listened to that bullshit.

Mullin took the stand on Tuesday, August 14, 1973. He was cross examined by Chris Cottle on the 15.

Herbert Mullin, 1973:
Every hour people die. There is a steady flow of death in order to keep the coastal areas free of cataclysmic earthquakes and to keep the earth in orbit.

He blamed everyone in his life but himself.

Herbert Mullin, 1973:
I have a feeling I was a scapegoat, an outcast they [his parents and sister] chose to carry all the guilts and fears of the rest of them, so I could not have a better life in my next life.

Herbert Mullin, 1973:
If I had been in prison, I would not have had a chance to kill those people.

Herbert Mullin, 1973:
I'm just like everybody else, I want to be worth something.

Chris Cottle, 2020:
Jim would have had a much better time on the Mullin case had it not been for Mullin's testimony in the courtroom.

Herbert Mullin, 1973:
William Mullin [his father] once told me that a wet dream was the stuff that comes from a mother's breast to a child and I believed that until I was a sophomore in high school when I learned about testes in biology class.

   If I had found a girl and got married and had a child, I could have had a normal life.

Chris Cottle, 2020:
You know about the half a head haircut that Frazier did. Mullin didn't do anything like that, but he got up and Jackson couldn't stop him, but he took the stand. I had a chance to cross examine him and the guy was totally out there. But he said enough to hurt himself in the course of it.

Jim Jackson disagreed, citing Mullin's belief that ninety percent of the world practiced "killjoy sadism" against Mullin himself.

James Jackson, 1973:
Since Mr. Mullin holds these beliefs we can see that he did not murder, he merely made necessary sacrifices; sacrifices he believed were expected of him by 90 percent of society.

Chris Cottle, 1973:
The definition of criminal insanity does not deal with mental illness, it deals with the state of mind when a defendant acts in violation of the law.

Chris Cottle, 1973:
There is so much evidence to indicate Mr. Mullin understood what he was doing was wrong.

Chris Cottle, 1973:
Mr. Mullin's acts support that he was thinking about what he was doing. His thought processes fall within the category of being legally sane and able to deliberate.

Chris Cottle, 1973:
He did it because they were witnesses and to cover up his crime of killing Jim Gianera.

Terry Medina, 2020:
Looking back, he was, in my opinion, the definition of criminally insane. And Jim Jackson just did a fabulous job defending him. I'll never forget the closing argument Jackson made. Had me convinced.

   And of course, you've got to put on top of all this: the jury might have thought the guy was absolutely nuts. But in the back of their head, which they're not supposed to do, but they can't help but ask themselves, "Do we want this guy to ever get out?"

After fourteen and a half hours of deliberation, on Monday, August 20, 1973, the jury returned their verdict.

James Jackson, 2020:
They found Mullin guilty of two counts of [first degree] murder and eight counts of second degree murder. The two counts of murder were thrown in there so they could give life in prison. They knew that. These jurors understand what's going on perfectly well. They're not dummies.

The first degree murder charges were for the crimes against Jim Gianera and Kathy Francis.

Chris Cottle, 2020:
I don't know how the jury could come to that conclusion on the degree of murder. I guess what they decided was that the pre-

meditation conclusion was the result of mental illness. It seemed to me, in the scheme of things, we only needed guilt on one of them. I did talk with jurors after these cases and I think there was a deal in the jury room. I think they almost had a unanimous first degree but there was one person and I think that the second degree was part of a deal.

Chris Cottle, 2020:

We may not have had the evidence to tie him to the first two crimes without his confession. It was thirteen murders and he was tried for ten over here. I came in so late, I'm not sure about why Mullin wasn't charged for those first two.

On August 22, 1973, the *Santa Cruz Sentinel* published a letter written by the foreman of Mullin's jury, Ken Springer, to California Governor Ronald Reagan, local representatives to the state, and the state mental health officer. Reagan's severe cuts to social programs in the mid-'60s resulted in many mental patients who were discharged onto the streets of California.

Kenneth Springer (Mullin jury Foreman), 1973:

I hold the state executive and state legislative offices as responsible for these ten lives as I do the defendant himself—none of this need ever have happened.

We had the awesome task of convicting one of our young valley residents of a crime that only an individual with a mental discrepancy could have committed.

Five times prior to young Mr. Mullin's arrest he was entered into mental hospitals. Five times his illness was diagnosed.

At least twice it was determined that his illness could cause danger to the lives of human beings. Yet in January and February of this year he was free to take the lives of Santa Cruz County residents.

According to testimony at his trial, Herb Mullin could and did respond favorably to treatment of his mental illness.

Yet, the laws of this state certainly prohibit officials from forcing continued treatment of his illness, and I have the impression that they, as a matter of fact, discourage continued treatment by state and county institutions.

In recent years, mental hospitals all over this state have been closed down in an economy move by the Reagan administration.

Where do you think these mental institution patients who were in these hospitals went after their release from institutions? Do you suppose they went to private, costly mental hospitals or do you suppose they went to the ghettos of our large cities and to the remote hills of Santa Cruz County?

We know where Edmund Kemper went when he was released from a state mental institution!

I freely admit that I write this at a time when my emotions are not as clearly controlled as perhaps I would like them to be, but I cannot wait longer to impart to anyone who may read this my convictions that the laws surrounding mental illness in the State of California are wrong, wrong, wrong.

Springer urged readers to write to Governor Reagan.

Kenneth Springer, 1973:

Don't let one other person in our country lose his life because our Governor needs a balanced budget…please, please write.

Herbert Mullin, 2020:

I met him [jury foreman Ken Springer] for the first time in October 1963. He owned a TV and radio and record player shop in old Felton town. I walked in and asked if I could purchase a portable record player. He tried to sell me a $300 living room furniture model, which I indicated I did not desire to purchase. Immediately he shouted something like, "…get out!"

I was startled and got up and moved toward the door. I asked, "Don't you have catalogs where we could purchase a portable record player for me?"

He screamed, "GET OUT!"

If you do interview him and/or Jim Jackson, you might want to question them as to why Ken Springer was chosen as jury foreman.

EDMUND KEMPER

Jackson had Kemper injected with Amytal Sodium, a form of "truth serum," on September 9, 1973 at Dominican Hospital.

James Jackson, 2020:
Don Lunde was involved in Mullin and Kemper. Kemper, he wouldn't say was insane. But he had a friend who was a psychiatrist from Fresno, whose name escapes me [Joel Fort]. He came over and would say that Kemper was a victim of irresistible impulse. I said, "That's fine, but it doesn't work here." At some point in time we—you ever hear about the truth serum story? It's funny. Lunde's buddy is a psychiatrist who's able to do something other than just chat. He can administer drugs. So we go to Dominican Hospital and they don't want to see us at all, but we got a court order saying we're going to inject him with truth serum. So he's lying in his bed shackled. Lunde and this guy shoot him up and Kemper's lying there telling the same stories as he's always told. Nothing new. But then he started getting agitated. He's got both hands cuffed to the bed, his legs are cuffed and he's rattling around. Pretty soon Lunde and the other psychiatrist are debating whether or not to give him another shot. I said, "Well, this isn't doing any good now. Give him another shot." The psychiatrist at this point doesn't know what the effects will be, so they don't give him another shot. The hospital people are all pissed because we've got this guy rattling his chains in there. That was the end of that. Another bullshit psychiatry thing.

Once the drug was injected, Kemper was laughing and dopey.

To James Jackson—

Edmund Kemper, 1973:
You gotta try this Jim.

Soon Kemper was crying and lamenting. The doctors and Jackson debated what to do next and what line of questioning to take.

Nothing new or insightful was revealed or discussed, and the debacle ended with Kemper and Dr. Fort arguing: Kemper saying he had so much to talk about and Dr. Fort telling him it would take weeks to hear it all and to be patient.

HERBERT MULLIN

On September 18, 1973, Mullin returned to Santa Cruz for the last time. He was sentenced to life for the two first degree murder charges and five years to life for the eight second degree murder charges. The terms were to run consecutively. Judge Franich stayed execution of the consecutive ruling pending the outcome of an appeal of the two first degree murder counts.

Mullin's parents were in the courtroom, but he did not look at them.

William Kelsay, 2019:
Jim Jackson defended all three of those mass killers. And you talk about the burden because the Mullin case ended in August of '73 and we started the Kemper trial around the middle of October.

KEMPER TRIAL
OCTOBER–NOVEMBER, 1973

Before the trial, on September 21, 1973, *Register-Pajaronian* reporter Marj Von B approached Kemper, requesting an interview.

Edmund Kemper, 1991:
I talked to her just briefly. She was hovering around the jury room in the courthouse talking to my lawyer, he hadn't shown up yet, she was up there talking to the officer that was with me and I said, "My lawyer does not want me talking to the media at all."

Marj Von B did convince Kemper to answer a couple of questions.

Edmund Kemper, 1973:
My lawyer says I'm not crazy enough.

Kemper was being housed next to Herbert Mullin in the Redwood City County Jail. Marj Von B asked if he felt Mullin was truly insane.

Edmund Kemper, 1973:
If you've been confined as closely to him as I

have, then you've got to know he's crazy.

Marj Von B, 1973:
You don't think it's a put on?

Edmund Kemper, 1973:
No, in my time at Atascadero I've seen a lot of them, and he's one of them.

The interview was cut short when Kemper spotted his attorney headed their way.

Edmund Kemper, 1991:
I see him [Jackson] coming way down the hall.

I said, "Let's set up a little scenario and act like I'm giving this really incriminating interview that screws everything up."

And she kind of laughed because it was breaking the tension in the room, you know. So we set up this little scenario, and she's busily acting like she's writing, and I'm talking about all of this hare-brained stuff that relates to the case and feelings, and he just starts turning bright red as he gets within hearing range. It's like a big clown that's got this huge forehead, hair standing out all over, and now he turns bright red and he says, madder than a wet hen, he stomps into the room, slammed his briefcase on the desk and we all start laughing, and he gets really mad now, and he says, "What are you laughing about?"

I said, "This was a setup just for you, I'm not doing an interview."

But later on I gave her an interview [printed in Front Page Detective magazine, March 1974] because she treated me so fairly up to that point, and also she gave me a pen that day. It was a cast aluminum ballpoint and I took it back to my high security jail cell up in Redwood City. It was really slammed down tight. I'm in a two-man cell by myself, they have a camera on me twenty-four hours a day, a videotape monitor. The lights are on. It's two sets of these four footers and it's as bright as day, all day long, all night long, twenty-four hours a day, and I was there for five months, and I brought this pen back in; I smuggled it in with me. And I get stripped shook leaving the cell. I get stripped shook coming back in. I brought this pen in and got it in with my legal papers…

Remember that pen.

Kemper's trial was given to Justice Harry Brauer. Brauer served in the Santa Cruz Superior Court from January 2, 1973, to November 2, 1984. He had served in the Municipal Court of Santa Cruz from 1962 to 1973. He had started his career as a lawyer in Watsonville in 1954.

James Jackson, 2020:
Brauer was my buddy. He was a very bright guy. Very fair. He was interested in having people do things legal and correct. He didn't like incompetence. I showed up in his courtroom and got up and cited a couple of cases off the top of my head and it impressed him because nobody in Santa Cruz did that. So we became friends.

In the pretrial, James Jackson tried desperately to get Kemper's statements after being arrested declared inadmissible. This would mean all physical evidence found from Kemper's statements would be stricken as Kemper had not had access to a lawyer.

James Jackson, 2020:
They picked him up in Pueblo, Colorado and drove him home via Billings, Montana, or something like that. Their excuse was that there were storms or some bullshit. They wanted to get him to talk. Well, they didn't realize he would have talked anyway. He talked and talked and talked and talked.

Jim Jackson, 1973:
He was literally held incommunicado. He was held overnight at the Santa Rita jail farm in Alameda County under the assumed name of Jameson the first night he arrived back in the state.

James Jackson, 2020:
Kemper would talk to anyone he could. He'd sign anything they asked him to sign. You couldn't get him to shut up if you tried.

Mickey Aluffi, 2019:
This probably was a pretty easy case for the prosecution because they had all the evidence.

And Jim Jackson, the only thing he could hang a hat on was the fact that the guy was crazy.

Right: Deputy Bruce Colomy escorted Kemper to and from court throughout the trial. Colomy and Kemper became close enough during their time together that Kemper later said of Colomy, "He's more like a father to me than anyone I have ever known …He's like the father I wish I had had." Kemper gave Colomy his J.C. pin before he left the Santa Cruz jail.

Edmund Emil Kemper, his wrists handcuf-
d to a chain around his waist, is led into
perior Court by sheriff's deputy Bruce
olomy. Kemper was arraigned on eight

counts of first - degree murder. Although h
sported a moustache at an earlier court date
Kemper appeared in court today clean
shaven. (Photo by Sentinel Photographer Bil
Lovejoy)

James Jackson, 2020:
My strategy was the psychiatrists. To have them say he was nuts. Who does this kind of stuff? The strategy couldn't be that he didn't do it after he confessed through nineteen states. Plus he killed his mother. You do this. You're insane.

William Kelsay, 2019:
It was a trial where everything was right for the prosecution. You had one of history's great monsters for the defendant. Jackson had a serious problem because he couldn't find a psychiatrist or any witness to suggest that Ed Kemper was legally insane per the M'Naghten Rule the state of California has. Additionally, the three psychiatrists that Judge Brauer appointed, their testimony at trial was devastating.

On Friday, October 12, Kemper testified for four and a half hours relating to his arrest, interrogations, road trip back, and assistance in identifying burial sites. Four law enforcement officers from Pueblo, Colorado also testified.

James Jackson was trying to get all the evidence revealed in Kemper's interview with Pueblo law enforcement stricken from the record, as Kemper had asked for an attorney and this request was not heeded.

Justice Harry Brauer disagreed. While Kemper did request an attorney, he continued talking of his own volition in a "monologue."

Harry Brauer, 1973:
Without any prompting or any further interrogations, questions, or even coherent speech from the two officers present, he [Kemper] goes on and admits he had killed his mother. This is inconsistent with the theory that he wanted counsel.

Also on October 12, Doctors Joel Fort of San Francisco and Donald Lowe of Palo Alto gave their report to Judge Brauer and testified. They found that Kemper was legally sane at the time

of the murders.

Joel Fort, 1973:
There is some tension and anxiety demonstrated but no guilt, remorse, or depression. He is not suicidal at the present time but remains homicidal particularly towards young, attractive, seemingly affluent college women.

Joel Fort, 1973:
The motives that have entered into his multiple murders, which he readily admitted and described in lengthy detail, include: extreme sexual curiosity and sexual inadequacy with fear of rejection leading to sexual acts with the dying or dead co-ed victims and with his mother's elderly friend who he also killed; revenge against those he hated for being better off in terms of material things and freedom than he was, including indirectly the families of the young victims; and rebellion against rejection and authoritarianism in the case of his mother and grandmother.

Donald Lowe, 1973:
Violent fantasies in 1970 and 1971, particularly as his efforts to become closer with women became unsuccessful.

Just before the first murders—

Donald Lowe, 1973:
[Fantasies of] killing thousands of girls and having sex with their bodies.
   "I saw beautiful girls as sacks of gold if I put out their brains."

Donald Lowe, 1973:
His decision, finally, to live out his fantasy appears to have been determined by ambivalent rage towards his mother generalized to all women, by strong sexual urges towards women which were blocked, and by his considerable intelligence and ability which approached a sense of omnipotence.

Kemper quoted by Donald Lowe on why he dismembered his victims—

Donald Lowe, 1973:
"I wanted to do the most violent thing possible. I blamed their bodies."

Donald Lowe, 1973:
Alcohol tended to reduce his violent sexual cravings and he often stayed drunk in order to avoid killing.

Fort agreed that Kemper did not use alcohol—

Joel Fort, 1973:
At the time of going out to pick up hitchhikers, deciding to kill them, shooting or stabbing them, hiding them, having sexual relations with them, decapitating them, or burying them.

Joel Fort, 1973:
But for chance and unknown factors there could have easily been twenty, fifty or even a hundred victims, as altogether he picked up some 200 young female hitchhikers over a period of many months.

After two days of private interviews, a jury was selected on October 18. The six men, six women, and one female alternate were sworn in. In an unusual move for the time, Justice Brauer asked reporters to keep the names of the jurors out of the press.

Harry Brauer, 1973:
I know that in the Mullin case some jurors were threatened and others received obscene telephone calls.

William Kelsay, 2019:
There were three stages to the trial, but it went quickly. It was all done and completed within three weeks. The first stage was to establish the corpus delicti of the crimes and to put the confessions in. The second stage was the confessions, of which he had a lot of hours in the court, detailing all of that. The third, and Peter Chang had emphasized this

in his opening statement, and Jim Jackson had no expert testimony from any alienist, which is a psychiatrist, to even remotely suggest that Ed Kemper was insane. And all three court appointed psychiatrists came to the same conclusion and it was devastating.

Prosecutor Peter Chang gave his opening statement on October 23. For some of the murders, the prosecution had to prove the corpus delicti, or that the murders did in fact occur despite the fact that—

Peter Chang, 1973:
…all of their bodies were never really found.

James Jackson deferred his opening statement.

Gabriel Pesce, father of Mary Ann Pesce; Louis Luchessa, the father of Anita Luchessa; and Skaidrite Rubene, mother of Aiko Koo, all testified. It was the first time seeing the murderer of their children.

William Kelsay, 2019:
At the beginning of the trial, Peter put on the evidence of the tapes from the Santa Cruz Police Department of Ed Kemper's phone calls to the police to confess, to try to have them pick him up and arrest him. And it took the third call to convince the police department, that hey this guy might really be the guy that did this. The hanging up by the Santa Cruz Police Department, was in a weird sense kind of funny.

On October 24, the prosecution played a recording of Kemper's 911 call from Pueblo—

Jim Conner, 1973:
Tell me about the killings.

Operator, 1973:
Your three minutes are up. Signal when through, please.

The courtroom laughed.

Richard Verbrugge and Mickey Aluffi testified about their road trip back from Pueblo.

Richard Verbrugge, 1973:
He [Kemper] wanted to avoid the press and he was also worried someone might want to assassinate him.

Mickey Aluffi, 2019:
When he actually went to trial, I got called to the stand. You have to give your name, your rank, and all that stuff. So I got up there and I told them, "My name is Sergeant yep yep."

He looked at me and kind of smiled and nodded. He took credit for me getting promoted.

Aluffi also testified about confiscating Kemper's pistol.

The morning of October 25 was spent listening to tapes of Kemper detailing the deaths of Alice Liu, Rosalind Thorpe, Sally Hallett, and his mother—

Edmund Kemper, 1973:
[I watched] hundreds and hundreds of rapists go through Atascadero and always being caught eventually, I decided to mix the two and have a situation of rape and a murder, and no witnesses and no prosecution.

From then on I did not pick up people for sport anymore; it was for possible execution.

I didn't pick up males anymore. It was all co-eds and it would only be if they were a possible candidate for death, which would mean they were young, reasonably good looking, not necessarily well-to-do, but say a better class of people than the scroungy messy, dirty, smelly hippie-type girls I wasn't at all interested in. I suppose they would have been more convenient, but that wasn't my purpose.

My little social statement was I was trying to hurt society where it hurt the worst and that was by taking its valuable members or future members of the working society, that was the upper class or the upper middle class.

Edmund Kemper, 1973:
I was striking out at what was hurting me the worst, which was the area, I guess deep down, I wanted to fit into the most and I had never fit into and that was the group, the in-group.

Edmund Kemper, 1973:
[I was] quite insane at the time I was committing the crimes…I felt fearful before…but when I'm actually beginning to get myself involved in a crime, it was a big thrill.

It was a very strong sensual, sexual excitement in some ways that replaced the sexual drive, let's say, but there was always a disappointment in not achieving a sexual rapport with the victim. That's why sex after death sometimes, because it's through frustration.

Edmund Kemper, 1973:
Considering the abilities I did have in say, creating a calm about me where people weren't excited or suspicious or nervous and had the trust of most people around me, I believed and I still believe that had I wanted to, just as a demonstration…and I thought of making this as a demonstration to the authorities in Santa Cruz, how serious this was and how bad a foe they had come up against…I had thought of annihilating the entire block I lived on…and the houses opposing it, which would have included as many as ten or twelve families…I would have done it and left, I think very unnoticeably by the other people that would still be there.

The afternoon was met with some drama when a female spectator caught Kemper's eye from the back of the court and drew her finger across her throat in a slitting motion. Kemper, already distressed from listening to his own confession tapes, alerted his attorney who approached the bench. Justice Brauer called for a recess, but the woman was not found.

Paul Dougherty, the Head Criminalist from San Mateo County Sheriff's Office, testified on the morning of Friday, October 26, covering his analysis of collected evidence. Dougherty also recounted his work at Kemper's house after Mickey Aluffi had summoned him.

Paul Dougherty (San Mateo County Criminalist), 2020:
When I was testifying, and I got to the part about finding his mother's head in the closet—and we had pictures of that—as I started to testify about that, Kemper started to get up out of his seat. Most people don't know this, but I saw him start to rise out of his seat. They had two of the biggest deputies I'd ever seen in my life and they were right there behind him. They both put their hands on his shoulders and he sat right back down. Up until that point, that was the only emotion they'd ever seen out of him.

The afternoon started outdoors with the jury examining Kemper's car. It ended with prosecution witness psychiatrist Dr. Walter Rappaport testifying about Kemper's mental health.

Walter Rappaport, 1973:
He had the mental capacity to formulate the specific intent to kill.

[Kemper] suffers from a behavioral disorder that has been called being a psychopath or sociopath. He follows the wrongful path rather than the rightful path.

Mr. Kemper could have conformed to the law had he wanted to and he did for a time.

The exchange between Dr. Rappaport and James Jackson grew heated, which drew giggles from the spectators. Two high school classes were in attendance for the day. One studying local government and the other a class called Man and His Behavior.

On the morning of Sunday, October 28 at 3:30 a.m., Kemper made his third suicide attempt using the pen he had smuggled into his cell, given to him by *Register-Pajaronian* reporter,

Marj Von B.

Edmund Kemper, 1991:
I smashed the pen on the floor with my boot, sharpened it, got a sharp edge on the metal and slashed my wrist and was bleeding all over the place. It was very messy, very exciting, and everybody is dragging me off to the hospital to get sewed up and all of that and I got maced. Shot up with industrial-strength bottle of mace they had, about a quart of it, and they gassed me with that whole thing and dragged me off to the hospital.

Kemper had severed an artery in his right wrist which required five stitches.

Robert Cancilla (San Mateo County Sheriff's Sergeant), 1973:
He fought like hell and said he would kill anyone who came into his cell to help him.

It took four deputies to get the leg irons and handcuffs on him.

Joel Fort, 1973:
It's my guess that he was trying to get more attention. I don't think he tried to kill himself. I think he tried a suicidal gesture.

He has sufficient strength, sophistication, experience, and intelligence and if he really wanted to kill himself, he could do it.

Fort had testified on October 12 that Kemper wanted to die in the gas chamber because he saw the gas chamber as a status symbol. Fort added that when Kemper was eight, he had been impressed by the execution of a woman, Barbara Graham, who had been involved in a notorious murder case in California in 1955.

While cross examining Dr. Fort, Jim Jackson informed the court that after killing his mother and beheading her, Kemper not only ground her larynx in the garbage disposal and yelled at her severed head, but he also threw darts at her head.

Harold Cartwright, 2020:
He [Kemper] was being held in Redwood City, and they'd bring him over every morning for court. The officers and I would joke that after court, we could give him a police car and tell him to check himself in to Redwood City, and he would do it! We could tell him to be in court the next morning at eight thirty, he would be there. The only thing none of us were really sure about was that when he killed his mother, if that was the last person he would ever kill or whether or not he might pick up a hitchhiker on the

way back to jail. As an academic discussion, it was funny.

Austin Comstock, 2020:

The law library was in the middle of the Superior Court building. If you went back there now, they are all little offices, but they used to have a holding cell down in the basement. It was designed that way to bring prisoners up to court. They would be moved from the jail to that little holding cell before the court was ready for them. But they would come right up through the law library, and the bailiffs would march them through and into court. One day I just happened to be there, and the photographer from the *Sentinel* knew that they were going to have Kemper in court that day. They had Kemper in chains. He was 6'8" and the photographer yelled at Kemper, "Look like a monster!"

Or words to that effect. Kemper raised his hands with his chains over his head.

Doctors Lowe and Fort testified before the jury on the twenty-ninth, thirtieth, and thirty-first.

Dr. Lowe commented on the fact that psychiatrists in Fresno declared Kemper "no longer a danger to society" and agreed to seal Kemper's juvenile records while Kemper had the head of Aiko Koo in his trunk.

Donald Lowe, 1973:

Their conclusions were that he was a competent, capable person even at that time when he had this private hell going on within himself.

Donald Lowe, 1973:

This is a mark of our psychiatric evaluations. They are only so good and they are not going to get at things so precious to people that they won't confide in them to anybody.

James Jackson, 1973:

I've rarely heard a psychiatrist say this.

Joel Fort (Appointed doctor by Judge Brauer), 1973:

[I am] not actually a psychiatrist, if that label means I restrict my work to middle-class neurotic women.

James Jackson, 1973:

Don't middle-class neurotic women need love too?

Joel Fort, 1973:

Definitely, but they don't need it from a psychiatrist.

Later in his testimony—

Joel Fort, 1973:

The murders were an explosive expression of hatred.

Chris Cottle, 2020:

Mullin and Frazier were not faking mental illness. However with the standard we have, they both were found sane by the law. The public defenders may disagree with me. With regard to Kemper, he definitely, I guess was a sociopath, but he is a clear thinking guy. Crazy, but with common sense. Organized thinking.

Harold Cartwright, 2020:

We knew these guys did something, but the question is whether or not they fit within the M'Naghten Rule. Were they legally sane, under the law, at the time. Jim had strong feelings about Mullin and Frazier. But Kemper was an enigma. I think that's why he's so popular today. He doesn't fit anywhere.

Joel Fort, 1973:

I would place him [Kemper] in the category—the broader category of personality disorder, specifically antisocial personality, which is no more or less than the old concept or diagnosis of psychopath or sociopath; and particularly I would refer to him as a sexual sociopath, or as I said earlier, in common language, a sex maniac.

Peter Chang, 1973:
Now, one of the diagnosis [sic] that he received at Atascadero was a diagnosis of paranoid schizophrenia. Do you agree with that?

Joel Fort, 1973:
No, I do not agree with the diagnosis, and in my extensive review of those records and the records that they used to arrive at that decision I found no basis whatsoever for that diagnosis.

Peter Chang, 1973:
What was—

Joel Fort, 1973:
It was one of the many mistakes that was made there.

Peter Chang, 1973:
What was the origin of the diagnosis?

Joel Fort, 1973:
The origin of the diagnosis, as far as I could trace it back, were two physicians, court examiners in Madera County who in a—without any explanation whatsoever, just a brief one or two-line statement put down paranoid schizophrenia, and that record, that statement by them then led to the commitment, the subsequent institutionalization at Atascadero.

Peter Chang, 1973:
Did the records at Atascadero support the diagnosis of paranoid schizophrenia?

> *Previous pages: Don Smythe, Kemper, Bruce Colomy, and Terry Medina on the way to court.*
> *Above: Bruce Colomy, Kemper, and James Jackson.*

Joel Fort, 1973:
No. What happened at Atascadero from the first diagnosis and evaluation that appears on the records on through to the end of an extremely voluminous record is that he came in with the statement from these two physicians in Madera County who may or may not have had relevant background and experience to make the diagnosis, and probably spent only a few minutes with him because that's usually what happens in these situations.

On the basis of that and without any of the usual kinds of things that a doctor should put down to justify a diagnosis, they simply began incorporating it as his diagnosis.

A paranoid schizophrenic should have marked feelings of unreality, deep personalization [depersonalization], meaning that you lose your sense of identity, and lose the boundaries between yourself and other people in your environment, and most of all has delusions, meaning false beliefs, beliefs that you are being persecuted, beliefs that can be grandiose where you think you have enormous powers, and hallucinations meaning seeing things or hearing things that aren't there.

So none of those things were found in the defendant. None of them are listed by anybody who saw him at Atascadero, and the only thing that is listed at several points is paranoid idealization, which is the long way of saying that the person has some thoughts that I, the examiner, that is, at Atascadero, interprets as paranoid, and when I track that down, those thoughts were that his mother and his grandmother were rejecting of him, did not like him, did not show him affection, which was total reality rather than in any way being paranoid idealization.

Kemper told Dr. Fort he had memorized twenty-eight psychological tests and administered them to thousands of inmates at Atascadero.

Fort reviewed his findings when giving Kemper "truth serum." Kemper had admitted to Fort—

Joel Fort, 1973:
—taking pieces of flesh from some of his victims, cooking it, and eating it.

Peter Chang, 1973:
Now, while we are talking about that, do you have any opinions as to why he killed his grandparents at age fifteen?

Joel Fort, 1973:
Again I don't think it was for any one reason, but the major things were that he saw them—particularly his grandmother as an extremely harsh, authoritarian-type lady who did not care for him, did not let him do any of the things that he wanted to do, was keeping him against his will because he preferred to be with his father, and if not with his father with his mother.

And another factor for the killing was that she was a symbol of two people that he hated and rejected for different reasons. Particularly she was very much like his mother in her personality and her reactions to him, came on in the same way to him, subjectively as his mother did, and she, of course, being the mother of his father was very closely tied together with his father who he resented for having abandoned him at an early age and having rejected him whenever he sought contact with the father.

Now, after killing his grandmother, I think the killing of the grandfather was again for several reasons. Somewhat different. He saw him, also, as not letting him do the things that he or other boys his age should have been allowed to do. He certainly didn't seem as harsh and punitive as the grandmother, but he shared some of the same dimensions of keeping him there against his will and making him do things that he didn't like. But also it was an effort to cover up. He was—he had just killed the grandmother. The grandfather came back home from shopping, and he was afraid that if his grandfather found out what he had done, the grandfather would become violent toward him. So one of the motives, in addition to what I have already stated, was self-protection, that is, to get rid of the grandfather so that he couldn't do anything about the grandmother's killing.

Peter Chang, 1973:
Did he tell you about any fantasies of killing his sisters at an early age?

Joel Fort, 1973:
Yes, and of other people.

Peter Chang, 1973:
Why did he want to kill his sisters?

Joel Fort, 1973:
Well, it was mainly his older sister, but sometimes it involved the younger one. She had friends, got more attention and respect, affection from the mother. In general had the things he didn't have.

But I must add, too, that that did not seem to be a predominant part of his thinking during that time, certainly as compared to his hatred of his mother, thoughts of killing her or thoughts he would often have about killing the boys who teased him or would not play with him, and so forth.

Kemper's younger sister, Allyn, took the stand on October 31. She testified that she suspected Kemper had killed Cindy Schall. Kemper responded—

Allyn Kemper (Edmund Kemper's younger sister), 1973:
"No, of course not, but don't say anything to Mom about it…she has already asked me and if you talk to her about it, it will just stir things up."

Allyn also recounted the murder of the family cats. The story was a bit different than Kemper's version, with Kemper being nine years old, wrapping the cat's corpse in a bathrobe and putting it in the garbage where their mother found it.

Allyn recalled Kemper saying he wanted to kiss his fifth grade teacher as a child, but that he could not—

Allyn Kemper, 1973:
"Because if I did, I'd have to kill her."

Allyn testified that Kemper had cut off the hands of one of her dolls and told the court about his lifelong obsession with guns. She noted that at one point Kemper had been cleaning a rifle and it went off, sending a bullet right past her. Lastly, she testified that weeks before Kemper murdered their mother, he had invited her into his room and playfully placed a pair of handcuffs on her wrists—

Allyn Kemper, 1973:
I didn't like that. I said to take them off now.

On November 1, 1973, James Jacskon, out of the presence of the jury, reserved the right to introduce photographs into evidence at a later time. The photographs concerned Kemper's most recent suicide attempt and their ability to discredit the testimony of Dr. Fort. Mr. Chang noted that Kemper lost two pints of blood in the suicide attempt. The court reserved ruling on the motion until the pictures could be evaluated as to their inflammatory nature.

Edmund Kemper took the stand late on October 31.

William Kelsay, 2019:
Kemper actually testified that he was two people. A good person and a bad person. He was trying to work that angle. But it was too little, too late with the overwhelming evidence and the establishment of all sorts of premeditation, thought, planning, and concealment.

Early in his testimony, Kemper talked about the first time he killed a family cat. He relayed the story of burying it and later digging it up and fondling the body, and talking to it.

Edmund Kemper, 1973:
I wanted the girls for myself, like possessions, they were going to be mine.

Edmund Kemper, 1973:
Alive, they were distant, not sharing with me. I was trying to establish a relationship and there was no relationship there…

When they were being killed there wasn't anything going on in my mind except that they were going to be mine…That was the only way they could be mine.

James Jackson, 1973:
Like the cat?

Edmund Kemper, 1973:
Like the cat.

Why did he dispose of the bodies in the way that he did?

Edmund Kemper, 1973:
Because they were rotting and I was losing them. […] When the girls died I kept them a certain length of time, but I couldn't keep them any longer. […] I still have their spirits.

He visited Mary Ann Pesce's grave.

Edmund Kemper, 1973:
I loved her and I wanted her.

Kemper talked about decapitating Cynthia Schall and burying her head in his backyard facing his bedroom window.

Edmund Kemper, 1973:
[I] talked to it many times, saying affectionate things.

When court was brought back after the lunch recess, the courtroom was again full of teenagers. A local high school had dismissed students early to attend the trial as a civics lesson. In a disturbing twist, Jim Jackson spent the afternoon questioning Kemper about his fantasies. Kemper

told the court about murdering a family cat for a second time.

Kemper also described his childhood fantasies about striking his mother with a hammer.

After Kemper detailed his cannibalistic fantasies he turned to Jim Jackson—

Edmund Kemper, 1973:
I can't believe this conversation.

Judge Brauer, 1973:
I'd be much happier if the courtroom weren't full of teen-aged girls.

Chang ended Wednesday by asking Kemper about why he had attempted suicide in jail.

Edmund Kemper, 1973:
I was thinking about the girls who died… their fathers…

Kemper broke down in tears but quickly recomposed himself.

Edmund Kemper, 1973:
I'm sorry….Their mothers and about what I did.

Kemper covered his face with his hands, unable to continue. Judge Brauer called it a day.

On Thursday, November 1, Kemper continued his testimony.

Chang asked Kemper if it was true that he told people he was going to kill Mullin.

Peter Chang, 1973:
Haven't you told people you will?

Edmund Kemper, 1973:
I would never get the chance.

Peter Chang, 1973:
Poor old Mr. Mullin…didn't you use to

throw water on him when he was in a cell next to yours?

Edmund Kemper, 1973:
Just to shut him up.

Kemper admitted to fantasizing about killing Peter Chang.

Peter Chang, 1973:
How would you diagnose yourself, Mr. Kemper?

Edmund Kemper, 1973:
I believe very dearly and honestly there are two people inside of me and at times one of them takes over.

Peter Chang, 1973:
You disagree with the court–appointed psy–chiatrist who diagnosed you as a sex maniac?

Edmund Kemper, 1973:
I don't believe I am.

Peter Chang, 1973:
Why do you tend to blame others for what you have done?

Edmund Kemper, 1973:
I feel there are others involved. I don't be–lieve I was born to be this way.

Peter Chang, 1973:
Do you think society thinks what you've done is grossly evil?

Edmund Kemper, 1973:
Right now, yes.

Peter Chang, 1973:
Horrendous?

Edmund Kemper, 1973:
Yes, but there are times those things don't even enter my mind.

When talking about the murder and dismemberment of Alice Liu, Chang asked Kemper to identify the large "Buffalo Skinner" he used. Kemper turned to Judge Brauer—

Edmund Kemper, 1973:
I don't imagine I'll be able to examine that evidence.
    If I keep my hands under the table, bring it closer so that I can look at it.

Chang asked Kemper when he had purchased the knife—

Edmund Kemper, 1973:
Nowhere near the time this offense took place.

Peter Chang, 1973:
Well, what did you buy it for, skinning buffaloes or what?

Kemper said he had a "penchant for knives." He bought the buffalo skinner at the same store where he bought some other knives which he had "killed some dogs with."

Kemper mentioned that he registered his hand strength at 235 pounds of pressure with his right hand at a machine at the Santa Cruz Beach Boardwalk.

At the Division of Highways, he said they called him "Forklift" because he could hold his arms straight out in front of him and they could load him up with two, ninety-eight pound bags of cement.

In the early morning of November 4, a fire gutted Jim Jackson's house. Jackson was hosting a party. He and his friends had been listening to music and dozed off.

James Jackson, 2020:
A log rolled out of the fireplace and lit the carpet on fire and the place burned. It was unlivable.
    Brauer said to me, "You don't think you're going to get a postponement because of this, do you?"
    "Can I get a day anyway? I don't have any clothes."
    "Well, I don't want anyone on the jury feeling sorry for him because of this."
    "I don't think you'll have any problem there."

Jackson lost his dog, Oliver, in the blaze.

At two o'clock in the morning on November 5, Kemper tried to commit suicide a fourth time by reopening the wound on his wrist from his last suicide attempt. A San Mateo County sergeant making regular rounds observed Kemper's bandage lying on the floor. He then saw blood on Kemper's shirt. He called for backup and the jail guards attempted to open Kemper's cell. However, Kemper had jammed the cell door with a small piece of wood from a tongue depressor.

Once deputies forced the door open, it took the sergeant, three deputies, a physician, and chemical spray in Kemper's eyes to restrain the inmate and deliver him to Kaiser Hospital in Redwood City.

After injecting Kemper with a sedative, a doctor determined there was no real damage and Kemper did not need his arm sewn back up.

Jailers found a small wire in Kemper's cell. It was this wire that Kemper had used to pull his stitches.

After the ordeal, Kemper was brought back and placed in a padded cell with leather restraints.

Final arguments began on the morning on November 7.

Peter Chang, 1973:
His super-sane, unclouded mind was able to recount every splintering detail.

Peter Chang, 1973:
The magnitude of evil goes beyond the pale of anything in the annals of murder…if these murders are not first degree, then nothing is a first degree murder.

William Kelsay, 2019:
Other than having a singular, perhaps unusual juror who perhaps would somehow find that he wasn't sane, we knew it was pretty much a slam dunk. We took a very low key as to the presentation and performance. Peter was excellent.

James Jackson, 1973:
Why does Mr. Kemper act as he does? Why, it does not suffice to say, as the psychiatrist said, he is a sex maniac, a deliberate, cold-blooded killer, a sadist. None of these things mean anything.

The jury started deliberations at 2:30 p.m. on November 7. Without having reached a decision, they retired for dinner and slept at the Islander Motel. They returned the next day, deliberated for a few hours, and had their verdict at 10:28 a.m. on the morning of the eigth.

William Kelsay, 2019:
After five hours of deliberation, which really isn't very long. Particularly when a judge will instruct you to consider all the evidence and review it, drawing conclusions and trying to arrive at a unanimous verdict.

In an unusual move, Judge Brauer read the decision himself.

Judge Brauer, 1973:
The jury finds the defendant guilty, sane, and guilty of murder in the first degree on all eight counts.

Brauer looked at the jurors—

Judge Brauer, 1973:
If I seem a bit excited, I am…I had some fear you might possibly arrive at a different verdict. I agree with your verdict entirely.

Kemper received sentencing on November 9.

William Kelsay, 2019:
Harry Brauer sentenced him to eight concurrent life sentences.

Judge Brauer, 1973:
The Penal Code does not permit consecutive life sentences. However, I will inform the state Adult Authority in the most direct language I know that you should not be released from prison during your natural life.

Kemper had told Pueblo investigators that he would kill again if released—

Judge Brauer, 1973:
You were not bragging…I know you were speaking in anguish and remorse and speaking nothing but the truth.
    May God have mercy on your soul, Mr. Kemper, but you have to understand, I have to protect the rest of the people from people like you.

Edmund Kemper, 1973:
Yes, sir. I understand.

William Kelsay, 2019:
After Judge Brauer sentenced him, he asked him if he had anything to say and Kemper said something to the effect of, "I should be tortured to death."

Kemper approached Peter Chang and the two shook hands.

Edmund Kemper, 1973:
Thank you, Mr. Chang, for your restraint and your help.

Kemper faced reporters.

Edmund Kemper, 1973:
Well, it's all over now…all I have to look forward to is my life in prison.

Jim Jackson faced reporters.

James Jackson, 1973:
Psychiatrists can't help him because they don't know anything…Who knows why he did what he did? It's a rotten waste. He's intelligent and a nice guy.

Edmund Kemper was taken to the California Medical Facility at Vacaville to serve out his term.

HERBERT MULLIN

On December 8, 1973, psychologists dueled in Santa Clara Superior Court over Herbert Mullin's sanity in his trial for the November 1972 murder of Henri Tomei.

On the morning of December 11, 1973, Judge William Ingram ruled Mullin mentally competent to stand trial. Mullin entered a plea of innocent and innocent by reason of insanity. But late that afternoon Mullin conferred with his attorney, public defender C. Randall Schneider, and decided to settle the case. Mullin changed his plea and was found guilty of second degree murder by Judge Ingram.

On December 21, Mullin was sentenced to five years to life for the murder of Henri Tomei. With Mullin's sentences from August, he was set to serve the two first degree convictions concurrently and the nine second degree convictions consecutively. In addition to the new sentence, Mullin received a box of Christmas cookies sent by his mother. Mullin was then sent to the California Medical Facility at Vacaville for observation.

Herbert Mullin, 2020:
We [he and Kemper] were housed on the same tier at California Medical Facility at Vacaville, California. It was/is a prison built in 1955. I spoke with him maybe five or six times. I would talk about science, he wanted to talk about crime. We did not talk much after that became clear.

At Vacaville, Mullin and Kemper attended group therapy with Dr. Morton Felix.

Susan Felix (Widow of Dr. Morton Felix), 2020:
My husband died nine years ago. […]
    Mullin and Kemper were in the group and so was that other man. It was, uh… Charles Manson. I thought that was pretty amazing.

Previous page and this page: Kemper in court.

Above: Kemper shakes the hand of attorney Roland Hall. Hall was Kemper's attorney before the trial and for the first few days. When Kemper could not afford Hall, Jim Jackson, from the public defender's office, was appointed the case.

PRISON LIFE AND PAROLE HEARINGS

All male prisoners on death row in California are housed at San Quentin State Prison. While John Linley Frazier was there, he socialized with Charles Manson. After the death penalty was struck down in 1972, Frazier and all the prisoners on death row had their sentences commuted to life in prison. Frazier moved around the state prison system and was denied parole several times.

While at Folsom Prison, Frazier ended up in protective housing after being stabbed twice by members of the Aryan Brotherhood in retaliation for a letter Frazier wrote to prison officials complaining about violence at Folsom. Frazier was also cited for making his own shiv.

Frazier was later moved to Mule Creek Prison in Ione, California—the same prison where Herbert Mullin was, and is currently housed.

Herbert Mullin, 2019:
I spoke to him a couple of times. I did not know he was involved in the Santa Cruz dentist [eye surgeon] crime until after he passed on.

At his 1990 parole hearing, Frazier refused to enter the hearing room; instead he released a typewritten statement asking not for parole, but to be emigrated to another country. One section read—

John Linley Frazier:
After twenty years of observation I have realized that the status quo of authority which governs and manipulates it is only concerned with the continuity of power as evidenced by the occupation of the land and machinations throughout the world. The results of this tradition and current practice of Social Darwinism will mean ever increasing deterioration of the quality of life and consequently more turmoil and repressive action.

From Frazier's 2008 parole hearing—

Ariadne Symons (Santa Cruz Deputy District Attorney), 2018:

Santa Cruz has had in its history three serious killers, two serial killers and one mass murderer. John Linley Frazier is the mass murderer. Although this crime happened in 1970, years ago, it still has an impact on our society and on our citizens, which can be told by the people who have written letters when once again it became possible that Mr. Frazier would be released. Simply the heinous nature of his crimes and the number

of people that he actually murdered compels him to be stayed behind bars. He was convicted of five counts of first degree murder. He stalked these people, he terrorized them, he planned the killing, the little boys were killed after their parents were killed. I note that there were two little girls in the family,

Above: An undated picture of John Linley Frazier released by Mule Creek Prison after his suicide.

they were at boarding school at the time so they were not killed by Mr. Frazier, one of them committed suicide, as did Dr. Ohta's mother. I think one can say those are attributable to Mr. Frazier, if not legally, certainly morally. I noticed in his papers, he claims to have killed two other people, he seems to be proud of killing those other people. There's no expression of remorse of any kind throughout the papers, so he doesn't begin to understand the impact of what he has done.

On August 13, 2009, Frazier killed himself in his cell. He died by hanging.

On learning of his suicide—

Lark Ohta, 2009:

Obviously, shock. It's just sort of overwhelming news, very confusing news. I'm not sure how I feel. I'm just trying to integrate it all now.

HERBERT MULLIN

Bob Lee (Santa Cruz County District Attorney 2002–2014), 2011:

And, of course, in looking at the commitment offenses, it affected their entire community. He [Mullin] changed the way people live in Santa Cruz County. Just front and center. He changed the way parents raised their kids. He changed the way kids played in the streets. He stopped kids from, you know, going into the forest and the way the whole community treated strangers. You know, it's ironic one of the reasons Mr. Mullin killed people, he claimed at the very beginning was to prevent a catastrophic earthquake. Mr. Mullin actually killed more people in Santa Cruz County than the last terrible earthquake in Santa Cruz County in 1989. The irony of that is

CONCERNING DR. Gordon Haiberg's & DR. Morton Felix's REMARKS in 1975 & 1976.

Both DR. Haiberg & DR. Felix told me that my parents had deliberately refused to teach me how to become a self-confident and competant, mature young man —.

Both of them agreed with me that my family and friends had been practicing some form of kill-joy sadistic witchcraft on me, and that they are the people responsible for causing me to committ the crime spree —.

DR. Haiberg & DR. Felix agreed that my family & friends knew when each crime happened, and that they did nothing to stop me from committing the next ones — nor did they attempt to notify the police or sheriff authorities —

My meetings with DR. Haiberg & DR. Felix took place from October 1925 thru to approx. Thanksgiving 1976.

Neither DR. Haiberg nor DR. Felix would put those ideas into writting when asked to do so —.

stunning.

Herbert Mullin, 2019:
He [Dr. Gordon Haiberg] also talked to me and my parents together in the prison visiting room at CMF Vacaville prison in, probably, late summer 1976. After the interview between me and my parents, Dr. Haiberg told me during our next psychotherapy session that he believes that I am accurately describing and explaining what happened. My parents and family and former friends did keep me very naive, gullible, and immature; they did cause me to become paranoid undifferentiated schizophrenic; they did cause/urge me to commit the thirteen

victim crime spree; and that they knew when those crimes happened and did not notify the Sheriff or police in order to stop the series of crimes from happening and/or continuing.

Dr. Gordon Haiberg told me to stop associating with my family; my parents, he said, were not in any way beneficial to my efforts to get over the mental illness. He encouraged me to continue striving to become a

Above: Page six of Herbert Mullin's 2011 rebuttal to a pscyhological evaluation in 2010.
Next two pages: Mullin in 2019 and some of his recent drawings.

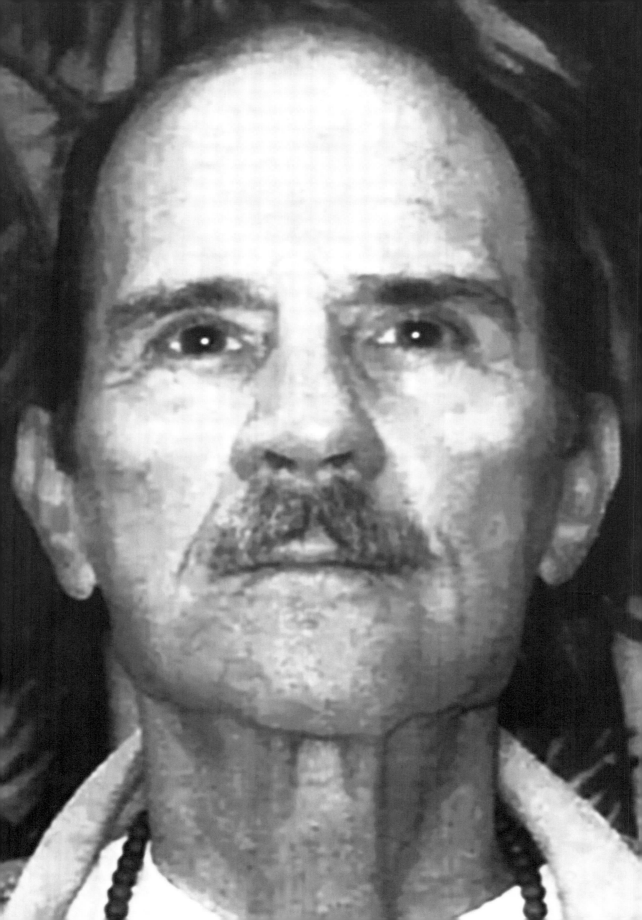

GOOD HEALTH AND GOOD WEALTH FOR THE UNITED STATES OF AMERICA ____.

HM

It was interesting to watch the dance of the moon and planets during October, November, December of 2019 —
Then they continued dancing in January, February, March, and April, of 2020 —
♄·Saturn, with, ♃·Jupiter, & ♀·Venus, & ☽ moon, in the southwestern sky at/after sunset in late 2019 —
then ♃·Jupiter, ♂·Mars, ♄·Saturn & moon in early 2020!; them dancing in the southeastern skies before the rising of the sun ——.

April 3ʳᵈ 2020
Friday —

Herbert W. Mullin —

ASTRONOMICAL OBSERVATIONS

5/2/2002 — Thurs.   c. 8:47 p.m.

5/10/2002 — Friday   After Sunset —

5/15/2002 — Wednesday — After Sunset

♉α = Taurus Alfa star ..... oka Aldebaran
♃ = planet Jupiter
♄ = planet Saturn   ☿ = planet Mercury —
♂ = planet Mars
♀ = planet Venus

H.W.Mullin —
11·29·2020 —

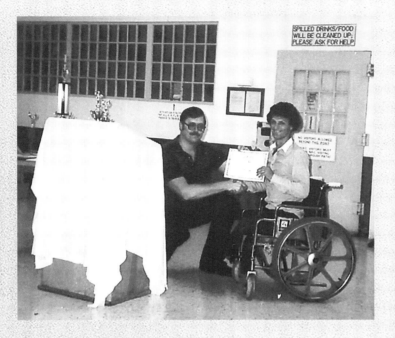

over 80 percent of Americans believe in God and over eighty percent of Americans are Christian. We've all been taught that there is life after death and we will live again and I hope that means that those people will enjoy the beauty of Santa Cruz County. I mean, if they're going to grow up again I think they should graduate from the University of California at Santa Cruz. I think wow, that would be a great experience for them.

good, healthy, beneficial, worthwhile citizen of America.

Dr. Haiberg passed away in 1987.

The last time Mullin saw his parents was in the fall of 1976.

Herbert Mullin, 1981:
They kept writing me letters, but they were full of bullshit. They'd write and tell me how they really prayed that I would be a healthy child, how all they wanted was for me to be a successful person. It was obviously bullshit.

Herbert Mullin, 2019:
One thing I want to emphasize is that I am very sorrowful and very remorseful for having committed the crimes. I hope and pray every day that the God of America will somehow reimburse the victims and their loved ones for the loss and tragedy! I hope that God will guide, protect, and improve them in their afterlives.

Herbert Mullin, 2020:
I don't think any human being knows exactly what's happening but statistics say that

Bob Lee, 2011:
So after looking at the family, look at Mr. Mullin. And you literally need a scorecard to determine Mr. Mullin's numerous excuses over the years of why these crimes were committed. He was compelled to commit these murders to prevent earthquakes. He then said it was family members conspired him to commit these murders which has been basically a similar statement for thirty-eight years. That homosexuals and bisexuals made him commit these crimes. He read a book in the '80s about pre-medicated murder. It was then that he said that his pre-medications he took for mental illness which compelled him to commit these murders. He then got involved in witchcraft because he believed that peers put a spell on him which caused him to commit these crimes. And, of course, his dad has always been this killjoy sadist that has made him naive, immature, and gullible, who intended for him to commit these murders. And then finally in 2006, he said the psychedelic drugs contributed to make him do these crimes. He's got no insight. He doesn't take responsibility. And one doctor back in 1988, I think it's Dr. Allison, said that Mr. Mullin switches back and forth. He goes from at least an awareness now that he's responsible although it's an awareness that

he immediately switches and says no, it's my parents. It's my fiancée. It's my sister. It's my mother. It's my peer group. It's the Catholic Church. It's even my aunt who made me fall off a horse when I was seven years old that kept me immature, naive and gullible that was part of this general conspiracy that wanted me to commit these crimes. He's basically had 38 years of, in essence, blaming others.

Herbert Mullin, 1981:
You tell people that Herbert Mullin says he's only five percent guilty. Tell 'em I'd like them to write the governor. That I deserve a retrial. Maybe they'll hear me. I know people would accept me if I got out.

Mullin is up for parole again on March 18, 2021.

EDMUND KEMPER

William Kelsay, 2019:
I've handled, I can't count the number of murder cases, particularly as a judge, all over the state of California. I've never seen anything quite like Ed Kemper. That is to say, how he was capable of such monstrous crimes and still act absolutely normal.

Edmund Kemper, 1988:
I wrote a letter to a local judge asking for permission to get what is called multi-target neurosurgery, stereotactic surgery. Lobotomies have not been legal in this country for a long time. A modified lobotomy is called a leukotomy, and that is only practiced by one man in this country, and his peers, to my understanding, are trying to persuade him to stop doing that. It's considered too gross a procedure.

The media took a lot of attention to that issue when I raised it in 1975. And it became a national issue, it was on the Tom Snyder show late at night, discussing whether prisoners should

be operated on and then released.

What I was trying to get was an operation that I was—I had been in dialogue with a practitioner of that surgery in Southern California for two years. At the end of that two-year period I determined that I was willing to put my faith in a surgical procedure that would, to my satisfaction, assure that I would not be violent again, that this would break the conditioning I had put my mind through for years. It would not affect my IQ, it would not affect my personality. I had a lot of documentation on that.

At the time, what was called the Bethesda Study was being carried on in Bethesda, Maryland, by Senator Kennedy's Subcommittee on Health. The media term "psychosurgery" is a misnomer, it's supposed to be applied to surgical approaches to relieving intractable pain. It's a popular term with the media. It went from psychosurgery all the way to, "He wants a lobotomy to cut violence out of his brain." And that is so gross a simplification as to be incorrect completely. I would not ask for a lobotomy, I would just as soon kill myself, as to pull a Jack Nicholson out of a popular TV movie, being a vegetable, which did happen to some lobotomy patients.

I—I just want to expand on it a moment here. I finally dropped that issue when it went to the State level of appeal. I had a falling out with the doctor because during the letter-writing process, the letter portion of our relationship, he assured me that the extent of the procedure, was going to be the relieving of any violent tendencies on my part. When I met the man face-to-face two years later and we talked, during an examination of me, it came to light that he intended to pursue this on a political level beyond the operation itself, that he was going to use all of this political influence and medical influence to achieve a release for me. And I got in an argument with the man at that point, as it relates to the families.

At any rate, we had an argument. And rather than resolve the thing here, in the heat of emotion, I went back to my cell, I thought on it, and I wrote him two inquiring letters, asking him questions that had been raised in our—in this finding of mine, that he had other motives on top of just the surgery. And it's not ulterior motives, they're fine motives, but it was not shared with me during that entire length of our relationship. I wrote these letters, I got his responses, I felt them to be evasive and not on the issue,

Left: Murder Can Be Fun #8 zine written and published by John Marr in 1987. The issue covered Frazier and Mullin as well. After hearing the stories for years, this was my first real indication that they were all true!

Right: A graphic novel biography on Ed Kemper was published in France by Hachette Comics/Robinson in 2020. It was written by Thomas Mosdi and the art was beautifully done by David Jouvent.

Next few pages: A collector's books, magazines, and videos related to Kemper. Candace's Kemper tattoo.

...C'EST UNE CONNERIE, IL NE FAUT JAMAIS CHASSER PRÈS DE CHEZ SOI, JE ME RELÂCHE DANGEREUSEMENT ! EN DEHORS DE ÇA, LA SITUATION SE PRÉSENTE BIEN, IL PLEUT BEAUCOUP...

...CE QUI REND CES DEMOISELLES PEU REGARDANTES SUR LEUR CHAUFFEUR ! J'EN REPÈRE DEUX, MAIS LAISSE TOMBER CAR ELLES SONT ENTOURÉES PAR CE QUI SEMBLE ÊTRE QUELQUES AMIS...

LA NERVOSITÉ ME GAGNE...

JE ROULE SUR MISSION AVENUE QUAND JE L'APERÇOIS...

CINDY, UNE BLONDE MENUE...

À PEINE EST-ELLE MONTÉE QUE JE BRAQUE MON AUTOMATIQUE SUR ELLE...

...ET JE LUI FAIS LE COUP DU MEC SUICIDAIRE, ÇA MARCHE SI BIEN !

OH ! DÉRAPAGE MENTAL, QUE VIENT-IL FAIRE DANS MA VOITURE, CELUI-LÀ ?!

HERBIE, JE TE VEUX PAS DANS MA TÊTE MAINTENANT, FOUS LE CAMP !!

BON, VISIBLEMENT, IL VA FALLOIR FAIRE AVEC !

JE NE SUIS PAS LE SEUL À JOUER LES MEURTRIERS DANS LA RÉGION À CETTE ÉPOQUE-LÀ, ÇA ASSASSINE À TOUR DE BRAS, À TEL POINT...

...QUE SANTA CRUZ REÇOIT LE PRIX PEU CONVOITÉ DE CAPITALE DU CRIME !

ET HERBERT MULLIN, AVEC SA DOUZAINE DE VICTIMES, N'EST PAS ÉTRANGER À L'AFFAIRE !

LE HASARD FAIT QUE CET EMMERDEUR DE PREMIÈRE DEVIENT MON VOISIN DE CELLULE...

PETIT ET TEIGNEUX, CINGLÉ, IL FAIT CHIER TOUT LE MONDE ET NE M'AIME PAS BEAUCOUP..

MAIS JE TROUVE UN MOYEN INATTENDU DE L'AMADOUER LORSQUE JE DÉCOUVRE QU'IL RAFFOLE DES CACAHUÈTES PLANTERS...

...UN VRAI MACAQUE !

MA TENDRE CINDY, J'AI FAILLI T'OUBLIER ! JE TE RACONTE N'IMPORTE QUOI, T'EMBOBINE, INOFFENSIVE SOURIS ENTRE LES GRIFFES DU MÉCHANT CHAT ! ET PUIS...

...UNE BALLE DANS LA TÊTE ET TOUT EST FINI !

JE RESTE FIGÉ DE SURPRISE ! D'HABITUDE, ELLES S'AGITENT AVANT DE FAIRE LE GRAND SAUT, AU MOINS UN PEU. LÀ, RIEN...

...LA FAUCHEUSE L'A SOUFFLÉE COMME UNE BOUGIE !

PAW !

SOIS SAGE, HERBIE, OU TU N'AURAS PAS TES FRIANDISES !

which further clouded my trust for this man. And I'm not naming him, but I subsequently told him that I was withdrawing any efforts to make—to pursue this on a legal issue. My understanding is that it would have been the United States Supreme Court because it met all the criteria as a constitutional case. And it wasn't on whether or not I have the right to ask for brain surgery but any kind of surgery period, since I'm an incarcerated inmate in a prison.

Since 1960, the Blind Project employs prisoners to record books onto tape. The project also provides braille transcription and repairs braille devices. It is well publicized that Kemper recorded thousands of hours for the project.

Edmund Kemper, 1988:
I began with The Blind Project as a volunteer in February of 1977. It was not a work assignment until—1985. […]

I'm an inmate coordinator there, sir. I used to—when I started there, and when I was a volunteer for years before, I read books onto tape for the blind.

Kemper also made mugs.

Edmund Kemper, 1988:
I've been working on ceramics over the years, I've developed a technique in ceramic arts that I took an award for in 1982 at a statewide prison arts competition. And I've been offered two different opportunities to publish my technique in Ceramics Monthly, and I've declined on both occasions because I take that very seriously, and to really pursue that I would have to resign from my job over to the hobby shop and work there full-time on the clay work, devote myself to that to really do it justice. So I've kept it as a more-or less low-key hobby.

James Jackson, 2020:
I wrote to him [Kemper] periodically in prison. He sent me a coffee cup he made. I'm sure he did it on purpose, but it's this twisted thing, which I'm sure went to depict his crazy mind.

William Kelsay, 2019:
In the '80s, there was actually one member of a parole board that actually found that he would be perfectly safe to be released. But that was Ed Kemper. He could act so normal.

Segments from a June 1988 report from Kemper's prison therapist were read at Kemper's

1988 parole hearing—

Jack Fleming (Prison therapist), 1988:
Invitations from the media arising from the notoriety in his crimes continue to pose a conflict for him. Certainly there is much to be learned from his life and he is willing to share what he can. On the other hand, he is aware that society is disposed to view him as a "monster" and this rekindles feelings of rejection. [...]

...be able to open up in a therapy group and not react defensively. This concern has been adequately dispelled. He has demonstrated that he can discuss his case, his childhood and other relevant personal matters with the group. Moreover, he can do this without dominating the group, thus allowing for constructive or concentrational feedback with others. Progress in therapy is considered satisfactory.

With respect to his psychological readiness, appropriateness of the social interactive conduct, as well as vocational skills, I have no reservation with that in his parole readiness.

Obviously, the recommendation was not considered.

For several years, author Leonard Wolf visited and wrote to Kemper.

Joey Tranchina, 2020:
Dr. Leonard Wolf, father of Naomi Wolf, he was a very well known writer. Born in Transylvania. Very well known. I taught a class called "Writers on Writing" at San Francisco State and that's how I got to know so many writers because I could give poets a paycheck.

He [Wolf] wrote a book, I'm not sure if it's still in print, called *A Dream of Dracula* about how the vampire was the central myth of twentieth century American culture. It's a brilliant essay about bloodsuckers. I was never a student of his, but we worked together. He visited Kemper many many times. Probably more than anyone else. He knew Kemper very well. I started out as a grad assistant but by that time our relationship had evolved, and I was a paid photographer working for him when I took the photographs of Kemper.

Tranchina recalls his first meeting with Kemper in Vacaville—

Joey Tranchina:
As I mounted my Nikon on the tripod, I asked a question: "Kemp, we waited for an

hour while you were with that German film crew. How does it make you feel that people come from all over to interview you?"

Kemper's words are burned into my memory—"How do you think you'd feel, if people came from all over the world to speak with you and all they EVER wanted to talk about was the ten worst things you EVER did in your life."

William Kelsay, 2019:
We all suffered varying degrees of nightmares over our experiences with Kemper because what he did was so vicious and unbelievable.

Mickey Aluffi, 2020:
As an interesting aside, about—I don't know—three or four months ago, I got a letter from some lady. I can't remember where she's from. It's like Pennsylvania or someplace on the East Coast. And she goes on this dissertation on how she's so interested in Kemper. She just wants to be able to visit him and marry him and just love him to death and all this stuff. And then she wanted me to respond to her. I never did.

The public's fascination with Kemper has soared in recent years. Without a doubt, part of the attraction comes from Cameron Britton's amazing portrayal of Kemper in the Netflix series, *Mindhunter.*

In October 2017, the first episode of *Mindhunter* hit televisions. The series tells a fictional account of the formation of the FBI's Behavioral Science Unit. Early on in the actual FBI program, agents interviewed Edmund Kemper for his professional insights. Kemper was featured on several episodes of the series.

David Dozier, 2020:
I watched the show with Kemper [*Mindhunter*] and the actor who played Guy was nominated for an Emmy. The actor does a very good portrayal of Guy Kemper as he appears in those documentaries and videos online. But that isn't the Guy Kemper I knew.

The Guy Kemper I knew was reasonably articulate and personable. The guy in the documentaries is someone in a very strange place, in my mind anyway.

Mindhunter was based on FBI profiler John Douglas' book of the same name. In part, the book details Douglas' experience interviewing serial murderers.

> *Preceding and above: Joey Tranchina took these shots when visiting Kemper with writer Leonard Wolf.*

Douglas was a thirty–two–year–old FBI Academy instructor traveling with his partner, Robert Ressler, teaching experienced, hard–nosed police and deputies around the country—

John Douglas, 2018:

I said, oh my goodness. There is no way I'm going to get up at thirty-two years of age—even though my background was pretty solid—and have all these experienced cops in class. So the only way I thought to accelerate the training was that we had to do—like in the show, these two week road schools. You spend maybe a week in LAPD and then maybe you switch over and go to Boise, Idaho, and we had all this downtime. "So while we're in California, Bob [Robert Ressler], let's go in. Let's go interview Edmund Kemper. Let's see if he'll talk. We've got the badge. We've got the creds. We can get into these prisons. Let's go talk to Charles Manson. Let's see what they'll tell us about their crimes. Their pre-offense behavior. Their post-offense behavior. Victim selection. Why did they confess, if they confessed to the crime at all?"

So it was because of that and because Ann [Burgess] had recently conducted a heart attack study, predicting men who had certain variables would get a heart attack. I saw this as a reverse engineering type of thing. Our illness is the offender. So we've got to back track. We've got to reverse the engineering. What are the variables if you are looking at a homicide? What's going on there that we can interpret? And how can we interpret these variables? We must go talk to the experts. And the experts are these guys sitting around in prison.

Edmund Kemper was one of the first offenders to open up to Douglas and Ressler about all aspects of his crimes and thinking.

More recently, Kemper apparently suffered from a stroke and lost some motor skills. He is confined to a wheelchair and his eyesight is rapidly failing.

IMPACT

Richard Verbrugge, 2020:
After all this, I think the people that lived in Santa Cruz realized, "Oh my God. We've caught up with the rest of the world." This stuff can happen to any city, any size, anywhere.

Harold Cartwright, 2020:
It was hard. It was hard on all of us. Within two years after all three of the murders, Peter Chang was divorced because of his alcoholism. Jim Jackson was divorced. Some of the deputy sheriffs and police officers were divorced. I was divorced. It wasn't the sole cause of those, but it played a big role in our lives and in our families' lives. I worked thirteen months without a day off. That's hard on a marriage.

I would have been a much better adjusted, happier person if I hadn't met these people. If I would have just been on vacation those four or five years.

Terry Medina, 2020:
It put things in my head that I can never get out. Still sometimes it just comes back in ways that make me feel pretty…I don't know if the word is "sad." You know, when you're doing it, it's all business. But looking back on my life, it has definitely affected my life. All the murders in my career, there's been hundreds, it never surprises me what human beings can do to one another anymore.

There's times that it—like, Aiko Koo still bothers me a lot. The two kids at the Mystery Spot, it's hard to get that out of your head.

Mickey Aluffi, 2019:
It's kind of hard to realize how you are changing; it's probably more obvious to somebody else. But I can tell you from my perspective it has affected me in kind of a desensitization. Dealing with so many homicides and bodies, it does have an effect. Also, you notice that your friends are mostly law enforcement. You don't have friends on the

outside. Whether that's a trust issue one way or the other, I don't know. But at one point in my career, I noticed that in me. So what I did was make a conscious effort to change. I didn't divorce myself from the Santa Cruz Sheriff's Office, but I left in good standing and went to Watsonville Police Department where I was in a little better position to work more with the community than against it. That did a lot for me.

Mickey Aluffi, 2020:
I also developed this gallows humor that just wasn't appropriate. I mean, sure, we can sit here and talk and there are funny and interesting aspects to it all. And sometimes it protects you. But you have to think about the families involved as well.

Peter Chang on Jim Jackson having to defend all three killers—

Peter Chang:
It was a thankless task for a man who was only doing his duty, especially in the Frazier case. […] Everyone was buying guns for their self protection…and then threats were made against Jackson's life and those of his family. Even socially, Jackson was ostracized. He went to a dinner party one night, and a doctor there spat on him in contempt for his legally defending Frazier.

Joel Fort, 1993:
After my testimony in the Kemper trial, I received a serious death threat and was guarded by the police overnight and had to carry a body alarm for a long time.

Chris Cottle, 2020:
I ran for district attorney as he [Peter Chang] was leaving. He was running for a judgeship.

Austin Comstock, 2020:
He [Peter] had two terms as the DA which expired in '74, and Peter ran against Don May for superior court judge.

James Jackson, 2020:
Chang ran for judge against May and lost.

Austin Comstock, 2020:
After he lost the election, Peter became a defense attorney. His drinking got worse.

Peter Chang, 1991:
[By] 1982, I had lost my practice, my family and everything that had been dear to me. I would still walk five miles in the rain, if necessary, to be at a bar when it opened.

Peter Chang died of lung cancer in December 2004.

Terry Medina, 2020:
Like Chang, he [Doug James] drank too much. And then the job started to get too big, too much. James wasn't managing his budget. His undersheriff was a guy named Paul Terra.

Paul Terra was another homegrown Santa Cruz guy. He was about five foot five. Small guy, but a hunter fisherman and kind of a tough guy. But neither one of them had the background to manage the budget and in the early days they didn't really have to. It just wasn't a factor early on. Time went along and it got to be too much for James. So the Board of Supervisors, as we were learning some time later, told them, "Look, you got to hire somebody that knows what they're doing." And so he winds up hiring a lieutenant from the LA County Sheriff's Office named Davis—I can't remember his first name—and that started a revolt in the sheriff's office because Davis was a complete asshole. And that's what prompted Al Noren to run for sheriff. So that's kind of the story.

In 1974, Al Noren defeated Doug James and became the Santa Cruz County Sheriff.

Chris Cottle, 2020:
Law enforcement here became more sophisticated in the investigation of violent crimes. Many things that are standard procedures

For fifteen years Doug James has effectively served the people of Santa Cruz County. Doug James is THE MAN proven equal to the task!

Vote For Performance

RE-ELECT
SHERIFF
DOUG
JAMES

Paid for by the committee
to re-elect Doug James Sheriff
George Barsi, Co-Chairman
John Burdick, Co-Chairman

now were never even thought of before the Ohta murders.

Chris Cottle, 2020:

Most of the crimes were in the county, but some were in the city of Santa Cruz. The police department was involved, Scotts Valley Police Department was involved. But again, no one was prepared or experienced in crimes like this. The training wasn't out there at that time.

Ben Seibel, one man, was *the* scientific evidence department at the time. You put it in a paper bag and bring it down to him. That was it.

Now it is damn good. Everybody would acknowledge that it's one of the results of this period. Santa Cruz has a highly rated forensics lab.

The "Hippie Mayor" Pat Liteky resigned from the Board of Supervisors in March 1975, after a contentious relationship with the press. He was baited into revealing closed session details from a supervisors meeting and resigned that night.

Most of the people I talked with expressed a

loss of trust.

Chris Cottle, 2020:

For me personally, these crimes changed a lot about how I live my life. When I go to Africa, I don't worry about some yo-yo coming and giving me trouble. I worry about other things, but not that. That's from Carpenter [The Trailside Killer] as well. I won't go into Nisene Marks unless I'm with someone else.

Terry Medina, 2020:

Things changed after all this. People didn't trust. I mean, they thought there must be all these wackos out there killing everybody, which is why everybody bought all the guns, which is what we're seeing today. Something happens and people go out and buy guns.

Chris Cottle, 2020:

I, to this day, will never pick up a hitchhiker after all this. Maybe if I know the person, but actually there are a lot of things I won't do because of my experiences.

Along with everything else, a certain degree of

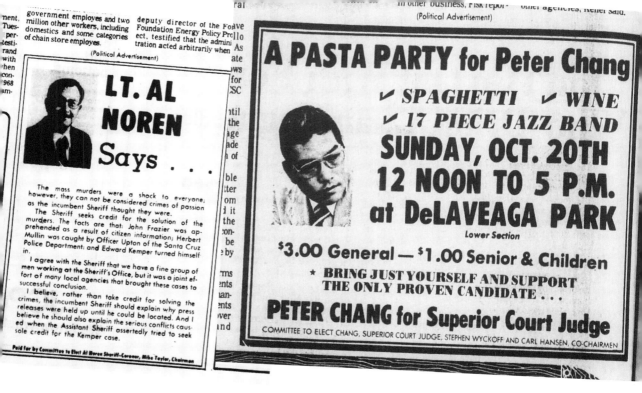

(Political Advertisement)

LT. AL NOREN Says . . .

The mass murders were a shock to everyone; however, they can not be considered crimes of passion as the incumbent Sheriff thought they were.

The Sheriff seeks credit for the solution of the murders. The facts are that: John Frazier was apprehended as a result of citizen information; Herbert Mullin was caught by Officer Upton of the Santa Cruz Police Department; and Edward Kemper turned himself in.

I agree with the Sheriff that we have a fine group of men working at the Sheriff's Office, but it was a joint effort of many local agencies that brought these cases to successful conclusion.

I believe, rather than take credit for solving the crimes, the incumbent Sheriff should explain why press releases were held up until he could be located. And I believe he should also explain the serious conflicts caused when the Assistant Sheriff assertedly tried to seek sole credit for the Kemper case.

Paid for by Committee to Elect Al Noren Sheriff-Coroner, Mike Taylor, Chairman

(Political Advertisement)

A PASTA PARTY for Peter Chang

✔ SPAGHETTI ✔ WINE
✔ 17 PIECE JAZZ BAND

SUNDAY, OCT. 20TH
12 NOON TO 5 P.M.
at DeLAVEAGA PARK
Lower Section

$3.00 General — $1.00 Senior & Children

★ BRING JUST YOURSELF AND SUPPORT THE ONLY PROVEN CANDIDATE . . .

PETER CHANG for Superior Court Judge
COMMITTEE TO ELECT CHANG, SUPERIOR COURT JUDGE, STEPHEN WYCKOFF AND CARL HANSEN, CO-CHAIRMEN

notoriety came for some of those involved.

Mickey Aluffi, 2020:

I think the weirdest thing is that all of this stuff happened in '72 and '73. And then after he [Kemper] was convicted and sent to state prison, there was no interest for like thirty years. And then, I'm thinking, it must have been about twenty years ago. I got a call from A&E to do a documentary. And then the calls started coming in. The BBC. I'm doing another one now. Another group from the United Kingdom.

Terry Medina, 2020:

I don't know how many TV shows Mickey [Aluffi] has done. I've done about ten or twelve, and some of these well-funded production companies have done very good research and others are horrible. So I've had this second career as a TV star.

Chris Cottle, 2020:

I was talking to a guy who kind of lost interest, but he's working on a play involving Peter Chang. Peter's a central figure in all this.

Terry Medina, 2020:

There were several books and documentaries. Lunde's book, *The Die Song*, treated me pretty favorably. The book *The Die Song*. They called me a twenty-five-year-old, handsome young detective.

One of the books was written by a San Francisco reporter using a pen name.

Urge to Kill came out very quickly. That was a good one.

James Jackson, 2020:

Listen, the first one [Frazier's crimes] had the *London Times*, *The New York Times*, and all those reporters hanging around, standing in front of the jail, and all the rest of it. Television stations from around the world. But it became apparent not long after that the press was a bunch of idiots. The questions were just horrible. No research.

THE OHTA AND CADWALLADER FAMILIES

Taura Ohta, the oldest of the two surviving Ohta daughters, married her high school sweetheart a month after the murders. They divorced

two years later and she remarried. The couple had a daughter.

Lark Ohta, 2020:
For Taura it was hard. My sister felt it all so deeply and it was tough for her to move forward and to acclimate. She needed my parents a lot. And she also didn't go live with a family, which I think made it worse. She had no new family.

On May 26, 1977, Taura Ohta took her own life.

Taura Ohta was buried next to the rest of her family in Santa Cruz.

Two years after that, Dr. Ohta's mother committed suicide as well.

Lark Ohta, 1990:
After twenty years, you think the pain has got to end, but it doesn't really go away.

Above: The San Lorenzo Valley High School football field is named the "Dean Richardson Memorial Field."

Lark Ohta, 1990:
People say, "Don't you want to put it all away?" But how could something that big in your life go away? If you don't talk about it, it's like it never happened, like my family wasn't real.

Lark Ohta, 2020:
I have two sons that are exactly a year apart, just like my little brothers were. My oldest son is named Derek Taggert.

I didn't come straight out and tell my children what had happened, when they were little. How do you tell little children about that?

Though, when they asked, I was always completely honest with them. I said that I had had a different family, and that they had died when I was young. And as they got older, they would ask more, and I would tell them a little more. But they could only take in so much information at each age, and I wanted the news to be delivered as organically as possible.

That was all that I could do. This was their family, too, and they had lost them just as I had.

My sons have now lived longer than my two brothers, and that always startles me.

When I came to the age where I had lived longer than my parents had, it was very hard to imagine. I realized how young they had been. I thought they were old when they died, but they were only forty. And now fifty years have passed and I am sixty-five—well past their ages and it always feels strange to me. Confusing, I guess.

Melinda Cadwallader, 2020:
It happened when I was eleven.

By the time I was twelve we moved to Hawaii.

Lark Ohta, 2020:
It makes me feel good to remember things with you. Good things. Because they were real people. They did great things and had wonderful lives, all five of them. They should be remembered, not just because they were killed.

LIST OF WORKS CONSULTED

Urge to Kill book by Ward Damio

Sacrifice Unto Me by Don West

The Die Song by Donald T. Lunde and Jefferson Morgan

Peter Chang Application for Appointment as Santa Cruz County District Attorney, January 22, 1999

Peter Chang Obituary

Santa Cruz Sentinel newspapers

Register Pajaronian newspapers

Valley Press newspapers

Independent newspaper (Long Beach, CA)

Los Angeles Times newspapers

The San Francisco Examiner newspapers

The Stanford Daily newspapers

The Fish Wrap Live! Volume 9, Issue 3 November 11, 1998 "Surf City mystery" By Karina Ioffee

Sundaz newspaper, February 1973

Murder Can Be Fun: #8 Shut Up Ma!

The Champion Magazine, November 1991. Profile of Peter Chang.

The Champion: Journal for the National Association of Criminal Defense Lawyers

Social Psychology Quarterly 1991, Vol. 54, No. 4, pages 343-352: Fear and Loathing: Archival Traces of the Response to Extraordinary Violence by Dane Archer and Lynn Erlich-Erfer

Newsweek November 26, 1984. The Random Killers by Mark Starr with George Raine and Daniel Pedersen in California, Daniel Shapiro in Texas, Nancy Cooper in New York, Holly Morris in Atlanta, Patricia King in Chicago, and John Harris in Washington.

Mickey Aluffi and William Kelsay: Giant Hunter presentation for the Aptos Historical Society, November 9, 2019

Trial transcripts of Herbert Mullin trial

Trial transcripts of Edmund Kemper trial

John Linley Frazier Life Term Parole Consideration Hearing, November 19, 2008

Handgun crime control, 1975-1976: hearing before the subcommittee to investigate juvenile delinquency of the Committee on the Judiciary, United States Senate, Ninety-Fourth Congress. April 23, July 22, October 28, 1975

Bay Area Television Archive: https://diva.sfsu.edu/collections/sfbatv

edmundkemperstories.com

The Crime Piper

ancestry.com

classmates.com

Yearbooks

The Insanity Offense: How America's Failure to Treat the Seriously Mentally Ill Endangers Its Citizens. By E. Fuller Torrey

Joel Fort, M.D. PUBLIC HEALTH PIONEER, CRIMINOLOGIST, REFORMER, ETHICIST AND HUMANITARIAN With an Introduction by Dorothy Smith Patterson Interviews Conducted by Caroline C. Crawford in 1991, 1992, and 1993 UC Berkeley. Copyright 0 1997 by The Regents of the University of California

A Legal History of Santa Cruz County by various authors. Published by the Museum of Art and History

Front Page Detective Magazine March 1974. Interview with Marj Von Beroldingen

Gathered police reports, files, and documents from the Santa Cruz Sheriff's Office.

Collected documents of Donald T. Lunde.

Dr. Lunde interviews with Allison Ayers, Bert Bongiovanni, Dolores Frazier, June Aries, Mike Wark from November 20, 1973. Undated interview with Pat Pascal

Dr. Lunde interview with Allyn Kemper on June 12, 1973

Harold Cartwright interview with Susan Swanson on May 23, 1973

Harold Cartwright interview with Michelle Ann Sims on May 25, 1973

Harold Cartwright interview with Sue Crissman on September 27, 1973

Harold Cartwright memos relating to many interviews he had

Several witness statements

Undated statement from Susan Swanson

Kemper's full file from his time in Atascadero

Hundreds of DA, public defender, police and deputy sheriff reports with notes on interviews they conducted

Herbert Mullin quotes from interviews:

    Correspondence with Herbert Mullin

    Herbert Mullin Life Term Parole Consideration Hearing, February 17, 2011

    Herbert William Mullin v. John J. O'Connor & The Archdiocese of San Francisco, i.e., Archbishop Levada. Petition for Appointment of Competent Legal Counsel &/or Petition for Writ of Habeas Corpus

    An interview he did with the Valley Press in 1981.

    April 10, 1973 interview with Dr. Lunde

Edmund Kemper quotes culled from:

    Santa Cruz County Sheriff interview with Edmund Kemper April 24, 1973

    Santa Cruz County Sheriff interview with Edmund Kemper April 28, 1973

    Santa Cruz County District Attorney interview with Edmund Kemper April 29, 1973

    Edmund Kemper Life Term Parole Consideration Hearing, June 15, 1988

    Edmund Kemper Life Term Parole Consideration Hearing, July 25, 2017

    Grand Jury testimony: Edmund Kemper

    Various interviews with Edmund Kemper posted on YouTube

    Dr. Lunde interviews with Kemper on June 12, 15, 20, 1973

    Dr. Lunde, Dr. Fort, and Jim Jackson interview with Kemper on September 8, 1973

    Harold Cartwright interviews with Kemper from May 21 and 30, 1973; August 24, 1973; October 1, 1973

    Handwritten notes by Herbert Mullin

All quotes from 2020 and 2021 were taken from interviews conducted with the author.

IMAGE CREDITS

Every effort has been made to trace the ownership or source of all images for the purpose of giving proper credit. I regret any inadvertent error regarding the attribution of images and will be pleased to make the proper acknowledgement in any future printing.

All copyrights are held by the photographers.

Mickey Aluffi: 189, 460

Pete Amos: 19–20, 49, 59–60, 65, 69–71, 74, 76, 78, 80, 84–85, 107, 114–116, 122, 164–165, 223, 247, 251, 262, 266–267, 287, 291, 313, 347, 349–350, 373, 386, 389, 405, 408, 427, 430, 436, 450, 457–458, 462–463, 492–494, 497, 499–502, 506, 509, 511–512, 519, 530, 546, 552

Peter Breinig / San Francisco Chronicle / Polaris: 15

Candace Caspers: 522–524

Nancy Guilfoyle: 214–215, 217, 552

Hachette Comics/Robinson: 521

Jenny Kennedy: 131

Ann Lobner: 5

John Marr: 520

Liz Morales Photography: 537

Herbert Mullin: 515–517

Eileen Murray: 134

Nate and Amanda Murray: 321

Roger Murray: 132–133

Lark Ohta: 56–58, 552

John Perez: 298, 300–302, 552

The Santa Cruz Public Library: 224

The Santa Cruz Sentinel: 6–7, 12, 36–37, 40–41, 46–47, 52–53, 61–63, 87–88, 90, 97, 134, 151–153, 155, 159, 161, 216, 218, 221, 227, 239, 245–246, 250, 252, 256, 276, 288–289, 298–299, 314–315, 331, 338, 348, 366, 384, 456, 491, 530–531, 552

The Santa Cruz Sheriff's Office: 7, 182–183, 186, 296, 391, 453–456, 552

Forrest Schall: 235–236, 238, 552

Joey Tranchina – transparentpress©2021: 525–526

The Press Banner (formerly the Valley Press): 7, 39, 47, 79, 117, 128, 210, 212, 220, 287, 289, 317, 470–471,

Sam Vestal (Photos courtesy of Vestal Family Trust): 16, 45, 64–65, 95, 106, 118–119, 137–138, 141–144, 146, 149–150, 153–154, 156, 158, 166, 332, 476, 479–480, 482, 484, 540, 545

Rita Wright: 311, 356–357

THE AUTHOR

This is Emerson Murray's second book. The first, *Bruiser Brody*, is a primary source biography published by Crowbar Press. He has written articles, he paints, and he makes noise cassettes and CDs.

Emerson grew up in the San Lorenzo Valley and still lives in Santa Cruz County with his wife, two kids, and two dogs. He has been collecting material for this book for over thirty years.

For more information about Emerson and his projects, visit emersonmurray.com

INDEX

Symbols

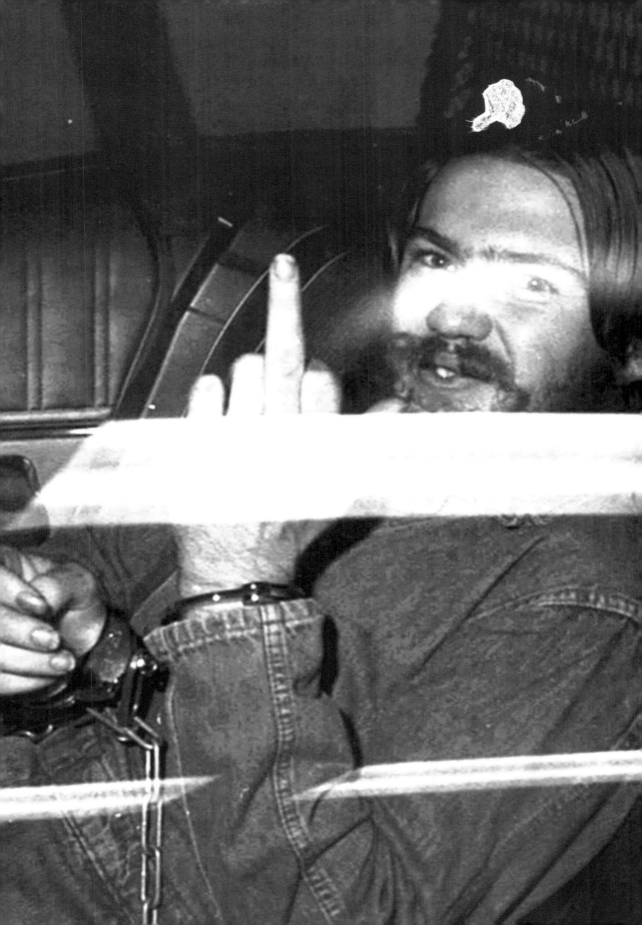

> *Right: A note and transcript of a cassette tape found in Mullin's apartment after he was arrested.*

```
                    *** SING ***
```

I am the hitchhike KILLE

The Music of

J. S. BACH

FOR FUN
(Bach Courus)
Monday 4 - 5:30
Wednesday 4 - 5

OR

CREDIT

CHAMBE

Call J. Zaust

in my insanity and I broke from my, from my certificate of sanity and
I hope to see the day when, when the people whom I'm thinking of ah well
also be in a, in a sense in a similar sation, station, you know, as they,
as they, as they are now probably, just to say you have, you have not done
your job, you have not protected me, I ah preacher of the Gospel, you
have not protected me and that's why/am sort of not going to believe in
your, in your games, cause it, it's awfully cold, it's ??????
Arrividerchiero (sp) I will not sing those songs, they are, they are
Indian songs, I saw the moon, I felt very bad, I was not afraid as some,
afraid of some but I think/very very courageous, that is an old trip,
whomade that place, it was not made by man, no it was not made by man,
it was made by everyone. Reminiscence, logically,?? diversity ?? It is very
amazing.
He died so that I could have longevity, I have created you so that you
would die for me. I pray that you will receive longevity. ???

just be when you get here, just be, learn how to ah just exist on the air,
like some many of those that I enjoy do, this just sound his voice, be
with him, if you can, he's wonderful, man, ah, the City is a nice place
to live,nothing wrong with the City, a good life, it's all groovy, man
it's groovy, very, very groovy. Congratulations Mr. JEFFREY F. SEAGULL
ah, are you married, you have a house, yeah, a color television set, you
have a nice stereo, record player, tape recorder cassette, way ahead of me,
man, way up there ahead of me, good luck on your journey through time, you
did a very good job of raising me, I'm awful proud of you. Our only hope
is to not teach people military ways, that was a long time ago you said that.
Does it have any significance now? It has alot of significance, one, two,
three, I am me, ha   END OF SIDE ONE.

MULLIN IS SINGING THESE WORDS.

Five hundred miles, five hundred miles, five hundred miles, five hundred
miles, Lord, I'm five hundred miles from my home. Not a shirt on my
back, not a penney to my name, Lord, I'm five hundred miles away from
home. This away, this away, this away, this away, Lord, I'm five hundred
miles away from home. Lord, I'm one, Lord, I'm two, Lord, I'm three,
Lord, I'm four, Lord, I'm five hundred miles away from home. This away,
this away, this away, this away, Lord, I'm five hundred miles away from
home.

Hey, Jude, don't make it bad, you were made to go out and get her, remember
to let her into your heart and you can start to make it better. Hey, Jude,
don't be a fool, you were made to live by the rules and when you come on the
bay and you will start to learn to pray. Hey, Jude , don't mess around,
cause he's been laid under the ground, remember to let her into your heart
and you can start to make it better.
                          (Spelling ?)
Hare Krishna, Hare Krishna, Krishna, Krishna, Hare, Hare. Hare Rama, Hare
Rama, Rama, Rama, Hare Hare. Hare, Krishna, Hare Krishna, Krishna, Krishna
Hare Hare. Hare Rama, Hare Rama, Rama, Rama, Hare, Hare. Clemka maday
I did my heed, buspa a una dek ma he, tunna numga procho di at. Oh Money,
pardon me, um um um. Shanti,hie,hie ,hie, hie, hie, hie.

JimmyCrack Corn, and I don't care, Jimmy Crack Corn and I don't care,
Jimmy Crack Corn and I don't care, I don't know what to say. Who are you
and why did you go, who are you and why did you stay, who are you, are you
really there, really, I don't care. Jimmy Crack Corn, and I don't care

3. A large crowd *CAN SOMETIMES CAUSE TROUBLE.*

4. A person is most helpless when *HE IS PUT UP AGAINST SOMETHING HE KNOWS HE CAN'T HANDLE.*

5. The hardest decisions *COME WHEN A PERSON HAS NO ONE TO HELP THEM*

6. Parents would worry less if *CHILDREN COULD LEARN TO COPE WITH THEIR PROBLEMS SOONER.*

7. When fire starts, *MOST OFTEN IT IS PUT OUT*

8. Fathers should learn that *THEIR CHILDREN NEED THEM MORE THAN THEY THINK.*

9. One's closest friends *ARE NOT ALWAYS HONEST WITH THEM SELVES OR YOU*

10. It is easy to get into trouble when *SOMEONE STARTS DRINKING LIQUOR*

11. Few children fear *LARGE CROWDS OF PEOPLE.*

12. He drew back from the touch of *FIRE*

13. The most pleasant dreams *CAN SOMETIMES BE MISLEADING*

14. A drunken man *CAN LOSE MOST OF HIS MORALS VERY EASILY*

15. No one can repair the damage caused by *A PERSON WHO THINKS NO ONE WANTS TO UNDERSTAND HIM.*

16. The nicest thing about being a child *ARE THE SIMPLE PLEASURES OF LIFE THAT THEY ENJOY.*

17. To be without shame *MUST BE AWFUL*

18. Worse than being lonely *IS BEING SCARED*

19. Children are most annoying *WHEN THEY KEEP ASKING THE SAME THING OVER AND OVER AGAIN.*

20. If people only knew how much *COMMON UNDERSTANDING THERE IS LEFT IN THE WORLD, THERE WOULDN'T BE AS MUCH TROUBLE*

21. The worst thing about being sick is *THE WAY NORMAL PEOPLE LOOK AT YOU.*

22. It is hard to sleep when *I START WORRYING ABOUT MY OWN PROBLEMS.*

23. People shouldn't *THINK THAT THE WHOLE WORLD IS AGAINST THEM.*

24. A masculine* woman should *CONCENTRATE ON THEIR PERSONALITIES.*

1. Are you right or left handed? *LEFT*

2. What is the age of the person you drew? *TEENAGE*

3. What is the sex of the person you drew? *MALE*

IQ 116

Left: Various tests from Kemper's time in Atascadero, January 1966.

W

Y

Z

Lark Ohta, 2020:
  It makes me feel good to remember things with you. Good things. Because they were real people. They did great things and had wonderful lives, all five of them. They should be remembered, not just because they were killed.